Teaching Gifted Children

Teaching Gifted Children

Principles and Strategies

Aimee Howley
University of Charleston

Craig B. Howley
University of Charleston

Edwina D. Pendarvis
Marshall University

Little, Brown and Company
Boston   Toronto

Library of Congress Cataloging-in-Publication Data

Howley, Aimee.
    Teaching gifted children.

    Bibliography: p.
    Includes index.
    1. Gifted children—Education—United States.
2. Gifted children—Education—Curricula.
I. Howley, Craig. II. Pendarvis, Edwina D. III. Title.
LC3993.9.H68 1986   371.95´6´0973   85-19875
ISBN 0-316-37585-3

Library of Congress Catalog Card No. 85-19875

ISBN 0-316-37585-3

9 8 7 6 5 4 3 2 1

ALP

Published simultaneously in Canada
by Little, Brown & Company (Canada) Limited

Printed in the United States of America

Text Credits

Adapted text from C. Heilman (1977), ''Baby-sitting costs vs. schooling costs'' in *Phi
Delta Kappan*, 58 (9), 707, used by permission of Phi Delta Kappan and the author.

Quotes from R. Feynman from *Nova*, series program #1002, coproduced by BBC (London) and WGBH (Boston). Used by permission of the British Broadcasting Corporation and R. Feynman.

We dedicate this book to our children.

Our children dedicate this book to Snake Pliskin, Stephen King, Gollum, Josh Walls, and Susan.

PREFACE

Teaching Gifted Children: Principles and Strategies, as the title suggests, is primarily a text for courses that consider curriculum and instruction of the gifted. Such courses are sometimes called "methods" courses, and this text presents a method of teaching the gifted. It is not, however, a sourcebook of classroom activities or of curriculum options.

Our familiarity with schools has directed our attention primarily to practical alternatives for the gifted. Our experience has, however, suggested the need to relate practice to a sensible theoretical structure. We have therefore tried to illuminate issues related to gifted education as well as to define strategies most suitable for teaching gifted children.

Although this text reviews the characteristics of gifted children and the history of gifted education, it does not do so in depth. We have written the text on the assumption that students will already have encountered the material covered in a special education survey course and in an introductory gifted education course.

The method of this text affirms several notions relevant to gifted education, and proceeds in its work on that basis. These assumptions concern

fair and accurate identification procedures,
special gifted populations,
exceptional child status,
differentiated instruction,
effective teaching,
academic learning, and
intellectual and social context.

Together these assumptions constitute a lens through which to examine gifted education and, as articulated in discussion, a strategy for conducting school programs for gifted students. No single approach to pedagogy, however, can satisfy all parties, and we have tried to make our preferences explicit so that readers can challenge both our assumptions and our conclusions. We use several formatting techniques in an attempt to make ideas and procedures both more accessible and easier to remember.

Chapters are grouped into three sections: preparation (overview and evaluation); instruction (developing placement alternatives, negotiating program plans, acceleration, enrichment, curriculum, instructional formats, teaching techniques, arts programming); and social context (under-achievement, equal opportunity). The first part contains Chapters 1 and 2. The second part contains Chapters 3 through 10. The third part contains Chapters 11 and 12.

Each of the three parts is preceded by a content overview that introduces the most important concerns and previews their role in the subsequent discussion. Each chapter is preceded by an outline of its content. Continuity of discussion is reinforced by chapter introductions and summaries. Boxes, tables, figures, and other such devices clarify and amplify points in the text.

A note on citations: statements, opinions, and findings are explicitly attributed to cited works when a portion of text is referenced without a preceding abbreviation. When a citation is preceded by *e. g.* ("for example"), the cited work exemplifies the statement, opinion, or line of argument in text. When a citation is preceded by *cf.* ("compare"), the cited work comments on the same issue, usually from a perspective that differs from ours.

A book is a wonderful thing, and we have had a good time with this one. Writing is hard work, however, and we are in debt to a number of associates for various sorts of help and support: Aaron Anton, Joan and Frank Badger, Treasa Brown, Dennis Clarkson, Geoff and Leslie Clifton, Susan Ferrell, Alice Holstine, Pat Howard, Bill and Lorie Howley, Jim and Lorna Howley, Dick Hunt, Barbara Jones, Betsy Kent, Luanne McCown, Mark Scarpelli, Elizabeth Scobell, and Caryl and Powell Toth. The staffs of the Drain-Jordan Library at West Virginia State College, the Marshall University Library, and the Andrew S. Thomas Memorial Library at the University of Charleston were gracious and helpful.

We are indebted to our reviewers, especially the one who tutored us in the use of nonsexist language: William Durden, The John Hopkins University; Jerry Flack, University of Colorado at Colorado Springs; Barbara Ford, Learning Dimensions; Anne K. Golin, University of Pittsburgh; Reva Jenkins-Friedman, The University of Kansas; and Dorothy Sheldon-Shrader, Central Washington University. We also thank Sally Lifland and her associates for their work in readying the text for the press. Finally, we thank our sponsoring editor, the redoubtable Mylan Jaixen, who kept cutting off our limbs so we wouldn't have to go too far out on them.

BRIEF CONTENTS

CONTENTS

PART II   Instruction   65

Teaching Gifted Children

PART I

Preparations

Part I of *Teaching Gifted Children: Principles and Strategies* comprises a discussion of the aims of gifted education and the identification of gifted students. These and related topics are treated in Chapter 1, "Genus and Species: The Taxonomy of Gifted Education" and Chapter 2, "Assessment and Interpretation: The Function of Evaluation."

This part of the text affirms two assumptions that, together, distinguish it from other textbooks on gifted education. These two premises concern (1) the place of academic learning and (2) the methods of identification. These assumptions will, in turn, underlie discussions in Part II about placement options, program negotiation, acceleration, curriculum, teaching strategies, and instruction in the arts.

The Place of Academic Learning.   School learning is the context in which the definition of giftedness has become a priority. School learning can be measured quite well in normative terms, both as achievement and as potential. Academic content, the primary object of school learning, is instrumental in defining and characterizing gifted children. It therefore makes sense to us that academic content be emphasized in instructional programs for gifted children.

Methods of Identification.   Gifted children usually display advanced academic potential and advanced academic achievement. Eighty years of child study has confirmed the need to differentiate the school program for gifted children. Like the handicapped, the gifted are *exceptional children*.

Unresolved matters concern *not* the necessity of a different program, but the nature of children to be served in school gifted programs. For this reason we discuss in some detail the process of individual assessment. Such assessment involves primarily individual norm-referenced testing of potential and achievement, but group testing, criterion-referenced testing, and other assessment alternatives should also be considered. Identification should relate to academic program goals and instruction.

1

CHAPTER 1

Genus and Species: The Taxonomy of Gifted Education

INTRODUCTION

This chapter has two main purposes. First, it reviews the broad outlines of the field of gifted education. Second, it introduces the reader to the authors' orientation and approach to the instructional issues that challenge those who work with apt students.

This chapter reviews the characteristics of gifted children in the context of the development of the field. It then examines three typical categories of giftedness. These categories are (1) generalized intellectual ability, (2) specific academic ability, and (3) ability in the arts. Both here and throughout the text, these three categories are explained and compared with other notions of giftedness. Finally, this chapter examines various conceptions of the aims of gifted education.

During the course of the development of the field of gifted education, some consensus has emerged concerning the characteristics of gifted students, the sorts of categories around which such characteristics can be organized, and the aims of gifted education. The field, however, is still vigorous and growing, and there are, fortunately, many areas of contention.

FROM GALTON TO RENZULLI AND BACK AGAIN

The histories of many fields show signs of a cyclical evolution. Perhaps this is because the important problems of a field are never completely solved, and progress in the field depends on the willingness of workers and thinkers to reexamine significant problems.

A number of important problems of this nature persist in gifted education. We bracket our consideration of these problems with the work of Sir Francis Galton and Joseph Renzulli. The persistent problems considered by these two men, and those we will address in this section, are

1. the nature of talent,
2. the measurement of talent,
3. the significance of eminence, and
4. the contribution of effort.

Both Galton, who is most often credited with raising the issue of giftedness in modern times and Renzulli, whose model of identification and programming is widely used at present in U.S. schools, spoke clearly about these issues. So of course did many other researchers and writers in the field, and we shall draw on their work also to help illuminate these problem areas. This treatment is not strictly chronological, though it is historical; its purpose is to synthesize important contributions to the study of talent.

Musicians, Statesmen, and Generals

Galton's *Hereditary Genius* (1869/1962), like many influential works that have founded a line of inquiry, defined and addressed a problem in ways that have profoundly influenced subsequent inquiry. Galton's problem was the origin of talent.

Like other advanced thinkers of his day, Galton had read Darwin's *The Origin of Species*, which first appeared in 1859, and he had been impressed with its social implications. Darwin's basic premise, the premise that so shocked his contemporaries, was that species, including the species *homo sapiens*, rose and fell according to natural laws in the vastness of geological time. This observation was a severe blow to the notion of humankind as the center of the world.

Galton and many others (most notably the conservative philosopher Herbert Spencer, see Chapter 7) believed that if Darwin's theories about evolution were correct, the implications for a science of human social evolution were momentous. The significant concepts from Darwin were *natural selection* and *survival of the fittest.*

These terms seemed to Galton to explain the origin of human talents. Galton believed, and set out to prove, that particular talents—for example, talent in music, in statesmanship, and in military leadership—had been developed through natural selection and were therefore passed on genetically through survival of the fittest. To prove his contention, Galton collected data on families' performance over several generations in selected fields of endeavor. His history of the musical talent of the Bach family is interesting and complete.

Galton claimed to have proven that rare talents of many sorts were transmitted genetically. What he actually proved is more difficult to say. His work strongly suggests that families of musicians, for example, do tend to produce more musicians than other families. His method, however, was totally incapable of *proving* his contention.

First, he did not study the presumed genetic trait or combination of traits directly. He simply did not have the theoretical or technical means to do so. (Despite the comparative scientific sophistication of our time, we still lack the means to identify precisely those genetic components which might determine talent.)

Second, Galton's sampling technique was poor. (The statistical notion of random sampling had yet to be developed.) His data were biased from the start, since he chose families that were already eminent.

Third, Galton failed to take sufficient account of purely social influences. During the middle ages, the Renaissance, and even into the late nineteenth century, occupations in many places tended to be socially "hereditary." The son of a woodcutter became a woodcutter, the son of a military man became a military man, and so forth. Galton's data were thoroughly contaminated by what we would now call *design error.*

Finally, Galton used secondary and tertiary sources that tended to be obscure or unreliable. He did not control the conditions of observation upon which his data, and his judgments, were based.

Why then, was Galton's contribution so influential and so original? Galton's contribution was not so much the establishment of truth as the airing of issues. The issues he raised concerning heredity, kinds and components of talent, and degrees of talent remain pertinent to the field of gifted education today.

One of Galton's contributions, however, has had a great deal of influence technically: his concept of *degree of eminence.* Galton defined eminence not in terms of quality (excellent in what way) but in terms of quantity (excellent to what degree). Galton conceived of the degree of eminence as a mathematical expression. The degrees of eminence (given letter names in Galton's scheme) were based on rarity per unit population—1 in 1000; 1 in 10,000; 1 in 100,000, and so on. Though his sense of statistical accuracy left much to be desired his notion of comparative statistical rarity is the basis of most contemporary identification efforts. This notion is one way to express *deviation* from the mean on the normal curve.

The Nature of Talent.   The persistent questions regarding the nature of talent have been

What is intelligence? (See Chapters 2 and 12.)

What are the component *talents* of intelligence? (See Chapters 2 and 7.)

What is the difference between intelligence and talent? (See Chapters 2 and 6.)

What is creativity? Is it a component of intelligence? (See Chapters 2, 6, and 10.)

What is the source of differences in individual intelligence? (See Chapters 11 and 12.)

What is the effect of culture on efforts to define mental traits? (See Chapters 2, 6, 11, and 12.)

Many answers have been given to these questions, and many techniques have been used in an attempt not only to define but to measure talents and intelligence accurately. Distinctions among talents, "gifts," aptitudes, intelligences (cf. Gardner, 1983), IQ, and even intellect are common in the literature of giftedness and mental testing.

The variety of interpretations is impressive. Hofstadter (1963), for example, notes that *intelligence* has an active and practical orientation, but that *intellect* has a reflective and scholarly orientation. Jensen (1980) believes the matter of the inheritance of IQ to be beyond doubt, whereas Scarr (1981), using similar research techniques, and Jencks et al. (1972), using different techniques, believe the genetic influence on IQ to be much less strong. Renzulli (1977) maintains that the element of effort needs to be considered in identifying gifted students, whereas Whitmore (1980) notes that many gifted children are poorly motivated. Gallagher (1975) notes that all notions of giftedness are culture-bound, but much effort has been directed toward developing tests that are culture-free (e.g., Kaufman & Kaufman, 1983).

The Measurement of Talent.   In order to address the special needs of talent in the schools, it has been necessary to develop measurement instruments that can be used to identify individual children. The necessity of doing this accurately and fairly is a great burden. Sometimes it seems as if it is impossible for such instruments to be both accurate *and* fair. Important questions regarding the measurement of talent include

How can talent be measured? (See Chapter 2.)

Can intelligence be measured separately from talents? (See Chapter 2.)

Is it fair to compare students to one another using a single scale? (See Chapters 2, 11, and 12.)

How can creativity be measured? Is it distinct from IQ? (See Chapters 2, 6, and 10.)

Can we use absolute or criterion-referenced instruments to identify giftedness? (See Chapters 2 and 4.)

Psychologists, building on Galton's notion of degree of exceptionality, began to apply statistical measurement techniques early in the twentieth century. Alfred Binet (1857–1911) was among the first to develop a test to identify particular children for a school system. At the turn of the century, he used his test to find children who would probably have difficulty in the French public schools.

Shortly thereafter, Lewis Terman, working at Stanford University, adapted the tests for use in the United States and produced what has been known ever since as the Stanford-Binet Intelligence Scale. Terman was interested in bright children rather than slow children (cf. Gallagher, 1985), and he used his adapted Binet scale to study such children (see Box 1.1).

Since Terman's day, the reliability of norm-referenced measures such as the Stanford-Binet has increased as a result of the continuing evolution of statistics as a technical field. The issue of fairness, however, persists. Some minority groups (notably blacks and hispanics) have been found to have IQ test group means that are lower than the national average; other minority groups (notably Jews and orientals) have been found to have higher group means. When scores based on a nationally normed sample are used to identify individuals as gifted, the low-scoring groups are penalized and the high-scoring groups are given an advantage. This phenomenon explains the poor representation of blacks and hispanics and the strong representation of Jews and orientals in gifted programs.

The use of reliable norm-referenced tests has therefore been replaced or augmented in some locales with rating scales such as the one developed by Renzulli and his colleagues (Renzulli, Hartman, Smith & Callahan, 1977). Research has not yet addressed whether or not this sort of instrument results in *fairer* assessment practices. It does seem likely that these instruments measure different sorts of characteristics than do traditional norm-referenced tests and that they may make these measurements *less reliably* (see Chapter 2 for a full discussion of this issue).

Eminence and Effort.   Eminence is akin to renown. Although in itself it is not necessarily significant, eminence can nonetheless be construed as performance on the "test of life." Galton, for example, spoke of life as a series of tests to be undertaken. He did not doubt the validity or the reliability of such life tests. According to this logic, if we want to find a gifted person, we need merely find one who is eminent.

Galton believed that people became eminent through a combination of effort and talent. Neither, alone, was sufficient to ensure eminence or accomplishment, perhaps the more significant precursor of eminence.

According to a contemporary logic, that of the Renzulli programs (Ren-

---

BOX 1.1 Lewis Terman

Shortly after revising the Binet scale for use in the United States, Lewis Terman (1877–1956) used his new Stanford-Binet Intelligence Scale to identify 1528 gifted children. Terman identified as gifted those elementary school children who scored 140 and above (ratio IQ, see Chapter 2) on his test. At the time of their identification, the subjects were students in grades K–12. Their mean IQ on the Stanford-Binet was 151. High school students were tested with the Terman Concept Mastery Test; their mean IQ on this measure was 143.

Terman continued to study his sample until his death (e.g., Terman, 1925; Burks, Jensen & Terman, 1930; Terman & Oden, 1947, 1959). Melita Oden and others continued the study thereafter (e.g., Oden, 1968). Terman's work is the most extensive longitudinal study ever conducted in U.S. educational research. The studies cited above contain detailed reports of the subjects' school performance, careers, and adult accomplishments. The data include information on marriages and divorces, offspring, publications, patents, and physical and mental health.

On the average, this large sample of gifted individuals *excelled in academic performance* and at least equaled the normal population on every measure used. Terman's study effectively discounted popular sentiment that gifted persons' exceptional intellectual endowments are counterbalanced by physical, social, or emotional deficits.

Applying Galton's concept of statistical infrequency as a criterion of giftedness, Terman included in his study only about four children out of every thousand. Later research suggests that perhaps one-third to one-half of the children who *could have qualified for inclusion under Terman's criteria* may well have gone undiscovered because their teachers failed to nominate them for testing.

Terman's selection methods, like those of any research study, defined the parameters of the population to whom the findings were most applicable—in this case, high-IQ scorers from homes with middle- or upper-class values and resources. Nonetheless, Terman's study continues to yield implications for the education of a sizable portion of the student and adult population who are identified as gifted under current definitions.

---

zulli, 1977), if one wants to educate very productive, committed workers in various fields, one first looks at eminently successful adults in those fields. Next, one locates students who demonstrate a mixture of talent, creativity, and task-commitment resembling that of the eminent adults. Finally, one provides these students with a program of study that consists of successive approximations of adult performance.

An alternative logic (Whitmore, 1980) emphasizes the fact that talent and task-commitment exist independently of each other. This logic asserts the need to cultivate talent wherever it is found. In this view, effort and motivation are concomitants of talent development, not prerequisites. Proponents argue that this view is fairer than one that includes task commitment, because op-

pressed minorities (blacks and the poor especially) often lack task-commitment in school even when they demonstrate exceptional talent.

Genius, Genes and Genus

Although it may seem from the above historical circuit that the field of gifted
education is beset by a thicket of opposing half-truths, there is a common
root of consensus. This consensus can be summarized as follows:

1. The broad category of rare potential characterizes the genus known as
   gifted children.
2. Gifted children, though not so rare as eminent adult "geniuses," are
   unusual.
3. This comparative rarity can be used to identify such children.
4. The comparative rarity of giftedness necessitates unusual educational
   arrangements.

The consensus does not extend to the question of the origin of giftedness.
Some workers in the field probably favor a hereditarian interpretation. The
majority, hedging their bets, probably ascribe equal influence to heredity and
environment. Still others ascribe a major influence to environment and a minor influence to heredity. This last group probably comprises the smallest
group in the field with an opinion on the question. This is, however, the
group to which the authors belong. It may come as a surprise, therefore, to
the reader that we endorse the use of norm-referenced tests (including IQ
tests) to identify and develop programs for gifted children. This combination
of positions is perhaps just another way to hedge bets. Let us explain.

Genius and Genes.   Galton, as we noted above, was the first to consider the
origin of special talents in a scientific mode. His scientific approach did not,
as we also noted, prevent him from assuming his conclusions and from bias-
ing his data. As is apparent from the title of his 1869 work *Hereditary Genius*,
Galton credited a strong hereditary influence. The application of Galton's
statistical techniques to Binet's test, however, put the question on a more
reliable empirical footing. It was Terman, at Stanford, who adapted the test
for the United States, gathered data, and analyzed it (see Box 1.1).
    There was little doubt in Terman's mind about the genetic origin of what
has been called intelligence, intelligence quotient, or simply IQ. Terman called
his series of studies of gifted children *Genetic Studies of Genius*. Terman, like
Galton, was nonetheless unable to study genetics per se. Like Galton, Terman
assumed his consequent (cf. Gould, 1981).
    In recent years Arthur Jensen has brilliantly defended the hereditarian po-
sition, starting with his now-famous 1969 article in the *Harvard Educational
Review*. For anyone interested in the question—and it is hard to believe that
anyone in the field of gifted education or mental retardation remains unin-

terested—Jensen is required reading. Important books by Jensen are *Educability and Group Differences* (1973) and *Bias in Mental Testing* (1980).

Galton, like Jensen, was aware of group differences. He suggested in *Hereditary Genius*, for example, that different "racial stocks" possessed different degrees of talent. Moreover, he suggested that Teutonic "races" were superior to Mediterranean "races," and that within the "races" different classes possessed varying degrees of ability. In a revealing passage of *Hereditary Genius*, Galton justified nineteenth-century British territorial acquisitions in Africa and China as a kind of manifest destiny inherent in the superiority of the British racial stock.

Today these passages in Galton's work seem preposterous to any but the most bigoted reader. Talk of the fine distinctions of racial stock is too reminiscent of Nazi fascism. Jensen (1973) himself notes that any racial group produces very capable individuals, as different from the average as are similar individuals in other groups. Yet in Jensen's work the notion persists that important racial differences in mental ability exist, and when they concern the organization of our own nation and society they do not seem so preposterous. We are perhaps too willing to accept the proposition that, because the United States is a paragon among nations (so the legend runs), its social distinctions, and even its racial distinctions, are confirmed by nature.

An exposition of equal brilliance from the opposition is to be found in Stephen Gould's (1981) *Mismeasure of Man*. Gould's concept of evolution is of general interest, and his account of the history of mental measurement and of Terman's activities is of specific interest to educators of the gifted. Gould takes a very dim view of IQ testing, which he regards as supportive of hereditarianism.

The essential social bias of hereditarianism, to which Gould and others object, is this: if intelligence is largely hereditary, then both blacks and "lower-class" children are naturally less apt, on average, than white upper-middle-class children. Such group differences, in an hereditarian interpretation, tend to be used to justify the social stratification and distribution of wealth and power of existing society.

The Authors' Orientation. We find that Gould's position on hereditarianism makes sense in a pedagogical context. Rather than affirm the existence of "intelligence" as a single-trait, adequately measured, biologically determined IQ, we prefer to believe that academic talent, however it may come into being, can—and must—be nurtured. This position necessarily implies that environment plays a very important role in talent development. Recent work by Bloom and his colleagues (Bloom, 1982; Bloom & Sosniak, 1981) indicates that the nurture of talent, even in prodigies, is undertaken before the presumed gifts become evident.

This view also acknowledges the reality of both individual differences and group differences in intelligence-test performance. It recognizes that poverty and black skin reduce an individual's life chances in our society (e.g., Duncan, 1968; Ryan, 1976). It also acknowledges the injustice of the fact that poor people and blacks are thus rendered less valuable and less valid as human beings.

If we could make the world anew, would we, however, really choose to turn all children into prodigies? Probably we would not, because our educational thought has traditionally placed a strong emphasis on moral, spiritual, and emotional growth (Cremin, 1961; Katz, 1968, 1971). Similarly, giving credence to environmental influences as a pedagogical principle is not an indication of belief in the ability of humankind to remake the world. That is, we cannot *assume*, like the educators of the time of Horace Mann, that education is necessarily a significant force for social change, even if we *hope* that it can make some difference.

Genus.   Who are the gifted children? What shall we do with them when we find them?

Though a number of definitions have been offered, none is acceptable to everyone. The definition adopted by the U.S. Congress in 1978 follows:

> The term gifted and talented children means children and, whenever applicable, youth who are identified at the preschool, elementary, or secondary level as possessing demonstrated or potential abilities that give evidence of high performance capabilities in areas such as intellectual, creative, specific academic, or leadership ability, or in the performing and visual arts, and who by reason thereof, require services or activities not ordinarily provided by the school.
>
> (From Section 902 of PL 95-561)

The current federal definition may well change in coming years. Moreover, state education agencies (SEAs) have generally adopted their own definitions, which they revise as they deem appropriate from time to time. Teachers in the various states must implement these local definitions, of course. We believe the following analysis and synthesis identifies the commonalities of many definitions and programs as they have been promulgated in recent decades. It relates them to goals that are particularly germane to gifted education.

As the federal definition indicates, however, there is a good deal of question about which talents a definition should include. To identify talent (after the Guilford Structure of Intellect model) in 120 separate mental functions, or an even greater range of combinations, would be impractical (see Box 1.2).

On the other hand, defining giftedness by the global IQ score may not take sufficient account of intraindividual differences. An individual may be quite talented academically, yet obtain scores that do not reach the two-standard-deviation IQ criterion necessary for placement in many programs. Single-factor theories of intelligence provide few clues about such a common phenomenon.

Thurstone's concept of primary mental abilities (Thurstone, 1938) may provide useful clues. Thurstone identified first four and later seven categories of mental ability: (1) verbal, (2) number, (3) spatial, (4) memory, (5) reasoning, (6) word fluency, and (7) perceptual speed. More recently, Howard Gardner

---

BOX 1.2   Guilford's Structure of Intellect Model

In the 1950s the psychologist J. P. Guilford began to report about a new model of intelligence, which he called "the structure of intellect" (SI). Guilford's model differs from other conceptions of intelligence in several ways (Guilford, 1959).

Guilford postulates three dimensions of intelligence. His model is conceived as a three-dimensional solid with x-, y-, and z-axes labeled to represent (1) contents, (2) products, and (3) operations. Subdivision of the three dimensions into four kinds of contents, six kinds of products, and five kinds of operations yields a structure of 120 combinations, or specific mental factors. Guilford (1959) reported that 50 specific factors had been identified. The SI model is the most extreme example of a multiple-factor theory of intelligence.

(1983) described a theory of intelligence organized around seven "frames of mind": (1) linguistic, (2) logical-mathematical, (3) spatial, (4) musical, (5) kinesthetic, (6) interpersonal, and (7) intrapersonal.

Many of the abilities or areas of intelligence postulated by Thurstone and Gardner relate to school learning. Tests currently available measure aptitude for or achievement in academic areas. Since schools have traditionally addressed certain types of learning, it may make more sense to define giftedness with respect to school learning than with respect to all the possible activities of the mind or the person.

ON BEING GIFTED: THE SPECIES

Although giftedness has been historically defined in terms of the notion of intelligence, we have said above that giftedness is better defined in terms of school learning, including the arts. The notion of arts talent accounts for student behaviors that have previously been inadequately addressed through the construct *creativity*. (See Chapters 2 and 10 for an extensive discussion of this issue.)

This portion of the chapter discusses three species of school-related giftedness: high-IQ giftedness, specific academic talent, and talent in the arts.

General Intelligence as Giftedness

As we have noted, traditional views of intelligence were developed primarily by psychologists interested in mental measurement. Early notions of intelligence were based on a theory of IQ as a unitary trait. In 1927 Charles Spearman proposed a two-factor theory of intelligence which was based on the notion that any mental test that measured intelligence contained two types of information, the information specific to the test (or "s") and the information representing an underlying general factor (or ''g''). This general factor was what Spearman and later Wechsler believed to be the best representation of the trait intelligence (Sattler, 1982).

Multiple-factor concepts of intelligence originated with Thorndike, who proposed three kinds of intelligence. Thurstone and Gardner, as we noted above, each defined seven, though not the *same* seven. Guilford proposed 120 independent mental abilities (see Box 1.2). Intelligence has also been conceived of in terms of fluid vs. crystallized intelligence (Cattell, 1963), as well as in terms of simultaneous vs. sequential intelligence (Kaufman & Kaufman, 1983).

The limitation of multiple-factor theories of intelligence (and certain other psychological constructs) is their problematic relationship to school learning (Guilford, 1959). Many theories, like Guilford's SI, seem more concerned with uncovering basic cognitive mechanisms than with discovering academic talent. The utility of IQ, by contrast, is that it has been shown consistently to predict school achievement, a utility that is lost when the general construct is infinitely subdivided.

Psychologists still do not know much about the cognitive processes required for learning science, mathematics, language, and the arts. They are not sure what processes, for example, are involved in mathematical analysis as opposed to literary analysis. They do not know if there are overarching processes that apply universally to learning.

Intelligence as represented by the IQ construct is certainly not an intellectual *process*. As a measurement paradigm, however, IQ successfully relates the construct intelligence to educational purposes. The use of IQ test scores is compatible with an educational definition of giftedness.

What is an educational definition of giftedness? The school curriculum forms a legitimate context in which to define giftedness. The curriculum addresses a relatively narrow spectrum of human endeavor: academic learning. Definitions that adhere closely to the academic context of schooling are the most likely to characterize a type of giftedness that schools actually can accommodate. IQ provides one practical means of predicting academic performance and therefore is a legitimate focus of such a definition.

Specific Academic Talents

IQ, as we noted, *predicts* academic achievement at least moderately well; it also embodies a sense of *potential*, which may not yet be realized as achievement; and it is a sort of global measure of academic functioning. All of these characteristics of IQ contrast with the more specific notion of academic talent.

Academic talent does not predict academic achievement—it *is* academic achievement. Present achievement, which defines academic talent, does not contain the same sense of potential that characterizes IQ. Of course, *present* achievement in one area predicts *future* achievement in that area, in much the same way that IQ predicts general school achievement. Its implications for talent development in the context of schooling are, however, clearer. Finally, exceptional talent (achievement) in one area does not, in itself, implicate students' total academic performance, though talent in one area is often associated with talent in other areas.

Qualitatively, the distinction between general intellectual giftedness and academic talent is slight. Both specific talent and general intellectual talent relate to significant portions of the school curriculum. We characterize these talents as (1) mathematical, (2) verbal, and (3) artistic. The first two are treated immediately below. The third is considered separately because its identification and nurture pose special problems in the context of schooling.

Mathematical Talent. Talent in mathematics has been studied from a number of different vantage points and in a number of different academic contexts. Ability in science in particular is often conceived of as being strongly related to the exercise of mathematical talent. Among the researchers who have studied math and science talents in the last thirty-five years are Roe (1952/1981), Brandwein (1955), Mackinnon (1962/1981), Taylor (1968), and Stanley (1974, 1976, 1977, 1981). Julian Stanley's Study of Mathematically Precocious Youth (SMPY), begun in 1971, has generated a great deal of interest in very apt young mathematicians. This project has not been limited to research, but has actively undertaken advocacy on behalf of talented young mathematicians.

Researchers have studied the personality traits and cognitive characteristics of talented mathematicians and scientists. Personality traits that correlate with mathematical ability include independence, reserve, and preference for abstract pursuits (e.g., Brandwein, 1955; Roe, 1952/1981). Weiss, Haier, and Keating (1974) found that mathematically talented boys studied by SMPY shared the following traits: flexibility, malleability, intelligence, quick-wittedness, even-temperedness, and foresightedness. An early interest in science, avid reading, and enjoyment of intellectual and solitary pursuits characterize the gifted scientist (Roe, 1952/1981).

In general, research suggests that individuals talented in mathematics and science exhibit the following cognitive traits to an exceptional degree:

1. *spatial visualization*—the ability to imagine and transform points, lines, and figures;
2. *manipulation of abstract symbols*—the ability to understand and apply symbol systems which describe processes and concepts; and
3. *reasoning skills*—the ability to conceptualize, organize, and solve problems in an orderly fashion.

The cognitive characteristics of gifted mathematicians and scientists are quite similar. In fact, since science is not a discrete discipline (but contains several separate disciplines), it is more practical to conceive of talent in science as a particular form of mathematical talent. We find that this view clarifies a number of difficult issues related to the identification and instruction of students who are talented in these fields. Suitable tests of science aptitude and achievement, for example, are not widely available, particularly at the elementary level. The tests that do exist frequently measure factual recall rather than conceptual sophistication.

Because students with exceptional mathematics ability differ considerably from other students, they require special instruction. Programs for these students may resemble those for high-IQ students, especially when the students' mathematical precocity is associated with high verbal ability. Programs for students whose talent is primarily mathematical may include rapid acceleration only in mathematics and related subjects. These students may not, for example, require special instruction in language arts.

Verbal Talent. Unlike mathematical talent, verbal talent is difficult to distinguish from general intellectual ability. Like high IQ, verbal precocity implies aptitude for most school learning. In the elementary grades, mastery of reading, spelling, and other language arts skills depends on verbal ability. Mastery of other subjects at this level, such as science and social studies, involves reading and listening comprehension almost exclusively. At the secondary level, aptitude for science depends more on mathematical talent.

Because IQ and verbal ability are so closely linked, few studies have selected subjects on the basis of *verbal talent* alone. Nevertheless, there are children whose verbal abilities are much more pronounced than their spatial and mathematical abilities.

Most studies of individuals with verbal talent have looked for personality correlates specific to that group. Such studies sometimes contrast personality traits of verbally apt students with those of mathematically talented students. Although there is much that these groups share, there are a few traits that seem to distinguish the two.

Bright children who score well in reading but poorly in arithmetic, for example, may be reluctant to express their feelings openly and lack self-confidence in comparison with children who score higher in arithmetic (D'Heurle, Mellinger, & Haggard, 1959). Other studies suggest a greater dependence on adults and less social interaction with peers among students of high verbal but low or average mathematical ability (McCarthy, 1979). When subjects are selected on the basis of high verbal achievement rather than on the basis of the contrast between high verbal and low mathematical achievement, the personality correlates are less negative. McGinn (1976) found verbally gifted youth, identified by SMPY, to be creative and interested in writing, reading, and other intellectual pursuits. Independence, imagination, originality, and spontaneity characterized the verbally gifted children in this study (McGinn, 1976).

Special education for children with high verbal ability should, in general, consist of modifications similar to those made for children identified as gifted because of their high IQ scores. For those children with *significant discrepancy* (see Chapters 2 and 11) between verbal achievement and mathematical achievement, however, acceleration in quantitative subjects (i.e., math, natural sciences) may not be appropriate. In fact, remedial work in mathematics may be an important element of individualization of instruction for such students.

Visual and Performing Arts

One of the most interesting areas of study to emerge in recent years is the early education of child prodigies, primarily in the arts. Studies of child prodigies and adults who have achieved worldwide acclaim as artists suggest the types of learning environment and instruction that are effective in the development of talents in the arts (Bloom, 1982; Bloom & Sosniak, 1981; cf. Pressey, 1955). Bloom and his fellow researchers were surprised to find that recognition of unusual potential typically came after early instruction, rather than prior to it (Bloom, 1982). Because instruction was begun so early, these children's outstanding abilities were acknowledged before they were out of their teens.

Educationally relevant correlates of prodigious talent have been found to be:

1. *Early identification:* Of over 400 adults recognized as musical prodigies, almost half were recognized as talented before the age of five and about 85 percent before the age of ten (Fliegler, 1961).
2. *Expert instruction:* After initial instruction, progidies were taught by *master teachers* in a tutorial setting. Bloom (1982) emphasizes the importance of the close match between ability and instruction which characterizes prodigies' education.
3. *Familial support:* The families of prodigies enjoy and participate actively in the field in which the children excel (cf. Galton, 1869/1962). Typically, they value the field to such an extent that they make unusual arrangements to nurture their children's interest in it. At least ten years of devotion to the talent area preceded eminent status in all of the artistically gifted adults studied by Bloom.

Other talented children may not benefit so much from instruction as do prodigies, but it is *almost certain* that their talent can be developed to a *much higher level* by providing expert instruction in a stimulating environment as early as possible (cf. Gould, 1981).

This research is provocative in light of the provisions for the nurture of artistic talent in the schools. School programs do not typically accord an important place to arts instruction. Often art and music programs, as the areas in which self-expression is emphasized, are considered *antidotes* for the way in which math and language arts are taught. In this sense, art and music serve a therapeutic or affective function, not an intellectual one. This conception of the arts cannot provide the context in which to nurture artistic talent (see Chapter 10 for an extensive discussion of the problems of education in the arts). The arts have a long academic history and a sophisticated intellectual content; these qualities of the arts necessitate special arts programs for students talented in the arts.

The specialized arts school provides a context in which the arts are valued earnestly and in which materials, resources, expert instruction, and opportunities for sustained work abound. It is a challenge to approximate this environment in most public schools. Before much change can occur in our schools, educators will need to understand better the important place of the arts in cultural and intellectual life.

Because the arts are considered to be more "creative" than math and literature, much that is known about arts talent comes secondhand from creativity research. Much of this research does, however, address the personality correlates of arts students. In general arts students are found to be

- *Intelligent:* Though not necessarily high-IQ gifted students, many score close to the gifted range, and others well within the gifted range. Most commentators believe that exceptional arts talent implicates general intellectual ability, and that an IQ of 120 or so is necessary for such talent to emerge and mature.
- *Nonconforming:* They do not always do what they are told; their ideas may appear odd to others. They are less concerned with pleasing others than are most children.
- *Engaged:* They are involved intellectually with their specialty and are exceptionally sensitive to its emotional nuances.

The growth of special programs has been slower in the visual and performing arts than in other academic areas. Traditionally, arts programs have been viewed as something of a luxury both by the public and by many educators. This view appears to be changing, however, and the number of programs to identify and develop giftedness in the arts is increasing (see Chapter 10).

Having explored the characteristics of children who can best be viewed as gifted *in the school context,* we turn our attention to the characteristics of school programs that serve these youngsters. Our particular emphasis in this introductory chapter is on the aims of such programs. Affirmation of the schools' traditional role in assisting cognitive development guides this discussion.

THE AIMS OF GIFTED EDUCATION

Educational aims express the general expectations of our society for its initiates, the children in schools. The aims of gifted education, therefore, articulate the sentiments of society toward the nurture of its most capable members. Some difficulties arise in specifying the aims of gifted education, however, because the most capable children do not always become the most innovative or productive adults. Nevertheless, gifted education attempts to serve children whose exceptional abilities distinguish them from their classmates.

The ways in which capable children are identified and the strategies used to develop their talents are determined by the values and goals of the educational community that serves these youngsters. The various approaches to gifted education reflect different views concerning the nature of giftedness and the goals of educating the population of gifted children.

This portion of the chapter explores the varying aims of gifted education. It considers aims that are primarily oriented toward social utility and those that are primarily directed toward individual talent development. Although these two sorts of aims are not mutually exclusive, their differences account, in part, for the considerable variation in current approaches to gifted pedagogy.

The Social Utility of Gifted Education

One rationale for educating gifted children is to provide society with highly trained leaders. Leaders in medicine, technology, and the arts, as well as in politics, are thought most likely to emerge from among the ranks of the gifted. Programs for gifted children that are based on this view emphasize both cognitive and affective development. This balanced approach is believed to enable such youngsters to develop the leadership skills necessary for their future roles.

Many different sorts of programs for gifted children are based on the premise that leadership training is the *principal* goal of gifted education. Programs stressing creativity and problem-solving, social and emotional development, and career education all share this aim. Although the theories behind them differ somewhat, these approaches are often combined in practice. Enrichment programs for gifted children frequently contain elements from all three approaches. We will now examine the origin and character of these approaches.

Creativity and Problem-Solving. Early in the progressive era, educators (e.g., Dewey, 1916/1961) began to concern themselves with children's problem-solving abilities. Brueckner (1932, p. 13), for example, believed that one important goal of instruction was "to develop in the individual a mind sensitive to problems and skilled in methods of solving them."

Later, methods of creative problem-solving (e.g., Crosby, 1968; Osborn, 1953) were developed in industry and applied to pedagogy. The expressed goal of these techniques was to ensure "that the economic supremacy of our country [be maintained] by the creative ability of our citizens" (Osborn, 1963, p. x).

Since that time, many approaches to gifted education have focused on developing the creativity and problem-solving skills of bright children. Some have emphasized the more rational processes of productive thinking (e.g., Covington & Crutchfield, 1965; Rogers, 1969). Others have stressed the intuitive processes that are presumed to condition creative production (e.g., de Bono, 1967; Gordon, 1961; Gowan, 1978; Khatena, 1978; Torrance, 1962). Still others have focused on developing the cognitive structures presumed to underlie all thinking processes (e.g., Gowan, 1972; Meeker, 1969; Myers, 1982; Norton & Doman, 1982).

Social and Emotional Development. The progressive era in U.S. education was responsible for a child-centered approach to instruction. This child-centered pedagogy was based on three educational principles which continue to influence gifted programs today. First, instruction was predicated on an understanding of child development. Second, the fundamental aim of education was viewed as the cultivation of the "whole child." Finally, the curriculum was determined (at least in part) by what the child was interested in studying.

The first two of these principles, in particular, promoted an approach to instruction that emphasized affective as well as cognitive aims. The affective portion of the school program was concerned with the moral, emotional, and spiritual development of children. As early as 1865 educators were concerned that "heart culture [i.e., affective education] . . . be paramount to brain-culture [i.e., cognitive education], moral culture to intellectual culture" (cited in Katz, 1968, p. 108).

Although child-centered education may on the surface stress concern for the development of individual talents, we classify this approach as being primarily oriented toward social utility. Our rationale for this classification is the persistent linkage between affective education and goals of socialization, citizenship, and leadership.

Three current approaches to the affective education of the gifted reflect the concern for developing the "whole child." One approach provides special counseling services to gifted children to offset pressures and adjustment difficulties that may accompany giftedness. Programs based on this approach may reflect psychoanalytic, behavioral, or ecological perspectives.

Another approach is based on developmental principles and is "concerned with the on-going growth of the child and not with *putting out fires* as they occur within the child's life" (Culross, 1982, p. 24). This perspective underlies programs that provide training to improve children's recognition and acceptance of emotions, communication of feelings, group interaction, and self-esteem (Clark, 1983).

A final approach combines cognitive and affective components to improve students' awareness of their values and actualization of their potential. Sisk (1982) considers values clarification particularly important for gifted children because of their advanced reasoning and critical sensitivity. By integrating discussion of issues with consideration of values, emotions, and aesthetic tastes, this approach to affective education is intended to help students become self-directed and well-integrated learners (cf. Lyon, 1971).

Career Education. Preparing students for adult vocations is an educational practice that also can be traced to the progressive era. Progressives emphasized both manual (i.e., vocational) training and life adjustment. Hofstadter (1963, p. 352) characterizes the life adjustment movement in secondary education as an attempt to "better equip . . . all American youth to live democratically with satisfaction to themselves and profit to society as home members, workers, and citizens."

Career education programs for the gifted are founded on several assumptions concerning both the nature of gifted students and the nature of work in our society. First, "the gifted and talented [are seen as] those who tend to do best in the labor market" (Hoyt & Hebeler, 1974, p. 63). Second, the gifted are defined by their "social contributions, productivity, and usefulness" (Hoyt & Hebeler, 1974, p. 192). Third, the encouragement of individual career choice is considered necessary for developing a satisfied and productive work force (Ottina, 1973). Finally, the marketplace is viewed as a fair testing ground, capable of both motivating excellence and rewarding merit (Eysenck, 1973).

Some gifted education programs are explicitly designed to provide career awareness or vocational training. Others are implicitly involved with developing noncognitive skills related to career performance. Mentorships and executive internships enable gifted students to have direct experience with work roles. Leadership training provides orientation to the affective expectations associated with particular roles in the employment hierarchy.

The career development goals of gifted education are conceived sometimes narrowly and sometimes broadly. In the narrow view, career education is considered an adjunct to other instruction (e.g., Fox, 1979a). In the broad view, all educational provisions for the gifted are seen as part of career preparation (e.g., Van Tassel-Baska, 1981). This broad conception of career development, in particular, reflects a view of gifted education shared by Galton and Renzulli and many others in between. It emphasizes the nurture of students most likely to become eminent adults. Since only a very few such children will become truly eminent, this view of gifted education also focuses on cultivating leaders in various fields of endeavor.

Individual Talent Development

A somewhat different goal orientation in gifted education emphasizes the development of talent regardless of its social utility. Those who view gifted education from this perspective generally have two goals: (1) to perpetuate an intellectual legacy and (2) to provide the kind of instruction that is most likely to develop students' demonstrated aptitudes. In this portion of the chapter we will explore the ramifications of these two goals. Together they justify an approach to gifted education that challenges traditional offerings.

Literacy and Rationalism.   Literacy is familiarity with the written word; rationalism is a method of applying reason to human endeavors. Together, literacy and rationalism define an intellectual tradition that underlies western civilization. From classical times through the modern era, literacy and reason have provided continuity in our cultural record. Although not all members of society have had equal access to the written word, some individuals in each era have inherited, enriched, and passed on the literate tradition.

In U.S. education today we like to think that all students have equal access to all opportunities. In reality, however, individual differences and social inequities limit the opportunities of some students and enhance those of others (Jencks et al., 1972). In spite of the unequal opportunities afforded some students within our schools, it is nonetheless important to sustain the traditions of literacy and rationalism.

In previous times, only particular constituencies had *any* connection to the literate tradition. Although access is more fairly distributed now, this tradition faces challenges posed by popular culture. Communication is no longer dependent on the written word; television, telephones, computers, and other electronic innovations have all hastened the process of communication and increased the quantity of information conveyed (McLuhan, 1964; Toffler, 1970, 1979). Nevertheless, if our culture is to have any record at all, written language must be valued by at least some constituency. For this reason, many private and some public schools continue to offer a ''classical'' curriculum to academically apt students.

This type of program is sometimes criticized as elitist. The criticism probably reflects an accurate assessment of the *history* of the literate tradition. In previous eras the cultural record was perpetuated by a small wealthy class. Even fundamental literacy (i.e., the ability to read and write) was conditioned by economic and social variables (Watt, 1957). In spite of this history, it is not necessary to link the ownership of the literate tradition with its content. In a more equitable society, that ownership can be shared by all those able to participate in it, through understanding, appreciation, and contribution. For this reason, the preservation and cultivation of an intellectual legacy should be at least one of the aims of public education.

Gifted children, moreover, have a special aptitude for participation in the traditions of literacy and rationalism. In fact, they are defined as gifted because of aptitudes that predispose them to formal learning: verbal precocity, reasoning ability, previous success in school subjects, talent in the arts.

Identifying children who demonstrate these aptitudes and providing them with an academic curriculum is not an elitist approach to education. Various artifacts of schooling, however, cannot be easily divorced from the history of literacy and rationalism in particular or the economic and social history of our culture in general. IQ tests, for example, are biased in favor of particular groups in society because their construction and use reflects that history. Because of their historical antecedents, many practices in gifted education are elitist to some degree. The goals of gifted education, however, need not be elitist, even considering the inequities of our society.

Development of Demonstrated Aptitudes.   Gifted children deserve differentiated instruction because they are likely to suffer without it. The characteristics that distinguish gifted children from others clearly have academic implications. Although the gifted are not granted the right to a special education by federal statute, they are acknowledged as exceptional by federal definition (see Box 1.3). Some states classify the gifted along with the handicapped; others provide for them separately (see Chapter 4). In either case, however, the method of identifying the gifted is analogous to the method of identifying the handicapped—they are located because of their deviation from

---

BOX 1.3   Public Law 94-142, The Education of All Handicapped Children Act of 1975

The Education of All Handicapped Children Act of 1975 (PL 94-142) established a national mandate to provide appropriate schooling to the handicapped. It also established detailed procedural safeguards to promote adherence to the law.

PL 94-142 mandated for handicapped children an education based on a child-centered pedagogy. These children were to be identified because of their individual differences and educated in accordance with their individual needs. To this extent, at least, special education for the handicapped parallels differentiated programming for the gifted.

Other provisions of PL 94-142 are not applicable to the gifted. In particular, the goal of normalization (i.e., least restrictive environment) does not apply to students who exceed normal performance. When the least restrictive environment principle is interpreted broadly to mean "environment least restrictive of cognitive development," however, it can be applied to the gifted as well as to the handicapped.

A knowledge of the provisions of PL 94-142 can help teachers of the gifted establish appropriate programs for bright children. These provisions include

- a free, appropriate public education,
- an individualized education program,
- education in the least restrictive environment,
- nondiscriminatory testing,
- parental notification and consent provisions, and
- procedures to ensure confidentiality.

Clearly, a federal law similar to PL 94-142 would make differentiated instruction for gifted children more accessible. Incorporation of PL 94-142 principles into state or local regulations may strengthen gifted services in particular regions. Some components of PL 94-142, however, have been difficult to implement for handicapped children. Legislation for gifted children might benefit from a critical review of the implementation record of PL 94-142.

---

the norm. Similarly, the goals for instructing the gifted can be equated with those for instructing the handicapped. Individualized education based on demonstrated need is an educational principle that applies equally to gifted and handicapped populations.

Implications for Gifted Programming

The need to develop talent suggests certain instructional principles that differ from those used to develop the *social utility* of gifted students. The goal of developing the strengths of academically talented children leads directly to a pedagogical tradition rooted in the history of literacy and rationalism.

Gifted children are particularly adept at school learning and should therefore be initiated into an intellectual tradition. Our conception of school learning includes

- *Literature as a discipline:* including the school subjects of reading, writing, oral language and the formal study of literature, history, and social sciences;
- *Mathematics as a discipline:* including the school subjects of arithmetic, precalculus higher mathematics, calculus, physics, and the mathematical aspects of natural and social sciences; and
- *The arts as disciplines:* art and music, primarily, since these are addressed by most public school programs.

It should be obvious that specific and generic skills such as spatial ability, perceptual speed, problem-solving ability, leadership, and creativity all have a role in the work of literature, mathematics, and the arts. Similarly, interpersonal intelligence has a good deal to do with the empathic understanding of literature, and intrapersonal intelligence with the traditional academic valuation of reflection and contemplativeness (cf. Gardner, 1983).

Thus, all these abilities can be addressed in the context of the above disciplines. Copley (1961), among others, has noted that creativity and problem-solving skills cannot be taught in isolation from an organized body of knowledge in which to apply them. It appears that in order to apply such skills, students need to work in a well-defined intellectual context (Bruner, 1960).

Another important element of giftedness is the notion of potential. Whereas talent is a demonstrable, but not fully mature skill, potential has more predictive connotations. The notion of measuring potential involves gauging not *typical* performance, as in the assessment of talent, but *optimal* performance. In this distinction lies the value of a global academic measure like IQ. In fact, the achievement of gifted children is *often* less extreme than their measured IQ.

From this perspective on talent and potential talent, two purposes can be construed for gifted programs:

1. to discover, fairly and accurately, children with academic potential and talent and
2. to advocate for and to provide appropriate education for such children.

SUMMARY

This chapter recapitulated historical and conceptual developments in gifted education. It highlighted issues of enduring importance, including the nature, measurement, and origins of talents of all sorts. It also examined IQ as a useful, but hardly ideal, global measure of academic talent.

Several species of giftedness were identified as belonging to the genus: high-IQ, verbal, mathematical, and artistic. The chapter reported differences and similarities among these species in terms of cognitive traits and personality traits. In general, it was apparent that, at least in descriptive terms, substantial commonalities do exist.

Finally, characteristics and history were related to the aims of gifted education, viewed through the two lenses of social utility and individual talent development. The concluding discussion related the aims of gifted education to curriculum and to program goals.

CHAPTER 2

Assessment and Interpretation: The Function of Evaluation

INTRODUCTION

Individual assessment includes procedures for determining program eligibility, designing appropriate instructional plans, and monitoring student progress. This last phase of assessment contributes significantly to program evaluation as well, since the aggregate of individual student progress reflects the instructional success of the program.

This chapter considers aspects of individual evaluation. In particular, it addresses concerns related to the determination of eligibility. The discussion focuses on three areas of giftedness: general intellectual talent, specific academic talent, and arts talent. We will consider assessment for program evaluation in Chapter 3 and assessment for individual program planning in Chapter 4.

Throughout this chapter, we emphasize the interrelatedness of various academic measures and the limitations, in particular, of the Intelligence Quotient (IQ). IQ may, we believe, reflect some aspects of academic potential. It does not, however, appear to be a unitary trait that reflects human worth or potential in general (cf. Gardner, 1983; Gould, 1981; Sternberg, 1977).

REFERRAL FOR ASSESSMENT

The identification process consists of several levels of decision-making. At each level, decision-making procedures must be carefully designed to select gifted children, while minimizing the number of children who are assessed but do not ultimately qualify for placement. If the persons responsible for identification at any level lose sight of requirements for placement, expenditures of effort, time, and money will be misdirected.

Definitions

Assessing children who do not later qualify is unavoidable; however, each "false positive" represents potential damage to the child and to the gifted program. No matter how much reassurance they are given, children who fail to qualify for the program are likely to suffer embarrassment and self-doubt. Although this is only a temporary source of discomfort to most children, it is a negative effect of the identification process and should be avoided not only for the sake of individual children but also for the sake of the program.

The way in which giftedness is defined, however, can sometimes make development and use of clear-cut eligibility criteria difficult. If a school system has adopted the federal definition provided in the Gifted and Talented Children's Act of 1978 (Section 902 of PL 95-561), a variety of placement requirements must be established based on the type of gifted program offered. The federal definition supports identification and special education for several categories of ability:

> The term gifted and talented children means children . . . who are identified at the preschool, elementary, or secondary level as possessing demonstrated or

potential abilities that give evidence of high performance capabilities in areas such as intellectual, creative, specific academic, or leadership ability, or in the performing and visual arts and who by reason thereof, require services or activities not ordinarily provided by the school.

(From Section 902 of PL 95-561)

States that have established programs refer to the gifted in statutes and define the term in regulations governing school districts' gifted programs.

However the gifted are defined, many children for whom special programs are intended will not be identified if assessment instruments fail to reflect the definition and eligibility requirements. Inappropriate referral, screening, or evaluation measures result in a waste of resources and damage to the credibility of the gifted program. Most important, the types of children selected for the program will not match program goals or methods. If academic criteria—IQ and achievement test scores—are used to identify children, it is logical to provide such children with a program that emphasizes academics. If children are selected for leadership ability, the program should provide leadership training primarily.

The most common reason for referral of children for gifted assessment is exceptional academic talent of some sort. An important part of many assessments is the comprehensive individual IQ test, although both the nature and the use of this sort of test have been criticized (e.g., Gardner, 1983). Because of the emphasis on identification of academic talent, however, discussion in this chapter will deal with issues related to IQ, academic aptitude, and achievement testing.

Characteristics and Referral Sources

About half the children who could score two standard deviations above the mean on a comprehensive individual intelligence test (the ninety-eighth or ninety-ninth percentile) are lost at the first level of the identification process (i.e., referral for testing). This significant loss results from problems with referral sources and procedures.

Effectiveness versus Efficiency. The purpose of referral and screening procedures is to locate students who will later be determined eligible by a qualifying evaluation measure. In the case of gifted students, the evaluation measure may, for example, be an IQ score of 130 on the Stanford-Binet. Screening and referral procedures select a comparatively small sample of students who are likely to meet the standards established by the evaluation measure. The Slosson IQ test may, for example, be used to select this sample. Following screening or referral, the (more thorough) evaluation measure is administered to the sample to develop information that will figure prominently in the determination of eligibility.

Referral and screening procedures attempt to maximize two variables simultaneously. First, they try to include *all* students who *will* score above the standard on the evaluation measure. This is effectiveness. Second, they try to select *no* students who will *not* score above the standard on the criterion measure. This is efficiency. The financial point of screening and referral procedures is to save school systems the expense of having psychologists administer lengthy individual tests to all students. Screening and referral procedures are never completely effective or efficient, of course. If they were, they would be unnecessary.

Effectiveness and efficiency are expressed as ratios. The two ratios that represent effectiveness and efficiency are constructed from three statistics:

1. all students who would be identified as gifted on an evaluation measure (e.g., Stanford-Binet),
2. all students selected for further evaluation by the screening or referral procedure (e.g., Slosson IQ Test), and
3. the intersection (overlap) of these two sets.

Effectiveness is the ratio of the number of students in set 3, above, to the number of students in set 1. *Efficiency* is the ratio of the number of students in set 3 to the number of students in set 2. Effectiveness is the number of students in set 3 as a percentage of all students who score above the standard on the criterion measure. Efficiency is the number of students in set 3 as a percentage of all students who are selected by the referral or screening procedure. When optimal effectiveness is about 100 percent, optimal efficiency is about 50 percent (see Box 2.1).

BOX 2.1 Effectiveness and Efficiency of Referral and Screening Procedures

A = set of students actually identified as gifted by criterion measure
B = set of students selected by screening or referral procedure
C = set of students common to both sets A and B

$$\frac{\text{number of students in } C}{\text{number of students in } A} = \text{effectiveness of referral or screening}$$

$$\frac{\text{number of students in } C}{\text{number of students in } B} = \text{efficiency of referral or screening}$$

The most common source of referrals is the classroom teacher (Marland, 1972). Studies show, however, that teacher referral excludes from 20 to 90 percent of the children who meet a high-IQ criterion of giftedness (Borland, 1978; Ciha, Harris, Hoffman & Potter, 1974; Jacobs, 1971; Pegnato & Birch, 1959; Rubenzer, 1979a; Terman, 1925). (These figures represent the effectiveness of referral.) The younger the students and the more mixed the racial and ethnic composition of the class, the less likely teachers are to recognize gifted pupils.

The effectiveness of teacher nomination is hampered by the stereotype of gifted children as highly motivated and well adjusted to school. The image of the gifted child as a physically superior, popular, enthusiastic participant in both academic and extracurricular programs was propagated by longitudinal research begun in the early 1920s by Lewis Terman (1925). Terman set out to discover whether adult "genius" could be predicted on the basis of childhood performance on the intelligence test he developed (i.e., the Stanford-Binet scale) and to identify characteristics common to the gifted throughout childhood, adolescence, and adulthood.

Recognizing that the selection process limited the degree to which results could be generalized, Terman (1925) speculated that gifted children not nominated for testing were not so positive, motivated, adaptable, or accelerated as children who were nominated. Terman in fact obtained a *subset* of the group of children who could score high above the mean on the Stanford-Binet Intelligence Scale (Terman & Merrill, 1973). Although the sample shares some characteristics with the entire gifted population, some of these children's traits, as Frierson (1965) notes, are *not* common to the group (e.g., high grades, parental aspirations for college attendance, interest in reading for pleasure, and superior physical development).

The nature of the school curriculum contributes to identification problems (Stanley, 1974). At each grade level, academic expectations are too low to differentiate gifted students from conscientious students of average or above average cognitive development. Bright children can make A's in most class work, since the personality traits of above-average children affect classroom performance at least as much as do cognitive factors (cf. Glidewell, Kantor, Smith & Stringer, 1966). Reliance on observed class work may cause teachers to refer average students instead of gifted students. Studies show that the percent of nonqualifying children referred by teachers ranges from about 90 percent (at the kindergarten level) to 30 percent (Borland, 1978; Jacobs, 1971; Weise, Meyers & Tuel, 1965). (These figures represent referral efficiency.) *Thus, success on assignments is not a good criterion for distinguishing those children who are highly capable from those who are appropriately challenged in the regular classroom.*

Recognizing the importance of finding sources and procedures to locate gifted children, Pegnato and Birch (1959) compared the relative effectiveness and efficiency of several referral methods (see Table 2.1). Their criterion for giftedness was an IQ score of 136 on the Stanford-Binet Intelligence Scale (a score that represents the highest 1 percent in ability as measured by that test at that time).

TABLE 2.1 **Effectiveness and Efficiency of Screening Procedures**

Screening Methods	No. Selected by Screening Method	No. Identified as Gifted by Stanford-Binet	Effectiveness[a]	Efficiency[b]
Teacher judgment	154	41	45.1	26.6
Honor roll	371	67	73.6	18.0
Creativity	137	14	15.5	10.2
Art ability	66	6	6.6	9.1
Music ability	71	8	9.9	11.2
Student council	82	13	14.3	15.8
Mathematics achievement	179	50	56.0	27.9
Group IQ test cutoffs				
IQ 115	450	84	92.3	18.7
IQ 120	240	65	71.4	27.1
IQ 125	105	40	43.9	38.1
IQ 130	36	20	21.9	55.5
Group achievement tests	335	72	79.2	21.5

[a]Percent of gifted located, $N = 91$.
[b]Ratio of number selected by screening to number identified as gifted, in percent.

From "Locating gifted children in junior high school" by C. Pegnato and J. Birch, *Exceptional Children*, 25 (7), 1959, pp. 300–304. Copyright 1959 by The Council for Exceptional Children. Reprinted by permission of The Council for Exceptional Children and J. Birch.

The study was conducted in a large urban junior high school with a predominantly middle- and upper-middle-class student population. The teachers were instructed to nominate gifted students in their classes. The researchers did not suggest qualities to consider when nominating students. Six other sources of referral were included in this comparison study: honor roll students, students on the student council, students who scored 115 IQ or above on a group test, students who averaged three or more grade levels above their grade placement on mathematics and reading subtests on a group achievement test, and students identified as gifted in music or in art by teachers in those fields. The Stanford-Binet was administered to all 781 children referred by these methods; of these, only 12 percent (91) had IQs of 136 or higher. (The comparatively large sample size—for a study administering individual IQ tests—explains the continued relevance of this study, now over twenty-five years old.)

Based on the comparisons of these referral methods, Pegnato and Birch

(1959, p. 253) concluded that "teachers do not locate gifted children effectively or efficiently enough to place much reliance on them for screening." Table 2.1 summarizes the results of the various methods of referral examined in the study. It provides only an index of the relative values of common referral methods.

Children who were referred by teachers comprised only 45.1 percent of the children identified as gifted; of the children referred, almost one-third were in the *average* range of intelligence. Of the children referred on the basis of grades, *82 percent failed to meet the criterion for giftedness.* Of the 371 children who were on the honor roll, only 67 (18.1 percent) were found to be gifted.

The most effective referral method involved a dual criterion. IQs of 115 or above on a group intelligence test *or* reading and math achievement scores three or more grade levels above grade placement located 96.7 percent of the gifted children.

Referral Alternatives.   Reliance on teacher perspective rather than on more objective measures seems unwarranted when placement in the gifted program requires an individual IQ or achievement test score in the ninety-eighth or ninety-ninth percentile. Instead of using subjective criteria based on stereotypes of giftedness, teachers could simply refer those children who have above-average group IQ or achievement test scores. According to Pegnato and Birch (1959), using a group IQ score of 120 in this dual-criterion approach yields *efficiency* comparable to that of teacher nomination. However, since these two criteria are considerably more *effective* than teacher nomination, locating about 75 percent of children with IQs of 136 or above (on an individual IQ test), this combination of measures is preferable to teacher referral. It also has the advantage of reducing the risk of teacher disappointment or distrust inherent in use of teacher-generated referrals.

Using parents as the referral source also shows promise. Parents provide better referrals than teachers, especially for young (i.e., preschool, kindergarten, and primary) children. Instead of overnominating children, as educators might expect, parents in general provide realistic estimations of their children's abilities. Parents in upper socioeconomic neighborhoods, however, tend to underestimate the likelihood that their children might require special programs because of outstanding academic ability (Roedell, Jackson & Robinson, 1980).

Peer referral has *not* been established as an accurate means of locating children who score in the top percentiles of individual IQ tests, although it is a commonly recommended identification method. The major benefit of peer referral is that children may know another student's particular hobbies or abilities (such as mechanical expertise) of which teachers may be unaware.

Though self-nomination has occasionally been used with apparent success in gifted programs, we know of no study that has investigated its effectiveness or efficiency. This method is one of the least researched, and probably least used, identification processes.

Consistency of Referral and Placement Requirements

No matter what the source of the referral, guidelines are needed to ensure that nominations and placement requirements are consistent. The guidelines most commonly used are checklists of personality traits or behaviors supposedly characteristic of gifted children.

Checklists as Referral Guidelines.   Many school systems use checklists that are conglomerates of items describing traits of children identified as gifted according to diverse criteria. Gleaned from research studies that have defined giftedness in different ways, some items are associated with children who score high on tests of divergent thinking, some are associated with students who score high on IQ tests, and some are associated with pupils who succeed on achievement tests.

Though one of their strengths is that they are easily administered, checklists often fail to address placement criteria; they include irrelevant items. Items that are helpful in identifying one type of giftedness may be useless in identifying another.

The practice of using checklists that are composites of research findings is likely to promote referral of the above-average, well-rounded child and to suppress referral of the gifted child who is not well-rounded. For example, the Scale for Rating Behavioral Characteristics of Superior Students (SRBCSS) (Renzulli, Smith, White, Callahan & Hartman, 1977) is used in its entirety by many districts regardless of whether all of its sections are applicable to the type of giftedness the schools wish to identify. Lowrance and Anderson (1977) found that only the learning characteristics sections of the SRBCSS correlated with superior IQ scores on the Wechsler Intelligence Scale for Children–Revised. If a high score on a comprehensive IQ measure is required for entry, use of other sections of the scale (e.g., leadership characteristics) confounds the selection process.

Some checklists include items of questionable validity for identifying *any* type of giftedness (Berg, 1980, p. 32):

> uses a lot of common sense,
> is friendly and outgoing, and
> likes to play.

It is unlikely that these items will help discriminate gifted children from children with average intelligence.

Still another problem with checklists is inclusion of items so general that inter-judge reliability is likely to be low—for example, "has a wide range of interests" (Berg, 1980, p. 32). Items as general as this are subject to many influences that have nothing to do with the child's ability, such as whether the respondent observes representative behavior, whether the respondent has a positive attitude toward the child, or whether the respondent is familiar with behavior typical of children of that age.

Hagen cautions educators that none of the referral checklists available has been established as valid and reliable:

> Many of them are what the writer would call pseudopsychometric instruments. Many of them consist of series of ambiguous statements to be checked yes or no for each student and then tell the user to add the yeses to obtain a total score. The total score is meaningless and useless because the . . . statements do not represent a scale and therefore cannot be added together.
>
> (Hagen, 1980, p. 26)

Referral Compromises.   Teachers, parents, and peers need guidelines to refer children for testing. In order to avoid unnecessary expense, counterproductive testing, and dissatisfaction with the identification process, guidelines *must* be valid, reliable, and unambiguous (Roedell et al., 1980).

On a parent questionnaire designed to identify gifted children ages two through five, Roedell et al. (1980, p. 58) included the following items:

- Does your child read, not just listen to, books such as *Winnie the Pooh* or *Little House on the Prairie*, which contain long stories and few pictures? Examples of sentences found in these books are "He split each log straight down the middle," and "Nothing had ever been so tempting as that watermelon on that hot day."
- Does your child comment on words that have two or more meanings?

If children are to be placed on the basis of academic criteria, items similar to those above are appropriate. If children are to be placed on the basis of other criteria, such as expert judgment of artwork, then checklists should include only items that reflect artistic skills and interest.

We recommend that those who select or develop questionnaires and checklists *for referral* (not for screening or evaluation) consider the problems common to these informal measures and collect evaluative data concerning their use in particular instances.

A combination of standardized tests and referral checklists can offset the limitations of each type of measure *as a source of referrals.* Since group standardized tests are based on dominant-culture values, the abilities of poor children, bilingual children, and handicapped children may be underestimated. Nomination on the basis of observed performance at home or in the classroom is especially critical as an alternative route *to referral.*

Good referral procedures are based on an awareness of gifted children's characteristics and educational needs. Support for referral efforts will develop once teachers, parents, and administrators become convinced that exceptional arrangements for the gifted constitute good pedagogy. Equally important for acceptance of gifted programs is the understanding that differentiated instruction that is appropriate for the gifted is inappropriate for the average student. This implies that both parents and teachers need to understand (1) the kinds of children who require exceptional arrangements, (2) the reasons they require such exceptions, (3) the types of programs available for them, and (4) the procedures by which students are declared eligible.

EVALUATION OF INTELLECTUALLY AND ACADEMICALLY GIFTED STUDENTS

As we have seen, referral identifies a pool of candidates who might be eligible for special programming. More comprehensive assessment practices, often termed evaluation, are used to select gifted students from this pool of candidates. Evaluation procedures differ according to the type or types of programs available. In Chapter 1 we examined three categories of giftedness: IQ giftedness, academic talent, and artistic talent. We will now consider methods of evaluating candidates in each of these domains. Since it is difficult to make a clear distinction between IQ giftedness and academic talent, we will consider evaluation procedures for these aspects of giftedness together.

Evaluation of academically and intellectually advanced students to determine their eligibility for differentiated instruction should involve a comprehensive process of assessment. Assessment is defined by Salvia and Ysseldyke (1981, p. 4) as "the process of understanding the performance of students in their current ecology . . . [as] an evaluative, interpretative appraisal of performance." Testing, on the other hand, is considered a "tool" for assessment (Sattler, 1982, p. 6), and tests are viewed as "sampling device[s] within a larger strategic framework" (Swanson & Watson, 1982, p. 6). Evaluation is assessment directed to a particular end; testing is one technique of assessment. (See Figure 2.1.)

Protection in Assessment

Before we consider specific evaluation practices, it is important to review procedures for protecting students who are being evaluated. Although various types of mental tests have been used with increasing frequency during the last eighty years, their use has not been monitored until recently. Litigation and legislation have now defined some of the boundaries of appropriate testing practice, but the mystique of mental testing continues to obscure abuses in test administration and interpretation.

In general, protection-in-assessment procedures are less widely established for the gifted than for other exceptional children. This is because the gifted are not protected by the provisions of PL 94-142 (the Education of All Handicapped Children Act of 1975) and are not necessarily protected or provided for by state mandate (cf. Mitchell, 1981b). Additionally, the issue of equal education opportunity for handicapped students has tended to eclipse concern for appropriate educational opportunity for advanced students.

PL 94-142 Protection.   Provisions for protection in the assessment of handicapped students are specified in the federal regulations for PL 94-142. These provisions set minimum standards for the appropriate assessment of hand-

FIGURE 2.1 Assessment, Evaluation, and Testing

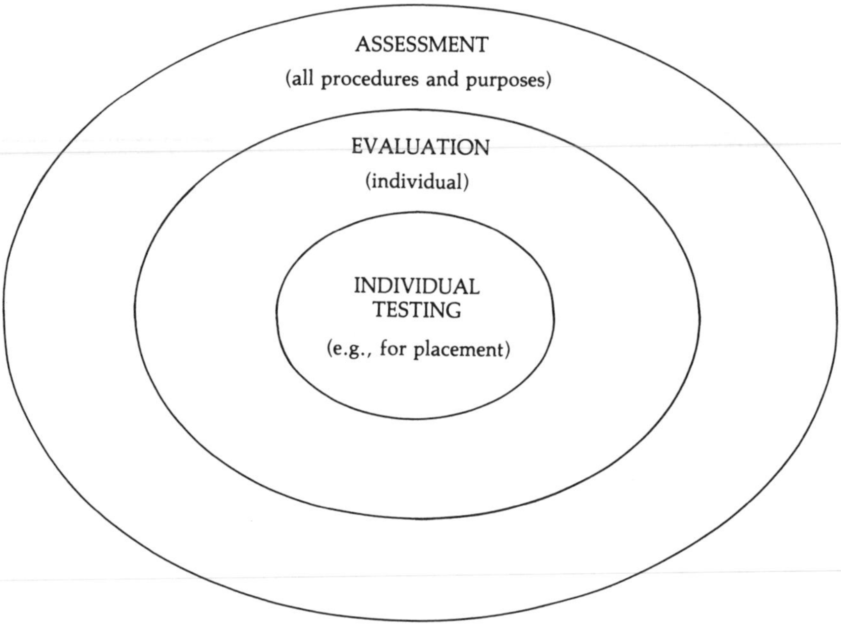

ASSESSMENT
(all procedures and purposes)

EVALUATION
(individual)

INDIVIDUAL
TESTING
(e.g., for placement)

icapped students but are equally applicable to the evaluation of gifted and potentially gifted students.

These provisions include the right to a multidisciplinary assessment at public expense, the requirement that testing materials be nondiscriminatory, and the stipulation that testing be administered in the child's native language. In addition, the regulations require that tests be administered by trained personnel, following the instructions provided by the test constructors, and that tests be used only for the specific purposes for which they have been validated.

Other provisions of PL 94-142 may contribute little to protection in the *evaluation* of the gifted. These include the requirement that tests other than IQ tests be used to determine a student's specific educational needs and that no one test be used as the sole criterion for determining a student's educational placement (45 CFR 300.532). Such provisions protect handicapped children from erroneous placement in restrictive programs. Since gifted programs are not restrictive in this sense, eligibility determination might be based on criterion-level performance on one of several equivalent sorts of instruments (e.g., IQ tests, aptitude tests, *or* achievement tests). Assessment for program planning, however, should always consider achievement, classroom performance, and other characteristics as well as IQ.

Procedural safeguards included in PL 94-142 specify the rights of exceptional students and their parents in relation to notification of referral for evaluation, consent for testing, and notification of evaluation results. These procedural safeguards include the right to an impartial due process hearing if parents do not agree with the decision of a local education agency (LEA) concerning their child's referral, evaluation, placement, or instruction in a special education program (see Chapter 4).

Parents and/or exceptional students also are afforded the right to an independent educational evaluation, results of which must be considered in any meetings concerning the child's educational placement. Parents must be reimbursed by the LEA for this independent evaluation if the LEA's evaluation is found to be inadequate or incorrect by the impartial hearing officer. However, in order for parents to obtain this reimbursement, they may have to initiate a due process hearing to prove that the assessment procedures or results were unsatisfactory (Martin, 1979).

In general, the federal regulations governing protection in assessment provide a reasonable framework for conducting multidisciplinary assessments in all special education programs. Adherence to these regulations is often perfunctory rather than substantive, however, because local policy concerning the assessment process frequently prescribes *efficient* testing practice rather than *optimal* testing practice (cf. Poland, Thurlow, Ysseldyke & Mirkin, 1982).

In addition, evaluation of IQ is sometimes given inordinate status in the multidisciplinary assessment process (cf. Gardner, 1983). Psychologists may overestimate the significance of intelligence tests because of the training required to use them. Although IQ may be an important component of a gifted evaluation, information provided by other members of the assessment team (e.g., teachers, educational evaluators, and parents) is valuable for placement or program planning (Ysseldyke, Algozzine & Mitchell, 1982). The equal participation of all team members in making decisions is the rationale for multidisciplinary assessment.

Optimal Evaluation Practices for the Gifted

Although federal regulations governing protection in assessment have improved evaluation practice, these requirements may not be sufficiently specific. Certain additional guidelines may increase the comprehensiveness and the fairness of evaluation practices for the gifted. Evaluation procedures that are based on these guidelines, as well as on PL 94-142 provisions, are optimal for evaluating gifted students. The guidelines most important for optimal evaluation of the gifted are specified in the following procedures.

Optimal Evaluation Practices

1. using criteria from *either* an aptitude, achievement, *or* IQ test to determine placement in gifted programs,

2. using individual tests rather than group tests,
3. using tests suitable for their designated assessment function(s),
4. using qualified examiners to administer tests,
5. using culture-fair testing and placement practices, and
6. obtaining parental consent for testing.

Using Achievement Tests for Placement.   As we observed in Chapter 1, a primary function of schools is to transmit the formal knowledge that represents our culture. Gifted *students* are those with at least the potential to develop intensive and extensive repertoires of academic behaviors.

It seems clear, however, that if IQ tests measure potential and if potential represents how well individuals *can* perform, then accurate IQ testing must depend on eliciting optimal samples of whatever behaviors reflect *maximum performance* (Lyman, 1968). Achievement tests, on the other hand, measure actual accomplishments and *typical performance.*

To demonstrate achievement reliably without, however, possessing the potential to do so is a logical impossibility. In cases where achievement has been reliably demonstrated, low IQ test results are unreliable measures of students' giftedness.

Similarly, it is possible for students to demonstrate academic potential (i.e., high IQ) without academic achievement if they have not encountered an environment that adequately engages their potential. Some high-IQ students do not demonstrate the criterion behavior of giftedness, and their scores on achievement tests fall below their scores on IQ tests.

For these two reasons, both achievement and IQ tests should be used in the identification of gifted students. This provision protects two sorts of children. First, it grants access to advanced work to students with the demonstrable readiness for such work, regardless of IQ scores. Second, it grants access to an intellectually nurturing and emotionally supportive environment to gifted students who are not achieving well.

In effect this provision parallels the PL 94-142 requirement that placement not be based on the results of any single instrument. The idea behind gifted education is to identify and serve children who can excel in school. IQ measures capture some, but not all, of these children. Achievement measures capture some, but not all, of these children. Since both sorts of measures are useful for program planning, and since both apply to academic aptitude and learning, it makes sense to look at both when students are evaluated.

Using Individual Tests Instead of Group Tests.   The use of individual rather than group tests is supported in most literature on assessment, especially when the purpose of testing is to make educational placement decisions (e.g., Anastasi, 1968; Rubenzer, 1979a; Salvia & Ysseldyke, 1981). In general, the practice of using individual tests for evaluation of students is advocated because these tests are more likely to provide a true representation of students' abilities or levels of achievement.

Limitations of group tests include both technical problems (such as the inappropriately low ceiling resulting from the inclusion of only those items specific to a particular level) and problems in administration (such as the examiner's inability to establish rapport in a group setting). These difficulties reduce the likelihood that a group test will provide a valid or reliable assessment of a child's performance. According to Rubenzer (1979a), gifted children are actually penalized by group intelligence testing (see the discussion earlier in this chapter on the use of group IQ tests for generating *referrals*).

Using the Appropriate Assessment Instrument. A related guideline involves the use of appropriate assessment instruments in making different types of educational decisions. Salvia and Ysseldyke (1981) identify five purposes of educational assessment: (1) screening, (2) placement (i.e., individual evaluation in our discussion), (3) individual program planning, (4) program evaluation, and (5) evaluation of individual progress. The use of tests that are appropriate for the specific purposes intended is crucial to valid and effective assessment. "If we fail to consider the purposes for which a test was administered, we may use that test inappropriately" (Salvia & Ysseldyke, 1981, p. 14).

The misuse of screening test data to determine educational placement occurs frequently, especially in the identification of the gifted. Duffey, Salvia, Tucker, and Ysseldyke (1981, p. 431) define screening as a procedure for collecting data "to help professionals identify the extent to which a student's behavior differs from 'normal' or 'average' behavior. Students whose behavior sufficiently deviates from the 'normal' are typically identified as candidates for further assessment."

Only comprehensive, individually administered tests of ability, aptitude, and achievement are sufficiently accurate to be used in determining educational placement (Martinson, 1979). Marland's (1972) comparison of "experts'" recommendations with actual school practices for identifying the gifted indicates that whereas 90 percent of the experts recommended the use of individual intelligence test scores, only 23 percent of school districts used this method of identification. The situation has improved in recent years, no doubt, but some school systems still choose less costly screening procedures for the educational placement of the gifted.

Using Qualified Examiners. Another practical guideline which seems almost self-evident is the PL 94-142 requirement that tests be administered by qualified examiners. Since the single most accurate method of identifying the gifted is the individual, comprehensive intelligence test (Martinson, 1979), assessment teams often must rely on psychologists to administer and interpret the examinations that determine students' eligibility for placement in gifted programs.

The ability of psychologists to carry out this critical evaluative role depends on a thorough understanding of the range of responses to testing commonly exhibited by gifted children. Psychologists should be able to determine when extraneous characteristics such as fear of failure, perfectionism, fear of appearing different, or divergent thinking affect test performance adversely. In addition, they should be willing to probe (during testing) or research (after testing) atypical or even seemingly absurd responses to test items. Such responses from apt students may result from thinking that exceeds the normal range.

Finally, psychologists should be aware of the limitations of accepting scores derived from performance at or near the ceiling of a test or subtest. Salvia and Ysseldyke (1981, p. 125) caution, "Tests often lose their power to discriminate near the extremes of the distribution."

An understanding of assessment considerations peculiar to the gifted might be obtained through course work, practicum experience with the gifted, or a reading of the literature on the assessment of the gifted. At least one of these approaches should be included in the required training of any psychologist or psychometrist who is permitted to evaluate students for possible placement in a program for the gifted.

Using Culture-Fair Evaluation Practices.   The stipulation of PL 94-142 that school systems provide nondiscriminatory evaluations is reflected in two specific guidelines. The first requires that tests be administered in the child's native language or other mode of communication and the second requires that tests be used solely for the purposes for which they have been validated (45 CFR 300.532). These guidelines may not be sufficient, however, to ensure that evaluation is culture-fair.

Simply asking children test questions in their native languages does not account for the culture patterns that condition their responses. In addition, it may not even reflect "the language . . . minority children speak [which] is an adulterated Spanish [or other language] resulting from the constant interaction with an English-speaking school and a Spanish-speaking [or other non-English-speaking] home" (Samuda, 1975, p. 93).

The use of specifically validated instruments may not eliminate discriminatory assessment practice. The tests most frequently cited as discriminatory are statistically validated for use with minorities. These tests are standardized on a normative sample that includes minorities. This procedure is thought to validate tests such as the Stanford-Binet and the WISC-R for minority children (see Chapter 11).

Those who argue against the use of these validated instruments often cannot propose more valid alternatives. The culture-free tests advocated by some are merely nonverbal IQ tests. To consider these IQ tests free from cultural content because they do not include verbal items or require verbal responses is to underrate the extent of cultural influence on the *entire* behavioral repertoire of children. In fact, minority students "have been shown to perform, if not more poorly, at least just as badly [on culture-free] tests as they do on conventional intelligence measures" (Samuda, 1975, p. 142; cf. Jensen, 1973).

Another alternative to culture-biased tests involves the use of culture-specific measures. They measure what Scarr (1981, p. 443) refers to as the "social competence" of children within their cultural or subcultural group. Since significant within-group cultural variation occurs among children of the same race, nationality, ethnic heritage, or socioeconomic class, one measurement instrument would not even be applicable to all children from one group. Even if a variety of such tests were available, the development of methods to assess the fairness of a particular instrument for a given child would be a technical nightmare.

Mercer (1981) has developed a culture-specific assessment system that evaluates scores from the WISC-R in terms of students' socio-cultural backgrounds. She suggests using this system for identifying gifted as well as handicapped children from minority cultures (Mercer, 1981). Mercer's System of Multicultural Pluralistic Assessment (SOMPA) has been criticized by Salvia and Ysseldyke (1981) for its lack of technical data, by Samuda (1975) for its reliance on a dominant-culture-specific test, and by Sattler (1982) for its failure to account for a sizable portion of the variance in the WISC-R scores of blacks and Hispanics. In the absence of other approaches to culture-fair assessment (e.g., locally derived norms, minority-group quotas), the Mercer technique may provide minority students the access to gifted programs they deserve.

The most promising approach to culture-fair assessment, however, involves the use of local, regional, or minority-group norms. The rationale for using local or minority-group norms is to identify the children with the highest potential or achievement from a particular school or a particular subgroup of the population. Since the purpose of culture-fair testing for gifted placement is to provide suitable cognitive instruction to members of all subgroups, it seems reasonable to look to artifacts of culture and of testing to explain the lower mean performance of blacks and other minorities (notably the poor) on standardized tests. Given the premises of culture-fair testing, the most cognitively apt children in population subgroups require differentiated instruction *even if they are not among the highest-scoring children in the population as a whole*. Specific techniques for establishing local norms are described by Messick and Anderson (1974). The advent of microcomputer hardware and statistical software programs should make the derivation of local norms much easier. (See also Chapter 11 on cultural underachievement.)

Obtaining Parental Consent. A final guideline for conducting fair evaluations of gifted and other exceptional children involves obtaining parental consent for such evaluation. PL 94-142 requires that parents of handicapped children be notified prior to any evaluation and that they give consent prior to an initial preplacement evaluation. In many states these requirements are not stipulated for evaluations of gifted and potentially gifted students. In the absence of consent provisions, parents are unable to monitor or influence testing practices.

Norm- and Criterion-Referenced Tests: General Concerns

Although in general we recommend the use of norm-referenced measures for determining the eligibility of children for placement in gifted programs, we recognize the importance of criterion-referenced tests as well. These two types of measurement are distinguished in the following way: "norm-referenced devices . . . compare an individual's performance to the performance of his or her peers; criterion-referenced tests measure a person's development of particular skills in terms of absolute levels of mastery" (Salvia & Ysseldyke, 1981, pp. 29–30).

The choice of a norm- or a criterion-referenced measure is determined by the need of the assessment team to consider a particular type of information about a student. In current practice, norm-referenced tests are frequently used to evaluate eligibility and criterion-referenced tests to assess skills for individual program planning.

Determination of eligibility based on the most accurate norm-referenced measures available is a requirement when schools can provide individual programs to only a few students. If schools, however, were designed to allow children to "learn at their own rates . . . pursue ideas and activities to whatever depth possible, . . . those children with special needs would begin to emerge very early. An education program designed to meet each person's needs from the beginning of school [would] better show us those children with high cognitive ability than any single test instrument" (Clark, 1979, p. 13).

In such schools, criterion-referenced tests could be used by educators to assess the actual competence of individual students rather than to try to predict their likelihood of attaining competence (McClelland, 1980). However, until our society changes schools to accommodate the needs of every individual student, the use of criterion-referenced tests for determining eligibility may be *more discriminatory* than the use of norm-referenced measures. In the context of current pedagogical practice, criterion-referenced tests measure differences in exposure to educational advantages, not differences in the ability to benefit from such advantages. In fact, *no measurement tool yet devised* has been able to transcend the cultural, political, social, and economic import of schooling.

The selection of appropriate assessment instruments involves a process of *approximating* objectivity and *attempting* fairness. Use of these instruments involves an imperfect resolution of the contradictions between (1) the principle of standardized test administration and interpretation and (2) the need to evaluate optimal learning potential.

Testing Intelligence

Since eligibility for placement in a gifted program often depends on high performance on an IQ test, it is important to understand the uses, misuses, and varying interpretations of evaluation instruments designed to measure intelligence. We will therefore explain both the IQ construct and methods for deriving IQ scores before we attempt to describe the use of such measures in assessing giftedness.

History.   Much has been written on the nature of intelligence, its origin, its malleability, and its representation as a quantity. Historically the IQ originated not as a ratio (or quotient) between mental age and chronological age but as the difference between age level performance and chronological age.

The first IQ test was referenced directly to the school curriculum: Binet developed test items from exercises that teachers used in French schools. He used these sample items to predict how well students would perform on similar tasks in the school setting (McClelland, 1980). Binet's procedure was not unlike that used by teachers in developing criterion-referenced tests for measuring skill and content mastery. The scope of Binet's test was large, however, with items spanning many areas of cognition as well as many performance levels. On his test, items were used to represent the ability to master skills rather than as proof of previous mastery.

On the 1908 version of his scale, Binet assigned age levels to each item, thus establishing a basis for quantitative comparison of relative performance. By subtracting the total age level score or mental age (MA) from the chronological age (CA), Binet was able to locate those students who were functioning significantly below the expectation for performance at their chronological age. This procedure for determining discrepancy did not account for the relative significance of score disparities at various chronological ages (Gould, 1981). This technical difficulty was solved in 1912 by Wilhelm Stern, who proposed that the disparity be expressed not as a difference but as a quotient. Thus, he developed the formula for calculating the ratio IQ:

$$\frac{MA}{CA} \times 100 = IQ$$

Binet probably did not believe that his scale measured intelligence. He wrote, "The scale, properly speaking, does not permit the measure of intelligence, because intellectual qualities are not superposable, and therefore cannot be measured as linear surfaces are measured" (Binet, cited in Gould, 1981, p. 151).

In fact, Binet articulated the notion of IQ as an *inference* from a sample of behavior when he indicated that a larger sample of items would be more accurate than a smaller one. This belief is similar to a defensible contemporary view of intelligence testing: "intelligence tests are samples of behavior. Regardless of how an individual's performance is viewed and interpreted, intelligence tests and items on those tests simply sample behaviors" (Salvia & Ysseldyke, 1981, p. 244).

Key Issues. Since Binet's time, arguments concerning the measurement of intelligence have depended on several key issues. The first of these relates to the source of variations in intelligence among individuals and among subgroups of the population. Ultimately, this issue devolves to a consideration of the origin of intelligence, with opposing positions being the hereditarian (or biological determinist) view that intelligence is a genetically transmitted trait (e.g., Jensen, 1981) and the environmentalist view that intelligence is a behavioral repertoire acquired during the critical period of child development (e.g., Scarr & Weinberg, 1976). A mediate position explains differences in measured intelligence as resulting from the interaction between inherited traits and environmental conditions (e.g., Jencks et al., 1972).

A second related issue is the degree to which IQ measures sample one unitary trait. Both single-factor and multiple-factor theories of intelligence (see Chapter 1) regard intelligence as a thing or collection of things that can be quantified, standardized, and assigned differentially to individuals and groups of individuals. This process is aptly described by White (1977, p. 34) as "a technology for directing an uncertain measurement paradigm toward an undefined entity."

If one views intelligence as a trait or an aggregate of traits, one must establish a method for ensuring that mental tests actually measure the trait or that the subtests adequately represent the salient constellation of traits which comprise intelligence. Ironically, the same conclusions about the nature of abilities are used both to verify the existence of mental traits and to justify the use of particular tests to measure those traits. The reasoning is tautological, since the identification of these mental abilities depends on the factor analysis of those constructs (or vectors) most thoroughly resolved in performance on a particular mental test or subtest (Gould, 1981). Thus, the abilities measured by intelligence tests are actually the same abilities defined by those tests.

This circular reasoning is apparently justified by the adherence of mental-test performance to the normal curve. But since the assumption is made that intelligence in the population is distributed in conformity with the normal curve and since the items comprising mental tests are "selected after trial for conformity with the normal distribution" (Morrison, 1977, p. 84), this rationale is equally tautological.

In comparison to the questionable *construct* validity of intelligence tests, their *predictive* validity (though only moderate) is fairly well established. Even some critics of IQ testing (e.g., Lyman, 1968; McClelland, 1980) admit that these tests predict school success, but they contend that this predictive accuracy occurs not as a result of the technical adequacy of IQ tests but as a result of the social variables that influence both IQ and school performance. Nevertheless, as we saw in Chapter 1, the relationship of IQ tests to school learning is clear. When IQ tests are used to measure the potential for school learning, they identify students with particular aptitude for school learning.

Measures of Optimal Performance: Recent Trends. The identification of gifted children depends on the use of tests to evaluate optimal performance. Operationally, this means using information about what children have learned to judge what they are capable of learning (cf. Bloom, 1964). However, the procedure used to assess learning may interfere with an accurate determination of learning potential. Testing may intimidate some students so that performance suffers (cf. Haggard, 1980). Test items may be phrased in unfamiliar language so that errors are made by children who would respond correctly if items were worded differently. In addition, scoring procedures may not account for intelligent responses that differ from prescribed responses.

As a result of these and other limitations of standard test administration procedures for assessing optimal learning potential, several theorists have recently suggested techniques for revising test administration practices (Lidz, 1981). These techniques include (1) the development of different types of tests, to assess, for example, "nonentrenched" tasks and concepts (Gardner, 1983; Sternberg, 1982, 1984), (2) the use of specific interview procedures to evaluate the reasoning underlying students' responses (Alvino & Wieler, 1979), (3) the training of students in tasks similar to those encountered on IQ tests (a procedure called "trial programming" by Karnes and Bertschi, 1980), and (4) the use of a verbal praise procedure during testing (Saigh, 1981). The goal of such testing techniques is an appraisal of the likelihood that a student would benefit from a particular type or level of instruction.

If procedures designed to assess optimal performance are used to evaluate children for placement in gifted programs, the norms derived from the standardization of the tests used will be meaningless for interpreting the results of these alternative test administrations. Therefore, school districts must develop local, regional, or subgroup norms based on the nonstandard testing practices they adopt.

Circumspect Use of IQ Tests.   The fair use of IQ tests depends on an interpretation of their limited utility. The process of assessing giftedness is, by its very nature, a process of identifying those children whose educational needs substantially deviate from normal educational needs. Since only some children can be provided instruction in individualized special programs, those served should be those whose educational needs are the most different from the norm.

Because the determination of average educational needs depends on regional, cultural, ethnic, and socioeconomic variables, such needs will differ from school to school. The more the local sample used to renorm a test is representative of a particular subpopulation, the more accurate locally derived norms will be in providing criteria for discriminating between normal and deviant performance in the subpopulation. Thus, the assessment of optimal performance coupled with local norming data would do a great deal to increase the accuracy and the fairness of procedures used to determine gifted program eligibility in atypical locales.

The Tests Themselves

Tests that assess academic talent (i.e., giftedness) can be divided into two general categories: those applicable for screening and those applicable for evaluation. Screening instruments are useful for identifying children who might score at a particular criterion level on an evaluation test. Evaluation instruments are used to determine eligibility for placement in a special program.

Although the classification of particular tests as either screening or evaluation instruments is somewhat arbitrary, it reflects two psychometric principles worth consideration. First, screening tests generally sample fewer behaviors than evaluation tests and are, therefore, less sensitive to qualities (like intelligence) that are characterized by a complex set of behaviors. Second, because many screening tests require no more than thirty minutes to administer, the examiner is often unable to assess noncognitive student responses that may influence test performance, such as test anxiety, degree of rapport with the examiner, frustration, or perfectionism).

Measuring IQ. One category of IQ tests is of particularly questionable value in the evaluation or even screening of gifted children (though we have discussed the way in which such tests can be useful for generating referrals). This category includes group IQ tests such as the Otis-Lennon School Ability Test (Otis & Lennon, 1979), the Lorge-Thorndike Intelligence Test (Lorge & Thorndike, 1966), the Cognitive Abilities Test (CAT) (Thorndike, Hagen & Lorge, 1974), the Primary Mental Abilities Test (PMA) (Thurstone & Thurstone, 1962), the Boehm Test of Basic Concepts (Boehm, 1971), the Culture-Fair Intelligence Test (Cattell, 1950; Cattell & Cattell, 1960; Cattell & Cattell, 1963), and the Raven Progressive Matrices (Raven, 1938). (The Raven test is designed for either individual or group administration; however, we do not recommend it even as a screening test because its norms are out of date.)

These tests, which can be administered to a group of students, rely on a multiple-choice format, are frequently interpreted by grade-level norms, and are particularly unreliable in assessing giftedness (Alvino & Wieler, 1979). Some school systems screen potentially gifted students by administering group tests on a one-to-one basis. This procedure allows the test examiner to evaluate relevant testing behavior and to monitor the student's adherence to test directions. However, by altering the standard administration methods specified for these tests, this procedure invalidates the tests' norms, thus making obtained scores *more* unreliable than those derived using standard administration practices.

Individual screening tests of intelligence vary in their suitability for identifying potentially gifted children. The Peabody Picture Vocabulary Test (Dunn, 1959), for example, has been reported by some researchers to overestimate intelligence and by others to underestimate it (Gensemer, Walker & Cadman, 1980). Its revised version, the PPVT-R (Dunn & Dunn, 1981), has been shown to be less functional than the PPVT for identifying gifted children; it tends to provide scores that are approximately ten points lower than PPVT scores for this population (Pedriana & Bracken, 1982).

The Slosson Intelligence Test (SIT) (Slosson, 1971), another popular screening device, was developed using items similar to those on the Stanford-Binet. Therefore, it appears to correlate highly with the Stanford-Binet (Slosson, 1971). Although the test manual reports correlation coefficients of .90 to .98, other studies seem to be less favorable (Swanson & Watson, 1982). Additionally, the correlation of scores within a restricted IQ range (e.g., the gifted range) may well be smaller than that for the population at large. The Slosson shows a moderate correlation with WISC-R verbal and full-scale scores within the restricted gifted range (Karnes & Brown, 1979) and seems to be approximately 100 percent effective and 50 percent efficient (an excellent record, see Table 2.1) in discriminating between gifted and nongifted students when a criterion of 130 is adopted for both the Slosson and the WISC-R. (Rust & Lose, 1980).

These reports may no longer be accurate, however, since the 1981 renorming of the SIT established a new set of technical specifications for the test. These are purported to conform more closely to specifications for the 1972 version of the Stanford-Binet (Armstrong & Jensen, 1981). The 1971 SIT has a mean of approximately 100 and a standard deviation of about 24; the 1981 SIT has a mean of 100 and a standard deviation of 16 (Armstrong & Jensen, 1981; Slosson, 1971). (This *may imply* that a screening cutoff of 120 on the 1981 SIT will yield results similar to those of a screening cutoff of 130 on the 1971 SIT.)

The Woodcock-Johnson Psychoeducational Battery Tests of Cognitive Ability (Woodcock & Johnson, 1977) include twelve subtests measuring various verbal and nonverbal abilities (see Table 2.2). This test, which is almost as time-consuming to administer as the WISC-R (Wechsler, 1974), is of questionable value as a screening instrument for giftedness, since it has not been studied with gifted samples. A preliminary study with average-IQ-range students (who were identified as learning disabled) indicates a strong correlation between W-J Tests of Cognitive Ability scores and WISC-R scores. According to this study, the W-J scores tend, however, to be an average of one standard deviation below the WISC-R scores (Reeve, Hall & Zabreski, 1979).

Other individual screening tests of intelligence include the Test of Concept Utilization (Crager & Spriggs, 1972), the Ammons Quick Test (Ammons & Ammons, 1962), and the Pictorial Test of Intelligence (French, 1964). One screening test that is particularly suitable for secondary-level students is the Concept Mastery Test (Terman, 1973).

A method of screening that is not used as often as may be warranted involves administering a short form of the WISC-R (Wechsler, 1974) as a predictor of performance on the full WISC-R battery. Various groupings of WISC-R subtests have been recommended for use in screening gifted children. The Block Design/Vocabulary dyad and the Similarities/Vocabulary/Block Design/Object Assembly tetrad appear to be highly accurate predictors of the WISC-R performance of gifted students (Karnes & Brown, 1981). Goldberg (1965, p. 8) cites another combination: ''The administration of only four subtests . . . Vocabulary, Information, Block Design, and Similarities, is sufficient for effective prediction. If a cut-off point of 53 (an average [subtest] standard score of approximately 13) is used, 60 percent of non-intellectually superior children are eliminated and 100 percent of the gifted are included.'' This record of effectiveness and efficiency is excellent. (The WISC-R subtests have

TABLE 2.2 Behaviors Sampled by Intelligence Tests

Verbal Behaviors

Tests	Vocabulary—receptive	Vocabulary—expressive	Auditory recall	General information	Similarities-differences	Verbal analogies	Abstract reasoning (verbal)	Classification-induction	Verbal fluency	Practical comprehension	Verbal sequencing	Numerical reasoning	Following directions	Sentence completion
Screening (Group)														
Otis-Lennon School Abilities Test	X				X	X		X				X	X	
CAT	X					X		X				X	X	
Culture-Fair Intelligence Test	X				X									
Raven Progressive Matrices														
Lorge-Thorndike	X					X		X				X		X
PMA	X											X		
Screening (Individual)														
PPVT/PPVT-R	X													
Slosson Intelligence Test		X	X	X	X	X				X		X		
W-J Cognitive Abilities Test	X	X	X											
Evaluation Tests														
WISC-R		X	X	X	X					X		X		
WAIS		X	X	X	X					X		X		
WPPSI		X	X	X	X					X		X		
Stanford-Binet	X	X	X	X	X	X	X	X	X	X	X	X	X	X
McCarthy Scales	X	X	X			X			X			X	X	
CMMS														
Leiter International														
K-ABC			X											

Note: Construction of this table involved analysis of subtests or tasks measured on the instruments listed. This catalog of tasks was organized by combining similar tasks from different tests into one category. Since the list of tests was not inclusive and their analysis was not statistical, we consider the table to be more illustrative than descriptive. Tests listed as sampling a particular

Perceptual-Performance Behaviors

Visual recall	Nonverbal sequencing	Figural analogies	Spatial relations	Puzzles	Coding/motor speed	Mazes	Abstract reason (nonverbal)	Design copying	Draw-a-person	Classification-deduction (nonverbal)	Classification-induction (nonverbal)	Discrimination (nonverbal)	Series completion (nonverbal)	Picture completion	Analysis (nonverbal)	Synthesis (nonverbal)
	X	X									X					
		X									X			X		
					X	X	X			X	X		X			
		X					X						X		X	X
		X									X		X			
			X			X	X									
								X			X					
X			X				X					X				
	X		X	X	X	X								X		
	X		X	X	X											
			X		X	X	X							X		
X			X	X		X	X	X	X	X	X		X	X		
X	X		X	X					X	X	X	X				
												X				
	X	X								X	X	X				
X	X	X	X								X			X		

behavior do not necessarily include items which assess that behavior at all levels. Similarly, the indication that a behavior is sampled does not reflect the quantity or quality of the tasks used to measure it.

standard [scaled] scores with a mean of 10 and a standard deviation of 3, so a subtest score of 13 is approximately equivalent to a full-scale IQ score of 115.)

Similar short forms have been developed for use with the Stanford-Binet (Terman & Merrill, 1973). One shortened test, proposed by Terman and Merrill, enables the examiner to administer the Stanford-Binet in about one-third less time (Sattler, 1982). Another short form uses items from both the Cattell Infant Intelligence Scale and the Stanford-Binet. This Cattell-Binet Short Form (Alpern & Kimberlin, 1970), however, does not seem to be as effective in predicting Stanford-Binet IQs as the short forms of the Wechsler are in predicting WISC-R IQs.

Measuring IQ—Evaluation Tests. Students who score at an established criterion level on an IQ screening test should be administered a comprehensive test of intelligence such as the Stanford-Binet or one of the Wechsler scales. It is important to note that the criterion established for screening tests *should typically be lower than that established for eligibility,* since screening test scores may not correlate perfectly with evaluation test scores and since screening tests usually have a larger standard error of measurement (SEM) than evaluation tests (see Table 2.1).

Although there are several comprehensive tests of intelligence available, especially for young children, the Stanford-Binet and Wechsler-scales are used most frequently. Because of their prevalent use in school assessments, we must carefully appraise their applicability for evaluating giftedness.

Although the original Binet scale was developed for assessing learning problems, the revision prepared by Terman in 1916 for use in the United States was designed to evaluate the learning potential (IQ) of average, below-average, and above-average subjects. Terman was particularly interested in giftedness and contributed greatly to its study (*Genetic Studies in Genius,* volumes 1–5, Terman's longitudinal study of gifted individuals). Perhaps this interest informed Terman's choice of test items that tended to emphasize verbal rather than perceptual-performance capabilities.

Although the Stanford-Binet has been criticized for its heavy weighting of verbal skills (Sattler, 1982), *this* characteristic of the test probably *improves* its applicability for the identification of superior academic ability. Terman and Merrill (1973) contend that the eight types of tasks most sensitive to intelligence (operationalized as problem-solving ability) are vocabulary, abstract words, sentence building, similarities and differences, analogies, sentence completion, verbal absurdities, and reasoning. These skills, sampled on the Stanford-Binet, relate to the cognitive import of scholastic learning (including its contemplative aspects) and are therefore especially suited to the identification of superior students (Miller, 1969).

The Stanford-Binet provides a continuous scale of items ranging from the 2-0 age level to the Superior Adult III level. The nature of tasks sampled varies from level to level. At the younger age levels, the test samples behaviors related to visual-motor skills, spatial relations, general knowledge, picture vocabulary, recall, and classification. Near the test ceiling, behaviors sampled include verbal fluency, abstract reasoning, expressive vocabulary, arithmetical reasoning, and general knowledge. The test is scored by crediting items between the lowest basal and the highest ceiling.

In 1936 David Wechsler developed a test designed to measure the intelligence of adults. This Wechsler-Bellevue Intelligence Scale was composed of separate subtests intended to sample the many manifestations of intelligence.

Wechsler expanded his original scale downward to develop a test for measuring the intelligence of children. This test, the Wechsler Intelligence Scale for Children (WISC) (Wechsler, 1949), was revised slightly and renormed in 1974 to account for the general upward trend in IQ scores since the original standardization of the WISC in 1949 (Pedriana & Bracken, 1982). In 1955 the Wechsler-Bellevue was revised and reissued as the Wechsler Adult Intelligence Scale (WAIS) (Wechsler, 1955), and in 1981 this test was again revised and renormed to account for the same population phenomenon that necessitated renorming of the WISC. The Wechsler Preschool and Primary Scale of Intelligence (WPPSI) (Wechsler, 1967) was developed in 1967 for use with children from 4 to 6.5 years of age and includes eight subtests similar to those on the WISC-R.

All of the Wechsler scales sample two broad domains of cognitive functioning, the verbal domain and the performance domain. A full-scale IQ score is derived by computing the sum of the scaled scores on both the verbal and performance batteries. Therefore, the full-scale IQ is not so much an averaging of verbal and performance IQs as an inclusion of both domains to provide a larger sample of items for evaluating "global intelligence."

This notion of intelligence as a global phenomenon (Wechsler, 1974) makes the Wechsler scales less suitable than the Stanford-Binet for assessing intellectual giftedness. Because of the importance given to performance items (e.g., spatial relations, visual-motor skills, visual sequencing) on the Wechsler scales, academically gifted students frequently score 10 points lower on the WISC-R than they do on the Stanford-Binet (Miller, 1969; Rubenzer, 1979a). In addition, the multiple-subtest format of the Wechsler scales makes them less suitable for identifying gifted students whose superior intellectual functioning is not generalized. Whereas the Stanford-Binet allows students to continue to attempt items as long as they have one correct item at each successive level, the Wechsler scales require that students achieve a ceiling on each subtest. This causes difficulty when students fail to achieve a ceiling on subtests measuring cognitive strengths, since students may be unable to demonstrate the full range of those strengths.

IQ measured on the Wechsler scales is less related to the criterion performance expected in gifted programs than is IQ measured on the Stanford-Binet and is probably less accurate as a measure of the academic learning potential of superior students (Miller, 1969). Because of the scoring technique, which involves adding scaled subtest scores, calculation of students' general intelligence may not reflect the extent of their strengths but rather may overemphasize the significance of their relative weaknesses. This phenomenon is contrary to the practice of eliciting optimal performance.

Other evaluation tests of intelligence are useful with special populations. These include the Arthur Adaptation of the Leiter International Performance Scale (Arthur, 1950), a completely nonverbal intelligence test applicable for assessing the learning potential of hearing impaired, bilingual, or certain learning disabled students; the Hiskey-Nebraska Test of Learning Aptitude (Hiskey, 1966), a nonverbal battery for use with hearing and deaf individuals (Swanson & Watson, 1982); and the Columbia Mental Maturity Scale (Burgmeister, Blum & Lorge, 1972), a less comprehensive, nonverbal intelligence test useful only with preschool and early-primary-level gifted children. In addition, the Blind Learning Aptitude Test (Newland, 1969) is designed to evaluate the learning potential of blind children between the ages of six and twelve.

Several comprehensive intelligence batteries that include both verbal and nonverbal items are available for assessing young children. These include the Minnesota Pre-School Scale (Goodenough, Maurer & Wagenen, 1971), the Cattell Infant Intelligence Test (Cattell, 1940), the McCarthy Scales of Children's Abilities (McCarthy, 1972), and the Bayley Scales of Infant Development (Bayley, 1969). These tests may have only limited applicability for assessing giftedness because a strong correlation between precocious *infant development* and superior intelligence later in life has not been documented (Carter & Kontos, 1982; Goldberg, 1965; Smolak, 1982).

One new comprehensive test, the Kaufman Assessment Battery for Children (K-ABC) (Kaufman & Kaufman, 1983), is intended to measure intelligence and achievement. This battery samples behaviors related to both problem-solving, or fluid intelligence, and acquired learning, or crystallized intelligence (cf. Cattell, 1963; Kaufman & Kaufman, 1983, p. 2). The K-ABC excludes behaviors that reflect crystallized (or verbal) intelligence from its assessment of intellectual potential. This characteristic of the K-ABC is considered sufficient by the test authors to establish the test as a culture-fair measure. However, the notion that minority students perform better on nonverbal than on verbal tasks has not been demonstrated empirically (Jensen, 1973; Samuda, 1975). Jensen (1973), in fact, reports that minority children (blacks in particular) perform better on verbal tests than on nonverbal tests. In addition, the contention that perceptual-performance skills are ascribed and verbal skills are acquired is merely speculative.

The K-ABC is applicable for use with children from 2.5 to 12.5 years of age and so would be useful only for evaluating superior students of preschool and primary school age. Since the K-ABC does make an attempt to provide *minority group norms*, its use in evaluating gifted children from culturally different backgrounds warrants further study. In particular, however, its intelligence portion seems not to address the criterion measure most suitable for gifted program eligibility. (We caution the reader to recall that *both* IQ and achievement comprise valid parameters within which to assess eligibility.)

IQ Test Selection, Administration, and Interpretation. The procedures that circumscribe testing are as important to thorough and fair assessment as are the tests themselves. In general, IQ tests should be selected to emphasize student strengths, since their use as optimal measures of learning potential is advocated for gifted students (Saigh, 1981).

Therefore, a student who shows verbal precocity should be administered the Stanford-Binet, whereas one who is more apt mechanically should be administered the WISC-R or the Leiter (see Table 2.2 for an enumeration of behaviors sampled by the intelligence tests discussed in this chapter). Special circumstances, such as a student's handicap, bilingualism, or lower-class background warrant extra care in test selection, modification in test administration, and caution in test interpretation (McFarland, 1980). Modified testing procedures may also be required for students scoring at or near the ceiling of individual IQ tests. In all of these cases, procedures such as off-level testing and trial programming, which are not typical testing practices, may be justified.

In most cases, however, tests should be administered following standard procedures. The adherence to specified test instructions provides for similar test reliability among examiners. However, scores on complex tests such as the WISC-R or WAIS-R may vary from examiner to examiner both as a result of examiner error (Franklin & Stillman, 1982) and as a result of examiner interpretation.

Establishing and maintaining rapport throughout a testing session is important in order to provide a suitable, psychologically safe climate for testing. Physical conditions may affect test performance. The evaluator should make sure not only that tests are administered in quiet, well-lighted, private rooms but also that the examinee is neither hungry, tired, nor excessively distressed. In the case of potentially gifted children, the examiner should provide ample time for test administration, should not rush students' responses, and should encourage responses to high-level items. Because some children will answer only questions that are familiar, the examiner should be sure to stress the importance of attempting difficult items and the advisability of guessing on questions about which the student is somewhat uncertain.

In interpreting the test results of superior students, evaluators should appraise the applicability of the test as well as the performance of students. They should report this information, with particular regard to the range of students' successful responses, reaching or failure to reach a ceiling on the test or on particular subtests, the relevant test behaviors of the students, and the relative strengths and weaknesses in students' cognition, suggested by scatter in subtest performance.

Occasionally, an aberrant pattern of performance can be effectively analyzed by using one of several schema developed for this purpose (e.g., Bannatyne, 1974; Kaufman, 1975). Bannatyne (1974) and Kaufman (1975) have provided methods for analyzing cognitive factors by grouping WISC-R subtests, but such analyses are not as well articulated for the Stanford-Binet. The Binetgram does, however, provide a visual representation of student performance in the cognitive areas sampled by the test (Sattler, 1982). In difficult cases, this type of profile analysis may be useful for verifying the giftedness of a handicapped or culturally different child.

In general, however, the discrepancy among subtest or factor scores must be extremely large in order to be considered statistically significant (Salvia & Ysseldyke, 1981). *Therefore, the interpretation of apparently discrepant scores in determining strengths and weaknesses should be quite guarded.*

Another schema for test interpretation, proposed by Meeker (1969), is the classification of test items using a matrix based on Guilford's structure of the intellect (SI) model (Dyer, Neigler & Millholland (1975). This approach attempts to make tests that were developed from a unitary-factor perspective conform to an extreme multiple-factor theory. The use of SI categories for assessing the aspects of student performance on an intelligence test is considerably less valid than the use of the Bannatyne or Kaufman categories.

Finally, evaluators should keep in mind that testing is just an approximation of performance. An interpretation of an IQ score of 132 on the Stanford-Binet should reflect an understanding of test reliability and standard error of measurement. An obtained score of 132 signifies that 68 percent of the time the student's true score will fall within the 127–137 range; that 95 percent of the time the true score will fall within the 122–142 range; and that 99 percent of the time the student's true score will fall within the 117–147 IQ range. (These probability determinations are based on the hypothetical, repeated administration of the test and are therefore an artifact of the test's coefficient of reliability.)

Thus, we can be quite certain that the criterion performance of 132 on the Stanford-Binet indicates above-average to highly superior potential. *The task of discriminating between the gifted and the almost gifted is made difficult by the imprecision of even the best tests available for identification of exceptional students.*

Measuring Aptitude.   As we have indicated above, the distinctions among measures of general intelligence, aptitude, and achievement are arbitrary and are based on theoretical constructs that cannot be justified empirically. Since certain tests are, however, classified by their authors as aptitude measures, we will review the use of such instruments with respect to their theoretical premises.

Among those tests categorized as measuring aptitude, there seem to be three general types of test: those designed to measure capacity to perform certain types of tasks, those designed to distinguish various skills for the purpose of making vocational plans, and those designed to measure scholastic aptitude.

The first type, and the simplest to differentiate from intelligence tests, measures the capacity to perform specific tasks or types of tasks. The SRA Mechanical Aptitudes Test (Richardson, Bellows, Henry & Co., Inc., 1947–1950), for example, evaluates skills related to the performance of various mechanical tasks, for the purpose of assisting in vocational counseling or placement.

The second type of aptitude instrument relies on a multiple-factor definition of mental abilities. Tests of this sort provide separate scales for evaluating various capabilities including spatial aptitude, verbal reasoning, numerical aptitude, clerical ability, mechanical aptitude, dexterity, perceptual aptitude, abstract reasoning, and written language aptitude. On most tests of this type, skill domains are evaluated independently and are not combined to provide a general-factor mental ability or IQ score.

An exception to this rule is the Primary Mental Abilities Test (PMA), a group test for assessing verbal meaning, perceptual speed, number facility, spatial relations, and reasoning. On this test, a total score is derived from the separate subtest scores to provide an IQ measurement.

In general, however, tests such as the Differential Aptitude Test (Bennet, Seashore & Wiseman, 1947–1973) comprise this class of measurement instruments. Their intention is to differentiate among various skill domains for the purpose of assisting students in choosing courses of study or making career decisions (Lyman, 1968). Other such tests include the General Aptitude Test Battery (United States Employment Service, 1946–1973) and the Flanagan Aptitude Classification Tests (Flanagan, 1957–1960).

The final category of aptitude tests includes those that purport to measure scholastic aptitude. Since one rationale for using intelligence tests is that they are accurate in predicting school success (Butcher, 1968), these scholastic aptitude measures seem almost indistinguishable from intelligence tests. One difference, however, between the espoused purpose of these tests and that of certain IQ tests is the explicit acknowledgment that previous learning substantially influences test performance. Scholastic aptitude, as a concept, relates previous learning to future learning without postulating a general intellective factor which mediates the transaction. The Detroit Tests of Learning Aptitude (Baker & Leland, 1967) and the Analysis of Learning Potential (Durost, Gardner & Madden, 1970) represent this type of aptitude test.

The aptitude tests most suitable for use with gifted students are probably the College Entrance Examination Board's Scholastic Aptitude Test (SAT) (Educational Testing Service, 1926–1983) and Preliminary Scholastic Aptitude Test (PSAT) (Educational Testing Service, 1960–1983). Both the SAT and the PSAT are issued annually in different forms. They are group-administered, multiple-choice tests designed to measure aptitude for verbal and mathematics learning. The SAT is intended as a predictor of the scholastic achievement of entering college freshmen and is used extensively by colleges in selecting candidates for admission (Linden & Linden, 1968). The PSAT is a short form of the SAT designed to give eleventh-grade students an opportunity to evaluate their probable performance on the SAT.

An unusual application of the SAT for identifying precocious junior high school students was developed at Johns Hopkins University (Stanley, Keating & Fox, 1974). The procedure involves administering "difficult high school and college tests to elementary and junior high school pupils . . . [to] aid in identifying a significant number of children who have already learned—usually on their own—far more than their classmates" (Laycock, 1979, p. 77). Cutoff scores are established in order to determine students' eligibility for special Johns Hopkins programs, including summer programs and early entry into college.

Although the use of the SAT for the off-level testing of students younger than those for whom it was designed is considered an assessment abuse by some critics (e.g., Alvino, McDonnel & Richert, 1981), it does seem to be justified. The rationale for this unusual testing practice is twofold. First, the applicability of other tests such as the Stanford-Binet for very bright intermediate-level children and above-average adolescents is somewhat limited by failure to achieve a ceiling on the test (Sattler, 1982). Second, aptitude tests in general and off-level tests in particular are valuable for predicting the probable performance of gifted students in programs that have specified objectives.

Since success in a rapidly accelerated math program may require a particular level of math performance on a test like the SAT, performance criteria can be established to determine program eligibility (Stanley & Benbow, 1982). Similarly, a program that addresses the needs of mechanically apt students would most appropriately select those students on the basis of a test of mechanical aptitude. Although our cautions concerning the use of group tests are still pertinent in these situations, the relevance of these particular tests for the purposes specified counterbalances those concerns. These very restricted applications of group instruments in no way justify the use of group tests when appropriate individual tests exist for meeting assessment needs.

Measuring Achievement.   The assessment of achievement may be the only evaluation function delegated to the teacher of the gifted. Achievement tests sometimes are used to determine program eligibility but more frequently are included in an assessment battery to assist in appropriate instructional planning. We endorse both applications of achievement testing and will consider each in turn.

Achievement testing may be used in place of ability testing or in addition to it. When it is used as the sole criterion for determining gifted placement, it excludes many underachieving gifted children from programs that might improve their achievement (Fearn, 1982). When eligibility for special programs depends on criterion performance on *either* an ability *or* an achievement measure, however, capable students who for some reason do not achieve sufficiently high scores on IQ tests can be included (see Chapter 1). Additionally, achievement testing is the most appropriate technique for evaluating specific academic talent in areas such as mathematics or science (Consuegra, 1982). Programs that are designed to provide accelerated subject area instruction should employ selection procedures directly related to the subjects being taught. For determining eligibility for such programs, norm-referenced or criterion-referenced achievement tests seem most appropriate.

Like tests of intelligence, achievement tests can be classified by their method of administration (group or individual) and by their applicability for screening or evaluation. The factors that govern the choice of an achievement test are, however, somewhat different from those that determine the selection of an intelligence test. Depending on the purpose of testing and the student's age, a group achievement test may be as appropriate as or more appropriate than an individual measure. For example, if the purpose of testing were *to screen* a large number of junior high school students for an accelerated reading program (perhaps as one element of a comprehensive program for scholastically talented students), a group test would probably be as accurate as and would certainly be more economical than an individual test. In general, individual tests of achievement do not discriminate the performance levels of advanced students beyond the sixth or seventh grades. Therefore, group tests may be the only alternative for assessing the achievement of older gifted students.

Group Achievement Tests. Several group tests of achievement are particularly applicable for use with gifted students. The Sequential Tests of Educational Progress (STEP) (Educational Testing Service, Cooperative Test Division, 1956–1972) constitute a multilevel achievement battery designed to measure communication skills and content knowledge. They are quite suitable for evaluating the advanced skills of academically gifted students from elementary through secondary grades. This type of test differs from many comprehensive group achievement tests in that it can be used to test the limits of a student's knowledge.

Other sequential achievement tests applicable for use as *off-level* measures include the California Achievement Tests (CTB/McGraw-Hill, 1977), which use a locator test to determine students' appropriate levels; the Iowa Tests of Basic Skills (Hieronymus, Lindquist & Hoover, 1978), which include multilevel as well as single-level test batteries, and the Metropolitan Achievement Tests' Survey Test (Prescott, Balow, Hogan & Farr, 1978), which provides an alternative to the instructional batteries of the original Metropolitan Test.

Many other group achievement tests, such as the SRA Achievement Series (Naslund, Thorpe & Lefever, 1978), the Metropolitan Achievement Tests' Instructional Batteries (Farr, Prescott, Balow & Hogan, 1978) and the Stanford Achievement Test (Madden, Gardner, Rudman, Karlsen & Merwin, 1973), are intended to measure *grade-specific* mastery of skills.

The College Entrance Examination Board Achievement Tests (Educational Testing Service, 1901–1983) and the American College Test Program Examination (American College Testing Program, 1960–1983) may be used for the off-level achievement testing of advanced secondary school students in the same way the SAT is used for off-level aptitude testing. However, the administration schedule and the cost of testing may render this test inconvenient for public school use in routine screening efforts.

Individual Achievement Tests. The two individual screening tests of achievement currently published are quite limited in their scope and usefulness with superior students. The Wide Range Achievement Test (WRAT) (Jastak & Jastak, 1978) is often used because it can be administered in about ten minutes. This test, however, has "limited behavior sampling, inadequate standardization, and absence of reliability and validity data" (Salvia & Ysseldyke, 1981, p. 176) and should be scrupuously avoided in any legitimate screening effort.

The Peabody Individual Achievement Test (PIAT) (Dunn & Markwardt,

1970), on the other hand, is a well-standardized test showing sufficient reliability and validity to justify its use as a screening instrument (Swanson & Watson, 1982). The PIAT has five subtests: Mathematics, Reading Recognition, Reading Comprehension, Spelling, and General Information. Norming is provided for both age and grade levels, and scores are reported as grade (and age) equivalents, percentile ranks, and standard scores (mean = 100; standard deviation = 15).

It is important to note that the grade equivalent score, which is misleading on any test, is especially deceptive on the PIAT. Greatly inflated grade equivalencies, for example, translate into only above-average percentile ranks and standard scores. Care should be exercised in interpreting these results for classroom teachers and parents.

An additional use for the PIAT recommended by one researcher (Simpson, 1982) involves employing the General Information subtest as a brief screening test to predict the IQ performance of students. Simpson bases this recommendation on a .60 correlation between the performance of average and above-average subjects on the General Information subtest and their full-scale WISC-R scores.

Individual tests for evaluating the achievement of superior elementary school children include comprehensive tests of acquired skills and diagnostic tests specific to one subject area or skill. The Woodcock-Johnson Psycho-educational Battery (Woodcock & Johnson, 1977) includes tests of achievement in four areas: mathematics, reading, written language, and knowledge.

The Kaufman Assessment Battery for Children (Kaufman & Kaufman, 1983) also includes an achievement scale which evaluates achievement in areas somewhat different from those measured by the Woodcock-Johnson. These achievement subtests assess a combination of skills acquired either at home or in school. The following list of subtests illustrates this point: Expressive Vocabulary, Faces and Places (naming famous people and places in drawings or photographs), Arithmetic, Riddles (naming a general principle defined by its characteristics), Reading/Decoding, and Reading/Understanding. The applicability of this type of scale for verifying mastery of school learning has not yet been demonstrated.

Several individual, single-subject achievement tests may also be applicable for evaluating the skill mastery of gifted children. These tests, which are intended for educational diagnosis, are valuable for appraising the academic strengths and weaknesses of gifted children. They may also be helpful in the assessment of learning disabled and other underachieving gifted children who exhibit discrepancies between their ability and achievement. Among these specific tests are several worth mentioning.

The Woodcock Reading Mastery Tests (Woodcock, 1973) are a norm-referenced battery combining five subtests claimed to sample several different reading behaviors. Subtest reliabilities do not confirm the diagnostic value of these subtests, so scatter should be interpreted with particular caution.

The Key Math Diagnostic Arithmetic Test (Connolly, Nachtman & Pritchett, 1971) is a norm- and criterion-referenced instrument that evaluates performance in fourteen areas of elementary arithmetic. Because the test content is restricted to basic arithmetic skills, it is not applicable for evaluating mathematical precocity. It is useful instead for assessing the skill deficits of students to determine instructional objectives (see Chapter 4 for a more detailed discussion of this process).

Finally, the Test of Written Language (Hammill & Larsen, 1978) is a norm-referenced test that claims to evaluate various aspects of written expression. Because the written language of gifted students frequently is not as well developed as their spoken language (Pendarvis, 1983), performance on this test may assist educators in designing group or individual writing programs for gifted elementary students.

Two tests have been developed recently to assess the academic achievement of preschool, kindergarten, and primary-grade students: the Test of Early Reading Ability (Reid, Hresko & Hammill, 1983) and the Test of Early Mathematics Ability (Ginsburg & Baroody, 1983). These two tests should be useful in documenting precocious academic performance and in individualizing instruction.

EVALUATION OF STUDENTS GIFTED IN THE ARTS

We suggested in Chapter 1 that arts are a part of school learning. Children talented in the arts are viewed as academically talented, and programs for them are cognitive in nature (see Chapter 10 for a complete discussion of arts talent in the schools). Since art and music are the arts usually included in the school curriculum, the discussion here and in Chapter 10 considers talent in these areas.

Traditionally panels of experts have chosen students talented in art and music. This procedure still dominates in private arts programs, such as camps, music festivals, and art schools. For teachers of gifted students in public schools who must, however, assess arts talent, we present some alternatives.

Standardized Tests

Music. Buros's *Eighth Mental Measurements Yearbook* (1978) and *Tests in Print II* (1974) list four times as many tests in music (24) as in art. Among the music tests are the Iowa Tests of Music Literacy (Gordon, 1970–1971), for grades 7–12; the Music Achievement Tests (Colwell, 1967–1970), for grades 3–12; the Music Aptitude Profile (Gordon, 1965), for grades 4–12; and the Seashore Tests of Musical Talent (Seashore, Lewis & Saetveit, 1960/1919).

Of the above tests, the Music Achievement Test seems, according to Buros, to have the largest norming samples and to give a variety of grade norms. Any of these tests, or some of the others discussed by Buros, could prove useful in identifying children gifted in music. As we noted in our discussion of the identification of intellectual giftedness, the sort of program into which children are to be placed should relate reasonably to the evaluation techniques used (cf. Glass, 1983). Children identified primarily by written standardized tests will not in general prove to be *gifted* performers, much less gifted composers, though they may prove to have *some* facility for performance.

It is more likely that children assessed as gifted by written group tests will prove capable of *understanding* musical language when they are provided instruction in music theory and history. Thus, standardized tests should prove more useful in helping to select students for classes in music history, theory, or general appreciation than in helping to select students for classes related to specific instrumental or vocal performance.

Art. According to Alexander (1981), interest in identifying students gifted in art is slight. In fact, the literature on students gifted in the visual arts and the humanities is itself very small (Chetelat, 1981).

Among the six art tests cited in Buros (1978), none is intended for use in grades lower than grade 6. The two tests mentioned by Alexander (1981) are the Barron Welsh Art Scale (Welsh & Barron, 1963) and the Graves Design Judgment Scale (Graves, 1948), for grades 7–16. Saunders (1982) discusses the Meier Art Test (Meier, 1963, originally 1929), intended also for grades 7–16.

These group tests purport to measure "art judgment" or "aesthetic perception." They are, however, actually tests of taste, subject to very wide cultural and subcultural differences. They are quite probably inappropriate for their intended use. Alexander (1981, p. 39), for example, says of the Meier tests, which are now nearly sixty years old, that they "appear culture bound" and of doubtful use with children under age twelve. Helmstadter (1972, pp. 83–84) reports that the prototype of the Barron Welsh Art Scale was originally developed "for use with clinical patients who didn't speak English." Welsh and Barron (1963) claimed it distinguished various aspects of creativity; however, according to Buros (1972), other studies have questioned the test's ability to distinguish creativity either among art students or among the general population. One would hesitate to use as assessment tools for any grade or talent level such outdated and invalid instruments.

Creativity Tests

Inasmuch as creativity (or divergent thinking) tests are often used as proxies for criterion-referenced or norm-referenced tests specific to art or music (e.g., Saunders, 1982), we need to discuss the most popular of them briefly. The most commonly recommended battery is the Torrance Tests of Creative Thinking (Torrance, 1974), which comes in two verbal and figural forms. Thinking Creatively with Sounds and Words and Thinking Creatively in Action and Movement are also available (for a total of six forms).

With a bit of semantic interpolation one could propose that these instruments were identification tests for fiction writing, art, music, and dance. These instruments were not, however, designed to evaluate arts aptitude. The figural tests, for example, are probably no more useful in this regard than the Bender Gestalt, House-Tree-Person, or Goodenough-Harris Draw-a-Man tests (mentioned by Saunders, 1982, in the context of art identification).

Wallach (1970) suggests that because the Torrance tests are confounded by their measurement of convergent skills, they are simply less accurate measures of intelligence. Gallagher, Aschner, and Jenné (1967, pp. 90–91) found that personality and, in particular, sex differences—not differences in cognitive thinking (i.e., divergent vs. convergent thinking)—accounted for differences in classroom performance within the high-IQ range. Reisman (1981) found that Thinking Creatively in Action and Movement significantly predicted cognitive performance in young children.

In related research, Hocevar (1979) found that

> It is likely that ideational fluency [i.e., the ability to generate many ideas in a short amount of time] is the factor that causes creativity tests to be highly intercorrelated and factorially distinct from intelligence tests. . . . but this does not mean that the broader category of creative thinking will be factorially distinct when the effect of ideational fluency is controlled.
>
> (Hocevar, 1979, p. 194).

Moreover, Hocevar (1980) found that when three measures of ideational fluency and a high-level intelligence test were correlated with an inventory of creative activities, differences in the predictive·ability of the measure of ideational fluency versus the IQ test were not significant.

The above research suggests that creativity tests do not in general distinguish between creativity and intelligence, nor do they predict creative behavior better than IQ tests. In particular, creativity tests are not specific to art or music, nor do they contain enough items related to art or music to represent a set of sample behaviors necessary to predict aptitude for particular kinds of art or music instruction.

Biographical Inventories

Some instruments use biographical data to extrapolate prospective giftedness from personality and past accomplishment. Whiting (1976) found that inventory ratings of past accomplishment predict subsequent accomplishment. Three such instruments are the Group Inventory for Finding Creative Talent (GIFT) (Rimm & Davis, 1980), the Group Inventory for Finding Interests I and II (GIFFI I and II) (Davis & Rimm, 1982), and the Biographical Inventory (Taylor & Ellison, 1966).

There are three problems with the inferences derived from biographical inventories. First, a strong motive in all identification efforts is to find talent that *may not be corroborated by demonstrable achievement*. It is hardly surprising that past achievements predict future achievements. Past academic achievement, for example, also predicts future academic achievement. Biographical inventories may fail to identify children with arts *potential*.

Second, the validity of items on biographical inventories may not depend on their ability to discriminate creative children from high-IQ children. GIFFI I, for example, includes the statement "I have taken art, dancing, or music lessons outside of school because I wanted to " (Davis & Rimm, 1982, p. 51). The validity of such items is established through ratings by teachers and researchers of children's personalities and their original short stories and drawings. IQ tests also correlate highly in the general population with ratings of personality and ratings of original stories (Gallagher, 1975). The positive correlation between creative personality traits and IQ scores indicates that we cannot be sure that there are major benefits to be derived from using biographical inventories as opposed to IQ tests.

Finally, personality characteristics of children may predict neither adult personality nor adult accomplishment. MacKinnon (1978) suggests that the personality type of children with records of creative achievement differs from that of creative adults. He says that creative adults may be more unconventional and uninhibited than they were as children. Personality characteristics of children may therefore be an obscure guide to arts talent or potential.

Evaluation of Performance and Production Aptitude

Whereas children who can benefit from arts history, appreciation, and criticism courses may be located through a combination of IQ tests and group arts tests, children with specific arts talent must be identified by other means. For the assessment of musical performance ability or aptitude for studio art work, a combination of techniques is recommended by most writers (e.g., Alexander, 1981; Chetelat, 1981; Petzold, 1978). Basically, such alternative methods devolve to a special kind of *expert* criterion-referencing.

Chetelat (1981) relied on three methods: (1) personal observation of children in his art classes, (2) nominations by teachers, parents, child, and child's peers, and (3) portfolio analysis. In effect, Chetelat relied on his expertise and intimacy with art media, technique, and children to evaluate both process and product. Chetelat (1981, p. 157) says that teachers who work with the gifted in art must be art specialists, and that "the art specialist who works with . . . the gifted must be a lover of art, an exhibiting artist/teacher, a museum attender, a reader of art books and periodicals, a traveler, and especially, an addict for working with children and understanding them." Such teachers are the only professionals likely to have the skills, knowledge, or community contacts necessary to conceive the project, identify the children, and provide the instruction (cf. Goodlad, 1970; Koch, 1970, 1973).

For jury judgments, local experts should be chosen carefully. It may be wiser to use a single expert judge if a knowledgeable panel cannot be assembled. If a single expert is used, most of the identification burden should probably fall on the person chosen to implement the program, i.e., the art or music teacher (see Chapter 10 for reports of model programs).

COMMON EVALUATION AND ASSESSMENT COMPONENTS

Though much of the preceding discussion has concerned instruments and techniques specific to the assessment of certain talents or certain kinds of children, assessment efforts share two important components. Most assessments, including placement evaluations, benefit from formal and informal classroom observations. Additionally, after data from tests, other instruments, reports, and observations have been collected, they must be analyzed and then synthesized in an assessment report. These common components are examined below.

Formal and Informal Observation of Superior Students

The effects of school environments on learning are more difficult to measure than individual performance. Since the goal of gifted program placement is to improve the appropriateness of a student's educational environment, an evaluation of the student's current learning environment is imperative.

The ecological tenet that environment interacts with performance should be considered in any observation of students in the classroom context. (See Swanson & Watson, 1982, for a discussion of ecological models. Also see Lidz, 1981, for a discussion of a related model of psychosituational assessment.) The comparison of performance in the regular classroom with performance at home, at music school, or in a special class may be enlightening.

Informal assessment of performance usually depends on data provided by an informant such as a parent, classroom teacher, special subject teacher, or guidance counselor. Techniques for assembling this type of information may include anecdotal records, running records, work samples, sequence analyses, and rating scales.

Formal observation is usually conducted by a specified observer who identifies and quantifies target behaviors. Target behaviors may be quantified in various ways such as through measures of the accuracy of a student's performance, or the frequency, duration, or latency of a particular behavior. Whole interval, partial interval, or time sampling techniques are used to generate observation data.

The aspects of the learning environment that are important to assess vary from year to year for each student, because they are dependent on the particular nature of a teacher's instructional adaptations for bright students. Therefore, observation should be part of a yearly program revision process, especially in the earlier grades when the child has only one classroom teacher, as well as part of the initial evaluation.

Curiously, most observation that occurs as part of a preplacement evaluation focuses on the degree to which the student's characteristics conform to the characteristics of other gifted children, creative adults, talented scientists, gifted mathematicians, or other gifted individuals (e.g., Consuegra, 1982; MacKinnon, 1968; Renzulli et al., 1977; Rimm & Davis, 1976). The use of checklists based on personality characteristics to make educational placement decisions contravenes principles of psychometrics, cultural relativism, and, ultimately, due process. ''Rating scales provide only a first level of information and must be followed by more extensive assessment. . . . '' (Kerr & Nelson, 1983, p. 16). Unless we heed this caution we will fail to identify superior and even highly gifted students who do not choose or happen to appear able (as not infrequently happens). In addition, we may falsely select students who demonstrate good study habits but lack exceptional academic talent.

Assessment Reports

Following any assessment of a student, the examiners prepare reports describing the results of the assessment. Such reports include discussion of

1. the background of the student,
2. the purposes of the assessment,
3. the results of the testing,
4. significant behaviors exhibited during the testing session,
5. the data obtained through observation,
6. interpretation and integration of the findings, and
7. recommendations for further assessment, placement, and instruction.

These reports provide the formal documentation necessary to support the placement of a student in a special program. This documentation may be crucial if parents disagree with and wish to contest the findings. It may also prove helpful should the family move to another state or district.

When assessments are conducted by a multidisciplinary team, several team members may contribute reports summarizing various assessment procedures. The psychologist may record the results of the intelligence testing; the teacher of the gifted may report the results of achievement testing; the classroom teacher may document results of observations of the student. This multidisciplinary approach is optimal for providing a thorough assessment of the student's performance in various settings (Golin & Ducanis, 1981). However, multidisciplinary assessment can be just as misleading and biased as an assessment completed by one examiner (Ysseldyke & Algozzine, 1982b). The same rules of testing practice apply in both situations.

Case Study Approach. Although case study techniques such as behavior rating, product evaluation, and nomination procedures do serve the legitimate function of assisting in appropriate program planning, they should not be used to guide placement decisions. The case study approach to the assessment of gifted children is advocated by a number of authors in the field (e.g., Jenkins-Friedman, 1982; Renzulli, Reis & Smith, 1981). When the purpose for using informal, subjective, and technically inadequate measures is confused with the purpose for using formal, objective, well-validated procedures, protection in assessment cannot be guaranteed. The case study techniques listed above are not evaluation instruments, they are not culture-fair, and they are not constructed to account for error in measurement (see Chapter 4).

SUMMARY

This chapter has presented methods for the identification of three species of school talent: intellectual talent, specific academic talent, and arts talent. The discussion emphasized the most defensible assessment practices and cautioned against less valid approaches.

Several general principles have guided our consideration of assessment. First, we suggested the importance of careful referral procedures. Second, we affirmed the need for due process in determining eligibility. Procedures related to due process include the selection of nondiscriminatory tests as well as the establishment of measurable criteria for admission to programs. Third, we acknowledged the merit of statistically reliable measures in spite of some theoretical and practical limitations. Finally, we stressed the need for multidisciplinary assessment providing information from several sources.

The thrust of this chapter has been on assessment practices for *identifying* gifted children. We have used the term *evaluation* to refer to this type of assessment. Other assessment practices are considered in Chapter 3 in the discussion of program evaluation and in Chapter 4 in the discussion of assessment for individual program planning.

PART II

Instruction

Part II of *Teaching Gifted Children: Principles and Strategies* addresses instructional concerns: issues of placement, program, curriculum, and teaching. From the perspective of historical and empirical foundations, we provide guidelines for evaluating and implementing teaching methods for the gifted. As in Part I, our discussion focuses on the development of intellectual, academic, and artistic talents.

Chapter 3, "Identifying and Developing Placement Alternatives: The Continuum of Services," examines the various settings in which differentiated instruction for the gifted can occur. Two important notions are *least restrictive environment* and *continuum of services*. These concepts apply to gifted education in an unusual way.

Chapter 4, "Individuals and Systems: Negotiating Program Plans," shows how individual program planning, in a structured format, can provide opportunities for overall program development, in spite of persistent constraints.

Chapter 5, "Pace and Content: Acceleration," and Chapter 6, "Quality and Quantity: The Dilemma of Enrichment," review placement alternatives, instructional practices, and model programs.

Chapter 7, "Form and Content: Curriculum," views gifted curriculum in the context of traditional academic studies. Its primary object is curriculum content, not curriculum development procedures. This approach articulates the curriculum features of a program for academic talent development in a public school setting.

Chapter 8, "Teaching Gifted Children: Instructional Formats," offers practical methods for providing the academic content of gifted programs. A review of relevant research guides the discussion of how to employ both inductive and expository instructional formats with gifted students.

Chapter 9, "Teaching Gifted Children: Techniques for Concept and Skill Development," considers specific techniques that can be used in teaching the gifted. Question-asking techniques are discussed with particular reference to inductive learning. In addition, techniques for concept and skill development are examined, as are exemplary enrichment techniques. Finally, the chapter explores the relevance of behavior modification to gifted underachievers.

Chapter 10, "Aesthetics and the Gifted: The Arts in the Schools," explores objectives and methods for arts instruction that address the needs of both academically gifted and artistically talented students. It provides a rationale for emphasizing arts instruction in a public school setting and contrasts arts instruction with creativity training.

Part II also suggests cautions in applying instructional principles and practices that are not supported by research. Gifted education is a relatively new pedagogical specialty; its practitioners are experimenting with various instructional approaches as it develops. Our reluctance to endorse heartily many of the current practices in the field reflects our concern for practices of enduring value.

CHAPTER 3

Identifying and Developing Placement Alternatives: The Continuum of Services

INTRODUCTION

Determination of an appropriate learning environment should be the result of all evaluation, program development, and placement efforts. That it sometimes is not, that less appropriate rather than most appropriate placements are common, that there is confusion as to what constitutes least restrictive alternatives in *all* exceptionalities (e.g., Evans & Marken, 1982; Heron & Skinner, 1981; Kuo, 1981; Norton & Doman, 1982) is apparent. Nonetheless, improvement in placement practices is both necessary and possible (see Chapter 4).

Some consensus ought to be possible about methods of determining appropriate alternatives for gifted students. Principles for constructing such a consensus can be adduced a priori from the cognitive nature of giftedness, discovered from empirical research, and inferred from existing, if inconsistently implemented, alternatives.

In this chapter we will consider (1) the concept of the appropriate environment, including its relation to mainstreaming, normalization, and the least restrictive environment for particular students, (2) existing alternatives in the public school system, including regular class modifications and special education, (3) institutional priorities in placement alternatives, and (4) program evaluation.

THE CONCEPT OF THE LEAST RESTRICTIVE ENVIRONMENT

Giving students the opportunity to achieve to potential is the essence of the concept of the least restrictive environment. However, the least restrictive environment concept does not apply to the gifted in the same way that it applies to the handicapped. Gifted children are at risk academically, not socially. The gifted need suitably paced instruction, appropriate cognitive work, realistic (i.e., not age-appropriate) standards of performance, and the opportunity to interact with intellectual peers. These needs, when met, amount to the opportunity to achieve to potential. The question that confronts teachers of the gifted is how best to nurture the abilities of gifted children in the context of available options in public schools. Contradictory suggestions have been made on the basis of disparate local definitions and practices.

For example, Whitmore (1980) describes how the curriculum, teaching style, and social context of the regular classroom can damage both the academic and the social development of gifted children. Henson, on the other hand, claims that the regular classroom is the most appropriate setting for gifted children:

> We do not want to make the same mistake with the "gifted" that we have made in other areas of education, i.e., social isolation. Social awareness comes with experience. If these children are going to provide potential future leadership they cannot grow up in a "make-believe" world where everyone is "gifted" and one only deals with problems at a theoretical level.
>
> (Henson, 1976, p. 110)

As the quotation above illustrates, disagreement over what constitutes the least restrictive environment for gifted children is not based on concern for their *academic* development. The concern for social adjustment causes many educators to refuse to place gifted children in any setting except the regular classroom with their chronological peers. There is no reason to believe that gifted children do not benefit academically from special programs, including self-contained classrooms, though few such classrooms exist in the United States (cf. Kuo, 1981).

The discussion below assumes that the potential of gifted children with which we are primarily concerned is academic ability (see Chapter 1). The discussion below also assumes that the gifted are exceptional learners and that differentiation of their instruction is advisable.

The Inappropriateness of Normalization

Normalization and its prime placement strategem, mainstreaming, are *not* principles that maximize the potential of the gifted. Throughout this text we document the serious problems gifted children encounter in the regular classroom.

Mainstreaming the Gifted. Normalization represents a maximization of potential for handicapped persons and is of undoubted value to them. The principle of normalization refers as much to noncognitive adaptive behavior as it does to cognitive functioning. To promote normalization, PL 94-142 directs that whenever possible handicapped students be educated in the regular program. Only when appropriate results cannot be achieved with assistance are these students to be placed in more restrictive environments. However, even in restricted placements, normalization (or cultivation of behavior that is "normal" or permits interaction with "normal" people) for the handicapped remains a goal that is directly related to curriculum.

Because the gifted are not handicapped, however, normalization is not an appropriate goal for them. Gifted students do not suffer the same sort of isolation as the handicapped. Nor is their adaptive functioning subnormal. More importantly, the gifted have not historically been removed from the mainstream, and seldom has such removal been successfully proposed in the United States. Thus, surprisingly, normalization, inappropriate as it is, can be said to be a universal principle governing the education of the gifted. This circumstance, however, is without design; it represents the indifference that schools have until recently shown toward the gifted.

Self-interest may be a factor in preventing schools from being equally indifferent to the education of the handicapped. Sapon-Shevin (1982) reminds us that there are two possible reasons for separation of any minority group, including exceptional children: (1) it may benefit the separated population, or (2) it may benefit the majority. The adults in the school system benefit from the separation of handicapped children. Although separation of mildly handicapped children has not been demonstrated to be beneficial, efforts to include them in regular classrooms meet with resistance. When the brightest students leave the regular classroom, however, teachers may fear that less apt students will no longer have the opportunity to emulate more apt learners (cf. Katz, 1968, on emulation). Since gifted children are rarely behavior problems, there is little cause for teachers to insist they be removed from the classroom. In fact, teachers perceive gifted students as an asset to the regular classroom. The climate of the regular classroom may actually suffer when gifted children are placed in separate classrooms.

The schooling of the gifted will improve only if a wider array of options is open to them. Unfortunately a general feeling exists that the regular classroom is the best place in which to make any necessary adjustments required for gifted children. Thus, several strategies have been reported for accomplishing this task (e.g., Colon & Treffinger, 1980; Treffinger, 1982; Ward, 1981). For instance, New York, a state with a small appropriation for the gifted and a large number of identified gifted students (see Box 4.4, p. 122), has prepared a 400-page manual entitled *Educating Gifted Pupils in the Regular Classroom* (N.Y. State Department of Education, 1982). These efforts help teachers recognize and perhaps make allowances for some needs of the gifted, but they cannot transform the regular classroom into the most appropriate environment for gifted children.

To claim that the regular classroom is the most appropriate environment, or to assert that mainstreaming (i.e., normalization) is necessary for the gifted, is at best somewhat misleading. The fear of elitism restrains educators from promoting extensive alternatives for the gifted. We shall, however, conceive of elitism in terms somewhat different from those typical of most discussions (see Chapter 12).

Critical Variables. The issue of most appropriate environment relates not so much to the particular setting that maximizes potential as to the instructional practices that accomplish this end (Leinhardt & Pallay, 1982). After reviewing studies dealing with the influence of alternative settings for handicapped students, Leinhardt and Pallay (1982, p. 572) conclude that nine variables "are important to student growth." Four of these variables are especially relevant to gifted education:

1. small class size (10–15 students),
2. increased time spent in cognitive activities,
3. reasonably rapid pacing, and
4. increased teacher instructional time, permitting higher on-task rates and greater cognitive press toward learning.

These variables of instruction address most of the problems related to regular class placement for the gifted. Gowan and Demos (1964, p. 138), after citing changes necessary to bring about enrichment (their generic methods term, following Hollingworth, for gifted education) in regular heterogeneous classes, state that implementing their suggested changes will "practically insure that enrichment in the heterogeneous classroom will become the most expensive way of ministering to the needs of the gifted."

Although setting per se does not determine the most appropriate environment, *setting is a means to operationalize the principle.* In making placement decisions, the aim should be to increase program alternatives for the student. Too often segregated settings have in the past damaged handicapped children and restricted their options. Exile to special classes was *for them* permanent and academically harmful. The four important variables cited above (Leinhardt & Pallay, 1982) seemed generally not to be associated with special class placement for the handicapped.

The same history does not characterize the education of the gifted, however. Because many gifted children *seem* to be good students (Are they good students if the work is too easy to them?), whereas none of the handicapped *seem* to be good students (Are they bad students if the work is too difficult for them?), the gifted seem favored. Sometimes gifted programs do provide spurious rewards to children so identified (Weiler, 1978), thereby entrenching such a notion.

The isolation that intellectual concerns impose on academically capable students goes unnoticed, however keenly these students may feel it. The possibility that the gifted need increased academic options and more flexibility in programs is often dismissed or discredited, because their needs are less visible than those of other "special" student populations.

Although setting is not the only variable that effectively determines the least restrictive environment, we still need some sense of preferred settings. One way to approach the problem is to determine which of the settings on the continuum of alternative placements are unlikely to foster the variables noted above (see Box 3.1). These settings can then be conceived of as the *most restrictive* and, therefore, *least appropriate settings.*

Gifted Children in Regular Classrooms. Whole-group teaching is probably the single most durable practice of the regular classroom (cf. Cuban, 1982). This practice necessitates the provision of other options for both the handicapped and the gifted, who differ greatly from their peers. Teachers can be expected to make some changes for students, but the gifted are so different that many significant changes must usually be made in order to provide them appropriate schooling (cf. Leinhardt & Pallay, 1982). According to Cuban (1982), these changes have not proven possible, and are not imminent, in the regular classroom.

To mainstream a gifted child is, in effect, to state that either (1) no alternative placements are available, or (2) this particular gifted child is in need of very little differentiation of instruction, *in contrast to the majority of gifted students.* In general neither of these statements is explicitly acknowledged by those proposing mainstreaming as the least restrictive environment for the gifted.

Normalization of the gifted amounts to reducing the influence of their potential on their (academic) achievement. Jencks et al. (1972, p. 74) somewhat facetiously suggest that one way to promote equality is to restrain the achievement of bright students. As Jencks et al. (1972) note, this is an inef-

BOX 3.1 Two Representations of the Continuum of Placement Alternatives

The concept of placement continuum underlies the notion of least restrictive alternative, which figures so prominently in legislation for the handicapped. As this notion has been applied to the handicapped, the least restrictive alternative is that which is least isolated—that is, the regular classroom. The most restrictive alternative is that which is most isolated—that is, full-time residence in a treatment facility such as a state hospital or mental retardation center. The principle of least restrictive alternative implies that students' placement should approximate regular class placement as closely as possible. The principle also implies that *fewer* students should be served in the most restrictive environments than in the least restrictive environments. This sense of continuum is illustrated below:

Traditional Notion of Continuum of Services (originally conceived to improve socialization of handicapped students)

regular class	(least restrictive)
resource room (½ time)	
self-contained special class	
special day-school or center	
home-bound instruction	
residential treatment center	(most restrictive)

To apply the preceding continuum of services to the gifted does not seem warranted. We do not anticipate that instruction will diminish the severity of their condition. Therefore, it makes sense to conceive the entire continuum somewhat differently, in cognitive terms. In the following continuum, *developmental placement* refers to advanced placement at higher grade levels based on cognitive characteristics. Resource rooms that offer only enrichment programs are not included below. Simultaneous placement in two or three environments is possible, and likely, for older gifted students.

ficient way to promote equality. This proposal, however, describes what often happens to the gifted in schools. No one pays too much attention to them; in general they are erroneously thought able to do well enough without any unusual provisions (Gallagher, 1975).

Assuming that normal students are receiving a more or less appropriate education and that the same is now true for handicapped students, it is only fair that the instruction of the gifted be differentiated. When cognitive goals are emphasized, the equity of differentiated services becomes apparent. In a

Alternative Notion of Continuum
(conceived to address
cognitive growth of students)

special school — advanced program	(most advanced)
special class — advanced program	
resource program — advanced program	
regular class, developmental placement	
regular class, enriched curricula	
regular class, regular program	
regular class, mainstreamed placement	
resource room — remedial program	
special class — remedial program	
special school — remedial program	(least advanced)

The basic principle of this continuum of placement is *cognitive press*, a notion that is appropriately applied to the handicapped (Leinhardt & Pallay, 1982) as well as to the gifted. This principle implies that children should be placed so as to maximize their learning, a notion that suggests more advanced placements are generally preferable to less advanced placements.

differentiated program, gifted children are able to receive an education predicated on their exceptional characteristics.

This view of the status of education does not deny that a great deal of improvement in the educational system is needed for students who come from backgrounds structured by impoverishment, oppression, and exploitation. These backgrounds, however, are social expressions of pressing political economic problems which the educational system is powerless to remedy alone.

In summary, then, the notion that undergirds normalization for the handicapped is *maximization of potential*. Normalization for the gifted, however, amounts to a *diminution of potential*. Similarly, mainstreaming is not an innovation of any particular benefit for the gifted. Moreover, because of the enduring and perhaps inevitable practices of the regular classroom, full-time placement in the regular classroom is usually the least appropriate alternative for gifted students (cf. Lewis & Kanes, 1980). Restraining the academic achievement of the gifted causes personal damage of uncalculated intellectual import. This fact should cause considerable pedagogical concern. Additionally, cognitive aptitudes and skills are, on a personal level, irrelevant to the way in which social inequality is structured. Therefore, the charge of elitism does not apply to differentiated academic instruction for the gifted (see Chapter 12).

Determination of Appropriate Environments

The most appropriate environment is the one that maximizes opportunities for students to develop cognitive excellence. Because appropriate placements must be based on individual characteristics, PL 94-142 "specifies that a continuum of programs and services be provided. . . . Thus public schools can no longer decide special education placements based on the availability or unavailability of a variety of school program options" (Fiscus & Mandell, 1983, pp. 12–13).

States, however, have implemented this principle reluctantly, even for the handicapped (Martin, 1979). For gifted students, this principle has been almost totally ignored (cf. Clendening & Davies, 1980). In gifted education one hears, at present, that this district serves gifted children in resource rooms, whereas that district serves them in the regular classroom. When the needs of gifted children are addressed *in some manner* by a system, seldom are other alternatives considered.

Nevertheless, we agree with Feldhusen (1982, p. 38), who writes, "meeting the needs of the gifted calls for a diversity of educational offerings. It seems unlikely that any one program offering will meet the needs of all the different types and levels of giftedness." This viewpoint implies that there are ways to measure different aspects of giftedness as well as to evaluate the effects of various instructional programs on individual attainment.

The degree to which it is possible to meet all the needs of many different gifted students depends on the accuracy of parameters for measuring student characteristics, the effectiveness of establishing precise instructional programs, and the relevance of research on aptitude-treatment interactions (Cronbach & Snow, 1977). We will examine research efforts that consider these questions and will suggest methods for applying research findings in school settings.

Research on Aptitudes and Treatments.   Aptitude-treatment interaction (ATI) and other related research compares the effects of instuctional treatments on learners with varying characteristics, which are usually represented as dichotomous variables. For example, a simple ATI study might assess the effect of rote drill on the achievement of learners with high and low intelligence. A more complicated variation of the study might compare the effects of rote and discovery learning methods on the achievement of low- and high-ability students (e.g., Snow, 1980). More recent studies attempt to discern aspects of individual functioning that differ from scholastic aptitude but may nevertheless contribute to the information processing skills necessary for academic achievement. The aptitudes most frequently studied include previous achievement, cognitive style, locus of control, conceptual tempo, achievement motivation, learning style, and personality variables (Carrier & McNergney, 1979; Holtan, 1982).

ATI Methods and Results.   Perhaps the most useful ATI research for determining instructional options for gifted students is that which considers effects of various programming and teaching strategies on the achievement of students with high scholastic aptitude scores. Although the evaluation of achievement as a function of IQ × treatment does not contribute to the development of new methods for assessing and instructing less efficient or less culturally validated learners (cf. Cronbach & Snow, 1977), it is consistent with eligibility criteria for gifted programs. In addition, application of this research may be possible in schools as they are presently conceived. The more specific ATI research, examining interactions between subskills related to information processing, may be too problematic to be put into practice at this time.

Some interesting trends emerge in the analysis of treatments effective with high-IQ students. Ability grouping, which has been found to have a negligible effect on the achievement of handicapped (Leinhardt & Pallay, 1982) and average students (Findley & Bryan, 1971), is effective in improving the achievement of the gifted (Kulik & Kulik, 1982). Inductive teaching (i.e., the inquiry or discovery method) appears advantageous only for high-IQ students (Cronbach & Snow, 1977), whereas programmed instruction and drill seem less effective (Snow, 1980). Academically able students also seem to benefit from more permissive classrooms in which they are allowed to express opinions, ask questions, and make comments. In addition, ATI studies have found that when the ability level of the teachers resembles that of their students, the students' achievement tends to be about two-thirds of a standard deviation higher than when students and teachers are unlike in ability level (Cronbach & Snow, 1977). This supports the notion that teachers of gifted students should be highly intelligent.

ATI studies dealing with previous learning or previous achievement may be useful in planning for gifted students. Several of these studies show that previously acquired knowledge of a subject or skill may mitigate the differential effectiveness of a particular treatment (e.g., McGivern & Levin, 1983; Stinard & Dolphin, 1981). A high degree of instructional support may be more important when students are first learning a skill or subject than when they already have some background in the area of instruction (Holtan, 1982). These results may influence decisions made about the placement of young gifted children or about instruction provided to older gifted students preparatory to independent study or other self-directed projects.

More Tentative Research. Less significant for gifted education are studies comparing the effects of the interaction between cognitive style and various instructional techniques. Cognitive style is frequently determined on the basis of one's approach to information processing (field-dependent or field-independent) or one's conceptual level (high or low). That these "styles" are reminiscent of the concept of intelligence makes their distinction from intelligence spurious; that the measurement of these cognitive styles is far less rigorous, precise, or valid than the measurement of IQ weakens the results of studies based on their measurement. However, since such studies abound, we will briefly consider their implications.

Conceptual level (CL), as quantified by scoring subjects' essays for conceptual complexity, measures the degree of sophistication and abstractness of thought. High-CL subjects "perceive their environment as differentiated and integrated . . . They are flexible and creative, inclined to explore, and relatively tolerant of stress" (Cronbach & Snow, 1977, p. 376). Low-CL subjects, on the other hand, are more rigid, less mature, and think less abstractly than high CL subjects. Considering their similarity to high IQ subjects, it is no surprise that high-CL subjects also learn better by inductive methods and in less structured, more self-directed settings than low-CL subjects (e.g., Tomlinson & Hunt, 1971).

The field-dependent/field-independent dichotomy was operationalized by Witkin (1973) to distinguish between global thinkers and analytical thinkers, respectively. Although the distinction is typically made on a test of perceptual performance, it is assumed to imply differences in information-processing strategies, modes of communication, personality, and even interests (see, e.g., Frank & Davis, 1982; Mahlios, 1981). Cronbach and Snow (1977) consider the notion of field-independence equivalent to that of fluid ability. They write, "Perhaps workers such as Witkin . . . are only demonstrating what Binet built into his definition of intelligence: the principle that weakness in analysis or self-discipline is a cause of poor intellectual performance. Then 'field-dependence' is a deficit rather than a style" (1977, p. 382).

For the purpose of planning the education of gifted students, however, it would be questionable either to assume that high IQ and field-independence are the same ability or to consider them different abilities and test for them separately. However, many of the treatments found effective for high-IQ students also prove advantageous for field-independent subjects (McLeod & Adams, 1979).

Generalizing about conceptual tempo is troublesome. This characteristic, represented by the impulsive-reflective dichotomy, presumably differentiates between those learners who "move quickly to conclusions, often settling on the first response that occurs to them [and those who] . . . spend more time carefully considering various possibilities" (Charles, 1976, p. 46). The relationship of this trait to other cognitive attributes is questionable.

Distinctions between left-brain and right-brain processing have also been considered in the ATI literature (Rice, 1980). Since these attributes are not easily measured, however, research relating them to instructional treatments is inconclusive. Although neurophysiological research has localized areas of the brain that control certain processes, such as language, it has not determined how thinking, remembering, or imagining occur. More importantly, it has not validated a theory of laterality in which one side of the brain is shown to dominate over the other (Springer & Deutsch, 1981).

Like other research, ATI studies sometimes rely on questionable measurement paradigms; others employ treatments that are shortlived, poorly conceived, or themselves dependent on inadequate measurement tools. In addition, the statistical processes normally recommended by ATI researchers for making instructional placement decisions have been criticized (Van Der Linden, 1981). Although aptitude-treatment interaction research provides a methodology for understanding the ramifications of various attributes in many educational settings, not all studies are equally valid or equally clear in their implications for practice.

Using Results of ATI Research in Individual Planning. The ATI research most useful for planning instruction for gifted students involves the comparison of various educational treatments for high-IQ subjects. Although the study of the interactions between cognitive subskills and instruction improves the understanding of intellectual processing, it is not of practical value. Rice (1980, p. 99) quotes Messick, the head research psychologist at the Educational Testing Service (ETS), on this point: "Diagnosing each ability separately doesn't help much, because life doesn't present challenges to only one ability at a time. Most tasks require several different abilities simultaneously."

The ATI research that considers general cognitive ability as one of the independent variables, however, presents several significant conclusions relevant to the placement of gifted students. This research also tends to corroborate results of studies evaluating the instruction-technique preferences of gifted students (Stewart, 1981).

Major Implications of ATI Research

1. Gifted students appear to benefit from ability grouping or from the type of intensive, rapid-paced instruction that is possible in a homogeneous group. Therefore, their placement in resource rooms, self-contained classrooms, and honors sections for a sizable portion of the day is justified because of its effectiveness (see Box 3.1, above).
2. High ability students seem to be the only students capable of gaining more from inductive teaching than from didactic teaching, according to ATI research. This finding supports differentiation in the approach to instruction chosen for the gifted. Such differentiation is probably not routine in regular classroom placements.
3. Gifted students learn more in an environment in which they can assert their opinions, ask questions, and control some features of their own education.
4. Since all students appear to benefit from instruction prior to independent study, optimal programs for gifted students provide them with intensive, relevant instruction before requiring them to pursue self-directed study.
5. Since students appear to learn more from teachers with cognitive ability similar to their own, teachers of the gifted should be recruited from among the most academically able.

ATI research has also explored how various aspects of personality interact with different treatments. The results are somewhat startling. For example, discouragement interacting with the extroverted personality produces academic gains, and encouragement interacting with introversion produces similar gains (Cronbach & Snow, 1977).

The conscious manipulation of personality and treatment interactions seems well beyond the resources and the purview of schools (cf. Bronfenbrenner, 1970). Nonetheless, familiarity with this research may change teachers' attitudes toward providing corrective or neutral feedback to students. *Praise may not be reinforcing to all students.* On the other hand, to exclude corrective feedback, as is sometimes recommended, from the repertoire of acceptable teaching practices may be parochial, especially if the goal of gifted education is to maximize the academic potential of highly able students (cf. Good & Brophy, 1984).

In addition, ATI research has shown that the use of motivation (e.g., task commitment) as a criterion for selecting students for programs may not be defensible, since motivation varies with personality. Motivation exhibited in school may reflect only the interaction between students' personalities and their present learning environments. Some of the eminent persons who have been studied in order to ascertain aspects of "genius" were not motivated in school (cf. Hollingworth, 1942; Wright, 1932). Since schools have not changed substantially over the years (Cuban, 1982; Katz, 1971), we suspect that motivation in school represents neither hypothetically intrinsic motivation nor motivation out of school (cf. Bloom & Sosniak, 1981; Coleman, 1961; Hollander, 1978). Therefore, placement in programs designed to develop cognitive strengths should depend on the evaluation of cognitive characteristics. If task commitment is considered important for improving the productivity of gifted students, it should be developed by gifted programs, not used as a criterion for access to them (Haensley, Shiver & Fulbright, 1980).

Finally, ATI research may have an important role in validating computer-assisted instruction (CAI) in fields such as mathematics. If computers can be programmed to diagnose learning characteristics from error analysis, they can provide sequential instruction that is compatible with students' favored information-processing strategies. Until such techniques have been developed and validated, however, we recommend that individualization strategies involving CAI be viewed as cautiously as other forms of instruction (e.g., programmed instruction) that have been shown to be less effective with gifted children. In general, individualization for gifted students should rely on what is known about their learning in various settings and with various types of instructional intervention.

ALTERNATIVES FOR GIFTED STUDENTS IN THE PUBLIC SCHOOL SYSTEM

Like handicapped children, gifted students require a variety of placement alternatives to meet their individual learning needs. This provision is in keeping with the concept of least restrictive environment which "affirms the individual's right to develop and pursue personal freedom with as few as possible imposed restrictions on the individual's development and freedom" (Suran & Rizzo, 1983, p. 187). The placement option(s) selected for particular gifted students should depend on their age, aptitudes, previous learning, and personality characteristics. The alternatives available to the student should be prioritized based on a determination of their effectiveness in addressing the "optimal instruction goals" for the learner (Jeter & Chauvin, 1982, p. 2).

Regular Classroom Modification

Although regular class placement is not the optimal setting in which to differentiate instruction for the gifted, this option is frequently adopted by schools in order to serve gifted students inexpensively (cf. Gowan & Demos, 1964). Those districts that provide part-time resource room services may also offer instructional modifications in the regular classroom. Colon and Treffinger explain the situation as follows:

> Gifted students are found in regular classrooms. It seems doubtful that we are on the verge of removing those students extensively from the classrooms of typical schools in our country. The most serious implication of this fact is that, given their presence in regular classrooms and their characteristics, their needs are also present and unavoidable.
>
> (Colon & Treffinger, 1980, p. 18)

When gifted children are assigned to regular classrooms on the basis of chronological age, it is difficult to provide either acceleration or enrichment. Acceleration may become a perfunctory exercise, with students working through one textbook after another and receiving little guidance from the teacher or stimulation from intellectual peers. Enrichment may "degenerate into a disjointed use of unrelated bits and pieces" (Shufelt, 1981, p. 46).

Nevertheless, the regular classroom can be modified to meet *some* of the needs of *some* gifted children. Feasible alternatives in the regular classroom include independent study options, ability grouping strategies, and developmental placement. Our discussion considers each of these approaches in isolation, although some combination of them is required to accommodate the needs of many gifted students.

Independent Study Options

Various independent study options can be arranged for gifted students in regular classrooms. These include teacher-designed learning contracts, individualized activities completed in classroom learning centers, correspondence courses, programmed instruction, personalized systems of instruction, and computer-assisted instruction (CAI). All of these alternatives, when used correctly, have the advantage of providing gifted students with advanced-level materials, but each option has some particular disadvantages. In addition, these independent study arrangements all limit gifted students' access to direct teacher input and interaction with other students.

Learning Contracts. The use of learning contracts to guide independent study is suggested by several authors as an appropriate strategy for instructing gifted students (Clark, 1983; Colon & Treffinger, 1980; Sisk, 1979; Treffinger, 1982). To use this technique effectively, teachers must assess students' skills or knowledge prior to instruction, delineate suitable instructional objectives, and evaluate progress in mastery of the skills or content studied.

This procedure is complex and time-consuming, especially if it must be repeated several times throughout the year for a number of students. It requires a teacher who is knowledgeable in several fields, who is willing to allow students to direct aspects of their learning, and who is able to design evaluation procedures that elicit evidence of students' integration of skills and knowledge, not just their recall of factual information.

Since the development of learning contracts can be tedious, teachers sometimes rely on available resources which may not be suitably paced or sufficiently advanced for gifted students. Arranging for students to complete entire textbooks at their own rates or work through commercially developed enrichment activities does not constitute appropriate individualization, since it does not eliminate repetitive drill or provide relevant feedback (Shufelt, 1981). Despite these drawbacks, use of independent study contracts is preferable to whole-group instruction on a level too elementary or superficial to benefit gifted students.

Classroom Learning Centers. Classroom learning centers are usually intended to provide reinforcement or enrichment activities that supplement direct instruction by the teacher. They are most applicable to instruction in elementary classrooms serving children of varying ability levels. The use of learning centers has been advocated for individualization, but their frequent misuse has also been noted (Cooper, 1981).

In general, learning centers allow teachers to control the difficulty of activities provided to children of different skill levels. Classroom management systems, based on the completion of numerous learning center activities each day, are difficult to establish and monitor, however. Their use as the principal instructional strategy in a classroom is questionable, because teaching involves more than the administration and grading of educational materials. Learning centers often include worksheets, games, puzzles, and reinforcement activities which are inappropriate for initial instruction and which may be particularly unsuitable for the instruction of gifted students. Usually the types of advanced-level activities that can be included in learning centers provide enrichment experiences removed from a coherent academic context. Acceleration is very difficult to accomplish through the use of learning centers.

Correspondence Courses. An instructional strategy appropriate for middle school and high school gifted students placed in regular programs is the completion of correspondence courses in addition to or in lieu of required courses. This approach is effective only with students who are highly motivated and unlikely to be distressed by the delay in feedback associated with correspondence instruction.

Placement teams that choose this option for gifted students should consider including some form of extrinsic motivation, such as a contractual agreement between the student and the school (e.g., DiSilvestro & Markowitz, 1982) or course credit toward graduation. This external source of motivation increases the likelihood that the student will complete the correspondence course. *Completion of an accredited correspondence course, especially if it evidences mastery of advanced skills, should be recorded on students' transcripts and used to satisfy requirements for graduation.* In addition, students may benefit from a modest amount of directed instruction in study techniques prior to beginning their first correspondence course. One method provides students with a system for deriving and fulfilling instructional objectives pertinent to private study (Morgan, 1981).

Programmed Instruction (Regular Classroom Only). Although aptitude-treatment interaction research has indicated that programmed instruction is not an optimal strategy for teaching gifted students, its use in regular classrooms may be preferable to other learning alternatives *in that setting* (Parke, 1983). This instructional technique involves the presentation of sequenced material in textbook, workbook, filmstrip or computer software formats (see the discussion of CAI below). The student responds to frequent questions provided in the programmed material and is given immediate feedback concerning the accuracy of answers.

The sequential nature and linear presentation of programmed materials make them particularly applicable to instruction in formal logic, grammar, mathematics, computer programming, and typing. This technique does not seem to be suitable to fields in which the conceptual content is more significant than the factual content, or in which the concepts are more global and less sequential (e.g., literature, sociology, history). Although Feldhusen, Elias, and Treffinger (1969) suggest that programmers could provide materials that develop higher-level cognitive skills, such materials have not yet been developed. Gallagher suggests one way to use programmed materials:

> If the teacher participates extensively in the presentation of the program, if the materials are spaced rather than concentrated so that there is time available for additional synthesis and practice, and if the criteria used to evaluate the effect of this material are similar to the objectives of the material itself, there is evidence that such materials can be useful in stimulating the thinking abilities of the student.

> (Gallagher, 1975, pp. 223–224)

Personalized Systems of Instruction. Personalized systems of instruction (PSI), another independent study option, use instructional modules prepared to present the content of entire courses. This course format, which can be substituted for the traditional lecture/discussion format, depends on the following components (Boileau, 1983, p. 140):

1. self-pacing,
2. unit perfection,

3. former students as proctors,
4. emphasis on written materials,
5. criterion-referenced testing and grading, and
6. re-testing for achievement mastery.

Frequently, PSI courses prepared by college instructors are videotaped and housed in auto-tutorial learning labs where students can have access to them. Such videotapes could provide gifted middle and high school students with course work appropriate to their instructional levels and interests. These tapes might be rented from colleges and used like correspondence courses, or portions of videotaped courses might be adapted to provide enrichment.

Regular classroom teachers at any grade level can develop their own PSI modules using filmstrips, cassettes, study guides, tests, and review materials. These modules might provide more comprehensive coverage of topics considered by the total class, or they might involve instruction in areas not considered by the entire group. The PSI approach, if it is carefully monitored by the teacher, might be a suitable vehicle for offering accelerated instruction to gifted students in a regular classroom.

Computer-Assisted Instruction. Computer-assisted instruction (CAI) extends the applications of programmed instruction by providing more pacing and branching alternatives. In addition, computers programmed to interact with student input can analyze students' errors, prescribe remedial sequences, and evaluate progress (Eisele, 1980). As with students receiving other forms of programmed instruction, achievement of students participating in CAI courses improves when they meet occasionally with the teacher to ask questions and review difficult problems (Tsai & Pohl, 1981).

Although computers are being touted as the panacea for all educational ills, CAI courses are a form of programmed instruction; cautions that apply to programmed instruction apply also to CAI. Consideration of computers' value as motivators should not be confused with appraisal of their ability to offer appropriate instruction. CAI should not replace accelerated instruction in subjects not adaptable to a programmed format (e.g., humanities, arts, social sciences, and some aspects of natural science).

Grouping Arrangements

Several grouping arrangements that can be implemented as part of the regular education provisions of a school or district may benefit gifted students. These include tracking, departmental (or flexible) grouping, cluster grouping, ungraded school placement, and open classroom arrangements. The most restrictive of these—tracking in particular—seem to be detrimental to low-ability and minority-group children and are avoided by some school districts (cf. Drowatzky, 1981; Leinhardt & Pallay, 1982; Snow, 1980).

Although homogeneous grouping is more suitable for gifted students than heterogeneous grouping, schools are not often arranged to accommodate this need of gifted students. However, teachers can still group students within their classrooms or can arrange with each other to exchange students for instruction in some subjects. In addition, classroom teachers can provide peer tutoring and cooperative learning experiences that benefit gifted as well as other students (Bronfenbrenner, 1970; Good & Brophy, 1984; Slavin, 1981).

Tracking. Tracking involves "placement . . . into groups that remain the same for instruction in all subjects" (Drowatzky, 1981, p. 47). This procedure, which does not account for intraindividual differences, may be more suitable for the gifted than for other students whose general scholastic aptitude is not so deviant from average. Gifted students, especially those scoring in the top 2 or 3 percent on individual intelligence tests, usually perform within the top 10 percent of their class in most subject areas.

The high performance of gifted students, however, can also be accommodated in a flexible or departmental grouping arrangement, which may be more equitable for other students. This arrangement is accomplished by grouping students according to their achievement levels in academic subject areas. Flexible grouping is practicable in subjects like language arts and math because standardized aptitude and achievement tests in these areas actually differentiate among students of varying skill levels. However, determining aptitude for or achievement in subjects like social studies or natural science may be more difficult since achievement tests in these areas usually measure recall of factual information, not conceptual sophistication. Nevertheless, both tracking and departmental grouping arrangements allow gifted students at all grade levels to receive instruction *more* suitable in pace and content than that which can be provided in a heterogeneous group.

Cluster Grouping. Cluster grouping is a placement alternative in which several elementary-level gifted students *in a particular grade* are grouped together in a classroom that also contains a number of average and above-average students (cf. Findley & Bryan, 1971; Good & Brophy, 1984; Sisk, 1979). This type of grouping makes it possible for teachers to engage in a reasonable amount of individualized planning because it requires them to develop appropriate activities for only two or three levels instead of the four or five levels normally represented in a heterogeneous self-contained classroom.

Some educators of the gifted (e.g., Clark, 1979, p. 140) caution against cluster-grouped classrooms since "these classrooms rely on group instruction and a set curriculum." Problems occur when this curriculum does not vary significantly from that prescribed for all students at the particular grade level. Although cluster grouping allows for interaction with intellectual peers, it may not permit sufficient differentiation to accommodate the cognitive needs of gifted students.

Ungraded Schools. Ungraded schools permit flexible grouping alternatives within age categories defined more broadly than those in conventional schools. In ungraded schools students can progress at a more rapid pace than is possible in graded schools, which do not encourage grade-skipping. This administrative arrangement eliminates traditional distinctions among grades and facilitates departmental grouping by ability.

Open Classroom/School Arrangements. In open classrooms in public schools, students are typically housed in one large room and instructed by several teachers working as a team. This approach allows for flexible grouping within a grade and provides gifted students with more opportunities for independent study (Gallagher, 1975). Open schools combine the open classroom concept with that of the ungraded school to allow for flexible grouping, student mobility, and self-directed learning.

Developmental Placement

Perhaps the least difficult but most effective regular classroom modification for gifted students involves acceleration in grade level (or "developmental placement," Christopherson, 1981). In spite of the ease of this approach and its demonstrated success, "the practice of acceleration is probably the least used administrative arrangement for providing services for the gifted" (Sisk, 1979, p. 375).

Developmental placement is based on theories of learning that view gifted children not as different from normal children, but simply as more advanced in their development (Christopherson, 1981). Early entry, grade-skipping, and cross-grade placements provide strategies for developmental placement (see Chapter 5 for a full discussion of accelerative strategies). Christopherson suggests the following criteria for determining a student's readiness for above-grade level placement:

Christopherson's Criteria for Developmental Placement

The child's level of intellectual development should exceed the 80th percentile for the older children. . . .

To place the child with . . . older children in one subject area . . . the child should exceed the 70th percentile for the older children's achievement in that subject area. . . .

To place the child with older children in all subject areas, achievement should exceed the 50th percentile in five-sixths of the subjects and the 30th percentile in the rest. . . .

[The child should] exceed the 33rd percentile of older children for social and emotional development and the 10th percentile for physical development.

(Christopherson, 1981, p. 41)

Special Provisions

Interest in gifted children spread rapidly in the early 1920s as a result of the general enthusiasm for intelligence tests. The "Terman classes" established in the Speyer School in New York (Hollingworth, 1926) segregated high-IQ students for the entire school day. The Colfax Elementary School in Pittsburgh (Newland, 1976) and the Cleveland Major Work classes (Hall, 1956) segregated children in academic subjects only. These prototypes were based on the assumption that the heterogeneity of the regular classroom works against the best interests of gifted students.

Educators expected that increased homogeneity would make instruction more effective. Teachers, it was argued, could prepare their lessons and materials to suit a narrower range of ability. Bright students would not have to repeat material they had already mastered, and less able students would not have to cover material they were not ready to learn. These goals were to some extent accomplished through ability grouping, but there were important qualifications.

A meta-analysis of fifty-two studies of grouping at the secondary level found differential effects for slow and gifted groups. Kulik and Kulik (1982) report the effects of grouping on the achievement of average and below-average students as near zero, but they found the effects of grouping on high-ability students to be clearly positive. (The investigators also found that students who are grouped for a particular subject have a better attitude toward the subject than ungrouped students.)

Grouping may be mildly detrimental to the social acceptance of gifted students by other students (Gallagher, 1975). Maddux, Scheiber, and Bass (1982) found this effect in fifth grade children newly placed in a gifted program; the effect was not, however, found in sixth graders who had been attending a similar gifted class for a year. Decline in social acceptance on entry into a gifted program may be only temporary (cf. Fund for the Advancement of Education, 1957). There certainly is no indication that serious problems in social adjustment result from participation in a segregated gifted program. Maddux et al. (1982), for example, found more positive self-concepts among gifted fifth and sixth graders enrolled in a special class than among nongifted classmates in a regular classroom (cf. Gallagher, 1965).

According to Tremaine (1979), the benefits of special classes for gifted students include higher grades (in spite of the fact that they are taking more difficult, advanced-level classes) and more scholarships. These outcomes cannot be explained as effects of selection for the program studied by Tremaine because there were no significant differences between non-enrolled gifted students in the control group and gifted students in schools that did not have a gifted program. Ability grouping of bright children, according to Whitmore's review of the research (1980, pp. 67–68), "results in the highest academic achievement without negative social and emotional effects on the individual."

Endorsement of ability grouping should be tempered by an understanding of the many variables that influence achievement. Grouping in itself is not sufficient to cause much change (Clark, 1983; Kulik & Kulik, 1982; Leinhardt & Pallay, 1982). Other associated variables are probably responsible for the positive gains attributed to grouping. Academic gain may be a function of the quality of the school. Marked gains in performance resulting from ability grouping, for example, occur more visibly in poorly funded schools (Evans & Marken, 1982). Where the general quality of instruction is low, special classes may play a crucial role in the education of exceptional students.

Special classes are commonly used to provide for gifted children in public schools. Part-time placements include resource rooms or centers, itinerant teacher programs, advanced classes, and school-within-a-school programs. Full-time segregated placements include self-contained classrooms, special schools, and home schooling. The demography of the school district and of the gifted population guides the development of program alternatives.

Resource Programs.   In many districts the resource program is the only special placement available at the elementary school level and is referred to as "the gifted program." In these districts, placement in the resource room program is often mistakenly considered an adequate way for schools to fulfill their obligation to exceptionally able students. Most educators of the gifted, however, agree that in view of the limitations of any single approach, it is only a partial response. The diversity of the children's needs requires several types of special classes.

Three variations of the resource program are (1) the resource classroom, attended only by the children in the school building; (2) the resource center program, attended by gifted children from several schools; and (3) the itinerant teacher program, in which the teacher travels from school to school to serve gifted children. Each variation lends itself differentially to the demography of particular school districts (see Box 3.2).

The chief advantage of the resource program is flexibility of scheduling. School administrators may also believe that resource programs are less expensive to implement than self-contained programs, but a study by Gallagher and his associates shows this belief to be inaccurate (Gallagher, Weiss, Oglesby & Thomas, 1982).

Flexibility of the resource approach is greatest when the teacher serves a single school. Resource rooms are most effective when the caseload for the teacher of the gifted is reasonable (e.g., twenty to thirty students). Where a resource room operates in one school, gifted students can be scheduled according to their individual ability levels and classroom situations. The other resource variations are limited by extraneous factors such as transportation (House, 1981). The problem of continuity and weak content is most serious in itinerant teacher programs. Not only do logistical difficulties (classroom space, transportation, scheduling) contribute disproportionately to a lack of continuity, but itinerant teachers have little time to establish credibility with co-workers.

The needs of individual children will vary from year to year, depending, in part, on the regular classroom program. It should be recognized, however, that two to five hours of enrichment or accleration per week cannot meet the needs of children who are significantly advanced in verbal comprehension, memory, and reasoning. Many high-IQ students should not spend *any* time working at their chronological-age grade level.

BOX 3.2   Enrichment Centers for Underachievers

An interesting application of the resource program model is one adopted in Israel to develop academic skills of bright children living in poor neighborhoods. Based on the premise that talented children in poor communities are the group of students most disadvantaged with respect to their potential, two regional enrichment centers were established to serve high-ability students in elementary schools in the poorest areas of Jerusalem and Tel-Aviv. The purpose of the centers was to counteract the negative effects of low teacher expectations and an anti-intellectual social climate (Smilansky & Nevo, 1979).

Sixth graders who scored in the upper quarter of their group on a battery of tests were invited to attend the enrichment centers for two afternoons a week during the school year and for a month in the summer. About 90 percent of the eligible students participated in the program from sixth through eighth grade. Enrichment took the form of systematic tutoring in critical reading and study methods, science courses, foreign language studies, and enrichment in the humanities.

A follow-up study determined that 66 percent of the children in the Jerusalem enrichment program reached the twelfth grade of an academic secondary school as compared to 32 percent of the control group. Comparable results were found for the Tel-Aviv center. Smilansky and Nevo (1979) report that the enrichment center program was inexpensive and easy to organize. Centers were housed in public buildings: a museum, a high school, a public library. At relatively little expense, the rate of bright, disadvantaged students' completion of college-bound high school programs was doubled.

Students who are provided accelerated work in the regular classroom may need the resource room only for individualized instruction in a subject not offered in the regular program, such as algebra in the fifth grade, or for a special class, such as a class in literature for high-ability readers. On the other hand, gifted children who are not being challenged by classroom work or who are having achievement problems may need to spend a larger portion of their time in the resource room.

An efficient use of the resource room is to provide accelerated classes to high-IQ students and to students who are especially apt in particular subjects. Resource centers can also serve high-IQ and academically talented students in populous areas where staff and equipment can be concentrated in one center that serves children from several schools. Provision of resource centers is also possible in more rural areas if districts combine resources and if transportation problems are not prohibitive.

Itinerant teachers in rural districts sometimes serve just a few students in each school, especially when they serve only high-IQ children (Witters & Vasa, 1981). If these teachers are also permitted to serve children who score in the 98th percentile or above on achievement tests, they can arrange scheduling to meet the needs of all the advanced students in a rural school (e.g., high-

IQ students and gifted mathematics students during one time period, high-IQ and gifted language arts students during another). If the programs are sufficiently rigorous, this approach can improve instruction for both groups.

Including academically talented children in the rural resource program allows discussion, debate, and lecture; these options are impossible with only one or two students in a class. Since interaction with other gifted students is an advantage of the special class (Alexander & Muia, 1982), a dual-criterion approach is particularly appropriate in rural districts. When a high IQ score is the only criterion for placement, rural districts may spend much more per gifted child to provide special instruction than urban and suburban areas.

Resource programs may have difficulty when they depend on cooperation from individual teachers in scheduling children for instruction outside the regular classroom. Although daily attendance in a resource program is ideal, students in most programs rarely attend a resource class two days in a row, and instructional continuity is difficult to maintain.

If children stay in the regular classroom for a special event or if a holiday intervenes, resource teachers may find that two or three weeks elapse between class meetings. This is an intolerable teaching situation. When teachers find themselves in competition with regular class special events, they often try to make disjunctive instructional time entertaining to induce students to *choose* to attend the resource program. The result of this tactic may well be further loss of support for the program. To objective observers the program will seem irrelevant because it is neither challenging nor related to the academic curriculum nor designed to accomplish long-term goals. In this situation students will not be willing to do serious academic work. The pull-out nature of resource programs is a critical failing at the junior and senior high school level.

The establishment of policy governing scheduling is essential to forestall the development of such a predicament. Scheduling decisions must be made during the negotiation of individualized education programs (IEPs), based on information from both the classroom teacher and the resource teacher. Administrative support must ensure that once the schedule has been established, it is followed. If these precautionary steps are not explicitly taken, the resource program can *very quickly* degenerate into an optional extracurricular activity. Within schools there are many forces at work that precondition this eventuality, and alert administrators and teachers must take steps early on to circumvent them.

The resource program model contributes to gifted education's reputation as more entertaining than educational (Renzulli, 1977). Lack of supportive policy and the pull-out format of resource programs promote reliance on loosely related learning activities, games, and projects. The threat to continuity posed by lack of support for programs can be alleviated through conscientious delivery of substantive, relevant instruction, which should characterize all special education efforts for the gifted (Stanley, 1981).

Advanced Classes.   Seminars, independent study classes, honors programs, fast-paced classes, and a variety of other advanced class options are the most common alternatives for gifted junior and senior high school students (Silverman, 1980). The need for greater diversity in programs for adolescents than in programs for younger students stems from the greater differentiation of aptitude among gifted students (Keating, 1979). Advanced classes address this need (Feldhusen, 1982). Any subject can form the content of a special class, and criteria for eligibility can vary. For example, an honors biology class can be offered to high achievers who want in-depth study of a subject in which they are interested. Students of the highest ability can enroll in honors classes as well as in fast-paced, intensive classes.

Coordination at the district, regional, and state level can articulate programming for students whose needs become more intense and more diverse as they get older. Otherwise, gifted students who are accelerated in elementary school may have to repeat work in junior high school because there is no comparable program at that level (Van Tassel-Baska, 1981). A coordinator at the state and district levels can assist in identifying types of programs needed, developing plans and procedures that take into account local demographic characteristics, locating resources to implement programs, and evaluating the effectiveness of programs for the gifted. At the school-building level, large high schools may assign a teacher of the gifted the responsibility for coordinating and scheduling individual gifted students' programs. Whether or not the consulting teacher provides direct instruction to gifted students depends on the nature of the program.

Without provisions for college level instruction, gifted programs for adolescents are incomplete. Although teachers at the secondary level are more specialized than elementary teachers, some gifted high school students are more expert within a subject area than their teachers (Renzulli, 1982). The Advanced Placement Program (APP), discussed in Chapter 5, is the most widely used means of offering college level instruction to public school students. (Other options for college instruction are treated in the discussion of dual enrollment in Chapter 5.)

Less well known than the APP is the International Baccalaureate program, a curriculum developed for children of diplomats and other mobile populations. International Baccalaureate credit, awarded on the basis of performance on written and oral examinations, is accepted by many universities in Europe and the United States, including Columbia, Johns Hopkins, MIT, Princeton, Stanford, the University of Michigan, and the University of Pennsylvania, (Peterson, 1972). The program requires students to be tested in six subjects: a first and second language, mathematics, an "exact" science such as physics, a "human" science such as anthropology, and an elective (Peterson, 1972). Syllabi describing the objectives of each course of study, the requirements for higher or subsidiary level examinations, and the course examinations guide students' programs.

School-within-a-School. The school-within-a-school concept is varied in application. In some cases, it involves nearly total separation, with the gifted students grouped for all of their classes. In some instances, it resembles a college honors program in that classes are limited to superior students, though the students take other classes as well. But whereas college honors programs offer more opportunities for individualized work and greater access to libraries and other instructional resources (Gold, 1979), public schools-within-schools, although they provide advanced curricula, may have access only to regular school resources (Clark, 1983). Whether there is a specific, designated physical location or whether the school-within-a-school program is accomplished through scheduling alone depends on the district. A slightly larger population than the typical rural school is probably needed to implement this option; in suburban or urban areas it is a cost-effective means of providing gifted education (Fox, 1979b).

Self-contained Classes.   Although total separation is viewed with suspicion by most educators, it may represent the best approach to education for some gifted children. Lamping (1981), a teacher and parent of a gifted child, identifies and rebuts common arguments against self-contained classes for the gifted. These arguments are that (1) gifted children should learn to associate with all kinds of people, (2) grouping the gifted promotes snobbish attitudes, encouraging the gifted to see themselves as an elite group, and (3) gifted children will succeed regardless of the education provided them. The first concern, notes Lamping, can be addressed in a variety of ways that do not entail holding gifted students back academically such as through clubs and other extracurricular activities. The latter two arguments are not supported by research.

When individualized education programs are implemented for several children in self-contained gifted classrooms, age spans must be limited, probably to no more than three years, although there will be exceptions (e.g., a highly gifted six-year-old may be placed in a self-contained classroom that usually serves nine- through eleven-year-old students). Small caseloads, though expensive, are critical. A maximum caseload of twelve gifted students per self-contained classroom has been established in one state (West Virginia State Department of Education, 1983). Although this caseload may seem small, it is not unheard of as a regular class size in rural schools.

Most importantly, the amount of differentiated service thus provided should be much greater than is possible through the combination of part-time regular grade placement and part-time resource class placement. If some academically talented students also attend the self-contained class for instruction in their areas of strength, a self-contained program can be more cost-effective than a resource program, not only in terms of cost per benefit but also in terms of gross expenditures alone (see the discussion of cost-effectiveness later in this chapter).

Special Schools.   Most practicable in large metropolitan areas, schools for the gifted concentrate, within a single building, resources and programming efforts that serve a large number of students (Fox, 1979b). Schools for the gifted and alternative or magnet schools specializing in fields such as foreign languages, science and engineering, science and mathematics, or performing arts are found primarily in large cities—the Bronx High School of Science, the Cincinnati School for Creative and Performing Arts, and the Houston

High School for the Performing and Visual Arts are among the best-known. State-funded residential schools such as the North Carolina School of Science and Mathematics, a tuition-free school for gifted eleventh and twelfth graders (Cox & Daniel, 1983), are a recent phenomenon.

Although most specialized schools enroll only high school students, a few schools, such as the Cincinnati School for Creative and Performing Arts and the North Carolina School of the Arts, accept some younger talented students. The residential school has been advocated as a means of addressing the needs of gifted disadvantaged youngsters. Two examples are Kentucky's (short-lived) Lincoln School (Ecton, 1979) and the boarding-school "fostering programs" in Israel (Smilansky & Nevo, 1979).

Home Schooling.   Although in placement models for handicapped children the home is considered to be a restrictive educational setting, the use of home schooling as an instructional alternative for the gifted is increasing, especially in rural areas (cf. Kearney, 1984). Parents adopt this option for a number of reasons including disagreement with values promulgated by the school system and dissatisfaction with the quality of instruction in the schools (Holt, 1981, 1983).

Recent litigation and legislation lend support to home schooling. For example, Arizona has passed a law allowing parents to teach their children at home without the permission of the local school board (Divoky, 1983). Although the majority of school districts approve home schooling grudgingly, there is incentive for cooperation between districts and parents: if districts provide textbooks and other materials, they justify continued receipt of state allotments for students educated at home (Holt, 1983).

SCHOOL SYSTEM PRIORITIES IN PLACEMENTS

Because schools are bound together by many common pedagogical and administrative conditions, they share some tendencies in the placement of exceptional students. In general, the more unusual a child's need (e.g., the lower the incidence of the child's exceptionality), the less flexible school arrangements are likely to prove; this is, after all, the reason that special education has been developed as a school option.

In light of these facts, teachers need to develop some sense of the conditions that influence school priorities in placement alternatives for gifted children. Obviously particular schools and districts will vary. There are, however, some general approaches that teachers may employ to cope with a variety of school system responses, since in general these responses will be predicated on a common logic of management. We discuss three possible administrative concerns: (1) program effectiveness, (2) cost-effectiveness, and (3) child-appropriateness.

Program Effectiveness

The evaluation of gifted programs in the public schools has been, understandably, a low-priority concern. Demonstration of accomplishment is one of the major purposes of evaluation. Experimental programs and model programs funded by outside agencies include evaluations to demonstrate the validity of their premises. Funding agencies have invested money to test these hypotheses and require evidence of their validity, or at least documentation of their accomplishments.

Public school boards are primarily concerned, however, not with testing hypotheses, but with providing instruction. Their limited funds are expended on personnel, buildings, textbooks, and school buses. In 1971, only about 4 percent of the estimated school-aged population in need of gifted education was receiving any special instruction or programming (Marland, 1972). By 1976, about 33 percent of the gifted school-aged population was reported as participating in gifted programs (Erickson et al., 1978).

School boards have considered evaluation an extravagance until recently, when dissatisfaction with the public schools—together, ironically, with tighter budgets—has made accountability an issue. In this context program evaluation has become a political necessity. The more an evaluation system is integrated into a program, the more likely it is to guide the improvement and document the cost-effectiveness of the program.

Program Evaluation: Groundwork. Evaluation considerations should be taken into account from the inception of a program. The goals of the program should guide evaluation efforts. In order for the results of instruction to be assessed, plans for collecting both formative and summative feedback are needed. Formative evaluation refers to analysis of the instructional process; summative evaluation refers to analysis of the products of instruction (Scriven, 1967). The former gives corrective feedback while the program is in progress, and the latter gauges the accomplishment of program goals.

The most critical activity in program evaluation is the selection of tests and instruments that address specific evaluation concerns. Selecting appropriate measures is important to ensure collection of valid and reliable data. Despite the fact that the only justification for initiating and maintaining gifted programs is positive change in student achievement, the effectiveness of gifted education programs is rarely documented in terms of positive gains in student performance as measured by objective tests. Too often it is expressed as satisfaction with the program (e.g., using survey or rating scale data only). Although student, parent, and teacher perceptions about programs constitute a legitimate kind of feedback, they cannot demonstrate accomplishment of instructional goals.

Program goals should be broad enough to subsume goals for individual students, but specific enough to guide instruction. Although many gifted programs are individualized, they usually have broad instructional goals common to all of the students. Evaluation concerns and selection of evaluation instruments should be determined at the time program goals are being developed; evaluation procedures should be specified in the program description. Standards for input (e.g., materials, facilities, personnel) and process (i.e., instruction) need to be developed. Responsibility for collection of input and process data is usually assigned to administrative personnel.

Program Evaluation: Instrumentation. Teachers should read the critical reviews of tests they are considering for use in evaluating programs in order to ensure that the tests measure what the program was designed to teach. When the broad goals relate to academic growth, standardized and criterion-referenced achievement tests can be used to evaluate programs. When the broad goals of programs involve measuring such notions as higher-level thinking skills, problem-solving, or critical thinking, special care in choosing program evaluation instruments is necessary.

For example, the Ross Test of Higher Cognitive Processes (Ross & Ross, 1976) has been suggested for both screening students for gifted programs and evaluating the effects of instruction (Callahan & Corvo, 1980). Most screening instruments sample a spectrum of general abilities rather than skills within a particular domain. If the Ross test measures general aptitudes derived from a variety of experiences, it may not reflect student growth resulting from a semester's or year's instruction in the gifted program. An evaluation summary discussed by Maker (1982a) showed significant gains on only one of several subtests of the Ross as a result of a year's instruction in a gifted program. Whether the equivalence of pretest and posttest scores on the other subtests reflects inadequate instruction or inadequate measurement is moot, since the test was not sensitive to what was taught in the program.

The Watson-Glaser Critical Thinking Appraisal (Watson & Glaser, 1964) is also used as an evaluation instrument in gifted programs (Maker, 1982a). However, relatively high correlations of scores on this test with IQ scores (.55 to .75; Watson & Glaser, 1964) suggest that there may be problems in using it as a program evaluation instrument. The authors recommend it as a research tool for efficacy studies of programs designed to teach critical thinking skills; however, decisions about its use should be based on review of the test, test manual, and articles about the test.

When goals are not common to most children in a particular gifted program, the comparison of pretest and posttest scores on a specified instrument is not feasible. The use of a variety of commercial or teacher-made criterion-referenced tests is preferable for highly individualized programs. Results can be summarized and included in evaluation reports as demonstration of program effectiveness.

Whether a norm-referenced or criterion-referenced test is used, a sufficient number of difficult items must be included. Using tests that are too easy may result in inflated pretest scores (Renzulli, 1975). Off-level testing is a solution to this problem if there is a test available that measures advanced-level skills taught in the gifted program.

Inclusion of a large sample of difficult items will help to offset the effects of regression toward the mean as well. We recommend the use of advanced-level criterion-referenced tests in evaluating instruction unless there is some compelling need to compare gifted children's performance to that of other children. Tests appropriate for routine program assessment include college placement tests, teacher-made tests, or tests that accompany textbook series. Teachers can select, modify, or design these tests to measure application, analysis, and synthesis of information (cf. Bloom, 1956).

It sometimes seems that what is taught in gifted programs is of such an advanced or esoteric nature that it defies measurement. Subjective impressions of instructional gains, however, are not compelling proof of program effectiveness. In spite of the difficulties associated with objective program evaluation procedures, the clear conceptualization of instructional goals, detailed specification of evaluation concerns, and careful selection of tests make objective evaluation procedures the only means of discovering and documenting program effectiveness. Thus, they constitute the most reliable basis for developing improved programs.

Cost-Effectiveness

Cost-effectiveness amounts to getting a good buy for one's money. Thus, when schools or businesses purchase equipment, the departments making the purchasing requests are generally asked to write specifications that precisely describe the functions and features of the equipment needed. The more precise the description, the more likely the department is to get what it wants, and the more meaningful is the comparison between competitive bids.

Public schools are run as if they were businesses (Counts, 1930), though they sell neither goods nor services on an open market. Schools are run as businesses because it is in the nature of our economy for them to be run that way. Construction of school buildings, employment of staff, and purchase of instructional materials are large expenditures—fiscal accountability is the inherent condition of administration.

Cost-effectiveness is very important to the establishment, survival, and growth of gifted programs for several reasons: (1) interest in gifted education has been sporadic; (2) many programs are not mandated; and (3) declining enrollments have decreased school revenues. Unless programs can be substantiated as cost-effective, their funds may be jeopardized. Because the gifted are effective learners, however, programs that address their demonstrated abilities can readily prove themselves cost-effective. Teachers *can* defend their programs against the above threats. They can exert a helpful influence, even when the determination of cost-effectiveness is not one of their responsibilities.

Using Cost-Effectiveness Studies.   Teachers can use cost-effectiveness studies to help establish the worth of their programs. Such studies are no more difficult to conduct than other empirical studies; in fact, they can be considerably less complex statistically than the typical research studies with which most teachers should be familiar. As with research studies, the relevance of cost-effectiveness studies depends on the appropriateness of the quantifications and the cogency of discussion. There is considerable latitude for defining variables and making judgments about how and what is relevant both to measurement and to discussion.

Cost-effectiveness can be used to defend existing programs from budget cuts, to improve programs, or to propose new ones. The teacher of the gifted who has collected data and given the matter some thought can influence study parameters. Even if no particular changes are anticipated, this sort of reporting to the principal or program director can help ensure that the assistance of the teacher of the gifted is sought when changes *are* anticipated.

Compared to benefits, costs are easy to determine. Costs are measured in dollars; one need only account for them consistently. Storms (n.d.) notes that costs in several areas (e.g., physical plant, salaries, and instructional materials) can be prorated in a number of ways. Some programs, depending on their complexity, may not need to account for all costs (e.g., building rent or maintenance). Gallagher et al. (1982) found that personnel costs amounted to 74, 85, and 75 percent of program costs for consultant, resource, and special class services, respectively, for gifted students.

Benefits cannot be construed in dollars because education does not produce a profit for the school system or a product that is sold on the open market. The determination of cost-effectiveness nonetheless requires that benefits be quantified. Gifted teachers should, therefore, remember that valid measures of substantial educational parameters are more likely to be viewed by all parties as meaningful benefits (see the preceding discussion of program effectiveness.)

Cost per Benefit. The proper measure for determining the cost-effectiveness of gifted program alternatives is cost per benefit, or the cost-benefit ratio. According to Gallagher et al. (1982), consultant programs cost (per pupil) 16 percent, resource rooms 30 percent, and special classes 27 percent more than regular programs. Since, in their study, median time in class was largest and pupil-teacher ratio smallest in the special class placement, Gallagher et al. (1982) concluded that cost per benefit was minimized in the special class delivery model, and it was therefore the most cost-effective model.

Note, however, that these conclusions were based on data from current practices as reported in a national survey, and not from a controlled investigation of similarly implemented and consistently defined consultant, resource, or special class models. For example, most special classes in this study were part-time placements, caseloads varied dramatically, and there was even some confusion over the distinction between class size and caseload. The information obtained was so variable that the researchers used the semi-interquartile range to derive their descriptive statistics. Therefore, these findings are only suggestive of the different possibilities for establishing the cost-effectiveness of these delivery models.

Child-Appropriateness

Our discussion of the research in Chapter 4 will indicate the degree to which schools have found it difficult either to determine child-appropriateness or to implement individual programs based upon its determination (cf. Poland et al., 1982; Ysseldyke & Algozzine, 1982a; Ysseldyke, Algozinne & Mitchell, 1982). Schools have not done well, even under the requirements of PL 94-

142. Nationally, the situation of gifted students, without the protections of PL 94-142, is much worse than that of handicapped students. Even in the fourteen states that apply PL 94-142 regulations to the gifted (Mitchell, 1981b), gifted programs are covertly viewed as an agenda item of lesser importance. Nonetheless, the poor performance of placement teams is not due to the desire of individuals to subvert the consideration of what is child-appropriate. Instead, decisions seem to emerge on the basis of what is most conveniently arranged.

Drowatzky (1981) has noted the difficulty schools have faced in the courts when called upon to relate the learning needs of individual children to particular administrative arrangements for accommodating those needs, especially as the needs and the arrangements interact with race and sex bias. Child-appropriateness is a pedagogical ideal seldom realized in specific provisions. The gap between theory and practice in education may in fact have widened as research methodology (i.e., the ability to make accurate empirical observations) has grown more sophisticated (cf. Good & Brophy, 1984).

In contrast, cost control and fiscal accountability are compelling everyday administrative priorities. The budget process ensures that these priorities will have real effects. In the face of the lack of improvement in the financial conditions of schooling, it is unlikely that consideration of child-appropriateness will make much progress.

Indeed, it is unclear how the consideration of the learning needs of individual children (which can be particularized almost indefinitely) can be reconciled with the need to provide extended universal schooling. The priorities of our economic system impose definite limits on the former task (Baer, 1980). Special education is one way to balance these forces, but it is only one possible response out of many.

PL 94-142 has established that schools must make some attempt to consider child-appropriateness in dealing with exceptional children. That the gifted are somehow implicated is evidenced by the fact that half the states house gifted education in the same administrative section as special education (Mitchell, 1981b). For gifted children, child-appropriateness implies not only that elitist curricula be avoided (cf. Christopherson, 1981), but that the equal access of all groups be ensured. The prospect that all the white, upper-middle class schools of a region will have gifted programs while poor white schools and black schools will have none is insupportable (Baer, 1980). Such a prospect is not a corollary of child-appropriateness, but of our economic and political system.

SUMMARY

If the goal of gifted education is to maximize the academic potential of gifted children, then normalization is an inappropriate strategy for gifted education. The chief method of accomplishing normalization, mainstreaming, which *has* been seriously proposed for gifted children, is also inappropriate. The long history of unchanging regular classroom practices suggests that mainstreaming the gifted is largely a way to pretend to improve their education while accomplishing nothing.

The limitations of regular class placement notwithstanding, the public school system can still supply at reasonable cost the variety of differentiated placements needed to maximize the academic potential of gifted students. A gifted program, however, cannot consist of only one such option. A program for gifted children must be composed of all the options that are potentially available to differentiate education. A gifted program should be predicated on the intellectual needs of children, not on a school's degree of responsiveness to those needs.

Teachers must realize that schools prefer cost-effectiveness to any other criterion of program performance. This fact of life needs to be reckoned with realistically. Programs that are based on activities irrelevant to the main academic goal of gifted education can establish their cost-effectiveness best through public relations efforts. Academically oriented programs that address the salient characteristics of gifted children can expect to justify their cost-effectiveness in purely conventional terms. The necessity for such a justification need not limit what gifted programs can accomplish.

CHAPTER 4

Individuals and Systems: Negotiating Program Plans

INTRODUCTION

The most effective education for children is that which is commensurate with their abilities; however, a number of elements work against the achievement of a match between instruction and student ability. Individualization, through either gifted programs or modification of instruction, depends on counter-acting those elements. For both philosophical and pragmatic reasons, the most promising means to address the individual needs of gifted children is to align efforts on their behalf with efforts to address the needs of handicapped children. This chapter presents a rationale for employing special education principles in the education of gifted students and details practices for negotiating programs that match the level and pace of instruction to students' level and rate of achievement.

SPECIAL EDUCATION AS THE BASIS FOR DIFFERENTIATED SERVICE

The most traditional means of accommodating student ability levels is to group children of similar age; however, it is generally conceded that grade placement fails to address significant individual differences in the development of children of approximately the same chronological age. The more students differ on variables related to academic performance, the less likely is grade placement to accommodate their needs. Instruction in the regular classroom assumes commonalities that do not hold for some children.

The consequent inadequacy of grade-level materials and activities for those children is sometimes obvious; for example, students reading far below grade level clearly have a need for lower-level books. With gifted students, the inadequacy of regular classroom materials and assignments is not always apparent. As a result of a mismatch between their aptitudes and the materials provided in regular classrooms, gifted students may appear to be either diligent students or underachievers. Even when the discrepancy between instructional level and the student's ability level is apparent, other variables influence efforts to accommodate students with unusual learning needs. Surprisingly, ease of accommodation is not necessarily a determining factor.

Basic Conflicts in Special Education

The quality of individualized instruction, designed to accommodate individual abilities, interests, or learning styles, depends in part on the resolution of three basic conflicts in educational ideation: (1) whether universal or special education takes priority, (2) whether or not gifted education belongs under the category of special education, and (3) whether gifted education should be controlled by the local, state, or federal government.

Universal versus Special Education. The conflict between universal education, which requires attention to utility and efficiency (i.e., educating the greatest number at the least expense), and special education, which focuses on optimal development of each student's ability, is unavoidable. As Kirk and Gallagher (1983) note, pressure for special education for the gifted is, in part, a response to the heterogeneity that universal education brings to the classroom. Unfortunately, resistance to this pressure is usually proportional to the level of our society's confidence in its "superiority." In periods of public confidence in the country's ability to maintain the status quo, interest in the needs of gifted students is minimal. In periods of uncertainty, interest in academic talent, "our most valuable natural resource," increases (Whitmore, 1981). Economic pressures in this decade may have created enough societal self-doubt to generate increased interest in gifted education once more (cf. The National Commission on Excellence in Education, 1983).

Gifted Education as Special Education. Commitment to universal education and equal opportunity for all students is not incompatible with gifted education when it is conceived of as a category of education for exceptional children. Though some educators decry the connection between handicapped and gifted students, this connection does supply a better rationale for differentiating education for the gifted than does the "natural resource" argument. Like handicapped students, the gifted, because they deviate from the norm, are poorly served by instruction that is based only on chronological age (Sapon-Shevin, 1982). If one accepts this fact and the principle that all children should be provided an education appropriate to their developmental level, then special education for the gifted is a necessary component of the concept of equal education for all.

The advantage of the exceptional child argument over the "natural resource" argument for differentiated education for the gifted is that it does not promote elitism. The contention that gifted children should be provided special instruction because they, more than other children, represent our future political, scientific, and artistic leaders is correctly perceived as elitist. First, we cannot predict who will be the country's future leaders. (It is not even apparent who the country's leaders are at any particular time. In fact, those judged by history as the leaders of an era are often vilified during their own lifetimes.) Second, the future-leader rationale for gifted programs excludes some children from a different curriculum not because they are incapable of mastering it, but because they are not being groomed as future leaders. We wonder if there is really any sound basis for selecting some children for and excluding others from gifted programs for potential leaders. The resentment that such gifted programs engender may be warranted (see Chapter 1).

The Problem of Local Autonomy. The local autonomy that characterizes the U.S. education system increases the difficulties involved in obtaining special programs for the gifted (cf. Counts, 1930, p. 57). The lack of centralized educational decision-making is one of the social barriers to provision of special education for the gifted (Kirk & Gallagher, 1983). Duplication of effort, inefficient use of resources, and inadequate long-range planning (cf. Counts, 1930, pp. 55–56) occur when gifted education is not coordinated at a regional or state level.

Advocates for handicapped children have lobbied for federal legislation to govern both state and local exceptional child programs. In states where gifted services are provided as special education programs, gifted children benefit from federal regulation of inconsistent local initiatives for the handicapped. One of the most controversial pieces of federal education legislation is PL 94-142. Several provisions of this law were previously discussed in Box 1.3, in the section on protection in assessment in Chapter 2, and in the section on the least restrictive environment in Chapter 3. We will continue to refer to this law, and its possible applications to gifted education, in this chapter.

INDIVIDUALIZING INSTRUCTION

We have shown that gifted as well as handicapped students need a continuum of services. No single placement alternative can meet the educational needs of all the gifted students in a school district or even in a school building. Chapter 3 presented a number of options that make individualization for gifted students feasible. This chapter identifies approaches to individualization that can be used within the continuum of services.

Approaches to Individualization

There are two basic approaches to matching instruction to learner needs: special placement and modification of instruction. The former is usually accomplished on the basis of chronological age, special program eligibility, achievement level, or interest. The latter involves manipulation of instructional variables, such as pace, level, and content of instruction. Individualization of instruction is usually conceived as a continuum ranging from marginal to very extensive instructional adaptations.

Some Early Examples. Early individualization systems allowed students to determine the pace of instruction. The Dalton Plan, initiated in Dalton, Massachusetts in 1920, allowed secondary school students to work at their own pace on monthly assignments. The Winnetka Plan was proposed to allow elementary school students to determine the rate of their learning in ungraded schools. At the college level, the Keller Plan (Keller, 1968) provided instruction that was mastery oriented and individually paced (Gage & Berliner, 1975). In the Keller Plan students not only determined the pace of instruction but also selected strategies for mastering objectives.

Some individualized instruction systems allow students to select the objectives they pursue. For example, a commercial system, Program for Learning in Accordance with Needs (PLAN), includes a set of instructional objectives at various levels of difficulty and covering several topics in language arts and reading for high school students (Flanagan, Shanner, Brudner & Marker, 1975). This computer-managed system was developed in response to results from the 1960 survey, Project Talent, which collected achievement and interest data on 440,000 high school students in the United States (Flanagan et al., 1964). Individual differences in achievement presented compelling reasons for individualized instruction; about 30 percent of the ninth graders scored as high in English and social studies as the average twelfth grader (Flanagan et al., 1975).

Student-Centered Instruction. Proponents of individualization for gifted children usually advocate student-determination of most variables of instruction. One of the espoused goals of gifted education is to produce independent learners (Treffinger, 1975). Treffinger (1975) maintains that the means of achieving that goal is to plan a graduated approach which moves students from teacher-controlled to student-controlled learning as students master independent study skills. Renzulli (1977) considers accommodation of instruction to student interest to be a feature that distinguishes gifted education. A major portion of his enrichment program model is based entirely on student interest.

Education for middle- and upper-class children (which constitutes much of gifted education) has been more influenced by child-centered movements such as progressivism (e.g., Dewey), humanistic psychology (e.g., Maslow), and alternative schooling (e.g., Holt). According to many observers (e.g., Bowles & Gintis, 1976; Rosenbaum, 1975; Wilcox & Moriarity, 1977; Wilcox, 1982) upper-class children are taught to question and analyze; lower-class children are taught to accept authority. Individualization based mainly on student interest is often justified on the grounds that gifted students will become society's eminent scientists, engineers, and doctors, and that they need to practice their roles early. Such individualization achieves, in effect, a curriculum for an elite. In contrast, individualization in accordance with individualized education program (IEP) provisions implies modification of accepted curriculum goals, not establishment of separate curricula.

The Diagnostic-Prescriptive Model. The individualization model on which individualized education programs are based is diagnostic-prescriptive teaching (cf. Hayes & Higgins, 1978). Although its title is reminiscent of the medical model of handicapping conditions, the strategy is recommended as an effective approach to instruction for all students, handicapped, gifted, or average (Stephens, Blackhurst & Magliocca, 1982). Four steps make up this instructional method.

1. *Assessment:* Before teaching a new skill, unit, or course, the teacher tests students to determine what they already know. Commercial or teacher-

made criterion-referenced tests containing skills or information to be taught are administered during this pre-instruction phase.

2. *Planning for Instruction:* Based on the assessment results, the teacher determines the level at which instruction should begin and the skills the student needs to learn.

3. *Instruction:* The teacher provides instruction that is geared to the student's learning needs.

4. *Evaluation:* The teacher conducts evaluation procedures to determine if stated objectives were accomplished. If they were, the cycle begins again. If not, alternative instructional strategies may be tried and/or the objectives may be evaluated in terms of their appropriateness for the student at that time.

Comparing Two Diagnostic-Prescriptive Models. Ysseldyke and Salvia (1974) compare two diagnostic-prescriptive teaching models. One is based on constructs of mental processes that are presumed to underlie academic performance. This model purports to diagnose weaknesses in such processes as visual sequencing and auditory memory. A "prescription" to remediate these weaknesses is developed as a guide to instruction. The allegedly improved mental processes are expected to translate into improved academic performance. Research does not substantiate the claims that have been made for this individualization model (Hammill & Larsen, 1974; Ysseldyke & Salvia, 1974; cf. Kavale & Glass, 1982).

A second model of diagnostic-prescriptive teaching, the task analysis model, assesses academic skills needed to accomplish learning objectives and identifies unlearned skills without postulating underlying mental-processing problems. It is a more direct approach to individualization and has gained acceptance as the more productive of the two models. According to Kavale and Glass (1982, p. 6) exceptional children need an "effective program of *academic* remediation . . . to overcome *academic* deficits." In fact, they conclude that *programs that do not keep this goal in mind are harmful to children.* Glass (1983, p. 73) suggests that the process approach (ability training) may be a major reason for the failure of special education to demonstrate measurable improvement in the academic performance of students in special education classrooms. Of the two models, the task analysis model appears to be more useful for gifted education programs as well as for other special education programs.

The Case Study Approach to Individualized Planning

In gifted education the case study approach is discussed most often in terms of its usefulness for helping to make placement decisions (see Chapter 2). It usually refers to the collection of two types of information, standardized test results and results of nonstandardized measures such as teacher checklists. A matrix is often used to organize the information; performance may be weighted by level or by type (e.g., Baldwin, 1978). Simpler case study approaches involve placement on the basis of student attainment of a cut-off criterion on, for example, three out of five measures. The purpose of using the case study approach in this way is to include children whose abilities are not adequately represented by the more traditional criterion for placement, a high IQ-test score.

Dirks and Quarfoth (1981) compared two case study approaches. One approach places children on the basis of breadth of ability. In this approach children must score in the top 10 percent in at least three of five areas. The other approach places children on the basis of depth of ability. In this case children must score in the top 2 or 3 percent in at least one of the following areas: school grades in basic skill subjects, achievement test scores, creativity test scores, behavior checklist scores, and intelligence test scores. Children selected by both models were given the WISC-R. The researchers found that the breadth model identified moderately bright children (mean IQs in the upper 120s) who made good grades; it identified no gifted underachievers. The depth model included more high-IQ children. Approximately 36 to 70 percent of the children identified in a depth model scored 132 or higher on the WISC-R, whereas only 15 to 40 percent of those identified by a breadth model scored 132 or above.

Although advocates of the case study approach argue for its effectiveness in identifying underachievers (Baldwin, 1978), the value of case studies for such a purpose depends on the type of information collected. Pegnato and Birch (1959) discovered that use of the single-criterion referral cut-off score of IQ 115 on a standardized group IQ test was the only referral method that identified some very bright underachievers. These children would still be missed in many case study approaches.

Renzulli and Smith (1977) question the use of individual intelligence test scores as the standard against which to measure various identification approaches. They compared the case study approach to the traditional approach (administration of group ability tests followed by administration of individual tests to those students who score above a certain level). Using teacher judgment of students' success in the gifted program as the standard for determining the relative success of the two identification methods, they concluded that the case study approach was a less expensive and more effective means of determining program eligibility.

These findings raise several questions:

1. Were the teachers on the selection committees the same as those who evaluated the success of students selected? If they were, what effect would this have on their objectivity?
2. What were the goals of the programs for which children were selected? Were they similar to programs in which IQ and achievement criteria were used for placement?
3. What was the criterion of "success" in the program? Was it academic growth or classroom performance?

Criterion-Referenced Tests.   Renzulli and Smith (1981) recommend the use of criterion-referenced tests in "compacting" gifted students' regular education programs. [Renzulli defines curriculum compacting as the construction of an accelerated curriculum (see the discussion of the combined-grade type of acceleration in Chapter 5). Renzulli, however, conceives of compacting as an arrangement for individuals.] Assessment of specific skills prior to instruction allows students to demonstrate mastery and thus avoid repetition. A more thorough discussion of the use of criterion-referenced tests in individualizing instruction follows this section.

A caution regarding the use of these tests to determine *placement* is, however, in order at this point. The cut-off scores required as demonstration of readiness to progress are often set unjustifiably high for gifted students. For example, gifted students are sometimes required to demonstrate up to 95 percent mastery on criterion-referenced tests before being allowed to accelerate their learning whereas other students may be required to demonstrate only 65 percent mastery before proceeding to more advanced work (cf. Christopherson, 1981).

Other Case Study Information.   Other types of information that may be included in case studies are biographical inventories, checklists of various sorts, and classroom observations based on behavior sampling. Reports of persons who know the child outside of school may also be useful. Such observations increase the possibility that anomalies in norm- and criterion-referenced data may be explained. As we have noted frequently, however, *any information gathered should relate to the locale's definition of giftedness and to the goals of its gifted programs.*

Care in Applying the Case Study Approach.   A multiple-criteria approach to placement is strengthened by the use of objective measures. Culturally different students and underachievers are better served by locally normed or culturally normed tests than by subjective instruments that measure how well they conform to the values of the middle-class culture of teachers or, worse, how well they conform to middle-class stereotypes of minority subcultures. A high IQ score should not be the single criterion for entry into gifted programs; high achievement and aptitude test scores should qualify students as well (see Chapters 1 and 2).

In spite of their limitations, standardized tests reduce the variance that examiner qualities introduce. Since norm-referenced tests yield information about general areas of strength, they can be used both to determine appropriate placements and to help teachers determine the kinds and levels of criterion-referenced tests that are applicable for specific instructional planning.

A case study approach is better conceived of not as a means to determine whether or not to place students in gifted programs, *but as a means to individualize their education.* Norm- and criterion-referenced test scores, grades, awards, interests, and information about students' behavior in various settings are all sometimes useful in making decisions about the form and content of instruction.

DEVELOPING INDIVIDUALIZED EDUCATION PROGRAMS

As important as program alternatives are for gifted students, they are not always sufficient to meet their educational needs. Individualized instruction, even within special classrooms, is also necessary (Mitchell, 1981b).

Individualized education programs (IEPs) were established by PL 94-142. IEPs specify the services the school will provide in order to promote accomplishment of annual goals established for the student. They are appropriate for exceptional children, including the gifted, and they can coordinate both program and instructional modifications. The development of individual program plans for gifted children, however, is not required by federal law as it is for the handicapped. Even states that mandate services for gifted students do not necessarily require IEPs (Karnes & Collins, 1978). Nevertheless, program planning procedures that have improved the specificity and accountability of programs for the handicapped are applicable for developing plans for gifted students.

PL 94-142 does not dictate the format of the IEP, but it does require certain components and procedures, which in theory constitute an effective way to individualize instruction:

- parental participation in educational planning for children,
- nondiscriminatory assessment to determine eligibility for placement in special education programs,
- specially designed instruction based on individual levels of performance, and
- ongoing evaluation of educational progress.

The meeting at which the IEP is developed is part of the diagnostic-prescriptive teaching process. Prior to the meeting the school (or parent) obtains an assessment to help determine whether or not the child is eligible for special education and to gather information about the child's learning characteristics. After the results of the assessment are reviewed, the child's level of performance is summarized in a statement that lists relative strengths and weaknesses. Based on this summary, the IEP sets learning goals to be addressed through special education placement and individualized instruction.

The federal law mandates a team process for developing IEPs and specifies the required members of the IEP multidisciplinary team. These include

1. a supervisory representative of the school district or agency,
2. the child's teacher,
3. the child (when appropriate),

4. other individuals at the discretion of the parents or the school, and
5. the evaluator or someone capable of interpreting evaluation data, if the child is being evaluated for the first time.

The school must make an effort to include parents in educational planning by informing them of the need to develop an IEP and by considering the parents' schedule in setting up the meeting (Wolf & Troup, 1980). The participation of parents is perhaps the most progressive element of PL 94-142. The full participation of parent and teacher helps to ensure that the persons who work closely with the child understand and agree on what needs to be accomplished. (The roles of parents and teachers in placement teams will be discussed further in the section on negotiation in this chapter.)

Though school personnel expect parents to provide information about their child, they too often do not accept parents as legitimate partners in the decision-making process (Yoshida, Fenton, Kaufman & Maxwell, 1978). The value of their contribution may be rated low relative to that of other members of the committee (Gilliam, 1979). This is probably a function of territorial attitudes among educators, lack of assertiveness among parents, and the historical alienation of parents and schools. Both groups often become impatient with the sometimes lengthy planning that IEP development entails. Parents and education personnel need training in order to make the most effective use of the IEP process (e.g., Muir, Milan, Branston-McLean & Berger, 1982).

The development of an IEP hardly *guarantees* good education. An IEP does, however, make appropriate education a more visible goal and renders progress toward that goal, as well as progress in learning, more verifiable.

Since we consider the use of IEPs beneficial for gifted students, we will examine their application with this population. Other types of program plans (e.g., Colon & Treffinger, 1980; Renzulli, Reis & Smith, 1981) specifying differentiated instruction for superior students resemble IEPs, although they differ somewhat in the information included.

PL 94-142 requires that the IEP provide the following information (45 CFR 300.346):

1. a statement of the child's levels of educational performance,
2. a statement of annual goals including short-term instructional objectives,
3. a statement of the specific special education and related services to be provided to the child and the extent to which the child will be able to participate in regular educational programs,
4. the projected dates for initiation of services and the anticipated duration of the services, and
5. appropriate objective criteria and evaluation procedures and schedules for determining, on at least an annual basis, whether the short-term instructional objectives are being achieved.

Making Long-Term Plans for the Gifted Student

Whether or not gifted program plans are developed along federal guidelines, teachers of the gifted are usually involved in some process for developing program plans (Lewis & Kanes, 1980). Therefore, procedures for determining instructional sequences are necessary for the provision of appropriate differentiated instruction (Hedbring & Rubenzer, 1979).

The development of an instructional plan for the gifted student frequently involves a process distinct from the curriculum planning process. This disjunction unfortunately perpetuates gifted programs that are "tacked-on" to the regular curriculum.

Such programs acknowledge their subordinate status by not addressing the core of educational responsibility. They often restrict their operations to the nurture of creativity, the development of critical-thinking skills, and the exploration of feelings and values (Feldhusen, 1982). Gifted programs sometimes attempt to develop these skills in isolation from specific academic disciplines. Such programs assume a supportive role in the development of talent, but they relinquish any claim to primacy in the long-range planning for gifted students. This is a problem because teachers of the gifted are apt to be the only people specifically concerned with long-range plans for these students.

Annual plans outlining services provided in an enrichment program do not generally encompass the full scope of educational offerings nor do they articulate an instructional sequence in any one academic context. Curricula, which are inclusive and developmental, are rarely formulated or even adapted for the individual.

The principles of differentiated gifted education, which legitimate its relationship to all education, are pertinent to long-range planning. These principles are

1. that knowledge is hierarchical,
2. that learning is developmental,
3. that schools should allow students to pursue formal learning experiences commensurate with their previous learning, and
4. that the purpose of formal schooling is to maximize the learning potential of students in order to allow them as much freedom of choice, when they are adults, as our society permits.

The implications of each of these principles for individual program planning will be discussed in turn.

The hierarchical nature of knowledge should be reflected in the development of any curriculum, whether it is designed for an individual or for a class of individuals. Mastery of certain fundamental skills is required prior to learning more complex skills. Command of a body of factual knowledge frequently must precede the ability to analyze and integrate learning in a particular field (Bloom, 1956; Copley, 1961). Plans for gifted students should account for the hierarchical structure of knowledge, not only by incorporating activities that span the cognitive sequence from lower- to higher-level skills (Maker, 1982a), but also by incorporating in the early grades fundamental learning necessary for more complex instruction in the later grades. This principle, though often overlooked in plans for gifted students, is presupposed in the development of typical school curricula (e.g., Ausubel, 1980).

Because of the hierarchical nature of knowledge, the rapid mastery of basic academic skills should be a priority in plans for gifted students. These skills are required for most other learning (Feldhusen, 1982). Similarly, plans for primary level gifted students should outline instructional sequences necessary for advanced learning in later years. Thus, for children who show an aptitude for math, rapid mastery of arithmetic in the early grades should precede algebra instruction in the intermediate grades. If systematic preparation for instruction in algebra does not occur in the primary grades, these students may not be capable of handling algebra when it *is* offered. Often schools identify children's aptitudes in particular fields and then ignore these aptitudes instructionally. Later, teachers cite students' failure at higher-level learning in these fields to discredit the validity of their previously identified aptitudes.

Since most knowledge is sequential, program planning should involve the selection of options for instruction at the child's levels of functioning in particular subjects. "The developmental view sees each child as proceeding through several sets of stages, each stage succeeding the one before it . . . Because the developmental framework emphasizes progress within specific fields or domains of knowledge, it leads to selection criteria and program features directly related to particular kinds of excellence" (Feldman, 1979b, p. 662). For example, suppose a student selected because of intellectual giftedness does not yet demonstrate excellence in reading. A program plan consistent with the child's current level of functioning would provide for rapid mastery of reading skills, but *not* for a "gifted" literature curriculum which would be of greater benefit to a more apt reader.

Once we accept the first two principles of long-range planning for the gifted, the third and fourth principles appear self-evident. That schools should allow students to progress at a pace and to a depth commensurate with previous learning is a truism. The inability of the regular classroom to provide this opportunity to exceptional learners justifies the provision of individualized instruction in special education programs (e.g., Kirk & Gallagher, 1983). For gifted children this principle can be actualized only when a variety of alternative placements are available (see Chapter 3).

Thus, long-term plans for gifted students should include advanced instructional options commensurate with previous learning. The implications of this notion for the secondary school instruction of gifted students may tempt some educators to limit elementary school gifted programs to the enrichment provisions to which we alluded above. However, in order to *educate* bright students rather than merely reward them, we must provide a full range of options throughout the school years.

The fourth and final principle addresses our *underlying* concern for the education of gifted students. In order to maximize the potential of these superior learners, we must not limit their options for further learning by restricting their present instruction.

> Children with talent potential should have an opportunity to develop across the arts, sciences, and literature. Premature concentration in one area may prevent individuals from developing the broad base of experience they need prior to intelligently focusing their potential . . . If others insist on premature concentration in one area of endeavor, this may hinder a potentially talented person from full realization of personal capacities.
>
> (Perrone & Male, 1981, pp. 45–46)

The focus on a liberal education, which has been overshadowed by emphasis on minimum competency, is an essential tenet of gifted education.

Individual program plans for gifted students should address those aspects of the curriculum that provide the skills and knowledge necessary for the pursuit of advanced learning. Limitations of the broad curriculum should be considered only when the student demonstrates extraordinary aptitude for and commitment to one particular field. Program plans that justify *restricted* offerings on the basis of superficial student "interest" are potentially irrelevant to later academic pursuits.

Developing Appropriate Goals for the Gifted

The formulation of annual goals for a gifted student involves consideration of the areas specified in the school's curriculum. Students identified because of superior scholastic aptitude usually require differentiated instruction in most academic areas; those identified because of specific academic talents require differentiated instruction in their areas of strength.

The distinction among handicapped children between mentally retarded and specific learning disabled students is analogous. Whereas mentally retarded children demonstrate general deficiencies in scholastic performance, specific learning disabled students exhibit particular deficiencies in one or more areas of scholastic achievement. Thus special education programs for mentally retarded children usually provide instructional modifications in most academic areas, whereas special education programs for specific learning disabled children provide instructional modifications only in areas of weakness (Lewis & Doorlag, 1983).

Determining Cognitive Goals.   In determining goals and objectives for high-IQ gifted students, it is easy to mistake discrepancies in academic achievement for demonstrated strengths and weaknesses. Since such discrepancies may exist because of the student's lack of exposure to a subject, this type of profile analysis may be unfounded. Rather than being based on the apparent strengths of the individual child, annual program goals should reflect the academic goals of the school's adopted curriculum.

These goals may include statements intended to describe the long-range purpose of a particular program. For example, a regular curriculum goal in mathematics might be "students will master the basic operations of addition, subtraction, multiplication, and division." This goal may encompass one component of the school's mathematics program for grades one through four. Including this goal in an annual plan for a gifted first grader ensures that this child's program is related to the general academic curriculum and specifies suitably paced instruction.

This type of program development has two implications. First, it requires the statement of product goals. Since high-level cognitive processing results from intensive study in particular fields (Copley, 1961), product goals can address many of the concerns of process-oriented programs (e.g., Hedbring & Rubenzer, 1979; Lewis & Kanes, 1980; Maker, 1982a; Meeker, 1979a). Because the development of goals implies the measurement of their attainment (Hudson & Graham, 1980) and improvement in processing defies accurate measurement (Lewis & Kanes, 1980), we suggest the establishment of product-oriented goals and process-oriented instructional methods as a creative solution to the dilemma.

The second implication of this type of program development is its dependence on a district's long-range planning for gifted students. A program that offers students algebra instruction in the fifth grade cannot stop providing for their advanced math needs in the sixth. Considering the diverse academic needs of gifted students in a school district, elementary school programs that promote significant academic growth will necessarily create a need for numerous middle school and secondary school options, including advanced subject area classes and early college entry. These planning concerns transcend the scope of what is normally included in the IEP development process. Nevertheless, these types of alternatives should be established.

Determining Noncognitive Goals. Annual goals such as "improves self-concept," "accepts strengths and weaknesses," and "understands available career options" sometimes are included in IEPs for gifted students. These concerns may be part of a school counseling program (Walker, 1982) but should not *typically* be included in an individual plan designed to provide differentiated instruction for the cognitively advanced student.

Certain gifted students, however, legitimately require special assistance in integrating cognitive and affective experiences. These students, including many underachieving, learning disabled, emotionally disturbed, physically handicapped, and culturally different gifted children, may need guidance counseling or therapy in order to maximize their cognitive potential (Whitmore, 1980). These needs stem more from the students' adjustment difficulties than from their giftedness. Some gifted educators (e.g., Whitmore, 1980) suggest that schools' typical responses to gifted children may exacerbate their emotional vulnerability. Affective goals are, therefore, more appropriately included in program plans for these youngsters.

Therapeutic concerns should be addressed only in the development of IEPs dealing with students' handicaps. Counseling, on the other hand, should be available to all children. Listing this service in the gifted child's IEP may misrepresent the nature and severity of the child's affective need. Certainly, providing for therapy or counseling services to be given by teachers of the gifted involves incorrect assumptions about such teachers' role and expertise.

Determining Specific Objectives

PL 94-142 requires that the IEP include short-term objectives articulating the sequence of skills necessary for completion of specified annual goals. These "short-term objectives are subordinate to goals and should therefore reflect a hierarchical relationship to the goals" (Tymitz-Wolf, 1982, p. 199). The development of these sequences poses difficulties in planning for the education of the gifted.

Because the IEP development process was initiated as an educational planning vehicle for the handicapped, it is assumed that the purpose of goals and objectives is to delineate those modified portions of the curriculum that can be accomplished by the impaired learner (Turnbull, Strickland & Brantley, 1982). Since a gifted student can complete course work at an accelerated pace, modifications should be extensive. Annual goals for the gifted should, therefore, be more inclusive than curriculum goals established for particular grade levels. Short-term objectives may, in turn, be no more specific than those broad goals of the curriculum specified for average learners.

Although the nature of objectives may differ greatly for gifted as opposed to handicapped learners, the procedure for developing them is the same. Assessment data generated as part of the eligibility determination process can provide some information about the student's learning characteristics and instructional needs. Additional data, however, may be required in order to ensure that the level and pace of instruction are suitable for the individual child.

In general, the most significant data generated in the identification process are derived from norm-referenced measures. Scores obtained on such instruments indicate the student's performance relative to that of others. This information, however, also provides generalizations about the student's performance relative to the curriculum. If a sixth grade student scores at the 98th percentile in reading, we can be reasonably certain that the student has mastered the decoding skills necessary for studying works of literature. Further inquiry to determine annual goals and short-term objectives would focus on the student's previous readings and familiarity with techniques of literary analysis. A sequence of literature courses could then be planned that would, over a period of several years, increase the student's literacy and improve ability to analyze literature.

Criterion-referenced testing also may be used in program development although it has certain limitations peculiar to its use with superior students. Criterion-referenced tests measure mastery of subskills in a particular domain or curriculum. They do so by analyzing tasks or by sampling performance on those subskills found to represent the domain. By providing "information about the individual's mastery of the domain, [a criterion-referenced test indicates] . . . readiness to address the next level of instructional objectives'' (Lidz, 1981, p. 58). Criterion-referenced assessment is especially applicable for the evaluation of the mastery of basic skills. Several commercially prepared tests have been developed for this purpose:

- The Brigance Diagnostic Inventories (Brigance, 1977; Brigance, 1978; Brigance, 1980) provide multiple-skill criterion-referenced measures of basic and functional skills.
- The Key Math Diagnostic Arithmetic Test (Connolloy et al., 1971) can be used as a criterion-referenced measure of basic arithmetic skills. Its application is limited to the assessment of elementary level gifted students because of its low subtest ceilings.
- Criterion-referenced reading tests include the Criterion Reading Battery (Hackett, 1971), the Fountain Valley Teacher Support System in Reading (Zweig Associates, 1971), and the Prescriptive Reading Inventory (CTB/ McGraw-Hill, 1972).

In addition to these criterion-referenced measures are tests provided by textbook companies to evaluate mastery of the scope and sequence of skills presented in their reading, mathematics, language arts, and other subject area series. Teachers can also develop criterion-referenced tests in any field, providing they adopt consistent methods of task analysis, domain sampling, and item construction. Unless such tests actually sample tasks representative of the sequence presented in the adopted curriculum or on the gifted child's IEP, they *cannot* reveal mastery of objectives in that sequence.

The difficulty of obtaining or constructing sufficiently difficult measures in virtually every subject area constitutes the major limitation of the use of criterion-referenced testing for determining instructional objectives for gifted students. This problem leads to the widespread use of the less appropriate tests accompanying textbooks. These instruments must be used judiciously because they vary in the sophistication with which they measure skill or content mastery (see Lidz, 1981, for cautions in interpreting results of criterion-referenced tests).

Cautions for Program Planning

Certain assessment practices used in developing IEPs for gifted students should be viewed cautiously. In particular, some applications of norm-referenced assessment seem unwarranted both theoretically and procedurally. Three such practices recommended by gifted educators are (1) Structure of Intellect (SOI) analysis of performance on the intelligence-scale subtests to determine cognitive strengths and weaknesses (Hedbring & Rubenzer, 1979); (2) the use of complex matrices to analyze students' strengths and weaknesses (Maker, 1982a; Renzulli & Smith, 1978); and (3) the analysis of achievement test profiles to determine strengths and weaknesses (Feldhusen, 1981; Gallagher, 1975).

The use of SOI analysis in determining programming alternatives for the gifted depends on several questionable assumptions. This technique assumes that Guilford's (1967) Structure of the Intellect actually represents the discrete categories of mental processing. It also assumes that the purpose of gifted education is to strengthen these processing skills by remediating weak areas of functioning (Hedbring & Rubenzer, 1979; Meeker, 1979a), as well as by focusing on the development of strengths (Maker, 1982a). Since this approach relies on assumptions that have not been demonstrated empirically, its application should be restricted to research (e.g., Gallagher et al., 1967). This criticism of SOI analysis applies equally to the application of SOI matrices for interpreting WISC-R and Stanford-Binet performance and of the Structure of Intellect Learning Abilities Test (Meeker, 1979b), which uses 24 of Guilford's 120 cognitive domains to determine specific academic aptitudes (Khatena, 1982).

Complex matrices have the strength of bringing together various sources of information. The use of matrices for *analyzing* students' strengths and weaknesses (Maker, 1982a; Renzulli & Smith, 1978) is, however, even less reliable than the application of informal techniques for determining the subtest scatter on one test. The difficulty arises when such matrices are *scored*. By incorporating various subjective and objective measures in one assessment score, this approach implies that such measures have similar reliability and validity. Since these measures actually vary greatly in their reliability and validity, composite *scores* obtained by combining information from these instruments have extremely limited technical relevance.

The analysis of achievement test data to characterize the learning aptitudes of gifted students seems reasonable considering the similar type of test interpretation recommended for the handicapped (Fiscus & Mandell, 1983; Turnbull et al., 1982). This application of assessment data, however, has been criticized for both the handicapped (Duffey & Fedner, 1980) and the gifted (Perrone & Male, 1981) for several reasons:

1. The relationship between norm-referenced achievement tests and particular curricula has not been established, although some achievement tests do provide information concerning their measurement of specific curriculum components.
2. The determination of intraindividual differences or scatter between subtests frequently relies on the analysis of apparent discrepancies rather than on the calculation of statistically significant discrepancies (Gardner, 1977; Salvia & Ysseldyke, 1981).
3. The performance of a superior student may be close to the ceiling of an achievement test, in which case the apparent variability in derived subtest scores will be exaggerated.
4. Even a statistically significant discrepancy may result from the student's lack of exposure to a particular field or from poor instruction in that area, rather than from an *inherent* weakness in cognitive functioning.

Gifted students learn much about literature, history, and science as they read for pleasure, watch movies and television, and participate in adult conversation. *Other subjects must be taught.* Few families linger at the dinner table to discuss the nature and application of trigonometric functions. Mathematics and foreign languages, particularly, do not lend themselves to learning through typical sources of general information. Some instructional continuity in writing skills is also required to promote parity between the student's ability to communicate and to understand.

Although average or slightly above average test scores on mathematics or language subtests do not necessarily indicate a lack of ability, they may indicate that more modest acceleration is advisable in those areas until test scores improve. For example, acceleration through compacting rather than grade-skipping may be advisable. A combination of moderate acceleration and tutoring could also be used to ensure that the student masters all the required skills for success in a higher grade.

Program Planning for Gifted/Handicapped Students. Some gifted children, however, are so far behind in one or two areas (e.g., math or reading) that they may qualify for programs that serve learning disabled students (cf. Whitmore, 1980; see Chapter 11). Program plans for these students should emphasize the development of strengths as well as the remediation of weaknesses (Whitmore, 1980).

Educational assessment and planning for gifted handicapped children must be multidisciplinary, and several different placements may be required. A gifted handicapped child may spend part of the time in a regular classroom, part in a program for gifted students, part in a program for handicapped students, and perhaps part in a related service program, such as speech therapy or counseling. The IEP serves as the management plan, coordinating the provision of all the services needed to offer an appropriate education to gifted handicapped children. The comprehensiveness of the IEP goals may vary according to the needs of the student. The education of gifted handicapped children obviously demands extensive planning.

Scope of Plans for All Gifted Students. Equally important, if less obvious, is the need for extensive planning for gifted children who are not handicapped. Whereas IEPs for talented children address only the specific areas in which they are exceptionally able, IEPs for high-IQ children should usually specify goals and services relating to every aspect of a child's education except nonacademic subjects (see Box 4.1). Just as a retarded child's delayed conceptual development affects learning in almost every subject, the intellectually gifted child's conceptual precocity influences performance in almost every subject and necessitates a comprehensive plan for education.

Establishing Criteria for Mastery of Objectives

"Writing instructional objectives requires that the specific criteria for completing the . . . task be included in the objective. By including such criteria, the measurement of the objective is implied" (Turnbull et al., 1982, p. 162). In the sample objective in Box 4.2, "After reading a 5.0 level passage, Susan

BOX 4.1 Inappropriate and Appropriate Goals

Goals are major IEP objectives. Goals should reference measurable content and individual needs of particular gifted students. They should address cognitive needs.

Inappropriate Goals	Why They Are Inappropriate
1. To increase self-confidence and feelings of self-worth.	This is a general concern of good teaching. It is appropriate for all students.
2. To expand research skills, explore topics of interest, develop creative problem-solving skills.	These goals are not specific to individual students and not referenced to a content area; they are appropriate for all students.
3. To identify personal strengths and weaknesses.	This goal is irrelevant and not measurable.

Appropriate Goals	Why They Are Apppropriate
1. To complete the first half of Algebra I through instruction in a two-hour weekly tutorial.	This goal is academically relevant, an appropriate accelerative strategy, and useful in planning.
2. To develop expository writing skills as measured by pretest and posttest writing samples.	This goal is measurable, relevant, and referenced to the individual student.

will recall significant details as indicated by her score of 90 percent or better on a written test of reading comprehension,'' both the task and the criterion for mastery are specified. What is not indicated is the nature of the test used to verify mastery. This should be determined in the IEP meeting and documented on the IEP.

In addition, estimated timetables for mastery of objectives should be included in the IEP. Gifted students' superior scholastic aptitude, coupled with appropriate instruction, enables them to acquire many skills very rapidly. Therefore, timetables should be established to indicate the school district's need to provide these students with progressively more advanced and more individualized instruction.

Evaluating Mastery: Techniques. Various techniques exist for evaluating mastery of goals and objectives. Selection of the most appropriate techniques depends on the characteristics of the student being evaluated and on the nature of the content being mastered. The recall of multiplication facts, for instance, can be assessed by oral and written examinations of several types.

BOX 4.2 Writing Behavioral Objectives Appropriate for Gifted IEPs

---

1. Specify the task to be accomplished.
   Appropriate Case: Susan will recall significant details in a 5.0 level passage.
   Questionable Case: Michael will demonstrate an understanding of the differences among Renaissance, Baroque, Classical, and Romantic styles.
2. Specify the conditions under which the behavior will occur.
   Appropriate Case: After reading a 5.0 level passage, Susan will recall significant details on a written test of reading comprehension.
   Questionable Case: After completing a course on music history, Michael will demonstrate an understanding of the differences among Renaissance, Baroque, Classical, and Romantic styles.
3. Specify criteria for mastery.
   Appropriate Case: After reading a 5.0 level passage, Susan will recall significant details as indicated by her score of 90 percent or better on a written test of reading comprehension.
   Questionable Case: After completing a course on music history, Michael will demonstrate an understanding of the differences among Renaissance, Baroque, Classical and Romantic styles by identifying eight out of ten selections representing each style.

The choice of the most suitable type of examination depends on the student's preferred mode of learning and on the teacher's minimum requirement for adequate mastery.

Of the possible evaluation techniques, norm- and criterion-referenced tests and examination of products seem to be the most relevant for assessing progress in gifted programs. Norm- and criterion-referenced tests may also be part of the more comprehensive monitoring process which includes assessment of the student's general academic growth and determination of program effectiveness (Turnbull et al., 1982).

In general, teacher-made criterion-referenced measures are favored by IEP teams for the evaluation of the mastery of short-term objectives (Fiscus & Mandell, 1983; Hudson & Graham, 1980). However, with gifted students, whose short-term objectives may be quite comprehensive, commercially prepared norm- or criterion-referenced tests may be preferable. Because frequent administration of the same test reduces the reliability of the results obtained, mastery of short-term objectives should not be assessed using these instruments more often than twice a year (Stanley, 1964).

If commercially prepared tests are selected for evaluating progress, certain guidelines for determining their suitability should be considered. Norm-referenced tests should measure the skills they purport to measure and should have an item pool sufficient to discriminate adequately between different levels of performance. Criterion-referenced tests, on the other hand, should have adequate content validity, should be systematically sequenced, and should include items representative of the domain(s) sampled.

Product evaluation is often included in IEPs for gifted students as a means for assessing their attainment of annual goals and short-term objectives (e.g., Wolf & Stephens, 1979). This type of evaluation involves measuring students' growth by evaluating samples of their work, including products such as term papers, paintings, original stories, exhibits, and oral presentations. This assessment technique depends on the subjective judgment of the evaluator, a potential difficulty that can be mitigated by the inclusion of several "expert" raters in the evaluation process (Khatena, 1982, p. 343; Stanley, 1964). Also, since the process of evaluating the mastery of objectives is predicated on the anticipation of students' progress, product evaluation should involve comparison of the students' work before and after instruction (Fiscus & Mandell, 1983).

Using Formative and Summative Assessment

Program planning implies two types of ongoing assessment. Formative assessment involves the "assessment of ongoing progress," and summative assessment involves "the assessment of learning outcomes at the end of instruction" (Lidz, 1981, p. 67). Formative assessment is integral to the diagnostic-prescriptive teaching process because it verifies the immediate effects of instruction. Summative assessment is required in the IEP monitoring process in order to validate the success of the individual program. In addition, summative assessment data are compiled to substantiate the effectiveness of programs.

In general, formative assessment involves the teacher's observation of students' mastery of knowledge and skills (Loe, 1980). The process of developing good tests to document mastery is more complex than is normally supposed (see Box 4.3). However, this means of verifying progress is more appropriate for the assessment of gifted students than the less complex process of charting classroom performance, which is considered most appropriate for the handicapped (e.g., Lewis & Doorlag, 1983; Loe, 1980).

Summative assessment, on the other hand, may be used to rate students, though this application presents many problems. Theoretically, summative assessment of differentiated instruction should substantiate the long-range effectiveness of teaching, which has been guided by formative assessment.

The routine assessment of gifted students' mastery of IEP goals and objectives should include formative assessment as appropriate, and summative assessment at least annually. The annual review of the IEP is conducted for the following reasons:

> To outline the child's progress with the current IEP; to revise the child's IEP and plan for the next school year; to determine if current goals and objectives, placement, personnel involved and other special education concerns continue to be appropriate; to decide if further assessment is necessary, and, if so, what procedures should be involved; and to establish the date for the next annual review.

(Fiscus & Mandell, 1983, pp. 235–236)

For gifted students especially, the annual review may reveal substantial prog-

---

BOX 4.3 Constructing a Good Test: Stanley's Advice

According to Stanley (1964, p. 171), "constructing a satisfactory test is one of the hardest jobs a teacher has to perform." Stanley says there are four steps in constructing a good test:

1. *Plan the test*: Review curriculum and instructional content, determine important concepts, apportion relative value of content (i.e., weighting).
2. *Prepare the test*: Choose format, compose questions, apportion subsections (i.e., according to content weighting), edit.
3. *Try out the test*: Give to other teachers for review, revise, administer to pilot groups.
4. *Evaluate the test*: Determine reliability and content validity, standardize.

The format of a test and the specific items on it may influence students' performance as much as their knowledge of the subject matter. That formative tests are intended to improve instructional precision militates against their use for grading or comparing the progress of a group of students. Although formative tests may be administered to a group, their interpretation should involve consideration of the suitability of instruction for each individual student in the group. This notion reverses conventional logic about the purpose of testing; accountability shifts from the student to the teacher.

---

ress which implies the need for increased differentiation, higher-level course work, and more comprehensive planning for future instruction.

PL 94-142 mandates that comprehensive reevaluation of handicapped children occur at least every three years, and more often if it is requested by the child's parent or teacher (Turnbull & Turnbull, 1978). This requirement is based on two principles related to the equal treatment of handicapped students. The first involves consideration of possible error in the original assessment and eligibility determination. The second involves the stipulation that handicapped students be placed in a setting as close as possible to the regular classroom. *Neither of these reasons is compelling in the case of gifted students.*

Although measurement error may occur in the original evaluation of a gifted child, correction of that error by subsequent intelligence testing generally would be of no benefit to the child. In fact, it might be damaging to the child's self-concept and possibly to the child's educational progress.

Further, a statistical phenomenon known as regression toward the mean (the tendency of scores from repeated test administrations to cluster progressively nearer the mean) may penalize gifted students. Certainly the continued placement of a gifted child in a special program *that does not appear to meet the child's instructional needs* should be investigated. This inquiry, however, should focus not only on measurement of the child's IQ but also on assessment of other factors that may be impeding the child's progress, such as (1) unsupportive school arrangements, (2) specific learning problems, (3) emotional problems. A child's failure to benefit from differentiated services is at least as likely to result from inappropriate instruction as it is to result from inaccurate testing to determine eligibility.

The interpretation of the least restrictive environment principle for the gifted differs from the application of that principle for the handicapped (see Chapter 3). Therefore, reevaluation of a gifted student should not involve the assessment of progress toward normalization. The goal with the handicapped is to "break the relationship between intelligence and achievement" (Salvia & Ysseldyke, 1981, p. 481). With the gifted, it is to *maximize* that relationship.

The previous discussion suggests that comprehensive reevaluation of the gifted should involve team assessments of progress aimed at planning for these students' future education. Except in very unusual circumstances, it should not involve the revision of eligibility determinations. Assessment and planning at this phase of the process can aid school districts in developing long-term strategies for accommodating the needs of gifted students. They can also assist students and their parents in evaluating and selecting relevant extracurricular, out-of-school, summer, and postsecondary alternatives.

SEEKING VIABLE SERVICE DELIVERY OPTIONS

The ways in which programs come into existence and the ways in which children are placed in those programs determine the character of the group of children served and the fate of individual children in those programs. In fact, these basically procedural issues influence both the quality and the quantity of services accorded gifted students.

Eligibility Determination, Placement, IEPs

Following evaluation of students, decisions must be made about whether students qualify for the gifted program (eligibility determination), how to serve them in the program (placement), and what to include in their instruction (IEPs). Practices vary widely from state to state.

Federal regulations for the handicapped have allowed states considerable latitude in making these decisions. The permissive quality of PL 94-142 has actually benefited gifted education, since fourteen states (i.e., Alaska, Alabama, Florida, Georgia, Idaho, Kansas, Louisiana, North Carolina, New Mexico, Nevada, Pennsylvania, South Dakota, Tennessee, and West Virginia) have so far chosen to administer programs for the gifted under the provisions of PL 94-142 (Mitchell, 1981a).

Once a child is found to be eligible, it is likely that goals will be determined by the available placement option (often there is only one). Nonetheless, the intent of the federal law is that the full continuum of least restrictive alternative options be at least *potentially* available. In the states cited above, the intent applies also to the gifted.

The distinction between potential availability and actual availability is difficult to determine. If a child requires services that cannot be provided in existing placement alternatives, other alternatives must be made available, even though the school has not previously implemented them. This is the primary rationale for developing IEP goals prior to placement in a particular setting.

Many districts are already under the impression that federal and state regulations, and particularly the extension of due process rights to exceptional students, have wrongfully eroded local prerogatives (McGehey, 1982). These districts are unlikely to pursue expansion of services for the gifted. However, this situation does not reflect a contradiction between the needs of the handicapped and of the gifted, but a general contradiction between the goals of schooling and the principles of educating exceptional children. See Box 4.4 for a summary presentation of state provisions for gifted education.

BOX 4.4   Overview of State Provisions for Gifted Education

State	Sp Ed	W/ Han	Local	$1M	$5M	$/Child	Certif
Alabama	X	X	X	n/a	n/a	n/a	X
Alaska	X	X	X	X	O	X	O
Arizona	O	O	X	n/a	n/a	n/a	O
Arkansas	X	O	O	O	O	O	O
California	O	O	O	X	X	O	O
Colorado	O	O	O	O	O	O	O
Connecticut	X	O	O	X	O	O	O
Delaware	X	O	O	O	O	O	O
Florida	X	X	X	X	X	X	X
Georgia	X	X	X	X	X	O	X
Hawaii	X	O	O	O	O	O	O
Idaho	X	X	X	n/a	n/a	n/a	O
Illinois	O	O	O	X	X	O	O
Indiana	O	O	O	O	O	O	O
Iowa	O	O	O	O	O	O	O
Kansas	X	X	X	X	O	O	X
Kentucky	O	O	O	X	O	O	O
Louisiana	X	X	X	X	O	O	X
Maine	X	O	O	O	O	O	O
Maryland	O	O	O	O	O	O	O
Massachusetts	O	O	O	O	O	O	O
Michigan	O	O	O	O	O	O	O
Minnesota	O	O	O	O	O	O	O
Mississippi	X	O	O	X	X	X	X
Missouri	O	O	O	X	O	O	O
Montana	O	O	O	O	O	O	O
Nebraska	O	O	O	O	O	O	O
Nevada	X	X	X	O	O	O	O
New Hampshire	X	O	O	O	O	O	O
New Jersey	X	O	X	O	O	O	O
New Mexico	X	X	X	X	O	X	X

(Continued)

BOX 4.4 *(Continued)*

State	Sp Ed	W/Han	Local	$1M	$5M	$/Child	Certif
New York	O	O	O	X	O	O	O
North Carolina	X	X	X	X	X	O	O
North Dakota	X	O	O	O	O	O	X
Ohio	X	O	O	X	O	O	O
Oklahoma	O	O	X	X	O	O	O
Oregon	X	O	O	O	O	O	O
Pennsylvania	X	X	X	X	X	O	O
Rhode Island	O	O	O	O	O	O	O
South Carolina	O	O	O	X	O	O	O
South Dakota	X	X	X	O	O	O	O
Tennessee	O	X	X	X	O	O	X
Texas	O	O	O	X	O	O	O
Utah	O	O	O	O	O	O	O
Vermont	O	O	O	O	O	O	O
Virginia	O	O	X	X	O	O	O
Washington	X	O	O	X	O	O	O
West Virginia	X	X	X	X	O	X	X
Wisconsin	O	O	O	O	O	O	O
Wyoming	O	O	O	O	O	O	O

Sp Ed = gifted programs administered as part of special education
W/Han = gifted programs closely tied to mandates for handicapped
Local = gifted programs locally mandated by state
$1M = state appropriations in excess of $1,000,000 in fiscal year 1981 *or* 1982
$5M = state appropriations in excess of $5,000,000 in fiscal year 1981 *or* 1982
$/Child = state appropriations amount to $500 or more per reported child.
Certif = teacher certification mandated for gifted education as of June, 1981
n/a = not applicable

Caution

Information in the funding categories is not necessarily comparable across states, because patterns of local and state funding vary. For example, in the South, state governments bear a heavier burden of school support than they do in the industrial Northeast. The analysis that follows attempts, however, to group data for comparison across *program type*. The figures should be taken as approximations only.

Summary Statistics (See Caution Above)

Seventeen states mandated programs.

Of these seventeen, fourteen (82 percent) also administer gifted programs as part of special education.

Of these seventeen, thirteen (76 percent) tie gifted programs closely to the mandates for the handicapped, (i.e., accord gifted students the same due process rights mandated for the handicapped under PL 94-142).

Of these seventeen, nine (53 percent) appropriated more than $1,000,000 in 1981 or 1982.

Of these seventeen, four (24 percent) appropriated more than $500/child in 1981 or 1982.

Of these seventeen, three (18 percent) appropriated *nothing* in 1981 or 1982. (Three other states did not report funding information.)

Thirty-three states did not mandate local programs.

Of these thirty-three, eleven (33 percent) also administer gifted programs as part of special education.

Of these thirty-three, *none* tie gifted programs closely to the mandates for the handicapped, (i.e., accord gifted students the same due process rights mandated for the handicapped under PL 94-142).

Of these thirty-three, eleven (33 percent) appropriated more than $1,000,000 in 1981 or 1982.

Of these thirty-three, one (3 percent) appropriated more than $500/child in 1981 or 1982.

Of these thirty-three, twenty-one (64 percent) appropriated *nothing* in 1981 or 1982.

Of the fifty states, six reported providing service to more than 50,000 students. [Students in these six states accounted for 39 percent of all gifted students served (N = 357,030). These six states appropriated a total of $71,771,010 for gifted education.]

Of these six states, two (North Carolina and Pennsylvania) mandated gifted programs *and* administered gifted programs as special education *and* extended the protections of PL 94-142 to gifted students. Per child appropriations in these states (FY 1982) were $288 and $500, respectively. *These states appropriated fully 34 percent of all monies spent on gifted students in 1982, yet their programs served only 12.7 percent of all identified gifted students in the United States.*

Of these six states, four (California, Illinois, Minnesota, and New York) *neither* mandated gifted programs *nor* administered gifted programs as special education *nor* extended the protections of PL 94-142 to gifted students. Per child appropriations in these states (FY 1982) were $103, $93, $11, and $28, respectively. *These states appropriated 19 percent of all monies spent on gifted students in 1982. Their programs, however, served 42 percent of all identified gifted students in the United States.*

Summary Conclusions (See Caution Above)

1. Mandated gifted programs are most often administered by special education. They most often extend the due process rights of PL 94-142 to gifted students.
2. Mandated gifted programs that are administered under special education and that extend due process rights to gifted students are apparently the best funded in the nation.

Adapted from P. Mitchell (Ed.), *A Policymaker's Guide to Issues in Gifted and Talented Education*, Alexandria, VA, 1981, pp. 3–7. Reprinted by permission of National Association of State Boards of Education, Alexandria, VA.

Objects of Negotiation

Educational decisions involving gifted children are negotiated; they should not be presumed to occur spontaneously. Consensus, on the rare occasions on which it is attempted (cf. Ysseldyke et al., 1982), usually is not easily achieved, nor are many decisions final. The law, in fact, provides for many kinds of review.

We will consider the objects of negotiation in three categories: (1) assessment of student characteristics and programs to address them, (2) intensity and quantity of service, and (3) continuity and quality of service.

The use of restrictive eligibility determination criteria (such as IQ above 145) is an example of the first category of negotiable issues. Another might be the exclusion from a gifted program of those who are academically gifted as opposed to intellectually gifted; such a subtle distinction may have little to do with how such children function in their areas of strength.

The availability of alternative placement options relates to our second category, intensity of service. Gallagher et al. (1982) have suggested that, although consultative alternatives for the gifted are slightly cheaper to operate than self-contained classes, they offer *much less* service and are therefore more expensive in terms of cost-per-benefit. By offering self-contained programs to some children, especially if the alternative includes accelerative strategies, school districts may in fact save money over the course of a child's public school tenure.

Our third category, which is closely linked to the second, relates to the notion that a gifted child's education should be guided by a continuous plan and not a succession of ad hoc arrangements. For example, when a child is still in the intermediate grades, tentative plans for later instruction and arrangements for the accrual of credit can be made. These might include early completion of the work of such higher-level courses as algebra, foreign languages, and history.

In the context of negotiation, teachers of gifted children should function primarily as advocates for the needs of their children, with the understanding that the effect of negotiations for individual children is cumulative. If for a full year teachers tolerate poorly functioning placement teams, or prepare IEPs in advance of meetings with parents, or remain silent on matters of professional opinion clearly within their domain (e.g., interpretation of IQ test results), then the cumulative effects on gifted programs will be harmful. If, however, teachers take principled stands which, though they may cause temporary problems with colleagues, advance the needs of both individual gifted children and the group of gifted children in the program, then the cumulative effect will be to permit growth in the quality and quantity of services.

In any situation some aspects of a program will be more amenable to improvement than others. The appropriate place at which to start improvements depends on student characteristics, the nature of identification procedures, the assignment of evaluation functions, the quality of administrative support, parent relations, and so forth. It also depends to a large extent on the personality of the teacher.

A teacher who wishes to propose changes in some aspect of a program should assess the importance of the change as well as the likelihood that the proposal will be accepted. Obviously, a teacher may also have personal priorities that interfere with professional priorities (e.g., the need to retain a job in a particular community, the need for privacy, or the need not to jeopardize certain professional or personal relationships). *These reflections are among the most difficult responsibilities of special education teachers.*

Negotiation, then, has a good deal to do with a teacher's developing sense of mission in the field. Doubtless some teachers will leave the field before developing (or after losing) a sense of mission. Some teachers will "weather well" and develop such a sense in spite of initial reservations or subsequent bad experiences. Some fortunate teachers may also enjoy a secure situation and feel that a sense of mission more general than the hard work of relevant teaching is not germane to their experience.

Negotiating for Regular and Special Education Programs

Most school systems already have or are initiating some gifted programs. A school system's programs may be a result of state mandates for gifted services or of local initiatives. In either case, gifted education programs may be administered as part of special education or as part of regular education.

When gifted programs are not part of special education, serious problems are likely. These problems could be addressed by the notions of least restrictive environment (appropriately applied), due process, free and appropriate education, and protection in assessment procedures. Many states and administrations will base arguments against the inclusion of gifted programs in special education largely on the difficulties created by PL 94-142.

It will be said, as gifted programs are increasingly proposed, that gifted and handicapped childen have opposing needs, that gifted children are more similar to normal children, and that gifted children therefore can be better served in regular education programs. This observation conveys the impression that gifted children do not require the protection of due process. We believe, however, that because individualization is not easily accomplished, the gifted are better served when they are protected by due process (cf. Mercer, 1979).

If gifted programs are not part of special education, two courses of action are open. One is to advocate that they be placed under special education control. Legislative action may well be necessary, and only a representative and active statewide group can undertake this goal. The second option is to advocate the establishment of separate gifted education regulations under state authority. Mitchell's *An Advocate's Guide to Building Support for Gifted and Talented Education* (1981a) offers some guidelines for this sort of work.

We are not necessarily opposed to the administration of gifted programs outside special education, if the same procedural safeguards that characterize PL 94-142 apply. These safeguards are most relevant in assessment, placement, and program planning. The point of such safeguards, however, is to implement appropriate pedagogy. With modifications, regular education certainly has much to offer gifted students.

Where new programs are being implemented, there may exist opportunities unavailable in more firmly established programs. Typically, newly established programs offer minimal services. Teachers may be asked to travel to several schools, or even to provide consultative services to an entire district. Often such arrangements serve a function more evidently administrative than instructional. A teacher confronted with such a consultative-administrative assignment could adopt several strategies to improve the likelihood and quality of eventual instruction.

First, the teacher could mount a vigorous identification effort, which included meetings with parents to determine eligibility. This strategy would build expectations that identification would be followed by instruction at some specified future time. Second, building on this expectation, the teacher could start to exploit options within existing regular education programs to begin some services to gifted children whose parents were receptive to such suggestions. These options could include cross-class placements, work in more advanced texts in the regular classroom, or grade-skipping (see Box 4.5).

Where programs are permissive (i.e., not required by the state, but implemented at the discretion of the district), contact among gifted teachers may be restricted. Teachers should act quickly to meet *academic needs* of gifted children in this situation, and then build wider contacts with other schools in the district or with neighboring districts. Academic instruction will in general please parents (cf. Katz, 1971), and it is probably the parents who can best shape the administrative perception of the need for a gifted program.

Neuman (1980, p. 11) notes that "the gap between mandated programs and implementation is often a chasm. There are a large number of 'paper programs' for the gifted that have no reality beyond lip service, yet they permit institutions to receive monies meant, but not used, for the gifted." Where mandates exist but are poorly implemented, other strategies are called for. One way to increase the amount of service available to gifted children is to exploit the notion of a *continuum* of services (see Chapter 3). For example, if it is the routine pedagogical practice to assign every child to a resource program for two hours a week, the teacher might propose that two hours a week is insufficient—that the child should be seen two, three, or four times a week and/or that the child should spend half the day in a more advanced class.

Negotiating for Special Education for Individuals

The scene of negotiation most important to individual gifted children is the multidisciplinary team meetings at which eligibility determination, IEP development, and placement are considered. Indeed, most of the negotiation about suitable programs for particular children will occur in these meetings.

BOX 4.5 How to Change School Programs for the Gifted

School programs for the gifted can be influenced by group and individual responses to particular situations, some by teachers, some by parents, and some by both teachers and parents.

Individual Response on Behalf of One Child	Group Response on Behalf of Many Children
1. Ask for a trial arrangement such as an acceleration option with provision for assessing its effectiveness after an established interval.	1. Form a parent group.
2. Request mediation with the county or district superintendent.	2. Determine common concerns and hold discussions with the superintendent.
3. Ask for a due process hearing.	3. Prepare a proposal to present to the Board of Education (include needs assessment, costs, and staffing).
4. Request an appeal of the hearing decision by the state superintendent of schools.	4. Lobby state officials or local officials to gain support for proposals.
5. Initiate civil action.	5. Initiate a class action suit on behalf of many gifted children.

Where gifted education is part of special education, prospects for benefiting particular individuals are greater than they would otherwise be, largely because of the functions assigned to the multidisciplinary team (see Box 4.6).

PL 94-142 mandates the use of multidisciplinary teams on the assumption that some of the past abuses in the placement of handicapped children have been the result of the secrecy with which placement was conducted. Often placements were decided by a single person (such as a psychologist, principal, or teacher). Psychologists have exercised the greatest discretion, perhaps because of their relatively higher status ("level I professionals," according to Golin & Ducanis, 1981, p. 44) and probably also because of their closer proximity to administrative authority. The position of the federal law and of handicapped rights activists, is that teams including parents and teachers would be less likely to make merely expedient decisions than would individuals in authority, acting sub rosa.

The use of placement teams has not, however, solved all the problems associated with single-person placement procedures. Research on the function and performance of placement teams has been accumulating since before September 1978, when PL 94-142 regulations required that the law be fully

---

BOX 4.6   Some Tasks for Teachers at Team Meetings

In the following excerpt from a paper by Markel, Bogusky, Greenbaum, Bizer, and Rycus (1976), we have replaced "handicapped" with "gifted" and "charity" with "reward."

> To a large extent teachers act as models and resources for the parent. They need to be informed about federal and/or state laws, and local options regarding [gifted] children. Teachers should be aware of community resources so that they can give the parents advice on additional services or facilities needed by a child. Teachers will have to constantly reassure some parents that public education of a [gifted] child is a right and not a [reward]. Parents should not have to feel grateful for service nor should they fear that services might be withheld because they differ in opinion or ask questions. Teachers and administrators are facilitators for parents in the process of setting priorities and making educational decisions. The teacher can be an asset at conferences for parents and support assertive behaviors.

Markel et al. (1976) note that it is important to make the distinction between assertive behavior and aggressive behavior. Assertive behavior attempts, in an objective fashion, to clarify rights, laws, roles and responsibilities. It is task-oriented behavior. Aggressive behavior, on the other hand, attempts to fix blame. Sometimes assertive behavior may be no better received than aggressive behavior. The attempt to keep discussion on-task and objective is nonetheless appropriate.

---

implemented. Ysseldyke and his colleagues at the Institute for Research on Learning Disabilities at the University of Minnesota recently published a number of pointed studies of the performance of teams and team members, both in a naturalistic setting (i.e., real placement meetings) and in simulated placement activities (Algozzine, Ysseldyke & Hill, 1982; Christenson, Ysseldyke & Algozzine, 1982; Poland et al., 1982; Ysseldyke & Algozzine, 1982a; Ysseldyke et al., 1982; Ysseldyke, Algozzine, Rostollan & Shinn, 1981). These studies suggest a connection between past abuses and current abuses. They isolate many of the problems inherent in placement team functioning.

The summative study of this series of articles is Ysseldyke et al. (1982). This study reviews the literature on the performance of placement teams from 1974 forward. Typical studies reported that parents and teachers seemed to be the most disenfranchised members of teams, that members tended to avoid their responsibilities for making decisions, that goals were unclear, and that alternatives were not explored.

Ysseldyke et al. (1982) studied thirty-four videotapes of placement team meetings in predominantly suburban and rural elementary schools. Parents were present at fourteen meetings. Meetings were rated on specific items that the authors felt might reasonably be construed as characterizing effective team meetings. The researchers (1982, p. 312) found that "important procedures simply do not occur, and there is little effort to encourage all team members to participate." Moreover, the researchers discovered that decisions were not made by consensus, that decisions were indeterminately expressed, and that team members did not challenge decisions or the way in which decisions were made (Ysseldyke et al., 1982, p. 311).

Ysseldyke et al. (1982, pp. 311–312) suggest four measures to improve placement meetings:

1. *Structured separation of activities,* which provides a clear context in which to consider evaluation data, conduct orderly discussion, and arrive at decisions;
2. *Consensus decisions,* which provide the context for reaching resolutions accepted by all parties, a necessary condition for cooperation;
3. *Clearly stated goals,* which provide focus for the meeting (participants know why they have gathered and what they must do);
4. *Nonspecialized participation,* which provides the substance of multidisciplinary interaction, "occurring when all team members engage in . . . interpreting data, generating alternatives, [and] evaluating . . . without regard to role or specialty" (p. 312).

If these points are too complex to implement, then a *structured agenda, with time allotments for specific functions,* can still produce significant improvements (Ysseldyke et al., 1982).

Despite the fact that all of this research was conducted with handicapped exceptionalities, it is nonetheless extremely relevant to multidisciplinary meetings at which gifted children are considered. First, the general procedural habits of placement teams are much the same, regardless of the suspected exceptionality of the child. The findings support our belief that teachers of gifted children should attend meetings with their own goals well-defined and possible alternatives identified for individual children.

Second, the findings that (1) classroom behavior may dominate placement team meeting discussions (Poland et al., 1982) and (2) regular classroom teachers are the personnel most consistently present on placement teams (Ysseldyke et al., 1981) need to be especially noted by teachers of the gifted in light of the limited opportunities gifted children actually have to display excellence in the regular classroom.

Third, the finding that noncognitive traits (e.g., parents' occupations, attractiveness of child, race) influence members of placement teams, regardless of unambiguous cognitive traits (Ysseldyke & Algozzine, 1982a), is significant. It should alert gifted teachers to the need to exclude such irrelevant details from considerations of eligibility, program development, and placement.

This discussion may seem to imply that gifted programs would fare better without having to confront the problems of multidisciplinary teams that have been revealed by the research. Such, however, is not the case, as the same problems would be encountered in other forums. The teacher of gifted children in programs administered under special education is in a *good* position to anticipate some of these problems, to develop a plan of action based on reference to explicit regulations, and to make allies among teachers, parents, and others encountering similar problems. This is a tactical advantage in developing meaningful programs for bright students. Teachers otherwise situated will lack a definitional framework, a sense of how the problems are likely to develop, and influential allies.

RESOLVING DISAGREEMENTS

Because of the relative openness of the special education process, it is inevitable that direct negotiation between parties will in some instances fail to produce viable options. The teacher of the gifted may have to play a prominent part in the sometimes arduous process of resolving such differences.

The Context in Which Disagreements Arise

Laws and regulations assume that decisions regarding the appropriate placement and instruction of exceptional students can be formally negotiated. According to research, such negotiated decision-making is not characteristic of team placement efforts. In fact, the research suggests that in most meetings alternative placements are, for some reason, *not proposed by team members.*

Perhaps alternative placements are not generated because most of the parties involved wish to avoid the contention that is possible when conflicting views are dealt with openly. Gallagher (1975, p. 85) has found that intellectual controversy is little tolerated in public schools. In this context, school personnel are apt to feel they have the most to lose. Because schools are authority hierarchies (i.e., instructional personnel are directly subordinate to several supervisory levels; the lowest levels in the authority structure are typically female, and the highest are typically male), lower-level school personnel in general exercise a great deal of restraint to avoid appearing to contradict one another or jeopardizing one another's status.

When controversy does occur, authority structures are very likely to be brought to bear, not only to impose a solution, but also to forestall future incidents. For example, a school psychologist in one district was dismissed for refusing to participate in preplacement meetings which actually determined placements in the absence of parents. This psychologist was also ordered by the assistant superintendent not to voice disagreements with other staff members in meetings at which parents were present. On appeal to the state superintendent of schools, charges were dropped and the district was ordered to reinstate the psychologist (West Virginia State Superintendent of Schools Decision, September 30, 1982).

The Role of the Gifted Teacher.   In dealing with and resolving differences, the gifted teacher should remember that (1) conflicts of opinion are inherent; (2) if they are not considered openly, individual children (and eventually programs) will be harmed; (3) the law intends that differences of opinion be negotiated and consensus reached; and (4) if satisfactory consensus cannot be reached, review procedures exist to conclude decision-making.

Teachers of the gifted should expect that some school personnel will be very careful to guard against the appearance of dissension among school team members. In fact, effective teams may pose an organizational threat to some schools, so some educators will doubtless nurture the ineffectiveness of teams (cf. Boss & McConkie, 1981).

One of the least discussed but most important roles of the teacher of gifted students is the role of advocate (Whitmore, 1983). The Council for Exceptional Children (1981) asserts that the professional educator's primary responsibility is to the student. Securing appropriate instruction for children is virtually impossible without a knowledge of federal and state education laws. Too often teachers and parents are led to believe that they *cannot* understand such documents. We have observed in our work that this misconception often leads teachers and parents to accept practices that openly contradict the requirements of law.

Teachers of the gifted should, therefore, become very familiar with the regulations governing matters likely to involve disagreements. They should share their knowledge of these regulations with colleagues and parents so that *actual* differences of opinion can be clarified. Often, apparent disagreements merely involve differences in interpretation of regulations that are not fully understood.

The Role of Parents. Unfortunately, when school personnel do not propose appropriate alternatives, the responsibility for such necessary action devolves to parents. As many commentators have noted (e.g., Farber & Lewis, 1975; Holt, 1981; Katz, 1968, 1971; Moles, 1982; also cf. Bronfenbrenner, 1970; Keniston, 1975) parents are not likely to have much influence with school personnel. Moreover, research has demonstrated that school authorities are *especially resistant* to influence on matters of particular concern (i.e., curriculum development, instruction, and school governance) to parents of exceptional children (Moles, 1982). Parents in states that apply PL 94-142 to gifted children can resort to the use of due process hearings, if they feel acceptable alternatives are not being proposed.

Procedural Due Process

Though gifted children do not suffer the same lifelong hardships as the handicapped, their deviance from the academic norm and consequent lack of equal protection in educational issues are just as great. Schools in general do not validate intellectual endeavors (Coleman, 1961; Hofstadter, 1963; Katz, 1971; Wiener, 1950), and this fact is symptomatic of the pedagogical predicament of gifted children.

Without recognition of the necessity for procedural due process to protect the rights of gifted children in respect to their education, little can be accomplished to advance their individual needs. Mercer (1979), in a dissertation on the due process and equal protection rights of gifted public school students, notes that several Supreme Court cases (e.g., *Griswold* v. *Connecticut*, 381 U.S. 479 [1965]; *West Virginia Board of Education* v. *Barnette*, 319 U.S. 624 [1943]; *Pierce* v. *Society of Sisters*, 268 U.S. 510 [1925]) are applicable in the case of the gifted. According to Mercer (1979, p. 587-A), it would seem that the law requires schools "to provide educational services from which the child has the opportunity for a meaningful and appropriate education."

Another parallel between gifted and disadvantaged populations is in order. Katz (1971) notes that poor children do not need an education that addresses attitudes or emotions, but one that teaches them to read and to understand mathematics. Gifted children deserve similar respect from educators. Due process will be required in order to effect cognitive goals in gifted education and to provide access to appropriate education for all gifted children.

Hearings.   Due process procedures required by PL 94-142 make it less likely that an exceptional child's educational benefits will be mitigated by irrelevant factors such as administrative convenience. The following excerpt, from testimony that was delivered at a due process hearing on behalf of a child who is both gifted and learning disabled, illustrates the need for such procedures:

> In two and a half hours of class time yesterday, Sean did not learn one new concept or skill. He worked only fifteen minutes of the two and one-half hour period, five minutes on a math worksheet that was too easy for him and ten minutes on a spelling assignment that was too hard. . . . Of eleven interactions with classmates, only three were positive. From his peers, Sean is receiving primarily negative feedback. The other children appear to regard him as a nuisance. The majority of teacher comments directed to Sean were either negative or corrective. Because he is not behaving appropriately, Sean is receiving almost no positive response from anyone in school. Whether the "fault" is Sean's or a result of an inappropriate program, it is likely that six hours a day, five days a week in a place where he is receiving so little positive social response is damaging. . . . In the second grade, he is already the most "turned off" gifted child I have ever observed . . . Both Sean's time and the teacher's are being wasted. Because of his significant intellectual strengths and equally significant learning and behavior problems, the regular classroom program is not adequate to meet his needs.

> (Used with the permission of "Sean's" parents.)

Sean's parents requested a due process hearing because Sean was making poor grades in school and becoming increasingly reluctant to attend. Numerous meetings with the teacher, the principal, and the special education director had brought no real effort to provide education designed to develop Sean's intellectual ability. Attention was focused only on his learning and behavior problems. School personnel felt that Sean should earn the right to participate in a gifted program. Also, the district did not have a gifted program in the school he attended, and it was inconvenient to provide direct services to him. Regardless of the reasons that Sean was inappropriately served, the result was his failure to learn anything except how unpleasant school can be. Had Sean lived in a state that did not offer the protection of due process for gifted children, his parents would have had no recourse; they would have had to accept what the school was willing to offer or remove Sean from school.

In many ways, a due process hearing represents the ultimate attempt by the parties involved to reach accord at the local level. Due process hearings are not, however, the best means of achieving workable arrangements in individual situations. Hearings are subject to the same forces that render placement teams less than effective, and their record with respect to effecting change and following procedures correctly is not good (Lyons, 1982). Nonetheless, as Lyons (1982) notes, hearings have been occurring with increasing frequency.

When the conflict between schools and parents concerns significant unresolved differences of principle, or when the unresolved differences have important implications (e.g., early entry to first grade or kindergarten), then a hearing is probably warranted. Teachers of the gifted should realize that research has shown that parents who use the hearing process are generally of middle to high socioeconomic status, well informed, and highly empathic to parents of other exceptional children (Budoff, Orenstein & Abramson, 1981; Mitchell, 1976).

Hearing decisions are frequently appealed to the state educational agency (SEA) (Budoff et al., 1981). The decision of the SEA is the final attempt of the entire school system to reach a semblance of accord between the parties. If one party is still not satisfied by the appeal decision, it may bring a civil action. Some of the gifted advocacy associations sampled by Grossi (1981) reported that they were involved in litigation.

SUMMARY

The justification for special instruction for the gifted and for the handicapped is the same: both groups are significantly different from the norm on educationally relevant variables. This justification does not conflict with commitments to equal educational opportunities for children. When state law includes gifted children under directives for educating handicapped children, gifted children have a practical advantage in the form of legislative assurance of reasonable accommodation to their exceptional academic ability.

The differentiation of instruction for gifted children does not imply that, given special programs, apt children will engineer a better society (cf. Wiener, 1950). Similarly, individualization of instruction for the handicapped does not imply that handicapped children, given special programs, will grow up to be self-supporting, tax-paying adults; nor should it. The assumption is merely that if we assert the need to provide an education to all children, then the most academically different children require special scrutiny.

In this chapter we have discussed ways in which to promote differentiation in the context of program development for individuals and groups. Our task has been complicated by the lack of any national program regulating gifted education. The role of negotiation in program development and methods of resolving disagreements were also considered.

CHAPTER 5

Pace and Content: Acceleration

INTRODUCTION

The term *acceleration* is emotion-laden for many school administrators, teachers, and parents. The academic benefits of acceleration lead some people to support it emphatically, whereas others view it as a one-dimensional approach to the education of advanced students which ignores their presumed right to socialize with age-mates. Many associate this term with just one accelerative option, grade-skipping; only a few people are aware of other possibilities.

Many disputes have focused on whether enrichment or acceleration is the most appropriate strategy for academically capable students (cf. Gowan & Demos, 1964; Hollingworth, 1926, 1942; Renzulli, 1977; Stanley, 1976). An early worker in the field (Freeman, 1924) believed that, if the term *enrichment* meant work at a more advanced intellectual level, then acceleration was an easily implemented strategy for realizing such a goal. Acceleration might be construed to be an approach to enrichment defined in this broad sense. Unlike other enrichment strategies, however, acceleration alters the *pace* of instruction rather than the *content*.

The dispute continues among educators today. Those favoring acceleration maintain that regular curriculum *content* is appropriate for the gifted, whereas those opposing acceleration suggest that the gifted require a *qualitatively different* curriculum content.

This chapter reviews the literature on the practice of acceleration. It debunks various myths about acceleration in light of the research and suggests possible accelerative options in various school settings. The chapter also describes model acceleration programs and gives practical guidelines for establishing similar programs. Because the literature on acceleration is so supportive, we view acceleration as an essential part of educational planning for all academically gifted students. Whether or not acceleration is selected for an individual gifted child, it should be an available option.

ACCELERATION AND THE NATURE OF ACADEMIC TALENT

One of the most striking characteristics of high-IQ children is their precocious verbal development (Keating, 1976). For a variety of reasons, these children acquire understanding of more words and greater comprehension of the messages conveyed by oral and written discourse. According to Keating (1979, p. 217), the increased rate at which students integrate verbal information is the "single most compelling difference" between gifted students and students of average ability.

As a consequence of this rapid verbal development, gifted students are capable of mastering academic curricula at an accelerated pace. One of the early studies of gifted children (Hollingworth, 1942) maintained that a child with an IQ score of 140 could complete the twelve-year school curriculum in only six years, and a child with an IQ score of 170 would need only three years to accomplish the twelve-year curriculum. In a recent study of underachieving gifted children, Fearn (1982) found that the pace of learning for both achieving and underachieving gifted children not only was about double that of nongifted children, but also tended to increase over time.

When the level and pace of instruction are inappropriate, both the cognitive and noncognitive characteristics of gifted students may stand in the way of their success. Rapid understanding and superior retention of information, excellent powers of abstraction, curiosity about many things, and independence of judgment are among the most often cited attributes of gifted children. They all represent what would appear to be positive differences.

The interaction of these qualities with an unchallenging education program, however, results in minimized academic performance. Classroom performance may, therefore, lead teachers to underestimate the student's ability. That this dynamic is not the exception but the *rule* is borne out by research studies such as that of Pegnato and Birch (1959), who found that less than half of a sample of children with IQs greater than 130 were judged by their teachers as being of good or very good ability. Braga (1971) obtained similar results among the teachers of gifted children admitted early to first grade. As Braga (1971) notes, however, even in neutral environments (i.e., situations in which teachers are unaware of the presence of early entrants), accelerated students cannot be distinguished as inferior to nonaccelerated regular or gifted students. In general, teachers are not aware of what gifted children could do in accelerated environments.

Fears about Acceleration

"Consistently positive and consistently ignored" (Newland, 1976, p. 245) is an accurate characterization of the research on acceleration (cf. Benbow & Stanley, 1982; Braga, 1971; Horne & Dupuy, 1981; Karnes & Chauvin, 1982; Kulik & Kulik, 1984). Studies of accelerated students find them to be free from the problems popularly thought to result from moving through school at a fast pace (cf. Braga, 1971; Christopherson, 1981; Daurio, 1979; Horne & Dupuy, 1981; Karnes & Chauvin, 1982; Solano & George, 1976).

In spite of the positive research results, fears about acceleration persist. The most common concerns are that (1) standardized tests do not really reflect classroom achievement, so a high score on a test is not acceptable evidence of capability to move ahead; (2) acceleration results in gaps in academic skills; (3) accelerated learning is superficial; and (4) acceleration is detrimental to the social adjustment of younger students. In the following section, we present research related to the academic and social adjustment of accelerates; the positive findings constitute a potent argument against many of the fears voiced about acceleration.

Academics.   Most teachers who object to the use of standardized test scores as a basis for acceleration do so on the grounds that the test scores give an inflated estimate of the child's potential. Research has shown that well-constructed intelligence and achievement tests are both valid and reliable predictors of academic achievement, except in cases where poverty, cultural difference, linguistic difference, or poor pedagogy confounds the measure (cf. Anastasi, 1968; Salvia & Ysseldyke, 1981). In such cases test scores are likely to result in the *underestimation* of children's potential or performance. In fact, the argument has been made, from a variety of perspectives, that schools *consistently underestimate* children's abilities (e.g., Bowles & Gintis, 1976; Coleman, 1961; Durden, 1980; Holt, 1964; Katz, 1971; Meskill & Lauper, 1973; Wirszup, 1981).

As we noted in Chapters 2 and 4, standardized IQ and achievement tests can be used for placement and for program planning. When needed, criterion-referenced tests can be employed in conjunction with standardized tests in determining objectives suitable for individual gifted students. When acceleration is an option being considered during the development of the individual program plan, criterion-referenced tests can be used to determine the kind and rate of acceleration. If classroom teachers participate in the testing process, they are often more willing to acknowledge the accuracy of the results.

Neither the "gaps in learning" nor the "superficial learning" criticism of acceleration is documented by research. On the contrary, follow-up studies often have found that accelerated students outperform bright, nonaccelerated students (e.g., Braga, 1971; Fund for the Advancement of Education, 1957; Karnes & Chauvin, 1982; Pressey, 1967). This is true even in advanced course work in highly sequential subjects, such as mathematics, in which serious gaps or superficial learning would be most likely to impair performance (Keating, 1979).

A study by Kulik and Kulik (1984) offers the best evidence yet compiled on the effectiveness of acceleration. In their study, Kulik and Kulik used meta-analysis (Glass, McGaw & Smith, 1981), the statistical analysis of results from many studies. The technique allows quantitative results from different studies to be integrated reliably. When accelerated students were compared with *equally bright students of the same age* who had not been accelerated, the accelerates were found to be achieving about one year in advance of their non-accelerated age-mates (Kulik & Kulik, 1984). Moreover, Kulik and Kulik (1984) found that accelerated students performed just as well as *equally bright older students* who had not been accelerated.

From the earliest research on acceleration to the most recent, no matter what research method is used, no matter what comparisons are made, the results are nearly unanimous (cf. Kulik & Kulik, 1984): acceleration allows a closer approximation between the bright learner's cognitive development and the level of instruction. When conducted sensibly, it offers this better match without in general producing any of the serious academic problems feared by some administrators, teachers, and parents. Moreover, it is an option that can be effected in even the smallest, poorest, most rural school or the largest, poorest, urban ghetto school.

Social Adjustment. More than sixty years of research has yielded positive results concerning the social adjustment of young accelerates (see Box 5.1). The social adjustment of these students has been measured by considering the number of extracurricular activities in which they participate, counselors' opinions of their interaction with teachers and peers, teachers' evaluations, parents' judgments, and students' responses to questions about their ad-

---

BOX 5.1   Acceleration: The Obscurity of Success

The following observations and reflections are drawn from real-life reports. How many are familiar to you?

"I have yet to see a four-year-old do well in kindergarten."

"My experience is that younger children have difficulty in the upper grades."

"Early precocity does not hold up."

"None that I've had has been a success."

A fourth grade teacher accelerated a student once in her nineteen years of teaching. She now rejects all acceleration because the student's subsequent teachers found him immature and irresponsible.

A principal rejects acceleration as a viable strategy for gifted children because "most children would not be mature enough to handle the stress of adapting to an older peer group."

A parent worries about the future of a gifted sixteen-year-old high school graduate.

According to researchers (e.g., Birch, Tisdall, Barney, & Marks, 1965; Braga, 1971; Kulik & Kulik, 1984; Stanley, 1976a), most negative attitudes toward acceleration are founded on misinformation, misinterpretation of data, or a belief that any change from the conventional way of doing things is untenable. A discussion of acceleration never fails to yield at least one story about a brilliant student who was accelerated and became (1) a school drop-out (it has been claimed that about 20 percent of gifted children drop out of high school, incidentally); (2) a social misfit (Hollingworth, 1942, did note the "heterodoxy" of the gifted); (3) a drug addict; or (4) a combination of all of these. The narrator attributes all of this to the skipping of one or two grades in school.

The fallacy in this reasoning is that we can never know the cause of the student's problems. Acceleration may have contributed to the problems, had no effect, or, perhaps, kept them from being worse. Moreover, even if a particular student's problems were associated with grade-skipping, the case is atypical. Research shows that such cases are not representative of the fate of accelerated students. The reason that these stories abound is, in fact, that they *are* atypical. They get people's attention, stay in their memories, are repeated to others, and contribute to the folk mythology about gifted children and their problems. Researchers have found that teachers cannot identify the successful accelerates or early entrants in their classes. Therefore, they have no way of reporting or propagating the success of such children (cf. Braga, 1971; Solano & George, 1976).

---

justment. The conclusions are similar: the majority of accelerated students suffer no serious problems in social adjustment.

There is some evidence that a few problems may occur in an initial adjustment period, but there is no evidence of long-term negative effects. For any child, entering a new social setting, such as a new school or college, presents problems. The problems of most accelerates appear to be of this nature; they are manageable and transitory—in fact, normal. (See Austin & Draper, 1981, for a thoughtful review of the peer relationships of the gifted, and Tidwell, 1980, for supporting data. These reports put the question into a meaningful context.)

The belief that social maladjustment is likely to accompany acceleration fails to take into account not only the results of research on acceleration, but also the common characteristics of gifted students. For example, gifted children often choose older children as friends because they share similar cognitive interests. For this reason gifted students appear to benefit from placement with *mental* age peers (cf. Whitmore, 1980). There is much more research, in fact, to support this educational placement than there is to support placement with chronological age peers (Birch et al., 1965).

The argument that acceleration causes emotional trauma due to academic pressure also fails to take into account the characteristics of gifted children. Many students thrive on intellectual challenges (Durden, 1980; Hollingworth, 1942; Stanley, 1976). It is in many ways more frustrating for such students to endure the slow pace of their own grade level than to meet the demands of a higher grade level. Since many gifted children enjoy intellectual activity, work matched to their ability level is more likely to stimulate them than to traumatize them. Many researchers report that students do superlative work in accelerated placements (e.g., Fund for the Advancement of Education, 1957; Bartkovich & Mezynski, 1981; Durden, 1980; Kulik & Kulik, 1984; Solano & George, 1976).

In summary, a thorough review of the research on acceleration reveals acceleration to be "not guilty" of all of the popular indictments against it. It has not caused academic, social, or emotional problems. Assuming that the academic ability of the child is assured and that appropriate, supportive, and systematic instruction is provided in the new placement, acceleration can provide significant cognitive and noncognitive benefits to many children, including both high-IQ and academically talented students. There is every indication that acceleration should be vigorously promoted by teachers of the gifted.

TYPES OF ACCELERATION

Acceleration includes a variety of strategies, administrative and instructional, which can be implemented in both regular and special education placements. Acceleration is, for the apt student, the modification analogous to overteaching for the slow-learning student. The principle behind slow-paced instruction, task analysis, and repeated practice to mastery is the accommodation of the individual needs of slow-learning students. The accelerative principles and strategies discussed in this section accommodate the needs of apt students. Although a particular accelerative strategy may not meet all the needs of an individual gifted child, it can nevertheless play an important role in the student's total educational program.

An Analogy

Binding an apt child to the pace of the regular curriculum is much like misplacing a child of normal ability in a class for the retarded. (More normal children than we care to admit actually have been so misplaced.) A normal child in such a setting would make a number of adjustments. First, the child would try to adapt socially. That is, after a time the child's behavior would resemble that of the rest of the class. Second, the child would modify his or her academic performance to conform to the teacher's expectations. The child would perform the kind and amount of work expected. After a time the child's achievement would suffer as well. Any incentive to realize potential would be lost in an atmosphere of cognitive lethargy.

The above description is only an analogy. There are many important differences between the situation of a normal child in a class of retarded students and that of a gifted child in a regular classroom. Unfortunately for the gifted, one of the differences is that special education teachers may well be able to distinguish a normally apt child in a class for retarded children more easily than regular class teachers are able to distinguish a gifted child in their classes (cf. Braga, 1971; Freeman, 1979; Pringle, 1970). Also, a normally apt child in a classroom for the retarded may be better accommodated both instructionally (because of smaller class size) and administratively (there *is* a regular program to which a normal child may be sent).

A significant part of the dilemma of gifted children in regular classroom placements is that because work may be easy for them, educators assume that the children's intellectual needs have been met or, rather, that the gifted children are meeting their academic responsibilities (cf. Baer & Bushell, 1981). However, neither interpretation is correct. The visibility of this problem, like that of successful acceleration, is low (cf. Coleman, 1961, p. 304, on the visibility of average students' interest in academic learning).

Standard Presentation: The Appeal of the Lockstep

There is a common assumption behind the belief that acceleration will leave gaps in learning. This assumption is that all students must experience a standard presentation in order to learn particular academic skills properly. The notion of individualization for exceptional students contradicts this assumption. Parents and teachers of exceptional children should acknowledge that the need for differentiated instruction will cause some difficulties, even in the case of gifted children. In a noncognitive sense these problems are often no different in kind or degree from those the retarded must face with far less effective defenses. Even changes for the better can be somewhat disruptive. The concern about "gaps" seems to have more to do with the social acceptability of nonstandard arrangements.

A gifted child who endures unnecessary overteaching in an undifferentiated program is far more likely to develop detrimental gaps in his or her education than a child who is so fortunate as to be always working at an appropriate instructional level. Often children fail to learn material because schools do not give them the chance to learn it. Such losses will inevitably go unnoticed, no matter how serious they may be. Some educators are overly concerned with possible discontinuities in instruction caused by differentiating a program and ignore the true omissions that occur when the gifted are denied opportunities for more advanced learning.

Individual differences imply differences in the presentation of curriculum content. The standard presentation, or "lockstep," curriculum is not typically appropriate for students who have been identified as academically apt on the basis of advanced academic performance or potential to achieve at advanced levels. Thus, failure to *consider* the need for accelerated instruction of some sort is tantamount to denial of the characteristics that make gifted students exceptional.

Accelerated Regular-Class Curriculum

An accelerated regular-class curriculum is primarily an option for elementary programs. At the secondary level, other options make more sense instructionally and can be accomplished more readily. However, at the elementary level, instruction generally occurs in self-contained rooms, and parents and teachers will doubtless give some thought to ways to modify the regular-class placement for gifted children (see Chapter 3 for many practical examples).

A major difficulty with accelerated regular-class curriculum is the limitation inherent in the diversity of children found in most regular classrooms. To implement changes for every child in a regular classroom is virtually impossible. In a typical elementary school, a teacher may supervise thirty students; it is practically absurd to consider the possibility of arranging an individual program for each child. Arranging partially individualized programs for a substantial proportion (perhaps 25 percent) of these children is within the grasp of an energetic, devoted, experienced, and highly competent regular-class teacher.

It is, however, unreasonable to expect this kind of performance typically. Twenty or thirty students to one teacher is a ratio appropriate for group instruction, not individual instruction. Pretensions to the contrary serve no one well. (How much less reasonable is the expectation that individualization be carried out by secondary teachers who may see upwards of 100 students!)

Nonetheless, it may sometimes be possible for teachers to make arrangements of an individualized nature for some gifted elementary students. We would caution that such an arrangement is only wise for a particularly eager student. The student should be capable of working independently and should meet with a teacher of the gifted regularly. The student should also be willing to seek help as the inevitable difficulties arise. The supportive involvement of parents may also be essential. And unless the school, district, county, or state acknowledges in some way the appropriateness of this particular arrangement, its very tentativeness is a sure detriment.

In summary, the factors of critical importance to this type of acceleration are

1. the commitment of the student,
2. the accepting attitude of the regular-class teacher, who will have to defend the anomaly of the gifted student's program to the rest of the class,
3. the consistent services of a teacher of the gifted to help implement the changes,
4. the active support and counsel of the student's parents, and
5. procedural rights circumscribing the arrangement.

Clearly, such favorable conditions do not characterize the situations of all gifted children. Indeed, they are fairly rare. If all of the above criteria are met, however, an accelerated curriculum could be accomplished to some degree within the regular classroom. Gallagher (1975) considers this option the least effective means of modifying education for the gifted student. Gowan and Demos (1964) consider it the most expensive way of differentiating services for the gifted. Our guarded prognosis for the ultimate success of an accelerated regular-class curriculum reflects our intuition that the regular class may be the most restrictive environment for the gifted student. The regular classroom is often characterized by instruction quite sensibly directed toward what the teacher perceives as the average level (Freeman, 1979).

Cross-Class Placement

By cross-class placement we mean participation by a child in classrooms other than the normally assigned regular class (but see Chapter 3 for a discussion of cluster grouping). A fourth grader, for example, who is reading at the eighth grade level could be sent to the sixth, seventh, or eighth grade class for the reading lesson. A demonstrably ready kindergarten child identified as gifted could be sent for a period in the morning to the first grade for reading instruction.

Cross-class placements can be a very effective way of accommodating a variety of individual differences efficiently within the regular program at the elementary level. First, the arrangement can include all exceptional children, not just the gifted. Also, such an arrangement on a schoolwide basis can allow, for example, a fifth grade regular-class teacher to take a first or second grade reading group.

Cross-class placement may be quite drastic (for example, sending a third grader to the eighth grade for reading or math), or it may be minimal (for example, sending a third grader in one class to another third grade room in which a different text or method is being used, or in which the students are working on material that is a bit more advanced). We think of cross-class placement as the option most similar to an accelerated regular-class curriculum. Indeed, both these options may be implemented without actually accelerating the student's progress through school. They are accelerative options only if the responsible adults are struggling to make possible progress that is more rapid than usual.

Nonetheless, the more frequent cross-class placements are, the more likely that individual cases of cross-class placement will prove successful. A single such placement of only one gifted child is quite likely to be unsuccessful. The child may be made to feel uncomfortable in a variety of ways, and the success of the strategy may be determined solely on the basis of this one child's adjustment. Therefore, we caution against making the experience of a gifted child—or any lone child—a test of the utility of cross-class placement. It is preferable to make a modest commitment to the arrangement either for a number of exceptional children (from one or, better yet, many categories of exceptionality) or for a particular section of the general school population.

At the secondary level cross-class placement can and should be accomplished much more easily. The integrity of a class of chronological peers is not quite so rigid in high school as it is in elementary school. The chief impediment to cross-class placement in high school may be, ironically, the standards for graduation. If, for example, the standards require four years of English, then a gifted secondary student may have no statutory choice but to endure four years of undifferentiated instruction. For gifted children this is a foolish waste of time (cf. Durden, 1980). The problem is worst in locales in which honors or Advanced Placement courses are unavailable (cf. Voorheis, 1979). (The Advanced Placement Program is described later in this chapter.) There is, however, no logical reason, and less social pressure than in elementary schools, to contravene a gifted sophomore's attendance in junior or senior English classes. In such a case, the student should be exempted from sophomore English; mastery of the more advanced class should be accepted as proof of mastery of the less advanced one.

Another form of cross-class placement takes gifted children, part-time, across the traditional boundaries of elementary, middle, or high schools. These boundaries represent the belief that students share developmental commonalities that separate them from their older associates. Thus, not only students, but teachers and administrators as well, ordinarily tend to regard the transfer from building to building as a rite of passage (see also the section on early entry later in this chapter).

Cross-class placement is a good way to accommodate the needs of students with particular, rather than general, academic talent. It can be cost-effective and can help differentiate instruction for various types of students.

Special Accelerated Classes

Special accelerated classes are rapid-paced courses in particular subjects. Good examples are the mathematics courses offered to mathematically precocious youth through the auspices of Johns Hopkins University. Many of the mathematically gifted junior high students participating in a study conducted at Johns Hopkins mastered in 40 hours a series of precalculus math courses that usually requires 540 hours of instruction (Bartkovich & Mezynski, 1981). Though the Johns Hopkins case is an example of a very rapid pace, it is appropriate for some very talented students.

Special Provisions. Accelerated classes are equally applicable to all ages and all subjects (cf. Durden, 1980, for a version of compromise between acceleration and enrichment in the humanities). Rapid-paced courses should be taught by highly competent teachers who are intellectually sophisticated and empathetic to the gifted. College instructors may make good candidates. Formal identification and placement procedures must be established and maintained for such courses.

The content of accelerated classes may vary somewhat from district to district, but certain guidelines seem necessary. In the elementary school, an obvious academic division between basic skills (reading and math) and content areas (science and social studies) suggests itself. In any case, the instructional emphasis needs to be academic and the courses must be aimed at students' demonstrable capacities and functional levels.

The special accelerated class in reading or math should be an addition or an alternative to cross-class placement as described above. Even placement at a higher grade level may not fully address the capacity of most gifted students to learn rapidly. The pace and (intellectual) peer interaction of the special class distinguish it from cross-class placement. Special accelerated classes are special education classes in the sense that their aims and procedures differ somewhat from those of the regular program and so do their students.

A criticism of special accelerated classes is that their treatment of the subject tends to be superficial. Clearly, if students unequipped to deal with rapid-paced courses are placed in them, these students are likely to acquire only a superficial understanding of the subject. This situation, however, is not a result of the instruction, but of a mistake in student selection. Carefully selected students who have completed rapid-paced courses excel on standardized measures of achievement (Keating, 1979b; cf. Durden, 1980; Fund for the Advancement of Education, 1957; Karnes & Chauvin, 1982; Solano & George, 1976).

Elementary Humanities. Accelerated content area instruction at the elementary level presents an interesting problem. Science and social studies are generally treated in a superficial fashion in the elementary curriculum. The same is true of art, music, and the humanities. Durden (1980), a humanities professor, deplores this treatment of the humanities by public schools. In general, the opinion of many educators is that only the elementary aspects of these subjects are accessible to normal preadolescent pupils. There are, of course, developmental hypotheses to corroborate this notion, especially the Piagetian distinction between concrete and formal operations. We question the applicability of this logic to the gifted. Formal operations are identical to abstraction and language-based concept formation. In all probability, the gifted reach the realm of formal operations in advance of their peers (Carter & Kontos, 1982; Keating, 1976).

Providing special accelerated classes in the humanities, the arts, and the natural and social sciences (and mathematics beyond the basic computational skills) may be one way to cope with the barriers and rites of passage associated with cross-class placement. If such elementary school classes are provided, however, it becomes important to determine how knowledge gained in these content classes will be dealt with at the middle or secondary school level.

Early Entry

Early entry is the accelerative option that has been studied the most thoroughly. The mystifying barriers separating preschool from kindergarten, elementary school from middle school, middle school from high school, and so forth can work to the advantage of the gifted student, if the school system will allow early entry. It provides students access to instruction at an appropriate level while minimizing adjustment difficulties. For example, shuttling between the middle school and the high school to receive advanced instruction in a cross-class placement may be difficult for many reasons. Perhaps transportation is a problem; perhaps the scheduling grids of the two buildings are totally out of phase (e.g., forty-five-minute periods versus fifty-minute periods); perhaps the student must attend middle school English during the time plane geometry is offered at the high school; perhaps peers (at both the middle school and the high school) resent the student's apparent exemption from a significant rite of passage. If the student attends high school in toto, however, these objections vanish.

Research.   Research has found early entry to be an effective accelerative option. Both the academic performance and the social adjustment of early entrants equal or exceed those of classmates. The results are particularly impressive especially since in many of these studies the early entrants were not gifted children.

Early admission to kindergarten has been investigated extensively. The physical development, social and emotional adjustment, and scholastic performance of underage students have all been studied. Even when the average IQ score of accelerates is only a little above average (e.g., 110), little or no deleterious effect is apparent. When IQ scores average 130 or above, the findings are overwhelmingly favorable (Daurio, 1979).

Hobson (1963) and Worcester (1956) conducted follow-up studies in school districts in Massachusetts and Nebraska, respectively, to determine the effects of early entrance to kindergarten. In neither study was giftedness a criterion for early entry, although the average IQs of early entrants were above the mean. The students were about eight months younger than their classmates, but in both studies the underage students were found to be at least as well off scholastically, socially, emotionally, and physically as the nonaccelerated students. Hobson (1963) found that the underage students made better grades, were graduated from high school with more honors, and participated in more extracurricular activities. Worcester (1956) found no statistically significant difference in physical development. The early entrant is not necessarily, not even typically, the smallest child in the classroom. Braga's (1971) results resembled Hobson's and Worcester's.

These findings are further supported by a recent study conducted by Alexander and Skinner (1980), who obtained counselor, student, and parent comments on early entry. The counselors rated all the accelerated students positively on interactions with teachers and other students. Early entrants and their parents were generally satisfied with the decision to enter school early, despite the fact that about half of the group reported that in the early school years a teacher had "noticed some indications of immaturity."

Birch et al. (1965) collected evaluative data during the first school years of early entrants with IQ scores of 135 or higher. Teachers' and principals' judgments of these students' educational and socioemotional adjustment was completely positive for thirty of the children, mixed for eight, and negative for only five. The researchers found it interesting that some teachers who cited the negative effects of acceleration (see Box 5.1) gave positive ratings to students of whose early entry they were unaware. (Braga, 1971, reported the same phenomenon.)

Recommendations.   Early entry is an option that can be exploited at any point where the school system makes formal distinctions between schools. (An interesting corollary is that the advantages associated with early entry may also be derived from acceleration when, for whatever reason, a student changes buildings. For example, acceleration may be most easily implemented when a family moves.) Early entry should be considered for gifted children when they enter school, when they move from a primary center to an elementary school, when they move from an elementary school to a middle or junior high school, when they enter high school, or when they enter college.

The appropriate amount of acceleration via early school entry depends on the individuals and conditions involved. The primary consideration should not be the noncognitive characteristics of the student (cf. Christopherson, 1981), but rather the cognitive characteristics of the student. That is, students must be cognitively equipped to undertake the work expected of them, and the new school must encourage the effort. Even an administratively skeptical school, however, may be quite suitable if the receiving teachers are supportive. Since gifted students are often more mature than their age-mates (Austin & Draper, 1981), and since the new placement will not involve contact with the old peer group, possible negative peer group influence is not a significant factor in weighing early entry options (Christopherson, 1981).

Special Cases.   There are three difficult cases to be examined before we conclude this discussion. These are (1) the underachieving gifted child, (2) the child who faces hostile teachers, and (3) the gifted child with high achievement on standardized tests but poor grades in school. (See Chapter 11 for a more complete discussion of the importance of the distinction between a child with poor grades but IQ-commensurate achievement measured by standardized tests of subject matter and a bona fide underachiever, one whose achievement does not approximate IQ.)

The underachieving gifted child has been referred to elsewhere (e.g., Whitmore, 1980) as LD-gifted—that is, a child who exhibits the cognitive and noncognitive characteristics of learning disabled children. By definition such children may not be cognitively ready to undertake work in an advanced grade, depending on the severity of the problem. Given supportive school arrangements, however, even some of these children may benefit from early entry options. Teachers should realize that many gifted children do not present smooth evaluation profiles, because IQ is a general academic measure and specific academic talents vary widely. Certainly a difference between achievement and potential of two or three standard deviations *may* indicate serious problems, however.

Children who face hostile teachers are condemned to almost certain failure in the new placement (see Box 5.2). For a variety of reasons some teachers are unwilling to help gifted children. If no other teacher or school is available to such a child, early entry in this case needs to be viewed circumspectly. The willing parents of a student of strong character may undertake it with a sense of advocacy, on behalf of other gifted children and the development of program flexibility generally. If both administrative and teacher support are lacking, the outcome is, however, uncertain.

The older gifted child who has poor grades is the special case for whom early entry is of likely benefit, but unfortunately the option is unlikely to be proposed, either by parents or by school personnel. If the poor grades reflect severely discrepant academic achievement, then the option may indeed not be suitable. However, in all cases the degree of achievement should be measured formally, with standardized tests, *not by grades*. Grades must not stand as a proxy for achievement. (As Dowdall and Colangelo, 1982, note, the literature on underachievement reflects this confusion.) Although parents especially are accustomed to this proxy arrangement, it often makes little sense for exceptional children.

Fearn (1982) has, in fact, reported an enhanced rate of achievement for gifted underachievers in a special program. (In this study, underachievement was defined—for gifted children—as performance on standardized tests lower than 1.5 grade placements above published norms.) The gains made by such students might qualify them for accelerative options.

In summary, early entry is an accelerative option that modifies the regular program at its disjunctions. It speeds up the student's movement through the curriculum without altering instruction.

Dual Attendance

Dual attendance refers to the option of attending and fulfilling the requirements of two school programs at once. Dual attendance is a combination of cross-class placement and early entry. The basic principle of dual attendance is that a student receive credit in two places for the same course.

BOX 5.2 Ralph: A Case Study of Unsupportive Instruction

Newland (1976) described the ill effects of inappropriate instruction on a gifted child's performance. Ralph was accepted as an early entrant based on parental request and objective evidence of ability. The principal reluctantly agreed to place the child in a first grade classroom; however, the first grade teacher didn't believe in acceleration. Ralph was confined to reading first grade books even though his assessed reading level was higher. The teacher was quoted as saying that this was necessary in order that he learn to "read them real good" (Newland, 1976, p. 253). After he learned to "read them real good" he would be allowed to read first grade–level material to the kindergarten children.

Within three months, Ralph had become a problem. The teacher reported that he couldn't read even first grade books, and that he was sulky, withdrawn, and at times mean to the other children. His parents noticed a change in behavior at home; he had become less interested in his usual activities.

The situation and Ralph's problems grew worse, so his parents transferred Ralph to a second grade classroom in another school; the teacher in this class used accelerative procedures in instruction. In a few months, Ralph showed new interest in school and his behavior returned to normal at home.

Inappropriate instruction (especially the noncognitive content of the instruction) had, temporarily in this case, turned a bright child who was eager to learn into an unmotivated problem child.

According to Newland (1976), had Ralph stayed in the original placement, there was a high probability that he would have become one of the many bright underachievers in the schools. Timely action prevented such evolution in Ralph's case. Teachers of the gifted need to be alert to deteriorating situations such as Ralph's so that they can propose alternatives to options that are not working out.

Part of the truth about underachieving gifted students may be that they are taught their oft-cited laziness, lack of motivation, and unwillingness to take on intellectual challenges.

For example, a high school senior may fulfill the English requirement by taking a college English course at (or from) a local college. The student *should* earn college credit and high school credit at the same time. This goal is not always met (Voorheis, 1979); in such cases the student is being made to perform double labor for reasons that have nothing to do with mastering content.

Various arrangements that result in both high school graduation at the prescribed time and advanced standing in a post-graduate program can be considered dual attendance. However, the important difference between *advanced standing* (dependent, for example, on a score of 4 or 5 on Advanced Placement tests following a senior-year advanced placement high school course) and *dual attendance* needs to be recognized. Advanced standing in a higher education program can be earned in several ways, but dual attendance represents a definite cooperative arrangement, and includes, where practicable, campus attendance by a student at two institutions (Voorheis, 1979). Courses via cor-

respondence, television, and itinerating college instructors are also forms of
dual attendance (cf. Meskill & Lauper, 1973) that can be practiced when actual
campus attendance is not possible.

Administrators of advanced and accelerated classes need to make a systematic effort to include poor students and minority students. Research has
found blacks and females less likely to enroll in such classes (Fox, 1974), perhaps because of self-selection (Sanders, 1981) or inferior self-concept (Fennema, 1974). Even girls who achieve better than boys in mathematics tend to
rate themselves lower than their male peers in ability. Girls in accelerated
mathematics classes show better adjustment when there are several other girls
in the class (Fennema, 1974; Fox, 1977). Quotas for blacks, females, and various ethnic groups are only partial solutions, but they are important. Sanders
(1981) recommends beginning advanced courses with racial quotas in elementary school to counteract some of the effects of early social stereotyping.
We believe this to be sound pedagogy.

Advanced placement programs and dual attendance schemes, which enable students to earn college credit while still in high school, provide two
major benefits. For students from poor homes, the most important benefit is
probably the chance to enter college with advanced standing. Shortening the
college program results in significant financial savings. Plans that allow superior high school students to take college courses provide an opportunity
for the students to pursue interests that could not be addressed in the regular
high school program.

Some state education agencies have developed policies on dual enrollment. In Georgia, high school seniors may take all or part of their classes in
college and receive credit for both high school and college. North Carolina
encourages dual enrollment by enabling the school and the college to share
the attendance count for high school students taking college courses; i.e., any
student taking at least three courses in high school is counted as a full-time
student, and colleges can count every course a high school student takes as
one-third of a full-time enrollment. These are both highly laudable arrangements; the Georgia plan, however, is what we have in mind when we discuss
dual attendance.

Although the issue of formal credit is not usually germane until at least
junior high school, dual attendance need not be exclusively a secondary-level
option. In a case in which a very bright elementary child takes a calculus
course, for example, provision ought to be made so that the student receives
the credit earned by mastering the subject.

Combined Grades

In the combined grade program, students progress through the prescribed
curriculum in one year instead of two, two years instead of three, or three
years instead of four. For example, a junior high school with seventh, eighth,
and ninth grades might choose to offer the three-year curriculum in two to
a group of apt students. Alternatively, it might combine only the seventh and

eighth grades for students specifically identified as gifted. Combined grade programs should not be confused with split-grade regular classrooms, which are really a special case of cross-class placement.

The notion of the combined grade program implies the differentiation of all aspects of the curriculum to some degree. For example, graduation requirements for the select group may need to be altered. Special accelerated courses will obviously need to be developed, though not necessarily in all subjects. Some provisions may be made for the students to demonstrate competence by examination.

In any case, combined grade programs require more coordination between different parts of the system: from building, to district, and ultimately to the SEA, which will probably certify the program in some way. In such a program, different materials, different kinds of activities, select staffing arrangements, careful assessment of students, and special schedules may all be required.

The practice of tracking may present legal impediments to a combined grade program, particularly if the program serves white middle-class children predominantly. (See the discussion of grouping arrangements in Chapter 3.) Perhaps the combined grade approach is defensible in programs that adopt thorough and accurate identification practices to find exceptionally apt students from *all parts* of the general population.

Ungraded Elementary Schools

Systems adopted ungraded schools in an attempt to find an alternative way to address the wide variation in student achievement and ability. Gifted children within the ungraded school theoretically had the opportunity to learn at their own rates. However, the chief modifications involved in changing many graded schools to ungraded schools seem to have been removal of walls and superficial endorsement of open classroom pedagogy. (Kohl, 1969, offers a glimpse at the larger issues. His comments are still germane.)

All too often the construction of physically open schools seems to have been associated with little substantive change: pupil-teacher ratios, professional attitudes, administrative concerns, curriculum design, student assessment, and instructional practice, in general, remained the same. We have used the past tense in this discussion because the era of the ungraded school seems to have ended. That is unfortunate, we think, because ungraded schools (if not created primarily to save money) might work more completely for the benefit of all children, including exceptional children, than other alternatives.

Other Options

We have reserved until last discussion of three other accelerative options. The first, grade-skipping, is the most popularly acknowledged (and most popularly rejected) form of acceleration. The other two, enrollment in private schools and home schooling, are normally considered beyond the pale of public schooling because they call for arrangements outside publicly supported education.

Grade-Skipping. Grade-skipping was practiced quite frequently in most U.S. schools up through World War II (Freeman, 1924; Hollingworth, 1926, 1942). In the 1950s the notions of developmental psychology (e.g., Gesell, 1950) were interpreted to mitigate the advisability of grade-skipping (see, e.g., Hildreth, 1952). As a result of the success of the progressive education movement, schools saw themselves by this time as stewards of the development of the whole child. Pedagogical thinking became directed not only to the cognitive aspects of school, but also to the affective and psychomotor domains (cf. Cremin, 1961; Hofstadter, 1963; Katz, 1968, 1971; Keniston, 1975).

The notion of balanced development is the pivotal argument against grade-skipping. According to this notion, not only must a child be cognitively ready to handle the work of the higher grade, the child must also be socially and physically ready to adjust to the new placement. This argument sounds quite reasonable. The chief problem with it is that schools still have not come to terms with the affective domain. Educators cannot, any more than the general public, agree about what constitutes normal, adequate, or appropriate affect. A behavioral definition of inappropriate affect is unquestionably useful when it is applied to students identified as severely emotionally disturbed. Such a definition does not provide much guidance, however, in the case of an affectively functional, cognitively gifted elementary school student. Christopherson (1981) believes that social, emotional, and physical development should not be major concerns in the acceleration of gifted children. We agree.

Thus, the argument devolves to the issue of socialization, and the basic assumption is that a child can best achieve socialization through associating with his or her age-mates. In the case of grade-skipping, opponents tend to allow a peer-group difference of one year to assume monumental significance and a child's cognitive difference of many years to dwindle to insignificance! We have seen this view raised repeatedly against grade-skipping, and we suspect that it is behind much of the opposition to acceleration in general, however invalid it has been proven to be by research. (See Chapter 11 for further discussion of socialization.)

Often the concern for socialization with age-mates is phrased as a report of the child's alleged immaturity. The child in these cases is not actually assessed to be immature in comparison to his or her age-mates; rather, the imputed immaturity comes from the educators' impression that the child is unable to handle with ease the difficulties of adjusting to new peers. In almost all cases this assessment arises from a teacher's or principal's subjective impression of the child. Teachers have not done well subjectively assessing the salient cognitive nature of gifted children (Alexander & Skinner, 1980; Braga, 1971; Freeman, 1979; Pendarvis, 1985; Worcester, 1956). Teachers' subjective impressions of the noncognitive nature of gifted children are perhaps no better than their impressions of such children's cognitive nature.

There is, however, a distinction between socialization and maturity. Socialization refers to a poorly understood institutional role of schooling, a role that may serve bright children well or ill. Maturity is a state of advanced development; and advanced development, both cognitive and emotional, is *characteristic* of bright children. One of the characteristics of gifted children is their maturity (cf. Austin & Draper, 1981). It is, for example, often reported that gifted children tend to choose older friends (Birch et al., 1965; Clark, 1983; Freeman, 1979).

If the notion of maturity needs to be addressed by educators, then its assessment must conform a little more to reason and a little less to the unexamined assumptions of convention. Social maturity scales (e.g., the Vineland Social Maturity Scale) are available for such use, but they are rarely used in assessing the social maturity of the gifted.

No doubt grade-skipping *can* be socially difficult in terms of peer reactions. The same difficulties adhere, however, to retention, an ineffective and possibly harmful option exercised quite frequently (D. Clarkson, personal communication, November, 1983). We have no doubt that school personnel could defuse many of the socialization difficulties of children who skip a grade.

In summary, a strong case can be made for grade-skipping (cf. Kulik & Kulik, 1984). Teachers at schools receiving gifted students as new enrollees ought to suggest the option for parents to consider. Unfortunately, some situations may preclude grade-skipping; in general, as Khatena (1982) notes, the easiest grades to skip are those that precede promotion to grade levels housed in other buildings. (We call this option early entry.)

Private Schools as a Public School Option.   The expensive tuition of excellent private schools is beyond the resources of most families of identified gifted children; it is even beyond the resources of most *middle-class* families. For the less-often-identified gifted children from a working-class background, exploration of this option is even more unlikely, no matter how appropriate (cf. Young, 1958).

Private schools, especially the prestigious prep schools, provide unusual benefits to their students. Private schools are generally more willing to use accelerative and enrichment options to match instruction to students' ability levels (cf. Gerencser, 1979). They are aware of the credit that outstanding students can reflect on their programs and are ready to go to great lengths to provide an excellent education (Bridges, 1973). For example, we know of a parochial school English teacher who requires eighth grade students to read some of the difficult books recommended in this text in Chapter 7, even though the class has few identified gifted students.

The student population at private schools tends to be far more homogeneous than the general population. In fact, with comparatively little concern for due process, careful evaluation, or self-conscious discussion of gifted pedagogy, many of these institutions have become virtual academies for the gifted. A number of these institutions do provide scholarships for apt students outside their typical applicant pool. (The same concern is reflected in the minority search programs of prestigious universities in the United States.)

In any case, such schools do offer moderately accelerated, high-quality, flexible programs to apt students. Moreover, there is no reason except custom that prevents school districts from sending some few of their gifted students to these schools. Similarly, more parents might want to consider applying for scholarships to these schools, a process in which they could be assisted by special education or counseling personnel.

In addition to excellent preparatory schools, boarding schools, and day schools, there are a handful of private schools specifically for gifted students. Whether these schools offer more or less to their gifted students than the other private schools is moot. Private schools of any sort have traditions and particular characters that set them apart not only from public schools, but from each other as well. Parents or placement committees considering private options will need to fit the school to the student.

Home Schooling as a Public School Option.   Instruction at home has had numerous advocates in the 1970s and 1980s. Holt (1981) provides humanistic and practical pointers to parents seriously contemplating this alternative. Holt, however, does not treat the notion of exceptional children, and thus neglects many strategies that parents of exceptional children could use in their advocacy efforts. (Holt probably sees the categorization of children as a less-than-useful approach to educational problems.) We view the trend toward home schooling as part of a more diffuse social reaction by several quite different groups against the perceived failings of public education.

Home instruction has been considered by gifted educators. The home instruction reported by Hollingworth (1942) is described by her parent informants as incidental or occasional; nevertheless it resulted in rapid learning for these very bright children. Doubtless any child competently taught individually or in a small group at home could make rapid progress. Kearney (1984) reports a recent home-schooling effort by the parents of gifted children in Maine.

Although parents are often academically and pedagogically competent to educate their children, unfortunately, many parents of gifted children do not *feel* competent to do so. Even temporary home schooling can send a clear message to the school that the education of local gifted children needs attention. Boards of education tend to be very sensitive to this example (Divoky, 1983).

Home schooling needs to be attempted from the vantage of informed opinion, articulated principle, and attention to consistent instruction. In many districts home schooling is not legal, and parents may be liable to prosecution under local compulsory attendance laws if they remove their children from public school. However, where gifted education is mandated, home schooling ought to be available as an option covered by agreement with school officials (e.g., an IEP).

Applying Accelerative Strategies

Before we conclude our discussion of types of acceleration, we want to emphasize that *all of the options* should be considered at least cursorily for *every* gifted child. In all cases the aim ought to be to ensure the continuity of the gifted child's instruction.

Acceleration is important because the education of apt students of all classes and races appears, to different degrees, to be in shambles. Even in states where services are mandated, coherent programs have not yet been approximated. In this context acceleration provides the framework for the entire academic program for gifted children. Perhaps that is what some educators find so threatening about acceleration. Teachers and parents who are aware of the many options for acceleration, especially those that are implicit in the structure of the regular program, can propose options, negotiate specific provisions, and conclude serviceable accords even under quite trying circumstances (see Chapter 4 for a discussion of this process). Box 5.3 gives suggestions for applying accelerative strategies.

BOX 5.3 Applying Accelerative Strategies

The following suggestions provide examples of the ways in which various professionals and parents can develop and realize goals for implementing accelerative strategies. As the comparative lengths of these lists imply, acceleration is best accomplished through the efforts of both the gifted teacher and the regular classroom teacher. The support of other persons is, however, often vital.

What the Teacher of the Gifted Can Do

1. Give tests to demonstrate students' mastery of curriculum content.
2. Meet with the regular classroom teacher to assist with any difficulties in the accelerative placement.
3. Provide information about out-of-school accelerative options.
4. Propose accelerative options at placement/IEP meetings.
5. Discuss acceleration at in-service presentations.

What Other Special Education Teachers Can Do

1. Give norm-or criterion-referenced tests in schools that do not have the services of a teacher of the gifted.
2. Support accelerative options in both formal and informal meetings.

What the Regular Classroom Teacher Can Do

1. Learn about the appropriateness of acceleration for gifted students.
2. Look more carefully at the cognitive characteristics of particular students in the classroom.
3. Read evaluation reports of gifted children.
4. Provide review of by-passed material for accelerates (e.g., as independent work or as homework).
5. Tolerate the adjustment period of accelerates.
6. Meet with the teacher of the gifted to discuss the students' progress.
7. Compact material when possible and appropriate.

(Continued)

BOX 5.3 (*Continued*)

What the Coordinator of Gifted Services Can Do

1. Suggest acceleration at meetings.
2. Review accelerative options with district teachers of the gifted and placement committees.
3. Schedule in-services on acceleration.
4. Arrange for regular classroom teachers to observe successful acceleration sites.

What the Special Education Director Can Do

1. Develop local acceleration policy with other administration representatives.
2. Fund model acceleration programs.
3. Develop placement committee procedures for accelerating gifted students.
4. Influence SEA policy on acceleration.

What Parents Can Do

1. Ask for acceleration.
2. Emphasize mastery of skills and content instead of report-card grades.
3. Review test results carefully.
4. Schedule meetings with school personnel periodically.

ACCELERATION: MODEL PROGRAMS

A basic question underlies the controversy in the field of gifted education about whether acceleration can in itself comprise a sufficiently comprehensive alternative for apt students: Does enrichment include acceleration or does acceleration include enrichment? Among contemporaries, Renzulli (1977) argues for the former, for example, whereas Stanley (1976) argues for the latter. We tend to agree with Stanley on this matter, and we recognize that at a certain point differences in degree (rate, in this case) do imply differences in kind (quality).

There are relatively few model acceleration programs currently in existence. Aside from the Study of Mathematically Precocious Youth (SMPY), we discuss no specifically accelerative program. The Calasanctius School addresses the issue, according to Gerencser (1979), but, like the Program for Verbally Gifted Youth (PVGY), claims to occupy a middle ground between acceleration and enrichment. Perhaps, as provisions in a program become sufficiently clear, or sufficiently comprehensive, the distinction between enrichment and acceleration blurs. Most programs, however, are far from comprehensive. The model programs discussed below do not address all aspects of a gifted child's education, with the apparent exception of the Calasanctius program.

These programs are not models in the sense that we are recommending their replication. Nor are they necessarily models in the sense that they have achieved perfection. They are rather examples, some of the details of which may be of interest or use to others who are concerned about programs for the gifted.

Fund for the Advancement of Education (Early College Entry)

In 1951, the University of Chicago, Columbia, the University of Wisconsin, and Yale, concerned with the effects of the Korean War draft on their enrollments and on the academic careers of able young men, applied to the Fund for the Advancement of Education (established by the Ford Foundation) for special scholarships for early entrants. The Fund expanded the grant to include eight other institutions, which, over the four years of the project, served 1,350 "Scholars," of whom 24 percent were women and 86 percent were age sixteen or younger. Twenty-nine percent were younger than 16.

Initially most of the institutions made special arrangements for the Scholars. These arrangements varied widely from school to school. Yale required the Scholars to take a special program of directed studies, ostensibly to provide "a richer educational experience" (Fund for the Advancement of Education, 1957). Columbia required Scholars to live on campus, whereas other students at Columbia were permitted to commute from the parental home. By the end of the program all such special arrangements, except Yale's, had been dropped after being found to be unnecessary, overprotective, or detrimental. Except for temporary strictures, the Scholars were treated administratively and instructionally exactly as other undergraduates. In fact, two of the institutions allowed Scholars to accelerate through college without earning a minimum number of hours.

The Scholars were matched on ability with a comparison group of entering freshmen of normal entry age. On all measured parameters—grade point average, honors, extracurricular activities, drop-out rate, SAT and GRE scores, and faculty rating of adjustment—the means of the Scholar group were higher than those of the comparison group. Pressey (1967) found that Fund Scholars earned advanced professional degrees two years earlier than the comparison group.

The one difference was that the transfer rate of Scholars was about twice that of their nonaccelerated counterparts. The Fund attributed about two-fifths of the cases of Scholar transfer to the liberal arts character of the participating institutions. The transfers left to follow scientific or technical programs elsewhere.

The Fund (1957) reported that the 1951 group of Scholars experienced more adjustment difficulties of a temporary nature than subsequent groups. The Fund attributed these temporary difficulties to the pioneering effort of the first group. (This finding tends to support what was noted previously about the isolation of individual accelerates.) The extent to which these temporary difficulties might have been attributable to the equally temporary special arrangements of the schools in handling the first group of scholars was not investigated by the Fund.

After 1954, the Fund discontinued support for the project, but Karnes and Chauvin reported in 1982 that approximately 80 percent of private and public institutions had enrolled early entrants (Karnes & Chauvin, 1982).

Study of Mathematically Precocious Youth
(Special Accelerated Classes, Early Entry)

The Study of Mathematically Precocious Youth (SMPY) at the Johns Hopkins University in Baltimore is one of the best-researched talent development projects in the history of education. The founder and director of the study, Julian Stanley, is an eminent educational psychologist, expert in research and statistics.

Officially begun in September, 1971, SMPY has identified mathematically gifted students from Maryland and other nearby states and provided them with accelerated courses, as well as facilitated other appropriate educational alternatives for these students (Stanley, 1974). Competitive examinations are given annually to identify seventh and some eighth grade students who score at least as high as the average male high school senior on the Scholastic Aptitude Test mathematics section. Only children who score in the 97th percentile or above on any standardized aptitude or achievement test (or major subcomponent thereof) are eligible to enter the competition. All students who enter and take the SAT receive a written interpretation explaining their test scores and what they imply for educational programming.

High-scoring students are awarded scholarships or tuition waivers to take courses at one of several participating colleges or universities in their state. The most precocious children are invited to summer seminars, where they may take rapid-paced mathematics courses and other advanced work offered under the SMPY aegis. In recent years, an umbrella organization, the Center for Talented Youth (CTY), has been established at Johns Hopkins to coordinate the efforts of various university projects, including SMPY, to locate and provide services to talented youth.

Although SMPY offers *many* accelerative options to mathematically gifted students, it is notorious for its radical accelerations. Educators usually hesitate to accelerate even extremely bright students more than one or two grades. Stanley has shown that the most precocious students can benefit from placement in classes four to six grades beyond the one associated with their chronological age. The success of SMPY's radical acceleration provisions has created greater interest in, and some acceptance of, both radical acceleration and more moderate acceleration (see Box 5.4).

One of the unexplained phenomena uncovered by SMPY is the differential performance of boys and girls. Fox (1977, 1978) has stressed the influence of social differences, specifically the academic climate, in discouraging the participation of girls. Benbow and Stanley (1980) have discussed what they believe to be brain differences responsible for the differential performance. Boles

---

BOX 5.4   Radical Acceleration

Radical acceleration has been advocated and supported empirically by SMPY. The program offers many accelerative options to seventh and eighth grade students who are highly gifted in mathematics. One option suitable for the most talented in this group is the opportunity to take college courses or to enroll in college on a full-time basis.

One of the SMPY students entered college from the sixth grade. At fifteen, this extremely bright student was the youngest doctoral candidate in Princeton's history (Nevin, 1977). (In an earlier era, Norbert Wiener, the MIT mathematician who helped pioneer digital computers, began his Ph.D. program at Harvard at age fifteen also.) This degree of acceleration is appropriate only for the very brightest students; however, acceleration in some form is a necessary accommodation to the learning capability of virtually all gifted children.

Stanley worries about the effects of nonaccelerated instruction on children who score in the highest percentiles on cognitive tests:

He or she can daydream, be excessively meticulous in order to get perfect grades, harass the teacher, show off knowledge arrogantly in the class or be truant. There is however no *suitable* way to while away the class hours when one already knows much of the material and can learn the rest almost instantaneously as it is first presented. Boredom, frustration and habits of gross inattention are almost sure to result.

(Stanley, 1977, p. 35)

(1980), however, refutes a similar contention that women's comparatively poorer performance on spatial reasoning tasks is sex-linked. In any case, this new controversy seems to be growing. Like hereditarian explanations of racial differences in IQ, sex-linked explanations of mental differences are difficult to document in light of historical and cultural variables.

Advanced Placement (Accelerated Courses, Early Entry)

The College Board's Advanced Placement Program (APP) was established in the 1950s to enable bright students to do college-level course work while still in high school and, on the basis of AP examination qualifying scores, to earn college credit at the same time. In the 1980–81 academic year almost 2,000 colleges participated in the program by offering credit for AP courses in a variety of disciplines, such as mathematics, literature, sciences, languages, and music (Southern Regional Education Board, 1982).

AP classes are taught in the high school by a high school faculty member who is provided with a curriculum description for the course. Although the content and methods of the AP courses are established by the high schools in which they are offered, the certified quality of course work is controlled by the AP examinations. The examinations are developed and updated in cooperation with talented high school and college teachers.

Students pay a fee to the College Board (Educational Testing Service) for each examination they take. This fee is much less than tuition for a college course. Often a major portion of the fee can be waived in cases of economic hardship (Marland, 1976). The opportunity to enter college with advanced standing (which decreases the duration and expense of undergraduate education) and the opportunity for instruction at a level commensurate with ability are the primary advantages of the Advanced Placement Program (see Box 5.5).

Calasanctius School (Private School for the Gifted)

We have chosen to use the Calasanctius School to represent the private school option because not only is it a private school but it is an avowedly pluralistic school for the gifted. That is, the school counts as one of its most important achievements its record with less-than-affluent and ''ethnically disadvantaged'' students (Gerencser, 1979).

Calasanctius, named to honor a colleague of Galileo, was founded in 1957 in Buffalo, New York. In 1957 tuition was $660; in 1985 tuition ranged from $2175 to $5050 depending on the student's age. The curriculum at Calasanctius is seriously academic and emphasizes liberal arts. Language instruction begins at the age of five. Instruction in German, French, Russian, Spanish, Japanese, and Chinese is available. All students are required to study one foreign language, with the objectives of conversational fluency and acquisition of the literature and culture of the language. Most students, however, choose to study two foreign languages. History is considered to be the unifying field of what public schools call social studies (Gerencser, 1979). Starting at about age ten, students at Calasanctius are required to take six or seven years of history. The weekly schedule of classes for each student is composed of instruction in ten to fifteen subjects on the college model of scheduling (i.e., one to three hours per week per subject).

Acceleration is part of the program; all AP courses are offered, and credit in at least three AP exams is required for graduation. Moreover, students are credited for what they know, not for the amount of time they spend in a course (Gerencser, 1979). (Carnegie units, the typical units of high school credit, are based on hours of instruction.)

Because Calasanctius is a self-contained school, it probably comes close to being a program of the sort one might ideally imagine for gifted children. Emphasis on the liberal arts permeates the school curriculum and provides the gifted thirteen- or fourteen-year-old with a broad intellectual background from which to choose a particular field of academic endeavor. Most gifted children in any setting begin to feel the pull of one field or another at this time (Gerencser, 1979), but only a few will have been privy to an educational program of such rigor and depth as that fostered at this school.

It is interesting to compare the Calasanctius approach with that of SMPY.

BOX 5.5 Implementing Advanced Placement Courses

Participating in the College Board's Advanced Placement Program (APP) and developing AP courses is a fairly simple procedure. All students need to do to receive college credit is to pass the AP examinations. Still, some planning is necessary. What follows is a brief list, based on the experience of participating school systems, of the steps to be taken during one school year before the start of such a program:

1. Appoint an AP committee, including teachers and counselors.
2. Send for College Board materials. (See addresses below.)
3. Organize and appoint teachers for courses.
4. Establish a selection method for students.
5. Conduct a workshop for AP teachers, using College Board consultants or AP teachers from nearby school systems.
6. Plan and hold meetings for parents, students, and members of the school community to build support for the AP program.
7. Explore the possibility of cooperative arrangements with other schools and school systems for offering joint courses or for administering AP examinations at a single site.

To learn more about AP programs currently operating in schools, or to seek help in starting a program, write or telephone the director of the Regional Office of the College Board nearest you:

Midwest: 500 Davis St., Suite 605, Evanston, IL 60201; (312) 866–1700

New England: 470 Totten Pond Rd., Waltham, MA 02154; (617) 090–9150

South: Suite 200, 17 Executive Park Dr. NW, Atlanta, GA 30329; (404) 636–9465

Southwest: Suite 922, 211 E. 7th St., Austin, TX 78701; (512) 472–0231

West: 800 Welch Rd., Palo Alto, CA 94304; (415) 321–5211

The difference is similar to that between residential care and crisis intervention in psychotherapy; however, both these educational programs are impressively successful. SMPY intervenes on behalf of moderately to profoundly precocious youth, and, almost through sleight of hand, impresses on their schools, and quite often on their parents, the unique nature of brilliant youth. The result is greatly enhanced opportunity for brilliant young mathematicians. Calasanctius, by contrast, proceeds through nurture—from infancy through college entry—to cultivate a general sense of academic commitment and community. The result is very likely an unusually literate succession of mildly to moderately gifted graduating classes. The sense, purpose, and populations of the two projects differ. Both projects, however, serve important purposes as examples of options for the education of gifted students.

Secondary and University Education Abroad

Consideration of the education of the gifted in other countries may help U.S. educators to evaluate various pedagogical options. Although information available on the subject of foreign educational systems is scant, this limited information may still help us understand our educational dilemmas.

European secondary schools have tended to be quite class-biased. Students from affluent homes have attended the academic *gymnasia* or *lycees*, while working-class students have traditionally attended vocational or (in Britain, in some instances) comprehensive secondary schools, after the American fashion. In Britain "public" (i.e., private) schools like Eton and Harrow remain the upper-class prep schools. In the United States we have inherited the association of affluence and scholastic aptitude, but this heritage has not influenced overt educational practice in public schools.

The United States, in sharp contrast to Europe, has maintained a highly differentiated system of private and public universities. Although there are excellent public universities in the United States, renown, honor, prestige, and reputation for academic excellence are the province of the exclusive, highly competitive, and very expensive private universities. In Europe, higher education is state-funded, and places are awarded on the basis of academic merit, usually by examination. Brilliant but poor students stand a much better chance of receiving an excellent education in Europe and Japan than in the United States. In Britain, however, Snow (1969) states that it has always been extraordinarily difficult for working-class academic talent to get even passable schooling.

We include secondary education abroad in our discussion of acceleration because in both Europe and Japan secondary school students cover material that is usually covered in the first two years of college work in the United States (cf. Durden, 1980; Gerencser, 1979; Karnes & Chauvin, 1982; Meskill & Lauper, 1973; Voorheis, 1979; Wirszup, 1981). (In France, the culminating secondary exam is called the *baccalaureat*, which means the degree of bachelor.)

The European and Japanese systems are not necessarily better (especially in regard to the class issue below the university level), but they are *faster* than the U.S. system; this fact appears to be true even in the case of the ordinary student.

Program for Verbally Gifted Youth

Durden (1980) has reported on the Program for Verbally Gifted Youth (PVGY) established in 1978 at Johns Hopkins University. The same SAT administration is used to identify seventh and some eighth graders for both PVGY and SMPY. Qualifying scores can be earned on the SAT verbal portion and the Test of Standard Written English, administered as part of the SAT.

Although mature use of verbal skills depends on complex life experiences, Durden (1980) believes that neglect of verbally gifted children until they become undergraduates is wholly unjustified. Durden notes the (traditional) preference given to mathematical talent over verbal talent and the "rapid decline of the effective use of verbal skills in a majority of our nation's youth" (Durden, 1980, p. 34). (See our discussion of the humanities in Chapter 7 and of the arts in Chapter 10 for a view of this dilemma in the public schools, and see Chapter 12 for the social implications of the dilemma.)

Durden believes that little real writing is taught to students in public schools. Indeed, he reports that "many of the disciplines [PVGY] treats are either lacking at the secondary level, . . . or, as in the case of writing, skills and grammar are introduced too late in verbally gifted students' intellectual development" (1980, p. 36). He says, "For many youths, PVGY is the first educational setting in which their papers receive the least bit of criticism, and the shock can be devastating to students who have not developed enough self-confidence to deal with anxiety" (p. 35). In fact, much of what is taught in public schools as creative writing is concerned more with personal development and creativity than with writing skills (Durden, 1980).

Durden stresses the academic content of the PVGY program and notes that many of the qualities required by SMPY are essential to PVGY: fast response, good reading ability, and the ability to perform efficiently in stressful situations. He notes that though PVGY has found that "verbally gifted youth do not work well in the framework of interpretative thinking, they are very receptive to college-level work rigorously stressing mechanics (such as writing skills) and linguistic formulas (such as foreign languages, English grammar and etymology)" (Durden, 1980, p. 36). The teaching of creativity is not part of the PVGY program, though imagination and independence of thought are encouraged (Durden, 1980). Thus, the similarities between SMPY and PVGY are strong, particularly in their shared belief in acceleration as a pedagogical essential for bright children.

Major Works Program (Special Elementary Content Classes)

Begun in 1921, the Cleveland Major Works Program is not, in fact, a program of acceleration. The Major Works Program's special elementary classes are examples of content area programming for the gifted. They provide what the regular curriculum lacks in the social sciences, humanities, and natural sciences.

Its special classes, however, are viewed as acceleration in the context of enrichment (Epstein, 1979). The study of adult literature in the fifth grade—and, especially, of French starting in the second grade—is indeed a form of acceleration if the instruction is interpreted as essential and students are credited for what they have learned. The chief problem in such situations (e.g., where acceleration is part of an enrichment approach) is that, although an entering ninth grader, for example, may have acquired mastery of the material normally presented in two years of regular high school French, this student may not be accorded Carnegie unit or other formal credit, but may simply be placed in a French III class.

Such an arrangement, which introduces material or subjects normally considered appropriate only for an older age group, must be considered to be acceleration, even if its instruction (as in the case of foreign languages) would make sense for nongifted children of the same age!

Washington State (Early Kindergarten Entry)

Washington State (M. Schmidt, 1981) has compiled information on early entrance to kindergarten to assist local school districts in serving underage children who are ready for school. Administrators are often reluctant to allow early admission even in cases where there is no question as to its appropriateness for the child, because they do not want to create a precedent. They fear that if one young child is admitted, there will be a flood of requests from parents who want their children entered in kindergarten whether or not early entry is appropriate.

Data from school districts that have established early entrance identification programs indicate that this does not happen (M. Schmidt, 1981). Since in Washington's programs parents are charged for the cost of the assessment to determine readiness, requests are usually limited to those involving children who are likely to qualify for early entrance. (If not backed by waivers for indigent parents, this practice seems to deny equal educational opportunity.) Questionnaires or checklists of behaviors that indicate readiness are given to parents and serve as guidelines to help them decide whether or not to apply for early entrance. Parents are also informed as to the screening process and the substance of the kindergarten curriculum; this, too, helps them determine the appropriateness of applying for evaluation of their child's readiness. Most programs for early admission require assessment of intellectual, physical, social, and emotional development. The following statement of a Washington school district policy on early entrance is typical:

> Mercer Island School District No. 400
>
> Entry to kindergarten on the basis of age requires that a child be 5 years of age on or before midnight August 31 of the year of entry. Entry into first grade on the basis of age requires that a child be 6 years of age on or before midnight September 30 of the year of entry.
>
> The Director of Student and Special Services shall establish a screening process to allow for exceptions to the uniform entry age for younger children demonstrating development sufficiently advanced as to indicate success in such an educational program. This process shall include screening in the following areas:
>
> (a) mental ability
> (b) gross motor skills
> (c) fine motor skills
> (d) visual discrimination
> (e) auditory discrimination
> (f) emotional/social development
>
> and shall include an internal district appeal process for parents or guardians.

Assessment of these areas usually involves standardized comprehensive tests, behavior checklists developed by the district, and/or informal observation of the child. Christopherson (1981), as we have noted, does not believe social, emotional, and physical development to be important considerations.

Administration of a battery of standardized tests is time-consuming and is not necessary in every case. The age of the child determines the scope and depth of the assessment. (A child who is a month or so younger than the cut-off age will exhibit negligible differences.) Outstanding intellectual ability and apparent maturity suggest a reduced need for in-depth assessment of visual, auditory, and motor development. It is only in borderline cases or in cases where large discrepancies in development across the areas are suspected that an in-depth evaluation is crucial. Parents, the principal, and district specialists determine the assessment needs on the basis of the child's age, behavior, and experiences. A team approach to identification offers a cost-effective means of successfully placing underage children, both gifted and nongifted.

SUMMARY

This chapter has discussed various accelerative options available to implement or supplement appropriate education for the gifted. It has articulated the notion that acceleration is (1) a characteristic of gifted children and (2) a logical and productive educational response to this characteristic. We suspect that many of the accelerative options discussed in this chapter are being implemented informally in many schools, though these arrangements do not surface as model programs.

The report of the literature on acceleration has revealed clear and consistent indications of the benefits of acceleration for gifted children as practiced since the progressive era (Kulik & Kulik, 1984). In many instances acceleration can also benefit other apt children. The report also revealed the paucity of fully implemented durable examples. The most notable of those reviewed is SMPY, which serves a small fraction of mathematically talented achievers in one region of the United States.

Prospective teachers of the gifted have difficult and crucial work ahead of them in advocating the need of the gifted to deal with continuously challenging and legitimate content through accelerative strategies.

CHAPTER 6

Quality and Quantity: The Dilemma of Enrichment

INTRODUCTION

This chapter considers enrichment options which may constitute all or part of some gifted programs. Some educators view enrichment narrowly as a supplement to other educational provisions. Others view it broadly as the total program for gifted students. This chapter considers the implications of both perspectives.

In particular, this chapter examines three approaches to enrichment: (1) the process-oriented approach, (2) the content-oriented approach, and (3) the product-oriented approach. In the context of this discussion, the chapter reviews aspects of instruction typical of enrichment programs. These include training in creativity, problem-solving, and information processing; career education; affective education; mentorships; independent study; and academic mini-courses.

Current programs representative of the three types of enrichment are considered. The chapter suggests practical strategies for implementing various enrichment approaches and also presents cautions concerning some strategies.

Finally, this chapter considers a dilemma, the resolution of which is crucial to the success of enrichment strategies. This is the dilemma of maintaining standards for the quality and quantity of enrichment services. Programs that meet optimal standards of quality and quantity necessarily involve acceleration and total curriculum planning. Programs that meet minimal standards provide weak offerings. Methods of improving less than optimal enrichment programs are presented in the context of this discussion.

DEFINITIONS OF ENRICHMENT

Enrichment is a term used narrowly to define a particular set of supplementary educational activities or broadly to explain the general purpose of education. It is a concept that has been applied to the retarded, the average, and the superior learner. Enrichment in all cases denotes a benefit or an advantage. Usually this advantage is provided to learners by agents outside themselves (e.g., teachers, parents, schools). The opposite of enrichment is *deprivation*, which is often associated with a descriptor such as *cultural, economic,* or *environmental.*

Special education of gifted students has been criticized as the provision of advantages to the advantaged (e.g., Baer, 1980). This belief stresses the uniformity of educational offerings and the conformity of individual students (Bartel, 1978; Kirk & Gallagher, 1983). Castiglione considers the issue:

> Many Americans inappropriately *equate* ideas of political democracy and equality before the law by arguing that naturally occurring differences between individuals in ability and performance ought to be ignored in the name of equity. . . . The gifted and talented . . . by virtue of their exceptional abilities *require* enriching services and activities not ordinarily provided by schools. While enrichment is incontestably valuable for all, the fact remains that gifted and tal-

ented children *require* a higher level of intellectual or artistic stimulation than do average children.

(Castiglione, 1984, p. 40)

Castiglione (1984) does not view enrichment as an advantage to already advantaged students. He sees it as essential instruction based on exceptional needs. He also stresses the importance of identifying gifted students from all social classes and ethnic groups so that enrichment is not provided just to advantaged classes or groups. Others, however, have documented the difficulty in realizing the goal of equality of opportunity (Jencks et. al., 1972). (See Chapter 12 for a discussion of social factors that influence gifted programs.)

Various educators differentiate between horizontal and vertical provisions in their definitions of enrichment. Because vertical enrichment involves "added learning believed to be directly contributive to the child's progressing to a higher conceptual level" (Newland, 1976, p. 249), it is often classified as a form of acceleration. Horizontal enrichment, according to Epstein,

implies expanding sideways. The gifted children do not move up any faster, but their learning is enriched by different curriculum materials, individual instruction, emphasis on the higher mental processes of divergent thinking and creativity, independent study, problem-solving projects with real products, and any number of techniques that give youngsters a welcome change from the routine of the regular classroom.

(Epstein, 1979, p. 69)

Several authors have tried to clarify the relationship between acceleration and enrichment. Gowan and Demos (1964, p. 138), for example, view enrichment broadly, suggesting that it encompasses all provisions for the gifted. They write that enrichment "embraces all the curricular adjustments made for gifted students. These include experiences in breadth and depth, and those connected with grouping, acceleration, and individualization of instruction in heterogeneous classes." Others, such as Newland (1976), reason that good horizontal enrichment provisions inevitably produce higher-level learning. Stanley (1981) agrees with this view and strongly recommends that schools make administrative accommodations to allow such advanced students to progress rapidly through regular curricula.

There is a fundamental difficulty with comparing acceleration and enrichment because the terms do not seem to represent points along the same continuum. Acceleration usually is considered an administrative arrangement; enrichment, as typically defined, refers to a curriculum modification or addition. For example, minimal enrichment might consist of an extracurricular activity; only optimal enrichment can be viewed as a curriculum for the gifted. (See Chapter 7 for a discussion of gifted curriculum.) More accurate dichotomies are those between grade-skipping and lockstep placement, honors and regular classes, or *enrichment and curriculum*.

Unfortunately, too often enrichment is minimal both in quantity and in quality. Vernon, Adamson, and Vernon characterize this sort of enrichment as a provision that

> seems to consist in the gifted child being encouraged to study and explore things which are not usually included in the conventional curriculum, and in this way to provide more stimulating activities which compensate for the boredom and frustration of having to do most of his work at the same level as that of his average or below average age peers.
>
> (Vernon, Adamson & Vernon, 1977, p. 181)

Viable enrichment programs are those that are able to meet the exceptional academic needs of gifted children. Quality of offerings and quantity of services seem to be important considerations in planning for enrichment. In practice, there is great variability among enrichment programs. Such disparate practice contributes to difficulties in establishing consensus about the definition of enrichment.

THE HISTORY OF ENRICHMENT

Enrichment of the curriculum for gifted children emerged as a progressive alternative to the accelerative strategies adopted in earlier periods (Osburn & Rohan, 1931). Progressive educators, concerned with the whole child, believed that enrichment would enable students to mature emotionally in the company of peers, while developing intellectual skills commensurate with their abilities (Fowlkes, 1930). This notion has remained virtually intact since the progressive era and continues to guide the thinking of many educators (e.g., Sisk & Bierly, 1979) who recommend enrichment provisions for the gifted.

During the progressive era, not only were the objectives of enrichment programs articulated, but the content of such programs was also delineated. For example, Cremin (1961) indicates that interdisciplinary *unit* instruction was implemented by progressive educators; this approach to enrichment is still evident in the recommendations of contemporary gifted educators including Martinson (1968); Renzulli (1977); and Vernon, Adamson, and Vernon (1977). Although the progressives (e.g., Hollingworth, 1926) anticipated that this type of instruction would occur in self-contained gifted classrooms, current practitioners usually employ this approach in resource rooms and other pull-out programs. In many districts, the term *mini-course* has replaced the term *unit*, probably as a means of distinguishing between the special offerings available for the gifted and the typical units of instruction provided as part of the regular elementary curriculum (cf. Cook & Doll, 1973).

There are a number of other interesting connections between the approaches for the enrichment of gifted students suggested by progressive educators and those advocated by current authors. Many general principles, such as the importance of developing creative thinking skills, can be traced to pedagogical writers of the early part of this century (e.g., Stedman, 1924).

Numerous specific content recommendations made by early educators are reiterated in the modern literature. Hollingworth (1926) discussed the use of biography in the education of elementary gifted children; Maker (1982a) recommends the same strategy. Fowlkes (1930, p. 84) suggested a multiplicity of enrichment opportunities and projects for the gifted such as block printing, writing plays, developing games, originating dances, and designing stage sets. Similar enrichment activities are enumerated by Bidlack (1974), Campbell (1969), Kanigher (1977), and Lombard (1977). The current notions of individualization, independent study, consideration of real problems, student-directed learning, and out-of-school learning all had significant theoretical and practical antecedents in the progressive era.

Most educators in the early years assumed that gifted education involved both a moderate amount of acceleration *and* ability grouping (e.g., Hollingworth, 1926, 1938; Stedman, 1924). These provisions *in combination with* a qualitatively different curriculum for the gifted constituted enrichment. This view contrasts with the current practice of providing enrichment *in lieu of* acceleration or ability grouping.

Recent Enrichment Variations

During the 1960s enrichment acquired a new connotation. Rather than focusing on the enrichment of gifted children, educators concentrated on the enrichment of "culturally deprived" children (Kerr, 1981; Tannenbaum, 1981). Programs such as Headstart and Get Set were developed to enhance the verbal and social learning of ghetto children. Such programs resembled nursery school programs for middle-class children (Risley, 1970) and included activities such as field trips, training for cooperative play, and reading readiness exercises. In addition, cultural enrichment programs were established for working-class children who demonstrated above-average achievement. The children were provided with enriching experiences such as trips to museums, libraries, theaters, and concerts in order to increase the likelihood of their graduating from high school or attending college (Havighurst, 1963).

In the late 1960s and the 1970s enrichment programs with greater structure were designed for culturally deprived and mentally retarded children (e.g., Risley, 1970). These programs involved specific training in verbal and information-processing skills. The techniques used by one team (Feuerstein, Miller, Hoffman, Rand, Mintzker & Jensen, 1981) involved cognitive process training not unlike that recommended by others (e.g., Meeker, 1979a) for improving the cognitive processing of gifted students.

During the late 1950s and the 1960s, gifted education was influenced by the trend to develop and implement innovative curricula, particularly in science and math (Gallagher, 1975). This focus, coupled with schools' tendency to track students by ability or achievement levels, seemed to eclipse the earlier emphasis on enrichment. One gifted-education text from the mid-sixties (Gold, 1965) does not even mention enrichment as a program option for the gifted.

Renewed interest in teaching basics has characterized education in the 1970s and 1980s. Concern for the enrichment of culturally deprived students is no longer a priority; enrichment has once again become the province of gifted education. This enrichment is sometimes haphazard and tangential to the academic curriculum, and is criticized by some educators for not addressing the cognitive needs of apt students (e.g., Stanley, 1976). In fact, it has been claimed that some enrichment activities are appropriate for average students (e.g., Renzulli, 1977; Weiler, 1978).

Current Enrichment Approaches: Overview

A number of enrichment programs have been recommended to meet the needs of gifted students. Some are designed to be used in conjunction with other enrichment approaches. Others are suggested as comprehensive programs. For example, career education activities are not usually advocated as the sole enrichment provision for gifted students. The Enrichment Triad (Renzulli, 1977), on the other hand, is proposed as an approach to enrichment that encompasses a variety of student levels and interests. In the following discussion we will consider several of the most prevalent approaches to enrichment.

We consider three categories of enrichment: process-oriented, content-oriented, and product-oriented approaches. Programs emphasizing one or another of these approaches are sometimes provided during the school day. Often, however, they are made available after school hours, on weekends, or during the summer. Many programs are eclectic in nature and incorporate aspects of two or three enrichment approaches. For the purpose of clarifying the theoretical and practical distinctions among the approaches, however, we will discuss them separately. A graphic overview of the enrichment approaches and their relationships is provided in Figure 6.1.

PROCESS-ORIENTED PROGRAMS

Process-oriented enrichment programs are intended to develop students' higher mental processes. Some attempt to increase the creative production of gifted children as well. Although inspiration for these programs comes from a number of sources, the antecedents of many of these approaches can be found in the work of progressive educators (e.g., Brueckner, 1932; Stedman, 1924).

The development of certain process-oriented programs has been influenced by the work of psychologists concerned with mental measurement. With the advent of factor analytic techniques, psychologists began to identify increasing numbers of distinct cognitive abilities. Guilford, for example, postulated 120 potentially measurable cognitive processes. The ability to identify many distinct cognitive processes led some educators and psychologists to suggest that these abilities could be developed through the use of special instructional materials (e.g., Meeker, Sexton & Richardson, 1970).

FIGURE 6.1 Enrichment Variants

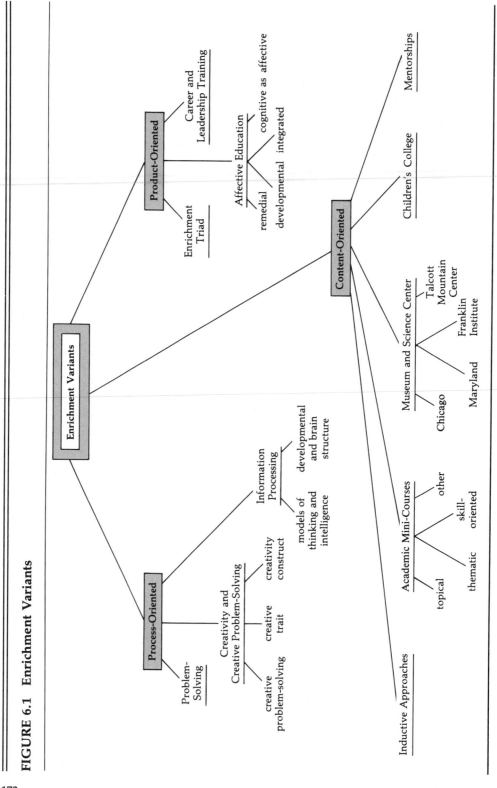

Some psychologists (e.g., Newell & Simon, 1972; Sternberg, 1977) proposed information-processing explanations of human cognition, some of which are equated with the functioning of artificial intelligences. The information-processing view of intelligence has also encouraged some educators to recommend methods for developing cognitive abilities. Some such methods are intended to remediate deficient mental processes, some to expand cognitive strengths, and others even to improve brain functioning.

The historical origins of process-oriented programs suggest a logical method for classifying these approaches. Table 6.1 categorizes various process-oriented approaches according to their pedagogical antecedents. In general, educators have tended to base their views of mental processing on a problem-solving, creativity, or information-processing model. The Venn diagram in Figure 6.2 suggests the relationships among the three categories and lists educators whose views are representative of the various possible combinations of these approaches.

Problem-Solving

Process-oriented programs that attempt to develop the problem-solving skills of gifted students are based on educational tenets emphasizing the active, volitional participation of the learner. Some proponents of instruction in problem-solving, therefore, regard presentation of factual information as irrelevant to the instructional process (e.g., Rogers, 1969). They believe that learning occurs only when the student takes the initiative to pursue instruction. Others (e.g., Bruner, 1960) consider factual knowledge necessary for the development of problem-solving skills in a particular field. This latter view will be discussed below as a content-oriented approach.

Problem-solving, as contrasted with creative problem-solving, is a strategy for developing reasoning skills; it involves (1) research to identify problems, (2) analysis of various perspectives on the problem, (3) evaluation of the merit of various perspectives, and (4) synthesis of findings. The development of these skills involves instruction in both research skills and critical thinking skills.

Cautions. Some problem-solving programs for the gifted involve the development of thinking skills in isolation from particular disciplines. Students select topics to pursue by independent study; they thereby acquire whatever research or reasoning skills are derived from their study of the topics (e.g., Bennett, Blanning, Boissiere, Chang & Collins, 1971). Thus, the thinking processes that are developed vary widely from student to student, depending on the topics selected. Teachers may not be able to document student achievement that occurs as a result of this type of program. They may also find it difficult to incorporate student-directed learning into long-range educational plans. This difficulty is intensified when students select topics that are not consistent with general curriculum goals.

Some problem-solving programs rely solely on activities developed or pur-

TABLE 6.1   Chronology of Representative Process Approaches

Problem-Solving	Creativity Training	Information Processing
Problem-Solving (Dewey, 1916/1961)		
	Creative Problem-Solving (Osborn, 1953) *Creative Perception* (Barron, 1958)	
Inductive Curricula (Bruner, 1960)		
	Synectics (Gordon, 1961)	
Inductive Teaching (Taba, 1962)	*Creativity: Divergent Thinking* (Torrance, 1962) *Drug-Facilitated Creativity* (Huxley, 1962)	
Kepner-Tregoe Method (Kepner & Tregoe, 1965)		
Productive Thinking (Covington & Crutch-field, 1965)		
	Lateral Thinking (de Bono, 1967)	*Structure of Intellect* (Guilford, 1967)
Learning-How-to-Learn (Rogers, 1969)		
	Purdue Creativity Training (Feldhusen, Treffinger & Bahlke, 1970) *Training Creative Thinking* (Davis & Scott, 1971)	*SOI Activities* (Meeker, Sexton & Richardson, 1970)
	Total Creativity Program (Williams, 1972) *Creative Imagination* (Gowan, 1978) *Imagination/Imagery* (Khatena, 1978)	*Developmental Stage Theory* (Gowan, 1972)
		Neuro-physiological Approach (Norton & Doman, 1982) *Hemispheric Integration* (Myers, 1982)

FIGURE 6.2 Relationships among the Three Process Approaches

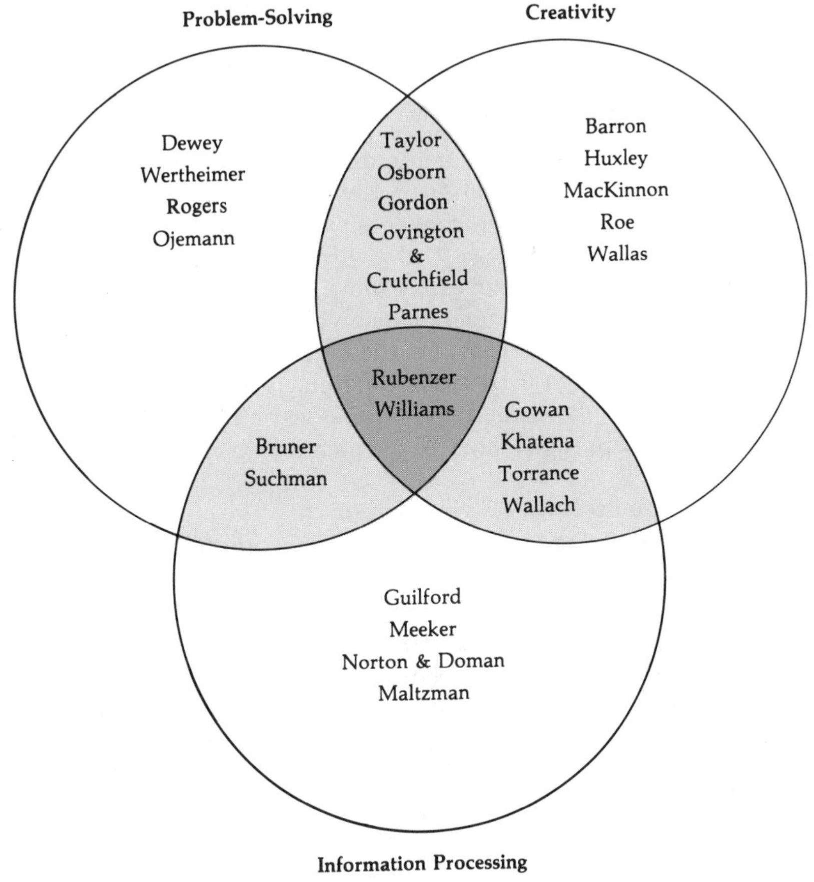

Problem-Solving   Creativity

Dewey
Wertheimer
Rogers
Ojemann

Taylor
Osborn
Gordon
Covington
&
Crutchfield
Parnes

Barron
Huxley
MacKinnon
Roe
Wallas

Rubenzer
Williams

Bruner
Suchman

Gowan
Khatena
Torrance
Wallach

Guilford
Meeker
Norton & Doman
Maltzman

Information Processing

chased by teachers or school districts to enhance the productive thinking of gifted students. The activities included in these programs range from programmed materials intended to teach problem-solving skills to games of strategy such as chess and backgammon. Self-paced problem-solving activities such as those provided in *Think-Lab* (Science Research Associates, 1974) are used, as are mind-benders, logic games, math games, puzzles, problem-solving competitions, and simulations.

These activities are not suitable just for gifted children. Average students may benefit equally or even more than gifted students from such activities.

Therefore, these types of programs have been criticized by Stanley (1981, p. 262) for providing "irrelevant academic enrichment."

Creativity and Creative Problem-Solving

Another approach to process training involves the development of creativity or creative problem-solving skills. This type of training differs considerably from that intended to increase reasoning or critical thinking skills (cf. Maltzman, 1960). Whereas the latter is directed primarily at convergent modes of reasoning, the former focuses on divergent patterns of thinking. Obviously, thinking *may* involve both convergent and divergent processes (cf. Guilford, 1959).

One of the difficulties in establishing creativity training programs in schools results from a fundamental confusion about the underlying aims of such attempts. The recent concern for the creativity of students actually seems to have emerged from three quite different realms. For the purpose of clarification these can be termed (1) the creative problem-solving approach, (2) the creative trait approach, and (3) the creativity construct approach.

The Creative Problem-Solving Approach. The creative problem-solving approach is represented by Osborn (1953), Gordon (1961), and Parnes (1981). This approach is concerned primarily with stimulating the creation of innovative products. Its focus on practical problem-solving has generated techniques such as *brainstorming,* which is defined as "a creative conference for the sole purpose of producing a checklist of ideas" (Osborn, 1963, p. 151).

Osborn was one of the first advocates of creative problem-solving. His 1953 book *Applied Imagination* influenced Parnes and others at the State University College at Buffalo. The Creative Problem-Solving Institute (CPSI) which they established there has continued to serve both business and educational interests. *Synectics* (Gordon, 1961), a related approach, was devised to increase the originality, fluency, and creative decision-making of corporate invention teams. Synectics provides a forced analogy method for stimulating inventiveness. Variations of the synectics method have been used in the development of instructional materials (e.g., "Making It Strange") applicable to public school enrichment programs. (See Box 6.1 for examples comparing the creative problem-solving and synectics approaches.)

The Creative Trait Approach. The creative problem-solving approach contrasts markedly with that derived from the work of MacKinnon (1962/1981), Roe (1952/1981) and others who have examined the characteristics of creative adults. Educators who base creativity training programs on this research generalize from the analysis of the traits of adult artists and scientists in an attempt to foster similar characteristics in children. MacKinnon (1962/1981, p. 117), for example, found that "the more creative a person is the more he reveals an openness to his own feelings and emotions, a sensitive intellect

BOX 6.1 Comparison of Creative Problem-Solving and Synectics

Suppose you teach a class of gifted children in a middle school that is having some problems with vandalism. You might have your gifted students develop possible solutions to this problem. Your problem-solving approach will determine the way you proceed with this problem-solving activity. Creative-problem solving suggests one process; synectics suggests a different one. Examples of how the class might solve the problem of vandalism based on these processes are presented below.

Creative Problem-Solving	Synectics
1. Fact-finding: Your students would ask themselves questions about the instances of vandalism. They would ask when these instances occur, where they occur, how they occur, and why they occur.	1. Your students might decide to develop an invention that would curb instances of vandalism.
2. Problem-finding: The class would compare the various instances of vandalism in order to find common elements. This process may help them define the problem.	2. They might consider developing an alarm system.
3. Idea-finding: The students would brainstorm as many possible solutions to the problem as they could.	3. The class would compare alarm systems with unrelated devices. They would try to make familiar things strange ("surprising metaphor"). This would be the process of *direct analogy.*
4. Solution-finding: The students would list criteria for determining which solutions are the best ones.	4. They might try to think like an alarm system in order to understand how to make an effective alarm system. This is the process of *personal* analogy.
5. Acceptance-finding: The students would rate their ideas based on the most appropriate criteria. They would choose several of the best solutions. Then they would devise plans for putting these solutions into action.	5. The students might try to develop phrases about alarm systems that express *compressed conflict*. An example might be "insider/outsider."
	6. Finally the students would make the strange familiar by formulating some of their strange ideas into actual plans for an alarm system.

and understanding self-awareness, and wide-ranging interests including many which in the American culture are thought of as feminine.''

The creative trait approach focuses on freeing children from constraints on their creative production. Gowan (1981b, p. 316), for example, supports ''Maslow's view that creativity results from mental health'' and holds that, therefore, ''we ought to strengthen the mental health of children.'' In addition, he asserts the importance of allowing children the freedom to experience their preconscious impressions, thoughts, and intuitions. This view is consistent with Kubie's (1961, p. 137) notion that ''the *preconscious system* is the essential implement of all creative activity.'' Creativity development programs based on this view emphasize the importance of enabling students to explore ''new realms or levels of awareness'' (Sisk, 1978, p. 135). This enhancement of creative incubation is accomplished through relaxation, meditation, yoga, visualization, and centering activities (Gowan, 1981b; Khatena, 1978; Rose, 1979; Sisk, 1978).

The Creativity Construct Approach. The creativity construct approach to creativity stems from the factor analytic tradition of mental measurement. Guilford's notion of the dichotomy between convergent and divergent production led to attempts (by him and by others) to measure divergent as well as convergent traits in children and adults. Maltzman (1960) attempted to measure and improve the originality of subjects in an experimental setting. Torrance (1974) developed a test of creative thinking based on four components of creativity identified by Guilford (1967): fluency, flexibility, elaboration, and originality. Recently this trend in the study and development of creativity lost some of its impetus when the tests of divergent thinking, which are integral to its implementation, were shown to be technically inadequate (see Chapter 2).

Cautions. It is not surprising that schools have difficulty integrating creativity training into their curriculum. Schools may not have any incentive to reward the creative behavior of students. In some cases the divergent behavior of students, including divergent production, threatens teachers. Schools may already find it difficult enough to garner the resources required for academic instruction that meets the needs of the academically and intellectually gifted.

More fundamentally, schools' efforts to encourage socialization may reinforce students' tendency to conform to expectations of normal behavior. Programs have been developed that promise to increase creative products, improve creative processes, and identify and nurture creative individuals (cf. Mooney, 1963). These programs, however, do not generally flourish in a school environment that does not reward the creative expression of students or teachers (Torrance & Myers, 1971). Some of the most highly creative youngsters in U.S. schools pursue the development of their talents outside the school environment (see e.g., Hollander, 1978; Wiener, 1950; Wright,

1932). Bloom and Sosniak (1981, p. 94) note, "We report very few instances in which talent development and schooling function to enhance each other."

Schools that tolerate diversity in the behavior of students are more likely to encourage divergent thinking and creative expression (Torrance, 1963). Increasing teachers' tolerance for ambiguity and acceptance of atypical behavior may reduce the need for enrichment programs specifically intended to encourage creativity.

Information Processing

A final process-oriented approach for gifted students attempts to strengthen their information-processing skills. This approach is based on the premise that

> if intelligence is the ability to acquire and apply knowledge, then intelligence must depend upon the underlying level of neurological organization and function. Intelligence . . . is thus open to change in direct relationship to variations in central nervous system function.
>
> (Norton & Doman, 1982, p. 250)

Programs based on this view attempt to develop higher-level thinking skills as well as to remediate deficiencies in information processing.

Information-processing approaches are not unique to gifted education. Mann (1979) reviews process training options that have been used primarily with mentally retarded and learning disabled students. Several authors (e.g., Glass, 1983; Hammill & Larsen, 1974) have found that process approaches do not promote academic learning of handicapped students; some of their concerns also apply to process training in gifted programs.

Models of Thinking and Intelligence. Some process-oriented enrichment approaches are based on schemes that categorize various kinds of learning or intellect. In program development for the gifted, Bloom's *taxonomy* is sometimes used as a definitive ranking of the processes of cognition. According to Maker (1982a, p. 38), "The taxonomies have enjoyed widespread use as schemes for making process modifications for the gifted." In general, these modifications have been directed toward developing gifted students' higher-level thinking skills, such as analysis, synthesis, and evaluation.

Bloom (1956, p. 10) indicates, however, that his "purpose in constructing a taxonomy of educational objectives is to facilitate communication" and that "this taxonomy is designed to be a classification of student behaviors which represent the intended outcomes of the educational process" (p. 12). Thus, the taxonomies classify the objectives of teaching, not the inherent or even hypothetical processes of learning. The taxonomy itself does not imply that higher-level thinking skills can be taught in a particular context or through a particular sequence of activities. Some educators (e.g., Bruner, 1960; Copley,

1961) maintain that higher-level thinking skills are best conveyed in the context of academic instruction.

Another classification system based on Guilford's (1967) *Structure of the Intellect* (SI) model has influenced both the development of programs and the application of particular teaching methods. Adopting Guilford's classification system, Meeker (1969) has developed a method for analyzing students' performance on various cognitive tests in order to determine their strengths and deficiencies. In addition, she has produced materials designed to remediate students' deficiencies in areas of cognition (Meeker et al., 1970). Although Meeker recognizes the importance of developing students' strengths as well as remediating their weaknesses, her diagnostic-prescriptive method lends itself to remedial instruction (see, e.g., Hedbring & Rubenzer, 1979).

Guilford's classification, however, is designed to identify components of intelligence and does not purport to classify these components for instructional purposes. Teachers who choose to use an approach based on the structure of the intellect model should be aware that similar process-training approaches for the handicapped have been criticized pointedly. Continued attention to the empirical research seems to be advisable.

Developmental Models and Brain Structures.   Other process-oriented approaches rely on a developmental view of cognitive processes. Building on the work of Erikson and Piaget, Gowan (1981a) postulated the existence of three developmental levels above Piaget's formal operations stage: the creativity stage, the psychedelic stage, and the illumination stage. According to Gowan, access to these levels depends on right brain–oriented teaching. This instruction evolves hierarchically to correspond with the stages of the child's development and concerns itself with ''three paramount issues . . . 1) Creative Fantasy or Magic Nightmare . . . 2) Teaching to Avoid the Creativity Drop . . . and 3) Establishing Verbal Creativity'' (Gowan, 1981a, p. 81).

An extension of this developmental stage theory leads to the assertion that cognitive structures correspond to brain structures. Some theorists (e.g., Andrews, 1980; Myers, 1982; Rubenzer, 1979b) suggest that the attainment of higher stages of cognitive development depends on the integration of brain function. They believe that, in general, our society emphasizes left-brain rather than right-brain development, and that a balance between the functions of the two hemispheres is rarely achieved. Rubenzer (1979b) further suggests that replication of the patterns of brain activity of effective learners will improve the problem-solving capabilities of less effective learners. To these theorists, reasoning and creativity are natural concomitants of healthy brain activity. In their view education involves releasing the brain from inhibiting forces rather than providing students with either content or process instruction.

Cautions.   Caution is advisable in applying the results of brain research to pedagogy. Efforts to categorize students as dominant in either right- or left-brain functioning or to improve their hemispheric functioning and integration may *seem* justified on the basis of the clinical data currently available. Dimond (1972, p. 198), however, writes, "It is not suggested that it will be possible in the immediate future to extend brain capacity in a practical sense by the full employment of both hemispheres."

Brain researchers are using new techniques and developing new hypotheses which may well contribute to an understanding of information processing. As with all new research techniques and hypotheses, however, applications based on limited findings may not be wise. According to Springer and Deutsch, for example, "our educational system may miss training or developing half of the brain, but it probably does so by missing out on the talents of both hemispheres" (Springer & Deutsch, 1981, p. 192). Too often the novelty of process-oriented approaches seems to have been used to compensate for the lack of substantive content in gifted programs. Since our society tends to equate the new with the good, such innovative programs may be exempt from careful scrutiny.

This portion of the chapter has considered process-oriented education for gifted students from three perspectives: problem-solving, creativity training, and information processing. Throughout the discussion we have cautioned against unreasonable or precipitous inference from limited or inconclusive data. Considering the speculative nature of much of the research in these fields, skepticism seems appropriate.

CONTENT-ORIENTED PROGRAMS

Whereas a process-oriented view emphasizes the development of thinking skills, a content-oriented approach to enrichment stresses the presentation of particular content. Through learning this content, students are expected to increase their knowledge of particular subjects or domains as well as to develop thinking skills. The substance of content-oriented instruction may differ greatly from that of process-oriented instruction, but they share the primary goal of developing thinking skills.

This portion of the chapter considers several enrichment variants based on a content-oriented perspective. These are inductive approaches, academic mini-courses, museum and science center programs, children's college options, and mentorships.

Inductive Approaches in Enrichment Programs

A comprehensive method for developing the problem-solving skills of gifted students involves instruction that emphasizes the structures or methodologies of academic disciplines. The inductive approach integrates the content and process of learning into a cohesive teaching method and curriculum structure.

Bruner (1960), for example, is concerned that students develop skills in analytic and intuitive thinking. However, he recognizes that the way to develop these skills is not to isolate them from a particular body of knowledge, for the development of these skills "rests upon a solid knowledge of the sub-ject, a familiarity that gives intuition something to work with" (Bruner, 1960, p. 57).

Just as the significance to students of factual information is limited by their inability to understand the structure of its context (i.e., the disciplines), the importance of reasoning and research skills is limited by their inability to ap-ply these skills appropriately within particular contexts of learning. Programs that develop problem-solving skills in the context of the disciplines (see Chap-ters 7 and 9) are more likely to encourage gifted students to pursue mean-ingful studies at an advanced level than are programs that stress problem-solving in isolation.

The integration of content and process has spawned various instructional alternatives. Curricula based on this integration were developed in the 1960s in the fields of mathematics, science, and social science. Bruner's (1966a) own curriculum unit, *Man: A Course of Study,* is in some ways characteristic of these efforts. Inquiry instruction evolved as the teaching method most suitable for developing the problem-solving capabilities of students. The effectiveness of this method with gifted students was considered in the discussion of ATI research in Chapter 3; its implementation is discussed in Chapter 9.

Consideration of inductive curricula may not be appropriate in a chapter on enrichment, since enrichment is often extracurricular. In fact, we view enrichment and curriculum as opposites. Although comprehensive curricula for the gifted are preferable to part-time enrichment provisions, schools fre-quently do not have such complete offerings. Academic instruction in an en-richment program, however, can integrate content and process instruction.

Stanley believes that such part-time academic enrichment, which he calls "relevant academic enrichment," is "likely to be both the best short-term and one of the worst long-term" approaches to the education of the gifted (Stan-ley, 1981, p. 263). Without the articulation of a comprehensive, accelerated curriculum, enrichment is likely to frustrate gifted students (Stanley, 1981, p. 263). Nevertheless, relevant academic enrichment is differentially suited to the needs of gifted students and, when provided, may impress the parents and teachers of gifted students so much that they request more comprehen-sive academic offerings.

Academic Mini-courses

An enrichment option provided by some school districts involves supple-menting regular curricula with various mini-courses. The topics presented in these mini-courses may differ from those considered in the regular curricu-lum or they may be similar to academic offerings normally provided at a later time in the regular sequence of courses. Mini-courses are generally used to expand the breadth of academic study. Even when they allow for some ac-celeration, mini-courses typically do not provide comprehensive instruction in a subject.

Kaplan (1975) considers three types of mini-course experiences:

1. the topical,
2. the thematic, and
3. the skill-oriented.

Topical Mini-courses. Topical mini-courses are most similar to regular academic courses and provide students with exposure to topics such as anthropology, current events, mythology, and solid geometry. The scope of the presentation of these subjects varies according to the length of the mini-course and the frequency of the sessions. A mini-course on cultural anthropology that meets an hour a day for nine weeks can consider a number of concepts and relate them to the characteristics of several different cultures. However, an anthropology mini-course that meets less frequently may be able to offer only a cursory overview of the anthropological method or a brief summary of customs in one culture. (See Box 6.2 for a sample mini-course plan.)

Thematic Mini-courses. Thematic mini-courses involve an interdisciplinary consideration of significant issues. For instance, a thematic mini-course dealing with the concept of tension between good and evil might include study of certain paintings, readings in philosophy, discussion of works of literature, and consideration of selected contemporary films.

Some suggested issues for consideration in thematic mini-courses are

- racial discrimination
- different views of "the beautiful"
- pollution
- war
- different views of justice
- technologies
- women's role in society
- ethical considerations in science

Skill-Oriented Mini-courses. Skill-oriented mini-courses usually provide intensive instruction in a specific skill or group of skills such as typing, research, or computer programming. Other less prevalent offerings include intensive foreign language instruction, musical instrument lessons, and instruction in various graphic arts. Yunghans (1981) described a mini-course program in art for gifted elementary school children in which children considered design problems in various media, such as oil painting, latch hooking, and weaving.

Other Mini-course Applications. Although gifted programs that rely on mini-course experiences are neither comprehensive nor sequential, they do provide gifted students with academic instruction related to their interests.

BOX 6.2 Anthropology: A Mini-course for Gifted Students (Grades Four to Six)

OBJECTIVES

1. To gain a general understanding of the nature of the study of anthropology.
2. To learn vocabulary necessary to an understanding of anthropology.
3. To become aware of the ethnographic method of studying a culture.
4. To view cultures from a relativistic perspective.
5. To experience the barter system in a simulation activity.
6. To discuss the customs, division of labor, and religious rituals in a West African culture through a simulation activity.
7. To analyze the differences among complex technological societies, peasant societies, agrarian tribal societies, and nomadic tribal societies.
8. To compare child-rearing and educational practices among Mexican villagers, Navaho Indians, Chinese peasants, South Indian villagers, Igboo tribal peoples, and modern Americans.

ACTIVITIES

This mini-course is intended to be presented over a six-week period. Students should meet with the teacher of the gifted for one hour each day during the six weeks. The mini-course activities are summarized below:

Day One: lecture and discussion concerning the nature of anthropology as a social science, an overview of the anthropological method, and an introduction of key concepts and vocabulary

Day Two: lecture and discussion about variations in cultures, the types of activities that vary from culture to culture; making of tortillas and comparison of this bread to previously prepared wheat bread, French bread, and pita as an example of cultural differences and similarities

Day Three: continued discussion of cultural variations; small groups compare brief readings about division of labor in three cultures

Day Four: lecture and discussion about cultural taboos; small groups develop list of possible universal cultural taboos; large-group discussion of universal taboos

Day Five: preparation for first simulation activity; discussion of objectives of the simulation

Days Six through Nine: simulation activity in which students become members of a peasant society that uses a barter system of exchange

Day Ten: debriefing; discussion of what was learned in the simulation activity

Day Eleven: lecture and discussion about the economies of different cultures; comparison of household economy, barter system, feudal economy, and complex exchange economies

Day Twelve: lecture and discussion of division of labor; small groups compare the division of labor changes between their grandparents' and parents' generations

Day Thirteen: discussion of religious differences between cultures; discussion of homework reading assignment about Mexican villagers' religious beliefs and Navaho religious beliefs

Day Fourteen: preparation for second simulation activity; selection of roles for the activity; discussion of men's and women's roles and religious roles

Days Fifteen through Twenty-one: simulation activities related to life in a West African village, including costume-making and simulation of religious rituals

Day Twenty-two: debriefing; discussion of what was learned in the simulation activity

Day Twenty-three: viewing of part I of "Roots"

Day Twenty-four: discussion of "Roots" including consideration of the native customs of the African tribe and the cultural dislocation caused by slavery

Days Twenty-five through Twenty-eight: small-group investigations of child-rearing and educational practices in a Mexican village, among the Navahos, and among modern Americans.

Day Twenty-Nine: group reports about child-rearing and educational practices; lecture about child-rearing and educational practices among Chinese peasants, South Indian villagers, and Igboo tribal peoples

Day Thirty: final exam

When mini-courses are provided in addition to acceleration or a comprehensive curriculum for gifted students, they allow for the study of topics, issues, or skills that may not be addressed even in the accelerated or honors program.

An additional application of mini-courses involves incorporating student-taught mini-courses into the regular or accelerated curriculum. This technique allows pupils to demonstrate knowledge obtained through independent study and can be used to enhance instruction in almost any subject (Demetrulias, 1982). This approach might be especially suitable for gifted students in the upper elementary through secondary grades.

Museum and Science Center Programs

Although a number of museums and science centers provide enrichment programs for gifted students, the nature and scope of these offerings vary widely. Some museums, for example, offer extensive programs integrated with the public school instruction of gifted students. Others provide workshops and seminars available to all motivated students in the community.

Chicago Offerings. In Chicago several museums and other cultural institutions have developed programs in cooperation with the Gifted Program Office of the city's public schools (Maxwell, 1980). These offerings include museology programs at the Field Museum, Art Institute, and Historical Society, as well as an architecture program at the Chicago Architecture Foundation, an ecology program at the Lincoln Park Zoo, an astronomy program at Adler Planetarium, and an aquatic science program at Shedd Aquarium. Although the goals, procedures, and target populations are different for each of these Chicago programs, they all maintain high academic expectations for the students who are selected to participate in them.

The Maryland Science Center Program. In conjunction with Maryland schools, the Maryland Science Center provides two types of advanced science programs (Hyman, 1982). These include a program of in-depth seminars for bright, motivated secondary school students and a similar seminar program for highly gifted middle school students.

These seminars allow students to participate in "courses above the level of those in the schools" (Hyman, 1982, p. 3). The courses, which are taught by college professors and research scientists, offer rapid-paced academic instruction and encourage students to become involved in independent research projects. As a result of these programs, "many students have . . . received additional recognition in the form of advanced placement, part-time or full-time employment offers from local science-related industries, or grant monies for their projects" (Hyman, 1982, p. 2). In recent years the seminars have considered topics such as digital electronics, architecture, astronomy, symbolic logic, cellular physiology, radiation biology, and microbial ecology (Hyman, 1982).

The Franklin Institute Program. The Franklin Institute in Philadelphia offers science workshops intended for "bright and motivated children . . . [not] solely . . . very-high-IQ youngsters" (D. Goldwater, letter of April 6, 1983). These workshops are not provided in conjunction with public school programs and there are no eligibility criteria. The science workshops provided by the Franklin Institute span a wide age range, with offerings for pre-school, primary school, middle school, secondary school, and adult learners.

Talcott Mountain Science Center Programs. A regional science center located at an abandoned NIKE radar site in Connecticut provides several science education alternatives (Atamian & Danielson, 1977). This center, known as the Talcott Mountain Science Center for Student Involvement, devotes about 30 percent of its resources to programs for gifted students. These programs include the following (Atamian & Danielson, 1977, p. 69):

1. classes during and after school hours, Monday through Friday, for students participating in special programs within their own schools;
2. Saturday research courses for students who are sponsored individually by their school districts; and
3. a summer research program.

In general, the programs for gifted students that are provided at the Talcott Mountain center either supplement instruction in the school gifted program or allow students to pursue independent research. Since the center staff is relatively small and the number of students served is quite large, the Talcott

Mountain programs, like the other museum and center programs described in this section, are best seen as adjuncts to other provisions for the gifted.

Children's College Options

Seminar and mini-course programs developed by various colleges and consortia of colleges also provide supplemental instruction for gifted students. The Super Saturday Program at Purdue University offers six-week enrichment courses for gifted elementary school students (Feldhusen & Wyman, 1980). Although the courses present academic content at a suitable pace, they are only "successful in meeting some of the needs of the . . . children" (Feldhusen & Wyman, 1980, p. 21). Feldhusen and Wyman, who have been instrumental in organizing this program, caution that although Saturday programs can "provide valuable instruction for the gifted . . . in the regular school setting full scale programming for the gifted calls for a variety of offerings and for acceleration" (1980, p. 21).

Unfortunately, not all college programs are as well conceived as the Purdue Program. One program, for example, enables gifted students to complete six-week courses on topics such as tee-shirt art, animal behavior, Kung-Fu, pottery, and disco dancing. Athough these courses are probably enjoyable, they do not further academic goals for the gifted.

The Catskill Saturday Seminars, offered to gifted high school students, are more academic in their orientation. Nevertheless, instructors of these seminars cannot assign any compulsory projects and cannot grade any work completed. The rationale for this policy is expressed by Porter (1978, p. 367) as follows: "Our students are already the busiest individuals, the leaders, the get-up-and-go-people of their schools. It is the philosophy of this program that no further burdens should be placed on them." This philosophy clearly articulates the extracurricular nature of this enrichment program. See Box 6.3 for a description of acceleration as enrichment.

Mentorships

Although mentorship programs are intended primarily as career exploration options, their value in enriching academic instruction has been emphasized by some educators. For example, Booth (1980, p. 11) writes, describing a middle school mentorship program, "We have evolved a program that achieves these important successes: students learn eagerly in an area of special interest to them, they develop a positive self-image . . ., they turn outward . . . by contributing to others in the community."

Runions (1980) discusses a Mentorship Academy Program in which gifted high school students both learn from mentors in the community and serve as mentors for younger gifted children. The program is designed to encourage the student to become "responsible for his learning" (Runions, 1980, p. 155). The implication of Runions's and Booth's view is that mentorship programs increase both the cognitive and affective competence of gifted stu-

---

BOX 6.3   Acceleration as Enrichment

Recently an eleven-year-old gifted child of my acquaintance was permitted to participate in a summer program at the college where I work. This program encourages gifted junior and senior high students to enroll in regular summer session classes. Some classes are recommended particularly for these students, but all classes are open to them. In addition, the gifted students are provided with a special option: they may change their status from credit-seeking to auditor at *any time* before the final exam.

This particular student was taking "Introduction to Philosophy," a college-level overview of the history and methods of philosophy. The five-week class met for three hours every day. Textbook readings were assigned, as were two papers, two tests, and a final exam. The material was difficult for this student, the pace was challenging, and the grading was rough. Nevertheless, the experience provided her with an intensive view of a difficult academic discipline. It improved her ability to reason, write, and voice her ideas.

The fact that this student got a B in the course is evidence of the appropriateness of its pace and content for her. She performed like an average college student and was motivated to perform by the challenging nature of the work.

Because this student is placed in junior high school, not in college, this radical acceleration effort has provided her with a form of enrichment rather than actual acceleration. It is the sort of enrichment, however, that will influence her achievement in other academic areas and will contribute to her literacy and her sense of rational expression.

By Aimee Howley.

dents. Others (e.g., Colson, Borman & Nash, 1980) emphasize the role of mentorships in allowing gifted students to explore career alternatives and select suitable vocational objectives.

Cautions.   Mentorships may pose certain difficulties to teachers of the gifted. First, the learning obtained through mentorship programs may be difficult to document. Since the academic content of these experiences varies from student to student and from mentor to mentor, teachers cannot be sure that what is provided to an individual student actually meets his or her cognitive needs.

Second, good mentors are hard to find. Mentorship arrangements depend on the voluntary participation of community members. Although the efforts of these citizens are commendable, their commitment to the program cannot be guaranteed. More pressing concerns may interfere with their ability to provide time and guidance to gifted students.

Finally, mentorships are difficult to monitor. Students may not be able to change mentorship placements if they are dissatisfied. Mentors may have no way to increase students' motivation or even to ensure their attendance.

In spite of these possible difficulties, long-term mentorships, like European apprenticeships, may convey knowledge, skills, and a sense of vocational purpose to some gifted students.

PRODUCT-ORIENTED PROGRAMS

Product-oriented enrichment programs primarily emphasize the products of instruction and not the content or processes conveyed. The products are sometimes tangible, as in the case of a student's painting, or intangible, as in the case of a student's increased mental health. Regardless of the type of product that results from instruction, the product justifies the program. Product-oriented programs vary considerably, but that variation often occurs because the products elicited are quite different.

This portion of the chapter considers three apparently distinct product-oriented program variations: (1) the Enrichment Triad, (2) affective education programs, and (3) career education programs. Although the Enrichment Triad is more concerned with cognitive products than are the other two approaches, it also involves career guidance. The product of affective education programs is ostensibly adjustment (or mental health), yet these programs may affect cognitive performance as well. Career education is a combination of cognitive and affective education; its product can most reasonably be identified as career choice.

The Enrichment Triad

A program model that combines several aspects of enrichment into a cohesive system is Renzulli's (1977) Enrichment Triad. This approach allows gifted students to experience three types, or levels, of enrichment. The enrichment activities provided in the triad reflect the interests of the students in the program and ultimately focus on real problems.

Type I enrichment "consists of those experiences and activities that are designed to bring the learner into touch with the kinds of topics or areas of study in which he or she may have a sincere interest" (Renzulli, 1977, p. 17). This exploratory phase of enrichment is intended to expand students' awareness of possible areas of study and the methods of inquiry associated with each area. Thus, Renzulli considers historiography a more suitable topic for consideration in a Type I enrichment program than the history of a particular era.

Type II enrichment provides group instruction in cognitive and affective processes. This process-training phase incorporates exercises and activities similar to those discussed in the sections of this chapter devoted to process-oriented education and affective education programs. Although Renzulli includes this component in the enrichment triad, he is not an advocate of process training. In fact, in an article entitled "What We Don't Know About Programming for the Gifted and Talented" (1980), Renzulli criticizes both the aims of process training and its outcomes. He writes,

> The process . . . models tend to impose rigidity on learning activities. In their
> effort to focus on particular processes (rather than content), such activities tend
> to split learning into the highly structured kinds of experiences that we criticized
> in the content-centered curriculum . . . Reliance upon process models has un-
> doubtedly resulted from a popular but completely unsupported belief that the
> gifted person is *process oriented.*
>
> (Renzulli, 1980, p. 602)

Perhaps Renzulli's apparently contradictory views about process instruction can be explained by considering the relative importance that he places
on Type III enrichment as compared to Type I and Type II enrichment. "Type
III enrichment consists of activities in which the youngster becomes an actual
investigator of a real problem or topic by using appropriate methods of inquiry" (Renzulli, 1977, p. 29). Renzulli writes that Type III enrichment is the
"one type of enrichment that is considered to be especially appropriate for
gifted learners" (p. 2). We can infer, therefore, that he considers Type I and
Type II enrichment to be appropriate for average students as well as for the
gifted. Although Renzulli incorporates Type I and Type II enrichment in the
triad, he values these enrichment approaches as programming for the gifted
only to the degree that they prepare gifted students for Type III enrichment.

The salient characteristics of Type III enrichment include its emphasis on
real problems, its independent study approach, its concern with products,
and its insistence that students present their products to appropriate audi-
ences. This type of enrichment encourages students to model their performance on that of professional researchers, scholars, and other productive
adults, according to Renzulli (1977).

Cautions.   There are several theoretical and practical problems associated
with the Enrichment Triad. First, Enrichment Triad programs assume that
Type I and Type II enrichment provide skills requisite for successful completion of Type III enrichment activities. The relationship among Type I, II, and
III enrichment has not, however, been established empirically. Many gifted
students who have not been exposed to Type I and Type II activities succeed
nevertheless with Type III enrichment projects. Performance at this phase of
enrichment may depend more on maturity than on previous experience with
other triad components.

Second, student interests are important influences in the choice of Type
III projects. Students may not be the best judges of the significant areas of
academic concern and so may choose projects that are not germane to their
cognitive needs (cf. National Commission on Excellence in Education, 1983,
pp. 18, 20, 24).

Finally, the Enrichment Triad in general and Type III enrichment in particular encourage students to mimic researchers, not to prepare for actual research. Copley (1961) criticizes school programs that give students the illusion
that they are able to perform real research. Without extensive knowledge in
a particular field, students cannot contribute significant or original work (cf.
Bruner, 1960; Wiener, 1950). Even highly gifted students rarely have the ex-

perience or knowledge to solve significant real problems. Those few who do function like adult researchers are able to do so because they have acquired expertise in their fields (Wiener, 1956). To expect that even a fraction of the most highly gifted students will exhibit this degree of involvement may be unrealistic.

Affective Education Programs

Although recent studies (e.g., Lehman & Erdwins, 1981) and reviews of studies (e.g., Austin & Draper, 1981) conclude that most gifted students are socially adept, well adjusted, self-confident, and independent, many educators nevertheless recommend programs for improving the affective competence of all gifted students. This approach, like process training, is derived from a concern for educating the "whole child." Some gifted educators seek to integrate the functions of the left and right brain; others (e.g., Gensley, 1973; Lyon, 1971) attempt to conjoin the intellectual and affective realms of functioning (see Katz, 1968, for historical precedents). Like process training programs for the gifted, affective education programs include remedial, developmental, and integrated efforts. An alternative to a specifically designated affective education program is a program of cognitive instruction that emphasizes associated affective concerns.

Remedial Affective Programs. Remedial programs such as the one described by Morton and Workman (1981, p. 457) "provid[e] services to intellectually gifted young people who are experiencing observable emotional or behavior problems." In general, the success of these programs depends on several factors. These include the student's willingness to alter the behavior, the flexibility of the environment that serves to reinforce the undesirable behavior, and the competence of the counselor or therapist. Sometimes the school environment reinforces the student's negative behavior. Teachers of the gifted or guidance counselors may not be able to modify that environment enough to alter its influence on the student (cf. Holmes, Holmes & Field, 1974).

Since the success of remedial affective programs depends on the skill of their implementers, problems arise when teachers of the gifted attempt to implement these sorts of programs. Teachers of the gifted, as well as many school guidance counselors, lack the training necessary to provide effective therapy.

Remedial affective programs may be most suited to the needs of emotionally disturbed gifted students or those with specific adjustment difficulties. For further discussion of this type of program for gifted underachievers, see Chapter 11.

Developmental Affective Programs. Developmental guidance designed to improve affective functioning usually involves group activities such as role playing, sensitivity training, and small-group discussion. These activities may be a routine or an occasional portion of the enrichment program for gifted students. They are often developed by the teacher or counselor to meet the specific affective needs of the children in a particular program. Commercially developed materials, such as DUSO, Developing Understanding of Self and Others (Dinkmeyer, 1970, 1973), have also been used with gifted students (Kelly & Terry, 1980).

Integrated Affective Programs. Integrated affective education programs are concerned with providing instruction that combines cognitive and affective components. Their features vary considerably, depending on their premises. In general, however, integrated programs can be classified into two categories: those concerned with values clarification and those concerned with students' self-actualization.

Values clarification is an approach to moral education that encourages students to develop an understanding of the origins and nature of their values. According to Raths, Harmin, and Simon (1966), values clarification activities help children

1. make free choices whenever possible,
2. search for alternatives in choice-making situations,
3. weigh the consequences of each available alternative,
4. consider what they prize and cherish,
5. affirm the things they value,
6. do something about their choices, and
7. consider and strengthen patterns in their lives.

Sisk (1982) suggests that values clarification is important for gifted students because of their advanced reasoning skills and their sensitivity to issues and feelings. Because values clarification combines affective and cognitive concerns, it is viewed as consonant with these characteristics of gifted students.

Affective education programs concerned with students' self-actualization usually integrate academic instruction with discussion of values, emotions, and aesthetic tastes. Frequently programs based on this combination of concerns are associated with "humanist" trends in education (cf. Lyon, 1971). These programs may vary in method and content, but their goal is usually the same: to develop self-directed, well-integrated learners.

Evyatar (1973) described an enrichment program at the Technion (technical college) in Haifa, Israel. This program, intended for eleven- to thirteen-year-old students classified as highly gifted (IQ of 140 or above), was designed to help the students achieve "a full realization of their potential and a better integration into society" (Evyatar, 1973, p. 115). Although the program was "intended as therapy directed at a lack of balance which manifests itself in the *negative-gifted-child-syndrome*" (p. 116), its therapeutic method did not involve specific affective training.

The provision of appropriate cognitive instruction was found to effect improvements in students' self-concepts and interpersonal relationships (Evyatar, 1973). "By feeding their hunger for knowledge and bringing them together with other children endowed with the same intellectual capacities, the course did seem to induce a better emotional balance" (p. 122). The results are consistent with the findings of Winne, Woodland, and Wong (1982), who concluded that academic climate is the school variable most important for sustaining the self-esteem of gifted students.

Cautions. Affective education may involve a remedial, developmental, or integrated approach. Because provisions for affective education are often made within the context of the gifted enrichment program, academic instructional time in the program may be reduced. Since affective education activities do not specifically meet the cognitive needs of gifted students, they may not represent the best use of the limited amount of time provided for differentiated instruction. In fact, affective education may be equally beneficial for average or below-average students.

Cognitive Instruction as Affective Education. As shown in the previous section, cognitive instruction is capable of producing affective gains. Therefore we favor providing gifted programs that emphasize the affective concerns associated with academic disciplines. The study of intellectual history, comparative religion, anthropology, sociology, and literature provides ample opportunity for discussion of ethical values. Aesthetic judgment and the emotional impact of the arts can be considered in courses on art and music history. Even courses in mathematics and science can effect changes in the emotional responses of students (see, e.g., Wiener, 1956, pp. 61, 86).

Fox (1979a), for example, described a program that offered a series of minicourses in applied mathematics to older elementary school students. These courses, which introduced mathematical concepts not normally considered in the elementary curriculum, were developed as a means of changing students' attitudes toward mathematics in general and toward careers in science and mathematics in particular. The success of such integrated programs speaks well for their adoption as enrichment offerings for gifted students. In addition, the integration of affective and cognitive experiences can enhance the learning within a suitably paced academic curriculum.

Career Education and Leadership Training Programs

Many schools, particularly at the secondary level, make some provision for career education. In addition, elementary social studies curricula often include career awareness activities which familiarize students with various types of adult work. Sometimes gifted students are also required, encouraged, or allowed to participate in supplementary career education experiences. These range from leadership training activities provided in elementary school enrichment programs to work-study opportunities offered in senior high school.

The significant characteristics of the most successful career education programs for gifted students seem to be (1) well-delineated goals, (2) a carefully defined client population, and (3) a socially acceptable challenge to certain social conventions. An example of the last (and most problematic) characteristic is the challenge posed by programs that encourage girls to enter traditionally male careers (see, e.g., Deutsch & Wolleat, 1981). Although these programs confront values maintained by a portion of our society, they reinforce values emerging in another segment.

Model Career Education Programs. All three of the above-mentioned characteristics of an effective career education program are evident in a pilot program established through the cooperative efforts of Johns Hopkins University, Towson State College, Essex Community College, and the Maryland Academy of Sciences (Fox, 1979a). This program for preadolescents focuses on developing cognitive skills necessary for an understanding of careers in applied mathematics (Fox, 1979a). It is designed to change attitudes toward mathematics and increase awareness of careers in applied mathematics only as a result of substantive content learning. This program is restricted in its goals, intended for a specified group of students, and oriented toward changing attitudes (especially girls' attitudes) toward mathematics. Because the program is geared to enrichment, the program coordinator cautions that it is "not sufficient for the development of . . . talent" (Fox, 1979a, p. 95).

A more comprehensive view of career education is provided in Van Tassel-Baska's model (1981). This model attempts to integrate career guidance and aptitude development. Kerr (1981, p. 331) suggests that Van Tassel-Baska's model is intended to meet the "psychosocial needs, skill development needs, and life career planning needs" of gifted students. Ambitious career education programs of this sort can perhaps be classified more aptly as global enrichment programs. They may not conform to the narrowly conceived criteria above.

Cautions. It is important to look carefully at the assumptions on which career education and leadership training programs are based. First, "the gifted and talented [are seen as] those who tend to do best in the labor market" (Hoyt & Hebeler, 1974, p. 63; cf. Hollingworth, 1926, p. 358). This may not actually be the case. In fact, within the restricted high-IQ range, "the correlation between ability and achievement [i.e., accomplishments] practically disappears" (McClelland, 1958, p. 13). In fact, "family background, social position, personal acquaintances, and mere chance itself are more likely to decide who receives social, economic, and political rewards" (Smith, 1977, p. 325).

Second, the gifted are defined by their "social contributions, productivity, and usefulness" (Hoyt & Hebeler, 1974, p. 192). This may be the general method by which society identifies its gifted members, but it does not relate to school identification paradigms. In fact, *no* mental measurement tool predicts leadership in the way that IQ predicts academic achievement. Since IQ does not seem to represent leadership potential, a focus on providing academically talented students with leadership training or career guidance for leadership positions may be misdirected.

THE DILEMMA OF ENRICHMENT

This chapter has listed cautions associated with particular enrichment approaches. In general terms, these cautions relate to two issues: (1) the quality of enrichment programs and (2) the quantity of enrichment services. Although these two concerns can be considered as discrete issues, they are interrelated.

Issues of Quality

Typically, enrichment is an extracurricular option made available to those gifted students who perform successfully in the regular classroom. Enrichment, therefore, may be based on the assumption that the regular classroom is an appropriate placement for gifted students. Enrichment may be provided as a salve or as a reward for gifted children's tolerance of inappropriate regular classroom instruction.

This trend seems inconsistent with cognitive goals for the gifted. Cognitive goals imply commitment to academic excellence. In order to make these goals operational, schools should provide superior students with progressively more difficult academic tasks as they demonstrate mastery of less difficult ones. They should expose academically apt students to accelerated curricula and encourage them to value academic learning.

Sometimes, however, schools provide just the opposite conditions for gifted students (cf. Baer & Bushell, 1981; Bronfenbrenner, 1970; Coleman, 1961; Hofstadter, 1963; Wiener, 1950). During the greatest portion of their time in school, gifted students may be given academic tasks that are too easy for them (e.g., Gambrell, Wilson & Gantt, 1981). They may not be accelerated, in spite of evidence of the benefits of this option; and their ability to excel academically may not even be recognized (cf. Whitmore, 1980).

In order to ensure the optimal academic performance of gifted students, schools should provide instruction that corresponds with the characteristics of these children. As we have seen above and in Chapters 3 and 5, these characteristics imply the need for advanced instruction. The provision of such instruction should not be limited to a few hours a week. The *quality* of instructional programs for the gifted ultimately depends on the *quantity* of appropriately advanced programming provided by schools.

Issues of Quantity

The success of enrichment depends on its inclusiveness. As was suggested previously, enrichment augments or replaces all or a portion of the regular curriculum. It should not be contrasted with acceleration; in its most limited forms, enrichment should be contrasted with curriculum.

Broad definitions suggest that enrichment should provide a curriculum for the gifted. In order to accomplish this task, however, enrichment provisions must be extensive and inclusive. Gifted students should spend most of their time in such a program.

A separate curriculum for gifted students, however, is not an alternative that is frequently adopted. For this reason, Chapter 5 listed the positive value of acceleration as a practical and expedient strategy for dealing with gifted students in contemporary schools.

Programs conducted in the framework of a curriculum that supports education for the gifted can, however, resolve the issues of the quality and quantity of enrichment. In Chapter 7, we explore curriculum for gifted students and suggest ways to develop extensive and inclusive programs for the gifted.

SUMMARY

This chapter has explored numerous enrichment options currently employed by school systems. It has reviewed three approaches to enrichment: (1) the process-oriented approach, (2) the content-oriented approach, and (3) the product-oriented approach.

The process-oriented approach to enrichment included provisions to develop the problem-solving skills, creativity, or information-processing skills of gifted students. In addition to summarizing the literature about these enrichment options, the chapter suggested some cautions to keep in mind about these enrichment approaches.

In this chapter content-oriented alternatives have generally been considered to be more consistent with the needs of high-IQ students, academically talented students, and artistically talented students. Several content-oriented enrichment approaches were presented. Comprehensive academic offerings, however, were seen as the province of the academic curriculum, to be discussed in Chapter 7. Programs for artistically talented students will be discussed at length in Chapter 10.

Product-oriented enrichment approaches were compared in terms of their goals and methods. The Enrichment Triad, affective education, and career education offerings were considered.

Finally, the related issues of quality of instruction and quantity of services were presented as the essential dilemma of enrichment. High-quality programs and extensive services were recommended. Such a recommendation, however, assumes that enrichment will have the status of curriculum rather than that of extracurricular activity.

CHAPTER 7

Form and Content: Curriculum

INTRODUCTION

Chapter 6 contrasted curriculum and enrichment and discussed prominent enrichment approaches based on creativity, affective options, and higher-level thinking skills. This chapter specifies important curriculum content for the gifted, and it also considers ways to implement this curriculum.

Other texts have viewed the curriculum as comprising all planned learning experiences, or both planned and unplanned learning experiences, or even the combination of all learning experiences and school arrangements that support learning (cf. Cook & Doll, 1973; Eggleston, 1977; McNeil, 1981; Oliva, 1982). This chapter defines curriculum as the course of study (in form) and as the disciplines of study (in content). Socialization and what has been called "the hidden curriculum" (see e.g., Eggleston, 1977) are discussed in Chapter 11.

The curriculum, as it is treated here, relates most directly to literacy and rationalism. These are goals of individual talent development that perpetuate an intellectual legacy (see Chapter 1). Only the two most basic aims are considered and the definition of curriculum is kept narrow in order that features of an academic program for gifted students may emerge. Selection of these aims and this definition of curriculum also reflects concern for the cognitive traits that distinguish the gifted. This chapter discusses only curriculum for the academically and intellectually gifted; curriculum for the artistically gifted is considered in Chapter 10.

Because intellectual ability is what characterizes gifted children (Pendarvis, 1985), a greater emphasis on the intellectual component of schooling may result in improvement in the schooling of gifted children (cf. Coleman, 1961; Katz, 1971; Stanley, 1976). Many recent reports on education recommend a stronger academic program (e.g., National Commission on Excellence in Education, 1983, pp. 19–21, 25–26).

CURRICULUM AS DISCIPLINED KNOWLEDGE

Even the narrow definition of curriculum adopted here requires some elaboration. Terms such as *knowledge, discipline, subjects,* and *courses* need to be defined and related both to one another and, for the purpose of this discussion, to the characteristics of academically and intellectually gifted children.

Knowledge and Disciplines

The quintessential curriculum question has been asked many times, perhaps most memorably by Herbert Spencer, a British philosopher. Spencer exerted a large influence in the United States on the emerging field of developmental psychology (Cremin, 1961). When Spencer (1860/1963) asked, "What knowledge is of most worth?" he had a remarkably ready answer: science.

Was Spencer referring to biology, or perhaps sociology? Spencer meant neither, of course. He was referring to a general way of looking at the world (Cremin, 1961)—in fact, to a discipline.

Phenix (1968) has defined a *discipline* as an organized, academic way of looking at the world. A discipline has a typical object of investigation, a way of investigating (a methodology), and an intellectual history that distinguish it from other disciplines.

Although this definition does not provide a clearcut means of distinguishing fields that are disciplines from fields that are not, in this chapter we do not need to make decisions about whether medicine, nursing, real estate sales, and creative problem-solving are disciplines, whether physics and biology are part of the same discipline, or whether physics is a stronger discipline than biology. It is the abstract notion of a formal body of intellectual knowledge—a discipline—that is important to a consideration of the academic curriculum. Disciplines embody the intellectual legacy, and they exemplify the aims of literacy and rationalism referred to above and in Chapter 1.

The remarkable thing about Spencer's answer to his own question is that he did not hedge. Today a teacher to whom this question is put might well answer something like, "It depends on the child. Interest is an important consideration." Seldom would a teacher make a choice even from among the obvious curriculum alternatives. Spencer's answer, however, was not original. Virtually all progressive thinkers of the nineteenth century (e.g., Darwin, Freud, Marx) agreed with Spencer about the importance of science, though they all conceived its mission somewhat differently.

The elementary and secondary curriculum for gifted children especially (and probably for all children) should introduce academic disciplines of substantial intellectual merit (cf. R. Mitchell, 1979, 1981). In addition to science (as considered by Spencer), literature, mathematics, natural science, history, and social science can also be recognized as comparatively strong academic disciplines. In the discussion below, literature and mathematics are taken to be the "knowledge of most worth."

Literature and Mathematics. Literature and mathematics (broadly conceived) form the basis of virtually all other academic disciplines. Both are applicable to a wide range of social sciences (i.e., anthropology, sociology, psychology). Mathematics is fundamental to all natural sciences, and it has become increasingly important in the social sciences as well. Literature is important for its role in cultivating verbal expression and comprehension, skills without which it is impossible to convey or receive meaning in any field.

Literature deals in the techniques of written expression and communication, such as reading, spelling, grammar, diction, style, and ideation. It also, particularly in fiction, deals with the spiritual, affective, and ethical value dilemmas that have concerned educators (cf. Kohlberg, 1966; Krathwohl, Bloom & Masia, 1964, Williams, 1972). Literature also properly includes imaginative and expository writing and the study of foreign languages. Literature is that component of the curriculum which corresponds most clearly to exceptional verbal ability, a characteristic of many gifted children.

Mathematics encompasses all quantitative aspects of enumeration, calculation, measurement, problem-solving, simulation, and theory. Mathematics is used in our culture to describe the world and to control aspects of it. Mathematics has also been said to be "the queen and handmaiden of the sciences" (Hardy, 1969). Mathematics provides exemplary logical procedures for the sciences and quantitative techniques that constitute the tools with which scientific investigation is conducted (e.g., Butterfield, 1957, pp. 108–128; Heisenberg, 1958, pp. 76–92; Korner, 1960, pp. 177–182; Wiener, 1954, pp. 13–21). Mathematics is the component of the curriculum that relates to those intellectual strengths of academically and intellectually gifted children commonly referred to as "quantitative ability."

In deciding to teach literature and mathematics (in their various subject and course manifestations) to the gifted, we are implicitly choosing to prepare students for future academic work (and not necessarily for complete living; cf. Spencer, 1860/1963). Such preparation, however, should not preclude provision of vocational training for the gifted at the high school level, starting as young as age twelve or fourteen. Recently vocational schools have begun to serve trainable mentally retarded students; there is no reason that gifted students, even at ages younger than sixteen, should not receive vocational training. (See Chapter 6 for a discussion of career, as opposed to vocational, training for the gifted.)

Subjects and Courses

Subjects and courses are the conventional means through which schools conduct instruction in the disciplines. Subjects—English, mathematics, history—are school versions of disciplines. Subjects are interpreted to students of different ages. Above the elementary level subjects are usually taught in a series of year-long or semester-long courses—English II, trigonometry, world history. A course may further be divided into sections, such as honors or remedial sections, to accommodate particular types of students. The disciplines are, however, the source of subjects and courses, and they are the intellectual rationale for teaching particular material at any level (cf. Bruner, 1960).

Ideally, the way in which a subject (English, for example) is divided into courses and sections reflects a coherent view of the discipline and its branches. Unfortunately, however, the courses English I–IV in high school often do not present a representative, current, or coherent image of the discipline of literature. A typical high school English course may involve remedial work in reading, simple grammar exercises, and spelling. In schools where students are grouped by ability, the instructional emphasis in the honors section of the course may be on reading above-grade-level material. Durden (1980) reports that writing, which is of course part of literature, is neglected in most classes.

Disciplines, Knowledge, and the Information Explosion

The "information explosion" has prompted some critics to claim that the conventional subject divisions of the curriculum are outdated. Toffler (1970, p. 157), for example, writes, "Today change is so swift and relentless in the techno-societies that yesterday's truths suddenly become today's fictions, and the most highly skilled and intelligent members of society admit difficulty in keeping up with the deluge of new knowledge."

McLuhan (1964, p. 301) writes that "the conventional division of the curriculum into subjects is already as outdated as the medieval trivium and quadrivium after the Renaissance." Despite these predictions, schools have not yet totally dismantled old subjects or made completely new ones, any more than post-Renaissance scholars cast aside the seven liberal arts: grammar, rhetoric, and logic (the literary trivium) and arithmetic, geometry, astronomy, and harmonics (the mathematical quadrivium).

Whitfield (1971, p. 8) astutely observes that "the factual burden of a discipline varies inversely with its degree of maturity." As disciplines mature, their significant theoretical structures emerge, and facts (bits of information) become much less significant in themselves. In a mature discipline facts become merely illustrative of a valid theoretical construct. The information explosion may represent the evolution of cultural chaos, rather than the growth of knowledge (cf. Wiener, 1950, pp. 41–66, on progress and entropy).

Although the implications of the information explosion for pedagogy are not yet clear, the continued existence of literature and mathematics is hardly to be questioned. In fact, literature and mathematics, as disciplines, comprise the two most coherent systems of symbols for dealing meaningfully with large amounts of information. We hope that curriculum development evolves in such a way as to accommodate to a greater degree the exceptional needs of gifted students for advanced instruction in verbal and quantitative disciplines.

THE ACADEMIC CURRICULUM

Curriculum development for the gifted is often based on the assumption that matters important for gifted children have been omitted from the regular curriculum. Developing qualitatively different programs with specially designed instruction becomes a curriculum development goal in gifted education (see, e.g., Maker, 1982a). Instead of trying to find elements that have been omitted from the regular curriculum, however, educators concerned with gifted children should recognize that the appropriate curriculum for gifted children *includes* elements of the regular curriculum (see Box 7.1).

The regular *curriculum* does contain the knowledge of most worth for gifted children. (This observation is *not* meant to deny that gifted students confront unique problems or that they possess unique strengths, but merely to affirm

---

BOX 7.1   Don't the Gifted Need a Gifted Curriculum?

The word *regular* is nearly synonymous in education with the word *normal*. Since the gifted are not normal, but exceptional, it is logical enough to assume that they require exceptional curriculum as well as exceptional placements (see Chapters 3 and 4).

In a sense, this perception is correct. The accuracy of the perception, however, depends primarily on the perceiver's view of what curriculum is, how it is made, and what its components are.

This text has adopted a narrow definition of curriculum. We believe that curriculum is rarely made anew and that the source of the curriculum is cultural tradition, and a very formalized cultural tradition at that—the academic disciplines. (It is possible and legitimate to view curriculum in other ways.)

Curriculum in the sense in which we have used it is composed not of instructional goals and objectives, but of content, of knowledge. It may comprise, for example, arithmetic (addition, fractions, place value), the skill of reading (decoding, fluent phrasing, comprehension), chemistry (valence, compounds, reactions), music (organum, homophony, twelve-tone row), and so forth.

The regular curriculum *in this sense* is the substance of learning, and regular-class placement is the context in which it is normally cultivated. In our view, the gifted need the knowledge of the regular curriculum as described here. But they also have other academic needs, including the need for a more rapid pace, greater conceptual detail, more frequent opportunities to read and write, alternative routes to demonstrate mastery, and access to advanced instruction.

Only if curriculum is defined to include all the activities of learning (non-cognitive and cognitive experiences; sequence, pace, and method of instruction; goals, objectives, and materials of instruction) is it possible to suggest that the gifted need a very different sort of curriculum. This is not, however, the manner in which we have used the term.

---

that there are certain areas of study that are "of most worth" for all students.) Regular-class *placement* (i.e., chronological age-grade placement) does not, however, deliver this curriculum effectively and efficiently to gifted children.

Programs for the gifted are more widespread today than they were in the 1920s and 1930s (cf. Mitchell, 1981b), but some of them have lost sight of the curriculum in its entirety. Though it is hardly possible to begin with a pedagogically clean slate, we should be able to cite the components that comprise a sound curriculum for the gifted. The task is essentially that of deciding what academic disciplines and related courses, subjects, and basic skills to teach and when to teach them. Chapters 8 and 9 will address in greater detail how such material might best be taught and will help distinguish the proposals of this chapter from their academic antecedents (i.e., the content-centered curriculum, with its burden of factual trivia and emphasis on lower-level thinking skills).

Gifted children do not think better than other children, or in different ways from other children, but they can in general deal with the symbols of academic work more directly and more efficiently. Instruction of gifted children should be concerned more closely with intellectual content and its implications. Typically, the focus of *implementation* of the regular curriculum is less on excellence (cf. Gardner, 1961; National Commission on Excellence in Education, 1983) than on minimum competence (R. Mitchell, 1981). Implementation of the academic curriculum in programs for the gifted should be designed to allow gifted students to use their strengths to maximum advantage.

Curriculum and Individual Differences

The discussion of curriculum development in this chapter focuses on the construction of a comprehensive curriculum, not on construction of individual programs for individual students (cf. Maker, 1982a, pp. 234–250). IEPs (individualized education programs) provide one way to *foster* appropriate education for individual gifted children in an inadequate educational environment. As such, they are crucial tools. The IEP process (see Chapters 3 and 4) should help teachers construct programs that incorporate some of the elements recommended here, even in difficult situations.

If the IEP process alone were sufficient to guarantee appropriate instruction, there would be no need for this chapter. School situations, however, often fall short of what is needed to attain IEP goals or to provide the kind and amount of instruction formally agreed upon in IEPs (cf. Ysseldyke, Algozzine & Mitchell, 1982). Most educators are also justifiably a little baffled as to what may constitute an appropriate curriculum for the gifted.

The curriculum described below is hardly a readymade formula, but it is more explicit than some proposals. The most productive approach to curriculum planning for the gifted seems to involve fitting individual students into appropriate components of a comprehensive curriculum, rather than developing multiple curricula to meet the needs of individual students. Therefore, the curriculum must be based on general characteristics of the gifted as well as on specific characteristics of different types of gifted students. Given such a curriculum, individual programming becomes a matter of flexible scheduling rather than of instructional design.

Curriculum and Types of Gifted Children.   Some student characteristics do need to be considered in applying this curriculum to certain kinds of gifted children. Among the gifted one sometimes needs to distinguish between the academically talented and the intellectually gifted child. In general, both groups share many characteristics (Pendarvis, 1985).

High-IQ gifted children can with reason (and the support of research, e.g., Kulik & Kulik, 1982) be tracked in all subjects or grouped together to allow accelerated programming. Such students can, for example, complete the elementary curriculum in four to six years (Fine, 1964). The curriculum suited to high-IQ children is also suitable for children whose *achievement* scores are two standard deviations above the mean in *several* areas, *whether or not they score in the gifted range on an IQ test*. (See Chapter 2 for a discussion of eligibility determination based on achievement.)

Children who score two standard deviations above the mean in *only one* achievement area and who are *close to the mean in other achievement areas and on an IQ test* will, however, probably have difficulty following a curriculum designed for students whose general academic aptitude is high. They should probably receive differentiated instruction in the area of strength only.

Model Proposals and Programs

Though academic curricula explicitly for gifted students have not been widely implemented in U.S. public schools, several have been proposed. One of the most notable proposals for public education was Conant's 1959 report, which was very influential two decades ago. Implementation of private programs has been reported by Fine (1964) and Gerencser (1979). Recently, academic high schools such as the largely black Banneker High School in Washington, D.C., have also begun to make a reappearance.

Conant's Proposals. James Conant, former chemistry professor and president of Harvard, studied U.S. high schools in the late 1950s. His report, *The American High School Today*, appeared in 1959. Though Conant distinguished between the academically talented and the "highly gifted" (pp. 62–63), his academic recommendations are relevant to the gifted. Conant was chiefly concerned with the top quartile of American high school students, whom he considered to be academically talented by definition. The "highly gifted" he considered to be "pupils of high ability who constitute on a national basis about 3 percent of the student population."

Conant did not believe it was necessary to identify such gifted children earlier than the seventh grade, nor did he feel they required much more than special guidance during high school. He did recommend that gifted students take part in the Advanced Placement Program in the twelfth grade.

Viewing Conant's distinction between the gifted and the academically able as a difference of degree, not of kind, we find value in the Conant proposals for academic content (we shall have more to say about his vocational proposals). Conant's specific proposal for the academically able (top quartile) is as follows:

> Four years of mathematics, four years of one foreign language, three years of science, in addition to the required four years of English and three years of social studies; a total of eighteen courses with homework to be taken in four years. This program will require at least fifteen hours of homework each week.
>
> (Conant, 1959, p. 57)

Conant believed that academically able students *could* take twenty or more academic courses with homework in four high school years. In fact, in his study approximately 4 percent of both male and female high school students (of the class of 1958) *had* taken twenty or more academic courses. Conant also recommended ability grouping for required courses, a minimum grade of C as a prerequisite for advanced academic electives, and election of at least one additional course without homework per year by the academically talented.

Conant's recommendations have not received much attention in curriculum development for the gifted in part because they were couched in terms of his recommendations for the academically able and in part because focus on academic curriculum fell into disrepute among gifted educators during the 1970s.

Report of the National Commission on Excellence in Education. Most of Conant's curriculum proposals have recently been reiterated by the National Commission on Excellence in Education (1983). Because of the decline in support for education, and because of the vitiation of academic programs (documented by the Commission), Conant's proposals suddenly seem more relevant to gifted education. The Commission reported the following findings about academic curriculum content:

> By content we mean the very "stuff" of education, the curriculum. Because of our concern about the curriculum, the Commission examined patterns of courses high school students took in 1964–1969 compared with course patterns in 1976–1981. On the basis of these analyses we conclude:
>
> - Secondary school curricula have been homogenized, diluted, and diffused to the point that they no longer have a central purpose. . . . The proportion of students taking a general program of study has increased from 12 percent in 1964 to 42 percent in 1979.
> - [The] curricular smorgasbord, combined with extensive student choice, explains a great deal about where we find ourselves today. We offer intermediate algebra, but only 31 percent of our recent high school graduates complete it; we offer French I, but only 13 percent complete it; and we offer geography, but only 16 percent complete it. Calculus is available in schools enrolling about 60 percent of all students, but only 6 percent of all students complete it . . . fewer than one-third of U.S. high schools offer physics taught by qualified teachers.
>
> (National Commission on Excellence in Education, 1983, pp. 18–19, 23)

Among the Commission's recommendations were improved offerings in (1) English, (2) mathematics, (3) science, (4) social studies, (5) computer science, and (6) foreign languages. The Commission's report, however, like the Conant report, did not specify academic provisions appropriate for the gifted.

Private Education. Examples of comprehensive academic curricula for the gifted in private schools have been reported by Fine (1964) and Gerencser

(1979). Both Fine and Gerencser have overseen the operation of special schools for the gifted, the Sands Point Country Day School and the Calasanctius School, respectively. Both schools at some point in their history offered K–12 schooling (the Sands Point School has closed; cf. Gonzalez, 1972).

The Sands Point curriculum was rapid paced, according to Fine. By approximately age eight, children were engaging in college-preparatory work at the junior high level, had been studying literature and writing for perhaps two years and had been studying French for five years. Senior high school, which began typically at age eleven (the equivalent of ninth grade), comprised Advanced Placement Program subjects, advanced lab sciences, independent study, and electives. Sands Point was founded with the lower grades, and a high school sequence was added as the school grew.

Sands Point attempted to integrate—or at least show the connections among—the disciplines, according to Fine (1964). He reports that English and social studies were treated as a core program, with the purpose of first introducing students to the culturally and politically significant events and circumstances of the modern and ancient world and then cultivating mastery of the basic tools "that are essential to all future study, both academic and day to day" (Fine, 1964, p. 248).

Music and art were the primary domains of creative efforts at Sands Point, and instruction included art and music history and theory. The music curriculum reported by Fine (p. 103) was excellent. It addressed the following seven goals: (1) recognition of orchestral instruments by sight and sound; (2) discrimination by ear of the musical styles of various periods; (3) ability to read music; (4) recognition and recall of outstanding compositions by a number of outstanding composers; (5) comprehension of musical forms, e.g., cantata, concerto, sonata; (6) comprehension of the history of music, its stages, personalities, and relation to the larger world; and (7) knowledge of the scientific and mathematical bases of music.

In Fine's (1964) account the Sands Point program achieves the status of paragon in many ways—reasonable identification procedures, clearly conceived academic instruction, excellent staff, flexible promotions, rapid pacing, and the sort of awareness of ideas without which meaningful education for the gifted is impossible (cf. Gonzalez, 1972, for a very different view of the school's performance).

This sort of education is, however, very expensive. According to Fine (1964, p. 51), though "many parents know what is best for their children . . . they simply do not have the funds to pay for their education." Fine claims fees were minimized, but reports no information on scholarships.

Gerencser (1979) reports similar work at the Calasanctius School, a private boarding school (see Chapter 5 for a discussion of acceleration at this school.) Its program has expanded from the upper to the lower grades. Promotion is flexible. Though Calasanctius does not *insist* on rapid pacing and early graduation, many students do graduate early, according to Gerencser. Advanced Placement credit *is* required for graduation, and a major final-year project, completion of which is approved by a faculty committee, is also required.

These final projects would probably be acceptable as junior or senior seminar papers in many U.S. colleges.

The curriculum emphasis at Calasanctius is academic. According to Gerencser, Calasanctius students take ten to fifteen subjects weekly, with one to three hours devoted weekly to each subject. The curriculum includes at least six years of history (not, Gerencser stresses, "social studies"), study of which is begun at about age ten. Chinese, German, French, Japanese, Russian, and Spanish are offered to all students from age five onward; upon graduation students are expected to earn AP credit in at least one foreign language. Senior high school seminars on a variety of academic issues are required in each of the three high school years. Colloquia on books replace school assemblies, according to Gerencser.

Though Calasanctius, like Sands Point, is a private school, it has managed to survive for over twenty-five years, and since 1972 has offered a full K–12 program. Since 1957 tuition has increased from $600 to over $2000, but some scholarship help is available. Gerencser (1979, p. 137) claims that "one of the most important achievements . . . was that a good number of children from middle and lower income families and from disadvantaged ethnic groups grew out from their environmental restrictions."

Cautions about Academic Models. The models in Chapter 5 were presented not as paragons or examples of perfection but as examples containing elements of interest for further development. Chapter 6 warned of the shortcomings of enrichment models; skepticism is also needed in examining academic models. Gonzalez (1972) suggests that Sands Point, for example, fell far short of its goals and failed to live up to its stated standards.

We caution the reader about our own model, also. It is, like the public school models above (Commission on Excellence, 1983; Conant, 1956), a proposal. The proposed curriculum that follows is merely *illustrative*. It is incomplete in many respects, for a great deal depends on local priorities and initiatives and on the characteristics of individual students. It is, however, important for teachers of the gifted to have a sense of the *academic options* that ought to be available for academically and intellectually talented students. Our discussion is divided between elementary and secondary levels.

ELEMENTARY CURRICULUM

This section deals with those concerns normally addressed in the first nine years of school (i.e., K–8); the next section, on the secondary curriculum, treats those concerns normally addressed in the last four years of public school (i.e., 9–12). This division is not, of course, the only way of segmenting the curriculum, but it is firmly entrenched in the conventional way of thinking about public schooling. Although junior high schools and middle schools (and even a few remaining ungraded schools) have replaced the traditional elementary/secondary division in some locales, most teachers probably still think of the subject matter covered by these various alternatives as either elementary or secondary in nature.

Another Caution

Studies, knowledge, and intellectual work are unified for an individual. Curriculum descriptions almost necessarily lose this sense of personal unity in the consideration of first this, then that course, strand, or topic. As Dewey (1902/1956) indicated, teachers and students alike should see that one thing leads to another intellectually, and that schools are at best an imperfect social institution for officially promoting learning.

Students need a healthy skepticism about their schooling. Teachers can best nurture this attitude noncognitively, in part by demonstrating their own status as fallible learners.

Pace

In several chapters we have observed that intellectually gifted children acquire concepts earlier and achieve more rapidly than is normal for their chronological age. Virtually every writer in the field has noted or corroborated the observation in some way. There can be little doubt that, as a group, gifted children can cover the same material as their age-cohorts in about two-thirds the time (if the mean IQ of the gifted group is about 130). If mean IQ is somewhat higher, perhaps Hollingworth's estimate of one-half the time is more accurate. Adjusting the pace of the curriculum so as to allow students to complete their work in two-thirds the time would reduce the number of years spent on elementary-level work from nine to six.

In actual practice, the elimination of even two years from the elementary curriculum is considered extreme by many educators. Our personal experience suggests that when parents and/or teachers have been insistent enough to negotiate IEPs that reflect this goal, the negotiated arrangement has been both appropriate and successful. We maintain that most gifted children (e.g., over 60 percent, depending on eligibility criteria) could undertake high school work starting at age twelve.

Gifted children can acquire virtually the same skills as their normal age-peers in a more flexible way. They can mediate more easily between conceptualization and simple drill at the elementary level. Indeed some writers (e.g., Payne, 1981) have suggested that such mediation is necessary for optimal learning among gifted children. This sense of learning may imply the appropriateness of a qualitatively different method of instruction (see Chapters 8 and 9). Instructional objectives used for regular children may not be appropriate for gifted children and usually should be modified.

Underachievement of gifted children in the context of regular-class placement, which is by no means a rare phenomenon, is the result of failure to provide optimal schooling for the gifted. The measured achievement of gifted children in schools is not an adequate guide to what can be expected of the children. Instead, it is a guide to what can be expected of schools at present. The potential of gifted children also represents the potential of schooling generally.

An elementary curriculum that follows a nine-year span is inadequate for gifted children. Curriculum planning for the gifted must take this fact into account. This does not mean, however, that acceleration alone is sufficient for the development of optimal programs.

Basic Skills

If the above position seems a bit extreme to the reader, then the position that most gifted children should acquire all basic skills by age ten may seem provocative. Basic skills are (at least today) what elementary education is all about; elementary education as we have defined it does not end before age thirteen in ordinary practice.

Reading and Arithmetic. By the chronological age of ten, gifted children may no longer require reading instruction per se. Gifted children older than ten should no longer need practice in decoding or general comprehension, as is provided in basal readers at elementary levels. At this age, gifted children should be ready to begin reading more extensive material in literature, history, geography, and natural and social sciences, in preparation for beginning secondary level studies at age twelve. Caution is in order, however, because possession of the perceptual skills needed to read successfully does not necessarily reflect verbal ability (Massoth & Levenson, 1982).

Many teachers believe that reading is the most important skill. This position makes a good deal of sense, regardless of how rapidly gifted children master the skill. Children may need some incidental instruction in how to cope with some kinds of written material, particularly the expository styles of history and science. Unfortunately, reading skills above the basic level are very rarely taught, even at the high school level (Vacca, 1981). Vacca (1981) gives suggestions (intended for secondary teachers) about the sorts of reading/study skills that are appropriate for older gifted elementary students. These reading skills consist of the same sorts of higher-level thinking skills that are often part of enrichment programs for the gifted, but which we believe are best taught in the context of a good academic program (e.g., Bruner, 1960).

Sometime between the ages of eight and twelve, gifted students should have acquired the fundamentals of math computation including decimals and percentages, long division, and the various topics of measurement. Age eleven is perhaps a good time for students to start a pre-algebra course.

Science and social studies are also part of the elementary curriculum, but ordinarily less attention is paid to them. First, many elementary students have not acquired the basic skills to the extent that they can deal effectively with more complex nonfiction texts. Second, teachers spend much less time preparing social studies or science activities than they do preparing reading or mathematics projects, centers, stations, enrichment activities, and so forth (Rosenshine, 1981). In many ways, science and social studies are quite incidental to elementary instructional practice, if not to the formalized curriculum plan. According to Rosenshine (1981, p. 18), "Other academic activities [i.e., other than reading, language arts, and arithmetic] namely, discussion and manipulation in social studies and science, occur for 8 minutes a day in second grade and 17 minutes a day in the fifth grade."

Handwriting.   Poor handwriting seems to be a characteristic of gifted children in general (Freeman, 1979). By the age of eight or ten, gifted children's handwriting may have fallen well behind their cognitive performance. Handwriting is a motor skill by and large, and it seems that motor development does not usually keep pace with intellectual development (cf. Gallagher, 1975). Programs for gifted children aged ten and under should probably not require more written work than the regular program. That is, even when children are studying at more advanced levels, where more written work is usually required, they should not be required to do more handwriting than other ten year-olds.

Required written work should not be busywork. It should have a purpose that is accessible to the student. Payne (1981, p. 20), in his discussion of the mathematics curriculum for gifted children, asserts a very reasonable rule of thumb for assigning written work: "Talented students should be expected to show enough work, presented in an orderly manner, to enable the teacher to follow easily what has been done."

Note that the process described by Payne (1981) is a dynamic one between student and teacher; the teacher should not require more information than is necessary to confirm learning or unmask problems. Typical classrooms require, as seatwork, more handwriting than is necessary to enable the teacher to work with small groups (Rosenshine, 1981). Box 7.2 differentiates between the purposes of handwriting and those of writing exercises.

Advanced Skills and Content Areas

Between the ages of eight and ten, gifted students need to begin to work more formally (i.e., less incidentally) on the content of disciplines. This phase of the curriculum might be conceived of as a presecondary sequence for gifted children, and should continue until students reach approximately age twelve.

Foreign Languages.   Our schools *should* introduce foreign languages at the elementary level. They lag behind the rest of the developed world *shamefully* in this regard; the shame is intellectual, not merely political and economic (Durden, 1980).

Foreign language instruction is, of course, appropriate for all students (see Chapter 5). In fact, courts in West Virginia have recently mandated foreign language instruction beginning in fourth grade. Because schools have not

BOX 7.2   Handwriting, Writing, and Advanced Work

A DISTINCTION: WHEN IS HANDWRITING NOT WRITING?

A distinction must be made between handwriting and writing. The two terms are often used interchangeably, though handwriting is a lower-order (visual motor) skill and writing is properly a higher-order (intellectual) skill. Handwriting is never writing.

Handwriting is the physical act of forming letters and words. The object of handwriting instruction is to shape habits of neatness, orderliness, attention to detail, and efficiency.

Writing, on the other hand, is concerned with expressing ideas, images, information, and preceptions. The instructional emphasis in learning to write is on grammar, diction, clarity, and style. (See pp. 217 and 282 for further discussion.)

Though teachers sometimes attempt things other than drill in handwriting lessons, they are not often successful in the attempt. Strict attention to neatness, orderliness, attention to detail, and efficiency (when a child is learning handwriting) are not compatible with clarity, style, and a concern for expression.

Writing is best carried out in a very different context from that which surrounds typical handwriting lessons. See Koch's (1970) *Wishes, Lies, and Dreams* for suggestions on teaching imaginative writing.

AN EXAMPLE: MATH AS THE PRISONER OF HANDWRITING

The assignment of a great deal of written work to a child who is under ten years old is not *necessary* in an efficient instructional sequence. For example, suppose an eight-year-old gifted child is working in a fifth grade math book at a rapid pace.

There is no reason for the child to complete every exercise in the book. Exercises can be sampled. Suppose fifty problems are included in the book to allow students to practice the skill. Depending on the teacher's understanding of the child's abilities, five, ten, or fifteen problems can be assigned to the gifted child who is progressing rapidly through the text.

This sample of the problems should, if the teacher's judgment is accurate, provide sufficient practice and permit the teacher to check the child's grasp of the principle involved. The assignment of all fifty problems not only would prove burdensome to the child, but also would make high-level learning the hostage of low-level learning.

generally implemented foreign language instruction, however, gifted teachers *must* advocate it.

Foreign language study for gifted students should begin when they are between six and eight years old (cf. Fine, 1964). Studies have demonstrated that younger students are more flexible in acquiring foreign languages than older students (Andersson, 1969; Bruck, Lambert & Tucker, 1977). Waiting until students master formal English grammar may be a dangerous delay (cf.

Sizer, 1984). Bright children especially need an early introduction to foreign languages (Durden, 1980; Fine 1964; Gerencser, 1979).

Ideally a choice of languages should be offered (Gerencser, 1979). However, the introduction of any foreign language is still such a novel idea that when schools do make the option available to young students, any choice among languages will be uncommon indeed.

A vigorous program in foreign language instruction at all levels would substantially improve the quality of our schooling, and it would benefit large numbers of children. For the gifted, however, such instruction is essential, even in the absence of a larger commitment from the educational establishment (cf. Durden, 1980). Foreign language study is not by any means a frill. The Japanese, the West Europeans, the Russians, and the Chinese are not in doubt about this issue.

The basic skill of foreign language competence can be exploited to deliver more advanced instruction. A completely implemented foreign language program could teach the basics and the presecondary content mentioned above bilingually. This option is clearly feasible in areas of the country in which there are a number of bilingual teachers, or in regions that have implemented bilingual programs for children acquiring English as a second language, such as the Southwest. Bruck, et al. (1977) have reported extensively on a successful French-English bilingual program. Bilingual content instruction was impressively successful with this sample, which, incidentally, was composed of normal, not gifted, students.

Andersson (1969), writing at the end of a period of intense growth (mainly in secondary schools) of foreign language instruction, said that the United States could hardly have devised a less efficient way to teach foreign languages, even by intention. He described the struggle for inception and support for good programs as a struggle against mediocrity. He too noted the need for longer-term and broader-based courses of study in foreign languages.

His suggestions for improvement are logical enough:

> Opportunity for the study of at least one foreign language should be extended to the high schools that still have no such instruction. The widely prevalent two-year sequence should be extended first to three years, in grades ten to twelve; then to four, in grades nine to twelve; then to six, in grades seven to twelve; and should finally be articulated completely with a program in the elementary school.
>
> (Andersson, 1969, p. 11)

Unfortunately the situation at present is probably worse than it was in 1969 (National Commission on Excellence in Education, 1983). Some critics still maintain that Foreign Language in the Elementary School (FLES) is inessential. The lack of many precedents or much interest among U.S. public schools in FLES is a serious threat, of course, to its commendation. There is *no way* to justify FLES empirically except to note the vigorous efforts of other nations.

Philosophically, culturally, and intellectually, however, foreign language instruction is fully justified.

English. The study of English (grammar, composition, and literature) should replace the study of reading (decoding skills) when gifted children are somewhere between eight and ten years old. Development of good writing skills (see Box 7.2), in particular, ought to be an early goal for gifted children.

Pendarvis (1983) found that at present gifted children's written language is virtually indistinguishable from that of average children. Nine- and ten-year-old gifted children ought to be writing short expository papers of perhaps 200 to 500 words. Imaginative writing is at least as important as expository writing for students eight to twelve years old. Longer prose pieces are probably easier to elicit in the imaginative format.

Gifted children ought to be schooled in the skills of editing and revising what they write. Too often these children (in regular placements, where creative writing may be confused with simple compositional grammar) see their work accepted and praised without understanding or criticism, just because it exhibits better grammar than that of their peers. The skills of writing cannot be learned without criticism and example (Koch, 1970, 1973; Koch & Farrell, 1981), and so it is no wonder that the writing of gifted children suffers (Durden, 1980). Writing, carefully reading and re-reading what one writes, and re-working material are essential cycles in learning to write, just as they are in writing. Children need adult models in this respect, and they need the example of adults who can work with their writing critically and yet with appreciative insight.

Children should begin to study American and British literature at about age ten, or even earlier if they are fluent readers (e.g., reading at the seventh or eighth grade level). (There is of course no reason except tradition and cultural accessibility to study American and British literature instead of European literature in translation.)

At age ten, fluent readers can appreciate some aspects of adult classics (see Box 7.3 for examples). Though children at this age will find portions of some works baffling, obscure, or only partially accessible (cf. Durden, 1980), dealing with such works and with such ambiguities will provoke intellectual growth. Difficult reading will, in fact, help children develop higher-level thinking skills. Adult works can, should, and *often will* be re-read at a more mature age. The re-reading will be a more fruitful, less naive venture because of the earlier introduction.

Unfortunately reading of some of the titles listed will not be viable in some communities. Our experience, however, is that fluent young readers often discover these works on their own when they begin to tire of Nancy Drew. *There are many alternatives to the titles listed.* Any attempt at a consistent treatment of literature is better than binding students to a basal text written below the students' instructional level.

The important point to remember in making selections is that books for

BOX 7.3   Illustrative Literature Selections (Novels Only: Ten Years Old and Older)

Classic—British

Austen	*Pride and Prejudice*
Bronte	*Jane Eyre*
Defoe	*Robinson Crusoe*
	Moll Flanders
Dickens	*David Copperfield*
	Hard Times
	Oliver Twist
Hardy	*The Mayor of Casterbridge*
Scott	*Ivanhoe*

Classic—American

Cooper	*The Deerslayer*
Dreiser	*An American Tragedy*
Twain	*Huckleberry Finn*

Contemporary—American and British

Fitzgerald	*The Great Gatsby*
Forster	*A Room with a View*
Heller	*Catch-22*
Hemingway	*A Farewell to Arms*
	For Whom the Bell Tolls
Vonnegut	*Cat's Cradle*
Waugh	*The Loved One*

Other Literatures

Hamsun	*Growth of the Soil*
Hesse	*Siddhartha*
Kafka	*Metamorphosis*
Solzhenitsyn	*One Day in the Life of Ivan Denisovich*
Zola	*Germinal*

These are ambitious selections, but many of these titles have been read by bright children of our acquaintance. Moreover, all of them deal with life situations with which gifted children are frequently concerned by the age of ten or twelve. There is no reason that they should not have these works as their official reading (literature) experiences, rather than juvenile or bowdlerized fiction.

Some school systems, however, are cautious in their selection of what might be considered controversial literature. In such cases, teachers of the gifted might select classic works of children's literature. For example, they might consider the following works:

Alcott	*Little Women*
Buck	*The Good Earth*
de Angeli	*The Door in the Wall*

Forbes	*Johnny Tremaine*
L'Engle	*A Wrinkle in Time*
	The Arm of the Starfish
Rawlings	*The Yearling*
Tolkien	*The Lord of the Ring*
Twain	*Tom Sawyer*

Teachers who are developing or designing a curriculum should realize that three or four such novels will suffice for a year's instruction at this level. Others can be assigned as independent reading. Students who have not been following an appropriate curriculum may find some of the illustrative works too difficult. Others (e.g., Alcott, Buck, Solzhenitsyn) ought to be accessible to most students reading at the seventh grade level.

this age group should not be too philosophical, too symbolic, or too experimental in their prose. For example, although *Wuthering Heights* would prove suitable in many cases, Thomas Mann's *The Magic Mountain* would not. Similarly, Ken Kesey's *One Flew Over the Cuckoo's Nest* presents complex issues in simple language, whereas the same author's *Sometimes a Great Notion* presents a tangle of profound issues in an enthralling web of narrative voice-changes that most ten-year-olds (and many adults) would find impenetrable.

Social Studies.   The progressives coined the term *social studies* to suggest the breadth of the effort necessary to understand and transform society (cf. Dewey, 1916/1961). Today the social reconstructionist content of the social studies has all but vanished. According to McNeil (1981, p. 284), ''The social studies curriculum is in disarray.'' We agree with Gerencser (1979) that history ought to be taught instead of an ill-defined social studies curriculum. Separate social science courses (i.e., sociology, psychology, anthropology, and political science) are best left until high school or college (see Chapter 6 for the place of mini-courses in enrichment programming, however).

Gerencser (1979) believes that gifted children should begin the formal study of history at about age ten. We concur; gifted children should be ready at about this age to read secondary history texts and some original sources as well. Instruction in the basics of geography should be started as a prerequisite to the study of history by age eight.

Systems of government can and should be taught in an historical context. Though the U.S. system of government is usually taught as the most significant achievement of history (Fitzgerald, 1979), the study of history should include a more objective consideration of other nations' histories and political systems.

Sciences.   Elementary science instruction is often more disjointed than instruction in social studies. For one thing, science lacks the overarching social intent of the social studies curriculum as originally conceived. Also, regular elementary school students do not have the intellectual or mathematics background to make sense of science in a disciplined way.

Much elementary science instruction takes place in unrelated topical discussions that introduce generalized concepts assumed to characterize the sciences. This sort of instruction is properly viewed as relevant enrichment. It is enrichment because it is not essential instruction (see e.g., Rosenshine, 1981); it is relevant because it addresses substantive concerns that will emerge as important later on.

Under the curriculum illustrated here, gifted students will possess the math calculation and conceptual fluency that are prerequisites for beginning a study of science based on the distinctions of discipline. Therefore, the curriculum should include a general science *course* that will introduce students of about age ten to the disciplined content of chemistry, biology, physics, and perhaps the social sciences. Bright children wonder what these disciplines do—they should get their answers early, in sufficient detail. The topical treatment of most elementary science programs obstructs the child's access to this knowledge by focusing on phenomena rather than disciplines.

Mathematics.   Because mathematics is an axiom-based logical structure with powerful theoretical organizing principles, considerable attention should be paid to that structure even in arithmetic instruction for the gifted (Kersh & Reisman, 1985). Introducing the ideas behind arithmetic algorithms and applications is essential to pique young students' interest in higher math. After children reach age ten, the conceptual content of mathematics (as opposed to arithmetic) should predominate in their studies. Gifted children should normally have completed acquisition of arithmetic skills by age ten or eleven.

One way to promote the transition from arithmetic (as a school subject) to mathematics (as a discipline) is through a course in pre-algebra. Though this may not be the ideal solution, it does seem practical for several reasons:

1. Algebra is normally the first secondary course in mathematics.
2. Even gifted ten-year-old students may find the combination of letters (variables and constants) and numbers, and the manipulations implied by the combination, confusing at first.
3. In many districts the "new math," which stressed concept acquisition and manipulation, is sadly defunct; many teachers may be teaching a basic (i.e., algorithmic) approach to math computation.

Teachers should choose a pre-algebra text that stresses *concepts*, not computation. For example, the Merrill pre-algebra text features a great deal of computation and is too repetitious for mathematically apt students; the Houghton Mifflin pre-algebra text has a more conceptual emphasis. Teaching arithmetic algorithmically to gifted students is dangerous. It conditions them to attend to procedures and to ignore the logical structure of mathematics.

Some—perhaps many—gifted children can do well in a complete algebra course at age ten or eleven. Mathematically precocious youngsters are often able to make rapid progress in conceptual math because of its sequential logic. Elementary programs should be prepared for this eventuality.

Additional Curriculum Elements. In discussing handwriting, above, we noted gifted children's typical difficulty with this skill. Therefore, we believe that both *typing* and computer *operation* should be taught to gifted students starting at as early as age eight. Typing is actually a prerequisite for efficient computer operation (Hofmeister, 1984). The juxtaposition of instruction in both areas should make learning of the two subjects mutually reinforcing. Students who receive consistent instruction (e.g., two to five hours per week in computer software use and typing) should be moderately proficient by age ten. Thomas (1982) believes that students are ready to learn *programming* about the same time they are ready to begin the study of algebra.

Curriculum Summary (Elementary)

See Box 7.4 for a summary of our illustrative elementary curriculum. We must stress again that the summary and our discussion are merely illustrative. We have tried only to suggest some of the possible academic alternatives. We hope that readers can create others, equally suitable.

We have not provided an exact scope and sequence because individual schools can develop such documents on their own. We have indicated the relevant subjects, the relation of these subjects to the disciplines of mathematics and literature, the approximate subject level for each age, and the pace of the overall program.

The parameters of the above curriculum (pace, ages, scope, sequence) will need to be adjusted to fit local circumstances. The development of a complete curriculum with objectives and materials based on our illustration is difficult, but familiar, pedagogical work.

The most pressing question we have, necessarily, left unanswered. That is, how does one induce the local board of education or state department of education to endorse, fund, and support the implementation of such a program? Consult Mitchell (1981a) for some principles of gifted education advocacy. A number of the curriculum texts cited in this chapter (e.g., McNeil, 1981; Oliva; Schaffarzick & Hampson, 1975) also provide extensive treatment of curriculum change.

SECONDARY CURRICULUM

The secondary curriculum for gifted students ought to be based on the skills that gifted children can be expected to have acquired in elementary school. (Again, by secondary curriculum we mean the sorts of material usually treated in public school grades 9–12.) As discussed in the section on elementary curriculum, these skills should include (for a typical twelve-year-old gifted student) reading and math achievement above the ninth grade level. Many gifted children of this age will be reading above the norm for twelfth grade students. If their program has followed some of our recommendations, it also will have included one year of introductory studies in literature, a first course in algebra, and instruction in a foreign language.

BOX 7.4 Illustrative Elementary Curriculum for Gifted Children (Ages Four to Twelve)

Chronological Age at IQ 130	Discipline	Basic Skills	Particulars
4 to 5	literature	reading writing	alphabet sight words (Dolch, etc.) manuscript handwriting basal readers 1^1–1^2 and up language experience reading
	mathematics	numeration addition money	counting 1–100$^+$ sets addition, sums to eighteen (subtraction) place value reading large numbers coins, money incidental introduction of advanced notions
6 to 7	literature	reading writing foreign language	graphemic irregularities word analysis, syllabication basal readers 2^2–5^2 and up poetry personal and business letters cursive handwriting foreign language

	mathematics	addition
		subtraction
		multiplication
		division
		measurement:
		  length, area,
		  volume,
		  time
			regrouping (subtraction, addition, multiplication)
			subtraction
			multiplication facts
			short division (beginning)
			word problems (including multiple solutions, no solutions, multiple steps)
			measurement (concept—including *rate*)

8 to 9	literature	(reading) grammar writing vocabulary foreign language typing	(basal readers 3^1 and up for those still in need of reading instruction) parts of speech/agreement creative and expository writing—no more handwriting, except in unusual cases JHS vocabulary-building basic geographical concepts foreign language: more reading and writing

Chronological Age at IQ 130	Discipline	Basic Skills	Particulars
8 to 9 (cont.)	mathematics	multiplication long division measurement fractions decimals graphing special topics	basic facts through 12s two- and three-digit divisors approximately fifth to eighth grade level addition, subtraction, multiplication, division place value; (beginning) metrics types, applications of graphs probability, variables, logic
10 to 11	literature	American and British literature grammar writing history foreign language	teacher selections; less preferably, seventh or eighth grade anthology phrases, diagramming, diction, effective sentences European and American history overview formal grammar, literature selections (excerpts, short stories), journals
	mathematics	review of basic skills (15 percent) pre-algebra (85 percent) science disciplines computer use	variables, equations, linear graphs introductions to biology, chemistry, physics, astronomy, and perhaps to sociology and psychology as social sciences BASIC, word processing

Algebra, literature, and foreign language courses taken in the elementary program should replace freshman English and Algebra I at the high school level. In addition, students should receive one to three years' foreign language credit, based on normative testing of their achievement (cf. Sizer, 1984). Students should also know how to type school papers and operate a microcomputer for at least routine uses (e.g., word processing and software applications).

If high school requirements are based on Carnegie Units or some other system of credit-toward-graduation point accrual, these lower-level courses *should be credited as if they had been secondary courses*. This will enable gifted students to start high school with advanced standing.

College Preparation and Academics

The postsecondary plans of virtually all gifted high school students include earning a college degree. Tidwell (1980) surveyed almost 1600 gifted secondary students. The mean IQ of Tidwell's sample was 137; the chronological age range was fourteen to seventeen. Personal needs and life goals of these students were overwhelmingly academic in nature (i.e., their needs were either in the achievement/intellectual or aesthetic needs category on Maslow's Hierarchy of Needs).

Tidwell (1980) found that 49 percent of the 1600 gifted high school students in her California sample planned to pursue advanced degrees (above the B.A. level). About half of those planning to get advanced degrees projected they would earn doctorates. About 10 percent of her sample aspired to skilled and semiskilled occupations. Most of these students *also* reported that a college degree was their educational goal.

The two goals are not incompatible. In fact, probably a greater proportion of gifted students would express an interest in vocational training (as distinguished from career education programs which have a professional or managerial content) if they believed there were room in their high school schedules for such training.

Distribution Requirements

In contrast to elementary schools, high schools usually have permitted some degree of student choice in the selection of a program. Selection of courses is conditioned by the way in which high school instruction has been traditionally offered, i.e., by specialized faculty in separately scheduled classes.

Conant (1959) presented a format for high school education for the academically talented that did not allow much room for choice. Our concerns are somewhat different from Conant's, though we share his concern and that of the National Commission on Excellence in Education (1983) for academic standards.

Our conception of the cognitive press necessary to promote high standards for the performance of gifted students has three provisions that affect education at the secondary level:

1. That gifted elementary students be accelerated an average of two years during the first nine years of school. (This provision permits gifted students to begin secondary-level work at age twelve.)
2. That they enter high school with, on average, one to three Carnegie Units or their equivalent of high school credit (in Algebra I, English, and/or a foreign language). (This provision is competency-based and it validates students' earlier work.)
3. That the curriculum be divided between disciplines of literature and mathematics, which allows us to address the question of program balance and distribution requirements.

The advanced standing credit referred to in item three constitutes one to three of the eighteen courses with homework recommended by Conant (1959). By Conant's standards, then, gifted students need to accumulate the equivalent, on average, of sixteen or more high school courses, which may be earned through any of the dual attendance arrangements discussed in Chapter 5, independent summer study, or formally organized summer programs.

In many, probably most, cases high school work could be accomplished in three years. It *could* be a common phenomenon, as it is in Europe and as it once was in this country, for gifted students to begin their undergraduate experience (or advanced vocational training) at age fifteen or sixteen.

The question of how to distribute secondary courses is addressed by the distinction between mathematical disciplines and disciplines of literature, by which we mean something more than the study of fiction and pure mathematics. These disciplines might more conventionally be called the humanities and the sciences (cf. Whitfield, 1971). We continue to use the terms *literature* and *mathematics*, however, both for their historical associations from Plato forward and their status as paragons among disciplines. We classify, for example, the following high school subjects under the rubric of literature: English, foreign languages, history, and social sciences. We classify the following high school subjects under the rubric of mathematics: mathematics, natural sciences, statistical aspects of social sciences, and history of science.

The preceding division, of course, is not the only one possible. We believe that the object of the social sciences (human beings) and its largely narrative exposition make it a discipline of literature at the high school level (particularly if its statistical aspects are not taught.) Similarly, since the object of the history of science is the study of science, we classify it as science. We could have classified these two fields differently, or left them out altogether. (They are, after all, rather uncommon offerings in high school). The point is that some division is possible and useful.

Our distribution recommendation is that imbalances in a student's program *not exceed a 2:1 ratio* between the more favored and less favored discipline. Such a proviso is required to enforce a compromise between the cultural pressures for technical specialization and the intellectual imperative to become well read. A 2:1 ratio allows a great deal of choice, if state and local requirements for graduation can be met flexibly. If a gifted program's developers thought it wise to promote less student choice, a 5:3 or even 1:1 ratio would make sense.

A typical high school student's academic program will include literature (as English), foreign language, history (most often U.S. history), perhaps a year of "civics" (i.e., U.S. political institutions), and several years of mathematics and natural science. Social sciences, statistics for social and natural science, and topical literature courses are less common. Box 7.5 gives some sample three- and four-year schedules for gifted high school students. Note that these schedules are constructed to reflect a range of student aptitudes, achievement, IQ, and interest. Courses with homework are calculated ac-

BOX 7.5 Sample Schedules (High School)

STUDENT A

Advanced Standing:

- Algebra I
- English I
- French I and II

First Year:

- Geometry
- French III
- U.S. History
- English II
- Biology
- Auto Shop I

Second Year:

- Algebra II
- Chemistry
- Auto Shop II
- French IV
- German I
- European History
- English III

Third Year:

- Transmission Repair
- Physics
- Calculus
- German III (German II in summer)
- Electronics
- English IV

Total courses with homework: 21
Literature/math ratio: 13:8

STUDENT B

First Year:

- English I
- Spanish I
- Biology
- Geometry
- Algebra II (Algebra I as Advanced Standing)
- Chorus
- Piano

Second Year:

- English II
- English III
- Physics
- Calculus
- Spanish II
- Statistics
- Chorus
- Piano

Third Year:

- Matrix Algebra
- English IV
- Electronics
- Spanish III
- Differential Equations
- Chorus
- Piano

Fourth Year:

- U.S. History
- Chorus
- Piano
- History of Science
- Russian I

Total courses with homework: 20
Math/literature ratio: 9:11

STUDENT C

First Year:

Honors English (I and II)
Algebra I
Biology
U.S. History
German I
Drafting

Summer (end of the first year):

Ancient Literature
German II

Second Year:

Geometry
European History
Ancient History
Latin I
Chemistry

Third Year:

Algebra II
English IV
Latin II
Statistics
German III
History of Science

Total courses with homework: 19
Literature/math ratio: 12:7

STUDENT D

Advanced Standing:

Algebra I, II
French I, II, III
English I

First Year:

Calculus
Physics
Statistics
Honors English (II)

Summer (end of the first year):

Differential Equations
English III (high school)
German I (high school)

Second Year:

U.S. History
Chemistry
German II
Thermodynamics*
Matrix Algebra*

Third Year:

German III
Organic Chemistry*
Hydraulics*
Logic and Boolean Algebra*
Humanities 101*

Total courses with homework: 23
Math/literature ratio: 12:11

*Dual attendance course

cording to the Conant conception (e.g., though student B practices the piano, the piano instruction is not counted as a class with homework).

Arrangements should be made to encourage gifted students to acquire a vocational competence in high school, in addition to pursuing the academic college-preparatory program. They should be permitted to elect a full training course, such as masonry or auto mechanics, starting at age fourteen. In general, vocational programs do not permit such specialization until age sixteen, i.e., not until the junior year in high school. Abbreviating a vocational course by eliminating the preliminaries that usually accompany such programs (cf. Jackson, 1981) can permit students to complete high school with both academic and vocational preparation by age seventeen or eighteen.

In actual practice, however, few gifted children are likely to pursue vocational programs without active recruitment (Micklus, 1981). If vocational training requires gifted students to spend an additional year or two in high school, following completion of a four-year academic program, the current poor representation of the gifted in manual training programs will persist.

Course Load

Conant (1959) found that 4 percent of students in his sample took twenty or more courses with homework during their four years in high school. Contemporary gifted students who took six such courses per year could match Conant's maximum figure in three years, provided they attained pre-entrance standing in English and algebra. The normal academic course load per year in U.S. high schools, where major classes meet for five sessions per week, is five courses. Students who took just one major course per summer session (or independently during the summer) could in three years take twenty major courses (again, counting advanced standing), eliminating one year from the high school sequence.

We know from the work of SMPY, however, that mathematics does not have to be taught in the rigid framework of five periods per week, one course per year. Very talented students who want to progress rapidly have done so in SMPY. Less talented students could doubtless progress somewhat more rapidly than they are now permitted—perhaps at twice the rate of ordinary precalculus classes.

Much of what is scheduled as work in English classes (especially when these classes are heterogeneously organized) may not be appropriate for gifted students. In high school, gifted students need practice reading advanced materials, not textbooks, and writing in a variety of modes. A coordinated history *and* English program with much reading and writing (i.e., perhaps one or two books per week and three or four papers per semester) which met five or six hours per week, yielding high school credit in both history and English, would be appropriate for the last two years of high school (i.e., for gifted students aged fourteen to sixteen).

It is important to remember that a program that requires a lot of reading must provide the time and the impetus for the reading to be done. Though ordinary textbook reading assignments in high school are not long, they frequently go unread (Rieck, 1977). In fact, Rieck believes that a sizable proportion of high school teachers model poor reading habits for their students. Rieck found, however, that students did read assignments when their teachers modeled good reading habits, by showing interest in and discussing readings, examining related sources, and directing students to pay attention to particular issues in the readings. It should therefore be possible to base courses in literature (used in the generic sense we have indicated) on wide reading, provided both teachers and students are given time in their schedules to do the reading and the expectation that the reading will be done is consistently iterated.

Ordinarily, of course, this sort of reading is not encountered until students begin college. Then bright students, who have been assigned an occasional complete novel in the high school curriculum, may suddenly find that they have to read as much or more than a thousand pages per week in literature, philosophy, and history. They may also find that they have to write ten or more pages per week to show their involvement in their readings. *At present, many gifted students are not prepared for such an experience.*

Advanced-Level Courses

In order to accommodate both gifted students and academically talented students in Conant's (1959) top quartile, some advanced-level courses should be included in the curriculum.

English. Elective alternatives to required courses are especially needed in English, where the electives should in many cases take the place of the nearly ubiquitous English I–IV sequence. Individual evaluation of bright students can provide the data necessary to determine the appropriateness of such alternatives. For gifted students, the results of such evaluations need to be considered in IEP development according to exceptional child procedures. An honors section for students apt in English is one popular and very practical way to address this need.

History. History courses for the gifted should reach beyond the required U.S. history. If enough alternatives were offered (the number would not have to be great; three or four would probably suffice), it would not be unreasonable to require three or four years of history of all academically talented students.

A year of civics and two years of U.S. history give students an unrealistic, ethnocentric view of both history and contemporary world affairs. By contrast, one year each of European history, U.S. history, South American history, and a topical course such as the modern history of the Far East, the industrial revolution, or historiography would introduce the scope of historical issues to academically talented high school students.

Foreign Languages. At a minimum, high schools ought consistently to offer a four-year course in two foreign languages (Andersson, 1969). Gifted students ought (at least until U.S. schools achieve a twelve-year fully articulated language program for all students) to be able to test out of one, two, or (in more rare cases) three years of foreign language at the high school level. They should receive high school credit for demonstrated achievement.

Ideally a high school ought to offer instruction in five or six foreign languages, such as Chinese, French, German, Japanese, Latin, Russian, and Spanish. Conant (1959, p. 69) advised, "The school board should be ready to offer a third and fourth year of a foreign language, no matter how few students enroll." This advice could be expanded to include the addition of more languages to the curriculum.

Mathematics. Mathematics through introductory differential and integral calculus (two semesters) should be offered in all high schools. It is imperative that it be available for gifted students. In addition, other courses aside from the typical secondary precalculus sequence of algebra, geometry, and trigonometry need to be offered. Possible additions could include statistics, differential equations, matrix algebra, and an additional calculus course.

Science. Many high schools do not offer physics on a regular basis. Like calculus, physics is a necessary subject for the gifted. In addition, science departments that offer the minimum sequence of biology, chemistry, and physics ought to consider adding electives in electronics, the history of science, or organic chemistry, for example (cf. Melzer, 1980).

Social Sciences. It is rare for a high school to have a social science department. We believe that a separate social science department might be necessary if the traditions of the social sciences are to be distinguished from those of history and social studies. The goal should be for students to acquire the content of introductory college courses in these subjects and to earn credit (college and high school) for such achievement. The best approach would include the use of a college text.

If the goal of such proposed social science courses is to introduce high school students to the nature and methods of several of these disciplines, however, an elective in the history of science is perhaps the best option. Such a course can usefully contrast the social and natural sciences. The Bronx High School of Science has, at times, offered a history of science course to its talented science students (Melzer, 1980).

Vocational Training

Though vocational training has been part of U.S. education for over a century, very little has been done to identify students who may have performance aptitudes relevant to particular trades. No doubt the difficulty arises in part from the changing nature of manual labor. Automation and the shift from an economy based on industrial production to one based on sales and service ("information") has diminished the need for manual labor. The level of skill required of manual workers has been lowered in some industries, whereas new skilled positions have emerged in other industries.

Continued economic changes tend to reduce the skill levels of even new positions rather quickly, however (cf. Bernstein, 1983; Bowles & Gintis, 1976; Poulantzas, 1975; Wright, 1979). Even the "high-tech" jobs associated with cybernetic trades will not be numerous; they are already becoming less secure and less well paid than was once the case (Bernstein, 1983; cf. Wiener, 1950).

Despite these difficulties with the job market, training programs should be available to students who have exceptional fine or gross motor skills, hand-eye coordination, dexterity, and task-organization skills and to students whose out-of-school interests or backgrounds might suit them to particular sorts of work.

Teachers of the gifted need, in vocational education as in academic education, to consider the issues of pace and valid content carefully. Perhaps as many as 25 percent of gifted students could be expected to elect an abridged vocational program; however, one should not expect the academically talented to seem nearly so talented manually as they are academically. The fact that such students may not make excellent grades in the vocational program should not be an impediment to their electing vocational training. Transcripts of gifted students who elect vocational training might contain a separate calculation of vocational grades, or academically talented students might receive pass/fail grades for vocational courses.

CURRICULUM CHANGE

The curriculum set forth in this chapter is illustrative. It represents an approach quite different from some of the enrichment provisions described in Chapter 6. The major concern of this chapter has been to illustrate the *content* of the curriculum, not the *process* of curriculum development. This focus reflects our view of eligibility, program development, and placement. The chapter indicates, among other things, what sort of academic knowledge ought to be taught to gifted students.

The chapter indicates the content that is appropriate for gifted students under *optimum* circumstances. Most situations are, however, less than optimal. This fact implies the need for curriculum coordination and development.

There are a great many texts available on curriculum planning and curriculum processes in general (e.g., Brubaker, 1982; Cook & Doll, 1973; Doll, 1982; Firth & Kimpston, 1973; Maker, 1982a, 1982b; McNeil, 1981; Oliva, 1982; Saylor, Alexander & Lewis, 1981; Schaffarzick & Hampson, 1975). Interested readers might consult several of these texts for additional suggestions about curriculum development after reading the following discussion.

Curriculum Coordination

Using the IEP process, teachers of the gifted in public schools should be able to *approximate* a curriculum similar to the one above for individual students. Keeping subsequent years in mind and making whatever ad hoc plans are possible will in some situations be all that the teacher can do by way of curriculum coordination.

One should expect that for some time to come gifted students will require special assistance if suitable programs are to be negotiated for them. Because of experience and interest, the teacher of the gifted may be the only adult keeping the child's entire public school progress in view. Regular classroom teachers and administrators may attribute too much importance to the value of keeping children with their age-mates; they may fail to understand the implications of cognitive competence; or they may be unwilling to take risks in making provisional placements. Parents may, to a lesser degree, share these propensities, misapprehensions, or misconceptions.

Teachers of the gifted need to remember that each exception that is successfully made for a gifted child will have implications for future options. For example, the issue of how high school credit can be awarded early may become palpable if a child completes just one year in a cross-class math placement, or if IEP goals for advanced math instruction in a pull-out program are completed. Repetition of such successes may eventually result in curriculum and policy changes. Until such changes are made, however, someone needs to take the responsibility for creating the conditions for small successes. Teachers of the gifted are the most likely—if not the only—institutional staff members to make this contribution.

It may sometimes be possible for a group of gifted teachers to agree to promote academically relevant programs for gifted children in administrative discussions, in addition to negotiating particular arrangements for individual children. Occasionally teachers of the gifted may be able to formalize and put into practice some of the academic options discussed above through participation in curriculum development, discussed below.

Curriculum Development

Although ideal academic curricula to support gifted education do not now exist in many places, many alternatives are possible if teachers of the gifted work cooperatively with regular educators to build on what *is* available. The fact that improved academic offerings can benefit many other students in addition to the gifted makes such a plan plausible. Both regular education and gifted education can gain from each other by working together on curriculum development.

Curriculum development is a delicate business (Oliva, 1982). It involves convincing various professional and lay constituencies (e.g., principals, program coordinators, teachers, school board members, parent activists, the voting public, and representatives of the SEA) of the necessity for a particular course of action. Teachers of the gifted may be asked to serve on curriculum committees, and coordinators of gifted programs will doubtless be asked to do so. The purpose of this section is to suggest opportunities for promoting curriculum that supports and implements gifted education. Four levels of curriculum development efforts are identified:

1. course development,
2. program development,
3. development of curriculum for the gifted,
4. regular curriculum development.

Course Development. One practical way to develop curriculum is to add courses of established academic worth to the curriculum. This addition can be undertaken quite straightforwardly by the gifted program.

For example, nationwide a strengthened calculus offering would be a major advance, both for gifted students and for other students pursuing an academic program. The gifted program could offer calculus if the school program does not already include calculus. The course could be opened to other qualified students, such as those who have completed Algebra II and trigonometry with a GPA of 2.6 or above. Such a choice might, of course, involve staff development as well.

At the elementary level a resource program might, for example, schedule ten or twelve mini-courses during the course of a year. Perhaps three of these could be full-year courses. These courses could present substantial instruction if each was offered for one hour daily. One of the authors conducted just such a program. The courses (accelerated reading, accelerated math, and French) attracted the interest of regular classroom teachers, who were then asked to send academically talented (but nongifted) students to the classes. The school developed a strong gifted program and subsequently established two self-contained gifted classes.

Program Development. Sometimes the gifted program consists only of eligibility criteria, a few eligible students, a teacher, and a workspace. In this case, the development of a written gifted program can contribute to the development of academic curricula.

The written program should specify

1. subjects in which instruction will be given, including course and mini-course descriptions;
2. rationales, goals, objectives;
3. evaluation instruments (summative and formative; see Chapter 3 on program evaluation and cost-effectiveness);
4. student population (academically talented regular education students should be included if possible);
5. amount of differentiated programming students may elect (e.g., the program may limit the participation of regular education students to areas of strength or it may develop IEPs for regular education students).

Often it will be possible for the individual teacher of the gifted to develop and implement such a program in a single school, with the support of the principal. In this case the delicate business of curriculum development involves convincing the principal and interested teachers of the value of enriched offerings for apt students. Depending on the local program and state regulations, it may be possible to arrange the schedules of selected regular class teachers so that they can be used as instructors.

Development of a Curriculum for the Gifted.   Writing a curriculum specifically for the gifted is difficult, in part because individual differences are important in special education and in part because gifted curriculum content must include many elements of the regular curriculum. Typically, gifted curricula tend to be inclusive, relying on broad definitions and endorsing many, if not all, sorts of horizontal and vertical programming options.

The rationale for this approach to curriculum development seems to be a humanist sensibility. Gifted programs correctly want to unfetter their students, to expand their intellectual and emotional horizons. As a result, when curriculum is written, the tendency is to include as much as possible in the belief that to exclude something is to limit student options.

Educators might consider, however, that formal education, although it may open intellectual and emotional vistas to gifted students, also limits and restricts their options at the same time. Gold (1965, p. 364) notes, moreover, that gifted students confront options "much more limited than implied in the blithe assumption that [they] can do anything." These limits and restrictions are also inherent in talent development of any sort. For example, when the gifted students studied by Bloom (1982) and his colleagues devoted up to ten years to their fields, they turned away from other options.

In any case, a written curriculum supportive of gifted education ought to address in some detail the need of the gifted for advanced study. It should specify options relevant to academic learning, including acceleration and developmental placement, curriculum content, and the availability of advanced courses.

Regular Curriculum Development.   Teachers of the gifted have an important function on committees that develop regular curricula. They can help promote standards of academic excellence by recommending advanced-level courses and watching that budget cuts do not jeopardize academic opportunities for advanced students (see Chapter 3 on cost-effectiveness).

Expansion of Curriculum Offerings

Teachers of the gifted and coordinators of gifted programs will most likely be involved not in overseeing complete curriculum projects, but in assuming various roles within a development project. Their chief interest and their chief assignment will probably be to increase opportunities for gifted students to undertake advanced work.

In order to determine the need for expanded curriculum offerings, teachers and coordinators should conduct needs assessments. Such assessments can include several series of questions to uncover areas of programming in need of development or improvement. The sample needs assessment in Box 7.6

**BOX 7.6 Sample Needs Assessment for Gifted
Curriculum Development**

---

1. Are gifted elementary students encouraged to acquire basic skills rapidly?
    A. If yes, how?
        1. grouping (regular-class placements)
        2. developmental placement
        3. special classes
        4. other
    B. If not, which options might be developed?
    C. If not, how can the gifted program help?
2. Are special content courses available to gifted elementary students?
    A. Which subjects?
    B. How frequently?
    C. At what levels?
    D. Are accelerative options included?
    E. Can older elementary students earn high school credit?
3. What is the *quality* of the basic skill and content offerings?
    A. Does instruction address concepts?
    B. Is enough writing required of students (ten years of age and older)?
4. Is rapid pacing possible at the secondary level?
    A. If yes, how?
        1. summer school courses for credit
        2. independent study
        3. honors or rapid-paced classes
        4. dual attendance
    B. If not, which options might be developed?
    C. If not, how can the gifted program help?
5. Which of the following courses are offered in the regular curriculum? (All
    of these are minimum requirements for the most academically talented
    quartile.)
    A. Honors English
    B. Trigonometry
    C. Chemistry
    D. Four years of two foreign languages
    E. Calculus
    F. Physics
    G. Computer science
6. What are the priorities for adding courses?
    A. How can additions be promoted?
    B. How can the gifted program help?
7. What is the quality of the existing offerings?
    A. Are they offered consistently?
    B. Are teachers of the gifted teaching some sections?
    C. Is enrollment adequate?

suggests questions to be considered in developing curriculum to support gifted education. Individual teachers can use their own answers to such questions to help guide their personal contributions to curriculum development.

SUMMARY

The major goal of this chapter was to illustrate the feasibility of developing a curriculum that supports the academic needs of the gifted. This chapter discussed the components of such a curriculum at both the elementary and the secondary level. It related the choice of curriculum to the question of knowledge of most worth, and it related the answer (mathematics and literature) to academic disciplines, school subjects, school courses, and the characteristics of gifted students. It also discussed the curriculum's relation to the information explosion.

The chapter discussed general issues related to an academic curriculum for the gifted, including the need for high standards (excellence), the role of individual programming, and student differences that are relevant to curriculum planning. Public and private school models of academic programming for the gifted were examined and cautions noted.

Elementary and secondary curricula were constructed on the basis of the examples and principles. An illustrative elementary curriculum keyed to chronological age, disciplines, and subjects was included in the discussion, as was a sample reading list of novels for gifted children aged ten and older. The importance of typing and computer use was noted.

Included in the discussion of secondary curriculum was consideration of the relationship of course distribution and requirements, course load, college preparation, and vocational training. Sample three- and four-year course schedules based on the implications of the discussion were included for four students of different abilities and interests.

The chapter concluded with a discussion of curriculum change. The necessity of curriculum coordination was considered in the context of both individual program development and more formal efforts to develop curricula. The discussion included guidelines for writing a program and conducting an academic curriculum needs assessment for gifted students.

CHAPTER 8

Teaching Gifted Children: Instructional Formats

INTRODUCTION

In general, instruction for the gifted is intended to result in what Taba (1965) calls "potent knowledge," by which she means learning that allows students to form abstractions and draw inferences based on those abstractions. This goal derives from the perception of intellectually gifted learners as being capable of advanced, original work in academic or artistic fields. Such characteristics of gifted learners suggest appropriate instructional formats for their schooling.

Although curriculum and instruction are presented separately in this textbook, they are interrelated. The content of education helps define the form of instruction, and, likewise, the form of instruction helps define the content of education. Practice in literary analysis is, for example, necessary in teaching the literature curriculum. Library research assignments result in learning somewhat different concepts and skills than do simulations, discussions, or field studies.

Although none of the practices discussed in this chapter is applicable exclusively to the instruction of gifted students, all are relevant to improving their academic achievement. Guiding our selection of particular instructional practices are several global principles:

1. Level of achievement is primarily a function of instruction rather than innate ability.
2. Formal and informal assessment of learning is the basis of effective instruction.
3. It is more productive to conceive of intrinsic motivation, or pleasure in learning, as a concomitant of instruction rather than as its goal.
4. Various instructional formats and techniques are appropriate for different types of objectives and students.

The first section of the chapter discusses the preceding principles and reasons for their application to the instruction of gifted students. The second section presents instructional planning as a process in which the teacher selects or develops objectives, tests, and instructional formats to teach the curriculum. This process requires knowledge of the characteristics, advantages, and disadvantages of a number of instructional formats such as those described in the final section of the chapter. Chapter 9 presents practical techniques related to the instructional formats discussed in this chapter.

TALENT DEVELOPMENT

It may seem gratuitous to begin a chapter on instructional methods with the reminder that a necessary assumption of education is that children are educable and that achievement reflects the quality of instruction. In looking for solutions to the difficult problems of instructing children, however, educators are understandably tempted to accept hypotheses that explain students' failure to achieve in terms of variables other than the quality of instruction (e.g., in terms of minimal brain damage, or diet). Application of these hypotheses in the classroom tends to undermine the instructional process.

The high positive correlation between achievement level on entry into an instructional program and achievement level on completing the program (e.g., Thorndike, 1973) can be interpreted to mean that ability is a constant (that is, a given that determines performance in any program). On the other hand, it can be interpreted as evidence of ineffective instruction. Research that has found exceptions to this rule, in the form of unusual achievement gains associated with certain instructional approaches, suggests the validity of the latter interpretation. The identification, use, and evaluation of promising methods are demanded by evidence that instruction can significantly affect achievement.

Accommodating Differences Instructionally

There is ample evidence that human abilities are quite plastic (Bloom, 1964; Dobzhansky, 1973; Gould, 1981; Piaget, 1970). Effective instruction is predicated on the implications of that evidence. (Defining human behavior in terms of innate characteristics carries the unavoidable risk of constraining behavior.) Each student does, however, bring a different set of attitudes and knowledge to the learning situation, and these must be taken into account when teaching techniques and materials are selected (Bloom, 1976). For example, students vary in the amount of instruction they need in order to learn a particular skill or concept; this is true even for very simple learning tasks. To learn complex materials, about 10 percent of the students need five or six times more practice than the 10 percent of the students who learn most rapidly (Bloom, 1976). Most school programs seem (because of time, personnel, and material restraints) to demand the same amount of practice and participation of all students, regardless of their needs.

The diagnostic-prescriptive teaching model asserts that individual differences must be considered in planning instruction. Instructionally this model implicates the use of mastery learning, a method that both acknowledges the importance of a well-defined curriculum content and respects children as learners.

Mastery Learning. Mastery learning is based on the assumption that most of the variance in student achievement is a function of instruction (Bloom, 1976). Thus, the teacher's response to students' failure to achieve high grades in a mastery learning program is to provide additional instruction. Educational research has shown that this approach dramatically decreases the variation in achievement represented by grades of C or lower on tests given at the completion of a course of study. A summary of research on mastery learning (Gage & Berliner, 1975) reports that mastery learning compares positively with traditional instruction. In two of the studies described by Gage and Berliner (1975), about 75 percent of the students in the mastery program reached the 80 percent criterion on a final examination covering course content, while only about 40 percent of the students in traditional programs reached that criterion. In a study at the college level, 65 percent of the mastery group earned a grade of A by meeting specified criteria for mastery of statistics, while only 5 percent of the nonmastery group earned an A according to those criteria. These findings are consistent with the results of other studies (e.g., Anderson, 1973; Binor, 1974).

Since gifted students are usually among the top 5 to 10 percent in achievement rankings in traditional programs, mastery learning may appear to be less relevant for them than for other students. The implication, however, of research on mastery learning is that, given improved instruction, gifted students can achieve at even higher levels. The research on acceleration (discussed in Chapter 5) supports this view. Evaluation findings from the SMPY project, which uses a diagnostic-prescriptive approach to teaching advanced mathematics to gifted students (Stanley & Benbow, 1982), demonstrate that talent is malleable and that it is rapidly developed, as Bloom (1976) contends, through instruction that is responsive to individual progress.

The essential elements of mastery learning are (1) specification of mastery criteria prior to instruction, (2) frequent diagnostic testing which is referenced to the curriculum, and (3) alternative learning routes (Bloom, 1976). The mastery approach differs from traditional instruction primarily in the extensive use of diagnostic feedback in planning instruction. Although feedback can take the form of class assignments, demonstrations, or written assignments for homework, most mastery learning programs include brief, formative tests at the end of each major learning step. On the basis of the tests, additional study is provided as needed. Additional study may take a number of forms: reviewing particular sections of the textbook, attending group study sessions, working with a tutor, or studying supplemental print or audiovisual materials. These procedures offer alternative presentation of concepts and additional practice to those students who need it.

A mastery approach to learning is most easily implemented with the convergent, highly sequential curriculum associated with mathematics, English grammar, or initial foreign language study. Although it requires more teacher time and effort than traditional instruction and may never fully address individual learning needs, we nonetheless find that the mastery approach shows the most promise for developing talent.

Competency-Based Education.   For optimal instruction of gifted children, we must borrow two concepts from competency-based education, another diagnostic-prescriptive approach to instruction. Competency-based education incorporates the principles of mastery learning and contributes an emphasis on (1) statement of competencies intended as outcomes of the course of study and (2) multiple entry and exit points in the course of study.

Although competency-based education has been criticized as specifying only those educational goals that can be measured easily (Cooper, 1981), it benefits gifted students *by offering them a means of demonstrating early mastery* of the goals of the program or course. Thus, it can provide a basis for allowing students to skip material that they have already learned. In competency-based programs, students can begin instruction at different levels, depending on their mastery level, and end the course when they have accomplished the learning objectives (competencies). All of the instructional techniques discussed in this chapter are compatible with mastery learning, which does not dictate specific materials or techniques but, on the contrary, requires diversity of both.

Task Commitment

Richard Feynman received a Nobel Prize for his work in quantum electro-dynamics. His response to a television interviewer's question about what the Nobel prize meant to him expresses a feeling common to many people who have made a significant contribution to their field. He said,

> I won't have anything to do with the Nobel Prize. I've already got the prize. The prize is the pleasure of finding the thing out, the kick in the discovery, the observation of other people using it. Those are the real things; the honors are unreal to me.
>
> (Feynman, 1983)

Sentiments like those expressed by Feynman abound in the autobiographical works of scholars and artists. Original work in any field has a longstanding association with intellectual curiosity and with finding intrinsic reward in intellectual activity. This association is reflected in the literature on gifted education in the commendation of goals that help gifted students develop love of learning for its own sake.

Task Commitment as Identification Criterion and Goal. The role of task commitment in gifted education is widely viewed in two different but not incompatible ways. They differ in that one focuses on intrinsic motivation as a *prerequisite* to gifted education, and the other focuses on the development of intrinsic motivation as an essential *aim* of gifted education.

In the former case, the concept of task commitment, which combines interest and willingness to dedicate much time and effort to a particular study, is used in *defining* giftedness, either explicitly, as in Renzulli's (1978) definition, or implicitly, as in items on behavior checklists used to guide teachers' referrals for possible placement in a gifted program. Items such as ''The student is a highly motivated learner'' and ''spends much time on projects'' reflect the correlation between achievement and pleasure in learning.

In the latter case, gifted programs espouse task commitment as a *goal* of instruction. In part, this reflects the belief that intrinsic motivation and high achievement are naturally related. Goals related to task commitment typically express an intention to develop students' enjoyment of learning.

Task Commitment as a Concomitant of Academic Achievement. Surprisingly, task commitment can also be viewed as a *function* of academic achievement rather than as a precursor to it. Studies of the effects of mastery learning have found that as students' competence in a subject increases, their enjoyment of the subject increases as well (Bloom, 1976).

Bruner (1966b) contrasts the limited effectiveness of irrelevant or unchallenging content in stimulating a sense of accomplishment with the motivational capacity of substantial, increasingly difficult material. He reports teachers' delight with the level of motivation exhibited by students working in the (then) new mathematics and science curricula. The teachers attributed students' eagerness to increased confidence in their ability to understand a difficult subject.

The effect of achievement on interest in school subjects appears to be cumulative. Whether a child has a history of successes or failures in a particular subject affects his or her willingness to undertake new learning tasks in that subject (Bloom, 1976). This is probably true across subjects as well. In working with gifted underachievers, Whitmore (1980) found that even at the primary grade levels children's classroom behavior derived from past experiences in school. These experiences influenced their expectations regarding the rewards and relevance of school work. Correlations between attitude toward school subjects and achievement in the subjects increase with time in school (Thorndike, 1973). This trend is most evident in mathematics (Husen, 1967). Such findings indicate the importance of early and continuing efforts to provide instruction that allows students to experience a sense of accomplishment.

It may be more productive to focus on cognitive gains rather than increased task commitment as an end of instruction in view of the fact that we do not know whether intrinsic motivation is a necessary ingredient of outstanding achievement (see Box 8.1). We do know that without advanced skills in academic or artistic disciplines, individuals cannot reach a level of outstanding performance. By emphasizing cognitive goals, teachers can ensure that students have the requisite academic skills for advanced scholarship.

INSTRUCTIONAL FORMAT SELECTION

Selecting the best instructional format, activities, and materials requires consideration of several variables: type of subject, instructional objectives, and learner characteristics. The study of some subjects, such as mathematics, must include individual practice in applying principles. Literature and social studies instruction must provide opportunity for discussion to compare views; and science cannot be taught properly without laboratory and field work to allow observation and description of relationships among elements and events. Instructional objectives guide selection of methods and materials by specifying the concepts and skills students are to learn. The students' developmental levels and aptitudes determine the level and pace of instruction. Group size and composition render some methods more feasible than others. In addition to all of these variables, availability of resources such as personnel, media equipment, facilities, and time further limits the range of instructional alternatives.

Analysis of Instructional Objectives

Since subject matter and approximate student developmental level influence the instructional objectives at the outset, preparation for teaching usually begins with consideration of the objectives that are to be accomplished through a particular unit of instruction. The source of the objectives is sometimes a curriculum guide developed commercially or by the school system. Objec-

---

BOX 8.1 Happiness and Hieroglyphics

We had certain hours allotted to various subjects but we were free to dismiss anything that bored us. In fact, it was school policy that we were forbidden to be bored or miserable or made to compete with one another. There were no tests and no hard times. When I was bored with math, I was excused and allowed to write short stories in the library. The way we learned history was by trying to re-create its least important elements. One year, we pounded corn, made tepees, ate buffalo meat and learned two Indian words. That was early American history. Another year we made elaborate costumes, clay pots, and papier-mâché gods. That was Greek culture. Another year we were all maidens and knights in armor because it was time to learn about the Middle Ages. We drank our orange juice from tin-foil goblets but never found out what the Middle Ages were. They were just "The Middle Ages."

I knew that the Huns pegged their horses and drank a quart of blood before going to war but no one ever told us who the Huns were or why we should know who they were. And one year, the year of ancient Egypt, when we were building our pyramids, I did a thirty-foot-long mural for which I laboriously copied hieroglyphics onto the sheet of brown paper. But no one ever told me what they stood for. They were just there and beautiful. . . . When we finally were graduated from Canaan, however, all the happy little children fell down the hill. We felt a profound sense of abandonment. So did our parents. After all that tuition money, let alone the loving freedom, their children faced high school with all the glorious prospects of the poorest slum-school kids. And so it came to be. No matter what school we went to, we were the underachievers and the culturally disadvantaged. . . . My own reading comprehension was in the lowest eighth percentile, not surprisingly. I was often asked by teachers how I had gotten into high school. However, I did manage to stumble not only through high school but also through college (first junior college—rejected by all four-year colleges, and then New York University), hating it all the way as I had been taught to. I am still amazed that I have a B.A., but think of it as a B.S.

Condensed from "Confessions of a Misspent Youth" by M. Wolynski. Copyright © 1976 by Newsweek Incorporated. Reprinted by permission.

tives that are listed in scope and sequence curricula, particularly those developed for advanced students, usually represent complex learning outcomes. Consequently, before instruction begins, the teacher must determine the component concepts and skills in order to develop a sequence of learning activities that organizes those concepts and skills into a logical progression (Bloom, Hastings & Madaus, 1971).

Although the distinction between them is moot, two types of analysis can be used to guide instruction: concept analysis and task analysis (Thiagarajan, Semmel & Semmel, 1974). Concept analysis is the process of clarifying important terms so that activities or materials designed to teach them will be effective and to the point. Concept analysis often begins with a look at a dictionary or textbook definition of a term and proceeds to a listing of critical attributes, examples, and "close-in" non-examples which help define the boundaries of the term (Thiagarajan et al., 1974). The more unfamiliar and complex the concept, the lengthier the process of analysis. Task analysis is the process of identifying and sequencing skills needed to accomplish the objective. Depending on the teacher's past experience, the analyses may take the form of a quick mental review or may involve checking source material.

Both task and concept analysis are hierarchical, beginning at the most complex level and moving to the simplest level (i.e., entry-level knowledge or skill). The precision with which the analysis of the instructional objective must be done depends on the importance of the objective and the potential difficulty it poses for the learners. Box 8.2 demonstrates the use of concept and task analysis.

Tests and Instructional Plans

Within the context of the curriculum objectives, teachers must consider the characteristics of the learners who are to meet the objectives. Their attitudes toward the subject and their maturity or developmental level will suggest the pace of instruction in the class, the level of difficulty, the effort needed to arouse and maintain student interest, and, in some measure, the content of instructional materials.

Educators who use a mastery learning approach to instruction suggest constructing tests before developing instructional activities and materials (Thiagarajan et al., 1974). Analysis such as that illustrated in Box 8.2 could form the basis for construction of tests that would assess component skills and knowledge as well as mastery of the objectives; thus it could be used to prepare both a diagnostic pretest and a final examination. The development of the tests will yield further information for planning instruction, and results of the pretest can be used to determine individual achievement relative to objectives.

Tests as a Component of Instructional Planning. Teacher-made and commercial tests are used in a mastery learning approach for several purposes. As mentioned previously, one purpose is to diagnose individual students' needs relevant to concepts and skills taught in a unit, course, or program. Like most instructional approaches, mastery learning also uses test results as a means of determining the effectiveness of instruction, both for individual students and for the class as a whole. These uses of testing generally require the comparison of performance on a pretest to performance on tests given subsequent to instruction.

Diagnostic testing serves the interests of the class as a whole. Through pretesting, the teacher may find that the students already know some of the material to be taught or that many of them lack skills which are prerequisite to those established as objectives. Based on information derived from pretesting, the teacher can eliminate planned activities that teach what has already been accomplished and can make provisions for students who need to work on prerequisite skills.

BOX 8.2   Concept and Task Analysis

For the following objective, the teacher might conduct concept and task analyses along the lines suggested below.

> The student will be able to identify common methods of development in expository writing and apply the method of choice in composing an original essay.

CONCEPT ANALYSIS

The major concepts in this objective are *expository writing, methods of development in expository writing,* and *essay.* In identifying the critical attributes of these concepts, the instructor might consult a literary dictionary, a lay dictionary, and the textbook for the class. The *American Heritage Dictionary* gives a general definition of *exposition* as follows: "a statement of meaning, an explication" (Morris, 1975, p. 463). A college-level textbook on essays defines the term as follows: "Exposition is the most commonly used of the traditional forms of discourse: exposition, argument, narration, and description" (Shugrue, 1981, p. 23).

Expository writing can be considered to possess three critical attributes: (1) prose form, (2) nonfictional content, and (3) explanatory or definitional intent. Topic, style, and length appear to be irrelevant to the concept. Literary examples that meet these criteria include books such as Darwin's *The Origin of Species* and essays such as Loren Eisley's "The Illusion of Two Cultures." Close nonexamples might include books, essays, or articles intended to persuade, such as Shirley Chisholm's "Women and Their Liberation," or to narrate, such as Thoreau's *Walden.* Analyses of the remaining important concepts in the objective would follow a similar procedure.

TASK ANALYSIS

The objective contains two major tasks: recognition of the methods of development in expository writing and application of one method in composing an original essay. Components of the first task are (1) identifying characteristics of each of the methods, (2) recognizing those characteristics as applied in written compositions, and (3) applying the characteristics as criteria in categorizing methods of development in written compositions. Components of the second task are (1) identifying the characteristics of an essay, (2) selecting a subject for exposition, (3) selecting a method of development, and (4) using the method to organize ideas about the subject. The first task requires reading comprehension skills, and the second requires skills of written expression.

An objective at an advanced level, such as this one, assumes basic skills as prerequisites; they are not included in the analysis. (The reader should note that this is merely *one* possible definition of exposition and *one* set of tools to develop *that* sense of exposition. There are many possible perspectives on expository writing.)

Because gifted students' skills are highly diverse and because they are advanced in academic level, pretesting is an important element of their instruction. They commonly require acceleration, independent study, or some other alternative to repetitive instruction. Teachers of gifted children who do not use pretests and frequent progress tests risk repeating the mistake for which regular education instruction has been criticized: teaching gifted children what they already know.

Pretesting for instruction to be provided in the resource room or self-contained classroom can usually be accomplished with little additional effort on the teacher's part. When instruction is given by a volunteer or another instructor, however, pretests, progress tests, and even final examinations are not so readily administered. When gifted students are enrolled in college courses, advanced grades, and mentorships, administering diagnostic tests may be more difficult. Nevertheless, in these situations the teacher of the gifted can confer with the other instructor and assist in the process of testing.

Although college courses and mentor programs typically include content with which the gifted education teacher is unfamiliar, diagnostic testing is still the best means of ascertaining whether the proposed instruction is appropriate in general and how it can be made most effective for the student or students.

Test Development. Mentorships and other alternatives for the gifted often have goals such as the development of original products or application of newly learned artistic or technical skills. In such cases, if tests are conceived of narrowly, as paper-and-pencil, multiple-choice or essay tests, testing may be neglected by dint of the apparent impossibility of administering a relevant pretest, progress test, or final examination. Familiarity with a number of test formats allows greater flexibility and precision in determining the effectiveness of instruction. Tests can take the form of written examinations, oral examinations, simulations allowing application of new skills, auditions, and jury reviews of the students' original work.

For example, a pretest based on the analysis of the expository writing objective presented in Box 8.2 could include items to determine whether students understand important concepts (e.g., *expository, essay*) and methods of development in expository writing (e.g., classification, example). Asking for definitions is the simplest and surest approach. The pretest must also discover whether students can recognize each of the methods of development and distinguish it from others in excerpts (e.g., by labeling each excerpt according to the method used). Finally, the pretest must determine whether the students can already write an essay using one of the methods to develop their exposition.

Those students who can complete the pretest successfully need do no more work in the unit; no students need to study what the pretest shows they already know. There are, of course, areas of ambiguity; some students may be able to write the required essay without knowing a particular version of exposition taught in the example. These students can practice identifying the methods by participating in instructional activities designed to achieve that end. Whether or not they should participate in other elements of the unit (e.g., writing another essay) might be decided on the basis of performance on the pretest and evidence of mastery of the concepts presented in class.

Bloom (1971) advises against giving grades on pretests and progress tests because a grade of C or lower might have a detrimental effect on the students' performance. If students believe prospects for success are low, they may allocate the time and effort required for success to other projects.

Extensive use of diagnostic tests to individualize instruction seldom occurs in large group instruction; it may be feasible only on a limited basis. Where placement or selection alone has failed to eliminate much heterogeneity and where the group size is fairly small, however, it is important and feasible. Many gifted classes are composed of only a few students, but these few may span a chronological age range of two to four years and demonstrate considerable variation in their abilities. Whether it is done formally or informally, individualization is necessary. Over a number of years, teachers can develop tests, learning activities, and instructional materials to help achieve this end. As we mentioned earlier, the match between learner and instruction will never be perfect, but close approximations can be achieved by careful planning.

INDUCTIVE VERSUS EXPOSITORY INSTRUCTION

One of the decisions a teacher makes in designing instruction is whether to use an inductive or an expository instructional format (or a combination of the two). Expository instruction is more direct and less time-consuming. The form of presentation may be a series of lectures, assigned readings, films, tapes, or a combination of these. Inductive instructional formats present students with examples of a particular concept. Students abstract the concept from the examples instead of having it presented to them. The inductive method has the advantages of engaging the students' attention overtly and of resulting in fuller understanding and longer retention of concepts (Bruner, 1966b).

Inductive Formats

There are so many concepts to be learned in school that, in general, the expository approach is used to teach all but the most important ones. In most regular education programs, induction is reserved for major concepts. Inductive methods, however, are common in gifted education. This is true for several reasons:

1. They are credited with teaching broadly applicable skills which form common goals of gifted programs (e.g., observing, questioning, and generalizing).
2. They are considered to be compatible with the cognitive strengths of gifted students (e.g., superior powers of abstraction, ability to perceive relationships, interest in cause-effect relationships).

3. Learning by discovery or induction is said to be gifted students' preferred mode of instruction (Clark, 1983; Gallagher, 1975).

Inductive formats range from the traditional Oxford tutorial course of study to inquiry training sessions designed to teach a single scientific concept. The common element in inductive formats is arrangement of the learning environment so that students will, by virtue of abstracting certain features from examples provided in the environment, arrive at general concepts or principles (Taba, 1975).

Tutorials. The tutorial is one of the oldest methods of instruction. Inductive in approach, the traditional tutorial combines directed reading, written assignments, and regular meetings between the student and the tutor (Highet, 1950). The tutor raises important issues and uses questions to help students clarify their ideas, refine arguments, and see the implications of lines of thought. The interaction requires intense and active participation by both the student and the tutor; the critical faculties and persistence of each are essential elements in this process (Highet, 1950). The depth and intensity of the tutorial necessarily limit its scope and the number of students whom the tutor can instruct. The tutor, directing primarily advanced specialized studies, seldom meets with more than one or two students at a time (Highet, 1950).

Although the expense of this method has prevented its extensive use, modified forms of the tutorial are employed in many high schools that offer special programs for students with unusual ability (cf. Gerencser, 1979). Student seminars and independent study courses, for example, borrow basic elements of the tutorial. In such programs learning proceeds through a combination of assigned independent work and periodic sessions in which students and teacher examine the conclusions the students have reached on the basis of their independent study.

Even the modified tutorial is demanding in that the teacher must have read all that each student has read (and written) and be ready to ask questions. These questions must reflect a sense of the relative importance of trends, ideas, and methods in the field in which the students are working and must be directed toward the broad instructional goals for the students. Unfortunately, they cannot all be prepared in advance. During the session the teacher must be able to adapt lines of questioning to students' responses (Highet, 1950).

Students selected for traditional or modified tutorial programs must be highly capable in their chosen field of study. Excellent reading comprehension and written expression are prerequisites. The tutorial is too difficult and expensive a method to be employed in teaching basic language skills. Also, the students must be capable of reading *primary sources* in the field (Highet, 1950). In order to arrive at the level of understanding at which this method aims, students need to confront ideas as expressed by their originators, not as summarized in secondary sources. This requires comprehension at the superior adult level, the level at which most gifted high school students are capable of reading. (Note that computer "tutorials" are not true tutorials, partly because of the impossibility of carrying on discussion and direct questioning, and partly because of the difficulty of presenting lengthy primary source material in video format.)

Because required work understandably takes precedence over extracurricular activities, the tutorial must be a part of the teacher's and the students' workloads. A tutorial conducted on an overload or volunteer basis is unlikely to be a worthwhile course of study. A tutorial taken as an add-on, with no credit toward graduation, is also unlikely to be a worthwhile course of study. In either case the time and energy that should be invested in the tutorial may be directed elsewhere (Freehill, 1961).

Whereas traditional tutorials are not feasible in many public school settings, essential elements of the tutorial can be incorporated into other instructional formats. The advanced student may be provided a directed reading program (see Box 8.6, pp. 256–257) in lieu of unnecessary review of basic skills in any content area. Even in a large-group setting, students can be given assignments that require them to formulate and defend their analyses of readings in literature, social studies, or science (Wallace, 1983). Group discussions or seminars afford gifted students an opportunity to practice expressing and defending their opinions.

Seminars. Although the term *seminar* is applied to a number of practices involving assembly of a selected group of students on a regular basis, the term as traditionally used connotes discussion aimed at problem-solving or discovery of new ideas (Minot, 1958). *Seminars are nearly always topical*, and they usually require preparation in advance of seminar meetings. Students prepare for seminar meetings by reading related books and articles and preparing reactions to them (Clendening & Davies, 1980).

There are three types of seminars for gifted students:

1. honors seminars, which are advanced sections of required or elective high school courses;
2. enrichment seminars, which are usually extracurricular and offered on Saturdays or after school; and
3. combination seminar/independent study programs, which take place during school time and usually carry elective credit (see Box 8.3).

Honors seminars typically offer students who are high achievers in a particular subject a course that is more intensive and demanding than others in the subject. An example of an honors seminar is included in a text by Clendening and Davies (1980) on programs for the gifted. The seminar focuses on the works of Ernest Hemingway. As in most honors programs, written composition is emphasized: seven position papers are required for the course. Two of these are read by the class and evaluated for clarity of position, support for the position, organization, and mechanics.

Since high school credit is usually awarded for honors seminars, achievement often carries greater weight in the selection of students for honors seminars than it does in the selection of students for enrichment seminars. The

---

BOX 8.3   An Independent Study/Seminar Program for Gifted High School Students

A combination independent study/seminar program offers high school pupils in New Haven, Connecticut, a number of different forms of advanced study in mathematics, science, English, and social studies (Blanning, 1978). Students selected for the program can earn credit for either required or elective courses by scheduling one period a day for independent work on projects in these subjects. One-to-one conferences with the teacher, lecture-discussions, and student seminars are scheduled during that time throughout the semester.

Mathematics students work on group or individual projects and, as part of the lecture-discussion component, report on articles in mathematics journals. Science students do independent work in quantitative chemistry, astronomy, or other branches of science and are encouraged to attend Yale's Saturday lecture series for high school youth. Creative writing workshops, part of the English program, are organized according to form (i.e., drama, poetry, short story). Students critique one another's work and discuss writing techniques in weekly seminars. To meet a U.S. history requirement by independent study, students read and outline the textbook and write short essays reacting to selected readings by specialists in particular periods in U.S. history (Blanning, 1978).

---

higher level of ideation and the heavier workload of most honors seminars demand consideration of achievement; interest alone does not ensure the appropriateness of this placement for a student.

Enrichment seminars often cover a wide range of subjects. They may be a series of lectures by experts, with each lecture followed by discussion, or they may be a series of informal symposia which encourage reflection, speculation, and discussion on diverse but related topics. If any homework is assigned between enrichment seminars, it is usually minimal. The purpose of these seminars is primarily to stimulate interest in diverse topics within a discipline (Porter, 1968). Participation is usually voluntary, with no grades assigned and no credit given for the course.

Since enrichment seminars depend on student interest for continued attendance, selection of participants is best accomplished by publication of basic prerequisites for the course and inclusion of all interested students on a first-come, first-served basis. There is nothing in the literature to suggest that students must exhibit unusual intellectual ability in order to benefit from enrichment seminars. If evidence of capability to understand and participate in a meaningful way is considered necessary, admission criteria should be related to the topic of the seminar and not to general intellectual ability.

Combination seminar/independent study programs are similar to the tutorial in that students read and do research on a subject, form generalizations on the basis of their readings, and meet with the teacher and other students to discuss their conclusions and to exchange ideas (Blanning, 1978).

Participation in combination seminar/independent study programs is often by agreement between student and teacher. Entrance is based on work requirements that are outlined prior to or at the beginning of the program. In a combination seminar/independent study, half of the total number of class periods might be devoted to independent study, about a quarter to films and group discussion, and another quarter to student presentations to the group (Clendening & Davies, 1980).

As we have seen, seminars can form the principal instructional method for an entire course of study or be used in conjunction with other methods of instruction. If the content of the unit or course is typically approached through a comparison of views and the development of generalizations through critical reading and discussion (e.g., literary criticism), the entire course may be conducted as a series of seminars. If some objectives of the unit do not lend themselves to this type of instruction, the seminar will be only one of the instructional techniques used.

Preparation for a seminar program is time-consuming, whether the seminar is used as the sole format for the course or in combination with other methods. Preparation involves the following steps:

1. selecting books, articles, essays, or stories to illustrate the generalizations to be developed and analyzed;
2. determining the sequence in which the readings should be assigned and discussed; and
3. developing questions to stimulate and guide discussion.

These steps are recommended even when seminars do not require outside reading. In this case preparation may include development of a bibliography for students who are interested in further reading on topics discussed in the seminar.

The popularity of seminars and group discussions is due in part to their applicability to resource room programs, which cluster children in groups of five to fifteen for instruction. This class size lends itself better to informal discussion than to formal techniques. Also, the discussion technique is credited with teaching critical thinking, communication, and social interaction skills.

The steps used in planning group discussions are similar to those used in planning seminars. The teacher must have read the material and formulated questions about the important points prior to the discussion. Students, too, must have read in advance of the discussion or experienced some common stimulus such as a film or play. (Readings, because of their comparative complexity, form the richest source of material for consideration in seminars; paramount intellectual value is derived from reading primary source material.) Discussion guides, in the form of organizing questions, allow students to collect their thoughts before class and make it more likely that they will become familiar with the material under discussion (Olmstead, 1974).

As we have stressed throughout this section, the instructional objective is critical in determining the teaching method. Topics that leave much room for controversy, argument, and debate, for example, suggest the use of discussion. On the other hand, highly convergent topics which have well-established principles and methods are usually taught through the use of lecture and practice. The humanities offer the broadest ground for discussion, although no field, including mathematics, should be construed to be so convergent that it disallows this method of instruction.

Independent Study.   This section is concerned with independent study undertaken by the student to gather and consider ideas from a number of sources in order to solve a problem defined in broad terms. It is much more open-ended than directed reading or independent programmed learning. Those types of independent study are examples of expository formats and will be discussed later in this chapter.

Independent study may constitute an entire course of instruction, or it may be one of a number of instructional formats used in a course. Although the instructional objective may be the same for several students studying independently, the readings, research methods, sources, and perspectives on the topics can be diverse. For example, given the objective of determining how economic factors influence the architecture of a society, one student might compare the architecture of two locales in the same country, another might analyze the architecture in only one city, and another might compare public buildings in different centuries.

The most obvious application of independent study is in research in science or the humanities, but it is a suitable method of instruction for any subject area. As suggested earlier, since learner characteristics have, to a large extent, been taken into account in development of instructional objectives in a scope and sequence curriculum, choice of instructional formats should be made primarily on the basis of those objectives (Olmstead, 1974). Student characteristics will determine the scope, procedures, and structure of independent study.

In general, the younger or less experienced the student, the more limited the scope and methods should be and the more tightly structured the study (Treffinger, 1975). Even at the graduate school level, students sometimes need assistance in conceptualizing the objectives of independent study, developing procedures, and locating sources. Treffinger (1975) points out that as students gain experience in this type of learning, they become more competent in designing, conducting, and evaluating independent work.

In the early grades, the most popular approach to independent study is to address a common instructional objective by relating it to student interests. During the intermediate years, library skills, reading comprehension, and composition skills can be applied in increasingly sophisticated independent studies. By high school, gifted students are often engaged in independent study courses. The Calasanctius high school program includes three years of independent research under the direction of a teacher in the school (Gerencser, 1979). Students are required to write a paper based on their independent work and present it to a committee of experts. This process is analogous to the thesis or dissertation-writing component of college work at the under- graduate or graduate level.

Even at the college level, students encountering independent study courses for the first time may not like this method of study. Any negative reaction may be due, at least in part, to lack of familiarity with this learning approach (Gage & Berliner, 1975). A five-year investigation at Antioch College showed that independent study courses which were highly structured by study guides, study questions, and reading lists resulted in improved attitudes to- ward independent study and in achievement equal to that of control students in traditional courses (Baskin, 1961). It is possible that without this structure the students' initial unfavorable reaction might have persisted and their achievement been less. We cannot, at any rate, expect gifted students to un- dertake independent study without considerable instructional support (Tref- finger, 1975).

The structuring of independent study for gifted students is usually accom- plished through a combination of individual conferences with the student and design of learning contracts (Markwalden, 1976; Renzulli, 1977).

Written contracts help in the organization, implementation, and evaluation of independent study. They guard against the fallibility of memory and en- sure that actual and projected timelines are reconcilable. Contracts also allow teachers and students to determine whether or not the aims or methods of the study should be revised. Although learning contracts vary in their spec- ificity and detail, they share a few basic components. They identify what is to be accomplished by what methods and by what date, and they identify the standard by which the success of the work will be evaluated (Gearheart & Weishahn, 1980). Resources are often listed on the contracts as well (Ren- zulli, 1977). Contingency contracts, used more often with handicapped or underachieving students, also specify a reward, such as a field trip or free time, to be granted on completion of the project (Gearheart & Weishahn, 1980).

With careful planning, independent study can be a valuable educational experience. Care must be exercised, however, to ensure that it does not de- generate into busy work. Independent reading and research materials cannot serve as full-time substitutes for a teacher. Gifted students who are so ad- vanced in a subject that they know more than the teacher knows cannot re- ceive much assistance from that teacher. Too often, when the school does not offer ready access to the instructional personnel needed by advanced stu- dents, independent study projects are assigned in the expectation that stu- dents can, with occasional help from the teacher or a volunteer mentor, teach themselves. *This type of study is unlikely to be effective.*

Independent study contracts should be developed by teachers who are ex- pert in the field that the student is investigating. Such teachers will be able to

1. frame meaningful research questions or learning objectives;
2. select the best of available literature or help the student make wise selections; and
3. evaluate student procedures and products.

Because teachers of the gifted are not expert in all fields, volunteer mentors are sometimes sought to assist in providing independent study to gifted students. This solution, however, poses some difficulties. Gold (1965) discusses the problem of finding expert tutors. His comments apply to volunteer mentors as well: "Sometimes they are able to involve students in their own scholarly pursuits. Sometimes, unfortunately, they are too preoccupied with their own concerns to regard the tutee as more than a burden" (Gold, 1965, p. 179). As we noted in the discussion of tutorials, the instruction of students engaged in independent study should be part of the teacher's workload. Volunteers cannot usually invest sufficient time.

Students can certainly benefit from wide reading in fields in which they are interested, but if they need instruction, the school should try hard to locate a qualified instructor. Because of the expense of formal tutoring, this effort will *nearly always* entail acceleration in the form of dual enrollment or early admission to high school or college.

Whether independent study is the principal method by which a student is to learn or only one of several activities within a course of study, it must be directed by a teacher who is knowledgeable in the discipline. This does not mean that students cannot explore relatively esoteric avenues of investigation within disciplines (see Box 8.4). Teachers do not have to be familiar

---

BOX 8.4 The Zoo School

A one-grade alternative school in Grand Rapids, Michigan, is designed to teach independent study skills to highly motivated students interested in science, specifically environmental science. Recognizing that even highly motivated students need assistance if they are to advance their conceptual and skill development in an efficient fashion, designers of the Zoo School program divided the year into three phases. The first phase consists of highly structured, teacher-directed projects that emphasize skills such as composition, taught within the structure of zoology and environmental science. The second phase offers greater scope for pursuing individual interests, but is still highly structured. Project outlines provided by the teacher guide students' work, but allow individual choices that result in different projects. The third phase is more individualized; students select from different project outlines and make more decisions about how they will proceed and with what materials. All of these steps are considered by the educators who designed the school to be *prerequisites to independent study* in which the students design and conduct their own projects (Schlemmer, 1981).

with every aspect of biology or history, for example, in order to assist students in individual work, but they do have to have a perspective that comes from an understanding of significant ideas, trends, and methods in the field and how students' projects relate to them. The best independent study projects provide for regular interaction with a qualified teacher and with students with similar interests.

Many gifted educators consider independent study to be a means of teaching both the content and the methodology of different disciplines (Gallagher, 1975; Renzulli, 1977). Independent study usually combines independent reading and solution of a selected problem. Whether the problem is "real" in the sense in which Renzulli (1977) uses the term or whether the problem is designed by the teacher, independent study can be considered a form of simulation, broadly conceived, in that the students are simulating the problem-solving behavior of adult mathematicians, scientists, and historians. The major distinctions between independent study and simulation activities are that (1) simulations are based on models of actual phenomena and (2) simulations often emphasize affective skills, such as cooperation in group activities and empathy for others, whereas independent study usually emphasizes reading, reflection, and written composition.

Simulation. A simulation is an operating model (Raser, 1969). As opposed to other models, such as blueprints, Guilford's (1967) SI model, or a model of the Chrysler Building, a simulation model can illustrate changing relationships (Raser, 1969). Whether static or dynamic, all models simplify a complex phenomenon. Heuristic models used in education focus on elements and relationships considered relevant to the instructional objective and omit those which are inessential.

The idea, event, or object modeled through simulation is responsive to student input, thus providing feedback which guides student interactions with the model. Feedback to students may take the form of alarms and flashing notices (in a computer simulation), of tokens representing money, or of verbal responses from other students participating in the simulation. The consequences of students' decisions are evident in the course of the simulation.

One of the oldest forms of educational simulation is the case method, which presents a problem, or case, for analysis by the students. This method was first used in law schools, but applications have been developed for medical schools, teacher education, and other programs (Olmstead, 1974). Although used less frequently in the public schools, the case method offers a good alternative to more traditional approaches, particularly in social studies, science, and literature (e.g., the "casebooks" sometimes used in college freshman English courses).

The case to be studied is typically a historical event such as a landmark court decision or a political crisis. Case materials for students may be purchased or developed by the teacher. They include a record of the case (with the resolution omitted), surrounding circumstances, relevant facts, and opinions of contemporary figures. Students read and analyze the case individually, arrive at a tentative conclusion or decision, and then come to class to discuss their solutions with other students. In this way critical events can be studied in terms of their influence on election campaigns, political economy, contemporary attitudes, law, or other fields relevant to the class. This method helps students understand the reasons for the outcome of the events and the interrelatedness of various elements in the case.

Simulations, such as the case method, and simulation games compress examples of the effects of social or psychological principles into a relatively short learning activity. Students can induce concepts and principles by seeing the effects of their decisions in the simulation. Like the case study method, most simulation games present the student with a scenario which gives background information, setting the stage for the game. Students select roles, given the rules or constraints within which they must play. After the game is completed, they engage in a discussion of what happened in the game, why things happened the way they did, and how the events relate to the real world. Simulation games may occupy one class period or may continue for several weeks.

Because they emphasize induction, simulations are popular in programs for gifted students. The benefits of simulation activities are common to other inductive methods. Simulations involve students actively by having them analyze events and arrive at their own conclusions. Students learn to test their conclusions and evaluate their correctness. Although some advocates of simulation games believe that the games develop transferable problem-solving skills, desirable affective behaviors, and skills of social interaction (Cline, 1979), this has not been clearly demonstrated.

Research *has* shown that students find simulation games interesting (Raser, 1969). Since, in general, they are no less effective than traditional methods, simulations offer a viable alternative that is likely to activate and maintain student interest. Simulations may be especially useful to teach skills and concepts that children find difficult or relatively uninteresting. They can also help break the routine of a series of discussions or lectures.

Simulation can be a valid instructional method for developing subject-specific concepts and skills—for example, understanding how archaeologists work and what they study. Finding a simulation or simulation game that shows promise of accomplishing particular instructional objectives can be difficult, however, even though there is a selection of simulation games available commercially. By reviewing descriptive and evaluative articles teachers can ensure that they do not order a game that, although it sounds appropriate, does not address the teacher's instructional objectives. *The Guide to Simulations/Games for Education and Training* (Horn & Cleaves, 1980) contains information about a number of simulation games.

When a good match between available simulations and the instructional objectives cannot be found, teachers may consider designing their own simulation game. Since game design is difficult and takes a considerable amount of time, an alternative solution is to select a commerical game as a model and modify it to suit the objectives. Some instructional games are designed expressly for this purpose (Thiagarajan & Stolovitch, 1980).

Inquiry Training Sessions.   Suchman (1975) developed a series of game-like science inquiry lessons and a procedure that can be used to develop similar lessons. Inquiry training sessions differ from other inductive methods in that only one example of a principle is given and the sessions are highly structured. Inductive methods usually provide several examples of a principle or concept so that students can, by comparing the examples, generate a rule.

Each inquiry session begins with a paradox. For example, a physical science lesson might begin with the teacher's filling a glass half full of water, placing a piece of cardboard over the glass, and then turning it upside down. The cardboard, instead of dropping off, stays in place, and the water, instead of pouring out, stays in the glass. The paradox is used to activate the students' interest. The assignment to the students is to discover, by asking only questions that can be answered ''yes'' or ''no,'' why the water stays in the glass. The use of a questioning procedure is intended to force the students to analyze the situation and form their own hypotheses rather than passively accepting an explanation given by the teacher. It is also intended to teach the students more efficient questioning strategies (e.g., to determine critical variables and to verify their perception of the situation).

Since the teacher knows the answer and students must confine their problem-solving to ''yes'' or ''no'' questions, this type of learning only simulates scientific inquiry. As with simulation and other types of games, its main appeal may be its motivational quality. There is no substantial evidence that it is superior to other methods in imparting science concepts and skills (Gallagher, 1975). Like other game-like formats, it should be used only occasionally; a steady diet may reduce the motivational appeal and hence the effectiveness of this relatively time-consuming method. If the motivational appeal is lost, the educational returns might not be enough to offset the cost in instructional time.

Laboratories and Field Studies.   Laboratories and field studies range from highly structured to open-ended in style. Foreign language laboratories usually consist of highly structured, convergent activities. Writing labs or workshops, though they may be designed to teach skills and concepts related to a particular type of writing (e.g., short stories), are open-ended. Some instructors use task sheets to give a great deal of structure to laboratory work at the beginning of a course and then gradually increase freedom for experimentation as students become more familiar with the subject and with laboratory equipment and procedures.

In the regular education program, laboratories often accompany lecture or discussion classes, but both laboratories and field studies can constitute an entire unit of instruction (see Box 8.5). Science centers and outdoor environmental programs for children who are talented in science emphasize labo-

BOX 8.5 Field Biology for Elementary Students

Science textbooks should serve only as reference and source books in elementary school science programs, where the objects of study are at hand: plants, animals, earth, and water. A field biology class for elementary-aged gifted students can teach science in the way naturalists learn about the environment—that is, through careful observation, recording, and organization of data.

Field notes are an important part of this approach to science. Riner (1983) suggests a team effort, with each child or a team of three or four taking turns as recorder. Each child copies all the observation notes into an individual notebook so that the child has a complete set of notes. These are referred to in class discussions and in writing reports (Riner, 1983).

"Describe the flying motions of the hawks we will see; include as much detail as possible" (Riner, 1983, p. 47). This instruction to students focuses attention and prompts them to observe more closely and record what they see. Questions like "Why are the ducks bobbing their heads under the water?" (Riner, 1983, p. 47) elicit tentative hypotheses which can be supported or refuted by observation.

Points along a transect line are designated by a coat hanger and inventoried for types of plant life, insects, temperature, time in the sun, and soil temperature. Students compare graphed results from different points along the line in order to discover similarities and differences and possible explanations for them. Long-term study, with inventories every few weeks, enables students to observe seasonal changes.

ratory work and hands-on experiences. The Talcott Mountain Science Center, which has equipment and personnel not usually available in the schools, is designed so that students spend most of their time in the laboratory (Atamian & Danielson, 1977).

Tutorials, seminars, independent study, simulations, inquiry training, laboratories, and field studies all have in common a predominantly inductive approach to instruction. They place students in a role in which they must abstract generalizations from questions asked, problems assigned, or examples given. All inductive methods offer the possibility for discovering relationships between the methods of a discipline and its content. Inductive approaches that do not fulfill that possibility, by virtue of neglecting methodology or removing meaningful content, weaken the justification for expending the additional time required by inductive formats.

Expository Formats for Instruction

Expository teaching does not usually involve much active student participation. Learner activity during expository instruction, such as a lecture, is covert most of the time. Thus, we are less sure of the students' attention and interest.

The major benefits of expository instruction are its directness and its greater potential for teacher control of the instructional process. It should be noted that these *benefits* are the same qualities that are cited as *drawbacks* of the expository method; whether they are benefits or drawbacks depends, of course, on the purposes of instruction. As mentioned earlier, objectives may suggest the appropriate mode. Learner considerations also apply, as we shall see in the following discussion of various forms of expository teaching.

Lectures. Students retain only about 45 percent of the content covered in lectures (Gage & Berliner, 1975)—about one-third of their thoughts during a lecture are irrelevant to the subject at hand. Most lectures could be written up and given to students as "handouts." Lectures are said to place students in a passive, receptive role, and gifted students are notoriously active, questioning learners. Nevertheless, it seems that lectures *can* be an effective means of instruction and should be incorporated *more often* into classes for gifted children.

Time is too short for students to discover by themselves all that they could benefit from knowing; indeed, this fact is what gives books their enduring value. Lectures allow experts to communicate in a short time some of the understanding that they have gained or the questions that they have come to face as a result of persistent work in their fields. Viewing something through the eyes of a specialist who has a deep understanding is an avenue to learning that may be more demanding and engaging than methods that involve students in overt activity. The key elements are (1) the uniqueness of the lecture content, which depends on the expertise of the lecturer, (2) the relevance of the lecture topic to the learners, and (3) the manner of delivery of the lecture.

Expertise in the subject matter of the lecture is necessary for originality and depth of content, but does not by itself ensure effective delivery. Laycock (1979), for example, recounts that Robert Oppenheimer, whose brilliance and look of erudition impressed students and colleagues, delivered lectures that apparently had equally impressive shortcomings.

What qualities, and what quantity of knowledge, constitute expertise is also open to question. The degree of expertise necessary usually depends to a large extent on student knowledge. For example, a teacher who understands and appreciates mathematics (or anthropology) may have all the expertise that is needed to teach Algebra I (or a mini-course on anthropology) in the typical expository mode to ten- or 11-year-old gifted students. Such a degree of expertise, however, would be less satisfactory if the students were in a senior high school honors program.

The superior verbal comprehension and enjoyment of reading common to gifted children suggest that they can benefit from listening to lectures as one of a variety of learning activities. For example, lectures could be (and often are) used as advance organizers (Ausubel, 1977) to prepare students for a group discussion or other type of activity.

In preparing a lecture, whether an outline or an entire script, the lecturer must identify important points, how they are connected, and how they can best be communicated to the particular class (Highet, 1950). The organization of major points is suggested by the nature of the topic, or at least the lecturer's perspective on the topic.

Even more than organization, the amount of enthusiasm evidenced by the lecturer appears to affect students' retention of the material (Gage & Berliner, 1975). How a lecture is delivered is one of the most important elements in determining the success of this method of instruction.

The adaptability of the lecture method is one of its strengths. It is responsive to different time constraints and to questions or issues that arise in class. It also gives the lecturer the opportunity to communicate personal views of a subject.

Directed Reading. *Directed reading* connotes more teacher control of the learning material and process than does the type of independent study discussed in the section on inductive instructional formats. Directed reading is an option for students who prefer learning through reading rather than through lecture, discussion, or other classroom activities. It is also an option for students who can work at a fast pace.

Directed reading (see Box 8.6) can be an instructional alternative in any subject area, but it is usually an inadequate substitute for systematic instruction at an advanced level. Like other forms of independent study, directed reading is sometimes selected as the primary form of instruction for a student who is advanced in a subject that the teacher of the gifted is not qualified to teach. When it or any other method is chosen not because it seems to be the best way for a particular student to accomplish the instructional objectives but because there is no qualified teacher available, the choice should be represented to the parents and the administration as only a stop-gap measure. A better means of meeting the needs of the student in question, and other students with similar needs, should be developed.

BOX 8.6   How to Direct Directed Reading

PROBLEMS SOLVED BY THE USE OF DIRECTED READING

1. Basal reading textbooks don't meet individual student needs and interests.
2. Students don't receive enough exposure to good literature for children and adults.

SELECTION AND PREPARATION

Compile a collection of books that will (1) challenge your students; (2) represent a variety of categories (for example, mystery, adventure, biography, fantasy, and history); (3) include authors who have proven popular with students (for example, Jack London, the d'Aulaires, C. S. Lewis); (4) include award-winning books (for example, Caldecott, Newbery, Pulitzer).

Prepare a reading guide for each book. The reading guide should contain questions about the book and perhaps a brief synopsis of the author's life and interests. Questions should include issues of style and method as well as content; for example,

- Based on your reading of *The Sword and The Stone*, what are your impressions of the author's opinions about how people should be governed and about how they should behave toward each other?
- What lesson do you think Merlyn wanted Wart to learn from his visit to the fish? the ants? the geese?
- Use drawings or sentences to illustrate the meanings of these words from the book: astrolabe, barbican, cauldron, recreant, cumbrous, peregrine, rout, dominion.
- Compare the two sorcerers, Merlyn and Morgan LeFay. How are they different? What qualities do they have in common? How did each influence Wart's life?

Make copies of the reading guides. Put one copy of the reading guide for each book into a looseleaf notebook, along with possible answers to the questions and key page numbers for each question.

GETTING STUDENTS STARTED

1. Give each student a brief synopsis of books that match his or her reading level. (The synopsis may be oral or written.)
2. Give each student an opportunity to look through the books.
3. After the student has selected a book, give him or her the reading guide for the book.

READING AND CONFERENCES

Assign at least two thirty- or forty-five-minute periods per week for reading, answering reading guide questions, and conferring with students about what they are reading.

Have at least two conferences with each student: a midpoint conference and an endpoint conference. The midpoint conference should check progress and comprehension and allow students to talk about what they are reading. The endpoint conference should include discussion of the book and review of the students' answers to reading guide questions.

If two or three students are reading the same book, schedule their conferences together. Make notes on the students' responses to determine their reading comprehension strengths and weaknesses, their interests, and their effectiveness in oral and written expression. Use the notes in planning group and individual instruction in literature.

Based on an article by Gail Gerlach in *Teacher*, February, 1981.

The amount of structure necessary for directed reading varies. At the college level, study may be guided sufficiently by a list of the instructional objectives to be accomplished and a bibliography keyed to the objectives (Thiagarajan et al., 1974). More elaborate instructions are usually required by younger students. Instructions typically include an annotated bibliography, a list of assignments to be done in conjunction with the readings, and a time-line establishing dates by which assignments should be completed. Depending on the objectives, both textbooks and tradebooks (including primary sources) may constitute the reading materials.

Regularly scheduled progress checks through one-to-one conferences with the teacher, tests, and evaluation of assignments are important to ensure that the student is benefiting from directed reading. The less able the student, the greater the need for gradual development of autonomy. For many students, particularly young students and underachievers, charting progress seems to improve achievement (Whitmore, 1980).

Programmed Instruction.   Whatever the purpose, programmed instruction is characterized by a pattern of alternating exposition, questioning, and feedback segments. Highly structured expository textbooks, workbooks, or computer software are often used for enrichment, acceleration, and remediation of basic skill problems.

In such materials, the student is provided with a statement defining a term, explaining an operation, or simply setting out a problem; this statement is followed by a request for students to respond (e.g., by filling in a blank or typing an answer on the computer keyboard). The materials then provide feedback by showing the correct answer or indicating the correctness of the response in some other manner. The success of programmed instruction depends on the quality of the materials, since they are often unsupported by discussion or practice. Student attitude toward programmed instruction also influences the success of this type of instruction. Students who have a positive attitude toward programmed instruction are, not surprisingly, more likely to complete the course of study successfully (McLain & Kovacs, 1967).

There is some disagreement over whether or not programmed materials are compatible with the learning style of gifted students (Gallagher, 1975). The repetitive nature of some programmed materials may bore bright students. The small learning steps intended to guarantee mastery of each step decrease intellectual risks. Successful students may prefer the intellectual challenge of greater content ambiguity. The following mixed reactions by bright students who were given the choice of using programmed instruction for enrichment illustrate this point:

> I found I had a very good start but have lost some of the enthusiasm that I formerly held.

> I really like this method. Sometimes when I get mad at my teachers, I wish all my courses were taught in this manner.

> I do not prefer this course to regular classroom courses because I would rather ask questions.
>
> (McLain & Kovacs, 1967, p. 41)

Forty-one percent of the students in this study indicated that lack of direction was a main disadvantage, and 10 percent simply found programmed instruction uninteresting.

One of the chief benefits of tutorial computer programs is the immediacy of the feedback they provide. Although the teacher's feedback to students can be more cogent and elaborate, teachers do not have time to provide immediate feedback to all students. Computer programs offer responses that are less dynamic than those of the teacher, but more dynamic than those of workbooks or programmed textbooks (Allee & Williams, 1980).

There is still much to be learned about effective uses of computers for instruction, but it seems that significant achievement gains can be made by students who have had difficulty with traditional approaches to instruction. Contributing to students' improved performance may be (1) the motivational appeal of the machine as a novelty, (2) student perception of the machine as a nonthreathening authority, and (3) the immediacy of feedback.

A study of Mexican-American students who participated in a computer-assisted-instruction remedial mathematics program for one to two years showed that these students from low-income homes saw the computer as fairer, clearer, and easier than their teachers (Hess et al., 1970). Ironically, the children whom research shows can benefit most from computerized remedial instruction are not often given a chance to use computers. In most schools only about 5 to 10 percent of the student population has access to the computers; these children are usually the high-achieving students (Martellaro, 1980).

Like their computer counterparts, programmed print materials should be reviewed carefully and their use supervised. Programmed textbooks are usually linear. Every student goes through every step of the learning sequence. The pace at which students progress is the only individual variable. However, if a student can benefit from advancement in basic concepts of a subject or basic skills, or if the student needs practice, programmed textbooks may be a viable option. They are available for a wide range of subjects including introductory statistics (Brown, Amos & Mink, 1975), English grammar (Blumenthal, 1981), and computer programming (Albrecht, Finkel & Brown, 1978).

One of the benefits of programmed instruction is that students learn faster than through traditional methods (Kulik, Bangert & Williams, 1983). Mathematical skills seem most amenable to improvement through computerized remedial programs, and underachieving boys seem to be most responsive to those programs (Merton, 1983). Whitmore (1980, p. 272) comments, "The use of programmed materials, commercial or teacher-made, allows failure to occur privately and diminishes competition between students for speed of learning or mastery."

Individual Learning Activities. Individual learning activities include learning centers, with a variety of materials and activities; learning kits; and auto-instructional units containing print materials or audiovisuals. All are used in gifted programs and in regular classrooms to provide enrichment or to offer alternative means of accomplishing instructional objectives. The materials, both commercial and teacher-made, range from lists of loosely related ideas for enrichment to sequential instructional programs designed to accomplish curricular objectives.

Individual learning activities based on materials designed for independent use have a legitimate place in the education of gifted students, but they are sometimes used simply as a means of keeping the students busy in the regular classroom or the gifted resource room. Like other independent study techniques, they are often used as a substitute for advanced instruction. Their most legitimate use is to provide an alternative activity within a unit of instruction that employs other methods as well.

When commercial materials are unavailable, teachers sometimes create their own auto-instructional materials. Following are suggestions (adapted from Thiagarajan et al., 1974, p. 108) for developing a learning unit that uses a taped script to guide the student's activities:

- List instructional objectives.
- Select media pertinent to the objectives (e.g., filmstrips, models, pictures, maps, worksheets, or textbooks).
- List a tentative sequence of activities using the materials.
- Write a draft of the script for the audiotape.
- Have another teacher and students read the script and tentative sequence of activities and make suggestions for improvement.
- Revise the script and instructional sequence list (which can serve as a checklist for students' activities).
- Make the audiotape.
- Assemble the materials.
- Field-test with students and revise as needed.

Techniques used primarily for expository teaching, such as lectures, directed reading, programmed instruction, and individual learning activities, emphasize comprehension of content and application of skills rather than the discovery of generalizations. Which expository or inductive format is best depends on the purpose of instruction, the topics under consideration, and group and individual learner characteristics. Research has found all of the above methods to be useful in some situations. However, none should serve as the single means of instruction (and probably *does not* in most situations). Feynman, the physicist cited earlier in this chapter, offers the following advice to teachers:

My theory is that the best way to teach . . . is to be chaotic and not to follow one particular philosophy, in the sense that you use every possible way of doing it, so as to catch this guy or that guy on different hooks as you go along.

(Feynman, 1983, p. 14)

SUMMARY

This chapter focused on instructional approaches and formats that are especially relevant to the education of gifted children. All of the methods presented were selected on the basis of their compatibility with several global principles. Mastery learning and competency-based instruction were identified as two diagnostic-prescriptive models that could operationalize those principles in teaching the gifted. Mastery learning is based on the view that achievement is a function of instruction and utilizes frequent testing to accommodate differences in learning level and rate. Competency-based education can permit gifted students to demonstrate early mastery of program or course goals. The chapter also discussed the use of concept and task analysis prior to instruction.

The chapter distinguished between two basic types of instructional format, inductive and expository, and found both to be suitable to various ends. Inductive formats were found to be particularly applicable to content of an ambiguous, controversial, or general nature; expository formats were found to be suitable to convergent subject matter. Inductive formats are best suited to situations in which shortness of instructional time is not a pressing concern; expository formats may be preferable when the utilitarian need for efficient instruction is paramount. The discussion noted that although inductive formats are often recommended for gifted pedagogy, they cannot supply all instructional needs and in fact probably should be used with some restraint.

CHAPTER 9

Teaching Gifted Children: Techniques for Concept and Skill Development

INTRODUCTION

Instructional techniques are the means by which teachers organize the classroom and educational activities to maximize learning. The utility of particular techniques depends, in part, on the instructional format of the class. Instructional techniques must also take into account individual student differences. Research indicates that some techniques are particularly suitable for the development of academic concepts and skills in gifted students. These include techniques that encourage inductive learning, techniques that promote teacher responsiveness, and techniques that reinforce students' efforts to master difficult concepts and skills.

The first section of this chapter describes conditions that permit these techniques to succeed. The second section focuses on techniques that support an inductive approach to teaching academic concepts to gifted children. Techniques that promote the acquisition of academic skills are discussed in the third section. The next section discusses techniques to use for enrichment goals. The final section explores the use of behavior modification techniques in working with gifted underachievers.

ANTECEDENTS TO EFFECTIVE INSTRUCTION

Before the students walk into the classroom, even before the teacher begins preparing for instruction, the likelihood of a productive school year has already been determined. The most promising instructional methods can be effective only if certain conditions are met:

1. Students must have been selected carefully to ensure that they have common learning needs.
2. Program elements should be flexible enough to address students' individual needs.
3. The level of the curriculum should match the children's achievement level.
4. The curriculum must be relevant to long-term educational goals for the students.
5. The role of the teacher as intellectual model should be established.

All of these conditions, except the last one, have been discussed in earlier chapters. It is time to look at the role of the teacher in some detail.

The Gifted Education Teacher's Role

The most important role of the gifted education teacher is that of the scholar-teacher (see Box 9.1). Teachers of gifted students should be sufficiently knowledgeable to carry out a direct instructional role. Otherwise, achievement gains made by the students are likely to be modest in comparison with their potential to benefit from instruction.

There are, however, many different sorts of gifted students and programs. Therefore, gifted education teachers will probably not be able to function in this role for all of their students. When the gifted education teacher is assigned the responsibility of serving students who are highly capable in areas in which the teacher is not trained, the teacher must assume the role of educational coordinator. Instructional techniques for the gifted teacher therefore include identification and evaluation of alternative instruction, such as college courses. The roles of teacher-scholar and teacher-coordinator are discussed below. Most teachers will probably fill both roles.

Teacher as Working Scholar.   Gallagher (1975) considers expertise in the disciplines as a basic requirement for instructors of the gifted. He believes this requirement to be more critical than training in techniques such as creative problem-solving. Gallagher notes that knowledge of enrichment strategies cannot substitute for subject-matter expertise.

BOX 9.1 Who Should Teach the Gifted?

Probably the best known study of the effectiveness of gifted teachers was carried out by Bishop (1968). He studied teachers who were identified as "most successful" by high school seniors attending the Georgia Governor's Honors Program.

Bishop found the teachers to be highly intelligent, within the top 3 percent intellectually, and to be high achievers, with a gradepoint average of 3.0 or better on their college transcripts. Other characteristics were similar to characteristics attributed to gifted students. These included being curious, creative, empathic, tolerant of ambiguity, and interested in literary and cultural matters.

Specific teaching approaches noted were student-centered instruction, teacher participation in the learning process, and an orderly, businesslike teaching style. The teachers also exhibited enthusiasm both for the disciplines they taught and for teaching bright youngsters (Bishop, 1968).

The Educational Policies Commission of the National Educational Association and the American Association of School Administrators had, nearly twenty years prior to Bishop's study, recommended identification of similar characteristics as qualifications for teachers of the gifted (Educational Policies Commission, 1950). The Commission stressed the need for teachers who were themselves "highly intelligent."

The teacher-scholar has been described as having an inquiring mind; powers of analysis and accumulation of knowledge; attributes of intuition and self-discipline; and tendencies toward perfectionism, introspection, and resistance to external authority (Brown, 1967, pp. 165–172). These traits closely reflect the cognitive and noncognitive traits often ascribed to gifted children. Since the cognitive traits form the basis for differentiating instruction for children identified as gifted and the noncognitive traits are generally considered potential contributors to achievement (e.g., Getzels, 1979), the teacher-scholar does seem to be an appropriate role model for gifted students.

One model program used teacher-scholars to improve the academic achievement of gifted students. Project F.U.T.U.R.E. (Facilitating Unlimited Talent Using Relevant Education) gave students advanced, fast-paced mathematics and language arts classes (Cohn, 1984). Unusually large gains in student achievement were due in part to the expertise of the teachers.

The language arts teacher for the fifth through eighth grade class in Project F.U.T.U.R.E. had published poetry, and during the second year of the project won a statewide poetry competition. The mathematics teacher for that age group had majored in mathematics in college, a relatively rare phenomenon among mathematics teachers. Cohn (1984) reports that these teachers contributed significantly to both achievement gains and more positive student attitudes toward mathematics and language arts. It thus appears that even in the elementary grades, the potential effects of teachers' scholarship on the achievement of gifted students are significant. The scholarship of prospective teachers should therefore be considered in teacher selection and preparation (see Box 9.1).

Although the tradition of having the apt pupil tutored by a teacher who is a working scholar is ideally suited to the education of the gifted, it is a method that many school systems cannot afford to utilize (cf. Bloom & Sosniak, 1981). Programs such as the Teachers' and Writers' Collaborative and other programs using working writers and artists (e.g., Ginandes, 1973; Koch, 1973; Szekely, 1981; Yeatts, 1980), however, prove that possibilities do exist for securing intellectual role models for talented students.

All communities can approximate this service by instituting more rigorous academic requirements for gifted education teachers, by recruiting teachers who are apt scholars, and by providing support for professional development efforts of teachers who are willing to continue their liberal arts education. The ease with which this task can be accomplished depends, of course, on the resources of the community.

Teacher as Coordinator of Instructional Resources. Gifted teachers commonly serve as coordinators of school and community resources needed in the education of gifted students. They generally have information and access to services, personnel, and materials. This information concerns:

- professional development and assistance to other classroom teachers;
- college instructors, mentors, and volunteers who can work with gifted students;
- instructional options for students who are talented in specialized areas such as the arts; and
- instructional options for students who are so capable in academic areas that the skills of even the best teachers in the public schools cannot meet their needs.

In order to meet the variety of gifted students' needs, gifted education teachers must locate and help develop community resources (Altman, Faherty & Patterson, 1978; Sellin & Birch, 1980). To perform this function effectively, teachers must be familiar with the services and resources of local and state facilities such as universities, museums, libraries, art galleries, performing arts companies, and historical societies.

Another component of the gifted education teacher's role is to help students identify information sources for their work. To do this, teachers must be familiar with specific library and museum holdings and with basic information sources, such as computerized information retrieval services, general library reference works, and government documents and services. This role is particularly important in independent study programs and is perceived by some educators as the primary role of the gifted teacher (e.g., Dubiner, 1980; Renzulli, 1977).

The gifted education teacher must also work with regular educators to modify instruction for gifted students. Although the regular classroom has been identified as the least cost-effective placement for gifted students (Gallagher et al., 1982), many gifted students do spend most of their time in a regular education program. In order to make that time as productive as possible, the gifted education teacher must work with the regular education teacher.

In order to make assistance to regular education teachers as effective as possible, gifted teachers should ensure that their responses to colleagues' questions and requests for help are prompt, specific, and complete. Whenever appropriate, gifted teachers should provide sample instructional materials and relevant literature. Whenever possible, they should demonstrate techniques about which the regular education teacher has asked. In fact, the most effective professional development format for changing teachers' methods is field-based training (Marotz & Nelson, 1978). Gifted education teachers may be able to provide just such help.

It is common knowledge among gifted education teachers, of course, that providing assistance and consultation is a delicate business. Classroom teachers may resent resource room teachers' freedom of movement and the small size of their classes. They are often not aware of all the responsibilities of the gifted education teacher. Gifted education teachers should avoid the pitfalls that are common in working with classroom teachers and other instructional personnel (see Box 9.2).

BOX 9.2 Consultation Pitfalls

The following pitfalls can heighten resistance to consultation (Kazanjian, Stein & Weinberg, 1976):

1. The consultant offers advice or solutions too readily or quickly without allowing the other teacher a chance to use his or her own problem-solving skills.
2. The consultant fails to listen carefully to the request or problem and so fails to provide an appropriate suggestion.
3. The consultant addresses too many issues at a time.
4. The consultant makes recommendations that conflict with administrative policy or with the values of the other teacher.
5. The consultant assumes the role of supervisor, administrator, or therapist.
6. The consultant introduces personal biases inappropriately (too obviously and without a convincing rationale).

Perhaps the most common consulting pitfall is failure to follow through on promised materials or actions; subsequent loss of credibility undermines future interaction between the gifted teacher and the classroom teacher who requested assistance.

The roles of the teacher, whatever they may be, are only one element of instruction. Another major element for which the teacher is responsible is the organization of classroom resources.

Instructional Facilities

It seems likely that the organization of the physical facilities in the classroom and the quality and amount of instructional equipment have some bearing on the success of instructional techniques. Learning activities deemed especially appropriate for the gifted, such as independent study, small-group discussion, and inquiry learning, can be carried out more readily with certain classroom organizations and the use of some special equipment. A critical component in the use of instructional facilities, however, is adequacy of the time allotted for students' use of the facilities.

Frequency and Duration of Instructional Time. Personnel providing direct instruction must work with students often enough to make a significant difference in the students' education. Otherwise, there is little point in having a program.

Scheduling efforts should take into account not only the amount of time but also the frequency of time allocated to special education. Generally, five hours of instruction per week is better provided in four or five daily sessions than in one long session once a week. Continuity of instruction is extremely difficult to achieve when students and teacher see each other only once or twice a week. Because of the low priority assigned to gifted education in some school districts, scheduling can be one of the most trying tasks for the gifted education teacher. *If the gifted education teacher does not insist on frequent class periods of at least forty-five minutes' duration, students may not learn enough to justify their leaving the regular classroom.*

Organization of the Classroom. In most regular education classrooms the teacher's desk is the focal point of the room. In gifted education classrooms there are usually several focal points: learning centers, displays, tables and chairs, and a library area. The teacher's desk is often set off to the side, creating a conference space where the teacher can talk or work with individual students in relative privacy. This difference reflects the student-oriented approach to education which is common to most gifted programs.

Feldhusen (1981), taking the vantage of a regular classroom teacher, maintains that individualization is more readily accomplished when the classroom is organized to include a number of learning centers and equipment that students can use independently. Examples of such equipment are typewriters, computers, tape recorders, headphones, and filmstrip viewers. Feldhusen recommends that elementary classrooms include an audiovisual media center and an arts and crafts center with a storage area for paints, paper, and construction materials; a math center with math games, calculators, computer, and math kits; and reading and spelling centers.

Individualization of instruction may also be encouraged by a profusion of "real things" in the classroom. Of course, books, pictures, and models should be abundant too, but they usually are. It is relatively uncommon to see plants, insects, rocks, machines, musical instruments, and other objects in the classroom. Such curiosities, however, offer more complex stimuli than pictures or models and are thus more likely to accommodate individual interests and aptitudes.

In addition, research shows that instruction which includes work with concrete materials results in higher achievement levels than similar instruction which includes only symbolic materials (Cooney, Davis & Henderson, 1975). The use of real objects as a basis for concept development is particularly important for elementary school students (Rowe, 1973), but it seems likely that it can make instruction more interesting and more effective at all levels.

Silberman's (1970) list of things he saw in a classroom for fourth through sixth graders offers one example of the assortment of materials that might be made available to young students:

- chick incubator,
- four cages with white mice,
- two microscopes,
- an internal combustion engine,
- a disassembled washing machine motor,

- a broken radio,
- parts for an intercom system,
- a collection of seashells,
- a butterfly collection,
- a display of fifty kinds of grains and seeds,
- a display of bark from different kinds of trees,
- shelves stocked with a miscellany of useful items (e.g., batteries, iron filings, magnifying glasses).

INDUCTIVE TECHNIQUES FOR CONCEPT DEVELOPMENT

According to Bruner (1966b), an early advocate of inductive instruction, learning requires three conditions: (1) activation of interest or attention, (2) maintenance of attention, and (3) direction of attention. The teacher's interaction with students, either directly or through instructional materials, engages and maintains students' attention, directing it toward certain ends. Critical elements of this process are based on the teacher's content knowledge, which allows the teacher to improvise as needed to meet changing conditions during instruction. The teacher's empathy for students and sensitivity to their responses are also important in activating and maintaining their attention.

A common activating device, used in both inductive and expository instruction, is the introduction of novelty or ambiguity. Novel events, words, colors, or sounds attract attention by violating expectations; ambiguity seems to ask for resolution. Suchman's (1975) inquiry training sessions (see Chapter 8) begin with a novel event—specifically, a paradox that demonstrates a scientific principle. The paradox establishes a problem that both activates and directs attention by violating students' expectations and increasing the salience of certain features of the environment.

Although this technique relies on surprise in order to gain students' attention, *familiar* ideas or objects can also activate attention. Activities in which new concepts are linked to familiar ones and new skills are applied to solve familiar problems, for example, both employ familiarity as an activator.

A constant mixture of novelty, ambiguity, and familiarity is required to direct learning efforts and help sustain them. Sensitivity to students' responses can help the teacher select examples, adapt activities, pace instruction, and change instructional formats.

Concept Development

A distinction can be made between instructional techniques directed toward concept development and those directed toward skill development. Instruction to teach new concepts is often characterized by features different from those used to teach skills. In gifted classrooms concepts are often developed in a way that engages children actively through inquiry and conjecture. In the regular classroom concepts are most frequently taught in an expository fashion.

Verbal and Nonverbal Concepts.   A concept is a definition. It is not necessarily a *verbal* definition, however. *Operational* definitions guide our behavior even when we have not verbalized them. Children learn many concepts before they learn to understand language or speak. They learn to throw a ball and drink from a glass and not vice versa. They learn to distinguish their family members from strangers. They learn to watch television and not the dryer. They learn to pound with a toy hammer, put a telephone receiver to their ear, and so on. Children's operational concepts are inherent in some way in the skills they learn.

Concept learning is usually described as if it were an objective process of noting similarities in objects or events and then forming categories based on those similarities. In reality, it may, however, be much less arbitrary:

> There is no clear reason why the child should know that when the parent identifies a dog by name, the parent is referring to the dog as an entity as opposed to the color, shape, action, head, or tail of the dog, or even the ground on which the dog is standing.
>
> (Palermo, 1978, p. 232)

When we learn concepts, either we form our own definitional rules based on patterns we have observed or others give us the definitional rules of the concept. (The extent to which the rules we form are constrained by our experiences or our physiology is an unresolved question.) These concepts are then used in forming new concepts—for example, to classify information, to discriminate between phenomena, and to generalize concepts (Cooney et al., 1975). Odd as it seems, concepts are acquired in large part by virtue of previously learned concepts.

Steps in Concept Development.   In expository lessons, students are *given* the definitional rules. A typical expository approach to teaching a concept entails the following steps (Cooney et al., 1975): (1) defining the concept, (2) giving examples of the concept, and (3) contrasting examples with non-examples.

In inductive lessons, students *abstract* the definitional rules by noting similarities in the examples and often contrasting them with the absence of those attributes in non-examples (Cooney et al., 1975). Inductive learning begins with identifying patterns in the environment. Based on those patterns, students form generalizations that can then be applied to relevant aspects of the environment. According to Taba (1965), concept formation consists of three basic processes:

1. differentiating the properties of objects and events,
2. abstracting shared characteristics and grouping on the basis of common properties, and
3. categorizing and labeling in order to organize diverse objects.

Observation is essential to differentiating properties of objects or events and to recognizing common properties. In order for observation to be an effective means of inquiry, three conditions must prevail (Suchman, 1975):

1. *Focus*: inquiry must be directed toward a goal.
2. *Freedom*: constraints on the search for a solution must be free of inhibiting fears about "right" and "wrong" answers or methods.
3. *Response (feedback)*: the environment must be sensitive to the students' probes or trials.

Concept development is most likely to occur if students are adequately prepared for observation experiences. Morsink (1984) describes a less-than-successful discovery lesson:

> My first experience with discovery learning was as a student in a physiology class. The teacher told us we would learn about the human body by dissecting fetal pigs. Then he brought the pigs into the laboratory, gave us our dissection kits, and told us to "see what we could discover." We discovered that preservative burned our eyes, that we didn't know how to cut the pig's skin without rupturing the internal organs, that dissection probes were great for poking each other, and that we didn't know what we were looking for.
>
> (Morsink, 1984, p. 100)

This lesson lacked two of the three conditions that Suchman says are necessary for inductive learning. It lacked focus because the students were not adequately informed about how to dissect the pigs, and it lacked response because the "environment" (the fetal pig and the teacher) did not respond to their search.

Morsink (1984) contrasts her experience in inductive learning with an inductive lesson she observed in a gifted program. Before the lesson, the teacher prepared her students by teaching them how to use the dissecting tools through a simulation activity—removing the skin from a tangerine and sectioning the fruit. The teacher also gave students a checklist to guide their observations during the dissection.

Inductive teaching is based on exemplars of the concept. Teachers must ensure that the exemplars are sufficient in number and that relevant attributes are salient enough to capture students' attention. When the natural environment does not supply such examples, simulations are good substitutes. Maximizing the usefulness of examples, in real or simulated conditions, is accomplished through a variety of question-asking techniques.

Question-Asking Techniques

Questions have several purposes in inductive teaching. They narrow the focus of students' inquiry, direct attention to particular dimensions of a problem, encourage inference, or gauge students' understanding. Effective question-asking techniques are based on knowledge of the results of different questioning procedures and of different types of questions.

Effective and Ineffective Question-Asking Patterns.   The development of effective question-asking patterns requires teacher planning and teacher flexibility. Teachers need to outline the content and hierarchy of possible questions in lessons. In class, teachers need to allow themselves sufficient time to think about student responses before they call on another student or rephrase the question.

Ineffective questioning techniques may inhibit students' induction of abstract concepts. Rowe (1973) studied the detrimental effects of two common patterns: rapid-fire questioning (two or three questions per minute with short waiting periods averaging nine-tenths of a second) and consistently judgmental comments following students' answers. These patterns have several undesirable results: students' answers are fragmentary and their arguments unelaborated, grasp of concepts is limited, and low-achieving students volunteer little. Good students learn to be more interested in teacher approval than in inquiry, and poor students are excluded from the instructional process. In such circumstances, teachers may fail to see when students make cogent points (Lipman, Sharp & Oscanyan, 1977).

With additional time to think, students ask more questions and volunteer more answers. Their responses also tend to become more elaborate. Participation by low-achieving students increases as well (Rowe, 1973). The flexibility of teachers' questioning increases with increased waiting time after asking questions and before commenting on students' answers (Rowe, 1973).

To learn inductively, students need the chance to integrate all relevant information and use it to develop concepts through their own efforts. There are no "flash card" responses in an inductive approach. In class discussions and other activities intended to stimulate reflection and discovery, terse judgments of correctness are counterproductive. Instead of judging the *correctness* of answers (with "very good," "right," "OK," and other brief judgments), teachers should use additional questions and more elaborate responses to help students redirect inquiry or revise ideas. When teachers decrease judgmental comments, student responses with approval-seeking inflections (which seem to say "That's it, isn't it, teacher?") tend to disappear.

Additional questions, called *probes*, can help by focusing students' attention on relevant dimensions of the problem. Probes can help students focus their thoughts and arrive at more original or perceptive insights (Robinson & Feldhusen, 1984). Probe questions also model techniques children can use in their own reading and thinking.

The use of apparently outrageous questions has also been suggested by the originators of a children's philosophy course. For example, a question like "Was there really a George Washington?" (Lipman et al., 1977, p. 76) causes students to evaluate the sorts of postulates needed to refute Washington's existence. Such questions are intended to help children examine their basic assumptions about reality.

Lipman et al. (1977) emphasize the importance of *not* answering some kinds of questions. Offering personal opinions can sometimes close off inquiry and development of student ideas. If, for example, a child asks "What is fair?" the teacher should respond with questions that stimulate the child to consider possible criteria for distinguishing fair from unfair treatment.

Questions to Elicit Different Cognitive Behaviors. Certain types of questions have been associated by a number of researchers with particular cognitive behaviors. This section treats three views of this relationship. Gallagher et al. (1967) studied divergent versus convergent thinking prompted by different types of questions. Taba (1965) classified questions in terms of their capacity to change the scope of class discussion or the level of its abstractions. Bloom (1956) devised a taxonomy of the cognitive domain based on a division of questions into different types. Bloom's taxonomy is often used in gifted education (see, e.g., Maker, 1982a, 1982b).

Gallagher et al. (1967) found that 50 percent or more of the questions asked by teachers of academically talented junior and senior high school students were cognitive memory questions. Questions requiring convergent productive thinking were the second most common type asked by the teachers. Less common were questions that required students to generate new ideas. The study found teachers' questions to be the determining factors in students' verbal productions in the classroom (see Box 9.3).

Taba (1965) categorizes questions according to several functions. She observes that at any level of thought questions may (1) focus the students' attention on a particular point or (2) extend the discussion. Focusing questions establish the topic to be considered. Extending questions encourage elaboration or clarification.

An example of a focusing question is "What is a nocturnal animal?" A related extending question would be "List and describe desert animals." Extending questions distribute participation so that more students are involved in the discussion. Taba (1965) views focusing and extending questions within one level of thought as preparing students for more difficult questions, such as questions that require hypotheses about cause and effect.

Taba's observation of different types of questions within one thought level highlights the importance of the notion of thought level. Bloom (1956) developed a taxonomy of questions based on this notion. According to Bloom's taxonomy, questions can be arranged from lower to higher level consecutively, as follows:

BOX 9.3 Common and Less Common Questions

Cognitive memory questions ask students to recall or recognize facts, generalizations, or previously learned rules that are applicable to the development of a new concept. Examples of cognitive memory questions are "What planet is closest to the sun?" and "What were some of the main points covered in our discussion about mercantilism?"

Convergent productive thinking questions ask for analysis and integration of learned materials; for example, "Can you sum up in one sentence what you think was the main idea in Paton's novel *Cry, the Beloved Country?*"

Evaluative questions, less frequently asked by teachers, ask students to make value judgments; for example, "What do you think of Captain Ahab as a heroic figure in *Moby Dick?*"

Divergent productive thinking questions, also less frequently used, allow students to consider multiple possibilities. One such question might be "Suppose Spain had not been defeated when the Armada was destroyed in 1588, but that, instead, Spain had conquered England. What would the world be like today?"

All types of questions can be used in an inductive approach to concept development. Because of their importance, questions should be guided by instructional purposes so that they move students toward accomplishment of objectives.

Adapted from Gallagher, Aschner & Jenné, 1967, pp. 19, 20.

Knowledge questions demand recall of previously learned material; for example, "What elements compose ammonia?" or "What is the formula for finding the area of a circle?" or "Conjugate the verb 'dormir'."

Comprehension questions require some understanding of content; for example, "What does Hemingway mean by 'grace under pressure'?" or "What incidents led to the papal schism in the fourteenth century?" or "How do earthworms help plants grow?"

Application questions ask students to use learned concepts or skills to solve problems or answer questions; for example, "Describe a phenomenon in the real world that is an example of an inverse proportion" or "Find the adjectives in the given paragraph." Many practice problems in precalculus mathematics require students to apply procedures explained in class.

Analysis questions ask students to identify similarities, associations, differences, and cause-and-effect relationships in an explanation; for example, "How did the author win the reader's sympathy for the protagonist in the story?" or "What is the significance of the stolen milk in Orwell's *Animal Farm?*" Word problems in mathematics require students to analyze similarities, differences, and relationships in a quantitative mode.

Synthesis questions focus students' efforts to integrate information; for example, "What arguments could you offer to support the position that man is inherently good? inherently evil? neither?'' or ''How can the persistence of poverty be accounted for?'' Word problems in mathematics also require students to synthesize the results of their analysis in arriving at an answer.

Evaluation questions ask students to make value judgments; for example, ''Was Oriental art important to the development of Whistler's work?'' or ''What was the most significant event in the Revolutionary War?''

Because they are easy to ask and respond to, knowledge and comprehension questions are the most prevalent. As the preceding discussion of effective question-asking techniques indicates, knowledge and comprehension questions do not promote inductive concept formation. The chief benefit of the Bloom taxonomy is that it gives examples of other sorts of questions (cf. Gallagher et al., 1967).

Good higher-level questions are not easy to create. Sanders (1966), for example, comments on one type of question generally considered to demand high-level cognition:

> There are weaknesses of synthesis questions that must be noted. One is the possibility of asking questions similar to puzzles in that they call for mental gymnastics but have no significance. The question asking the student to write titles for the story about the missionary being boiled to death is an example of a synthesis question having no real significance. Social studies are filled with genuine problems demanding creative thought, so there is no need to deal with trivia.
>
> (Sanders, 1966, p. 128)

Teachers should keep Sander's caution in mind when they use the Bloom taxonomy to plan questions. Higher level does not necessarily mean higher quality. Some questions designed to elicit higher-level processes may be as trivial as any rote-memory questions. As Taba sensed, questions at any level are not independent of relevant content. Perhaps the most important thing for teachers to do is to vary the kinds of questions they ask within a relevant content.

Evaluating Concept Mastery

The emphasis in this section is on the use of tests to assess students' mastery of concepts. Evaluating the results of inductive concept learning should not, however, be limited to measures of awareness or memory for concepts. The major justification for using an inductive approach is that it is supposed to develop transferable concepts or knowledge better than an expository approach (Taba, 1965). For a measure of concept mastery to be fully adequate, therefore, it may need to include assessment of students' facility in applying the new concepts.

Mastery of new concepts can be evaluated according to two basic criteria: completeness, or mastery of all important attributes of the concept, and understanding of the evidence that implicates the concept. Awareness of all the elements that define the concept can be tested—for example, by checking students' ability to discriminate examples of the concept from non-examples.

Robinson and Feldhusen (1984) have suggested some alternatives for evaluating how well students *apply* concepts. These authors rated students' short essays as "restricted" if they were inaccurate, irrelevant, or tautological; as "circumstantial" if they were bound by content, failing to take into account relevant possibilities; and as "imaginative-explanatory" if they used experience and integrated a variety of problem-solving viewpoints. According to Maker (1982a), Hilda Taba evaluated progress in concept formation and inference-drawing by considering whether students (1) selected the correct inference, (2) selected an unimaginative inference which seemed to relate to information in the question, or (3) selected an unsubstantiated inference.

Concept mastery is obviously difficult to evaluate. Some of the problems are the same ones that arise with other kinds of evaluation. Essay tests seem to give greater latitude to student expression, but they are more difficult to rate objectively. Factual tests do not permit students to innovate or to elaborate their answers, but they are easier to rate objectively. Assessment of either concept knowledge or concept application should, in any case, relate to the purposes of evaluation discussed in Chapter 3. The purposes selected can help determine the most appropriate sorts of questions and test formats.

Evaluation Questions Without Words.   Perhaps one of the best ways to evaluate understanding of concepts is to have students *apply* their inferences rather than *talk* about them. Using sophisticated vocabulary is easy for most gifted children: they have an unusual facility for picking up jargon. It sometimes becomes apparent, however, that their ability to use words differs from their ability to apply concepts.

This was the experience of teachers in a British primary grade school program for gifted youngsters (Tempest, 1974). In this program students manipulated electronic components; the staff were at first delighted to hear their young students using terms such as "transistors" and "diodes." Then the staff observed that, although the students were using components according to specific (rote) directions, they did not understand the functions of each component (Tempest, 1974). The staff realized that the students had not learned much about components of electronic circuits.

A solution to this problem was posed by early advocates of inductive learning (e.g., Hendrix, 1965). When application of the concept is the goal of an instructional activity, questions should present a number of exemplars for students to examine and discuss. Hendrix (1965), for example, stresses the need to separate the verbalization of a discovered concept from the insight itself. Premature verbalization, according to Hendrix, fails to ensure that the student really understands the concept; it is probably detrimental as well to formation of the concept.

Hendrix's (1965) research indicates that verbalization is not necessary even for the transfer of mathematical concepts. Students who were asked to verbalize a new mathematics concept did no better on tasks that required transfer of the ideas than did students who were not asked to verbalize the concept. Hendrix's observation may apply to instruction in other subjects also.

TECHNIQUES TO TEACH ACADEMIC SKILLS

The important components of instruction in any academic skill have been identified by Kaplan (1979) in a model of instruction in composition. Kaplan identifies three components: (1) exposure to models, (2) analysis of the models, and (3) practice in applying the techniques used in the models. Either an inductive or an expository approach can incorporate these components. That is, a learning setting may provide materials that allow discovery of techniques for writing poetry, adding numbers, multiplying fractions, or using a microscope, for example; or the techniques can be demonstrated and described. Whether the skills are introduced in an inductive or an expository manner, the value of practice in skill development parallels the value of application in concept development.

Basic Techniques

In order to impart skills, teachers must be prepared to use a number of different techniques in providing opportunities for exposure to skill models, analysis of the models, and practice in applying skills. Practice, however, implicates evaluation. Grammar, mathematical, and composition skills are measured not by asking students to recite rules, but by assessing the application of skills.

Exposure to Skill Models. Kenneth Koch's (1970, 1973) work as a teacher of poetry to regular-class elementary school children demonstrates the importance of exposure to appropriate models. The principles that Koch (1973) applied to the selection of poems to serve as models were excellence of material, relevance of material, and ability of material to challenge even the brightest students. These principles can guide selection of skill models for instruction in any area. (See Box 9.4 for an example of another challenging literature program.)

One of the first instructional decisions Koch made was to disregard the usual criteria for selecting poetry for children to read. These criteria (e.g., childlike subjects and simple vocabulary) would have resulted in the choice of models of "cloying sweetness," according to Koch (1973, p. 13). Koch exchanged the familiarity of stereotypic subject matter such as toys, school, and holidays for the familiarity of feelings expressed in the works of major poets like William Blake, Wallace Stephens, Garcia Lorca, John Donne, and William Shakespeare. He selected poems that were striking in imagery, had elements of fantasy and humor, and had easily modeled forms (e.g., sestinas).

By selecting poems that he knew the students would not completely understand, Koch avoided setting arbitrary limits on his students' understanding. His cues for selecting poems came not only from his intuition but also

---

BOX 9.4   Elementary School Literature Program

Biography, realistic fiction, poetry, and tragedy comprise the literary genres studied in a program for gifted sixth graders. Students selected on the basis of IQ scores, achievement test scores, and teacher recommendations attend the course one hour a day, three days a week, for the entire school year.

During the first part of the course, the students read three biographies, participate in small-group discussions of the biographies, and, as a culminating activity, write a research paper on the life of a famous person. In the second segment, students read three novels, complete directed reading activities, make five reports to the class, and write an original short story. Next, they read and study poetry. Skills learned in poetry are displayed in an anthology of the students' poetry.

The second semester of the school year is devoted to the study of tragedy. The sixth graders read three tragedies: Shaw's *Saint Joan*, Sophocles' *Antigone*, and Shakespeare's *Romeo and Juliet*. According to the teacher, Louise Vida (1979, p. 24), the study of tragedy enables the students to "enjoy the feeling of belonging to humanity." As part of their study, the students attend a live performance of a tragedy as well as a film of a tragedy. These activities, together with playing scenes from the dramas and writing their own plays, complete the students' literature program.

---

from his observation of the children's writing: "What I saw in my students' own poetry was helpful to me in choosing poems to teach them. . . . The extravagance of their comparisons. . . . The tone of secrecy in the poems my students wrote. . . . " (Koch, 1973, p. 12).

Central to Koch's method of teaching poetry was the relationship between understanding poetry and writing it. By writing poetry themselves, the children came to a clearer comprehension of what poets try to do and the methods they use to accomplish their purposes. Willingness to pay attention to the children's responses permitted Koch to arouse student interest and maintain it through the use of intellectually demanding models. These techniques are applicable to instruction in *every* subject area.

Analysis of Skill Models.   Optimal skill development depends in part on analyzing skill models: identifying components, techniques, styles, and forms. For the study of language arts, primary source material is recommended (Mindell & Stracher, 1980); the students should examine the work of respected historians, poets, scientists, and artists. Primary source material alone is not sufficient, however. Students should also analyze one another's work, with the teacher in the role of moderator.

For example, the analysis of a model can be used to teach sentence-combining skills to students. A lesson might begin with examination of a paragraph-long excerpt to study the author's use of different sentence patterns. The paragraph could be compared to samples of student writing, which is often full of choppy sentences (Stoddard & Renzulli, 1983) or nearly identical sentence constructions (Hunt, 1977). The teacher might point out that although variety in sentence length and construction is not a sure index of quality, control over these factors can help students improve their compositions. Finally, the students could analyze the excerpts, identifying all constituent statements contained in each sentence. Examples of this procedure are provided in Box 9.5.

Practice: Applying Skills.   Gifted children need less practice than other children to master most academic skills. The quality of the practice, however, is determined by the same variables that affect the quality of practice for other children. Practice is most effective when it is distributed over time and varied in format (Gage & Berliner, 1975). The immediacy and relevance of feedback also help determine the effectiveness of practice. Practice should, of course, be commensurate with the students' developing skill level.

Though appropriate practice ensures both development and retention of skill, rote drill is anathema to many gifted students. An incremental approach holds more promise for these children. In an incremental approach, subsequent lessons are designed to include tasks requiring previously learned skills. Research has shown much larger achievement gains with an algebra textbook (Saxon, 1979) that incorporated an incremental approach than with traditional

---

BOX 9.5   Sentence Analysis

The opening sentences from Doyle's *The Hound of the Baskervilles* and Lewis's *The Voyage of the Dawn Treader* are given below. Each sentence is followed by a list of possible component statements. (There are many other ways of breaking these sentences into their constituent ideas.) After analyzing these sentences, the students can recombine the component statements in new sentences, discuss their results, compare them with the originals, and then repeat the process using sentences from their own work.

Mr. Sherlock Holmes, who was usually very late in the mornings, save upon those not infrequent occasions when he was up all night, was seated at the breakfast table.

1. Mr. Holmes was seated at the table.
2. It was morning.
3. It was breakfast time.
4. Holmes was usually late to breakfast.
5. There were exceptions to his being late.
6. The exceptions coincided with his being up all night.
7. He was frequently up all night.

There was a boy called Eustace Clarence Scrubb and he almost deserved it.

1. There was a boy.
2. He was called Eustace Clarence Scrubb.
3. He almost deserved his name.

algebra programs (Klingele & Reed, 1984). The difference is surprising in view of the hierarchical nature of mathematics. A conscious effort to build in opportunities to practice recently developed skills may improve achievement in any skill area.

An opportunity for ungraded practice seems to be important also. In *Help Kids Write: A Practical Guide for Teaching Children to Express Themselves on Paper*, Bayne (1980) recommends techniques for giving feedback to students without the use of grades. These techniques are used in a six-part writing program that contains all of the previously mentioned features tending to make practice more effective. The program consists of these components:

- a weekly composition, assigned on Monday and due on Friday;
- a weekly sharing period in which students read their papers or parts of them and critique one another's work;
- time in which the teacher reads aloud to the students from literary works that would be difficult for them to read on their own;
- assignment of silent reading at home;
- free writing time in class; and
- evaluation (not always grading) of students' written work.

There are two means of evaluating students' work. These are (1) a weekly sharing period in which students critique one another's writing and (2) an individual editing conference with the teacher each week. Some papers are graded by the teacher, but not all of them. According to Bayne (1980), students who have struggled to write a composition, perhaps the best they've ever written, are not served well by being given the C the paper might merit in comparison with compositions written by other students. Instead, the teacher should find strengths to comment on and minor corrections to suggest. This program seems to be an excellent means for improving children's skills in literature appreciation as well as their skills in written expression.

Practice: Controlling Quality.   Teachers cannot always work with students on a one-to-one basis; they often have to use supplemental materials or volunteers. This text discussed some supplemental materials in the sections on directed reading, programmed instruction, and auto-instructional activities in Chapter 8. Some additional ways to provide more individualized practice are discussed below.

Practice: Peer Tutors.   One way to provide teacher-surrogates is to use peer tutors. This method compares favorably with other methods. In fact, students working with a peer tutor show greater achievement gains than those using computer drill (Hartley, 1977). Realistically, however, the limitations of peer tutoring are fairly clear. Most children can help other children on spelling, oral reading, and, in some instances, grammar exercises. Computer programming is, for the time being, also a notable example—many children know more about programming than do their teachers.

Gifted students' participation—sometimes as tutors, but primarily as tutees—in a cross-grade tutoring program may offer reciprocal benefits for all participants (Runions, 1980). For example, a sixth grader who needs more practice in multiplication could use flash cards and instructional games with a gifted second grader who is just beginning to learn how to multiply. Needless to say, the teacher must be alert to the possibility that misconceptions may be communicated by the tutors to their peers.

A study team is a form of peer tutoring that encourages students to work cooperatively to improve their performance (Bronfenbrenner, 1970; Swing & Peterson, 1982). Two or three gifted students in a classroom can work together on accelerated, individualized materials. This approach may offset some of the drawbacks of programmed instruction discussed in Chapter 8 (e.g., lack of opportunity to ask questions about the material).

Although achievement gains in terms of improved retention of material have been associated with *serving* as a peer tutor (cf. Demetrulias, 1982), the value of this use of gifted students' class time is questionable. Whenever surrogates substitute for the teacher, frequent assessments should be carried out to make sure that learning is occurring. In order to benefit from serving as a tutor, a gifted student should also need to review the skills being practiced.

Practice: Materials. When instructional materials substitute for the teacher, they must be thoroughly reviewed before use. It is a waste of students' time to use materials that are only tangential to objectives. If the match between materials and objectives is not reviewed prior to use, teachers may expect the materials to do more than they were designed to do.

In reviewing a math computer program, for example, one critic says that it, like most math software, does "not really teach mathematical concepts at all. A child who does not understand the concept of addition is not going to succeed in solving '12 + 12 = ?' despite the presence of colorful space maps" (Fox, 1982, p. 20). Good tutorial software can impart information, provide practice, keep records of student progress, and allow students to progress at their own rates (Herriott, 1982), but teachers should be aware that the quality of computer programs is highly variable (Fox, 1982).

Some logic puzzles, word searches, or games are more entertaining than instructional. For example, a lesson designed to teach principles of aerodynamics may include a logic puzzle using the names of famous pilots or a word search for the parts of an airplane. Such activities are fine if they are recognized as entertainment, but they should not be considered an integral part of the learning sequence. Unfortunately, they are sometimes (mistakenly) justified as teaching higher-level thinking skills.

Computer-Assisted Practice. Computers can be used to provide application and rehearsal of computer science skills and of traditional academic skills. The main advantage of computerized practice is that it allows children to practice at their own pace, thus reducing the average learning time by about one-third. This reduction is equal to the amount by which programmed textbooks reduce learning time (Kulik et al., 1983). Gifted students, like other students, can benefit from interactive drill and practice programs that assign problems based on the students' skill level. In order to accommodate gifted students' skill levels, however, practice software should go beyond the grade level of the students' age-peers.

Enrichment software, including simulation games, is also used for skill development in gifted education programs. Enrichment materials, such as those designed to accompany Newbery Award–winning books, include vocabulary development and comprehension skill-building activities. Simulations used for inductive teaching of social studies, mathematical, or scientific skills enable students to solve, in miniature, problems that would be too expensive or too time-consuming to arrange otherwise. For example, computer simulations have been used to teach skills related to such diverse topics as economic supply and demand, Thorndike's law of effect (that behavior is determined by its consequences), and safe maintenance of nuclear power plants.

Instruction in computer programming also begins early in many gifted education programs. Thomas (1982) notes that children who are ready to begin a study of elementary algebra are ready to grasp the fundamental concepts of BASIC. For gifted children, this may mean a chronological age of ten to twelve years. Many gifted children, however, begin using computers long before they reach this age. Even primary grade–level gifted programs often include instruction and practice in computer programming. LOGO is the programming language that is most commonly used in the early grades. An Advanced Placement study guide in computer science (College Entrance Examination Board, 1983) bases its instructional sequence on Pascal, a programming language that is more powerful than LOGO and includes concepts that are applicable to many programming languages.

Practice in using word processing programs and programs that analyze data is becoming more common in both elementary and secondary classes for gifted students. According to Papert (1981), composing on a word processor frees very young students from the laborious task of handwriting, which distracts children from their train of thought. Whether or not improvement in young children's composition actually results from using a word-processing program has not been established, but for students who have particular difficulty with handwriting, such provisions can make the composition and editing process easier.

Computer data analysis programs allow students to practice the management of information in a particular format. Computer data analysis programs can be used in mathematics, natural science, and social science courses that involve the determination of statistical probabilities. Statistical software may allow students more practice in applying statistical procedures to a set of data than can be gained by paper and pencil methods.

Evaluating Skill Acquisition

Evaluating students' progress in basic academic skills is relatively simple in comparision with evaluating mastery of concepts. The teacher's job is to assemble representative problems, present them to students, check to see if students know how to do each type of problem, and, if not, identify what kind of errors they are making. Testing students' mastery of highly complex skills that can be applied in divergent ways is more demanding. Regardless of the complexity of the skills being taught, evaluation is not only possible but necessary for optimal student achievement.

Skills may be tested by evaluating student products, such as a painting, story, mathematics problem, research report, or essay, or by evaluating performance, such as a dialogue between two students studying Spanish, an oral interpretation of a poem, a musical performance, a debate, or use of laboratory equipment. In either case, criteria for judging the students' mastery of skills must be identified.

Mastery Criteria. Criterion levels for successful mastery of a skill need to be established if gifted students are to receive credit for their academic work. Students in Project F.U.T.U.R.E. were required to demonstrate 85 percent mastery on an off-grade-level achievement test in mathematics or language arts (depending on which advanced, rapid-paced class the student had completed). The relatively high 85 percent criterion level gave a margin of safety to guard against the possibility that rapid coverage of the material might work against thorough integration of skills.

This mastery level and its rationale seem reasonable. Sometimes, however, gifted students in accelerated placements are required to achieve 90 or 95 percent mastery in order to move to the next level of instruction. Requiring such high scores on tests does not provide for testing error. The lower cutoff score of 85 percent on a criterion-referenced test or 85th percentile on a norm-referenced test encourages proficient students to move ahead at their own pace.

The criterion level should reflect the sequential nature of the subject. More sequential subjects seem to require higher criterion levels. In a highly sequential subject such as mathematics, a high criterion level (e.g., 85 percent) assures teachers that the student has mastered basic mathematical operations sufficiently well to understand more advanced concepts. In subjects that are less rigorously sequential such as English, social studies, or reading, a lower criterion level may be in order.

It is, for example, difficult to see why criterion levels for gifted students in subjects less sequential than mathematics should exceed those for students who are following the normal progression and pace. The normal passing criterion level in schools is about 70 percent. If a specified criterion level is sufficient to warrant passing regular students from one curriculum unit or grade to the next, the same level should be high enough to warrant passing gifted students to the next level.

A criterion of 70 percent may, of course, represent D-quality work. One alternative to this dilemma is to distinguish between grading criteria and skill-mastery criteria. That is, a 70 percent skill-mastery criterion need not be equivalent to a D grade; it may be deemed to represent a C or even a B in certain circumstances. The meaningfulness of the skill-mastery criterion level depends on the reliability of the measures employed as well as on educators' assessment of the essential prerequisites for the ensuing grade or unit. Reporting grades differs somewhat from determining skill mastery.

Grades. If the content of gifted classes is as challenging as it should be, it will be more difficult than that of regular classes. Students in accelerated placements will, for example, work harder than they would in a placement with chronological peers. Because grades are considered in admitting students to colleges and in awarding scholarships, some apt students may avoid difficult classes or placements that lower their high school GPA. This is an adaptive reaction of sorts: many students' financial status demands that they consider such factors in selecting the courses they will take. It is not, however, academically desirable. Some school systems have therefore adopted weighted grading systems to use when students elect difficult classes or placements. Under such systems, an A in an advanced course might count more than an A in a regular course. A B in an advanced class might equal, in quality points awarded, an A in a regular course. A C in an advanced course might equal a B in a regular course, and so on.

The same principle is applicable at the elementary level. Gifted students can easily make A's in a regular placement with chronological peers. In choosing accelerated placements, however, they may jeopardize their superior image in trade for doing work that is academically appropriate. Adoption of a weighted grading system is one way to help encourage more academically appropriate placements. It is important that gifted students be awarded credit for the work they do under the auspices of gifted education (Cohn, 1984). The weighted grading system allows credit without reducing students' chances of competing successfully for scholarships and admission to college.

TECHNIQUES ASSOCIATED WITH ENRICHMENT GOALS

The techniques discussed in the two previous sections of this chapter assume the goals for gifted education are academic. Other characteristic approaches to teaching gifted students were introduced in Chapter 1 and discussed in more detail in Chapter 6. These approaches teach concepts and skills related to creativity and problem-solving, social and emotional development, and career education.

Some techniques taught in these programs might be applied in academically oriented programs. Some concepts from these approaches lend themselves to the development of artistic, linguistic, and quantitative concepts and skills. Other concepts may be applicable in the development of discipline-specific skills. A brief catalog of some of these instructional models and techniques is presented next.

Creativity and Problem-Solving

The influence of Guilford's and Bloom's models of cognitive behaviors is apparent in virtually all creativity and problem-solving programs of instruction for gifted children. Guilford's notion of divergent versus convergent productive thinking and Bloom's categories of application, analysis, synthesis, and evaluation are used to organize process-oriented learning activities. Creativity training programs use techniques that would be classified as divergent and synthetic. Programs that emphasize critical thinking use techniques to promote convergent production, application, and analysis.

Techniques to Improve Creative Problem-Solving. Most creative problem-solving techniques emphasize idea production. Osborn (1953) recommended brainstorming as a means of improving creative efforts by pooling the ideas of several individuals. Osborn's guidelines for effective brainstorming are as follows:

1. Accept all ideas without judgmental comments.
2. Use other people's ideas to come up with new ones.
3. Encourage playfulness and "wild" ideas.
4. Try to produce as many ideas as possible.

Creative problem-solving models based on Osborn's (1953) work (revised and elaborated by Parnes, 1981) make explicit some possible steps to take in devising original solutions. These models are reminiscent of the formulaic treatment of the scientific method (e.g., stating the problem, forming the hypothesis, observing and experimenting, interpreting the data, drawing conclusions). Since methods and materials vary with different disciplines, however, models that present methods applicable to all disciplines are necessarily highly general.

Other problem-solving models suggest additional techniques to improve creativity. Synectics (Gordon, 1961; see Chapter 6) uses techniques that elicit different types of analogies to produce original ideas, but it incorporates brainstorming guidelines. Morphological analysis (Arnold, 1962; Callahan, 1978) also uses brainstorming, but it entails identifying various attributes of an object or situation and producing ideas to improve each attribute. Given, for example, the problem of improving their classroom, students would be asked to identify the attributes of a classroom (e.g., size, shape, equipment, materials, inhabitants, location, light, and sound). Brainstorming in morphological analysis is intended to discover ways to vary these attributes and produce ideas for improvement.

Idea production techniques are central to most creativity instruction, but other techniques are used to improve students' effectiveness in defining the problem to be solved, selecting among possible solutions, and verifying the value of the solution. Techniques related to each of these steps can be found in Callahan's (1978) *Developing Creativity in the Gifted and Talented*, Parnes's (1963) *Creative Behavior Guidebook*, Renzulli's (1973) *New Directions in Creativity* and his (1977) *Enrichment Triad Model*, and Torrance's (1965) *Rewarding Creative Behavior*.

Techniques to Improve Critical Thinking. In gifted education the term *critical thinking* generally refers to deductive reasoning, particularly the application of rules for determining the validity of arguments and for solving problems in logic. Instructional techniques range from occasional presentation of logic problems or puzzles to sequential presentation of logic rules and application problems in a formal logic course. The former approach predominates because few teachers have studied formal logic extensively enough to teach it.

By the fourth or fifth grade, many gifted students can benefit from introductory courses in formal and informal logic. By the time they are in junior high school, some gifted students are capable of successful participation in college-level logic courses. The content of courses in formal, or symbolic, logic is relevant for students who are especially able or interested in mathematics, philosophy, or computer programming.

When college courses are unavailable, computer tutorials or programmed textbooks can be incorporated into a teacher-made unit of instruction. An introductory college textbook such as Copi's (1978) *Introduction to Logic* can serve as a basis for the unit and as a text for interested students.

One of the best known courses for developing elementary and junior high school children's critical thinking skills is described in *Philosophy in the Classroom* (Lipman et al., 1977). Two novels written expressly for the course, *Harry Stottlemeier's Discovery* (Lipman, 1974) and *Lisa* (Lipman, 1976), raise questions of logic as well as other philosophical issues. These topics form the basis of class discussions and activities.

Lewis Carroll (1887/1958, 1897/1958) believed that logic was an important area of study for children of approximately thirteen years of age. His books *Symbolic Logic* and *Game of Logic* were written to introduce students to the study of logic.

Social and Emotional Development

Values clarification activities, counseling, and group discussions are the most common techniques in programs with social and emotional development goals. Many programs use the Krathwohl et al. (1964) hierarchy of affective behaviors to structure activities. That hierarchy organizes affective objectives into several categories: receiving, responding, valuing, organization, and characterization.

Presentation of Moral Dilemmas.   One of the most common techniques in programs to promote social development is the presentation of a dilemma for students to resolve. Kohlberg's (1964) research on the development of children's ethics forms the basis of this approach. Students are confronted with a problem, either by reading about a situation or by listening to the teacher's description. They then identify all of the important elements of the situation so that everyone in the class understands the problem. The teacher presents a possible solution, and students vote in favor of or against the proposed solution. Small-group discussions are conducted, in which students discuss the reasons behind their vote. Finally, another vote is taken. The purpose of this type of activity is to make students more aware of their values and to develop responses to ethical problems that are, according to Kohlberg's hierarchy, more mature.

Strategies for Emotional Development. In gifted education strategies to achieve goals of emotional development often attempt to encourage risk-taking and independence rather than adjustment. The Williams's model for affective and cognitive development includes teacher strategies that address these goals. Strategies to help students learn from their mistakes, see alternatives to adjustment, and express their emotions form an integral part of Williams's (1970) *Classroom Ideas for Encouraging Thinking and Feeling.*

Career Education. Mentorships and internships are the approaches to career education commonly used in gifted programs (see Chapter 6). A basic technique underlying these programs is modeling. The mentor provides not only information but also a role model for students to analyze in view of their own values and interests.

Such a model can expand students' notions of the acceptability of different careers. Other sections of this book describe applications of this technique to the education of gifted girls. The use of career role models is equally applicable as a means of overcoming sex-role stereotypes, social-class stereotypes, and stereotypes that limit the career choices of handicapped students. *Modeling can be especially helpful to gifted underachievers, who may have a narrow view of their options.*

BEHAVIOR MODIFICATION AND UNDERACHIEVEMENT

Few teachers of gifted children are educated in the use of behavior modification. The principles of behavior modification are based on analysis of the roles of antecedent conditions and the consequences of behavior in determining what students learn. Instructional techniques based on these principles are virtually ignored in the literature on gifted education. Nonetheless, by varying the antecedent and consequences, teachers can help some gifted students fulfill their academic promise.

Behavior modification tends to be used most frequently with problems of aggression or academic failure. Whitmore's (1980) program for young underachievers is one of the few programs in which behavior modification has been applied to the instruction of gifted children. It is in the area of underachievement, which has proven so resistant to intervention, that behavior modification now offers the greatest promise for gifted students.

Rationale for Behavior Modification Techniques

Although opponents of behavior modification object to its use because the adult consciously sets out to change the students' behavior, advocates of behavior modification point out that all teachers set out to change their students' behavior. Behaviorists note that teachers constantly manipulate students' behavior by giving and withholding approval, good grades, and privileges. According to the behaviorist viewpoint, behavior modification is simply a more explicit and systematic means of changing behavior.

External versus Internal Control. Behavioral psychologists and educators who use principles of behavior modification recommend that students be involved in determining the following (Gelfand & Hartmann, 1975):

1. whether there is a problem,
2. what the contributing variables are,
3. whether their behavior needs to change, and
4. what procedures should be used to accomplish the change.

The gifted child who is making poor grades, for example, in spite of appropriate educational goals and procedures may be asked by the teacher to help identify individual goals and rewards.

Care must be taken that external reinforcers do not encourage dependence on teacher approval. Wherever possible, the work itself should incorporate a reinforcing element, as do self-correcting materials which provide the students with immediate feedback. Only when there is a significant barrier to academic achievement is there a need to supply extraneous reinforcers. One universally accepted extraneous reinforcer, however, allows students to select enrichment or amusement activities after completing their work. Using activity reinforcers is known in the research literature as the *Premack principle*.

There is ample reason to believe that *arbitrary* imposition of rewards or punishments harms the development of internal control. Under such a circumstance, a child never knows what response a particular behavior will elicit. At times it may elicit punishment; at other times it may be ignored. When consequences are unrelated to their efforts, children may not gain a sense of control over what happens to them. A teacher's understanding and use of the logic of behavior modification may therefore actually help children internalize a sense of control.

Cautions about Behavior Modification. The two possible miscarriages of this method are not necessary concomitants of behavior modification. The same problems may also be associated with other teaching or counseling methods. These difficulties involve (1) causing students to adjust to an environment that does not serve their interests but serves the interests of others and (2) applying behavior modification without students' consent.

The second difficulty is easier to avoid than the first. The first may arise when behavior modification is used, for example, to encourage gifted children to comply with inappropriate instructional demands. This possibility can be guarded against, whenever a gifted child is having difficulty in school, by conducting norm- and criterion-referenced testing and informal observation. Educators should recognize that problems are generally the result of an interaction between student characteristics and classroom characteristics. In the usual case, elements of both must change. The demands of the academic setting must be appropriate; students should not be taught to meet academically inappropriate expectations.

Antecedents and Consequences

Consequences should be natural: seeing the completed picture after the last brushstroke, solving a difficult equation, reading a story aloud to an attentive audience. Tokens, candy, money, and other rewards that are unrelated to the task should be used only after other alternatives have failed. The teacher is usually the one who determines what behaviors are acceptable and what the reward will be. Teachers' expectations help establish antecedents to academic behaviors and help determine what behaviors will be reinforced. It is important that teachers of the gifted be aware of the possible effects of their responses preceding and following student behavior.

Teachers' Expectations. Teachers inform children of their expectations through the nature of the assignments they make and through their responses to students' performance on those assignments. Work that is too easy denigrates student effort instead of nurturing it. Accepting work that does not represent students' achievement and ability conveys to individual students the message that intellect is not valued.

Difficult assignments are usually considered threatening to students. They may, however, possess heightened motivational appeal for children who have experienced success in classroom activities in the past. Some research on gifted children suggests that, in comparison to other children, they prefer a higher probability of failure in intellectual tasks (Cronbach & Snow, 1977).

It is not clear how this general preference functions within subgroups of the gifted. Gifted underachievers may avoid risks in situations in which they have experienced failure, but seek them out in situations in which they have had success. Bright children who have had consistently negative experiences in school may avoid any new school-related activities for fear of failure (Whitmore, 1980). It is probably true that some gifted children are so anxious over their academic performance that they are unwilling to make an effort to perform. These children must first learn that they are capable of succeeding before they will be ready to test their limits (Torrance, 1965; Whitmore, 1980).

Teacher expectations should reflect the gradual improvement in underachievers' work. Students who have been performing far below their capacity, convinced that they are failures, cannot suddenly be confronted with standards that require skills they have yet to learn. For these children, intermediate academic goals must be established first (Durr, 1964; Whitmore, 1980).

Expectations that are too low, on the other hand, also inhibit the performance of gifted children (Durr, 1964). Educators who make learning risk-free may actually lower gifted students' interest in school tasks. For gifted children, success generally cannot be equated with ease.

The Effects of Praise.   Praise has been considered one of the teacher's most useful means of improving academic performance (Flanders, 1967; Gelfand & Hartmann, 1975). Its indiscriminate use, however, can hinder academic growth. Praise that is incongruent with students' perception of their work and praise for intrinsically rewarding work have been shown to be *detrimental* to achievement (Fulks, 1983). Praising students for activities that they undertake voluntarily may also decrease the students' voluntary participation in the activity, such as reading for pleasure (Maehr, 1976). Even play can be inhibited by providing extrinsic rewards for it (Gotz, 1977).

Judicious praise is honest and, above all else, informational. It may be indirect in that the teacher uses the students' ideas rather than praising them (Flanders, 1967; see also the previous section on question-asking). More effective than a gold star or "good job" written at the top of the paper are specific comments related to student performance (Fulks, 1983). Such comments are sometimes termed "corrective academic feedback."

Superior teachers give *reasons* for criticism and praise more often than other teachers. Most successful teachers in schools with high socioeconomic status, for example, tend to be demanding (Gage, 1978). They seem to use criticism sparingly, but in sufficient measure to communicate high expectations for student performance. Repeated use of student ideas and well-elaborated answers to students' questions appear to increase student participation in learning activities (Pankratz, 1967).

In general, teachers of the gifted can probably help their students by applying strategies commonly used by parents of high achievers (Tannenbaum, 1983):

1. setting high goals,
2. holding competence in high regard,
3. expecting children to be self-reliant and to assume responsibility for performance, and
4. employing consequences that reflect these expectations and attitudes.

Basic Techniques of Behavior Modification

All of the techniques teachers can use to modify students' behavior involve variations on four possible consequences: positive reinforcement, negative reinforcement, punishment, and response cost. Reinforcement, positive or negative, increases the behavior it follows. Both punishment and response cost decrease the behavior they follow. An excellent text on the practice of these techniques is *Strategies for Managing Behavior Problems in the Classroom* (Kerr & Nelson, 1983).

When teachers arrange consequences to change students' behavior, their treatment of choice should be reinforcement. It is efficient to reinforce desirable academic behaviors (e.g., completing math problems correctly, finishing class assignments, or attending to class discussions) that are incompatible with undesirable behaviors (e.g., wandering around the room, daydreaming, or disrupting class).

Punishment is generally a less effective means of behavior change. The anxiety, fear, and anger associated with the punishment are often generalized by the child to the teacher and the school setting. Punished behavior thus usually recurs.

Response cost involves removal of reinforcers for inappropriate behavior. Since reinforcers are taken away from the child in a response cost intervention, some theorists view this technique as aversive, like punishment. Response cost, however, can be used effectively in combination with positive reinforcement.

Two effective and commonly used means of improving academic achievement are (1) simple provision of positive reinforcement for small gains and (2) use of contingency contracts. Making sure the child earns something for improvements (e.g., for every math worksheet completed at least 85 percent correctly, for fifteen minutes of concentrated work on an academic task, for completing all the morning's assignments) is simple positive reinforcement. Contingency contracts are usually written agreements between the student and teacher stating what the student must do in order to earn a reinforcer.

Behavior modification looks simple, but its appearance is deceptive. There are many possible sources of failure. If a gifted child is a chronic underachiever, the teacher is likely to need help in identifying the sources of the problem and possible solutions. Behavior modification may not be needed at all if variables other than student behavior are the source of the problem. If behavior modification is required, the teacher may need to ask for help in planning and implementing the program.

SUMMARY

Techniques for teaching gifted students use the students' inclination to question and their ability to form abstractions readily. These characteristics suggest the need for teachers who have incorporated similar traits into their own scholarship and who can direct students to resources that can supply further data or instruction.

Gifted students' characteristic learning methods also require that their teachers be adept at using techniques of inductive instruction. Gifted children need less time to master material taught inductively than do other children. Techniques for asking questions to assist gifted students in the inductive process were presented in this chapter, as were considerations for evaluation of concepts acquired through inductive strategies.

Techniques for developing gifted students' academic skills were discussed in terms of three components of skill instruction: exposure to models, analysis of models, and practice. Suggestions and cautions regarding the quality of various practice methods were presented as well.

Exemplary techniques from enrichment models that address problem-solving goals, social and emotional goals, and goals for career education were briefly discussed and books for further reference identified. Finally, behavior modification, which is rarely used with gifted students, was examined as an alternative to consider in work with gifted underachievers. Possible difficulties with behavior modification techniques were pointed out.

CHAPTER 10

Aesthetics and the Gifted: The Arts in the Schools

INTRODUCTION

Art and music have not typically been treated with much respect by the schools, perhaps because they lack the utility and solid respectability of other disciplines (cf. Ziegfeld, 1961). In spite of their long academic history and their intellectual integrity, the arts are not easily integrated into the school program. They present special problems in the areas of assessment, planning, and curriculum. The relation of art and music to general cultural values shapes these problems and our discussion.

The domain of the arts is aesthetic expression and its criticism. Most aspects of life, including the disciplines of learning, can be understood aesthetically. Hardy (1969), Russell (1919), and Wiener (1956) demonstrate the vigor of an aesthetic sensitivity in mathematics.

Here we will use the term *arts* generically to refer to all arts, and the term *art* specifically to refer to graphic and plastic arts. Our attention will be focused specifically on visual art and music because U.S. schools do accord a place in the instructional sequence to these disciplines.

This chapter considers arts education programs for the gifted. The chapter reviews such offerings within the context of general school arts programs. It contrasts creativity training with arts instruction. Finally, the chapter examines model arts programs and suggests improvements in typical arts programs, based on the premise that the cognitive elements of the arts are the elements most capable of being conveyed pedagogically.

Because the emphasis of this text is on students and schools, the discussion focuses on art and music as academic disciplines. Surely, if "the relationship between intelligence and [artistic] gifts is close" (Hollander, 1978, p. 48; cf. Getzels & Jackson, 1962), schools should do a better job of providing music and art instruction for the intellectually gifted. In addition, the technical instruction of talented artists, musicians, dancers, and writers can occur within public school systems committed to that end (see e.g., Cox & Daniel, 1983).

THE SCHOOL ARTS CONTEXT

Within the context of mass education, arts instruction has served various ends. It has been used to train students in manual skills; it has been used to develop the moral sensibilities of students; it has been used to promote the development of the whole child (Eisner, 1972). In spite of its presence in school curricula, arts instruction is accepted hesitantly by many educators "who view the arts as an elitist and outdated source of learning" (Dimondstein, 1976, p. 14). The love-hate relationship that has been said to describe the nation's attitude toward intellectually gifted children (Gallagher, 1978) also characterizes its attitude toward artists. On one hand, they are regarded as threatening to the status quo; on the other hand, they are regarded as necessary to the country's continued vitality. The poorly funded, technically weak programs that constitute much of arts education today represent an unsatisfactory resolution of these opposing attitudes.

Lorin Hollander, the American musician and concert pianist, has recorded a personal parable of the relationship between the arts and the public schools:

> I gave my first concert, which was actually in the kindergarten class, and the whole day seems now rather—rather—metaphoric. It was called "circus" and the other members of the community pretended to walk tightropes, pretended

> to train animals, or were clowns and I played the two-part inventions of Bach. After the concert I had my first confrontation with the attitude of Arts & Lectures committees to all Bach performances: I was beat up in the schoolyard by my audience.
>
> (Hollander, 1978, p. 41)

Hollander's irony is edged with some resentment for our "Dating Game . . . [and] Gong Show mentality" with respect to the arts (Hollander, 1978, p. 49). He says further

> We as a community have chosen certain people to be the teachers and certain people to make the policy in what to teach these children. . . . But somehow these people . . . have made a gruesome mistake. They have decided to take the arts out of the schools.
>
> (Hollander, 1978, p. 49)

In such a context what shall we make of the fact that one of the recent TV serials most popular among preadolescents and adolescents romanticizes the events at one of the nation's most renowned performing arts high schools? Sadly, our "Gong Show mentality" has overtaken the schools. Regardless of how it may be distorted in video image, a stimulating atmosphere of artistic production represents an unattainable fantasy for millions; at the same time, in reality the arts are faulted for being elitist, impractical, and unconventional.

The Arts as Enrichment

Efforts to provide more substantial arts programs must counteract stereotypes of artists as starving and unstable and of the arts as elitist and inaccessible. Myths about the arts and artists have contributed to schools' difficulty in locating arts instruction within the regular curriculum. Often, schools view arts instruction as extracurricular or as enrichment. Careful consideration of the myths and realities of arts and artists may enable educators to accord arts instruction the priority that it deserves within an academic context.

Popular Stereotypes.   Many people experience discomfiture in the presence of art or music that is not familiar. Their difficulty in understanding works of art may make them feel less competent or less cultured than others. It may also indicate the degree to which aesthetic perceptions vary from common-sense representations of the world. Unfortunately, too many people, including educators, believe that they cannot understand the arts. The belief that the arts are inaccessible contributes to the confused state of arts education in public schools.

Educators concerned with the instruction of all children either may view the arts as inimical to the egalitarian principles of the common school or may consider the arts particularly well suited to the goals of developing the creative potential of all children (e.g., Chetelat, 1981; Lowenfeld & Brittain, 1964).

Both views are probably inaccurate, considering the various aims of public education (cf. Broudy, 1970).

One notion of the arts sees them as a palliative for excessive exposure to the sciences and other cognitive studies (cf. Langer, 1957). In this capacity, the arts seem to mitigate the mechanistic tendencies of a highly technological society (Ziegfeld, 1961). In pedagogy, this view attributes to arts instruction a *therapeutic utility*. When a small dose of the arts is provided to every child as an antidote to the dehumanizing effects of instruction in the other subjects, intensive arts instruction is apt to be considered an indulgence. This approach decreases the likelihood that relevant arts instruction will be available for talented students.

Arts as a Low Priority in Schools.   Parents and many teachers seem to agree that all students should receive some exposure to the arts to balance their school experience, but they do not recognize the legitimacy of the arts as subjects of academic study. Evidence of this attitude is reported by Szekely (1981) in his account of an artist-in-the-schools program. When parents and teachers were first told about the proposed program, they applauded the idea but suggested that the instruction be held after school so that it would not interfere with the students' academic studies.

Because of their low pedagogical priority, most arts education programs provide opportunities for participation in planned activities rather than formal instruction in either skills or content. Such programs are intended to encourage a minimal level of participation by all students. As a result, these programs allow for only rudimentary mastery of performance skills by those students who are especially interested or able.

Although basic arts programs are typically scheduled into the school day or week, many advanced arts programs are available solely through after-school art clubs, drama clubs, or choral groups. Even when advanced classes are available, they may not provide appropriate opportunities for talented students whose potential has not been developed. Because of the inadequacies of the basic arts program, many students' talents are neither recognized nor encouraged. The talents of others may be stifled through either neglect or the convergent emphasis of schools (cf. Torrance, 1963).

Since participation is the focus of most arts education classes, school arts programs rarely provide instruction in arts criticism and arts history (Munro, 1960). In practice, high school arts electives are frequently offered to students who are less capable in academic areas (Brown, 1983). Such students are channeled into arts programs because these programs are noncognitive in their orientation and do not have stringent standards for judging the merits of artistic performance (Eisner, 1965). Many talented students avoid arts electives because of their reputed noncognitive orientation (Brown, 1983).

In general, high school arts programs are so inconsistent that "the college teacher who faces a freshman class in either the history or the practice of the arts can hardly ever assume any specific knowledge or skill in that field on the part of high school graduates" (Munro, 1960, p. 9). The majority of college preparatory students who do elect arts classes are, in retrospect, dissatisfied with their high school programs in those subject areas (American Council for the Arts in Education, 1977).

Support for arts education is so limited that in less affluent communities arts teachers itinerate (Goodlad, 1970) and students are fortunate to have music or art for an hour a week. In these communities, there exist neither the resources nor the expertise to identify and serve the most talented students. The situation is analogous to, but more exaggerated than, that of the most intellectually gifted students of poor communities. Intellectually gifted students, no matter how poor the district, ought at least to have the inexpensive option of acceleration through the curriculum.

Acceleration, however, is not even a *potential option* for the artistically gifted, because most arts programs are not based on a sequential curriculum (Eisner, 1972; Stroh, 1974). Instead of presenting a coherent sequence of concepts and skills, arts programs typically reflect the interests of particular teachers (Wold & Hastie, 1965). Such programs expose students to a variety of experiences with different media or forms, but they do not consistently promote students' sense of control over any one medium (Eisner, 1965). In this way, school arts programs resemble enrichment programs for the gifted. Their low status in schools reduces the quantity of service provided and, potentially, the quality of instruction.

Convergence and Divergence in the Schools

Guilford's (1967) Structure of the Intellect model lists convergent production and divergent production as two of five mental operations. These two operations are similar because both involve retrieval of information from memory (Khatena, 1982). They differ, however, in that convergent production involves the statement of the one correct answer to a specific question, whereas divergent production involves the generation of numerous, varying responses to an open-ended question. Several authors (e.g., Guilford, 1967; Khatena, 1982; Torrance, 1974) associate divergent production with creativity and the presumed subskills of creativity: fluency, flexibility, elaboration, and originality. Art educators (e.g., Kaufman, 1966; Saunders, 1982) also associate divergent production with creativity. Kaufman (1966) considers the impact of schools' inhibition of divergent production:

> The average kind of teaching that occurs in the schools is geared to convergent learning, knowing the ''right'' answers, categorizing and systematizing what has been learned, producing acceptable imitations or specific syntheses in some particularized form. . . . The expressive qualities that are involved, on the other hand, in drawing, painting, or in sculpture are divergent in that they search out resolutions to problems and even cognitive tensions that may take any number of forms.

> (Kaufman, 1966, p. 265)

Although schools traditionally have encouraged convergent production (Lowenfeld & Brittain, 1964), their overt influence has not been wholly responsible for inhibiting the divergent production of children. Pressures for conformity arise in the social environment of schools as a result of the interactions both among children and between children and adults (cf. Coleman, 1961; Thelen, Frautschi, Roberts, Kirkland & Dollinger, 1981). The fact that the school environment encourages conformity probably does restrict the creative expression of students to some extent (cf. Torrance, 1963).

It is clear from an analysis of the content of the arts that instruction in these fields requires students to perform in both convergent and divergent modes. In fact, technical proficiency in the performing arts greatly overshadows creative expression, especially during the formative stages of skill development (cf. Bloom & Sosniak, 1981). The convergent production of correct notes on the violin precedes the creative interpretation of, for example, the Bach partitas and sonatas for violin solo. Even musical composition clearly requires a convergent, cognitive understanding of music theory (Thomson, 1962).

Creative arts that purport to require no technical competence are derived from a modernist aesthetic philosophy. These forms include plastic arts (especially painting and sculpture) and poetry. Neither abstract painting nor automatic writing, both of which represent departures from a representational aesthetic, constitutes a pedagogical mandate. These aesthetic views were never intended to legitimate a particular approach to arts instruction but rather to justify the departure by artists from traditional expressive modes. They cannot, in fact, be properly understood without this awareness. The interpretative license derived from these aesthetic views may allow students to explore media more freely. It does not, however, replace or supersede knowledge of technique, nor does it provide arts literacy.

The notion that all children are talented artists, which also relates to an abstract aesthetic, suggests a significant difference between learning processes in the arts and in the sciences. In the same sense, however, that all children are artists, they also are all scientists (Dulee, 1983). The fact that children are receptive to the world around them and can become inventive in a variety of media does not absolve schools of their educative responsibilities either in the arts or in the sciences.

Students Gifted in the Arts

The preceding discussion has significant implications for both the identification and the training of students gifted in the arts. If arts programs include hierarchical instruction in skills, students with particular talents can be recognized by their precocity or proficiency in developing those skills. Instruction can involve advanced technical training and, where appropriate, consideration of innovative solutions to artistic problems. Although some authors maintain that "facility with materials may not mean giftedness, but talent" (Salome, 1974, p. 16), we do not see the relevance of this distinction.

Of course childhood precocity, talent, or apparent giftedness (however defined) does not ensure adult creativity or excellence in a particular art form. Conversely, some adults demonstrate considerable artistic talent, even though they did not evidence childhood precocity (cf. Clark & Zimmerman, 1983).

In order to serve artistically gifted children, arts education programs must be strengthened. This will involve an increased emphasis on the cognitive aspects of the arts (Bernstein, 1982). According to Eisner (1966), arts education provides instruction in highly complex cognitive skills:

> Those who conceive of art as the expression or release of affect, misunderstand the nature of the artistic task. The artist's activity, far from being an unfettered discharge of emotion, is a controlled affair of the intellect, pervaded by emotions and functioning within the realm of the qualitative.
>
> (Eisner, 1966, p. 493)

A cognitive orientation in arts education is based on a concern for cumulative learning such as that found in the literature on language arts and mathematics learning (Engel, 1983). This approach allows for the development of sequential curricula in the arts, the provision of artistic literacy training to all students, and the initiation of special instructional programs for those students especially talented or interested in one or more of the arts.

PROGRAM DISTINCTIONS: INTELLECTUAL VERSUS ARTISTIC

The discussion in Chapter 2 indicated some of the difficulties inherent in efforts to identify students talented in the arts. In particular, it considered the dilemma of arts potential, a characteristic that was no better identified by creativity tests than by IQ tests. We concluded in Chapter 2 that many gifted students with IQs above 130 possess music or art talents. We can be no more certain, however, that these students possess the *most remarkable* music and art talents than we can be sure that they possess the most remarkable mathematics talent (cf. Stanley, Keating & Fox, 1974).

As with other academic programs for gifted students, we stress the importance of instruction related to identification paradigms. Therefore, in the arts, *as in other academic fields,* a distinction needs to be made between programs that serve children with general intellectual aptitude and those that serve children with specific academic aptitudes. Children with specific aptitudes in music need advanced courses in music performance, theory, and literature; those with specific aptitudes in art need advanced courses in media techniques, design, and art history. In practice very few school systems will seek to implement such programs; a few large systems may be able to establish specialized secondary schools for performing and creative arts, if they have not already done so.

More practicable are arts programs for students with general intellectual aptitude. Many of these students report a significant interest in aesthetic questions (Tidwell, 1980) and would probably qualify for the sort of arts program described above on the basis of both interest and specific talent (cf. Eisner, 1966). These students would very definitely profit from a program in the arts that developed a true literacy in the idioms of art and music through work in listening and viewing in the context of art and music history (Hurwitz, 1983). Most other gifted students should also be exposed to such instruction, regardless of interest, because of the intellectual significance of the arts. Rudimentary music and art courses offered to all students leave much to be desired in this regard (cf. Miller, 1979).

Although we recommend arts programs for all gifted students, we do not include these recommendations in the curricula presented in Chapter 7. That discussion focused on the fundamental (i.e., minimum) curriculum. Recommendation of arts instruction for all intellectually gifted students is based on the assumption that these students are already receiving instruction in the fundamentals discussed earlier. Arts instruction as well as elective options in many areas would be part of an optimal curriculum for the gifted.

The Two Components of the Arts Curriculum for the Gifted

The preceding discussion suggests the need to develop a program that includes two components, a basic program for all gifted students and a variety of electives for students with exceptional artistic talent (cf. Lehman, 1983). Effective programs to develop aesthetic literacy require daily effort toward learning arts idioms, concepts, and history. Such learning cannot take place in a series of unrelated activities featuring assorted media or visiting artists (Hope, 1983).

For the student with aptitude in the arts, aesthetic literacy is only a beginning. The amount of time devoted by such a student to the study of the art must be increased, as must the amount of instruction and materials; skill development in the arts, which is what distinguishes such a program from a general arts literacy program, requires an extraordinary amount of time and effort (Klein, 1983). In Box 10.1, Virgil Thomson comments on the extent of such training and its meaning to the musician.

Practice in a specific art field must begin early and become increasingly intensive in order for outstanding talent to emerge (Bloom, 1982; Bloom & Sosniak, 1981; Holton, 1983; Sward, 1933). Studies of prodigies and adults eminent in the arts indicate that instruction, practice, and performance take up increasingly more of the artistically talented students' time, until eventually most of their waking hours are spent in activities related to practice or performance of their art (Bloom, 1982). Students show a marked commitment to the field of their interest (cf. Hollander, 1978). Willingness to work and enjoyment of work are evident (Feldman, 1979a). Unfortunately, it is obvious that schools do very little on behalf of such students. Hollander (1978) implies that schools' best efforts have been to stay out of the way of their artistically talented students.

BOX 10.1   In the Midst of a Tawdry World

The eminent American composer Virgil Thomson (b. 1896) summarizes the significance of the musician's training in his *The State of Music* (1962, pp. 58–59):

> Of all the professional trainings, music is the most demanding. Even medicine, law, and scholarship, though they often delay a man's entry into married life, do not interfere with his childhood or adolescence.
>
> Music does. No musician ever passes an average or normal infancy, with all that that means of abundant physical exercise and a certain mental passivity. . . . I think that he is just more elaborately educated than his neighbors. But he does have a life different from theirs, an extra life; he grows up . . . to feel different from them on account of it. . . . Musical training is long, elaborate, difficult, and intense. Nobody who has had it ever regrets it or forgets it. And it builds up in the heart of every musician a conviction that those who have had it are not only different from everybody else but definitely superior to most and that all musicians together somehow form an idealistic society *in the midst of a tawdry world.*

[emphasis added]

We have added the emphasis above because we shall allude several times to this sense of difference which distinguishes the aesthetic viewpoint. Research (cf. MacKinnon, 1968) interprets such sentiments as personality differences characteristic of the creative temperament. We note that such sentiments are more pedagogically relevant when they can be seen as representative of intellectual differences (cf. Eisner, 1966, p. 493).

Sometimes schools justify their reluctance to provide arts education for talent development as concern for the whole child. This argument is based on apprehension about children's emotional development should their talents be "exploited"; the argument is not, however, applied to school athletes. This concern may in fact be legitimate in *parents* of a bona fide child prodigy in the performing arts; however, it does not warrant the conclusion that in all cases the best solution is repression of talent development.

Chandler (1980) reflects the prevalent attitude by recommending that parents of gifted children allow their children to determine when and if they wish to take music lessons. Working in the arts—and, to a more modest extent, enjoying the arts—demands rigor, discipline, and time (Greene, 1980; Thomson, 1962). Even prodigies (e.g., the cellist Yo-yo Ma) report that they were often reluctant students.

It is unwise to restrict children's aesthetic experience to what is conventional, safe, or preconditioned. The vision of the arts is a vision of what exists outside familiar experience. Educators do have the option of maintaining that the arts are pedagogically irrelevant because they lack utility. In the competition between aesthetics and utility, our schools *must* endorse utility. The dilemma, however, for gifted students and artistically talented students can still be sharp. Validation of their needs and their individuality will somehow address the aesthetic issues with which they are concerned.

PROGRAMS CURRENTLY AVAILABLE FOR ARTISTICALLY TALENTED STUDENTS

Programs for the artistically gifted are in even shorter supply than programs for the intellectually gifted. Advanced programs, defined as programs that go beyond basic instruction, are rare because coherent, sequential, basic instruction in the arts is rare. Those advanced programs that are available to artistically gifted students are usually found in large, comprehensive high schools and in schools that specialize in the arts. More generally available are various types of arts enrichment provisions. These take the form of learning centers in the classroom, mini-courses, artist-in-the-schools programs, volunteer programs, and summer programs. The effects of these part-time programs are necessarily more limited than those of more comprehensive, advanced programs. Arts centers, usually designed to serve children from several schools, combine some of the features of arts schools with aspects typical of enrichment programs.

Arts Enrichment Programs in the Public Schools

Even with the best intentions and a fair amount of ingenuity, the educators and volunteers who have developed arts education efforts in the public schools have not been able to approximate the instructional conditions that accompany prodigious artistic achievement. The primary benefit of some of the alternatives described in this section is that they offer enough instruction so that some children can be recognized as having artistic potential.

Learning Centers. Learning centers for independent or small-group activities in the regular classroom or the arts education classroom provide one means of addressing individual differences in level of artistic talent within a grade (cf. Chetelat, 1981). Like enrichment centers for intellectually gifted children, this approach does not offer significant modification in educational programming. As a result, the scope and nature of learning objectives that can be accomplished through this alternative are severely limited.

Of all the arts, the visual arts probably involve the skills with the greatest potential for development in the classroom learning center. Art history books, art supplies, and artistic problems individually assigned on the basis of students' interests and abilities can be included without too much difficulty (Chetelat, 1981). Self-study units can be organized to include study questions, slides, tools, and materials related to particular art media or topics of art history (Hurwitz, 1983).

Mini-courses. Mini-courses are used in both regular classrooms and gifted education classrooms to provide enrichment in the visual and performing arts. Those designed specifically for intellectually gifted students are often intended to teach creative processes rather than artistic skills. Activities that might be included in art-related mini-courses for gifted students are relaxation exercises, fluency exercises, and "cross-sensory" exercises (see, e.g., Khatena, 1981). There is little research to demonstrate that such activities are an effective means of developing artistic talent. Instruction in visualization, sensitivity, or brainstorming, for example, will not necessarily result in improvement in artistic performance.

A list of typical mini-courses for elementary school children includes titles such as "Masks," "Moving to Music," and "Method Acting and Interpretative Dancing" (Oliver, 1978). At the secondary level, one finds courses such as "Experimental Music" (music composition and performance), "Art and Music of the 20th Century," "Through History in Strings" (North American folk music), and "Music and Poetry" (Oliver, 1978). Such courses provide enrichment for interested students, but they cannot in any way be considered adequate for students who are capable of extraordinary artistic achievement.

Mini-courses that are scheduled into the school day like other courses and that last for at least one grading period may be as effective as other arts electives. The major drawback of the mini-course is that it is not a segment of curriculum that is intentionally related to academic goals. Thus, like other extracurricular activities, it is likely to be scheduled at irregular intervals or for unacceptably short periods of time. Like other extracurricular activities, mini-courses may not be evaluated for effectiveness. The major benefit of mini-courses is that they offer a means to introduce subjects which should be a part of the regular curriculum, such as music appreciation, art history, or aesthetic education.

Advanced Classes and Electives.   Electives for junior and senior high school students offer one means of meeting the needs of the artistically gifted. Although, as noted earlier, most such electives are not really advanced courses, a few are specifically intended for talented students. For example, a large public high school in Chicago requires students to audition for advanced technique classes in its highly structured dance program (Knowles, 1982).

Advanced Placement courses allow serious arts students to earn college credit by examination while they are still in high school. Advanced Placement courses available include two studio art courses, one art history course, and one music listening and literature course (Clendening & Davies, 1980; Dorn, 1976). Studio course students submit portfolios for review by experts in the arts, who consider the quality, concentration, and breadth of the students' work; ratings given by these experts determine the students' examination scores (Dorn, 1976). Examinations in the art history and music listening and literature courses are similar in format to the CEEB tests given in other academic areas; that is, they are composed of multiple-choice and essay questions.

Electives for elementary school children are relatively rare; however, one school system offers four years of piano instruction to students in this age group (Pardue, 1982). Students learn keyboard skills in classes that meet for forty minutes twice a week. No more than twelve students are enrolled in each class. Teacher applicants must audition in order to be considered for the program, and those who are accepted must complete a two-week workshop in order to learn group-teaching techniques for piano instruction (Pardue, 1982).

Because the children's parents pay a fee to cover the costs of the program, it is actually private instruction. This program model, however, offers public schools an option that can contribute significantly to skill development among artistically gifted students. One of its most important elements is that it begins early in the child's school career; another is that it is sequential and covers an extended period of time. Electives modeled after aspects of this group piano program could be developed in all of the arts.

Artists and Volunteers in the Schools. All of the alternatives described so far have used education personnel as instructors. Because of the specialized skills required for work in the arts and children's need to be exposed to experts in the field, several programs have attempted to bring artists into the schools, either as mentors for talented or interested children or simply as role models (see, e.g., Yeatts, 1980; cf. Koch, 1970). Shortage of funds has often meant that the artists could not be paid and thus their contact with students had to be minimal. In some cases federal funds have supplemented local monies, as in the Artists-in-the-Schools program (Harrod, 1979). Student artists and volunteers have added to the educational alternatives for all children; but, again, their impact is limited by the amount of time and other resources available to their programs.

Artists-in-the-schools programs are generally well liked by the teachers and administrators who are involved with them, but most programs have not documented changes in student behavior (Aquino, 1978). That these programs have potential to bring about measurable differences in achievement was demonstrated by a program that employed a novelist-actress as an artist-in-residence to work with gifted students (Yeatts, 1980). Junior and senior high school students worked half-days for a semester with the artist, critiquing and composing original prose. By critiquing the novelist's manuscripts, the students were able to develop criteria for making editorial decisions about their own writing. At the end of the semester, both formal and informal evaluation showed improvement in the students' written expression (Yeatts, 1980).

A variation of the artist-in-the-schools approach is the use of student artists in the schools. For example, an art partnership network was established in one school system to enlist college art majors as mentors for talented children (Szekely, 1981). The college students served as role models for the children and as mentors in helping them develop their own artistic ability. Before working with the children, college students in the art partnership network attended workshops to learn about the type of children with whom they were to form partnerships. The originator of the program claims that through this program artistically talented children can observe firsthand the solution of difficult aesthetic problems, and have a chance to discuss art and their own work with someone who is as intensely interested in the field as they (Szekely, 1981).

The Student-Artist-In-Residence program (SAIR) established in another school district received a federal grant to bring twenty-four college art students into the schools to practice their art (Norris, 1977). Students received a small amount of money and independent study credit to do art projects in the schools. Since the student artists were not commissioned to serve the schools by instructing children in art, the effects of this project were difficult for project personnel to evaluate (Norris, 1977). Teachers, administrators, and students all expressed both positive and negative attitudes toward the program. The positive comments attributed to the program the emergence of a more stimulating atmosphere and an increase of interest in art in the schools.

Some of the problems identified with the SAIR program are probably common to programs of this nature. For example, art professors who were supposed to supervise and assist the student artists working in the schools did not play as active a role as had been expected. Although Norris (1977) did not indicate what incentives were used to ensure the professors' participation, it is possible that they were not compensated for the additional workload. Failure to compensate participants is a common problem with many projects that seek to institute change in education.

Art teachers employed in the schools expressed some resentment toward the visiting student artists. They mentioned that the children saw the college students as real artists and their teachers as only teachers (Norris, 1977). This problem might have been alleviated had teachers been informal advocates and assistants to the project. Lack of space in which the college art students could work and lack of equipment and materials for them to use were also identified as problems.

An interesting question raised by the SAIR program was whether or not student artists and the schools were compatible. The administrators, at least initially, *did* disapprove of the student artists (Norris, 1977). One of the students most objectionable to school administrators had the highest GPA of the twenty-four students and was exceptionally talented. Basic differences in values affect not only the funding of arts education programs but also the implementation and effects of such programs.

Resolution of some of the problems common to artist-in-the-schools programs could be facilitated if programs were evaluated so that effective elements could be retained and strengthened and ineffective elements corrected. According to Eisner (1974), there are six areas in which evaluative data should be collected:

1. the number of students involved and the nature of their involvement in the program;
2. the project goals and measurement of their accomplishment;
3. continuance of the project by the school district;
4. successful elements of the program;

5. correlations among teaching ability, artistic competence, and personality of artists; and

6. flexibility of the system.

As they are currently conducted, most of these programs are more valuable as introductory experiences than as a means of serious study of the arts. It should be noted, however, that this is precisely the intention of most such programs.

Other volunteers can help provide alternatives for arts education in the schools. Parents, for example, can help in planning and implementing programs. One parent volunteer program presents art history and art appreciation lessons to elementary school classes (Ganley, 1983). Reminiscent of the picture study approach to art education used in the 1950s, this program features a painting a month. Parents research paintings, compile a bibliography for each one, summarize information about each painting, and suggest related instructional activities. The files are given to other parent volunteers to use in planning and conducting art lessons in classrooms at each grade level. Although this program is not the kind needed by artistically gifted children, it contributes a dimension of art education not found in many public schools. This approach, used in combination with seminars (such as those in the Junior Great Books program), could be used in a mini-course or elective for elementary school students if sufficient numbers of volunteers were available to support it. The main effect of the parent volunteer program just described is that it stimulates student interest in the visual arts (Ganley, 1983).

Artistic performances, such as symphonies, art shows, dance performances, and operas, have been presented in schools, partly for charitable reasons. Education is often seen by the public as a more legitimate enterprise than performance; thus, arts organizations may find that civic groups and foundations are more generous with their funds when the organization has an educational program (Hart, 1973). Although these educational outreach programs have the potential to make an important contribution to the education of all children, the quality of the instruction is not always high, because of a lack of coordination and communication between the organization and the schools (Hart, 1973; Schubart, 1972). Artists and educators need to consult with one another on content and methods. Some educators see the repertoire of opera or music companies as irrelevant to students' lives (Hart, 1973; cf. Cohen, 1981). However, many educators understand that the point of education is to extend students' perception of what is relevant (e.g., Postman & Weingartner, 1969). These educators and educators who are themselves involved in the arts should participate in planning cooperative programs with arts organizations.

Special Arts Curricula. One of the best known arts-related curricula is the Aesthetic Education Program developed by CEMREL, Inc., a private, nonprofit corporation. The curriculum consists of six levels designed to teach basic aesthetic concepts to elementary school children in kindergarten through sixth grade (Majeda & Onuska, 1977). The series, which is designed to be taught by the regular classroom teacher, discusses principles of aesthetics in several different contexts, as the titles of the six levels indicate: Aesthetics in the Physical World, Aesthetics and Art Elements, Aesthetics and the Creative Process, Aesthetics and the Artist, Aesthetics and the Culture, Aesthetics and the Environment. The forty-four units contained in the series include activities related to dance, film, literature, music, theater, and the visual arts. The Aesthetics Education Program benefits all children because it offers a better basic education in the arts than is typically available.

Another approach to curriculum revision to improve arts education is to make the entire education program arts-centered. Project IMPACT (Interdisciplinary Model Programs in the Arts for Children and Teachers), a federally funded program, established five model programs in schools in five states (Wenner, 1973). The goal of the project was to integrate the arts with other academic subjects in order to provide all students with a better basic education and to increase motivation through activities which allowed use of nonverbal skills, such as painting. Again, although this approach to art education is not intended specifically for artistically gifted children, it can improve their education by providing basic instruction that may allow recognition of their ability.

Off-Campus Programs for Artistically Gifted Students

Some programs for artistically gifted students require such specialized personnel and expensive equipment, materials, and facilities that it is not feasible to establish them in every school. Such programs are best offered on a district, state, or regional level (Fox, 1979b). Off-campus programs, such as centers, special schools, or programs that use university facilities, are relatively cost-effective because they avoid duplication of resources. These alternatives can provide early and increasingly challenging instruction by arts experts in appropriate facilities that provide adequate support.

Centers for Artistically Gifted Students. For the reasons just mentioned, arts centers for gifted students may prove to be one of the most popular means of providing programming for talented elementary and high school students. Such centers may be located in old homes, churches, libraries, or abandoned schools, which can be renovated and rented at low cost to the school district.

Most arts education programs do not have access to leading creative and performing artists (Schubart, 1972). Urban arts centers, however, sometimes allow talented students from several schools to work with outstanding artists and specialized teachers.

In most of these programs, gifted elementary and high school students are allowed release time from their regular school work to attend centers on a regularly scheduled basis (e.g., once a week, every afternoon, or every other week). In Connecticut, the Educational Center of the Arts allows talented students to attend special art classes for two hours each afternoon (Educational Facilities Laboratories, 1977). Only about half of the students who are recommended for participation in the program by their school art teachers and counselors can be accepted, however, because the program's resources are too limited to accommodate all of the students. In addition to the center program for artistically gifted students from the urban and suburban high schools in the area, the center staff provides an outreach program to talented handicapped students in nearby schools.

Some center programs for the artistically gifted are housed in a classroom in a local school to which children from other schools are bussed. For example, one such program for fifth through ninth graders who are gifted in the visual arts is located at an elementary school, but serves children from several elementary and middle schools (C. Toth, personal communication, December 12, 1983). Since the selection process that determines which children attend the center is representative of processes used in many similar programs, it is presented in some detail here.

As is common in identification procedures for exceptional children, there are three stages in determination of eligibility for placement in this program: referral, screening, and evaluation. At the referral stage, a child's teacher, a parent, or some other person knowledgeable about the child's artistic ability completes a referral form giving demographic information and information about the child's behavior relevant to the arts. The referring person also supplies three samples of the child's artwork. This file is submitted to the referral officer at the child's school, who then sends it to the district special education office. There, a screening committee reviews the file.

The screening committee that reviews referrals is composed of at least three of the following personnel: an education diagnostician or special education specialist, a teacher of the artistically gifted, an art teacher, a school psychologist, and a teacher of the gifted. Based on its review of the student's file, the committee decides if the apparent potential of the student suggests the need for further evaluation. If so, the committee informs the referring school and sends guidelines for compilation of a student portfolio.

Guidelines for selecting artwork for inclusion in the portfolio include recommendations that the work represent students' most original pieces, that a variety of media and subjects be represented, that the work submitted have a finished look, and that a childlike quality not be considered a reason for excluding a piece of work (C. Toth, personal communication, December 12, 1983).

After the committee reviews the portfolio, which includes at least fifteen works by the student being referred, the teacher of artistically gifted children observes and tests the student in a working situation which includes creative activities. The results of the observation, test, and portfolio review determine the placement decision.

At the center two teachers who are certified in both art education and gifted education work with groups of approximately twenty students; each group comes to the center twice a month for a full day. There they participate in activities that develop skills in art techniques and processes, art appreciation, and knowledge of art history and aesthetics (C. Toth, personal communication, December 12, 1983). Critiquing their own art work and that of others is a major element of the program as well (cf. Durden, 1980; Koch, 1970; Yeatts, 1980).

The same school district that offers this program for students in the visual arts also provides a center program for musically gifted students. The referral procedure for this program is similar to that for the visual arts program. Referrals may be made by anyone who is knowledgeable about the child's musical ability, and the referral form includes a behavioral rating scale to be completed by the person making the referral. Included with the referral information is the student's answer sheet for a music screening test that is administered at the child's school. The test, which is on cassette tape, measures receptive skills in music (M. Scarpelli, personal communication, December 12, 1983). The referral form, rating scale, and screening test answer sheet are sent to the special education office, where they are reviewed by a committee whose composition is similar to that of the committee for the visual arts program, except that teachers certified in music education are included instead of art teachers.

If, after reviewing the referral file, the committee decides that further evaluation is warranted, the student is invited to an audition and interview conducted by the teacher of the program for the musically gifted. The audition and interview are designed to elicit performance in broad areas of music: aural perception, aural imagery, musical understanding, sight-reading, and creativity. The teacher's ratings and observations based on the audition and interview are considered together with the referral information in the committee's determination of placement (M. Scarpelli, personal communication, December 12, 1983).

Most programs for artistically gifted children, whether they are center or in-school programs, are usually part-time provisions such as those just described. They combine a number of strategies in order to make the most effective use of limited resources. Flexible scheduling, the use of volunteers, the use of artists and art teachers as mentors or consultants, and the use of special materials that help teachers individualize within the classroom can all increase opportunities for enrichment in the arts and, to a lesser extent, development of artistic techniques. None of them can address fully the needs of students with outstanding artistic potential, however. The special instruction required by these students can be provided only through comprehensive programs such as those in specialized schools.

Specialized Schools. The most concentrated programs of study for artistically gifted students are offered in the specialized schools for the arts. In comparison with regular schools, these schools usually have more advanced courses, better facilities, and more opportunities for students to perform and to associate with others who are dedicated to the arts. In short, of all the public school programs, these approximate most closely the elements of recognition, expert instruction, and stimulating environment that typify the education of outstanding artists. The regional nature of these schools, however, restricts eligibility to students who live within the particular district. Hence, many areas of the United States are not served by such schools, and even within areas served by state, regional, or municipal units, some locales may be overlooked in talent searches.

Although most of the specialized arts schools are secondary schools, some allow for earlier entry. For example, the Cincinnati School for Creative and Performing Arts' program extends from the fourth through the twelfth grade, and the North Carolina School for the Arts, a residential school, goes from seventh grade through graduate school (Cox & Daniel, 1983).

Even though they specialize in the arts, these schools make provisions for students to complete both courses of general academic studies and concentrations in the arts. Academic standards for entering and remaining in these programs are high. For example, at the Houston School for the Performing and Visual Arts, the number of students who qualified as National Merit and Achievement Finalists has often equaled the number of students who qualified as finalists in the National Arts and Talent Search (Cox & Daniel, 1983). Students at these schools often are not allowed to perform unless they do well academically.

Performing is an essential part of serious artistic training (Quilter, 1977), and specialized arts schools usually include public performance as a major component of their program. The North Carolina School for the Arts mounts nearly 600 productions a year: dance performances, dramas, operas, chamber music concerts, and television productions (Cox & Daniel, 1983).

Course offerings in the arts are, of course, much more varied in specialized schools than in other schools. The Cincinnati School for Creative and Performing Arts has about fifty courses in the various arts (Cox & Daniel, 1983). Facilities, though not always better than those in other public schools, are in general superior in that practice and studio space is more adequate. The Houston School for the Performing Arts, for example, now has two ballet practice rooms, eleven music practice rooms, two art galleries, and a theater (Cox & Daniel, 1982).

The Houston School for the Performing Arts, the Cincinnati School for Creative and Performing Arts, and the North Carolina School for the Arts are among the best known of the public arts schools, but there are many other high-quality schools that specialize in the arts. The Duke Ellington School of the Arts in Washington, D.C., for example, has a student population that is highly able in the visual arts, dance, theater, and music (National Public Radio, 1981). Like students in other specialized arts schools, these students, 95 percent of whom are black, demonstrate the degree of commitment that Bloom (1982) found among internationally renowned performers. One of the teachers at the school comments on student commitment:

> They're getting up at five in the morning. Sometimes some of them travel 2 hours in the morning, 2 hours at night. They work all day long, the whole afternoon for the arts program, you know, so there has to be tremendous dream and vision to come here.

(National Public Radio, 1981, p. 8)

In reply to the interviewer's question "Well, aren't they missing just having fun and being silly?" the teacher answered, "No, they're having fun" (National Public Radio, 1981, p. 8).

Summer Arts Programs.   The peripheral role of the arts in public schools has encouraged the development of summer arts programs. The strong support that summer arts education has received from public and private funding agencies is due in part to the prestige associated with arts sponsorship. Support from legislators and other political figures (e.g., governors) may be increased because of the high status and visibility of arts programs.

Politicking notwithstanding, many summer arts programs provide excellent instruction and facilities. Often located on university or college campuses, the programs offer talented students access to studios, practice rooms, theater stages, darkrooms, and other facilities which are not available to them in most public schools during the school year. In many cases the university's art, dance, drama, and music faculty staff programs or serve as consultants.

The state of New York sponsors one of the most comprehensive summer arts programs for the artistically gifted. Component schools in dance, music, and the visual arts (including filmmaking and photography) are located at six sites across the state (Mills & Ridlon, 1980). The New York State Summer School of the Arts gives exceptionally talented high school students a chance to work with professional artists under optimal conditions: small student-teacher ratios, individualized instruction, and access to studio space during the day and evening.

One smaller-scale university program for artistically talented students provides a four-week summer session in which the students elect classes in drawing, painting, sculpture, or design (Walker, 1980). Another university-based program is more academic. In three consecutive summers, it offered workshops on the arts of the Middle Ages, the Renaissance, and Elizabethan England to students ages seven to fourteen (Fisher, Lavery & Hannum, 1982). Daily sessions were organized into classes in music, art, and science/drama of the period of history featured in the workshop. The Medieval arts program included instruction centered on the Bayeux Tapestry; the *Très Riches Heures* of Jean, Duc de Berry; Gothic architecture; and Gregorian chants.

Summer programs such as these, including state-sponsored honors programs, have both advantages and disadvantages. To the extent that they reduce pressure on the public schools to provide better arts education as a part of the regular academic program, they do a disservice not only to artistically gifted children but to all children. On the other hand, they represent some resistance to the forces that effectively militate against art in public education.

Programs for the artistically talented, like those for the intellectually talented, are commonly regarded as both superfluous and elitist. They are in greater danger than any academic program of being regarded as purely extracurricular. Because there are no comprehensive arts curricula in most public school systems, special options for the artistically gifted can never involve accelerated skill or content learning. At best, they involve enrichment. Until these problems are resolved, the major benefits of all but the most expensive provisions may be that they stimulate interest in arts education and offer some intersection of the children's talent and their schooling.

IMPROVEMENTS IN SCHOOL ARTS PROGRAMS

Significant improvements in service to artistically talented students depend on modifications in school arts programs generally. These modifications include provision of sequential curricula in both the techniques and the histories of various arts, flexibility in accommodating the special needs of talented arts students, and increased emphasis on arts instruction. These modifications are consonant with the recommendations of numerous artists and art educators (e.g., Chetelat, 1981; Eisner, 1972; Fine, 1964; Hollander, 1978; Munro, 1960; Read, 1960; L. Schmidt, 1981).

Arts Literacy

Arts literacy pertains to familiarity with and understanding of the idioms, concepts, and works of the arts legacy. We refer primarily to the legacy in art, music, and literature. We have dealt with the need of gifted children to begin to deal with significant literature at an early age (see Chapter 7), opposing the view of some commentators that children do not need to be "pushed" into adult literature. Gifted children do not need to be protected from aesthetic notions any more than they need to be protected from intellectual notions. This portion of the chapter will deal primarily with art and music literacy, from a perspective similar to that developed in Chapter 7.

The gifted need access to art and music knowledge generally, as distinct from performance or production skills in art and music. The two realms are not, of course, completely distinct: amateur arts skills make available insights that are not accessible to students without such skills (Smith, 1973). On the other hand, talented arts students who do not possess or who do not work toward acquiring the idiomatic, conceptual, and historical sophistication of their arts will exercise their skills with detrimental naiveté. Skilled artists understand their roots; in order to be part of the audience that understands such artists, one needs also to know something of those roots (cf. Puravs, 1973).

The contemporary practice of an art is strongly influenced, if not completely determined, by its history in a way that political or economic practices are not. The artists of one generation speak directly, through the legacy of their works, to the next. Sometimes the younger generation defines aesthetic issues very differently; sometimes a particular artist is anachronistic (e.g., Bach); sometimes an artist seems to anticipate the future (e.g., Shönberg). In addition to speaking to fellow artists, artists speak directly and meaningfully to those members of the public who concern themselves with the same aesthetic issues (Feldman, 1970).

The apparently independent existence of the work of art is what distinguishes arts history from the history of political and economic practice. In the history of the arts, original sources—works of art—exist to be dealt with directly by those who inherit them in the public domain. In political, economic, and social history, the substance of history (e.g., The Great Depression, the Boer War, the Spanish plunder of the Incas) has long since ceased to exist.

This difference captures the illusion of immortality to which the arts so often speak.

There is, within the field of arts history, a great deal for teachers to teach and a great deal for students to discover; the purely cognitive merits of instruction in the field are substantial. Unfortunately, the original sources of this history are very seldom dealt with on a consistent basis either in elementary school or in secondary school (cf. Miller, 1979).

History of Art. The influences of art since the eighteenth century are diverse. Modern works draw not only on the traditions of the West, but on the traditions of the East (for example, in the works of Van Gogh and Gauguin), on the traditions of Africa (for example, in the work of Picasso), and on various reinterpretations of contemporary experience or existence (for example, surrealism, pop art, and the imitation of child art) (Read, 1959). An appreciation of the sources of modern iconography, for instance, is what makes modern art accessible; ignorance of these sources means that one *cannot* (not simply "does not") like modern art.

In order to acquire a sense of these sources, one must begin one's studies somewhere. An historical approach based on the familiar "spiral curriculum" notion can constitute such a beginning. For example, by the end of secondary school, gifted students ought at the very least to have acquired a firm sense of the stylistic distinctions of Egyptian, Greek, Roman, Romanesque, and Gothic architecture; and of Byzantine, Renaissance, Manneristic, Rococo, Romantic, Impressionistic, and Expressionistic styles of graphic art and sculpture.

History of Music. Because of the growth of electronic media, people now have greater access to musical performances than at any other time in written history. Despite this fact, most musical tastes are quite narrow: at present, country-western is the norm for older fans and rock for younger fans.

Miller (1979) stresses the schools' neglect of the literature that constitutes the Western musical legacy. According to Miller, many students pass through high school without ever hearing the music of Duke Ellington or of Mozart. Very little time is spent listening to or discussing musical works in many music classes. One of the authors recalls a high school music appreciation class that consisted of (a) absolute silence and (b) a fill-in-the-blank workbook. Music appreciation class was a good time to do algebra homework in the 1960s. According to Miller (1979), the situation is no better today.

In some ways the music of previous eras or of unfamiliar traditions is less accessible than the art of previous eras or of unfamiliar traditions. The difference is perhaps due to the difference in media. A painting or sculpture remains complete before one's eyes, whereas music, like speech, is dominated by a temporal element. Musical events happen in time, rapidly and organically. As with an unfamiliar language, *only repeated hearings* can provide the familiarity requisite even to perception, let alone comprehension. Mozart, Bach, Dowland, and Coltrane are outlandish tongues to most people because the idioms (different for each artist) are totally unfamiliar to them. Moreover, the pain of acquiring these idioms seems so great and the reward at the outset so elusive that the effort appears pointless.

Fine (1964) believes that students ought to be familiar with the basic historical divisions of musical eras (Medieval, Renaissance, Baroque, Romantic, and Modern) and with musical works and styles of important composers. Listening must be a preponderant activity in music classes, but the listening of naive auditors must take place in sessions of involved discussion and response. Something like a truce must be established between the teachers, who can acknowledge the validity of students' tastes, and the students, who can suspend their disbelief. Like students beginning a foreign language, students encountering a new musical idiom will experience moments of intense resistance. These problems, in both music and art, must be met straightforwardly with the recognition that development of new tastes and new pleasures takes time.

Mastery of Technical Skills

The notion that arts instruction should be based on a hierarchical curriculum structure may distress some educators who do not wish to see arts education programs mirror the weaknesses of academic programs. Such educators may aptly resist arts instruction provided in a lockstep sequence to all students because such structured provisions are inimical to the child-oriented objectives of arts education. These educators see arts education as productive of creativity; their concern is with the creative process and byproducts of that process, such as increased self-esteem and improved problem-solving ability.

Our concern with the content of education, which in the case of the gifted includes academic considerations primarily, leads us to value arts education programs that encourage technical proficiency and prolific production. Such instruction provides increased artistic literacy to most students and allows talented students the option of accelerating their learning of rudimentary skills and concepts. This acceleration prepares the talented student for more advanced instruction in or out of the school setting.

The Music Curriculum.   Although much of elementary school music instruction currently involves rhythm exercises and group singing in unison, elementary school students should be capable of learning many other musical skills (Nitz, 1980). Seven-year-old Soviet children, for instance, are expected to achieve the following objectives in music (Morton, 1972, p. 151):

- discerning the character of music (gentle, gay, sad, humorous, serene);
- distinguishing elementary means for musical expressiveness: volume, register, tempo (fast, slow, moderate), dynamics (loud, soft, legato, staccato);
- distinguishing among a march, a dance, a song;
- learning the structure of the composition (its parts, phrases, couplets, refrains) and understanding these terms;

- distinguishing high, low, and medium sounds and whether they are long or short;
- understanding basic elements of musical notation (the staff, the positions of the notes on the staff; the symbols for half, quarter, and eighth notes);
- singing from music and naming the notes of separate phrases in the songs before they are learned;
- singing without accompaniment or the singing of the teacher;
- singing phrases in solfeggio.

Because secondary music instruction is frequently not mandatory, many students never acquire any music skills beyond those rudimentary techniques learned in elementary school. Others who receive private music instruction may miss opportunities for involvement in group efforts such as choirs, chamber groups, and orchestras. Although we will not suggest a particular sequence for music instruction, we will delineate elements of music that should be included in any program of technical training.

Music skills can be considered in various categories: listening, reading, playing an instrument or singing, and writing. In practice, musical skills, like language arts skills, are interrelated. The need for instruction that addresses each of these separate skill areas, however, should be recognized. Frequently, music programs that are good in other respects neglect several of these areas. Ear training, for example, is often overlooked in even the best school music programs. Ear training involves receptive skills not necessarily included either in music appreciation or in music theory classes.

Other important aspects of technical training in music include sight-singing (solfeggio), sight-reading on a particular instrument, part writing, counterpoint, form analysis, harmonic analysis, and orchestration.

All these elements should be combined into a meaningful, cumulative instructional sequence so that all students have an opportunity to become fully literate in music. Students who excel in particular aspects of this music curriculum can pursue advanced study in one or more of the components of the general program (L. Schmidt, 1981).

The Art Curriculum. As in music, techniques in the visual arts include many subskills. Unlike the skills involved in music, however, the skills particular to one medium in art are not so different from those of other media. Whereas keyboard technique in music cannot be adapted to a fretted instrument, the techniques involved in drawing and painting are not so remote from one another.

On the other hand, the visual arts are not connected by a language comparable to musical notation, which can be used to transcribe nearly all musical performance. The most closely analogous characteristic of the visual arts is the presence of the unifying elements of line, color, texture, shape, movement, balance, perspective, and iconography in art works.

The notion of scope and sequence in art curricula suggests numerous absurd possibilities. Restricting certain media to particular levels and limiting consideration of particular subjects to specific ages seem to be untenable alternatives. Ironically, however, arts programs often fail in practice to provide activities based on students' levels of competence. Eisner (1972) describes this practice in relation to his suggestion that students be provided a limited palette when they are first learning to paint:

> Many teachers go to the other extreme: the child has available to him a wider range of color than he can cope with adequately. The range of color has apparently been provided in the name of free expression and is considered a vehicle for maximizing the child's creative freedom. When such a range of color is combined with the use of large, nonresilient brushes and an upright easel on which is tacked a sheet of newsprint, one can only wonder how much freedom is in fact provided in such a context. The task of painting with fluid tempera paint on an upright surface using nonresilient brushes on newsprint is a task that would frighten most mature artists, yet nursery schools—in the name of creativity—are prone to make precisely these materials available to the young child.
>
> (Eisner, 1972, p. 160)

Structured alternatives to the license implied in Eisner's example are often overly prescriptive. The directed teaching method, for example, includes "stereotyped, step-by-step copying, tracing, or imitative procedures" (Conant, 1964, p. 36) which restrict students' imaginative options. One mediate position, which bears consideration, involves the application of Bruner's spiral curriculum to the teaching of art (Kaufman, 1966). This approach emphasizes the structural aspects of the discipline by repeatedly involving the maturing student in ever more complex experiences with the discipline. Kaufman (1966, p. 449) maintains that

> this teaching idea has special significance to art education because the main ideas of symbolic transformation are at one and the same time the essential learning substance of a serious work of art as well as of the schematic response to experience a first grader will create with crayons.
>
> (Kaufman, 1966, p. 449)

Although the application of the spiral curriculum principle to art education may be beneficial generally, it may pose some problems to talented art students who need accelerated learning experiences. "The spiral curriculum supports the teaching conception of presenting the most fundamental understanding of a field rather than teaching specific skills and topics" (Kaufman, 1966, p. 449). Unfortunately, evaluation of fundamental understanding is much more elusive than evaluation of the performance of skills or the knowledge of content.

Perhaps a solution to this problem would be to provide a spiral curriculum in art through the elementary school grades and selected advanced classes in the secondary school. Munro (1960, p. 24) alludes to such an arrangement when he suggests that "there is nothing in the present college introductory art courses which could not be successfully undertaken by the better secondary students." Through such provisions "gifted [art] students are not held back by crowds of mediocre ones" (Munro, 1960, p. 24).

Flexibility for Talented Arts Students

Talented arts students face serious educational problems because arts training is not provided by the schools. Serious students, particularly in music, may need to practice six or more hours per day as early as age ten or twelve; Hollander (1978) reports practicing eight to fourteen hours per day.

He reports further,

> When I was eleven I began to perform professionally, giving concerts, but I kept on with school. Often I'd have to turn in a paper late; . . . But I had Mozart and Bach, *to show me the real path.* [emphasis added]
>
> (Hollander, 1978, p. 46)

To Hollander the ordinary school experience was that "tawdry world" referred to by Thomson (1962; see Box 10.1).

It is not likely that many teachers of the gifted will routinely encounter students who achieve the sort of eminence Hollander has. Yet it is not the prospect of subsequent eminence that justifies a school response more flexible than that reported by Hollander, but the importance of the work that engages unusual talent, *regardless of its utility or acclaim.*

The sort of flexibility required depends on the particular student's artistic regimen. School activities may not be involved in this important regimen at all if there is no school program for students talented in the arts. In this case school inflexibility adds unnecessary burdens to the life of a serious arts student. Release time for practice or performance (music) or extended studio work (art) is probably the most widely applicable arrangement. *Since most artistically talented students are likely to be above average in IQ and achievement, accelerative options and credit by examination ought to be considered among release-time options.* Release time may also be affected on an occasional basis, so that some required assignments may be altered, eliminated, or made part of special arrangements (cf. Hollander, 1978).

Alternatives become possible, however, only if the student's strenuous out-of-school efforts are acknowledged as educationally significant and intellectually valid. Clearly it will be difficult for teachers of the gifted to convince fellow educators who may not be aesthetically literate to acknowledge such educational and intellectual significance. This situation is another indication that arts education needs to be accorded increased priority.

Increased Priority for Arts Education

Increased priority for arts education generally is in order for much the same reason that greater emphasis on academic subjects is in order for all students: the primary mission of schools ought to be to teach subjects of intellectual worth. Instruction in the arts clearly contributes to this mission; creativity training is more tangential.

Ironically, at the same time that our cultural legacy in the West has expanded to include a widespread perception of our aesthetic links to African, Asian, and Native American traditions, our intellectual sense of that culture has been displaced by a "tawdry world" (Thomson, 1962; see Box 10.1) of commercial culture which feeds largely on the ignorance and pliableness of its mass market. Schools may, through default, have assumed a role in conditioning and protecting this market (Kaufman, 1966, p. 362). This probable role is but one facet of the emasculation of the arts in the schools and in society at large.

The problem is not that of good versus bad art. For example, popular music of various styles has vigorous and knowledgeable representatives (cf. Puravs, 1973). Surely, for example, the Beatles, Jamaican reggae, and the work of Doc Watson and the Chicago Art Ensemble are legitimate aesthetic expressions of various sorts, not necessarily more or less wonderful than Japanese koto classics, the Balinese gamelan, or the piano concerti of Mozart.

The problem is that of aesthetic myopia. Many adults spend their lives pursuing the popular music of their youth: their tastes stagnate in the economic press of adult life. Oddly, these adults feel that knowledge of other forms or idioms (e.g., twelve-tone music, the nineteenth century art song) threatens their allegiance to a music repertoire that inevitably becomes quickly dated. The possibility that there exists a larger and richer context of which this repertoire is but a small part does not occur to most people. Their appreciation lacks an intellectual or cognitive element which can prompt aesthetic growth (cf. Kaufman, 1966, pp. 363–364).

In the visual arts, most people never develop the sort of stolid allegiances they do in the case of music: paintings, sculpture, and drawings have not been commercially exploited to the extent that musical performances have been. Popular tastes in the visual arts are more apt, at present, to be conditioned by commercial video images, mail-order catalogs, or retail arrays. Whatever the source, the effect of aesthetic myopia is similar: stagnant, commercially manipulated taste that eschews any sort of intellectual component (cf. Puravs, 1973).

The arts animate a humane vision of the world (Smith, 1973); the artistic impulse—the impulse to bring forth what is beautiful, meaningful, or true—is the point of rational life. Marcuse (1955) contrasted the productive, liberating impulse (*eros*) and the destructive, repressive impulse (*thanatos*) and asserted that the continued existence of our civilization was in jeopardy if we could not in our organization of *work* nurture a freer *eros*. This idea, which is perhaps the most thorough justification that can be given for arts education, requires some explanation.

The significance of this assertion cannot be considered "solely in terms of a future age of leisure and abundance" according to Read (1960, p. 55). Leisure provides only a frightening intellectual vacuum in the context of arts ignorance. Even if wealth arising from increased productivity can be redistributed and the work week shortened (cf. Leontief, 1982), the vacuum of leisure is more likely to be filled with unreflective consumption than with aesthetic production or reflection.

The problem is not simply pedagogical, however. Read (1960) notes that the intellectual-aesthetic vacuum raised by the specter of leisure and abundance *originates* in the organization of work. Clark (1983) has commented on the fragmentation that characterizes not only employment but also schools. The term for this fragmentation, this loss of completeness by the worker in the productive process, is *alienated labor*. Children are educated *for* employment (see Chapter 12) and adults *by* employment to accept the conditions of alienated labor. Unemployment is psychologically devastating even to those receiving public economic support, in part because valid activity to replace alienated labor is inaccessible; indeed, even the terms to define and accept the problem are lacking. Arts activity and intellectual activity are neither understood nor validated as an option in this context. They are, perhaps, seen to be dangerous.

Read (1960) concludes,

> Not only is "the cognitive function of sensuousness minimized" (Marcuse's phrase); but more seriously those repressed instincts upon which our civilization is built lack all constructive outlet. This negation to our technological civilization must be resolved; and since it cannot be resolved in work, it must be resolved in the development of the only impulse that is left undeveloped in our civilization, aesthetic play. The only development of the play impulse that is adequate for this task of reconciliation and reconstruction is its development into creative art.
>
> (Read, 1960, p. 59)

Our discussion thus far suggests that schools in general must make a greater effort to institute programs in the arts. Even though such programs may be worthy, they may not in themselves be sufficient to accomplish the above ends. Irrespective of the larger role of art within the human condition, however, both the ends (i.e., to improve the human condition) and the means (i.e., creative art) form a complete justification for academic arts programs within public schools.

SUMMARY

This chapter has shown how the arts play a utilitarian role in schools, a role antithetical to their nature. That nature has to do with the liberation of the imagination from the banal (cf. Chetelat, 1981; Fine, 1964; Hollander, 1978; Kaufman, 1966; Marcuse, 1955; Read, 1960; Thomson, 1962). Too often the arts are dismissed as merely impractical; even intense, expensive preparation does not guarantee graduates of arts programs any sort of employment in the arts. Even now, the supply of talent vastly exceeds the demand. The position of this chapter, however, has been that the terms of such a supply and demand concept are illegitimate, not that arts education is illegitimate.

The dreadfully possible prospect (cf. Read, 1960) that unemployment may become a universal experience lays to rest the problematic influence of utility. At present Ph.D.s go without employment; however, they resent not their intellectual work, but society's lack of esteem for it. We cannot predict the utility of an endeavor if our concept of utility is so poor as to exclude that which is most meaningful.

Arts instruction for all children needs to be a more intense experience in the public schools. Arts teachers' caseloads are absurdly high in most places. Curriculum is incoherent. We attribute this state of affairs to the lack of esteem and of financial support accorded the arts by public schools. In general, artistic talents have shared the fate of intellectual talents.

This chapter has distinguished between the sort of arts education appropriate to all intellectually apt students and the sort appropriate to arts students in particular. We examined some extant programs in the arts, noting in the process that the intellectual component of the arts is not distinguished or appreciated in practice in regular arts programs (Kaufman, 1966). Programs for artistically talented students, however, almost always include such an intellectual element.

Finally, the chapter has reviewed current arts programs for the gifted and has suggested a comprehensive arts program for intellectually gifted and artistically talented students. This program involves instruction in the important areas of arts literacy and arts technique.

PART III

Social Implications

Part III examines issues that relate to the social context of gifted education, including the controversial topics of underachievement, nature and nurture, elitism, and the utility of academic learning. Some readers will view these issues differently from the way we do. We recognize that there are no easy solutions to complex problems such as these. The problems must be examined, nonetheless. The tendency to identify mostly upper-middle-class, white children as gifted and the difficulty some gifted children experience in school, for example, are issues that need to be aired and continually reexamined. The examination of such problems here will, we hope, help teachers deal more explicitly with the inherent contradictions and ambiguities of gifted education.

Chapter 11, ''Underachievement: Luck, Effort, or Destiny?,'' examines probable causes of underachievement, particularly as they relate to the institutional effects of socialization. The individual effects of socialization are considered with respect to the affective hypothesis of gifted underachievement and the interpersonal relationships of the gifted. Chapter 11 is an attempt to deal with the question of underachievement in a new way. The chapter does provide information necessary for a more eclectic viewpoint, however.

Chapter 12, ''Equal Opportunity: Mediocrity or Excellence,'' extends the discussion of the hypothesis of institutional effects further. This chapter examines differing views of biology, equality, elite groups, and normative excellence in an institutional context. These ideas bear on some of the most troublesome questions of definition, identification, and instructional method in gifted education. In conclusion, Chapter 12 presents our view of this text's major implications for method in gifted education.

CHAPTER 11

Underachievement:
Luck, Effort, or Destiny?

INTRODUCTION

Children come to school with varying degrees of academic aptitude. Professionals in the field of special education, as well as educators generally, interpret this variability as constituting legitimate individual difference. This interpretation of individual difference, which forms the basis for determining those to be served by special education, is a response to several varieties of school failure (Eggleston, 1977; Ysseldyke & Algozzine, 1982b).

Typically schools seek to remediate or accommodate individual differences. Schools have not assumed or claimed much responsibility for the creation or amplification of individual differences, however. How does schooling mitigate individual differences, despite the acknowledgment of such differences in theories of pedagogy? What are the implications of this apparent dilemma for gifted students?

This chapter discusses achievement differences as a function of the socialization process of schooling. It conceives of this process both institutionally and individually. In particular, the discussion attributes a significant degree of responsibility for the individual failure of bright children to the priority accorded socialization as an important outcome of schooling. Certain types of bright children are more vulnerable than others.

DEFINITION OF ACHIEVEMENT AND UNDERACHIEVEMENT

The pedagogical literature has interpreted achievement in several ways. Grades have been used as a measure of achievement in many studies (Dowdall & Colangelo, 1982). Achievement has also been interpreted as performance on either group or individually administered standardized tests of achievement. In addition, past accomplishments (cf. Rimm & Davis, 1980) and vocational attainment (often measured as occupational status, cf. Duncan, 1961) have been used to study the achievement of students maturing into adulthood.

The discussion in this chapter adopts the second alternative—achievement tests. Norm-referenced achievement tests, however imperfect or diagnostically limited, have an established reliability and validity. Grades and grade point averages (GPA) are subjective assessments assigned on the basis of noncomparable criteria to samples of students who may have widely varying characteristics (Bloom, 1977).

Normative comparisons are implicit in the notion of underachievement. It is thus important that measurement error be accounted for. Measures of unknown bias and poor reliability obscure the definition of underachievement. Research suggests that bright average students are, in most classrooms, capable of earning high grades, and that "docile, industrious, polite, and conforming students . . . often get grades higher than their objective performance and aptitude merit" (Carrier, 1983, p. 963). On the basis of GPA, therefore, there is no way to distinguish between achievers who are gifted and achievers who are not.

If one chooses GPA as both an identification and an achievement criterion, one tautologically eliminates the question of underachievement. According to Dowdall and Colangelo (1982), this is Renzulli's position. The chief shortcoming of this position is the assumption that earning consistently high grades constitutes an achievement of intellectual worth. If one rejects the notion that a GPA of 4.0 should be an evaluation criterion in the identification of gifted students (see Chapter 2), one must also reject the definition of underachievement as a GPA of less than 3.0 or 2.5.

The only practical way to resolve this dilemma in the short term is to return to the normative notion on which identification is most often based. Normative achievement data can be compared to normative IQ data, and we can test the significance of the difference statistically (cf. Salvia & Ysseldyke, 1981). Moreover, the criteria and biases of such measures and the implications of their use are amenable to critical examination. When grades are used to define underachievement, any biases that affect classroom performance are inaccessible, since we cannot control the conditions under which classes are conducted, what is taught, how grades are compiled, and so forth. Grades are best viewed as a measure of classroom performance, a compound of behavior and comparative success on assignments.

A gifted student who is a severe underachiever by the GPA criterion (e.g., GPA below 3.0) may prove to be a high achiever on the basis of norm-referenced tests (e.g., scores above the 90th percentile). Such a student may have an intact intellectual life but be impervious to the sanction of poor grades (cf. Marolla, Williams & McGrath, 1980, p. 84). Conversely, a student who receives moderately good grades in the regular classroom may be discovered to be achieving consistently below expectancy based on IQ. Very bright children who have been socialized to classroom conformity may find noncognitive ways to keep active, or they may become uninvolved spectators. In either case their achievement suffers (Stanley, 1976).

Many factors affect the demonstration of achievement (as performance on normative measures) and potential (as IQ). Rosenbaum (1975), for example, suggests that tracking arrangements alone, at the secondary level, are sufficient to produce IQ changes even among groups of normal students. If the effects of the classroom on normal students late in their educational histories can be observed, it seems logical that the effects on students earlier in their schooling may well be strong.

What happens in the classroom is not isolated from forces ordinarily at work in society. Achievement and potential can be mediated by a host of sociological, psychological, and biological variables. Among the sociological variables are parents' education, mother's aspirations, family income, housing characteristics, and parental occupational status. Among the psychological variables are achievement motive, learning style, locus of control, behavior disorders, and emotional disturbance. Among the biological variables are organic brain damage, visual impairment, and physical handicaps. All these factors may contribute to underachievement.

Though Jensen (1973) notes that *in general* environmental variables have not been shown to exert much consistent effect on test scores, any environmental variable may in a particular case exert a statistically uncharacteristic influence. In fact, in a restricted population such as the gifted, anomalous effects may obscure the general trend. For example, though the correlation of IQs of parents and children is found typically to be about .50, Terman and Oden found that the correlation between the Stanford sample's IQs and those of its offspring was .08 (McAskie & Clarke, 1976, reporting a personal communication from Oden). This phenomenon can be conceived of statistically as the effect of restricted range. What it means is that the general observation does not hold for the special population.

In this chapter, however, we are concerned with the within-school factors that affect achievement, not the larger social and political issues. This topic is a very poorly researched aspect of education, but one that is critical to an understanding of the plight of apt students in the public schools. The process of socialization provides the context within which we view the classroom's mediating influences on achievement.

SOCIALIZATION

One definition of *socialization* renders it not very different from *education*. According to Otto (1975, p. 162), socialization is "the process by which individuals selectively acquire the skills, knowledge, attitudes, values, and motives current in the groups of which they are or will become members" (cf. Bronfenbrenner, 1970, for a similar definition). Others (e.g., Haggard, 1957) have considered socialization to be a process of internal, individual personality adjustment.

It may be instructive to use the term socialization more restrictively than does either Otto (1975) or Haggard (1957). One restricted definition describes socialization as the acquisition of those modes of behavioral or motivational control by which groups of individuals conform to expectations for performance of adult work roles (cf. Bowles & Gintis, 1976, p. 134; Spring, 1982). In contrast to formal learning, these controls are not acquired intellectually. Thus, socialization in this sense refers to noncognitive schooling in a particular economic context, rather than a universal social or psychological context.

Schools and Families as Forces for Socialization

In industrial societies socialization is often assumed to be the work of multiple agencies—for example, family, school, and age-mate peer group (Bronfenbrenner, 1970; Coleman, 1961; Haggard, 1957; Otto, 1975). In preindustrial societies, by contrast, the primary influence of the family is much stronger (Hanks, 1973; Schwarz, 1975). A logical conclusion would be that the socializing influence exerted by schools is different from that of the family or the peer group in industrial societies.

How can one characterize the origins of this sort of socialization? According to Katz (1968), in the United States schools began to emerge as an institution of changed import about 1850: "The role of the school became to break dependency, to wean the child from the parent to the real world: to perform aspects of the socialization process that parents had become unable to carry out'' (Katz, 1968, p. 119). According to Katz, early school reformers felt that parents had become unable to carry out these functions because temptations to softness abounded in the ugly, newly emergent urban world and, worse, these temptations were often foisted upon children by unsuspecting or ignorant parents. Increasingly, these were working-class and immigrant parents. Massachusetts passed the first statewide compulsory attendance law in 1852 under the influence of such thinking.

The school accomplishes its work by direct imposition of social norms in a setting quite unlike that of the family. This socializing work continues throughout students' public school experience, concurrent with formal cognitive instruction. The basic assumption in this text is that the work of the school as a socializing agent may not necessarily be congruent with its foremost instructional mission. That is, socialization involves primarily noncognitive schooling, whereas the promotion of formal learning, the foremost instructional mission, involves primarily cognitive schooling.

Chapter 5 noted that a recurrent argument against acceleration was the presumed need for socialization in the regular classroom with age-mates. The discussion in Chapter 5 suggested the possibility that socialization so conceived functioned to *normalize* gifted students. Hollingworth (1942) noted the tendency of gifted students to develop divergent beliefs and behaviors, a tendency she called *heterodoxy.* Hollingworth considered this to be a *positive* characteristic requiring nurture rather than extinction or suppression through normalization. Thus, in the case of gifted children, the emphasis of schools on socialization exerts a distinctly depressive effect. This emphasis, though explicit, is not well understood either by the public or by educators. In terms of within-school influences, socialization may be an important, but overlooked, factor in the phenomenon of underachievement.

The character of schooling as an intentional, rather than organic, institution points to another peculiarity of the socialization accomplished there. Schools, unlike families, do not socialize children to become part of the socializing institution for life.

The family is both the means and the end of one sort of socialization. Children elaborate their family roles, as prospective and as actual parents, in the context of the family. Ultimately, children perpetuate the organic institution of the family in many ways. It seems that life in our society cannot take place outside the context of the family without the most dire consequences. Personality disorders, character disorders, schizophrenia, manic-depression, a variety of neuroses, or persistent self-destructive behaviors profoundly damage many children who are not raised in a caring family.

Far from exhibiting the sorts of incapacitating disorders characteristic of children alienated from the context of the family, most students leave schools to become quite typical functional workers. In school, children are socialized not for a life of academic involvement in school, but for a life in the economic milieu outside school. Schooling is a very successful socializing agency, criticisms of its academic shortcomings notwithstanding (cf. National Commission on Excellence in Education, 1983).

School and Classroom Socialization Practices

One can begin to distinguish more minutely between the socialization intent and the socialization function of schools by examining school practice. A number of studies have examined school socialization practices, and some of these have implications of unique import for gifted children. In general these practices concern

1. custody (care-taking),
2. ranking (assigning a place on the success-failure continuum), and
3. compliance (cultivating habits of obedience).

Throughout this discussion, it is important to remember that these studies do not deal specifically with gifted students. Few studies have examined the socialization of gifted students; to our knowledge none has done so according to the definition adopted here. Our aim therefore is to understand how socialization is accomplished by schools and then to draw implications for gifted education. [If you review the notion of aptitude treatment interactions (Chapter 3), the discussion may prove easier to follow. In particular, it may be possible to understand better how some practices (such as tracking or normalization) may negatively affect some groups, but be suitable for others.]

The Coleman Report. The *Equality of Educational Opportunity Report* (Coleman et al., 1966), also known as the Coleman Report, seems to indicate that schools have very little effect on their students, once background variables are controlled. The report found that influences that had been thought to be strong were apparently of moot significance. Neither school funding nor teacher training nor physical plant nor amount of instructional materials nor teaching staff was found to influence student achievement systematically.

After 1966 researchers showed markedly less interest in pursuing the study of classroom social structure, a field that had elicited great interest during the first half of the century (Glidewell et at., 1966). Coleman (1961) had himself contributed significantly to this earlier literature.

Ironically, the Coleman report (Coleman et al., 1966) does provide circumstantial evidence indicating that the school functions *effectively* as a socializing agency because it acts *systematically in harmony with students' backgrounds.* Though the consistency of *this* relationship may have frustrated educators' traditional hopes for education, it is not paradoxical (Spring, 1982; cf. Counts, 1930). This institutional consistency implicates the general academic failure of students in schools, and the particular intellectual failure of some bright students.

Bloom (1977) carefully delineates this viewpoint. He articulates the difference between absolute and relative success criteria and shows how the difference is obscured pedagogically. Bloom (1977) claims that students are *socialized* differentially to success or failure by insistent success or failure experiences *not objectively related to learning*. This is a profoundly relevant observation.

Baer and Bushell (1981, p. 262) have noted that schools accomplish their socialization functions by "pos[ing] different kinds of problems to children which they must learn to solve for themselves [and then] sort[ing] . . . children into different social positions according to how well they teach themselves to solve 'academic' problems." They conclude that "effective advancement requires more resources than those normally available in school; in particular it requires many out-of-school aids" (p. 263).

The main question about socialization, therefore, is not so much what individual teachers can accomplish but how classrooms achieve their effective socialization functions so systematically, regardless of teachers' obvious good will. Schools perform these functions even while teachers and administrators ostensibly focus professional attention on cognitive goals (Bloom, 1977).

Socialization is an exceedingly complex topic, involving individuals, institutions, and their interaction. Several general conclusions regarding socialization processes are possible, based on the preceding discussion:

1. Socialization is different from formal cognitive learning.
2. Socialization outcomes are not consciously selected by schools.
3. Institutional practices and needs play a part in socialization outcomes.
4. Socialization serves noncognitive purposes.

Coleman's Earlier Work.   Coleman (1961) identified the priority of noncognitive over cognitive values in schools. He also located the origin of anti-intellectual influence outside the student subculture and ultimately outside the school itself.

Coleman reported that high school students could be ranked on participation in sports, sexual attractiveness, dressing habits, popularity, clique membership, car ownership, and family origin. He also confirmed, among other findings, that the influence of top athletes far exceeds that of top scholars:

> These results present a rude awakening for those who believe that high school constitutes an influence toward making the image of the brilliant student attractive. Whatever the effects of the curriculum, they are overbalanced, for freshman and sophomores, by the effects of sports and the adolescent culture's focus on athletic events. . . . The average boy, as an individual, appears to be more oriented to scholarship than is the social system of the high school. The norms of the system constitute more than an aggregate of individual attitudes; they actually pull these attitudes away from scholarship. The implication is striking: the adolescents themselves are not to be held responsible for the norms of their adolescent cultures.
>
> (Coleman, 1961, p. 304)

In short, Coleman concluded that school socialization practices actually work *against the valuation of intellectual pursuits*. Coleman even discerned a greater orientation to intellectual concerns among average students than was reflected in the school culture. The implications are indeed striking (see Box 11.1).

Interpersonal Relationships of the Gifted

Another concept of socialization involves peer relationships. The concept is especially relevant to the gifted because (1) the term socialization is often used colloquially to refer to the presumed need of gifted children to associate continuously with normal-IQ age-mates, and (2) it is sometimes assumed that the gifted ordinarily have difficulty establishing or conducting interpersonal relationships.

Box 11.1 James Coleman's *Adolescent Society*

Coleman (1961) published and analyzed carefully constructed sociograms to support some of his conclusions. The data came from four four-year high schools. Coleman identified three status categories for each class and for each sex. Thus, in each school there were twenty-four top status positions available.

The three top status positions charted by the sociograms are (1) top athlete (boys) and top dresser (girls), (2) top scholar (within each sex), and (3) individual most attractive to the opposite sex. In addition, cliques, defined as groups of four or more individuals bound by mutual selection to at least two other clique members, are charted. Also noted are the comparative ranks of cliques and the mean student ratings of clique members (on the parameters of "leading crowd," athleticism, scholarship, and sexual attractiveness).

This information allows one to compare the positions of attractive individuals, top athletes, and top scholars within the peer-group culture. Top athletes were generally members of a top clique; top scholars were more frequently not clique members than clique members. Of the thirty-two top scholars identified in the study, half the girls and about three-fourths of the boys were not identified as members of any clique. (In general, fewer cliques could be established for boys than for girls.)

Except in the case of top status positions, Coleman did not chart social isolates (i.e., those students who were mutually selected by no one). There were four top status isolates. Three of the four top status isolates were top scholar girls. Top scholars were, in fact, frequently charted on the outskirts of third- or fourth-ranked cliques (i.e., as having but one friend in the low status clique).

Best dressed girls (the analog of top athletes among the boys) were with one exception members of *top* cliques. The combination of athlete (dresser) and top scholar in the same person was rare for both sexes (i.e., two boys and one girl combined both attributes). Perhaps more meaningful, however, was the fact that no top scholar, of either sex, was also selected as most sexually attractive, in contrast to the selection of about one-half the top athletes and one-fourth the best-dressed girls as most attractive.

Hollingworth (1926, 1942) viewed peer relationships of the gifted circumspectly, with reference both to all gifted children and to very high-IQ gifted children. She felt that friendship choices became more limited as IQ increased and that gifted children with IQs above 150 experienced substantial difficulty in finding friends (Hollingworth, 1926).

Whereas intelligence has been found to correlate positively with peer acceptance in the general population (Glidewell et al., 1966), recent research does not indicate what distinguishes peer acceptance from popularity (cf. Coleman, 1961) or how to characterize the quality (rather than the quantity) of interpersonal relationships among different sorts of children (Austin & Draper, 1981).

Part of the problem lies in establishing the character of the relationship between gifted children and their nongifted age-mates, both in the cases of individual friendship and in general. According to Maddux et al. (1982), both the self-concept and the social distance of gifted children (fifth and sixth graders) are virtually unaffected by any placement, whether segregated, partially segregated, or regular class. These findings lend some support to Christopherson's (1981) assertion that social and emotional considerations *should not* be a major concern when accelerative options are considered.

Four summary observations about the interpersonal relationships of gifted children are discussed below:

1. *The gifted are not in emotional difficulty in general.* A number of investigations seem to indicate that the interpersonal relationships of the gifted are not much better or worse than those of intellectually average persons: Terman's gifted achievers were found to have more stable marriages and fewer emotional troubles as adults than the population in general. Haggard (1957), on the other hand, found high levels of free-floating anxiety and acquisitive competitiveness among school-age gifted achievers. This sort of variety in characteristics and definitions suggests that most measures of peer relationships among the gifted do not capture salient qualities of interpersonal relationships. Much work remains to be done to define and evaluate correctly the meaningful qualities of successful interpersonal relations before empirical studies can yield valid results.

2. *The gifted do not value popularity.* Tidwell (1980) recently published an overall impression of the peer relations of 1600 gifted secondary students from forty-six metropolitan California high schools. Tidwell's data strongly suggest that these students did not value popularity. Her data also indicate that gifted students are not unhappy with this state of affairs. Popularity, after all, is not a traditional intellectual value (cf. Getzels & Jackson, 1962).

3. *Peer acceptance and popularity are less than adequate measures for investigating further the peer relationships of the gifted.* The quality of interpersonal relationships may be better measured, if such measurement is pedagogically necessary, through criteria other than peer acceptance and

popularity. Maddux et al., (1982) approach the question more neutrally, for example, by treating peer relationships of the gifted in terms of self-concept and social distance. Persons making any assessment of the peer relationships of a particular gifted child should be aware of the *consistent* finding that gifted children quite frequently have some or many older friends, so apparent school friendship patterns may be misleading (Austin & Draper, 1981).

4. *The role of solitude, though noted, has been little investigated with respect to the social-emotional life of the gifted.* A very different perspective might be to recognize the traditionally valued role of solitude in contemplative life (cf. Bell, 1978, pp. 110–111; Copley, 1961; Getzels & Jackson, 1962; Hofstadter, 1963; Marcuse, 1964, pp. 242–244; Ortega y Gassett, 1968, pp. 80–86). Such a perspective, which may be unfamiliar to educators, would be consistent with the established finding that the gifted seek solitude in childhood (e.g., Freeman, 1979; Hollingworth, 1942; Terman, 1925). Intellectual pursuits seem also to require a modicum of solitude which may conflict with normal social aspirations to popularity and with the nature of schooling itself (cf. Baer & Bushell, 1981; Bloom, 1977).

CLASSROOM FAILURE OF GIFTED STUDENTS

Having considered the role of the school as an intermediate socializing institution, we need to look more closely at the classroom failure of particular gifted children identified as underachievers (see, e.g., Fine, 1967; Whitmore, 1980) and the role of socialization practices in that failure. (Please recall that *underachievement* in this chapter refers to achievement substantially below potential, as measured by norm-referenced instruments.)

The Affective Hypothesis of Gifted Underachievement

Most of the research on underachievement has sought behavioral or attitudinal correlates that distinguish gifted underachievers from gifted achievers, in the hope that knowledge of differences between the groups will suggest effective treatment. Unfortunately, the success of interventions grounded in research comparing these two groups on this basis has been extremely limited. Perhaps this is due to the fact that the causes of underachievement are too complex or too profound to be affected by the relatively superficial changes that most educational modifications and counseling programs have initiated.

There is also reason to believe that failure to recognize the extent to which achievement problems are exacerbated by certain aspects of the classroom can render efforts ineffectual (Whitmore, 1980). Although research comparing bright achievers and underachievers has failed to yield strategies for treating underachievement successfully, it has increased educators' understanding of relationships between academic performance and some aspects of socialization.

Research has demonstrated that the underachievement of an individual child may be a response to any of several variables. Because gifted children make high scores on tests of intellectual ability, it was assumed for many years that the problem lay entirely in the affective domain. Since the late 1960s, because of increased attention to handicapped children, researchers have framed questions about underachievement in terms of the cognitive domain as well.

Maker (1977) and Whitmore (1980) are among those who have advocated programs to identify and serve gifted children who underachieve because of specific learning disabilities. These researchers have recognized that high IQ scores and specific learning problems are not mutually exclusive, and thus underachievement in the gifted is not necessarily an affective problem. They acknowledge, however, the interaction between cognitive and affective factors.

Investigations of correlates of underachievement have considered both surface behaviors, such as study habits (Lum, 1960), and personality variables, such as level and direction of hostility (Shaw & Grubb, 1958). They have also identified possible sources of behaviors and attitudes that seem to increase the discrepancy between ability and achievement. Early research focused on family values and interaction patterns; more recent studies have emphasized the influence of societal values, communicated through the differential rewards that are offered to members of minority groups (Callahan, 1979). Because all of these approaches to the problem of underachievement have yielded partial answers, all must be considered in educating gifted children.

Early Interest in Underachievement. The discovery of underachievement is a corollary of the advent of modern intelligence tests. Early researchers discovered that some students who, according to the tests, should have been excelling in school were only mediocre students. Worse, some high-scoring students were making failing grades and dropping out of school early.

The most obvious cause of underachievement suggested itself first: a poor home environment. Such an environment was thought to be characterized by economic or emotional instability which left the family little time or energy to give adequate support to the child's educational efforts. Poor home environment continues to be cited as a major cause of underachievement (see, e.g., Smilansky & Nevo, 1978).

This explanation was not fully satisfactory, however, because it did not account for poor academic achievement among gifted students who came from stable middle or upper-middle-class homes in which parents typically place value on their children's education. Attention then turned to personality variables as inhibitors of achievement in children from middle-class families.

Personality Variables. Terman and Oden (1947) conducted follow-up studies to determine the scholastic and occupational status of participants in their longitudinal investigation of the characteristics of the gifted. They found that the men who failed to utilize much of their intellectual ability in school or in their careers shared some personality traits. According to ratings by parents, teachers, and wives, they (1) lacked the ability to persevere, (2) failed to integrate goals, (3) tended to drift rather than take action, and (4) lacked self-confidence. These characterizations appeared even in early ratings by parents and teachers, suggesting to researchers that the problem was chronic (Terman & Oden, 1947).

Since the time of Terman's findings, it has been noted repeatedly that underachievement is not a "surface" phenomenon (Gallagher, 1975; Shaw & McCuen, 1960; Kirk, 1952). It is often attributed, at least in gifted males, to a general pattern of maladjustment which affects both academic and social behavior.

Familial Influences

The view that underachievement is part of a syndrome of intrapersonal conflict has been explored primarily in a psychodynamic context in which the interaction patterns of the family play the prominent causal role. Underachievement is seen in this context as a form of rebellion against the parental authority by a child who is afraid to act in an openly aggressive manner.

One of the early reports on the personality development of underachieving college students described student explanations for academic failure as "unrealistic, superficial, and largely implausible" (Kirk, 1952, p. 214). Kirk saw underachievers' excuses and resistance to probing for deeper explanations as an effort to control hostility. She based this conclusion in part on counseling records that described underachievers as resistant to externally imposed tasks, self-derogatory, and depressive.

Similar descriptions, as well as the conclusion that underachievement is a means of satisfying hostility toward a parent who demands success, recur throughout the literature on underachievement. It was found, for example, in a study in which Kirk's report was cited, that on three of four personality scales underachieving males scored significantly higher on hostility measures than did achieving males (Shaw & Grubb, 1958). There was no significant difference between the scores of underachieving and achieving females in this sample of high school students. Since the items of the scale that elicited hostile responses were not school-related, Shaw and Grubb concluded that the genesis of the problem was not school, but the family. They also warned that counselors should not expect hostile persons to react favorably to demands for better performance; in fact, a demand for more or better work is likely to have a detrimental effect on achievement.

A study of high school boys given several sentence completion items as a personality measure found underachievers less likely to mention aggression (Kimball, 1952). Of the underachievers, 41 percent failed to give any responses that could be categorized as aggressive action toward removal of an irritant. Only 13 percent of the control group failed to give any aggressive responses. In a subsequent study, Roth and Puri (1967) found that underachievers given a projective test tended to verbalize intrapunitive action in response to a picture of a scene calling for aggressive action to resolve a problem situation, whereas achievers responded with verbalized extrapunitive action. Some underachievers responded with ideas that avoided any punitive action at all. This study too supports conjectures that underachievers turn their hostility inward or repress it.

In her work with over 100 gifted underachievers in England, Pringle (1970) found that her sample exhibited many of the characteristics just described. She attributed school difficulties almost exclusively to the home environment, as do most researchers who study the personality traits and attitudes of underachievers. Pringle claimed that one or both parents of underachievers were either overindulgent or unduly strict.

Parents of underachievers have been accused of being too insistent on high achievement. Similar judgments, however, have been made about parents of *achievers*. For example, a longitudinal study of bright children's school performance in the third through ninth grades found high achievers' parents to be too pressuring (Haggard, 1957). The high achievers in this study showed more resentment toward adults than did underachievers.

Discipline styles have also failed to distinguish underachievers' parents consistently. Although there seems to be a pattern of nonsupportiveness among fathers of male underachievers (Pringle, 1970), many achieving males also report perceptions of their fathers as unsupportive (McClelland, Atkinson, Clark & Lowell, 1953). Some studies have found mothers of female underachievers to be domineering (Fine, 1967); others have found them to be permissive (Raph, Goldberg & Passow, 1966).

When grade level, socioeconomic status, and intelligence were held constant, Raph et al. (1966) found no difference in parental disharmony, parental protectiveness, regularity of home routine, or parental pressure for achievement among male achievers and underachievers. Differences in the likelihood of parents' *sharing activities and ideas and providing encouragement with respect to achievement* were significant, however. Note that these significant factors, though affectively supportive, are cognitive in content and specific to performance.

Whether pressure to achieve is harmful may depend on whether or not parents (or teachers) provide the means for children to meet their high expectations for academic performance. High expectations for gifted children are necessary for their cognitive development, but high expectations in the absence of instruction to develop the attitudes or skills necessary to accomplish difficult tasks may condition failure. The persistent combination of high expectations and inadequate means to accomplish them is obviously debilitating to children. *This combination, in fact, is the persistent educational background of slow learners* (Bloom, 1977). Whitmore (1980) emphasizes the importance of teaching underachieving children that effort makes a difference in the outcomes of intellectual tasks. The availability of appropriate educational tasks is the fundamental prerequisite of such a strategy, however.

Some underachievers' parents may have failed to foster intellectual and social independence in their children. Pringle (1970) found that underachieving children in her sample were four or more years below norms of social maturity as measured by the Vineland Social Maturity Scale. She also found that despite above-average socioeconomic and educational levels, parents of bright underachievers provided average or below-average cultural and social opportunities.

Locus of Control.   Too little parental demand for achievement may leave children without incentive to persevere on arduous tasks (Fine, 1967; Pringle, 1970). Too great a demand may bring resistance. Underachievers' negative response to authority is often regarded as rebellion against overly demanding parents. Afraid to express their anger openly, underachievers simply fail to perform, often attributing their poor performance to factors beyond their control, such as lack of ability (Raph et al., 1966).

Attribution of failure to poor teachers, bad luck, lack of ability, or a boring curriculum is cited throughout the literature on underachievement as characteristic of bright children who make bad grades (Gallagher, 1975). Low achievers seem to feel that they cannot improve their performance because they lack control over the outcome of intellectual endeavors. Expressions of helplessness, such as these comments by underachieving teenagers, are common:

"Time just gets away from me."
"Luck's against me."
"I'm not much good, and there is no sense in trying to hide it."

High and low achievers attribute their success or failure to different factors (Kanoy, Johnson & Kanoy, 1980). Students' expressed reasons for success or failure on an academic task have been divided into four categories: ability, effort, luck, and task difficulty (Bar-Tal, 1978). These elements are categorized as (1) internal versus external and (2) stable versus unstable (i.e., they form a 2 × 2, four-cell matrix).

High achievers tend to attribute success to internal factors: ability or effort. They tend to attribute failure to an internal, unstable factor over which they have some control—that is, lack of effort (Bar-Tal, 1978). Low achievers, however, tend to attribute success to external factors: luck or an easy task. They often attribute failure to their own lack of ability. Consequently the low-achievement group denies its competence: it takes no credit for its successes and blames its failures on an internal, stable factor (that is, inability). That high achievers work more intensely and persevere longer at intellectual tasks is not surprising; they believe that effort makes a difference. Underachievers apparently do not.

Students' belief or disbelief in the proposition that effort affects performance may explain achievement to a greater degree than any other single variable that has been posited as an explanation. The mixed effects of family variables on achievement suggest that explanations based on degree of parental pressure to achieve, permissiveness, and authoritarianism are insufficient to differentiate achievers from underachievers.

Cautions about Counseling Results. Results of counseling interventions based on psychodynamic theories of underachievement, such as those discussed previously, have been for the most part unsatisfactory (Gallagher, 1975; Raph, et al., 1966; Whitmore, 1980). Although the explanation for the limited success of counseling efforts has often been that intervention was "too little, too late," there seem to be other difficulties as well.

Counseling assumes that the problem is within the children and, perhaps, the children's parents. It is based on the idea that if underachievers' attitudes are changed so that they are more like the attitudes of achievers, the underachievers will make better grades. This view (1) ignores the possibility that grades may not be a good measure of underachievement, (2) ignores the distinction between correlation and causation, and (3) minimizes the contribution the school makes to the problem. Although it appears that some children's personalities or attitudes place them, for some reason, at risk for underachievement, any intervention that fails to consider the influence of the school is unlikely to bring about significant long-term change.

The relatively few children for whom counseling may be needed are those who are so fearful, withdrawn, or aggressive that their behavior is far outside the normal range. Such children should be referred to a program that offers *intensive therapy*. For these students, poor academic achievement is a small part of the problem.

Most gifted underachievers' personal characteristics and behavior are within the bounds of normality; only in the classroom do they demonstrate comparative problems. This fact indicates that the point of conflict is the *classroom situation* of the child, either a particular placement or the details of that placement. It also suggests that intervention should include changing some elements of the classroom. Research supports this view. Educational interventions, modest as some have been, have proven more effective in treating underachievement than has counseling (Gallagher, 1975; Whitmore, 1980).

Underachievement as a Function of Schooling

About 20 percent of the students identified as gifted earn grade point averages of 3.0 or lower on grade-level work. This fact is surprising when one considers that on standardized tests gifted students usually score at least two grade levels above grade placement. Gifted kindergarteners score at about the second grade level, junior high students score at the high school and college level, and high school seniors score as well as the average college senior on comprehensive achievement tests (Marland, 1972).

One explanation for the relatively low grades is that school offers little reward for academic success. Some underachievers, in fact, complain that the only rewards for hard work in school are higher expectations for subsequent work (Raph, et al., 1966). If the work is not appropriate in level or in content, the resentment of these students is understandable, for such work can have no intrinsic meaning.

In the midst of a period in which personality problems were emphasized as the primary reason for underachievement, Raph et al. (1966) noted the need to consider the detrimental effects schools may have on some bright students. Their concern stemmed from studies such as those by Coleman (1961) and Tannenbaum (1962) which called attention to the unfavorable climate for academic development prevailing in most public high schools. Pringle (1970) also noted that teachers of underachievers greatly underestimated these students' abilities, and she suggested that this underestimate contributes to poor achievement. The schools' failure to provide relevant and challenging instruction has long been considered a primary cause of underachievement among gifted students (Hollingworth, 1942; Stanley, 1976; Whitmore, 1980; Young, 1958).

Emergence of Underachievement in School. Shaw and McCuen (1960) set out to discover when underachievement begins. They reviewed the grades of the upper quartile of a sample of eleventh and twelfth graders. Dividing the sample into male and female achievers and male and female underachievers, they found distinct patterns for the underachieving males and females. By the third grade, grade point averages of the male underachievers were significantly lower than those of the male achievers. The difference increased in significance at each grade level up to the tenth grade, where a decline in difference resulted primarily from a drop in the mean GPA of the achievers.

The female underachievers made *better* grades than the female achievers from first through fifth grade, although not at a significant level of confidence. In the sixth grade, the achieving females outperformed the underachieving females for the first time. This difference continued to increase in magnitude from sixth through tenth grade, but it was not statistically significant until ninth grade.

Although the investigators were puzzled by the underachieving females' tendency to earn better grades than achieving females in the first five grades, they did not see it as precluding the possibility that the females, like the males, entered school with a predisposition to underachieve; the authors of this study posited that underachievement was a chronic problem with both sexes.

Peer Socialization and Underachievement. Coleman's (1961) study suggests that scholarship may be subject to penalty in the public schools. Tannenbaum (1962) found that, among high school students, it was acceptable, even desirable, to be brilliant if one was athletic and not studious. On the other hand, being brilliant, studious, and not athletic was the least desirable combination. These studies make it clear that some gifted students, such as unathletic gifted boys, are not likely to achieve without suffering a penalty.

Classmates tend to disapprove of divergent thinking more when it is dis-

played by girls (Kurtzman, 1967). Classmates also tend to attribute more negative personality qualities (e.g., bossiness, snobbishness) to gifted girls than
to gifted boys (Solano, 1976). Perhaps this latter effect, however, is due to
the more widespread phenomenon of clique membership among girls of this
age (see Box 11.1).

Some studies have found gifted girls to be less confident in their abilities
than are gifted boys (Fox, 1976; Gallagher et al., 1967). In light of the attitudes
of their peers and teachers, it is understandable that gifted girls feel less secure and tend to attribute their failures to lack of ability. Among teachers who
have slightly negative expectations for gifted boys *and* gifted girls, the teachers' exposure to traits of gifted boys sometimes results in the teachers' having
a more positive attitude toward the boys. Exposure to traits of gifted girls,
however, fails to change teachers' negative feelings (Solano, 1976).

Traditionally masculine subjects such as mathematics are especially troublesome for girls. To the usual pressures inhibiting academic achievement are
added the taboo of ''acting like a boy'' and the sexual risk of competing with
male peers. The threat posed by competition in a masculine field may contribute to gifted girls' reluctance to participate in accelerated math classes.
Girls who are exceptionally able in mathematics often fail to persevere in their
study of advanced mathematics, despite their aptitude (Fox, 1976). Contributing to girls' drop-out rate is their failure to see mathematics as relevant to
their future. In this, girls reflect society's different aspirations for males and
females. It should not be surprising to find that gifted girls are more likely
than gifted boys to suppress their ability rather than risk displeasing teachers
and peers, particularly in a society that teaches girls that it is important to
please people (Blaubergs, 1978).

Work Roles.   As agents of socialization to adult work roles, schools are important participants in the noncognitive sorting of the sexes. Attitudes of
school personnel contribute to the discrepancy between ability and performance (Dowdall & Colangelo, 1982). Through teachers and counselors, inhibiting cultural values are inadvertently communicated to students. Although
this phenomenon affects all students who belong to minority groups, it has
been most discussed in the literature on gifted girls, perhaps because they
form the largest ''minority'' group identified as gifted (see below).

The effects of school personnel's values and their perceptions of students
are quite direct, as Casserly's (1979) interviews with high school counselors
show: ''Well, if they [girls] bring in their registration card [with an AP science
course] listed, I'll check to see if that's really what they meant, but I would
never encourage it. I mean, it's usually their last year and there are so many
fun things going on'' (Casserly, 1979, p. 364). Such attitudes acquired at school
correspond to those required in the workplace, where threats to traditional
sex roles can be even more disruptive than such threats in an academic context.

An example of how stereotypes affect teachers' behavior is provided by a
study comparing a teacher's directives in a working-class school with those

of a teacher in an upper-middle-class school. This detailed case study found that the teacher of upper-middle-class students encouraged internalization of academic discipline. Examples of her directives follow:

> Be fair to yourself, use your time wisely to help yourself become a better reader.
>
> Tommy, talk to yourself quietly and tell yourself where you are and what's expected of you.
>
> (To a child who has not completed his work during the allotted time:) Why do you do this to yourself?
>
> (Wilcox, 1982, pp. 289–290)

This teacher explained the reasons for the rules and admonished the students to consider their implications for academic progress.

The working-class students' teacher, on the other hand, emphasized external control in instructions for academic work:

> You have work to do and I want it done.
>
> Here's a star for everybody who finished.
>
> Sit down and do that work; this is a worktime.
>
> (Wilcox, 1982, p. 288)

If patterns like this one dominate teachers' behavior toward students from low socioeconomic status homes, they may explain findings that minority group students often fail to assume an internal locus of control for their achievement (cf. Bar-Tal, 1978). They also help to explain why counseling to change student attitudes has little effect on those attitudes.

The differences in teacher directives in Wilcox's study reflect differences in the types of adult roles the children are expected to fill. Upper-middle-class children are likely to assume professional roles that entail self-direction. Roles that the working-class children are likely to fill involve much closer supervision: "[A] worker (at this level of the work hierarchy) must come to work every day, be able to carry out the tasks within the assigned time, and accept task assignments without questioning them" (Carter & Carnoy, 1974, cited in Wilcox, 1982, p. 291).

Teachers can promote the development of different, more flexible roles for both boys and girls. An advocate for gifted girls contends that "the first task facing educators is to help gifted females gain the self-confidence, the sense of independence, and the positive image of themselves necessary for continuing achievement" (Schwartz, 1980, p. 115). This type of recommendation is best accomplished by improving the instruction provided to gifted underachievers. One must accept, however, that this solution will not necessarily improve the cooperativeness or mitigate the negativism of such students.

The Effects of Faulty Placement on Achievement. Early identification of exceptional ability and programs to develop ability have been considered important for optimal achievement since the time of the earliest studies of gifted children (e.g., Hollingworth, 1926). The more highly gifted the child, the more this is true. For the most precocious children, the likelihood of finding challenging work or classmates with similar interests is drastically lower in the regular school program than in a special program (Astin, 1974; Gallagher, 1975; Hollingworth, 1942).

In comparison with special classes for gifted students, many classrooms are unstimulating and confining to gifted students. A study reported by Marland (1972) found that in over half the regular classrooms, gifted students were not just neutral, but were negative and uninterested. In fact, research suggests that a sizable minority of gifted children do not like school and that the proportional size of this minority grows with increases in IQ (Astin, 1974; see Box 11.2). Perhaps students object to the fact that teachers talk 75 to 90 percent of the time in over half the regular classrooms. (This was the case in about one-tenth of the gifted classes.) Emphasis in most regular classes is on neatness, recall of factual information, and compliance. There is little room for reflection or for divergent thinking and behavior.

Even very young gifted children take offense at the same conditions that bright high school dropouts give as reasons for quitting school: too much pressure to conform, unfairness of teachers, and an irrelevant, unstimulating curriculum (French & Cardon, 1968; cf. Kenneth Rexroth's *An Autobiographical Novel*, 1966). Gifted first, second, and third grade underachievers report highly similar reasons for dissatisfaction in school: resentment or hostility from teachers and peers, social penalties for nonconformity, lack of opportunities to pursue individual interests, teacher criticism, teacher control, and an unrewarding curriculum (Whitmore, 1980, pp. 192–193).

Although schools underestimate the ability of most gifted children (Marland, 1972), some children are more likely than others to be the object of such faulty assessment. Gifted children who lack self-confidence and are reluctant to participate in new activities are particularly likely to be judged less intelligent than their IQ scores reveal them to be (Roedell et al., 1980). Active

---

Box 11.2 Frank Lloyd Wright's School Attitude

Frank Lloyd Wright, the eminent American architect, published the first volume of his autobiography in 1932. In part it is a lyrical tribute to the education given him on his uncle's farm. In Wright's mind this was his significant education; his distaste for formal schooling illustrates that highly gifted students may not like school much.

Of his early schooling Wright wrote that it "made not the slightest impression that can be remembered as of any consequence" (p. 13); of his secondary schooling, "it seem[ed] purely negative . . . [and] for that reason it may not have been positively harmful" (p. 35); and of his college years, "the retrospect of university years [was] mostly dull pain" (p. 51).

children who find it difficult to sit still for long periods of time or to comply with lengthy assignments are seen as problem children, no matter how bright they are. Schools may also underestimate the potential of gifted children whose achievement is not commensurate with their IQ scores.

Educational Interventions to Improve Achievement

Teachers and counselors can intervene effectively in the education of gifted underachievers, as several studies have shown. Successful interventions have combined several strategies: grouping bright students together, stressing academic skills, and gearing instruction to the ability of the students. One such program (described in Box 3.2) established boarding school programs and enrichment centers for bright disadvantaged secondary school students. Greater press for cognitive development and grouping for several years' instruction resulted in significant and long-term positive effects (Smilansky & Nevo, 1978).

Integrating findings from the literature on underachievers, Whitmore (1980) developed a program that included several important components:

1. early identification,
2. segregation in a psychologically safe environment,
3. emphasis on cooperation rather than competition,
4. diagnostic-prescriptive instruction, and
5. student involvement in selection of topics and activities.

The primary grade students in Whitmore's program were severe underachievers with IQs above 140. They had been labeled learning disabled or behavior disordered and referred for remedial education. When they were provided with a modification of their school situation based on individual needs, these children showed dramatic gains in achievement (Whitmore, 1980).

Whitmore's emphasis on cooperative goal structures is confirmed as a wise decision by Johnson, Maruyama, Johnson, Nelson, and Skon (1981). Johnson et al. (1981, p. 47) performed a meta-analysis of the effects of cooperative, competitive, and individualistic goal structures on achievement and found that cooperation "is considerably more effective than interpersonal competition and individualistic efforts . . . [and] that cooperation with intergroup competition is also superior to interpersonal competition and individualistic efforts" (cf. Bronfenbrenner, 1970; Popkewitz & Tabachnick, 1982).

The effectiveness of high academic expectations combined with basic skill interventions in accelerating the rate of academic growth in underachievers has also been documented with middle-class gifted students at the junior high level. Fearn (1982) reports longitudinal data collected in the sixth, eighth, and tenth grades which demonstrate improved performance of underachievers placed in gifted programs. The underachievers' academic growth rates prior to identification and placement ranged from 1.14 to 1.50 grade levels per year across subject areas of the Comprehensive Test of Basic Skills (CTBS). After intervention, the rates ranged from 1.75 to 2.45 on the CTBS. These rates were comparable to the rates of gifted achievers, which ranged from less than 1.70 to 2.40 across subjects. Fearn (1982) attributes the underachievers' improvement to the academic focus of the definition and treatment of the problem.

Early admission and accelerated school programs are considered to show promise for encouraging gifted girls to participate in advanced science and mathematics courses (Casserly, 1979; Fox, 1977). For optimal progress, gifted girls should be placed in an intellectually similar peer group.

Teachers of Advanced Placement classes report success in motivating girls (1) to participate in difficult science and mathematics courses and (2) to pursue college studies in these fields. This success corroborates the effectiveness of strategies recommended by Casserly (1979). These strategies include:

1. offering more AP classes in math and science;
2. actively recruiting girls for AP classes;
3. providing AP teachers with material on financial, academic, and professional opportunities for women in math and science; and
4. encouraging interaction between high school girls enrolled in AP classes and bright girls enrolled in junior high science and math classes.

As recently as the mid-1970s, prognosis for underachievers was guarded because of the failure of most interventions to affect performance significantly. Guidance efforts showed only small successes. Attempts to enhance self-concept (through placement with supportive teachers, for example) resulted in little improvement. Parental exhortations to work harder seemed only to make achievement problems worse.

The only interventions that have shown much promise on the basis of empirical data are changes in education programming. Though they have not been initiated widely or systematically, educational interventions have been conducted with some success. Such results suggest that underachievement, though difficult, is not an intractable problem.

SPECIAL CASES OF UNDERACHIEVEMENT: KNOWN ETIOLOGIES

In some cases, the agency of underachievement seems apparent. This is particularly true of gifted students who are handicapped and of those from oppressed classes of society.

This portion of the chapter considers characteristics of these students. It considers factors affecting their underachievement, modes of separating their potential from their weaknesses, and methods for remediating their academic deficiencies. Since these students' depressed functioning is partially conditioned by social variables that are not amenable to immediate change, remedial strategies may not be as effective in remedying the academic deficiencies of *these* youngsters as it is in remedying the underachievement of middle-class, white, nonhandicapped youngsters.

Handicapped Gifted Students

Children who are both gifted and handicapped are not *necessarily* underachievers. Some types of handicapped children are, however, *characterized* by their underachievement. These children are often categorized as specific-learning-disabled (LD) or behavior-disordered (BD) students. Underachievement is characteristic of these children, whether or not they are identified as gifted. Part of the process of identifying students with these handicaps involves the documentation of their academic underachievement (Cartwright, Cartwright & Ward, 1981; Lewis & Doorlag, 1983).

In general, the expectations that face gifted LD and gifted BD students in schools resemble those facing handicapped students. Whitmore (1981, pp. 109–110) considers several sources of the difficulties confronting these children, including expectations based on preconceptions about the handicapping condition, developmental delays that obscure exceptional performance, and lack of opportunity to evidence superior mental abilities.

Because gifted LD and BD students are usually underachievers, this portion of the chapter devotes particular attention to the nature of these students and their academic needs. Both specific learning disabilities and behavior disorders may be products of school and society (Carrier, 1983) or may result from some interaction between the individual and the environment.

The behavior disorders and learning disabilities of gifted children may be caused by psychological or social limitations on their ability to progress academically, express emotions, or pursue interests (Whitmore, 1982). These constraints may impede achievement or distort behavior to a significant degree and thereby bring these students to the attention of the teacher. Such constraints, however, may alter achievement or behavior only enough to mask students' giftedness. Rather than exhibiting characteristics of specific learning disability or emotional distress, some children may use their giftedness to compensate for their disabilities to such an extent that their performance resembles that of average students. In such cases, both giftedness and handicaps may go unrecognized (Wolf & Gygi, 1981).

Learning Disabilities and the Gifted Student.   Learning disabilities are often defined quantitatively. This is because "the label 'learning disability' includes the heterogeneous group of children who do not fit neatly into the traditional categories of handicapped children" (Kirk & Gallagher, 1983, p. 366). Although learning disabilities are presumed by many educators to relate to perceptual and/or conceptual deficiencies, they are not measured directly through assessment of neurological structures or functioning. Typically they are inferred from the presence of a severe discrepancy between students' measured intelligence and their academic achievement in any of several specified areas.

Although the original definition of learning disabilities provided by PL 94-

142 emphasized the necessity of determining a severe discrepancy between students' ability and achievement, a later definition stressed the underlying pathology presumed to cause that discrepancy. That definition refers to "a disorder in one or more of the basic psychological processes involved in understanding or in using language . . . spoken or written [manifested] in [the] imperfect ability to listen, speak, read, write, spell, or do mathematical calculations" (*Federal Register*, December 29, 1977). The definition further states that a learning disability is not primarily caused by "visual, hearing, or motor handicaps, . . . mental retardation, . . . emotional disturbance, . . . or environmental, cultural, or economic disadvantage" (*Federal Register*, December 29, 1977). These federal guidelines also restrict the identification of learning disabilities to the seven academic areas of oral expression, listening comprehension, written expression, basic reading skills, reading comprehension, mathematics calculation, and mathematical reasoning (*Federal Register*, December 29, 1977).

Although the 1977 federal definition does not operationalize the notion of severe discrepancy, identification of learning disabilities nevertheless depends on some determination of the discrepancy between ability and achievement (Algozzine, Ysseldyke & Shinn, 1982). The perceptual and conceptual processing deficits often presumed to cause learning disabilities are rarely accessible to direct observation or measurement. In addition, when processes can be measured, as in the assessment of auditory recall, results do not necessarily discriminate between achieving and underachieving students (McSpadden & Strain, 1977). The determination of a student's eligibility for special education in an LD program, therefore, depends almost solely on the quantification of the severe discrepancy between ability and achievement. Although in theory gifted underachievers should not necessarily be considered learning disabled, in practice their depressed performance on measures of achievement may make them eligible for placement in LD programs (cf. Wolf & Gygi, 1981).

Since the organic nature of learning disabilities often is assumed rather than verified (Chenoweth, 1965), indication of discrepancy in practice determines the diagnosis of a learning disability. The notion of discrepancy, however, has itself been challenged. Although "the latest federal guidelines . . . place importance on differences in ability and achievement . . . [they] include no discussion of ways to define severe discrepancies necessary for classification of LD" (Algozzine, Ysseldyke & Shinn, 1982, p. 299).

Many individuals exhibit discrepant performance that might be classified by some evaluators as "severe." The West Virginia State Department of Education (1982, p. 81), for example, proposed that a difference of 6 to 12 standard score points between ability and achievement represented a "fair probability that a significant discrepancy exists," and a difference of greater than 12 standard score points represented "a high probability that there is a significant discrepancy". Discrepancies of this magnitude, however, may fall within the standard error of difference between tests. An LD determination based on such a discrepancy may therefore be the artifact of test reliability rather than an indication of a real disparity between the student's potential and achievement (Salvia & Ysseldyke, 1981).

Students whose measured intelligence is two or more standard deviations above the mean are more likely than average students to evidence severe discrepancies in some academic areas as a result of developmental delays or school shortcomings. Consider the six-and-a-half-year-old whose IQ is 145. A severe discrepancy between this child's ability and performance in reading might appropriately be quantified as a 1.5 standard deviation discrepancy.

According to this formula, a student's standard score performance of 122 on the Peabody Individual Achievement Test might indicate that the student met eligibility criteria for placement in an LD program. The grade equivalent of a standard score of 122 on the PIAT reading comprehension subtest for a student of CA 6.5 is 3.3. The student's achievement in reading, which is actually 1.5 to 2.0 years *above* grade placement level, might qualify the child for placement in an LD program in which children typically perform 1.5 to 2 years (or more) *below* grade placement level. Although the gifted child's discrepancy may result entirely from lack of instruction in reading or from average perceptual-motor development, it nevertheless could be seen as indicating a learning disability based on the current federal definition.

In this case, however, the discrepancy would be used to make a placement only if the child were exhibiting inappropriate classroom behavior. The compliant, agreeable gifted student who achieved at this level in reading might be praised for accelerated progress; the rebellious, inattentive, or highly active gifted child who achieved at this same level in reading might be referred for special help and subsequently placed in a program for the learning disabled.

This scenario reflects Ysseldyke and Algozzine's (1982a) conclusion that special education classification decisions are based more on referral information than on child performance. These researchers suggest that "examiners hold and seek to confirm (with or without appropriate evidence) preconceived notions about the assessment outcomes based upon the child's *characteristics*" [original emphasis] (Ysseldyke & Algozzine, 1982a, p. 228). The atypical nature of gifted children may, therefore, ensure that certain gifted students will always be identified as learning disabled *primarily* as a result of their characteristics as gifted students.

Another, though perhaps less common, situation involves neurologically impaired (i.e., organically brain-damaged) gifted students who use conceptual strengths to compensate for processing deficiencies. These students may disguise their difficulties but may not reveal their giftedness (Whitmore, 1982). Hence, the underachievement of such students may be chronic, because they may never be provided a stimulating curriculum. This problem is compounded by the tendency of "teachers . . . to be easily satisfied with work of a good standard" (Pirozzo, 1982, p. 19). Because students demonstrate both average performance and the appearance of hard work, the teacher may overlook indications of giftedness, such as a large vocabulary and sophisticated reasoning.

The problems associated with the identification of gifted students with learning disabilities parallel the problems related to the education of these students. Since learning disability is not defined consistently either in the literature or in practice, findings generated from the observation of one sample of LD students cannot be presumed to apply to any other sample (Mercer, 1983). Since different states also use different criteria for evaluating giftedness, gifted students from one state may not be similar to those from another. Expanded definitions add to the confusion (cf. Glass, 1983). Therefore, considering the variety of identification paradigms for both LD and gifted students, variation among samples labeled both gifted and LD will be very great. One sample might, for example, include motorically delayed high-creatives, whereas another might include brain-injured leaders.

Use of a definition of giftedness that accounts only for students with superior academic potential or achievement (see Chapter 1) minimizes some difficulties in both identification and education of these exceptional children (cf. Glass, 1983). Similarly, use of a definition of learning disabilities limited to those students who exhibit "hard signs" of neurological impairment minimizes confusions about the education of these students (cf. Berko, Berko & Thompson, 1970). Carrier (1983, p. 952) cautions that definitions of learning disability should not assume that "because A (neuropathology) causes B (the signs of learning disability) all cases of B are cases of A." If narrower definitions are adopted for both giftedness and learning disabilities, identification of a discrete LD/gifted population may be possible.

Narrower definitions may also suggest appropriate instructional alternatives for those gifted students who actually have demonstrable neurological impairments. First, such definitions substantially reduce the number of gifted students who can be classified as learning disabled. This reduction, in turn, allows for increased precision in the diagnosis and remediation of the academic deficiencies of these LD gifted youngsters. Second, a limited definition guides school efforts to place into LD programs only those students whose academic or behavioral anomalies cannot be controlled by typical classroom management procedures.

Placement in LD programs may not be wise for gifted students (cf. Wolf & Gygi, 1981). Compounding the difficulty for gifted underachievers is the schools' frequent requirement that these children master basic skills before they proceed to more advanced content (Whitmore, 1982).

Remedial programs that require that students learn tasks to criterion levels, that instruction be highly sequenced, and that the learning environment be free of unnecessary distractions probably are detrimental to most gifted underachievers. Remedial programs designed to improve LD students' basic skills are not necessarily effective (Frauenheim, 1978; Haskell, Barrett & Taylor, 1977). Placement in a remedial program may further restrict the gifted child's access to learning experiences that are advanced, content-specific, or simply interesting. Structured programs may be essential, however, for the success of *neurologically impaired students,* regardless of their IQ (cf. Haskell et al., 1977; Reid & Hresko, 1981).

Just as there is no consensus about the identification of LD students, there is also controversy concerning their education. This controversy revolves around the distinction between process training and academic or skill training (Glass, 1983; Hammill & Larsen, 1974; Kavale & Glass, 1982; Mann, 1979).

Those who favor process instruction advocate "special training procedures that attempt to develop or ameliorate psychological deficits or developmental learning disabilities . . . such as attention, language, discrimination, thinking, memory, and so forth" (Kirk & Gallagher, 1983, p. 391). Those who recommend skill training suggest procedures for (1) remediating or (2) compensating for weaknesses in skill areas.

The skill training approach includes "direct instruction in either the terminal academic behavior or its immediate antecedents" (Mercer, 1983, p. 176). Sometimes this instruction involves the use of applied behavioral analysis to reinforce the learning of academic skills. Other times it entails the provision of instruction in skills that can compensate for weaknesses in areas of academic learning (see Box 11.3).

With a restricted definition of learning disabilities and a commitment to developing academic skills of neurologically impaired gifted students, educators may have more success in meeting the needs of LD gifted students. The articulation of the distinctions between underachieving and neurologically impaired gifted students may also enable educators to direct more appropriate services to those underachievers whose depressed academic performances reflect extrinsic influences rather than intrinsic handicaps.

Box 11.3 Remedial and Compensatory Skill Training

Consider the case of a student with a reading disability associated with a deficient visual memory. This impairment may manifest itself as the inability to recall sight vocabulary.

A *remedial program* designed to improve sight-word acquisition might employ techniques of applied behavioral analysis, such as systematic observation of the student's process of learning sight words, task analysis of sight-word learning, direct instruction using sight-word flash cards, systematic monitoring of student progress, and reinforcement of the student for improved performance in mastering sight vocabulary.

On the other hand, a *compensatory program* for instructing this student would concentrate on strengthening decoding skills so that the student would not need to rely so heavily on the recall of sight vocabulary.

In either case, the goal of instruction is to improve the student's reading skills, not to remediate the process deficit(s) presumed to underlie the reading difficulty. In the case of a neurologically impaired student, process training is particularly suspect, because the neurological structures governing particular processes may be damaged. Techniques of compensatory skill training probably are required in order to instruct such children (Berkow, 1977).

Behavior Disorders and the Gifted Student. Before Terman published the results of his longitudinal study, many people associated genius with insanity. The creative process was considered an outgrowth of conflict and distress, and scientific talent was personified in the image of the absentminded, reclusive, and antisocial researcher (cf. Mary Shelley's *Frankenstein*, 1818/1968).

Terman's studies replaced these stereotypes with new ones. Gifted individuals were soon envisioned as superior in all aspects of behavior. They were viewed as more intact than average individuals both physically and mentally. Creativity was redefined as the demonstration of healthy self-actualization (Kubie, 1961; Maslow, 1968); research and problem-solving were reframed as group processes (cf. Gordon, 1961; Osborn, 1953). Researchers have tended increasingly to substantiate the emotional normality of the gifted. In general, the view of the gifted as deviant was replaced with the view of the gifted as *exceptionally normal* (see Chapter 12). Neither conception accurately represents the gifted.

Although most studies tend to confirm the correlation between below-average IQ and behavior disorders (e.g., White, 1966), some studies suggest a correlation between behavior disorders and above-average IQ (e.g., Harvey & Seeley, 1984; King, 1981; Morse, Cutler & Fink, 1964). Many studies of behavior-disordered children do include subjects with IQs in the superior range (Kauffman, 1981).

The issue of deviance is of particular concern in a discussion of the emotional health or disturbance of gifted students. Teachers and administrators continue to be concerned with the emotional health or imbalance of gifted children. Perhaps this concern is responsible for gifted programs designed to improve the self-concept of gifted children or to improve their social interaction skills. (See Chapter 6 for a detailed discussion of affective education programs.)

Gifted children, however, appear to have fewer affective difficulties than average students (d'Heurle, et al., 1959; Lehman & Erdwins, 1981). Schools' insistence on remedial and developmental efforts intended to improve the affective competence of all gifted students seems, in the light of research, to be an inefficient use of limited resources.

A possible explanation of the prevalence of affective programs relates to the schools' role in socializing students. Gifted students, whose academic precocity sets them apart from others, are considered to be at risk for becoming socially deviant [see, e.g., "The Hippies" (author unknown), 1967; Hollingworth, 1926]. Affective education programs for these students may therefore be considered important preventive, rather than curative, measures.

Perhaps the logic of the schools' response to the emotional needs not only of the gifted but also of the emotionally disturbed (or behavior disordered) needs to be questioned. In theory, schools attempt to suppress the deviant behaviors of emotionally disturbed youngsters. In practice, special interventions are often no more successful, however, than regular-class placements in improving the behaviors of disturbed children (O'Leary & Schneider, 1977).

It is possible that this phenomenon confirms the hypothesis forwarded by "labeling theorists." These critics contend that society's or schools' response does not lead to the attenuation of deviant behavior but rather to its amplification (Hargreaves, Hestor & Mellor, 1975, pp. 5–6). Special placement, though hardly intended by teachers to function this way, may actually serve more as a warning to the compliant than as a benefit to the deviant. Perhaps this social control mechanism, together with the problematic phenomenon of student deviance, is responsible for the chronic underachievement of a sizable number of students.

One study found that classroom teachers perceived 20.4 percent of their students as exhibiting behavior disorders (Kelly, Bullock & Dykes, 1977). This study also indicated that teachers perceived behavior disorders in boys twice as often as in girls and in blacks twice as often as in whites. These findings support the view that the schools' tolerance for deviance is very low and that its social control function bolsters stereotypes concerning the various population subgroups. It is not a coincidence that the ranks of the underachieving gifted include disproportionate numbers of males and minority group children (Gallagher, 1975).

Although research studies have not specifically considered the phenomenon of behavior disorders among the gifted, many studies have validated a method for modifying the behavior and increasing the learning of all students. Considering the empirical documentation of the success of this technique, known as applied behavioral analysis, the failure of schools to reform misbehavior and to increase academic learning must, according to Baer and Bushell (1981), be attributed to schools' unwillingness to achieve these ends. See Chapter 9 for a discussion of behavior technology and the gifted.

Gifted Children from Economically Oppressed Groups

A consideration of gifted children from economically oppressed groups devolves immediately to fundamental issues of definition and causation. When giftedness is defined as IQ superiority, minority children (blacks and latinos, preponderantly) are found to be gifted less frequently than are white, mainstream children. Similarly, when giftedness is defined (more liberally) as superior performance of any culturally validated activity (see, e.g., Gallagher, 1975; Passow, 1972), activities valued by minority groups are judged less worthy than activities valued by the white middle class.

Issues of practical significance for such students, like quotas, content or level of instruction, or pursuit of mainstream careers, cannot be handled easily because the more fundamental questions have not yet been resolved. Groups of people who have been systematically oppressed by society are unlikely to demonstrate evidence of superior performance within the society. Nor are the institutions of a society, including its schools, likely to be responsive to the needs of such people. Those students who achieve in the face of the social preconditions for academic failure do so because of emotional, familial, or economic resilience (cf. Baer & Bushell, 1981).

Although gifted students are "found in all economic strata, and in all racial and ethnic groups . . . very small percentages of children from low-income families or minority groups are found in programs for the gifted'' (Maker, 1983, p. 140). In part, their underrepresentation results from biases in identification practices. Since many programs rely for eligibility determination on IQ calculated from national samples, economically oppressed students are at a disadvantage (cf. Khatena, 1982, p. 237; see also Chapter 2).

High performance on IQ tests suggests superior scholastic aptitude, as Chapter 1 argued, because IQ tests measure attainment of skills required for academic learning. Not all students with demonstrated potential to succeed in school actually realize that potential, however. The resources necessary to prompt achievement are most often available to middle-class and upper-middle-class youngsters. This phenomenon serves to strengthen the belief that academic excellence is a product of conformity to mainstream values and that intelligence is differentially distributed across social classes. This issue will be considered further in Chapter 12.

The *institution* of schooling functions to perpetuate mainstream values in addition to academic learning. It serves to reproduce economic hierarchies and inequalities (Jencks et al., 1972; Meyer, 1977). It accomplishes this function despite the personal intentions of many teachers. In such a context oppressed students are not likely to perform well either in school or on tests designed to predict school success.

Innumerable regimes have, over the millennia, justified their exploitation of subjugated peoples with a bogus presumption of such peoples' inferiority. The historical pattern is too familiar for the argument not to be suspect in our age. The failure of oppressed groups within a particular society to demonstrate mental capacity equal to that of others in society is not an indication of their biological or mental inferiority. Rather, it is more likely to be a measure of their underachievement, or *suppressed achievement.*

The underachievement of economically oppressed children is much more extensive than that of mainstream children because all aspects of their performance within the society are devalued. Thus, the underachievement of these youngsters cannot be viewed solely as an educational issue (Jencks et al., 1972). Changes in school provisions for these students are not likely to improve their achievement because the school has so far proven unable to function as an arena for resolving social and economic inequities (Jencks et al., 1972; Spring, 1982), contrary to the hopeful expectations of such thoughtful educators as Conant (1959) and Dewey (1900/1956). The belief that the school functions as a change agent for society is not verified by its performance (Popkewitz, Tabachnick & Wehlage, 1982).

Students who perform at the top of the range within a population subgroup but not in the superior range within the total population are not singled out through traditional identification practices (see Chapter 2). *The identification of these students as gifted underachievers would allow educators to offer them special education services that are otherwise denied to them.* Fearn (1982, p. 121) seems to describe just such an identification strategy in his discussion of a program for nonhandicapped underachieving gifted students.

The remainder of this chapter considers the achievement problems of the largest economically oppressed subgroups in the United States. These groups are women, workers, blacks, and those people (now predominantly of Latin American extraction) who speak English as a second language.

Women. Women constitute the largest group of economically oppressed individuals within our society. Their social role, however, has changed substantially in the last hundred years (cf. Hollingworth, 1926, for a concerned discussion of the plight of bright women sixty years ago). Economic discrimination on the basis of sex is a complex question because women's economic status is still not usually considered outside the family context. Though the situation is changing, women are usually accorded the economic status of their husbands or fathers.

Discrimination that affects primarily the *personal* initiative and role perception of a group is not of the same order as discrimination that invariably affects the economic status or *class* position of group members (cf. Duncan, 1968; Wright, 1979). The peculiarity of discrimination by sex probably accounts for the fact that women obtain IQ scores congruent with those of men within their ethnic, racial, or class group.

Because of the peculiar nature of discrimination against women, their underachievement is exhibited more often in the marketplace than in the schoolroom (Callahan, 1981). In fact, by conventional standards girls often appear to achieve better than boys academically (Torrance, 1965). Programs addressing the underachievement of girls have therefore been directed toward changing their attitudes about the pursuit of careers in traditionally male-dominated fields. These attitude changes in turn have improved girls' achievement in subjects needed for traditionally male careers (Fox, 1978).

A great deal remains to be done in equalizing the life chances of men and women. Teachers of the gifted should

- model interest and capability in all academic areas regardless of traditional sex orientations,
- use nonsexist language and teach students to use nonsexist constructions in oral and written language,
- suggest nontraditional career options for both male and female students,
- provide equal amounts and types of corrective academic feedback for male and female students (cf. Good & Brophy, 1984).

Workers. After women, the working class is the largest economically oppressed group. One researcher (Wright, 1979) has estimated the size of the working class in the United States at about 50 percent. Snow (1969, p. 505) addressed the issue of working-class children in an article defending strong academic programs: ''It has always been hideously difficult for children from the working-class to get any sort of tolerable education. It is in many respects difficult today. None of us has any right to be satisfied with the present position.'' Young (1958) also lamented the intellectual waste inherent in passing

over able working-class youngsters in favor of less able children of the affluent.

Because Young and Snow are British, however, their comments do not
specifically reflect the problem in the United States. Excellent universities are
not strongly supported by the government in the United States, as they are
in almost every other advanced industrial country. Moreover, in the United
States, working-class children are virtually excluded from schools with excellent academic programs below the college level, through lack of state support and local funding of public schools.

The children of skilled and unskilled workers are seldom identified as gifted
(Freeman, 1979; Hollingworth, 1926; Laycock, 1979; Terman, 1925; Young,
1958). The phenomenon is so striking as to require empirical and critical investigation. Unfortunately, because the terms of such an investigation have
not been laid down, no such investigation has occurred in the U.S. educational literature.

The concept of class is not familiar to U.S. educators as it is to British educators (cf. Dahrendorf, 1959; Gould, 1981; Robinson & Kelley, 1979; Whitt,
1979; Wright, 1979). In the United States the familiar concept is *socioeconomic
status* (cf. Blau & Duncan, 1967; Duncan, 1961, 1968; Duncan, Featherman &
Duncan, 1972). Socioeconomic status (SES) is an interval scale ranking (like
IQ) based on sociological measures of occupational status, educational attainment, or income attainment.

Socioeconomic *status*, rather than economic *class*, is thus the basis of what
is popularly referred to as lower, middle, and upper class in the United States.
Status refers to popularly perceived rank; *class*, on the other hand, refers to
position and function in the economic order.

In the absence of empirically descriptive data on working-class children,
we believe that the wisest plan is to identify as gifted the most academically
able 3 to 5 percent of children in working-class schools and to provide such
children an academic curriculum geared to their rate of acceleration (cf. Fearn,
1982). The ease with which such a logic could be applied to neighborhood
schools that are largely segregated by class and race (Jencks et al., 1972; Mosteller & Moynihan, 1972) makes this a practicable plan.

Blacks.   Blacks share the problems of the working class in the United States
(Wright, 1979) and encounter additional barriers as well. Duncan (1968) notes
that blacks are routinely and prejudicially assigned depressed occupational
statuses.

Blacks are oppressed in this way because they were once slaves. Because
of their peculiar economic and political history, blacks have not been assim-
ilated to the same extent or in the same way as other immigrant groups. As
a group, blacks, like women, are still not accorded the same rewards for similar work or qualifications as competing groups. The differential treatment of
these two groups cannot be obscured by inaccurate definitions: the characteristics on which discrimination is based (race and gender) are unambiguous.

Whites have made too much of the fact that blacks as a group achieve less well on IQ tests than whites. Different ethnic, racial, cultural, regional, and national groups *all* achieve different group means. For example, Chinese-Americans as a group score above white Americans, and yet no one has asserted that the education received by whites should therefore be less oriented to intellectual matters than that received by Chinese-Americans (cf. Jensen, 1973, on educational programming for blacks).

Because U.S. schools are largely segregated on the basis of race and class, we could make the same recommendation for black schools as for working-class schools. Blacks in the United States are in a more desperate position, however, than the working class. In the last thirty years, as the most oppressed ethnic and racial minority in the country, blacks have given the term *civil rights* a new meaning through an unprecedented advocacy of their own rights and needs. This struggle against the imposed role of slave will continue. It would be unethical and gratuitous for white authors, at present, to make recommendations about the education of bright black children. Black educators, black families, and black communities need to make these decisions.

In general, however, we believe with Katz (1971) and Cazden (1972) that poor people of all races want their children to learn to read and write and do mathematics. Moreover, we suspect that intellectual aspirations characterize all classes and races in literate societies, however particular societies may distribute knowledge (cf. Apple, 1982; Meyer, 1977).

ESL Students. Students for whom English is a second language (ESL students) are at a disadvantage both in testing and in schooling, which is why PL 94-142 stipulates that tests be administered in a student's native language. For the most part language difficulties are characteristic of recent immigrants to the United States; after a period of residence immigrants become natives (cf. Gould, 1981, pp. 220–233, for an account of the way in which IQ tests were used to confirm ethnic prejudices and exclude immigrants early in the twentieth century).

Of late, two issues have complicated the reception of immigrants: (1) the legal status of many recent immigrants and (2) the third world origin of many recent immigrants. In the United States these issues typically involve Spanish-speaking immigrants.

Some school systems have been ordered to enroll the children of undocumented workers. These are working-class aliens who do not possess documentation from the U.S. Immigration and Naturalization Service allowing them to hold jobs in the United States. Undocumented workers live a fearful, isolated, and transient life. This context jeopardizes the integrity of any educational effort on behalf of their children.

Many recent immigrants have come to the United States from the third world, particularly from nearby Central American and Carribean nations. Typically they leave their native lands because even a life that is destitute by U.S. standards is affluent by third world standards. They also come to the U.S. because political strife disrupts their lives.

Such immigrants raise in the imaginations of some citizens the specter that the United States will be overrun by the world's indigent. Now that the United States is fully settled, such resentments run deeper than earlier suspicions of the immigrant (cf. Riis, 1890/1971, for a description of immigrants' traditional lot).

The prognosis for finding and teaching the gifted among the children of undocumented workers is poor indeed. The prognosis for other immigrant children, however, is much better, particularly if native speakers are employed as teachers and examiners. With respect to gifted programs, both groups have difficulties similar to those of the working class.

SUMMARY

This chapter explored different notions of underachievement and suggested the need for care in defining the term with respect to gifted students. In particular, the comparison of normative academic achievement to IQ was related to previous discussions of giftedness.

Several definitions of socialization were discussed, and the relationship of both achievement and underachievement to socialization was examined. Socialization was examined primarily from an institutional, rather than an individual, perspective. The chapter cited a number of authors, including Benjamin Bloom and James Coleman, to help describe this sort of socialization.

Because socialization is often interpreted as pertaining to interpersonal relationships, the more ample literature on peer relationships of the gifted was also discussed. The conclusion was that, in general, the interpersonal relationships of gifted children are not at risk to any greater extent, on average, than those of nongifted children.

The chapter examined the affective hypothesis of the underachievement of gifted students, as well the possibility that underachievement is a concomitant of schooling. Discussion indicated that, in general, psychodynamic therapy and counseling, although interesting, were not nearly as effective in improving achievement as academic interventions directed to cognitive ends.

Finally, the chapter examined the special cases of underachievement with conventionally identified etiologies. These etiologies included handicapping conditions, especially learning disabilities and behavior disorders among gifted students. Economically oppressed subgroups of students were also discussed with respect to underachievement. In general, the discussion indicated that viewing socialization as an institutional effect provided a valuable perspective on the underachievement of gifted students.

CHAPTER 12

Equal Opportunity: Mediocrity or Excellence?

INTRODUCTION

This chapter examines the social context of gifted education. Its viewpoint, however, is political and economic rather than sociological. The aim of the discussion is to promote a critical approach to the understanding of the issues of elitism, egalitarianism, and hereditarianism and the role of academic instruction in the education of the gifted. Not all readers or instructors will agree with this analysis, but we hope the discussion provokes a sharp examination of the topics it treats; there is plenty of room for differences of opinion on these matters.

In order to examine the historical, economic, intellectual, and pedagogical implications of our discussion of gifted education, in the final section of this chapter we synthesize several lines of exposition and argument common to this and other chapters.

THE POLITICAL ECONOMY OF GIFTED EDUCATION

No one who has ever worked as a teacher or administrator can deny the seriousness with which bond issues, excess levies, and teacher raises are treated by all segments of the political community. Seldom, however, are the connections between local tax and election issues and the larger issues of the political economy examined. These larger connections concern not the maneuverings of national political parties, but the organization of political and economic life in general.

Economics in the United States today is divorced from political theory, though economics and politics were not originally conceived of separately. Heilbroner (1966, p. 49) notes, for example, that Adam Smith (author of *The Wealth of Nations*, 1776) himself was primarily a philosopher "with a philosopher's disdain of riches."

We use the term *political economy* in this chapter to refer to the unity of the political and economic system. Philosophically we view U.S. political institutions as but a specific instance of one sort of government, and forms of government do not themselves summarize political thought or political relations. Political economy accords structural and functional importance to how goods, services, and wealth are produced and distributed (cf. Heilbroner, 1966, pp. 46–50).

A grasp of the pertinent issues of political economy permits a critical approach to the problems of elitism, hereditarianism, egalitarianism, and educational opportunity as they relate to gifted education. The issues are indeed controversial, but, we believe, of such persistence as to require examination. Unexamined assumptions in this domain are particularly dangerous because they constitute our class, race, and cultural prejudices.

Legitimation

All nations need to propagate images of the legitimacy of their political economies (Turner & Starnes, 1976). The way goods and services are produced, how wealth is accumulated, how surplus of all kinds is distributed, and the way the power of the nation is used to maintain the political economy *must* be made to seem natural, proper, and just to citizens.

Meyer (1977) believes that legitimation of what we call the political economy is the chief function of education as an institution. He defines four types of legitimating effects:

1. legitimating specialized competence,
2. legitimating elite roles and the persons who occupy them,

3. legitimating the unexamined assumptions of collective reality through mass education, and
4. legitimating subordinate and superordinate relationships among citizens and between citizens and the state.

Meyer notes, "Modern education is seen . . . as a system of institutionalized rites transforming social roles through powerful initiation ceremonies and as an agent transforming society by creating new classes of personnel with new types of authoritative knowledge" (Meyer, 1977, p. 56). He comments further that "educational systems are thus, in a sense, ideologies. They rationalize in modern terms and remove from sacred and primordial explanations the nature and organization of personnel and knowledge in modern society" (Meyer, 1977, p. 66).

Meyer believes that educational systems in industrial societies produce significant effects that transcend particular influences on individuals. In part Meyer's formulation is a response to Coleman et al. (1966) and Jencks et al. (1972), who, as the reader will recall, found the effects of schools on students' destinies to be much less significant than previously thought (e.g., by the progressives of the 1920s). If schools are not an avenue of change for *individuals*, then might not the *institutional* effects of schools in fact be what sustains schools?

Such a possibility runs counter to the American ethos of individualism, hard work, free will, and mobility. Meyer (1977, p. 56) observes that such legitimating effects "transform the behavior of people in society quite independent of their own educational experience." That is, our subjective impressions and assessments of our own schooling do not capture the larger, objective reality of social institutions or of political economic relationships. This insight is new to education, although Dewey (1930/1962, pp. 101–102) glimpsed it when he stated that one could not suppose "that the pioneer gospel of personal initiative . . . could be maintained in an era of aggregated corporate capital."

The Coleman report (Coleman et al., 1966) confirms Dewey's insight empirically. Schools are not equal to the myths about them. The mechanisms of socialization seem to legitimate existing political and economic hierarchies rather than contribute to changing them for the benefit of individuals.

Socialization and Correspondence. As teachers we would like to assume that schools were institutions unto themselves. In that case the main function of schools would clearly be the cultivation and valuation of knowledge and intellectual work for its own sake. However appealing, this image is fantasy. The way in which the production of goods and services is organized necessarily has a profound effect on both the socialization intent and the actual function of schooling.

Bowles and Gintis (1976), among others, propound a "correspondence principle" which asserts a correspondence between the noncognitive outcomes of schooling (e.g., values, modes of self-presentation, disposition to organizational authority) and the sorts of noncognitive behavior and unreflective consciousness required in most work roles.

Carter (1976, p. 58) notes that "a particularly important insight embodied in the correspondence principle is the idea that . . . the school . . . is not in essence a thing in itself; its essence lies . . . in its relations to the institutions and processes of work."

The most critical implication of this line of reasoning for bright children is that learning is definitely not valued for itself. Moreover, noncognitive school behaviors are valued not because they promote learning but because they correspond to work destinies. Learning itself is also valued primarily for what it can accomplish in the economic system. Such attitudes are indeed to be found in the literature on gifted education. For example, Marland (cited in Hoyt & Hebeler, 1974, p. 22) espouses the belief that liberal arts colleges and universities should hold themselves "accountable for putting . . . knowledge to useful ends. And *knowledge must be useful . . . or it is nothing*" [emphasis added].

The intellectual community takes a quite different view, however, of the utility of knowledge. In general, scientific thinkers have pointed out that advances in knowledge usually follow investigations into matters that, precisely because they are not understood, seem to be trivial, esoteric, and unrelated to issues of established utility. Only after the replicable findings have been successfully disseminated does professional acceptance render the initial investigations valid. Utility validates the findings further when technical use popularizes them and makes them profitable. To judge knowledge and, ultimately, intellect for their utility is to misrepresent both the value of intellectual work and the nature of our political economy (cf. Adler, 1982).

Under a utilitarian scheme (cf. Marland, 1972), the best knowledge is that which is most efficient in the marketplace. Viable intellectual values are denigrated. The dedication of intellect to the goals of achieving corporate profit and maintaining social inequality may be legitimated in this way.

Reproduction.   The measure of the success of any legitimation structure is how successfully it helps reproduce the political economy underlying the social order. *By this criterion, the U.S. educational system appears to be in general quite successful.* This point underlies the discussions of many authors cited in Chapter 11 and elsewhere (e.g., Baer & Bushell, 1981; Bloom, 1977; Carrier, 1983; Coleman, 1961; Coleman et al., 1966; Fine, 1967; Jencks et al., 1972; Raph et al., 1966; Rosenbaum, 1975; Wilcox, 1982; Ysseldyke et al., 1982).

Traditional socialization theories (e.g., Schwarz, 1975) view the political economy (referred to euphemistically as "the adult world" or "the world of work") as a labyrinth of folkways to which the young adapt *individually*. By contrast, investigation based on the structure and function of institutions focuses especially on the *reproduction of class relations*. The notion of a class is not easily defined or captured empirically; the issues are of enormous magnitude and central political import. It is, however, apparent that reproduction of the U.S. political economy entails the reproduction of class relations in a way that preserves the prerogatives of corporate and private privilege and profit.

Bowles and Gintis (1976) note that schools assist such reproduction of the political economy by justifying social inequality and by shaping technical roles, market behavior, and authority relations.

If the political economy is seen to be ordered by objective merit, then the political economy is legitimated as a natural, proper, and just order—a *meritocracy* (see the discussion of hereditarianism in Chapter 1). Herrnstein's *IQ in the Meritocracy* (1973), for example, suggests that such is the case. Young's modern utopia, *The Rise of the Meritocracy* (1958), illustrates the degree to which the belief is compelling and ideologically quite complex.

One way in which schools justify inequality is through what Bowles and Gintis refer to as "IQism." The basic premise of IQism is "if you're so smart, why aren't you rich?" IQism is clearly at work when the mean IQs of professional groups are propagated as evidence of the association of intellectual merit, status, and high income (e.g., Hollingworth, 1926). The association of IQ and income, however, is much weaker than many persons believe. Bowles and Gintis (1973) found that the effect of IQ on income, when socioeconomic background and educational attainment were held constant, was slight indeed. On the other hand, when IQ was held constant, educational credentials were found to have a much stronger effect on income (more than four times as strong, in fact).

Equality. Thomas Jefferson, setting a prominently documented precedent for the United States, wrote, "We hold these truths to be self-evident, that all men are created equal, that they are endowed by their Creator with certain unalienable Rights, that among these are Life, Liberty, and the pursuit of Happiness" (*U.S. Declaration of Independence*, 1776). The French revolutionaries echoed this belief a short while later: "Men are born, and always continue, free and equal in respect of their rights. Civil distinctions, therefore, can be founded only on public utility" (*Rights of Man and Citizen*, 1789).

The *public utility* of civil distinctions is really the essential restriction on definitions of equality. In what ways are differences among sections of the public useful, to whom, and for what reasons? Scholars have noted frequently that the U.S. and French formulations about equality serve primarily to guarantee rights of property (see, e.g., Harris, Morgenbesser, Rothschild & Wishy, 1961; Hobsbawm, 1962; Palmer & Colton, 1965; Williams, 1966).

No one doubts that equality is a fine response to aristocratic despotism, yet many aver that extremes of equality are to be avoided (e.g., Gardner, 1961). The issue of equality is most often dealt with as if "equal" meant "same," so that the notion of "excellence" appears threatened.

Privileges, Rights, and Equality. Equality actually may refer to equivalent value rather than sameness. The French *Rights of Man and Citizen* places the concept of equality as equivalent value in a context that is meaningful to our argument. The concept that public utility is the only justification for civil distinctions (i.e., social inequality) contrasts the ideal of equality with the usefulness of inequality.

Under a utilitarian scheme (e.g., Osborn, 1963), any useful civil distinction takes precedence over "equal[ity] in respect of . . . rights"(*Rights*, 1789). Though everywhere in the United States equality is asserted to be a principle, everywhere private advantage proves more useful in practice (Dewey, 1930/1962). Useful inequality serves both to promote and to protect the privileges of property. To put it simply, we have not, as a nation and as a political economy, found equality to be practical.

The sort of value by which equality may be judged cannot be determined by cost-benefit analysis. The value of equality can be better understood as an *a priori commitment to the dignity and integrity of human potential*, manifested both in individuals and in a cohesive community. In the United States our commitment to utility and to the myth of "rugged" individualism has traditionally obscured our view of how a commitment to equality binds us to one another. Seeing the potential of humanity as an issue of equality is therefore somewhat alien to our way of thinking.

Human potential is the heritage of all humans, however, not of a particular class, nation, or race, as was thought in the nineteenth century (cf. Dobzhansky & Montagu, 1975; Galton, 1869/1962; Gould, 1981). Humanity, a species like any other, has biological limits as to excellence of all sorts. These limits are not best measured individually. This reality is the practical basis of our equality, though it cannot be reckoned in dollars. It may, unfortunately, be possible to so undervalue the species that the existence of even its most exemplary specimens is threatened (i.e., in holocausts of various kinds).

The value of equality is ultimate, absolute; the value of liberty is the immediate and relative practicality of "civil distinctions." In the United States we view liberty and equality as conflicting concepts. We have made them so by making the utility of liberty the criterion for defining equality. The sphere of liberty is wide; that left to equality is small indeed.

In the United States we have lost sight of the issue of equality as a shared social value with implications for the entire species and for our own society. We are therefore inclined to interpret equality as an individual issue. We point to the obvious physical and mental differences among individuals, and we claim that ideal equality in the face of such obvious differences is an absurdity. We buttress our claims with the assertion that—somehow—our individual differences ethically entitle us to the differing rewards of wealth, income, and social status. Thus we maintain that equality pertains solely to "equality before the law," despite our clear understanding that all do not have equal access to the law as an instrument of redress or protection (see Box 12.1).

Charity, "Gifts," and Equality.   The principle underlying charity has always been that some unfortunate individuals should be exempted from the scorn of the righteous because innate handicaps can preclude worthy efforts. Despite this sentiment, the struggle to provide organized and reliable social ser-

---

Box 12.1 Max Weber and the Logic of Merit and Wealth

Probably the best known theoretical examination of the meritocratic logic is Weber's *The Protestant Ethic and the Spirit of Capitalism* 1920/1958). According to Weber, the source of justification for such ethical beliefs derives from the notion that God has ordained the social structure:

> The phenomenon of the division of labor and occupations in society had . . . been interpreted . . . as a direct consequence of the divine scheme of things. . . . The perseverance of the individual in the place and within the limits which God had assigned to him was a religious duty.
>
> (Weber, 1920/1958, p. 160)

Within a particular divinely ordained calling "the most important criterion is . . . private profitableness. For if . . . God . . . shows one of his elect a chance to profit, he must do it with a purpose. Hence the faithful Christian must follow the call by taking advantage of the opportunity" (Weber, 1920/1958, p. 162). In this way differences in social position are usually ascribed to effort and divine ordination.

---

vices of any type to such individuals has been difficult. Charity ("volunteerism") is still put forward as an alternative during times when social services are reduced by the modern state. Often the impetus has been to protect society from the "defectives" (Gould, 1981). Such an argument was in fact used to promote early educational efforts on behalf of blacks and the working class (Bowen, 1981).

The vast difficulties of trying to ensure equality, even for the handicapped, are exemplified by the history of PL 94-142 before, during, and subsequent to its adoption. Surely, handicapped children must have the sympathy of the public. And yet implementation of the law has been fraught with contradictions, setbacks and evasion (cf. Pfeiffer, 1980; Poland et al., 1982; Ysseldyke et al., 1982; Ysseldyke & Algozzine, 1982b).

Exception based on defectiveness, however, certainly does not apply to individuals endowed with "gifts." In fact, Weber's (1920/1958) argument seems to imply that if such individuals are larger and healthier than others, if they are more academically apt than others, if subsequent to schooling they earn more money, have more stable marriages, and are more productive intellectually than others, then these characteristics can be interpreted as a mark of God's blessing. What damns the handicapped to charity and regret elevates the gifted to affluence and self-respect!

Privilege and Individual Differences.   When a political economy is, like ours, divided by class interests and by the historical practices of racism and sexism, the difficulty of confirming legitimate individual differences is immense. It is a futile task to derive the notion of equality from the human diversity apparent to common sense. Only when we see ourselves as a species do our resemblance to one another and the meaning of our equality emerge.

Unequal privileges obscure our concept of equality and confound our impression of legitimate differences. These unequal privileges are the afore-mentioned civil distinctions founded on public utility. *Individual differences in IQ belong in part to such useful civil distinctions.* (In part they relate to cultivation of the intellect for its own sake.) The association of affluence and IQ actually obscures the role of intellect in our society and its valuation by our society. Early commentators, for example, believed the association confirmed the social usefulness of intellect (cf. Hollingworth, 1926; Terman, 1925).

In the war of each against each, individual differences are not valued for themselves or even for the social good to which they may contribute. Individual differences are valued for the private privileges that they can secure. Curiously, it was the defender of absolutist rule, Thomas Hobbes, who noted (*Leviathan*, 1651/1962) that the *equality* of men, not their differences, was the source of conflict between them (see Box 12.2).

Hollingworth (1926, p. 358) stated the conventional view early in the history of gifted education: ''A competitive social-economic system does, so far as we can infer from present data, foster the interests of the intelligent through making it possible for them to obtain economic goods by the exercise of their

---

Box 12.2   Thomas Hobbes on Equality

Thomas Hobbes (1588–1679) is often contrasted with John Locke (1632–1704). In particular, Hobbes endorsed absolutist rule, whereas Locke is credited with influencing democrats like Jefferson. ''Life, liberty, and property'' were natural rights, according to Locke. Hobbes wrote of the struggle of each against each for security and justified absolutist rule as the best way of providing for security.

Ironically, Hobbes recognized the equality of humankind, an equality he found to be greater in intellectual than physical matters, as the following excerpt from his *Leviathan*, chapter XIII, indicates:

> Nature hath made men so equal, in the faculties of the body and mind; as that though there be found one man sometimes manifestly stronger in body, or of quicker mind than another; yet when all is reckoned together, the difference between man, and man, is not so considerable, as that one man can thereupon claim to himself any benefit, to which another may not pretend as well as he. For as to the strength of body, the weakest has strength enough to kill the strongest, either by secret machination, or by confederacy with others, that are in the same danger with himself.
>
> And as to the faculties of the mind, setting aside the arts grounded upon words, and especially that skill of proceeding upon general, and infallible rules, called science; which very few have, and but in few things; as being not a native faculty, born with us; nor attained, as prudence, while we look after somewhat else, I find yet a greater equality amongst men, than that of strength.

(Hobbes, 1651/1962, p. 141)

powers." Many of us, perhaps a large majority, probably still subscribe to this view.

Since 1926 researchers have, however, come to understand that this economic system is not necessarily so conveniently ordered. There is even evidence to suggest that the system identified by Hollingworth may in some ways disparage intellect (see, e.g., Baer & Bushell, 1981; Bowles & Gintis, 1973, 1976; Brandt, 1981; Coleman, 1961; Copley, 1961; Gardner, 1961; Hofstadter, 1961, 1963; Young, 1958).

Many writers have pierced the ideological veil obscuring the economic relations that effectively shape inequality (e.g., Counts, 1930/1971; Cummings & Taebel, 1978; Dewey, 1930/1962; Feldman, 1979a; Holt, 1964; Jencks et al., 1972; Kohl, 1967; Rosenbaum, 1975; Scarr & Weinberg, 1976; White, 1977). The belief that IQ is justly rewarded economically, however, persists because of its ideological utility for legitimation. Talent differences of all sorts are, thus considered, a matter of social inequality primarily because they are *thought* to bring and to require differential reward. In some instances, high IQ (i.e., one sort of talent difference) is associated with large economic reward; in other cases it is not. In general IQ brings differential economic reward only in conjunction with the more obvious civil distinctions of class, sex, skin color, occupational status, and educational attainment (Jencks et al., 1972; Olneck & Crouse, 1979).

As Jencks et al. (1972) noted, inequality is ultimately a social and economic issue (i.e., an issue of political economy), not an educational one. The possible existence of differences in academic talent no more threatens the notion of equality than does the existence of differences in athletic talent (see Box 12.2).

Elitism

Society has yet to confirm its valuation of intellect and intellectual talent as distinct from the uses of talent. The faulty association of intellectual excellence with social inequality serves to promote resistance to special education for the gifted. *More serious still*, it serves to promote gifted programs that do not address intellectual and academic concerns.

Gifted education has been criticized as the elitist provision of advantages to the advantaged. This criticism, based on the popular belief that differentiation of instruction is undemocratic, does not aptly reflect consensus opinion concerning political or economic elites (e.g., Guzzardi, 1965).

In a society in which income differences are praised as the reward for initiative and in which differences in acquired wealth are encouraged through both law and legend, schools' dedication to upholding values of democratic equality appears suspect (Bowles & Gintis, 1976). In fact, a number of authors (e.g., Apple, 1982; Baer & Bushell, 1981; Fine & Rosenberg, 1983; Giroux, 1983; Selden, 1983) have suggested that schools' "hidden curriculum" involves the maintenance or reproduction of conditions of inequality and stratification.

An examination of educational practice over the past eighty years reveals that modifications for the less academically apt not only have been permitted, but have been encouraged (Selden, 1983). Often these modifications take the form of segregated placements, a provision that seems to *limit*, not promote, the attainment and mobility of students from lower class and minority backgrounds (Findley & Bryan, 1971; Glass, 1983; Williams, 1983).

If educational practice has been found to serve political and economic ends in relationship to lower-class and minority students, why should we not expect it to serve the same ends in relationship to the ruling elite? It *is* possible that schools function in some significant ways to maintain the structural position of a ruling elite.

There is insufficient evidence (cf. Hollingworth, 1926) to conclude that this elite is endowed genetically with superior intelligence. In fact, because the children of the ruling elite are probably no more likely to be gifted than are children from the middle classes, the cultivation of superior intellect does not serve the interests of the most politically and economically influential. Historically, the interests of intellectuals have clashed with those of the ruling classes (Hofstadter, 1963; Lipset & Dobson, 1972). The historian Richard Hofstadter writes,

> The values of business and intellect are . . . eternally and inevitably at odds. . . . The intellectual is well aware of the elaborate apparatus which the businessman uses to mold our civilization to his purposes and adapt it to his standards. The businessman is everywhere; he fills the coffers of the political parties, he owns or controls the influential press and the agencies of mass culture; he sits on university boards of trustees and on local school boards; he mobilizes and finances cultural vigilantes; his voice dominates the rooms in which the real decisions are made.
>
> (Hofstadter, 1963, pp. 234–235)

Given the pervasive influence of the ruling elite, it is not surprising that this class would want to protect its position by attempting to suppress the possible ascendency of any competing group. The intellectual elite is a group that historically has challenged existing political structures (Lipset & Dobson, 1972).

The traditional antagonism between the power elite (cf. Mills, 1956) and the intellectual elite has been disguised, however, through the myth of the meritocracy. This myth maintains that the unequal distribution of wealth, income, and power in the United States is equitable because it reflects differences in innate ability and initiative (Bowles & Gintis, 1976; Karier, 1975; Olneck & Crouse, 1979; Young, 1958). In recent years this contention has been justified by statistical calculation of IQ heritability (Jensen, 1980; Scarr, 1971; but cf. Layzer, 1975). The myth obscures the difference between the most powerful and the most intelligent by suggesting that power and monetary success are the ultimate measures of intelligence (cf. Hofstadter, 1963; Selden, 1983). This was one of Galton's (1869/1962) basic assumptions (see Chapter 1).

Gifted programs may serve and justify the established disposition of power and control of resources under certain conditions. They must first, however, defuse the antagonism that traditionally characterizes the relationship of businessmen and intellectuals (cf. Hofstadter, 1963, above). One way to accomplish this end is to emphasize technical education and the technical aspects of science. This approach was, in essence, the nation's response to the apparent threat of the first Sputnik satellite. The emphasis on math and science had produced an overabundance of engineers by the mid- to late-seventies.

Another approach is to somehow direct critical thought to the solution of well-defined practical problems. Osborn's (1953) system of creative problem-solving, for example, was developed explicitly to help executives and industrial research and development teams deal more efficiently with business problems. Programs that treat various sorts of mental processes in isolation from consistent academic instruction also represent this approach.

Still another prospective way to defuse the antagonism of intellect and business is represented by the "life adjustment movement." According to Hofstadter (1963, p. 352), the purpose of this movement (ca. 1910) was to "better equip . . . all American youth to live democratically with satisfaction to themselves and profit to society as home members, workers, and citizens." According to Hofstadter (1963, p. 352), the essence of the plan was that "all pupils should in large measure get the kind of training originally conceived for the slow learner." The value of intellect is of course denigrated in such a plan; when a gifted program offers only counseling or training activities relative to life adjustment, anti-intellectual values are possibly implicated.

When publicly funded school programs for the gifted assume functions such as those suggested above, they are more likely to be considered elitist than are programs that cultivate intellectual values, interests, and aptitudes. When gifted programs do not identify samples of gifted students representative of the school population served in the district (cf. Fearn, 1982), they are also more likely to be viewed as elitist.

The Paradigm of the Normal Curve

The normal curve (often referred to as the bell curve) was first described mathematically by Abraham De Moivre (1667–1754) (see Glass & Stanley, 1971, for the equation of the familiar curve). De Moivre developed the equation for the normal curve as the algebraic expression of the likelihood of obtaining a given number of heads or tails in a given number of coin tosses. The normal curve therefore describes the probability of pure chance outcomes. One can use the curve to determine the probability of a particular chance event within measurable limits, depending on how one describes the event (e.g., with norm-referenced tests).

Such a probability is the mathematical content of an IQ score (or of any standardized score). An IQ of 130 can be interpreted mathematically in several ways. If a student's true IQ is 130 (a fact we can never know), then there is a 68 percent chance that the obtained score will (with a test reliability of .85 and a standard deviation of 15) fall between 124 and 136. We can be 95% certain that the obtained score will fall between 118 and 142 (cf. Swanson & Watson, 1982, pp. 71–72). Alternatively, one's chance—all things being equal—of obtaining an IQ score of 130 or above is one in thirty-three; of 115 or above, about one in six; and of 100 or above, one in two.

Ordinarily, we do not think of derived scores on norm-referenced instruments so abstractly. What concerns us as practitioners is the utility of scores for educational decision-making. Today, as a result of traditional practice, we interpret scores easily, with little thought about their mathematical basis. We can use the Binet categories—very superior, superior, above average—or the special education categories—trainable mentally retarded, educable mentally retarded, learning disabled (i.e., normal IQ), gifted.

There is little doubt that the paradigm of the normal curve can be a useful administrative tool. The general public acknowledges this usefulness (Lerner, 1981). Normative testing makes possible comparisons and descriptions of groups by criteria of measurable reliability. Some assumptions and projections based on the paradigm need to be examined, however, in order to understand both its applicability and its limits.

It is true, for example, that we do not know with even approximate certainty what causes the individual variability in performance on IQ tests or on achievement tests. Of course, it is related in some way to the difficulty of the test questions. What makes a question difficult is, however, problematic. Some writers have suggested that variability arises primarily from heritable inborn (or genotypic) traits (e.g., Burt, 1940; Hollingworth, 1926; Jensen, 1980; Spearman, 1904; Terman, 1925). Others have denied an important role to biological determinism (e.g., Dobzhansky & Montagu, 1975; Gould, 1981; Houts, 1977; Jencks et al., 1972; Layzer, 1975). Most educators, however, probably believe that such variability derives from a combination of specific environmental influences and genetic endowment (Laycock, 1979). The intermediate position may be more a matter of hedging bets than of evidence, reason, or knowledge (cf. Laycock, 1979, p. 152). At this time, there are no definite conclusions about the cause of individual differences. Therefore, one needs to be very careful in examining the ideological assumptions that guide application of the paradigm of the normal curve.

Normalcy as Paragon.   A paragon is a model of excellence or perfection. It is ironic, but quite true, that normalcy can be understood as such a model. Normalcy can be understood as a paragon because the diversity of characteristics (e.g., in IQ, thorax length of insects, shoe size) suggests that the normal (or the mean of a normal curve) represents an *ideal type*. Normalcy can thus be viewed statistically as a narrow band of scores around the mean of the distribution that describes a given trait. In the normal curve only 17 percent of all subjects will fall within three standard score points of the mean (i.e., within the average standard error of measure at IQ 100 on the WISC-R). That is, a minority of students can be reliably construed as typical of the mean; others deviate from the mean to greater or lesser degrees. This view emphasizes the uniqueness of the mean (i.e., its independence and its existence as a paragon). This range of ±3 standard score points closely corresponds to stanine 5, the one-half standard deviation centered on the mean, which includes 20 percent of the population.

If a person is to be described as the sum of traits measured individually, we should consider how those traits actually fit together to produce that person. Under these circumstances what sort of paragon is necessary to describe a whole person? It is clear enough that high IQ is a generally coveted (if resented and misunderstood) trait. But if we select five or six traits to describe a person academically, or ten or one hundred traits to describe the same person's "wholeness," will we necessarily select extreme positive characteristics in all cases? Shall we value the very emotional person? The very amorous person? The social isolate? The very talented thief? The very compulsive person? The choices are not at all clear.

Western thought has, however, a philosophical tradition that can resolve the dilemma in the absence of empirically compelling descriptions of wholeness. This is the Aristotelean tradition of moderation. Aristotle (1962, p. 43) wrote, "Virtue aims at the median. . . . Virtue is concerned with emotions and actions; and in emotions and actions excess and deficiency miss the mark, whereas the median is praised and constitutes success."

Excess and deficiency were to be avoided in all matters, according to Aristotle, though he was careful to warn that the standard for emulation ought to be chosen carefully (Aristotle, 1962, pp. 41–44). In his discussion of virtue as the mean, Aristotle created what we would call Likert scales. For example, for the trait of pleasure, the extremes of Aristotle's scales are self-indulgence and insensitivity, and the mean is self-control; for the trait of honor, the extremes are vanity and small-mindedness, and the mean is high-mindedness. Thus, under Aristotelean methodology, we could define a paragon gifted child, and we could base our identification efforts on the conformity of individuals to such a model. Matrix identification instruments could, if adequately standardized (a large project), be adapted to just this end.

The Aristotelean concept is doubtless one of the remote but fundamental cultural influences shaping our notion of the "whole child." The whole child is a paragon of the sort that would have appealed to Aristotle. The whole child notion implies balance of development. High-IQ children are at risk for developmental imbalance, and indeed, the research literature suggests that such imbalances often exist in individuals identified as gifted. Such imbalances are particularly evident in the motor and affective development of some gifted children. Thus, teachers and parents alike often assert that gifted children ought to remain with age-grade peers because of the presumed noncognitive benefits to be gained from such an association. Another way of putting this assertion, however, would be to say that normalcy (normal peers, normal procedures, and normal thinking) is the paragon.

Ultimately, the respect accorded normalcy transcends the individual to affirm the normal state of the political economy, the political and economic status quo. The tendency of intellectuals to question the status quo is troublesome to others (cf. Gallagher, 1985). When, however, intellectuals accept the status quo as perfectly natural, they betray their heritage, according to Hofstadter (1963). Becoming an intellectual, then, is a risky business.

Cummings & Taebel (1978) document the way in which children are socialized to accept the economic status quo. Though children enter school without significant economic prejudices toward trade unionism, private ownership of major industries, or state intervention in economic affairs, by the time they leave school most students take a negative attitude toward state ownership of major industries and a large plurality (41.2 percent) oppose state intervention in economic affairs. Cummings and Taebel (1978, p. 209) note that this kind of economic socialization legitimates "the general structure of social inequality in American life."

The aberration of intellectualism cannot charitably be forgiven, because it does not present itself as a misfortune or handicap (see the above discussion on charity). Moreover, since our political economy and our schools both denigrate intellect (Katz, 1971), intellect will be valued less, for example, than athletic ability, leadership ability, life adjustment, or belief in mainstream values (cf. Coleman, 1961; Hollingworth, 1942).

High IQ is a desirable attribute if conceived of as a possession that, like an expensive car or a fine home, bestows status only. When it leads either to the assertion of intellectual values or to claims of giftedness, it may be treated as a pretentious and undesirable aberration.

Teachers of bright students need to acknowledge that schools, as institutions of the political economy, regard gifted students as being at risk for heterodoxy (Hollingworth, 1942; Gallagher, 1975) and ultimately suspect as possible future intellectuals (Einstein, 1954, pp. 33–34; Hofstadter, 1963; Wiener, 1950, p. 157).

School Failure

For some reason, schools fail to educate a significant proportion of students (Bloom, 1977; Ysseldyke & Algozzine, 1982b). The conventional notion has been that the normal distribution of mental traits (created according to some hypothesized chance factor or combination of factors) is responsible for school failure. According to one version of this logic, a certain percentage of children will not succeed in school because they do not enter school with an aptitude for schoolwork and they are unlikely to develop such an aptitude during their stay in school.

Today the traditional view that some children are bound to fail while others are bound to succeed is not endorsed in special education: all children are presumed able to succeed to the limit of their abilities. Such a presumption, though necessary, is not sufficient to secure the desired end of maximum achievement. This is true in part because the assumption itself is purposely naive in terms of the political economy. Special educators have sometimes presumed to treat educational problems as if they were unrelated to the social milieu in which they exist. This tendency reflects a traditional belief that schools form an institution that can be understood without reference to the larger social context (cf. Carrier, 1983; Jencks et al., 1973).

As with other populations, both the failure and the comparative success of the gifted are often not believed to be related to broader social or economic issues. The reluctance to view the performance of children in the context of the political economy, which underscores the failure of less able children, serves to disguise the failure of gifted children. Many gifted children give the appearance of succeeding because they are seldom compared, for purposes of grading, with intellectual peers. Their presumed success is actually a disguised variety of school failure (cf. Bloom, 1977). Gifted children who fail more spectacularly as individuals, through poor grades, are frequently not identified as gifted. And most gifted children fail to do as well as they might were they not retained lockstep with their age-mates. Many others fail because optimal academic goals are not set for all children.

These related species of school failure are very much part of the academic experience of gifted children, yet ideological blinders make such failure difficult to recognize and difficult for teachers of the gifted to communicate to others. It is intellectually and practically *much easier* to deny the ability of able children than to confront the implications of this failure.

In the long term, it makes more sense to see school failure not as the burden of hapless children, but as one sort of failure of the institution of schooling in general (counterbalanced by its success of legitimation and socialization). It seems to be true that schooling is a pervasive social institution which reproduces the disposition of dominant social forces and ideologies. At the same time, however, it is these social forces and ideologies that condition what is popularly viewed as academic school failure.

Valuing Children.   Several authors have questioned the extent to which our society values children (e.g., Bronfenbrenner, 1970; Friedenberg, 1979; Keniston, 1975). Bronfenbrenner and Keniston compared the valuation of children in the United States to that in other industrialized nations. According to Keniston (1975, p. 18), ''We are the *only* [original emphasis] industrial democracy that lacks a system of income supports for families with children. In this area, we are an underdeveloped nation.''

Bronfenbrenner (1970) contrasted U.S. and Soviet childrearing practices. Bronfenbrenner, who cast his discussion in terms of socialization, not political economy, found that the Soviets were doing a much better job of socializing their children in conformity with *stated* goals than were Americans. He was surprised by the respect and affection accorded children and teachers by Soviet society (cf. Friedenberg, 1979). Bronfenbrenner concluded that

.

> If the institutions of our society continue to remove parents, other adults, and older youth from active participation in the lives of children, and if the resulting vacuum is filled by the age-segregated peer group, *we can anticipate increased alienation, indifference, antagonism, and violence on the part of the younger generation*

in all segments of society—middle-class children as well as the disadvantaged [original emphasis].

(Bronfenbrenner, 1970, p. 117)

Research indicates that teachers can implement some effective practices to provide some of what is missing. Bronfenbrenner's recommendations for improvements in the U.S. educational establishment derived from Soviet practices of group competition (competition for grades or other rewards among heterogeneous groups, rather than among individuals). These *practices*, he notes, parallel the findings of Western *research*. The Soviets practice an effective method they have not researched. In the U.S., we researched an effective method but do not practice it. A recent meta-analysis confirms that cooperative and group competitive efforts are more effective than individualistic and individual competitive efforts, as Bronfenbrenner suggested (Johnson et al., 1981).

Like applied behavioral analysis (Baer & Bushell, 1981), group competition remains unused in U.S. schools. Children could learn more; they could learn better, even if we were to accept their individual differences as totally determined on the basis of genetically encoded traits (genotype). Counterproductive pedagogical practices in U.S. schools seem durable (Cuban, 1982) for other than technical reasons. Keniston (1975) attributes failure in the schools to

the nature of our economic system and of our unthinking acceptance of the ideology that buttresses it. Our system, as it has worked, has needed a large pool of drudges—and we have provided them. . . . There are menial and boring jobs in every society . . . the question is whether they are to be filled by paying decent wages to those who do them or by impelling them to be done by those desperate souls we keep in chronic need. . . . This nation pays a moral and human price simply by tolerating a system that wastes the potential of many of the next generation.

(Keniston, 1975, p. 21)

The distinction between the intellectual elite and the economic elite reveals the way in which the political economy negatively affects gifted children from affluent as well as modest backgrounds. Complacency on these issues based on the belief that gifted children are relatively secure against such harm is completely unfounded. Indeed, such complacency is a significant part of their pedagogical problem. As Gallagher (1975) notes, the gifted do need assistance to make their schooling effective. They do not "make it on their own" for a variety of socially and intellectually complex reasons.

Social Distinctions and Evolution.   School practices and the apparent failure of schools to foster achievement even among the gifted are extensively influenced by social institutions. It may therefore also be possible that these same institutions influence the development of individual differences. For example,

Mercy and Steelman (1982) found that familial influences significantly contributed to intellectual attainment.

Dobzhansky and Montagu (1975) and many other anthropologists and biologists point out, more generally, that humanity's most astonishing evolution is cultural, not biological (cf. Gould, 1980, p. 266). Theories that attribute psychologically measurable mental variability to steady biological selection (especially in the last few centuries, cf. Jensen, 1973) completely misprize the notion of evolution, according to Gould (1980; 1981).

According to the anthropological and biological view, mental differences are indubitably real, but they are far more likely to be aspects of culture in a broad sense than of neurological eugenics or dysgenics. Ysseldyke and Algozzine (1982b) perceptively put the matter this way: "The differences among individuals are not the reasons children are not learning in school but are merely symptoms we have chosen to analyze, and they have not fared well in the analysis."

Gifted Education in the Schools

As officially instituted programs, services to the gifted are now more widely established than ever before. Many more children are served today than when Marland reported to Congress in 1972. Still, there are (as one should expect) many problems.

Among the problems this text has identified, some are amenable to direct solutions; others are not. Basically these problems pertain to

1. identification methods,
2. extent and kind of placement alternatives,
3. program content, and
4. the extent to which intellect is valued.

In general, we subscribe to the following basic principles

1. Identification should be based on talents pertinent to the main instructional purpose of schools: reading, writing, mathematics, and the arts; in short, verbal and quantitative intellectual skills in an academic context.
2. A variety of placement options, both regular and special, should be available to accomodate gifted children's ability to master academic material rapidly.
3. Essential programs should concentrate on teaching academic content.

One would expect that such programs and procedures will help produce an environment, perhaps limited to the gifted program, in which intellectual work is valued more than it may be elsewhere in the school. The extent to which this is possible, however, is unclear. The need to communicate such values and to nurture intellectual efforts in gifted children is, however, beyond doubt.

Reward versus Essential Education. When education for bright students does not address their intellectual and academic needs, it constitutes a pedagogy that intentionally cultivates the legitimacy of social inequality. A picture of such a version of gifted education (in California, where interest in the gifted has traditionally been strong) is reported by Weiler (1978). Weiler, a parent and teacher, recounts how prejudices and priorities operate instructionally:

> The MGMs [Mentally Gifted Minors] from our local school's second through sixth grades went to a computer center and played video display games such as tank battle. The children also named favorite colors, friends, pets, and pastimes; using this information, the computer printed out a personalized story for each child. When they returned to school, the children shared the excitement of their trip with classmates who had not been able to go. Some children wondered why everyone had not been included; most knew. . . . To establish leadership qualities, the MGMs are often expected to report to classmates about their special learning experiences. I've been told that this benefits the other children—a sort of trickle-down theory. It seems to me to be turning the knife.
>
> (Weiler, 1978, p. 185)

A bit further along in the article Weiler (p. 186) notes that ''it is both elitist and ignoble to accept the premise that our society must depend solely on the success of the [most academically apt] 2%.''

Weiler is not addressing the question of whether or not academically apt children should receive a differentiated program, or of what such a program should consist. Instead, her article is a critique of how the nation's largest gifted program at one time promoted the sort of useful (arbitrary and prejudicial) social distinctions described above.

Essential education for the gifted is probably quite another matter, and it is not dependent on the presumption that the gifted will find secure professional futures, provide for the national defense, or determine the fate of the nation. *Essential* education for the gifted does not concern self-concept, leadership, or moral development conceived of as pedagogical specialties.

It does involve consistent hard work at students' instructional levels on academic matters of intellectual worth. Moreover, on the grounds that mental traits are ill defined or equally distributed among ethnic, racial, and social class groups, such differentiated education ought to be available equally to all ethnic, racial, and social classes *as a matter of social policy*. This recommendation for gifted education is the analog of the presumption in handicapped education that, given optimal circumstances, all children are capable of making meaningful educational progress. Our current social policy is, however, based on the converse grounds, a fact that fully explains why so few economically oppressed groups (see Chapter 11) are to be found in most gifted programs.

Because injustice and social inequality are vital parts of our cultural consciousness, practical alternatives are likely to comprise an array of evils. If we propose pedagogical categories based on individual differences in norm-referenced test performance, even if we acknowledge all such differences to be culturally determined, then we will have endorsed in some measure the social inequalities and injustices referred to above. If we propose several categories of giftedness (e.g., as in the 1970 and 1978 federal definitions), then not only are we even *more likely* to be endorsing social inequalities, but we are likely to find that we are valuing the different sorts of giftedness unequally and that we cannot address such variety effectively or efficiently.

On the other hand, if we reject all notions of differences in aptitude, achievement, or IQ, ostensibly in the name of equality, then needed arrangements for the academically apt will not materialize. Nor will such restraint contribute to efforts to improve the schools in other ways.

Thus, it seems that the combination of factors calculated to do the least harm and the greatest good, using the tools at hand, includes:

1. circumspection especially about the nature and origin of group differences, but also about individual differences in IQ and academic talents,
2. fair identification of black working-class and ESL children, and
3. emphasis on academic goals.

IMPLICATIONS OF POLITICAL AND ECONOMIC ISSUES

The implications drawn below follow from our discussion of the larger issues as we have interpreted them, both here and in preceding chapters. We neither prognosticate amazing possibilities based on idealism nor make very limited projections from an empirical data base. Instead, we take our premises and our analyses to logical conclusions from which we may be able to examine alternatives consistently.

Historical Implications

Many writers (e.g., Cuban, 1982; Katz, 1971; Keniston, 1975) have noted how unchanging U.S. educational practices are. Others have commented on the apparent paradox of the failure to change in the face of research that substantiates viable alternatives (e.g., Baer & Bushell, 1981; Bronfenbrenner, 1970).

Gifted education needs to proceed with caution. First, though a base for program growth exists in many states, the opportunity to establish a federal mandate is slight. *Caution in particular needs to be exercised in using PL 94-142 as a model for future actions;* reservations pertain more to the legalisms and to the pedagogy implicated by the law than to the aspirations for full opportunity and equality of human potential embodied in the law. These latter concerns are just as applicable to the gifted as they are to anyone else.

Second, the presence of class and race biases threatens the future of special provisions for the gifted even more than those for the handicapped since programs for the handicapped have been thought anyhow to be compensatory. When gifted programs provide *noncognitive* benefits exclusively to bright children clearly not at risk, they seem to serve neither a legitimate pedagogical function nor a legitimate social function. The observation that "enrichment is valid as an educational technique only so long as it compels intellectual discipline" (Copley, 1961, p. 24) bears remembering.

The most bitter and *justifiable* opposition to the establishment or expansion of gifted programs in the future stems from a popular ideology (cf. Herrnstein, 1973) implicating gifted children from affluent backgrounds in the maintenance of the political economic status quo. In fact, badly conceived gifted programs *do* contribute to social injustice, sexism, racism and a devaluation of the dignity of all citizens. Intellectual aspirations cross the barriers of sex, race, and class. Aspirations for financial, professional, and social status often represent those barriers.

Economic Implications

Prevailing school practices and the phenomenon of school failure endure not because of the ignorance and incompetence of teachers, but because significant political economic structures require and maintain them (Keniston, 1975). It is nonetheless true that these structures seem to devalue the importance of intellectual work in schools (cf. Brandt, 1981; R. Mitchell, 1981; Schlechty & Vance, 1983).

Many writers, noting the intractable nature of school problems and the failure of school reform, have implicated the determining nature of economic factors (e.g., Baer & Bushell, 1981; Bowles & Gintis, 1976; Carrier, 1983; Coleman, 1961; Friedenberg, 1981; Jencks et al., 1972; Katz, 1968, 1971; Keniston, 1975; Rosenbaum, 1975; Wilcox, 1982; Wilcox & Moriarity, 1977; Ysseldyke & Algozzine, 1982b). The logic of such determinism suggests that schools change only in response to the prerogatives of the political economic order. Though accurate economic predictions are hard to come by, some reasonable generalities from a respected authority may suffice.

Leontief's Predictions.   Wassily Leontief, a Nobel-laureate economist, claims that by using input-output economics (a model he developed) it is possible to assess the impact of the new wave of technological (computer-based) innovation and its interaction with economic, social, and education policy choices. Leontief (1982) forecasts *greater wealth and income inequality* in the future, primarily because of the incursions into white-collar jobs of solid-state technology. As the service sector of the economy is automated, labor's share of income will decline, though automation will increase productivity, according to Leontief. He warns that if a portion of this increase in property income is not transferred "to . . . increase the real family income of wage earners and salaried employees" (p. 192), and if the length of the work week is not reduced, then increasing social disorder is likely. Leontief, however, claims that history "shows that societies have responded to such challenge with revision of their economic institutions and values" sufficient to forestall such disorder.

The Leontief forecast bears on our discussion of the determining nature of political economic forces on education. If jobs become more scarce, if productivity increases, and if labor income decreases as a result, then economic inequality will increase. This is the nature of the "profound challenge" defined by Leontief (1982, p. 204). Educators, policymakers, and citizens may find themselves confronting the following questions:

1. Will the work of schools as a sorting institution for scarce, desirable jobs intensify?
2. Will the utility (rather than the intellectual and human significance) of knowledge more thoroughly determine its pedagogical viability in the context of restricted employment?
3. Will the importance of education for social control functions increase?
4. What will be the role of intellectuals in society and gifted children in schools, if the above questions are answered affirmatively?

If gifted programs school bright children to believe that their endowment consists of differential access to valuable jobs; if the ideology that associates IQ, wealth, and social status is strengthened, and if the gifted are given an education that denies them the reasons for and the means of critical reflection, then their education will have betrayed them.

Intellectual Implications

It is probable that the schools do not cultivate the intellect of gifted children (Coleman, 1961; Hofstadter, 1963; Katz, 1971; R. Mitchell, 1979; Wiener, 1950). Indeed, this is the conclusion that suggests that differentiated instruction is a reasonable option for the gifted. On the other hand, it is possible to infer from our discussion that public schools are largely irrelevant to intellectual matters as we have defined them in the case of the gifted.

In general, the public has quite rightly resisted the provision of advantages to the advantaged. Mental attributes that are valued for their short-term utility in crises of various sorts but that are at the same time associated with the aberrations of heterodoxy and heresy will probably not receive the institutional endorsement of education. Schools do not deal particularly well with controversy, intellectual or practical; yet intellect thrives on the contradictions and ambiguities of controversy and the play of contention (cf. Gallagher, 1985).

Humanity, so long as it exists, will doubtless have a continued interest in what is beautiful, what is just, and what is consistent with stated premises. These are some of the important concerns of intellect which cannot easily be contained and directed toward precisely defined ends or predetermined problems. These are kinds of thought in which the intellectually and academically gifted ought to be encouraged to use their talents, regardless of the fact that such concerns may not enhance their careers, financial portfolios, or social positions. Although for students intellectual concerns are best expressed in the context of academic disciplines, it is nevertheless unlikely that these concerns will be without applicability in the practical world. The history of schooling seems to suggest just this conclusion (cf. Bowen, 1981).

Pedagogical Implications

The historical, economic, and intellectual discussion above, in the context of the rest of the text, suggests to us certain pedagogical implications in the areas of (1) definitions, (2) assessments, and (3) programs.

Definitions.   IQ is certainly not an adequate measure of intelligence (Gould, 1981; Sternberg, 1984). Nor, in a system that denigrates intellect (Coleman, 1961; Katz, 1971; Wiener, 1950), is it likely to be an adequate measure of intellectual giftedness (Hofstadter, 1963). It is, however, a statistically reliable general measure of adaptability to the academic regimen of school.

Multifactor definitions (e.g., the 1970 federal definition which included psychomotor, creative, and social categories of giftedness) are so lacking in specificity as to be inapplicable except as a post-hoc justification of intention and sentiment. In addition, such definitions place unwarranted demands on schools for flexibility and expertise (cf. Bloom, 1977; Bloom & Sosniak, 1981; Cuban, 1982; Katz, 1971; Schlechty & Vance, 1983; Torrance & Myers, 1971). The intentions and sentiments embodied in such definitions are admirable; the issues they raise are suitable topics for research, for criticism, and for philosophy. They provide, however, too contradictory a basis for program development in the context of universal schooling (cf. Glass, 1983).

Quite simply, IQ tests and other norm-referenced measures are about the best pedagogical tools we have from which to construct definitions that can be applied with some attention to fairness. In practice, however, IQ tests have *not* been used fairly. In fact, the misuses of IQ tests *far exceed* those noted by Jensen (1981). The ways in which IQ tests are used misrepresent biological, social, economic, cultural, and political reality and involve inflated assumptions about psychology (cf. Gould, 1981). It is to be hoped that better tests will emerge and that these new tests will be applied more fairly (cf. Gardner, 1983; Sternberg, 1977). New tests that undervalue language-based intellectual factors, however, will be more likely, not less likely, to contribute to the deterioration of cognitive schooling, in our opinion.

Assessment.   The overriding issue of assessment is the fairness and completeness of its results. Since black and white children perform very differently on standardized tests, the performance of individual black children should not be compared to means derived from largely white samples. When national norms, in which blacks may constitute approximately 10 percent of the norming sample, are used for comparative purposes, blacks are penalized by the preponderance of whites. It would seem that fairness in assessment practice demands that blacks be compared to blacks. Adoption of such a procedure would require, however, acknowledgment of the racism of our society. For some reason this alternative has been infrequently proposed and infrequently used.

The inequalities of our society offer educators a ready opportunity to institute gifted services in all neighborhood schools by identifying, as gifted, the top of the academic distribution on norm-referenced tests *in each school*. Such a step will mitigate the results of unfair assessment, though it will not eliminate them. Of interest is Armor's (1972) claim that the mean performance of blacks surpasses that of whites *when schools become 65 percent black*.

The completeness of assessment results is a more technical problem. Harried examiners often fail to collect all the data they should, whether in an effort to meet deadlines or to contain assessment costs. The quantity of research on the efficiency and effectiveness of screening and evaluation tools indicates the extent to which assessment costs are an important administrative concern.

For gifted children, the administration of a screening-level IQ test, a comprehensive IQ test, and one or more individually administered achievement tests does seem warranted (see Chapter 2). Supportive data may be required for controversial placement proposals.

Programs. Children with academic and intellectual talents are in possession of such talents all the time. Programs that seek to separate the special needs of gifted children from the regular needs of gifted children ignore this reality.

Ironically, it is just such programs that are most likely to concern themselves with nurturing the whole child, usually by providing programs centered on the affective domain. This sort of program does allow gifted children a needed opportunity to socialize with their intellectual peers. It does not, however, address the qualities by which gifted children have most often been identified.

Two principles emerge from our discussion. First, thinking about gifted children's programs must in some meaningful way address the issue of continuity in the yearly program and the educational tenure in its entirety. A gifted program that helps gifted children to tolerate their schooling (which seems to be all some programs do) is not meeting this requirement. A child who reads *The Lord of the Rings* or *Roots* at home but who is shackled firmly to the third grade reader in school needs advocates willing to confront the intellectual significance of this cognitive disjunction.

Teachers of the gifted will have to broach options: accelerative and enrichment alternatives (see Chapters 5, 6, and 7); adjustments in service intensity and continuum of service alternatives (see Chapters 3, 4, and 11); different instructional formats and techniques (see Chapters 8 and 9); and, perhaps, a multidisciplinary forum for decisions (see Chapter 4). Teachers should remember that in actual practice negotiations to promote recognition of the need for continuity in a gifted child's education are very hard work, requiring extraordinary resilience and skill in the context of employment (see Chapter 4). Parents and children are usually receptive to suggestions, however.

Second, programs need to be primarily academic in nature. They need to address academic goals, because academic aptitude is what distinguishes gifted children pedagogically (see Chapters 1, 2, and 10). If gifted children are also more creative, more social, and more emotionally sensitive, that is of course fine. But it would be optimistic even to say that such qualities will form the object of school curricula at the end of the twenty-first century. In this context, Michael Katz notes:

> Educational reformers should begin to distinguish between what formal school-ing can and cannot do. They must separate the teaching of skill from the teach-ing of attitudes, and concentrate on the former. In actual fact, it is of course impossible to separate the two; attitudes adhere in any form of practice. But there is a vast difference between leaving the formation of attitudes untended and making them the object of education.
>
> (Katz, 1971, p. 142)

Endorsing academic goals as the object of education cultivates an educa-tional purpose that is consonant with historical traditions of literacy and ra-tionalism. The value of such an intellectual legacy is *not* its practicality. To the extent that we value the traditions of intellect, we value the potential of hu-mankind. Our intellectual legacy describes our social evolution as a species within a particular culture.

A general educational response based on this value does not delimit the potential of any child. It provides all children with access to the heritage of the culture. When gifted education is practiced in this context, the academic potential of very apt individuals within all groups can be acknowledged and nurtured more consistently and with clearer, more legitimate purpose.

References

Adler, M. (1982). *The paidea proposal: An educational manifesto.* New York: Macmillan.

Albrecht, R. L., Finkel, L., & Brown, J. R. (1978). *BASIC: A self-teaching guide* (2nd ed.). New York: Wiley.

Alexander, P., & Skinner, M. (1980). The effects of early entrance on subsequent social and academic development: A follow-up study. *Journal for the Education of the Gifted, 3*(3), 147–150.

Alexander, P. A., & Muia, J. A. (1982). *Gifted education: A comprehensive roadmap.* Rockville, MD: Aspen Systems Corporation.

Alexander, R. (1981). An historical perspective on the gifted and the talented in art. *Studies in Art Education, 22*(2), 38–48.

Algozzine, B., Ysseldyke, J., & Hill, C. (1982). Psychoeducational decision making as a function of the amount of information reviewed. *Psychology in the Schools, 19*(3), 328–334.

Algozzine, B., Ysseldyke, J., & Shinn, M. (1982). Identifying children with learning disabilities: When is a discrepancy severe? *Journal of School Psychology, 20*(4), 299–305.

Aliotti, N. C. (1981). Intelligence, handedness, and cerebral hemispheric preference in gifted adolescents. *Gifted Child Quarterly, 25*(1), 36–41.

Allee, J. G., & Williams, R. L. (1980). A challenge for the language arts CAI developer. *Creative Computing, 6*(9), 120–125.

Alpern, G. D., & Kimberlin, C. C. (1970). Short intelligence test ranging from infancy levels through childhood levels for use with the retarded. *American Journal of Mental Deficiency, 75,* 65–71.

Alpern, M. (Ed.). (1967). *The subject curriculum: Grades K–12.* Columbus, OH: Charles E. Merrill.

Altman, R., Faherty, A., & Patterson, J. D. (1978). Project CITE: Gifted competency identification for teacher education. Jefferson City, MO: Missouri Department of Elementary and Secondary Education.

Alvino, J., McDonnel, R. C., & Richert, S. (1981). National survey of identification practices in gifted and talented education. *Exceptional Children, 48*(2), 124–132.

Alvino, J., & Weiler, J. (1979). How standardized testing fails to identify the gifted and what teachers can do about it. *Phi Delta Kappan, 61*(2), 106–109.

American College Testing Program, Inc. (1960–1983). *American college testing program examination.* Iowa City, IA: American College Testing Program, Inc.

American Council for the Arts in Education. (1977). *Coming to our senses: The significance.* New York: McGraw-Hill.

Ammons, R., & Ammons, C. (1962). *Ammons quick test.* Missoula, MT: Psychological Test Specialists.

Anastasi, A. (1968). *Psychological testing* (3rd ed.). New York: Macmillan.

Anderson, L. W. (1973). *Time and school learning.* Unpublished doctoral dissertation, University of Chicago.

Andersson, T. (1969). *Foreign languages in the elementary school: A struggle against mediocrity.* Austin, TX: University of Austin Press.

Andrews, M. F. (1980). The consonance between right brain and affective, subconscious, and multi-sensory functions. *Journal of Creative Behavior, 14*(2), 77–87.

Apple, M. (1982). Education and cultural reproduction: A critical reassessment of programs for choice. In R. Everhart (Ed.), *The public school monopoly: A critical analysis of education and the state in American society* (pp. 503–542). Cambridge, MA: Ballinger.

Aquino, J. T. (1978). *Artists as teachers.* Bloomington, IN: Phi Delta Kappan.

Aristotle. (1962). *Nicomachean ethics* (M. Ostwald, Trans.). New York: Bobbs-Merrill.

Armor, D. (1972). School and family effects on black and white achievement: A reexamination of USOE data. In F. Mosteller & D. Moynihan (Eds.), *On equality of educational opportunity* (pp. 168–229). New York: Random House.

Armstrong, R. J., & Jensen, J. A. (1981). *Slosson intelligence test: 1981 norms tables, application, and development.* East Aurora, NY: Slosson Educational Publications.

Arnold, J. E. (1962). Useful creative techniques. In S. J. Parnes & H. F. Harding (Eds.), *A source book for creative thinking,* (pp. 251–268). New York: Scribner's.

Arthur, G. (1950). *The Arthur adaptation of the Leiter international performance scale.* Chicago: C. H. Stoelting.

Astin, H. S. (1974). Sex differences in mathematical and scientific precocity. In J. C. Stanley, D. P. Keating, & L. H. Fox (Eds.), *Mathematical talent: Discovery, description, and development* (pp. 70–86). Baltimore: Johns Hopkins University Press.

Atamian, G. C., & Danielson, E. W. (1977). Programs for the gifted at Talcott Mountain Science Center. *Gifted Child Quarterly, 21*(1), 69–74.

Austin, A. B., & Draper, D. C. (1981). Peer relationships of the academically gifted: A review. *Gifted Child Quarterly, 25*(3), 129–133.

Ausubel, D. P. (1977). The facilitation of meaningful verbal learning in the classroom. *Educational Psychologist, 12*(2), 162–178.

Ausubel, D. P. (1980). Viewpoints from related disciplines: Human growth and development. In G. Hass (Ed.), *Curriculum planning: A new approach* (3rd ed.) (pp. 122–128). Boston: Allyn and Bacon.

Baer, D., & Bushell, D. (1981). The future of behavior analysis in the schools? Consider its recent past, and then ask a different question. *School Psychology Review, 10*(2), 259–270.

Baer, N. A. (1980). Programs for the gifted: A present or a paradox? *Phi Delta Kappan, 61*(9), 621–623.

Baker, H., & Leland, B. (1967). *Detroit tests of learning aptitude* (rev. ed.). Indianapolis: Bobbs-Merrill.

Baldwin, A. Y. (1978). The Baldwin identification matrix. In A. Y. Baldwin, G. H. Gear, & L. J. Lucito (Eds.), *Educational planning for the gifted: Overcoming cultural, geographic, and socioeconomic barriers.* Reston, VA: Council for Exceptional Children.

Bannatyne, A. (1974). Diagnosis: A note on recategorization of the WISC scaled score. *Journal of Learning Disabilities, 7,* 272–273.

Barron, F. (1958). The psychology of imagination. *Scientific American, 199,* 151–166.

Bar-Tal, D. (1978). Attributional analysis of achievement-related behavior. *Review of Educational Research, 48*(2), 259–271.

Bartel, E. V. (1978). *Getting your school ready for the gifted* (Bulletin No. 5485). Milwaukee: Wisconsin Department of Public Instruction.

Bartkovich, K., & Mezynski, K. (1981). Fast-paced precalculus mathematics for talented junior high school students: Two recent SMPY programs. *Gifted Child Quarterly, 25*(2), 73–81.

Baskin, S. (1961). Experiments in independent study (1956–1960). *Antioch College Reports,* No. 2, 571.

Bayley, N. (1969). *Bayley scales of infant development.* New York: Psychological Corporation.

Bayne, S. (1980). *Helping kids write: A practical guide for teaching children to express themselves on paper.* Cambridge, MA: Educators Publishing Service.

Bell, D. (1978). *The cultural contradictions of capitalism.* New York: Basic Books.

Benbow, C., & Stanley, J. (1980). Sex differences in mathematical ability: Fact or artifact? *Science, 210*(12), 1262–1264.

Benbow, C., & Stanley, J. (1982). Intellectually talented boys and girls: Educational profiles. *Gifted Child Quarterly, 26*(2), 82–88.

Bennet, G. K., Seashore, H. G., & Wiseman, A. G. (1947–1973). *Differential aptitude test.* New York: Psychological Corporation.

Bennett, F., Blanning, J., Boissiere, M., Chang, S., & Collins, W. (1971). Potentially gifted and talented high school youth benefit from independent study. *Gifted Child Quarterly, 15*(2), 96–108.

Berg, T. (1980). The smart man's burden. *Peabody Journal of Education, 58*(1), 31–33.

Berko, F. G., Berko, M. J., & Thompson, S. C. (1970). *Management of brain damaged children: A parents' and teachers' guide.* Springfield, IL: Charles C. Thomas.

Berkow, R. (Ed.). (1977). Learning disorders. In R. Berkow (Ed.), *The Merck manual of diagnosis and therapy* (pp. 1058–1062). Rahway, NJ: Merck, Sharp, and Dohme Research Laboratories.

Bernstein, H. (1983). The information society: Byting the hand that feeds you. *Phi Delta Kappan, 65*(2), 108–109.

Bernstein, H. T. (1982). Back to the basics in art. *Design, 83*(3), 4–9.

Bidlack, G. H. (1974). The special teacher/consultant for gifted pupils in the public school system: Two approaches. *Gifted Child Quarterly, 18*(3), 146–151.

Binor, S. (1974). *The relative effectiveness of mastery learning strategies in second language acquisition.* Unpublished master's thesis, University of Chicago.

Birch, J., Tisdall, W., Barney, D., & Marks, C. (1965). *A field demonstration of the effectiveness and feasibility of early admission to school for mentally advanced children.* Pittsburgh: University of Pittsburgh.

Bishop, W. E. (1968). Successful teachers of the gifted. *Exceptional Children, 34,* 317–325.

Blanning, J. (1978). An independent study and seminar program for urban gifted youth. *Roeper Review, 1*(1), 15–17.

Blau, P., & Duncan, O. (1967). *The American occupational structure.* New York: Wiley.

Blaubergs, M. S. (1978). Overcoming the sexist barriers to gifted women's achievement. In National/State Leadership Training Institute on the Gifted and Talented (Ed.), *Advantage: Disadvantaged gifted* (pp. 7–38). Ventura, CA: Office of the Ventura County Superintendent of Schools.

Bloom, B. (Ed.). (1956). *Taxonomy of educational objectives, handbook I: Cognitive domain.* New York: David McKay.

Bloom, B. (1964). *Stability and change in human characteristics.* New York: Wiley.

Bloom, B. (1971). Learning for mastery. In B. Bloom, J. Hastings, & G. Madaus, *Handbook on formative and summative evaluation of student learning* (pp. 43–57). New York: McGraw-Hill.

Bloom, B. (1976). *Human characteristics and school learning.* New York: McGraw-Hill.

Bloom, B. (1977). Affective outcomes of school learning. *Phi Delta Kappan, 59*(3), 193–198.

Bloom, B. (1982). The role of gifts and markers in the development of talent. *Exceptional Children, 48*(6), 510–522.

Bloom, B., Hastings, J., & Madaus, G. (1971). *Handbook on formative and summative evaluation of student learning.* New York: McGraw-Hill.

Bloom, B., & Sosniak, L. (1981). Talent development vs. schooling. *Educational Leadership, 39,* 86–94.

Blumenthal, J. C. (1981). *English 3200: A programmed course in grammar and usage* (3rd. ed.). New York: Harcourt Brace Jovanovich.

Boehm, A. (1971). *Boehm test of basic concepts.* New York: Psychological Corporation.

Boileau, D. M. (1983). Programmed instruction: A lull before the storm. *Communication Education, 32,* 137–143.

Boles, D. (1980). X-linkage of spatial ability: A critical review. *Child Development, 51*, 625–635.

Booth, L. (1980). Motivating gifted students through a shared-governance apprentice/mentorship program. *Roeper Review, 3*(1), 11–13.

Borland, J. (1978). Teacher identification of the gifted: A new look. *Journal for the Education of the Gifted, 2*(1), 22–32.

Boss, R., & McConkie, M. (1981). The destructive impact of a positive team-building intervention. *Group & Organizational Studies, 6*(1), 45–56.

Bowen, J. (1981). *A history of western education* (Vol. III). New York: St. Martin's.

Bowles, S., & Gintis, H. (1973). IQ in the US class structure. *Social Policy,* Nov.–Dec. 1972/Jan.–Feb. 1973, 65–96.

Bowles, S., & Gintis, H. (1976). *Schooling in capitalist America.* New York: Basic Books.

Braga, J. (1971). Early admission: Opinion versus evidence. *The Elementary School Journal, 72*(1), 35–46.

Brandt, R. M. (1981). *Public education under scrutiny.* Washington, DC: University Press of America.

Brandwein, P. (1955). *The gifted student as future scientist: The high school student and his commitment to science.* New York: Harcourt Brace Jovanovich.

Bridges, S. (1973). *Problems of the gifted child—IQ 150.* New York: Crane, Russak.

Brigance, A. (1977). *Brigance diagnostic inventory of basic skills.* North Billerica, MA: Curriculum Associates.

Brigance, A. (1978). *Brigance diagnostic inventory of early development.* North Billerica, MA: Curriculum Associates.

Brigance, A. (1980). *Brigance diagnostic inventory of essential skills.* North Billerica, MA: Curriculum Associates.

Bronfenbrenner, U. (1970). *Two worlds of childhood: US and USSR.* New York: Russell Sage Foundation.

Broudy, H. (1970). Quality education and aesthetic education. In G. Pappas (Ed.), *Concepts in art and education: An anthology of current issues* (pp. 280–289). New York: Macmillan.

Brown, F. L., Amos, J. R., & Mink, O. G. (1975). *Statistical concepts: A basic program* (2nd ed.). New York: Harper & Row.

Brown, J. C. (1983). Excellence and the problem of visual literacy. *Design, 85*(2), 8–10.

Brown, J. D. (1967). The development of creative teacher-scholars. In J. Kagan (Ed.), *Creativity and learning.* Boston: Beacon Press.

Brubaker, P. (1982). *Curriculum planning: The dynamics of theory and practice.* Glenview, IL: Scott Foresman.

Bruck, M., Lambert, W., & Tucker, G. (1977). Cognitive consequences of bilingual schooling: The St. Lambert project through grade six. *Linguistics* (187), 13–33.

Brueckner, L. J. (1932). The nature of problem solving. *The Journal of the National Education Association, 21,* 13–14.

Bruner, J. S. (1960). *The process of education.* New York: Vintage Books.

Bruner, J. S. (1966a). *Man: A course of study.* Washington, DC: Curriculum Development Associates.

Bruner, J. S. (1966b). *Toward a theory of instruction.* Cambridge, MA: Belknap Press.

Budoff, M., Orenstein, A., & Abramson, J. (1981). Due process hearings: Appeals for appropriate public school programs. *Exceptional Children, 48*(2), 180–182.

Burgemeister, B. B., Blum, H. L., & Lorge, I. (1972). *Columbia mental maturity scale* (3rd ed.). New York: Harcourt Brace Jovanovich.

Burks, B., Jensen, D., & Terman, L. (1930). *The promise of youth: Follow-up studies of a thousand gifted children* (Vol. III of *Genetic studies of genius*). Stanford, CA: Stanford University Press.

Buros, O. K. (Ed.). (1972). *Seventh mental measurements yearbook.* Highland Park, NJ: Gryphon Press.

Buros, O. K. (Ed.). (1974). *Tests in print II*. Highland Park, NJ: Gryphon Press.

Buros, O. K. (Ed.). (1978). *Eighth mental measurements yearbook*. Highland Park, NJ: Gryphon Press.

Burt, C. (1940). *The factors of the mind*. London: University of London Press.

Butcher, H. J. (1968). *Human intelligence: Its nature and assessment*. London: Methuen & Co.

Butterfield, H. (1957). *The origins of modern science: 1300–1800*. New York: Free Press.

Callahan, C. (1978). *Developing creativity in the gifted and talented*. Reston, VA: Council for Exceptional Children.

Callahan, C. (1979). The gifted and talented woman. In A. H. Passow (Ed.), *The gifted and the talented: Their education and development* (Seventy-Eighth Yearbook of the National Society for the Study of Education, Part II) (pp. 401–423). Chicago: University of Chicago Press.

Callahan, C. (1981). The gifted girl: An anomaly? In W. Barbe & J. Renzulli (Eds.), *Psychology and education of the gifted* (pp. 498–510). New York: Irvington Publishers.

Callahan, C. M., & Corvo, M. L. (1980). Validating the Ross test for identification of critical thinking skills in programs for the gifted. *Journal for the Education of the Gifted*, 4(1), 17–26.

Campbell, R. D. (1969). Special workshop for the gifted. *Today's Education*, 58(9), 32–33.

Carrier, C., & McNergney, R. (1979). Interaction research: Can it help individualize instruction? *Educational Technology*, 19(4), 40–45.

Carrier, J. G. (1983). Masking the social in educational knowledge: The case of learning disability theory. *American Journal of Sociology*, 88(5), 948–974.

Carroll, L. (1958). *Symbolic logic and game of logic*. New York: Dover Books. (Original works published 1887, 1897)

Carter, K., & Kontos, S. (1982). An application of cognitive-developmental theory to the identification of gifted children. *Roeper Review*, 5(2), 17–20.

Carter, M. (1976). Contradiction and correspondence: Analysis of the relation of schooling to work. In M. Carnoy (Ed.), *The limits of educational reform* (pp. 52–82). New York: David McKay.

Cartwright, G. P., Cartwright, C. A., & Ward, M. E. (1981). *Educating special learners*. Belmont, CA: Wadsworth.

Casserly, P. L. (1979). Helping able young women take math and science seriously in school. In N. Colangelo & R. T. Zaffrann (Eds.), *New voices in counseling the gifted* (pp. 346–369). Dubuque, IA: Kendall/Hunt.

Castiglione, L. V. (1984, June 6). The education of the gifted and talented: Nurturing a national resource. *Education Week*, p. 40.

Cattell, P. (1940). *Cattell infant intelligence scale*. New York: Psychological Corporation.

Cattell, R. B. (1950). *Culture fair intelligence test: Scale 1*. Champaign, IL: Institute for Personality and Ability Testing.

Cattell, R. B. (1963). Theory of fluid and crystallized intelligence: A critical experiment. *Journal of Educational Psychology*, 54, 1–22.

Cattell, R. B., & Cattell, A. K. S. (1960). *Culture fair intelligence test: Scale 2*. Champaign, IL: Institute for Personality and Ability Testing.

Cattell, R. B., & Cattell, A. K. S. (1963). *Culture fair intelligence test: Scale 3*. Champaign, IL: Institute for Personality and Ability Testing.

Cazden, B. (Ed.). (1972). *Language in early childhood education*. Washington, DC: National Association for the Education of Young Children.

Chandler, J. (1980). Music lessons: Andante. *Gifted Children Newsletter*, 1 (April 11). (Available from Dr. James Alvino, PO Box 115, Sewell, NJ 08080)

Charles, C. M. (1976). *Individualizing instruction*. St. Louis, MO: C. V. Mosby.

Chenoweth, A. D. (1965). The child with central nervous system deficit: The scope of the problem. In *The child with central nervous system deficit* (Children's Bureau Publication Number 432) (pp. 1–7). Washington, DC: United States Department of Health, Education, and Welfare.

Chetelat, F. (1981). Visual arts education for the gifted elementary level art student. *Gifted Child Quarterly, 25*(4), 154–158.

Christenson, S., Ysseldyke, J., & Algozzine, B. (1982). Institutional constraints and external pressures influencing referral decisions. *Psychology in the Schools, 19*(3), 341–345.

Christopherson, S. L. (1981). Developmental placement in the regular school program. *G/C/T* (19), 40–41.

Ciha, T. E., Harris, T. E., Hoffman, C., & Potter, M. W. (1974). Parents as identifiers of giftedness, ignored but accurate. *The Gifted Child Quarterly, 18*, 191–195.

Clark, B. (1979). *Growing up gifted*. Columbus, OH: Charles E. Merrill.

Clark, B. (1983). *Growing up gifted* (2nd. ed.). Columbus, OH: Charles E. Merrill.

Clark, G., & Zimmerman, E. (1983). At the age of six, I gave up a magnificent career as a painter: Seventy years of research about identifying students with superior abilities in the visual arts. *Gifted Child Quarterly, 27*(4), 180–184.

Clendening, C. P., & Davies, R. A. (1980). *Creating programs for the gifted*. New York: R. K. Bowker.

Cline, S. (1979). Simulation: A teaching strategy for the gifted. *Gifted Child Quarterly, 23*(2), 269–287.

Cohen, E. (1981). The arts from the inside out: Developing a performing arts curriculum. *G/C/T, 21*, 38–42.

Cohn, S. J. (1984). Project F.U.T.U.R.E.: A progress report after three prototype years of serving intellectually gifted students. *Journal for the Education of the Gifted, 7*(2), 103–119.

Coleman, J. (1961). *The adolescent society*. Glencoe, NY: Free Press.

Coleman, J., et al. (1966). *Equality of educational opportunity report*. Washington, DC: USGPO.

College Entrance Examination Board. (1983). *Advanced placement course description: Computer science*. Princeton, NJ: Advanced Placement Program.

Colon, P. T., & Treffinger, D. J. (1980). Providing for the gifted in the regular classroom: Am I really MAD? *Roeper Review, 3*(2), 18–21.

Colson, S., Borman, C., & Nash, W. R. (1980). A unique learning opportunity for talented high school seniors. In D. M. Jackson (Ed.), *Readings in curriculum development for the gifted* (pp. 140–141). Guilford, CT: Special Learning Corporation.

Colwell, R. (1967–1970). *Music achievement tests*. New York: Follett.

Conant, H. (1964). *Art education*. New York: Center for Applied Research in Education.

Conant, J. (1959). *The American high school today*. New York: McGraw-Hill.

Connolly, A., Nachtman, W., & Pritchett, E. (1971). *Key math diagnostic arithmetic test*. Circle Pines, MN: American Guidance Service.

Consuegra, G. F. (1982). Identifying the gifted in science and mathematics. *School Science and Mathematics, 82*(3), 183–188.

Cook, R., & Doll, R. (1973). *The elementary school curriculum*. Boston: Allyn and Bacon.

Cooney, T., Davis, E., & Henderson, K. (1975). *Dynamics of teaching secondary school mathematics*. Boston: Houghton Mifflin.

Cooper, A. (1981). Learning centers: What they are and aren't. *Academic Therapy, 16*(5), 527–531.

Copi, I. M. (1978). *Introduction to logic*. New York: Macmillan.

Copley, F. O. (1961). *The American high school and the talented student*. Ann Arbor: University of Michigan Press.

Council for Exceptional Children (1981). [Editor's note]. *Exceptional Children, 47*(7), 492–493.

Counts, G. (1930). *The American road to culture: A social interpretation of education in the*

United States. New York: John Day. (Facsimile reprint edition by Arno Press–New York Times, 1971)

Counts, G. (1932). *Dare the school build a new social order?* New York: John Day.

Covington, M. V., & Crutchfield, R. S. (1965). Facilitation of creative problem solving. *Programmed Instruction, 4,* 3–5, 10.

Cox, J., & Daniel, N. (1983). Specialized schools for high ability students. *G/C/T, 28,* 2–9.

Crager, P., & Spriggs, A. (1972). *Test of concept utilization.* Los Angeles: Western Psychological Services.

Cremin, L. (1961). *The transformation of the school.* New York: Vintage Books.

Cronbach, L. J., & Snow, R. E. (1977). *Aptitudes and instructional methods.* New York: Irvington Publishers.

Crosby, A. C. (1968). *Creativity and performance in industrial organization.* London: Tavistock Publications.

CTB/McGraw-Hill. (1972). *Prescriptive reading inventory.* Monterey, CA: CTB/McGraw-Hill.

CTB/McGraw-Hill. (1977). *The California achievement tests.* Monterey, CA: CTB/McGraw-Hill.

Cuban, L. (1982). Persistence of the inevitable: The teacher-centered classroom. *Education and Urban Society, 15*(1), 26–41.

Culross, R. R. (1982). Developing the whole child: Developmental approach to guidance with the gifted. *Roeper Review, 5*(2), 24–26.

Cummings, S., & Taebel, D. (1978). The economic socialization of children: A neo-Marxist analysis. *Social Problems, 26*(2), 198–210.

Dahrendorf, R. (1959). *Class and class conflict in industrial society.* Stanford, CA: Stanford University Press.

Darwin, C. (1958). *The origin of species.* New York: Mentor Books. (Original work published 1859)

Daurio, S. P. (1979). Educational enrichment versus acceleration: A review of the literature. In W. George, S. Cohn, & J. Stanley (Eds.), *Educating the gifted: Acceleration and enrichment* (pp. 13–63). Baltimore: Johns Hopkins University Press.

Davis, G. A., & Rimm, S. (1982). Group inventory for finding interests (GIFFI) I and II: Instruments for identifying creative potential in the junior and senior high school. *Journal of Creative Behavior, 16*(1), 50–57.

Davis, G. A., & Scott, J. A. (Eds.). (1971). *Training creative thinking.* New York: Holt, Rinehart, & Winston.

de Bono, E. (1967). *The five-day course in thinking.* New York: Basic Books.

Demetrulias, D. M. (1982). Student-taught minicourses. *The Clearinghouse, 55*(7), 330–334.

Deutsch, R., & Wolleat, P. (1981). Dispelling the forced-choice myth. *Elementary School Guidance Counseling, 16,* 112–120.

Dewey, J. (1956a). *The child and the curriculum.* Chicago: University of Chicago Press. (Original work published 1902)

Dewey, J. (1956b). *The school and society.* Chicago: University of Chicago Press. (Original work published 1900)

Dewey, J. (1961). *Democracy and education.* New York: Macmillan. (Original work published 1916)

Dewey, J. (1962). *Individualism, old and new.* New York: Capricorn. (Original work published 1930)

D'Heurle, A., Mellinger, H., & Haggard, E. (1959). Personality, intellectual, and achievement patterns in gifted children. *Psychological Monographs, 13,* 1–24.

Dimond, S. (1972). *The double brain.* Baltimore: Williams and Wilkins.

Dimondstein, G. (1976). Currents in the arts: Conflicts and contradictions. *Art Education, 29*(2), 14–16.

Dinkmeyer, D. (1970). *Developing understanding of self and others (D-1)*. Circle Pines, MN: American Guidance Service.

Dinkmeyer, D. (1973). *Developing understanding of self and others (D-2)*. Circle Pines, MN: American Guidance Service.

Dirks, J., & Quarfoth, J. (1981). Selecting children for gifted classes: Choosing for breadth vs. choosing for depth. *Psychology in the Schools, 18*(4), 437–449.

DiSilvestro, F. R., & Markowitz, H. (1982). Contracts and completion rates in correspondence study. *Journal of Educational Research, 75*(4), 218–221.

Divoky, D. (1983). The new pioneers of the home-schooling movement. *Phi Delta Kappan, 64*(6), 395–398.

Dobzhansky, T. (1973). *Genetic diversity and human equality*. New York: Basic Books.

Dobzhansky, T., & Montagu, A. (1975). Natural selection and the mental capacities of mankind. In A. Montagu (Ed.), *Race and IQ* (pp. 104–113). London: Oxford University Press.

Doll, R. (1982). *Curriculum improvement: Decision making and process*. Boston: Allyn and Bacon.

Dorn, C. M. (1976). The advanced placement program in studio art. *The Gifted Child Quarterly, 20*(4), 450–458.

Dowdall, C., & Colangelo, N. (1982). Underachieving gifted students: Reviews and implications. *The Gifted Child Quarterly, 26*(4), 179–184.

Drowatzky, J. N. (1981). Tracking and ability grouping in education. *Journal of Law and Education, 10*(1), 43–59.

Dubiner, F. S. (1980). Thirteen ways of looking at a gifted teacher. *Journal for the Education of the Gifted, 3*(3), 143–146.

Duffey, J. B., & Fedner, M. L. (1980). Educational diagnosis with instructional use. In R. Piazza & I. Newman (Eds.), *Readings in individualized educational programs* (pp. 102–106). Guilford, CT: Special Learning Corporation.

Duffey, J. B., Salvia, J., Tucker, J., & Ysseldyke, J. (1981). Nonbiased assessment: A need for operationalism. *Exceptional Children, 47*, 427–434.

Dulee, R. (1983) [Interview with John Holt]. *Aegis: Newsletter of the WVGEA, 2*(1), 6–8. Charleston, WV: West Virginia Gifted Education Association. (Available from Education Department, University of Charleston, Charleston, WV)

Duncan, O. (1961). A socioeconomic index for all occupations. In A. Reiss (Ed.), *Occupations and social status* (pp. 109–138). Glencoe, NY: Free Press.

Duncan, O. D. (1968). Inheritance of poverty or inheritance of race? In D. Moynihan (Ed.), *On understanding poverty* (pp. 85–110). New York: Basic Books.

Duncan, O., Featherman, D., & Duncan, B. (1972). *Socioeconomic background and achievement*. New York: Seminar Press.

Dunn, L. M. (1959). *Peabody picture vocabulary test: Manual of directions and norms*. Nashville, TN: American Guidance Center.

Dunn, L. M., & Dunn, L. (1981). *Peabody picture vocabulary test—revised*. Circle Pines, MN: American Guidance Service.

Dunn, L. M., & Markwardt, F. C. (1970). *Peabody individual achievement test*. Circle Pines, MN: American Guidance Service.

Durden, W. (1980). Gifted programs: The Johns Hopkins program for verbally gifted youth. *Roeper Review, 2*(3), 34–37.

Durost, W., Gardner, E., & Madden, R. (1970). *Analysis of learning potential*. New York: Harcourt Brace Jovanovich.

Durr, W. K. (1964). *The gifted student*. New York: Oxford University Press.

Dyer, C. O., Neigler, C., & Millholland, J. E. (1975). Rater agreements in assigning Stanford-Binet items to Guilford's structure of intellect operations categories. *Journal of School Psychology, 13*, 114–118.

Ecton, G. W. (1979). A history of the Lincoln School, Simpsonville, Kentucky, 1966–1970 (Doctoral dissertation, University of Kentucky, Lexington, KY, 1979). *Dissertation Abstracts International, 40*(6), 40/06, 3229A.

Educational Facilities Laboratories (1977). Arts center develops student talent. *Focus on Exceptional Children, 9*(7), 53–55.

Educational Policies Commission. (1950). *Education of the gifted.* Washington, DC: National Education Association.

Educational Testing Service. (1901–1983). *College entrance examination board achievement tests.* Princeton, NJ: Educational Testing Service.

Educational Testing Service. (1926–1983). *College entrance examination board scholastic aptitude test.* Princeton, NJ: Educational Testing Service.

Educational Testing Service (1960–1983). *College entrance examination board preliminary scholastic aptitude test.* Princeton, NJ: Educational Testing Service.

Educational Testing Service, Cooperative Test Division. (1956–1972). *Sequential tests of educational progress.* Princeton, NJ: Educational Testing Service.

Eggleston, J. (1977). *The sociology of the school curriculum.* London: Routledge & Kegan Paul.

Einstein, A. (1954). *Ideas and opinions by Albert Einstein.* S. Bargman (Ed.). New York: Bonanza Books.

Eisele, J. E. (1980). A case for computers in instruction. *Journal of Research and Development in Education, 14*(1), 1–8.

Eisner, E. W. (1965). American education and the future of art education. In W. R. Hastie (Ed.), *Art education* (Sixty-Fourth Yearbook of the National Society for the Study of Education, Part II) (pp. 299–325). Chicago: The University of Chicago Press.

Eisner, E. W. (1966). Arts curricula for the gifted. *Teachers College Record, 67*(7), 492–501.

Eisner, E. W. (1972). *Educating artistic vision.* New York: Macmillan.

Eisner, E. W. (1974). Is the artist in the schools program effective? *Art Education, 27*(2), 19–23.

Engel, M. (1983). Art and the mind. *Art Education, 36,* 5–80.

Epstein, C. B. (1979). *The gifted and talented: Programs that work.* Arlington, VA: National School Public Relations Association.

Erickson, D. (Ed.). (1978). *The nation's commitment to the education of gifted and talented children and youth: Summary of findings from a 1977 survey of states and territories.* Reston, VA: Council for Exceptional Children. (ERIC Document Reproduction Service No. ED 155 829)

Evans, E., & Marken, P. (1982). Multiple outcome assessment of special class placement for gifted students: A comparative study. *Gifted Child Quarterly, 26*(3), 126–132.

Evyatar, A. (1973). Enrichment therapy. *Educational Research, 15*(2), 115–122.

Eysenck, H. J. (1973). IQ, social class, and educational policy. *Change,* (September), 38–42.

Farber, B., & Lewis, M. (1975). The symbolic use of parents: A sociological critique of educational practice. *Journal of Research and Development in Education, 8*(2), 34–43.

Farr, R. C., Prescott, G. A., Balow, I. H., & Hogan, T. P. (1978). *Metropolitan achievement tests: Reading instructional battery.* New York: Psychological Corporation.

Fearn, L. (1982). Underachievement and rate of acceleration. *The Gifted Child Quarterly, 26*(3), 121–125.

Federal Register. (1976). Assistance to states: Proposed rulemaking (U.S. Office of Education). FR 41, 52404–52407. Washington, DC: U.S. Government Printing Office.

Federal Register. (1977). Assistance to states for education of handicapped children (U.S. Office of Education). FR 42, 65082–65085. Washington, DC: U.S. Government Printing Office.

Feinberg, W. (1975). *Reason and rhetoric: the intellectual foundations of 20th century liberal educational policy.* New York: Wiley.

Feldhusen, H. (1981). Teaching gifted, creative, and talented students in an individualized classroom. *Gifted Child Quarterly, 25*(3), 108–111.

Feldhusen, J. F. (1982). Myth: Gifted education means having a program: Meeting the needs of gifted students through differentiated programming. *Gifted Child Quarterly, 26*(1), 37–41.

Feldhusen, J. F., Elias, R., & Treffinger, D. (1969). The right kind of programmed instruction for the gifted. *NSPI Journal, 8*(3), 6–11.

Feldhusen, J. F., Treffinger, D. J., & Bahlke, S. J. (1970). Developing creative thinking: The Purdue creativity program. *Journal of Creative Behavior, 4*, 85–90.

Feldhusen, J. F., & Wyman, A. R. (1980). Super Saturday: Design and implementation of Purdue's special program for gifted children. *Gifted Child Quarterly, 24*(1), 15–21.

Feldman, D. (1979a). The mysterious case of extreme giftedness. In A. H. Passow (Ed.), *The gifted and the talented: Their education and development* (Seventy-Eighth Yearbook of the National Society for the Study of Education, Part II) (pp. 335–351). Chicago: University of Chicago Press.

Feldman, D. (1979b). Toward a non-elitist conception of giftedness. *Phi Delta Kappan, 60*, 660–663.

Feldman, E. B. (1970). Engaging art in dialogue. In G. Pappas (Ed.), *Concepts in art and education: An anthology of current issues* (pp. 352–359). New York: Macmillan.

Fennema, E. (1974). Sex differences in mathematics learning. Why??? *Elementary School Journal, 75*(3), 188–190.

Feuerstein, R., Miller, R., Hoffman, M. B., Rand, Y., Mintzker, Y., & Jensen, M. R. (1981). Cognitive modifiability in adolescence: Cognitive structures and the effects of intervention. *Journal of Special Education, 15*(2), 269–287.

Feynman, R. (1983). [Interview with physicist R. Feynman]. See WGBH Educational Foundation–British Broadcasting Corporation (1983).

Findley, W., & Bryan, M. (1971). *Ability grouping: 1970 status, impact, and alternatives.* Athens, GA: University of Georgia, Center for Educational Improvement.

Fine, B. (1964). *Stretching their minds.* New York: Dutton.

Fine, B. (1967). *Underachievers: How they can be helped.* New York: Dutton.

Fine, M., & Rosenberg, P. (1983). Dropping out of high school: The ideology of school and work. *Journal of Education, 165*(3), 257–272.

Firth, G., & Kimpston, R. (1973). *The curricular continuum in perspective.* Itasca, IL: F. E. Peacock Publishers.

Fiscus, E. D., & Mandell, C. J. (1983). *Developing individualized education programs.* St. Paul, MN: West Publishing Company.

Fisher, E. F., Lavery, B., & Hannum, C. (1982). Interrelated arts workshops and the gifted. *Design, 83*(4), 29–34.

Fitzgerald, F. (1979). *America revised.* Boston: Atlantic–Little, Brown.

Flanagan, J. C. (1957–1960). *Flanagan aptitude classification tests.* Chicago: SRA.

Flanagan, J. C., et al. (1964). *The American high school student.* Pittsburgh, PA: University of Pittsburgh, Project Talent.

Flanagan, J. C., Shanner, W. C., Brudner, H. J., & Marker, R. W. (1975). An individualized instructional system: PLAN. In H. Talmage (Ed.), *Systems of individualized education* (pp. 136–167). Berkeley, CA: McCutchan Publishing.

Flanders, N. A. (1967). Teacher influence in the classroom. In E. J. Amidon & J. B. Hought (Eds.), *Interaction analysis: theory, research, and application* (pp. 103–116). Reading, MA: Addison-Wesley.

Fleigler, L. A. (1961). *Curriculum planning for the gifted.* Englewood Cliffs, NJ: Prentice-Hall.

Fowlkes, J. G. (1930). Adjusting the curriculum to the needs of superior pupils. *Nation's Schools, 5*, 82–84, 86.

Fox, A. (1982). Quiz time in the classroom. *Creative Computing, 8*(10), 18–22.

Fox, L. H. (1974). A mathematics program for fostering precocious achievement. In J. Stanley, D. Keating, & L. Fox (Eds.), *Mathematical talent discovery, description and development* (pp. 101–125). Baltimore: Johns Hopkins University Press.

Fox, L. H. (1976). Sex differences in mathematical precocity: Bridging the gap. In D.

Keating (Ed.), *Intellectual talent research and development* (pp. 183–214). Baltimore: Johns Hopkins University Press.

Fox, L. H. (1977). Sex differences: Implications for program planning for the academically gifted. In J. C. Stanley, W. C. George, & C. H. Solano (Eds.), *The gifted and the creative: A fifty-year perspective* (pp. 113–138). Baltimore: Johns Hopkins University Press.

Fox, L. H. (1978). Gifted girls: Scientists and mathematicians of the future. In B. Johnson (Ed.), *Advantage: Disadvantaged gifted* (pp. 47–52). Ventura, CA: Office of the Ventura County Superintendent of Schools (National/State Leadership Training Institute on the Gifted and Talented).

Fox, L. H. (1979a). Career education for gifted preadolescents. In W. C. George, S. J. Cohn, & J. C. Stanley (Eds.), *Educating the gifted: Acceleration and enrichment* (pp. 89–97). Baltimore: Johns Hopkins University Press.

Fox, L. H. (1979b). Programs for the gifted and talented: An overview. In A. H. Passow (Ed.), *The gifted and the talented: Their education and development* (Seventy-Eighth Yearbook of the National Society for the Study of Education, Part II) (pp. 104–126). Chicago: The University of Chicago Press.

Frank, B. M., & Davis, J. K. (1982). Effect of field-independence match or mismatch on a communication task. *Journal of Educational Psychology, 74*(1), 23–31.

Franklin, M. R., & Stillman, P. L. (1982). Examiner error in intelligence testing: Are you a source? *Psychology in the Schools, 19,* 563–569.

Frauenheim, J. (1978). Academic achievement characteristics of adult males who were diagnosed as dyslexic in childhood. *Journal of Learning Disabilities, 11,* 476–483.

Freehill, M. F. (1961). *Gifted children.* New York: Macmillan.

Freeman, F. (1924). The treatment of the gifted child in the light of the scientific evidence. *Elementary School Journal, 24*(9), 652–661.

Freeman, J. (1979). *Gifted children.* Baltimore: University Park Press.

French, J. L. (1964). *Manual: Pictorial test of intelligence.* Boston: Houghton Mifflin.

French, J. L., & Cardon, B. W. (1968). Characteristics of high mental ability dropouts. *The Vocational Guidance Journal, 16*(3), 162–168.

Friedenberg, E. (1979). Children as objects of fear and loathing. *Educational Studies, 10*(1), 63–75.

Friedenberg, E. (1981). Deference to authority: Education in Canada and the United States. In E. Gumbert (Ed.), *Poverty, power, and authority in education* (pp. 45–64). Atlanta, GA: Center for Cross-Cultural Education.

Frierson, E. C. (1965). Upper and lower status gifted children: A study of differences. *Exceptional Children, 32*(2), 83–90.

Fulks, D. G. (1983). Using informational praise in reading. In *Selected articles on the teaching of reading* (Set F, No. 14). New York: Barnell Loft.

Fund for the Advancement of Education. (1957). *They went to college early* (Evaluation Report No. 2). New York: Fund for the Advancement of Education.

Gage, N. (1978). *The scientific basis of the art of teaching.* New York: Teachers College Press.

Gage, N., & Berliner, D. (1975). *Educational psychology.* Chicago: Rand McNally.

Gallagher, J. J. (Ed.). (1965). *Teaching gifted students: A book of readings.* Boston: Allyn and Bacon.

Gallagher, J. J. (1975). *Teaching the gifted child* (2nd ed.). Boston: Allyn and Bacon.

Gallagher, J. J. (1978, October). *Measurement issues in future programs for gifted students.* Paper presented at the Educational Testing Service Invitational Conference on Measurement and Educational Policy, Washington, DC (ERIC Document Reproduction Service No. ED 176 429).

Gallagher, J. J. (1985). *Teaching the gifted child* (3rd ed.). Boston: Allyn and Bacon.

Gallagher, J. J., Aschner, M., & Jenné, W. (1967). *Productive thinking of gifted children in classroom interaction* (CEC Monograph Series B, No. B-5). Washington, DC: The Council for Exceptional Children—National Education Association.

Gallagher, J. J., Weiss, P., Oglesby, K., & Thomas, T. (1982). *Report on education of gifted* (Report prepared for the Advisory Panel, U.S. Office of Gifted and Talented). Chapel Hill, NC: Frank Porter Graham Child Development Center (mimeo).

Galton, F. (1962). *Hereditary genius*. London: Fontana. (Work originally published 1869)

Gambrell, L. B., Wilson, R. M., & Gantt, W. N. (1981). Classroom observations of task-attending behaviors of good and poor readers. *Journal of Educational Research, 74*(6), 400–404.

Ganley, N. (1983). Art history alive. *School Arts, 8*(3), 21–23.

Gardner, E. F. (1977). Interpreting achievement profiles: Uses and warnings. *Journal of Research and Development in Education, 10*(3), 51–63.

Gardner, H. (1983). *Frames of mind: The theory of multiple intelligences*. New York: Basic Books.

Gardner, J. (1961). *Excellence*. New York: Harper & Row.

Gearheart, B. L., & Weishahn, M. W. (1980). *The handicapped student in the regular classroom*. St. Louis, MO: C. V. Mosby.

Gelfand, D., & Hartmann, D. (1975). *Child behavior analysis and therapy*. New York: Pergamon.

Gensemer, I. B., Walker, J. C., & Cadman, T. E. (1980). Using the Peabody Picture Vocabulary Test with children having difficulty learning. In *Evaluation of Exceptional Children*, (pp. 132–134). Guilford, CT: Special Learning Corporation.

Gensley, J. (1973). The gifted child in the affective domain. *Gifted Child Quarterly, 17*(2), 113–115.

Gerencser, S. (1979). The Calasanctius experience. In *The gifted and talented: Their education and development* (Seventy-Eighth Yearbook of the National Society for the Study of Education, Part II) (pp. 127–137). Chicago: University of Chicago Press.

Gerlach, G. (1981). How to direct directed reading. *Teacher, 98*(6), 72–73.

Gesell, A. (1950). *The first five years of life*. London: Methuen.

Getzels, J. W. (1979). From art students to fine artists: Potential, problem finding, and performance. In A. H. Passow (Ed.), *The gifted and talented: Their education and development* (Seventy-Eighth Yearbook of the National Society for the Study of Education, Part II) (pp. 372–387). Chicago: University of Chicago Press.

Getzels, J. W., & Jackson, P. W. (1962). *Creativity and intelligence: Explorations with gifted students*. New York: Wiley.

Gilliam, J. E. (1979). Contributions and status rankings of educational planning committee participants. *Exceptional Children, 45*(6), 466–468.

Ginandes, S. (1973). *The school we have*. New York: Dell.

Ginsburg, H., & Baroody, J. *Test of early mathematics ability*. Austin, TX: Pro-Ed.

Giroux, H. (1983). *Theory and resistance: A pedagogy for the opposition*. South Hadley, MA: Bergin & Garvey Publications.

Glass, G. (1983). Effectiveness of special education. *Policy Studies Review, 2*(special 1), 65–78.

Glass, G., & Stanley, J. (1971). *Statistical methods in education and psychology*. Englewood Cliffs, NJ: Prentice-Hall.

Glass, G., McGaw, B., & Smith, M. (1981). *Meta-analysis in social research*. Beverly Hills, CA: Sage.

Glidewell, J., Kantor, M., Smith, L., & Stringer, L. (1966). Socialization and social structure in the classroom. In L. Hoffman & M. Hoffman (Eds.), *Review of child development research* (pp. 221–256). New York: Russell Sage Foundation.

Gold, Marvin. (1979). Teachers and mentors. In A. H. Passow (Ed.), *The gifted and talented: Their education and development* (Seventy-Eighth Yearbook of the National Society for the Study of Education, Part II) (pp. 272–288). Chicago: University of Chicago Press.

Gold, Milton. (1965). *Education of the intellectually gifted*. Columbus, OH: Charles E. Merrill.

Goldberg, M. (1965). *Research on the talented.* New York: Bureau of Publications, Teachers College, Columbia University.

Golin, A. K., & Ducanis, A. J. (1981). *The interdisciplinary team: A handbook for the education of exceptional children.* Rockville, MD: Aspen Systems Corporation.

Gonzalez, N. (1972, July 31). The strange tale of the school for gifted children: Showdown at Sands Point. *New York,* pp. 36–43.

Good, T., & Brophy, J. (1984). *Looking in classrooms.* New York: Harper & Row.

Goodenough, F. L., Maurer, K., & Wagenen, M. (1971). *Minnesota pre-school scale.* Circle Pines, MN: American Guidance Service.

Goodlad, J. (1970). Advancing art in U.S. public schools. In G. Pappas (Ed.), *Concepts in art and education: An anthology of current issues* (pp. 274–279). New York: Macmillan.

Gordon, E. E. (1965). *Music aptitude profile.* Boston: Houghton Mifflin.

Gordon, E. E. (1970–1971). *Iowa tests of music literacy.* Iowa City, IA: Bureau of Educational Research and Service, University of Iowa.

Gordon, W. J. (1961). *Synectics: The development of creative capacity.* NY: Harper & Row.

Gotz, I. L. (1977). Play in the classroom: Blessing or curse? *The Educational Forum, 41*(3), 329–334.

Gould, S. (1980). *The panda's thumb: More reflections in natural history.* New York: Norton.

Gould, S. (1981). *The mismeasure of man.* New York: Norton.

Gowan, J. C. (1972). *Development of the creative individual.* San Diego, CA: R. Knapp.

Gowan, J. C. (1978). The role of imagination in the development of the creative individual. *Humanitas, 24*(2), 197–208.

Gowan, J. C. (1981a). The use of developmental stage theory in helping gifted children become creative. In J. C. Gowan, J. Khatena, & E. P. Torrance (Eds.), *Creativity: Its educational implications* (2nd ed.) (pp. 72–88). Dubuque, IA: Kendall/Hunt.

Gowan, J. C. (1981b). Some new thoughts on the development of creativity. In W. B. Barbe & J. S. Renzulli (Eds.), *Psychology and education of the gifted* (3rd ed.) (pp. 315–326). New York: Irvington Publishers.

Gowan, J. C., & Demos, G. (1964). *The education and guidance of the ablest.* Springfield, IL: Charles C. Thomas.

Graves, M. (1948). *Graves design judgment scale.* New York: Psychological Corporation.

Grossi, J. (Ed.). (1981). *Parent/advocate groups for the gifted and talented.* Reston, VA: Council for Exceptional Children—ERIC Clearinghouse on Handicapped and Gifted Children.

Guilford, J. P. (1959). Three faces of intellect. *American Psychologist, 14,* 469–479.

Guilford, J. P. (1967). *The nature of human intelligence.* New York: McGraw-Hill.

Guzzardi, W. (1965). *The young executives.* New York: Mentor Books.

Hackett, M. G. (1971). *Criterion reading: Individualized learning management system.* New York: Random House.

Haensley, P. A., Shiver, D., & Fulbright, M. (1980). Task commitment and giftedness. *Roeper Review, 3*(1), 21–24.

Hagen, E. (1980). *Identification of the gifted.* New York: Teachers College Press.

Haggard, E. (1957). Socialization, personality, and academic achievement in gifted children. *The School Review, 65,* 388–414.

Haggard, E. (1980). What do the tests test? In *Readings in identification and evaluation of exceptional children.* Guilford, CT: Special Learning Corporation.

Hall, T. (1956). *Gifted children: The Cleveland story.* Cleveland, OH: World.

Hammill, D., & Larsen, S. (1974). The relationship of selected auditory perceptual skills and reading ability. *Journal of Learning Disabilities, 7,* 429–436.

Hammill, D., & Larsen, S. (1978). *Test of written language.* Austin, TX: Pro-Ed.

Hanks, L. (1973). Indifference to modern education in a Thai farming community. In A. J. Ianni & E. Storey (Eds.), *Cultural relevance and educational issues* (pp. 357–371). Boston: Little, Brown.

Hardy, G. (1969). *A mathematician's apology.* London: Cambridge University Press.

Hargreaves, D. H., Hester, S. K., & Mellor, F. J. (1975). *Deviance in classrooms.* London: Routledge & Kegan Paul.

Harris, M., Morgenbesser, S., Rotschild, J., & Wishy, B. (Eds.). (1961). *Introduction to contemporary civilization in the West* (3rd. ed.; 2 vols.). New York: Columbia University Press.

Harrod, J. (1979). A fiddler in the schools: A folk arts residency program. *Design, 80*(4), 14–17.

Hart, P. (1973). The educational role of the symphony orchestra. *Music Educators Journal, 60*(4), 26–29.

Harvey, S., & Seeley, K. (1984). An investigation of the relationships among intellectual and creative abilities, extracurricular activities, achievement, and giftedness in a delinquent population. *Gifted Child Quarterly, 28*(2), 73–79.

Haskell, S. H., Barrett, E. K., & Taylor, H. (1977). *The education of motor and neurologically handicapped children.* New York: Wiley.

Havighurst, R. J. (1963). Metropolitan development and the educational system. In W. W. Kallenbach & H. M. Hodges (Eds.), *Education and society* (pp. 244–256). Columbus, OH: Charles E. Merrill.

Hayes, J., & Higgins, S. T. (1978). Issues regarding the IEP: Teachers on the front line. *Exceptional Children, 44*(4), 267–273.

Hedbring, C., & Rubenzer, R. (1979). Integrating the IEP and SOI with educational programming for the gifted. *Gifted Child Quarterly, 23*(2), 338–345.

Heilbroner, R. (1966). *The worldly philosophers.* New York: Simon & Schuster.

Heisenberg, W. (1958). *Physics and philosophy: The revolution in modern science.* New York: Harper & Row.

Helmstadter, G. (1972). [Review of Barron-Welsh art scales]. In O. Buros (Ed.), *Seventh mental measurements yearbook* (pp. 83–84). Highland Park, NJ: Gryphon Press.

Hendrix, G. (1965). Learning by discovery. In J. J. Gallagher (Ed.), *Teaching gifted students* (pp. 162–176). Boston: Allyn and Bacon.

Henson, F. O. (1976). *Mainstreaming the gifted.* Austin, TX: Learning Concepts.

Heron, T. E., & Skinner, M. E. (1981). Criteria for defining the regular classroom as the least restrictive environment for LD students. *Learning Disability Quarterly, 4,* 115–121.

Herriott, J. (1982). CAI: A philosophy of education—and a system to match. *Creative Computing, 8*(4), 80–86.

Herrnstein, R. (1973). *IQ in the meritocracy.* Boston: Little, Brown.

Hess, K. D., Tenezakis, M., Smith, I. D., Brad, R. L., Spellman, J. B., Ingle, H. T., & Oppman, B. G. (1970). *The computer as a socializing agent: Some socioaffective outcomes of CAI* (Technical Report No. 13, pp. 613–614). Stanford, CA: Stanford Center for Research and Development in Teaching.

Hieronymus, A. N., Lindquist, E. F., & Hoover, H. D. (1978). *Iowa tests of basic skills.* Lombard, IL: Riverside.

Highet, G. (1950). *The art of teaching.* New York: Vintage Books.

Hildreth, G. H. (1952). *Educating gifted children.* New York: Harper & Row.

The hippies. (1967). *Gifted Child Quarterly, 11*(2), 178–181.

Hiskey, M. (1966). *Hiskey-Nebraska test of learning aptitude.* Lincoln, NB: Union College Press.

Hobbes, T. (1962). *Leviathan.* London: Fontana. (Original work published 1651)

Hobsbawm, E. J. (1962). *The age of revolution, 1789–1848.* New York: Mentor Books.

Hobson, J. (1963). High school performance of underage pupils initially admitted to kindergarten on the basis of physical and psychological examinations. *Educational and Psychological Measurement, 23*(1), 159–170.

Hocevar, D. (1979). Ideational fluency as a confounding factor in the measurement of originality. *Journal of Educational Psychology, 71*(2), 191–196.

Hocevar, D. (1980). Intelligence, divergent thinking, and creativity. *Intelligence, 4*(1), 25–40.

Hofmeister, A. (1984). *Microcomputer applications in the classroom.* New York: Holt, Rinehart & Winston.

Hofstadter, R. (1961). *Academic freedom in the age of the college* (paperback ed.). New York: Columbia University Press.

Hofstadter, R. (1963). *Anti-intellectualism in American life.* New York: Knopf.

Hollander, L. (1978). Extemporaneous speech presented at the National Forum on the Arts and the Gifted, Aspen, Colorado, June 1978. In E. Larsh (Ed.), *Someone's Priority.* Denver: Colorado State Department of Education. (ERIC Document Reproduction Service No. ED 181 663)

Hollingworth, L. S. (1926). *Gifted children: Their nature and nurture.* New York: Macmillan.

Hollingworth, L. S. (1938). An enrichment curriculum for rapid learners at public school 500: Speyer school. *Teachers College Record, 39*(4), 296–306.

Hollingworth, L. (1942). *Children above IQ 180.* New York: Harcourt, Brace & World.

Holmes, M., Holmes, D., & Field, J. (1974). *The therapeutic classroom.* New York: Jason Aronson.

Holt, J. (1964). *How children fail.* New York: Dell.

Holt, J. (1981). *Teach your own.* New York: Delacourt.

Holt, J. (1983). Schools and home schoolers: A fruitful partnership. *Phi Delta Kappan, 64*(6), 391–394.

Holtan, B. (1982). Attribute-treatment-interaction research in mathematics education. *School Science and Mathematics, 82*(7), 593–601.

Holton, C. (1983). Producing a coherent world image. *Design, 85*(2), 14–17.

Hope, S. (1983). What counts is the individual. *Design, 85*(2), 45–47.

Horn, R. E., & Cleaves, A. (Eds.). (1980). *The guide to simulations/games for education and training* (4th ed.). Beverly Hills, CA: Sage Publications.

Horne, D., & Dupuy, J. (1981). In favor of acceleration for gifted students. *The Personnel and Guidance Journal, 60*(2), 103–106.

House, P. (1981). Programs for able students: District or regional alternatives. *Arithmetic Teacher, 28*(6), 26–29.

Houts, P. L. (Ed.). (1977). *The myth of measurability.* New York: Hart.

Hoyt, K. B., & Hebeler, J. R. (1974). *Career education for gifted and talented students.* Salt Lake City, UT: Olympus.

Hudson, F. G., & Graham, S. (1980). An approach to operationalizing the IEP. In R. Piazza & I. Newman (Eds.), *Readings in individualized educational programs* (pp. 50–67). Guilford, CT: Special Learning Corporation.

Hunt, K. (1977). Early blooming and late blooming syntactic structures. In C. Cooper & L. Odell (Eds.), *Evaluating writing: Describing, measuring, judging* (pp. 91–104). Urbana, IL: National Council of Teachers of English.

Hurwitz, A. (1983). *The gifted and talented in art: A guide to program planning.* Worchester, MA: Davis Publications.

Husen, T. (Ed.). (1967). *International study of achievement in mathematics: A Comparison of twelve countries* (Vols. 1 & 2). New York: Wiley.

Huxley, A. (1962). *Island.* New York: Harper & Row.

Hyman, M. B. (1982). Science museums and gifted students. *Chronicle of Academic and Artistic Precocity, 1*(2), 1–3.

Jackson, P. (1981). Secondary schooling for children of the poor. *Daedalus, 110*(4), 39–57.

Jacobs, J. C. (1971). Effectiveness of teacher and parent identification of gifted children as a function of school level. *Psychology in the Schools, 8*, 140–142.

Jastak, J. E., & Jastak, S. R. (1978). *Wide range achievement test.* Wilmington, DE: Jastak Associates.

Jencks, C., Smith, M., Acland, H., Bane, M. J., Cohen, D., Gintis, H., Heyns, B., & Michelson, S. (1972). *Inequality: A reassessment of the effect of family and schooling in America.* New York: Harper & Row.

Jenkins-Friedman, R. (1982). Myth: Cosmetic use of multiple selection criteria. *Gifted Child Quarterly, 26*(1), 24–26.

Jensen, A. (1969). How much can we boost IQ and scholastic achievement? *Harvard Educational Review, 39,* 1–123.

Jensen, A. (1973). *Educability and group differences.* New York: Harper & Row.

Jensen, A. (1980). *Bias in mental testing.* New York: Free Press.

Jensen, A. (1981). *Straight talk about mental tests.* Boston: Little, Brown.

Jeter, J., & Chauvin, J. (1982). Individualized instruction: Implications for the gifted. *Roeper Review, 5*(1), 2–3.

Johnson, D., Maruyama, G., Johnson, R., Nelson, D., & Skon, L. (1981). Effects of cooperative, competitive and individualistic goal structures on achievement: A meta-analysis. *Psychological Bulletin, 89*(1), 47–62.

Kanigher, H. (1977). *Everyday enrichment for gifted children at home and school.* Los Angeles: National/State Leadership Training Institute on the Gifted and Talented.

Kanoy, R. C., Johnson, B. W., & Kanoy, K. W. (1980). Locus of control and self-concept in achieving and underachieving bright elementary students. *Psychology in the Schools, 17*(1), 395–399.

Kaplan, S. N. (1975). *Providing programs for the gifted and talented: A handbook.* Reston, VA: Council for Exceptional Children.

Kaplan, S. N. (1979). Language arts and social studies curriculum in the elementary school. In H. Passow (Ed.), *The gifted and talented: Their education and development* (Seventy-Eighth Yearbook of the National Society for the Study of Education, Part I) (pp. 155–168). Chicago: University of Chicago Press.

Karier, C. (1975). *Shaping the American educational state.* New York: Free Press.

Karnes, F. A., & Brown, K. E. (1979). Comparison of the SIT with the WISC-R for gifted students. *Psychology in the Schools, 16*(4), 478–482.

Karnes, F. A., & Brown, K. E. (1981). A short form of the WISC-R for gifted students. *Psychology in the Schools, 18*(2), 169–173.

Karnes, F. A., & Chauvin, J. (1982). A survey of early admission policies for younger than average students: Implications for gifted youth. *Gifted Child Quarterly, 26*(2), 68–73.

Karnes, F. A., & Collins, E. C. (1978). State definitions of gifted and talented: A report and analysis. *Journal of Education for the Gifted, 1*(1), 44–62.

Karnes, M. B., & Bertschi, J. D. (1980). Identifying and educating gifted/talented nonhandicapped preschoolers. In J. S. Renzulli & E. P. Stoddards (Eds.), *Gifted and talented education in perspective* (pp. 185–189). Reston, VA: Council for Exceptional Children.

Katz, M. (1968). *The irony of early school reform.* Cambridge: Harvard University Press.

Katz, M. (1971). *Class, bureaucracy, and schools.* New York: Praeger.

Kauffman, J. (1981). *Characteristics of children's behavior disorders* (2nd ed.). Columbus, OH: Charles E. Merrill.

Kaufman, A. (1975). Factor analysis of the WISC-R at 11 age levels between 6½ and 16½ years. *Journal of Consulting and Clinical Psychology, 43,* 135–147.

Kaufman, A., & Kaufman, N. (1983). *Kaufman assessment battery for children: Sampler manual.* Circle Pines, MN: American Guidance Service.

Kaufman, I. (1966). *Art and education in contemporary culture.* New York: Macmillan.

Kavale, K., & Glass, G. (1982). The efficacy of special education interventions and practices: A compendium of meta-analysis findings. *Focus on Exceptional Children, 15*(4), 1–14.

Kazanjian, V., Stein, S., & Weinberg, W. (1976). An introduction to mental health consultation. In R. Clifford & P. Trohanis (Eds.), *Technical assistance in special education agencies: Negotiation, delivery, and evaluation* (pp. 53–69). Chapel Hill, NC: Mid-East Learning Resource System.

Kearney, K. (1984). At home in Maine: Gifted children and home schooling. *G/C/T* (33), 15–19.

Keating, D. (1976). A Piagetian approach to intellectual precocity. In D. Keating (Ed.), *Intellectual talent research and development* (pp. 90–99). Baltimore: Johns Hopkins University Press.

Keating, D. (1979). The acceleration/enrichment debate: Basic issues. In W. C. George, S. J. Cohn, & J. C. Stanley (Eds.), *Educating the gifted: Acceleration and enrichment* (pp. 217–219). Baltimore: Johns Hopkins University Press.

Keller, F. S. (1968). Good-bye teacher! *Journal of Applied Behavioral Analysis, 1,* 79–84.

Kelly, E. W., & Terry, P. J. (1980). Creative implementation of DUSO with gifted students. *Elementary School Guidance and Counseling, 15*(2), 114–119.

Kelly, T. K., Bullock, L. M., & Dykes, M. K. (1977). Behavioral disorders: Teachers' perceptions. *Exceptional Children, 43*(5), 316–318.

Keniston, K. (1975). Do Americans really like children? *Today's Education, 64*(4), 16–21.

Kepner, C. H., & Tregoe, B. B. (1965). *The rational manager.* New York: McGraw-Hill.

Kerr, B. A. (1981). *Career education for the gifted and talented.* Columbus, OH: ERIC Clearinghouse on Adult, Career, and Vocational Education (The National Center for Research in Vocational Education).

Kerr, M. M., & Nelson, C. M. (1983). *Strategies for managing behavior problems in the classroom.* Columbus, OH: Charles E. Merrill.

Kersh, M., & Reisman, F. K. (1985). Mathematics for gifted students. In R. H. Swassing (Ed.), *Teaching gifted children and adolescents.* Columbus, OH: Charles E. Merrill.

Khatena, J. (1978). Identification and stimulation of creative imagination imagery. *Journal of Creative Behavior, 12*(1), 30–39.

Khatena, J. (1981). The nature of imagery in the visual and performing arts. In J. C. Gowan & E. P. Torrance (Eds.), *Creativity: Its educational implications* (2nd ed.) (pp. 255–263). Dubuque, IA: Kendall/Hunt.

Khatena, J. (1982). *Educational psychology of the gifted.* New York: Wiley.

Kimball, B. (1952). The sentence completion technique in a study of scholastic underachievement. *Journal of Consulting Psychology, 16,* 353–358.

King, M. (1981). *Rural delinquency proneness: Its relationship to giftedness, environmental support, and environmental availability.* Unpublished master's thesis, University of Wisconsin, Platteville.

Kirk, B. (1952). Test versus academic performance in malfunctioning students. *Journal of Consulting Psychology, 16,* 213–216.

Kirk, S. A., & Gallagher, J. J. (1983). *Educating exceptional children* (2nd ed.). Boston: Houghton Mifflin.

Klein, R. A. (1983). The arts as a basic educational experience. *Design, 85*(2), 18–21.

Klingele, W., & Reed, B. (1984). An examination of an incremental approach to mathematics. *Phi Delta Kappan, 65*(10), 712–713.

Knowles, P. (1982). And what will happen on campus? *Design, 83*(5), 14–16.

Koch, K. (1970). *Wishes, lies, and dreams.* New York: Vintage Books.

Koch, K. (1973). *Rose, where did you get that red?* New York: Vintage Books.

Koch, K., & Farrell, K. (1981). *Sleeping on the wing: An anthology of modern poetry with essays on reading and writing.* New York: Random House.

Kohl, H. (1967). *Thirty-six children.* New York: Signet Books.

Kohl, H. (1969). *The open classroom.* New York: Vintage Books.

Kohlberg, L. (1964). Development of moral character and moral ideology. In M. Hoffman & L. Hoffman (Eds.), *Review of child development research, Vol. 1* (pp. 383–432). New York: Russell Sage Foundation.

Kohlberg, L. (1966). Moral education in the schools: A developmental view. *The School Review, 74,* 1–29.

Korner, S. (1960). *The philosophy of mathematics*. New York: Harper & Row.

Krathwohl, D. R., Bloom, B. S., & Masia, B. B. (1964). *Taxonomy of educational objectives, handbook II: Affective domain*. New York: David McKay.

Kubie, L. S. (1961). *Neurotic distortion of the creative process*. New York: Noonday Press.

Kulik, C. C., & Kulik, J. A. (1982). Research synthesis on ability grouping. *Educational Leadership, 39*(8), 619–621.

Kulik, J., & Kulik, C. (1984). Effects of accelerated instruction on students. *Review of Educational Research, 54*(3), 409–425.

Kulik, J. A., Bangert, R. L., & Williams, G. W. (1983). Effects of computer-based teaching on secondary school students. *Journal of Educational Psychology, 75*(1), 19–26.

Kuo, W. (1981). Special classes for the gifted and talented: A review of research in the Republic of China (Taiwan). Paper presented at the 4th World Conference on Gifted and Talented Children, Montreal, Quebec, Canada, August 21–25, 1981. (ERIC Document Reproduction Service No. ED 212 119)

Kurtzman, K. A. (1967). A study of school attitudes, peer acceptance, and personality of creative adolescents. *Exceptional Children, 34*, 157–162.

Lamping, E. (1981). In defense of the self-contained gifted class. *G/C/T, 17*, 50–51.

Langer, S. K. (1957). *Problems of art*. New York: Scribner's.

Laycock, F. (1979). *Gifted children*. Glenview, IL: Scott Foresman.

Layzer, D. (1975). Heritability analyses of IQ scores: Science or numerology? In A. Montagu (Ed.), *Race and IQ* (pp. 192–219). London: Oxford University Press.

Lehman, E. B., & Erdwins, C. J. (1981). The social and emotional adjustment of young intellectually gifted children. *Gifted Child Quarterly, 25*(3), 134–137.

Lehman, P. R. (1983). Excellence in art education: Does the nation really want it? *Design, 85*(2), 40–42.

Leinhardt, G., & Pallay, A. (1982). Restrictive educational settings: Exile or haven. *Review of Educational Research, 52*(4), 557–578.

Leontief, W. (1982). The distribution of work and income. *Scientific American, 247*(3), 188–204.

Lerner, B. (1981). Representative democracy, "men of zeal" and testing legislation. *American Psychologist, 36*(3), 270–275.

Lewis, C. L., & Kanes, L. G. (1980). Gifted IEPs: Impact of expectations and perspectives. In D. M. Jackson (Ed.), *Readings in curriculum development for the gifted* (pp. 70–76). Guilford, CT: Special Learning Corporation.

Lewis, R. B., & Doorlag, D. H. (1983). *Teaching special students in the mainstream*. Columbus, OH: Charles E. Merrill.

Lidz, C. S. (1981). *Improving assessment of schoolchildren*. San Francisco: Jossey-Bass.

Linden, J. D., & Linden, K. W. (1968). *Tests on trial*. Boston: Houghton Mifflin.

Lipman, M. (1974). *Harry Stottlemeier's discovery*. Upper Montclair, NJ: Montclair State College.

Lipman, M. (1976). *Lisa*. Upper Montclair, NJ: Montclair State College.

Lipman, M., Sharp, A., & Oscanyan, F. (1977). *Philosophy in the classroom*. Philadelphia: Temple University Press.

Lipset, S., & Dobson, R. (1972). The intellectual as critic and rebel: With special reference to the United States and the Soviet Union. *Daedalus, 101*, 137–198.

Loe, D. C. (1980). Informal assessment during clinical teaching. In R. Piazza & I. Newman (Eds.), *Readings in individualized educational programs* (pp. 113–116). Guilford, CT: Special Learning Corporation.

Lombard, T. J. (1977). An economical and simplified alternative for providing educational opportunities to intellectually talented students. *Contemporary Education, 48*(2), 85–89.

Lorge, I., & Thorndike, R. (1966). *Lorge-Thorndike intelligence test*. Boston: Houghton Mifflin.

Lowenfeld, V., & Brittain, W. B. (1964). *Creative and mental growth* (4th ed.). New York: Macmillan.

Lowrance, D., & Anderson, H. N. (1977). Intercorrelation of the WISC-R and the Renzulli-Hartman Scale for determination of gifted placement. Paper presented at the 55th International CEC Convention, Atlanta, Georgia, April 11-15, 1977. (ERIC Document Reproduction Service No. ED 135 173)

Lum, M. K. M. (1960). A comparison of under- and over-achieving female college students. *Journal of Educational Psychology, 51*(3), 100-114.

Lyman, H. B. (1968). *Intelligence, aptitude, and achievement testing.* Boston: Houghton Mifflin.

Lyon, H. C. (1971). *Learning to feel: Feeling to learn.* Columbus, OH: Charles E. Merrill.

Lyons, C. (1982). Due process hearings: Issues and recommendations. *Journal for Special Educators, 18*(2), 22-28.

MacKinnon, D. W. (1968). Personality correlates of creativity. In M. Aschner & C. Bush (Eds.), *Productive thinking in education* (pp. 159-171). Washington, DC: National Education Association.

MacKinnon, D. W. (1978). *In search of human effectiveness.* Buffalo, NY: Creative Education Foundation.

MacKinnon, D. W. (1981). The nature and nurture of creative talent. In W. B. Barbe & J. S. Renzulli (Eds.), *Psychology and education of the gifted* (3rd ed.) (pp. 111-127). New York: Irvington Publishers. (Original article published 1962)

Madden, R., Gardner, E. R., Rudman, H. C., Karlsen, B., & Merwin, J. C. (1973). *Stanford achievement test.* New York: Harcourt Brace Jovanovich.

Maddux, C. D., Scheiber, L. M., & Bass, J. E. (1982). Self concept and social distance in gifted children. *Gifted Child Quarterly, 26*(2), 77-81.

Maehr, M. L. (1976). Continuing motivation: An analysis of a seldom considered educational outcome. *Review of Educational Research, 46*, 443-462.

Mahlios, M. C. (1981). Effects of teacher-student cognitive style on patterns of dyadic classroom interaction. *Journal of Experimental Education, 49*(3), 147-157.

Majeda, S. S., & Onuska, S. (1977). *Through the arts to the aesthetic: The CEMREL aesthetic education curriculum.* St. Louis, MO: CEMREL.

Maker, C. J. (1977). *Providing programs for the gifted handicapped.* Reston, VA: Council for Exceptional Children.

Maker, C. J. (1982a). *Curriculum development for the gifted.* Rockville, MD: Aspen Systems Corporation.

Maker, C. J. (1982b). *Teaching-learning models for gifted education.* Rockville, MD: Aspen Systems Corporation.

Maker, C. J. (1983). Quality education for gifted minority students. *Journal for the Education of the Gifted, 6*(3), 140-153.

Maltzman, I. (1960). On the training of originality. *Psychological Review, 67*(4), 229-242.

Mann, L. (1979). *On the trail of process.* New York: Grune & Stratton.

Marcuse, H. (1955). *Eros and civilization.* New York: Vintage Books.

Marcuse, H. (1964). *One-dimensional man.* Boston: Beacon Press.

Markel, G., Bogusky, R., Greenbaum, J., Bizer, L., & Rycus, C. (1976, April). Assertive training for parents of exceptional children. Paper delivered at the 54th Annual International Convention of the Council for Exceptional Children, Chicago. (ERIC Document Reproduction Service No. ED 122 569)

Markwalden, W. (1976). Design for a process oriented learning contract appropriate for high ability students. *Southern Journal of Educational Research, 10*(3), 124-134.

Marland, S. (1972). *Education of the gifted and talented* (Report to the Congress of the United States by the U.S. Commissioner of Education). Washington, DC: U.S. Government Printing Office.

Marland, S. (1976). Advanced placement. *Today's Education, 65*(1), 43-44.

Marolla, J., Williams, J., & McGrath, J. (1980). Schools: Antiquated systems of social control. *Educational Forum, 45*(1), 77-93.

Marotz, B. A., & Nelson, C. M. (1978). Field based inservice special education teacher training. *Forum: Issues in special education, 1*(2), 1-4. (Material disseminated by the

Teacher Education/Special Education Project. Albuquerque, NM: University of New Mexico)

Martellaro, H. C. (1980). Why don't they adopt us? *Creative Computing, 6*(9), 104–105.

Martin, R. (1979). *Educating handicapped children: The legal mandate.* Champaign, IL: Research Press.

Martinson, R. (1968). *Curriculum enrichment for the gifted in the primary grades.* Englewood Cliffs, NJ: Prentice-Hall.

Martinson, R. A. (1979). *The identification of the gifted and talented.* Reston, VA: Council for Exceptional Children.

Maslow, A. (1968). *Toward a psychology of being* (2nd ed.). New York: Van Nostrand Reinhold.

Massoth, N., & Levenson, R. (1982). The McCarthy scales of children's abilities as predictors of reading readiness and reading achievement. *Psychology in the Schools, 19*(3), 293–296.

Maxwell, S. (1980). Museums are learning laboratories for gifted students. *Teaching Exceptional Children, 12*(4), 154–160.

McAskie, M., & Clarke, A. (1976). Parent-offspring resemblance in intelligence. *British Journal of Psychology, 67,* 243–273.

McCarthy, D. A. (1972). *Manual for the McCarthy scales of children's abilities.* New York: Psychological Corporation.

McCarthy, S. V. (1979). Differential V-Q ability: Twenty years later. *Review of Educational Research, 45*(2), 263–282.

McClelland, D. (1958). Issues in the identification of talent. In D. McClelland, A. L. Baldwin, U. Bronfenbrenner, & F. Strodtbeck (Eds.), *Talent and society: New perspectives in the identification of talent* (pp. 1–27). Princeton, NJ: D. Van Nostrand.

McClelland, D. (1980). Testing for competence rather than for "intelligence." In *Evaluation of Exceptional Children* (pp. 183–194). Guilford, CT: Special Learning Corporation.

McClelland, D., Atkinson, J., Clark, R., & Lowell, E. (1953). *The achievement motive.* New York: Appleton-Century-Crofts.

McFarland, S. L. (1980). The young gifted child: Guidelines on the identification of young gifted and talented children. *Roeper Review, 3*(2), 5–7.

McGhehey, M. (1982). The overextension of due process. *Education and Urban Society, 14*(2), 133–150.

McGinn, P. V. (1976). Verbally gifted youth: Selection and description. In J. C. Stanley, D. P. Keating, & L. H. Fox (Eds.), *Mathematical talent: Discovery, description, and development* (pp. 126–139). Baltimore, MD: Johns Hopkins University Press.

McGivern, J. E., & Levin, J. R. (1983). The keyword method and children's vocabulary learning: An interaction with vocabulary knowledge. *Contemporary Educational Psychology, 8,* 46–54.

McLain, J. D., & Kovacs, F. W. (1967). Programmed instruction for superior students in small high schools. Washington, DC: NDEA. (ERIC Document Reproduction Service No. ED 011 070)

McLeod, D. B., & Adams, V. M. (1979). The interaction of field independence with discovery learning in mathematics. *Journal of Experimental Education, 48*(1), 32–35.

McLuhan, M. (1964). *Understanding media: The extensions of man.* New York: McGraw-Hill.

McNeil, J. (1981). *Curriculum: A comprehensive introduction.* Boston: Little, Brown.

McSpadden, J. V., & Strain, P. S. (1977). Memory thresholds and overload effects between learning disabled and achieving pupils. *Exceptional Children, 44*(1), 35–37.

Meeker, M. (1969). *The structure of intellect.* Columbus, OH: Charles E. Merrill.

Meeker, M. (1979a). The relevance of arithmetic testing to teaching arithmetic skills. *Gifted Child Quarterly, 23*(2), 297–303.

Meeker, M. (1979b). *Using SOI test results: A teacher's guide.* El Segundo, CA: SOI Institute.

Meeker, M., Sexton, K., & Richardson, M. (1970). *SOI abilities workbook*. Los Angeles: Loyola-Marymount University.

Meier, N. (1963). *Meier art tests*. Iowa City, IA: Bureau of Educational Research and Service, University of Iowa.

Melzer, P. (1980). The real world of physics teaching at the Bronx High School of Science. *The Physics Teacher, 18*(4), 272–277.

Mercer, C. D. (1983). *Students with learning disabilities* (2nd ed.). Columbus, OH: Charles E. Merrill.

Mercer, J. (1979). The constitutional guarantees of due process and equal protection for gifted public school students (Doctoral dissertation, University of Minnesota, 1979). *Dissertation Abstracts International, 40*(2), 587A.

Mercer, J. R. (1981). The system of multicultural pluralistic assessment: SOMPA. In *Balancing the scale for the disadvantaged gifted: Presentations from the Fourth Biennial National Conference on Disadvantaged Gifted/Talented* (pp. 29–57). Ventura, CA: Ventura County Superintendent of Schools.

Mercy, J., & Steelman, L. (1982). Familial influence on the intellectual attainment of children. *American Sociological Review, 47*(4), 532–542.

Merton, A. (1983). Computers in the classroom. *Technology Illustrated, 3*(9), 38–46.

Meskill, V., & Lauper, R. (1973). Breaking the lockstep for the gifted. *NASSP Bulletin, 57*(370), 58–62.

Messick, S., & Anderson, S. (1974). Educational testing, individual development, and social responsibility. In R. W. Tyler & R. M. Wolf (Eds.), *Crucial issues in testing* (pp. 21–34). Berkeley, CA: McCutchan.

Meyer, J. (1977). The effects of education as an institution. *American Journal of Sociology, 83*(1), 55–71.

Micklus, C. (1981). The gifted and talented in our vocational schools. *NJEA Review, 54*(6), 10–11.

Miller, E. (Speaker). (1969). *Individual intelligence testing* (Cassette Recording No. 29233). New York: Jeffrey Norton.

Miller, S. D. (1979). Wolfgang Amadeus who? The neglect of music literature. *Music Educators Journal, 65*(8), 50–53.

Mills, C. (1956). *The power elite*. New York: Oxford University Press.

Mills, E. A., & Ridlon, J. A. (1980). A conversation about the New York State summer school for the visual arts. *School Arts, 79*(9), 62–68.

Mindell, P., & Stracher, D. (1980). Assessing reading and writing of the gifted: The warp and woof of the language program. *Gifted Child Quarterly, 24*(2), 72–80.

Minot, S. (1958). What a seminar is not. *American Association of University Professors Bulletin, 44*, 733–735.

Mitchell, P. B. (Ed.). (1981a). *An advocate's guide to building support for gifted and talented education*. Washington, DC: National Association of State Boards of Education.

Mitchell, P. B. (Ed.). (1981b). *A policymaker's guide to issues in gifted and talented education*. Washington, DC: National Association of State Boards of Education.

Mitchell, R. (1979). *Less than words can say*. Boston: Little, Brown.

Mitchell, R. (1981). *The graves of academie*. Boston: Little, Brown.

Mitchell, S. (1976). Parental perceptions of their experiences with due process in special education: A preliminary report. Paper presented at the annual meeting of the American Educational Research Association, April 19–23, 1976. (ERIC Document Reproduction Service No. ED 130 482)

Moles, O. (1982). Synthesis of recent research on parent participation in children's education. *Educational Leadership, 40*(2), 44–47.

Mooney, R. L. (1963). A conceptual model for integrating four approaches to the identification of creative talent. In C. W. Taylor & F. Barron (Eds.), *Scientific creativity: Its recognition and development* (pp. 331–340). New York: Wiley.

Morgan, M. (1981). Self-derived objectives in private study. *Journal of Educational Research, 74*(5), 327–332.

Morris, W. (Ed.). (1975). *The American Heritage dictionary of the English language*. Boston: American Heritage–Houghton Mifflin.

Morrison, P. (1977). The bell shaped pitfall. In P. L. Houts (Ed.), *The myth of measurability* (pp. 82–89). New York: Hart.

Morse, W. C., Cutler, R. L., & Fink, A. H. (1964). *Public school classes for the emotionally handicapped: A research analysis*. Washington, DC: Council for Exceptional Children.

Morsink, C. (1984). *Teaching special needs students in regular classrooms*. Boston: Little, Brown.

Morton, J. H., & Workman, E. H. (1981). Insights: Assisting gifted students with emotional difficulties. In W. Barbe & J. Renzulli (Eds.), *Psychology and education of the gifted* (3rd. ed.) (pp. 457–462). New York: Irvington Publishers.

Morton, M. (1972). *The arts and the Soviet child*. New York: Free Press.

Mosteller, F., & Moynihan, D. (Eds.). (1972). *On equality of educational opportunity*. New York: Random House.

Muir, K., Milan, M., Branston-McLean, M., & Berger, M. (1982). Advocacy training of handicapped children: A staff responsibility. *Young Children, 37*(2), 41–46.

Munro, T. (1960). The interrelation of the arts in secondary education. In *The creative arts in American education: The Inglis and Burton lectures*. Cambridge, MA: Harvard University Press.

Myers, J. T. (1982). Hemisphericity research: An overview with some implications for problem solving. *Journal of Creative Behavior, 16*(3), 197–211.

Naslund, R., Thorpe, L. P., & Lefever, D. W. (1978). *SRA achievement series*. Chicago: Science Research Associates.

National Commission on Excellence in Education. (1983). *A nation at risk: The imperative for educational reform*. Washington, DC: U.S. Department of Education.

National Public Radio. (1981). The Duke Ellington School of the Arts. *Options in education* (Program No. 287). Washington, DC: George Washington University, Institute for Educational Leadership. (ERIC Document Reproduction Service No. ED 211 435)

Neuman, E. (Ed.). (1980). *Reaching out: Advocacy for the gifted and talented*. New York: Teachers College Press.

Nevin, D. (1977). Seven teen-age math prodigies take off from Johns Hopkins on the way to advanced degrees. *Smithsonian, 8*(7), 76–82, 160.

Newell, A., & Simon, H. (1972). *Human problem solving*. Englewood Cliffs, NJ: Prentice-Hall.

Newland, T. E. (1969). *Manual for the blind learning aptitude test: Experimental edition*. Urbana, IL: T. Ernest Newland.

Newland, T. E. (1976). *The gifted in socioeducational perspective*. Englewood Cliffs, NJ: Prentice-Hall.

New York State Department of Education. (1982). *Educating gifted pupils in the regular classroom: Training manual*. Albany, NY: New York State Department of Education. (ERIC Document Reproduction Service No. ED 219 890)

Nitz, D. A. (1980). On the state of music education: The national malaise vs. the pursuit of excellence. *Music Educators Journal, 66*(8): 41–42, 61.

Norris, R. A. (1977). SAIR: The student artist-in-residence. *Art Education, 30*(2), 20–26.

Norton, R., & Doman, G. (1982). The gifted child fallacy. *The Elementary School Journal, 82*(3), 249–255.

Oden, M. (1968). *The fulfillment of promise: Forty-year follow up of the Terman gifted group*. Stanford, CA: Stanford University Press.

O'Leary, S. G., & Schneider, M. R. (1977). Special class placement for conduct problem children. *Exceptional Children, 44*(1), 24–30.

Oliva, P. (1982). *Developing the curriculum*. Boston: Little, Brown.

Oliver, A. L. (1978). *Maximizing minicourses*. New York: Teachers College Press.

Olmstead, J. A. (1974). *Small-group instruction: Theory and practice*. Alexandria, VA: Human Resources Research Organization.

Olneck, M. R., & Crouse, J. (1979). The IQ meritocracy reconsidered. *American Journal of Education, 88*(1), 1–31.

Ortega y Gasset, J. (1968). *The dehumanization of art*. Princeton, NJ: Princeton University Press.

Osborn, A. F. (1953). *Applied imagination*. New York: Scribner's.

Osborn, A. F. (1963). *Applid imagination* (3rd. ed.). New York: Scribner's.

Osburn, W. J., & Rohan, B. J. (1931). *Enriching the curriculum for gifted children: A book of guidance for educational administrators and classroom teachers*. New York: Macmillan.

Otis, A. S., & Lennon, R. T. (1979). *Otis-Lennon school ability test*. New York: Harcourt Brace Jovanovich.

Ottina, J. R. (1973). Career education is alive and well. *Journal of Teacher Education, 24*(2), 84–86.

Otto, L. (1975). Extracurricular activities in the educational attainment process. *Rural Sociology, 40*(2), 162–176.

Palermo, D. (1978). *Psychology of language*. Glenview, IL: Scott Foresman.

Palmer, R. R., & Colton, J. (1965). *A history of the modern world*. New York: Knopf.

Pankratz, R. (1967). Verbal interaction patterns in the classrooms of selected physics teachers. In E. J. Amidon & J. B. Hough (Eds.), *Interaction analysis: Theory, research and application* (pp. 189–209). Reading, MA: Addison-Wesley.

Papert, S. (1981). *Mindstorms: Computers, children, and powerful ideas*. New York: Basic Books.

Pardue, T. (1982). Group piano. *Design, 83*(3), 21–23.

Parke, B. N. (1983). Use of self-instructional materials with gifted primary-aged students. *Gifted Child Quarterly, 27*(1), 29–34.

Parnes, J. (1963). *Creative behavior guidebook*. New York: Scribner's.

Parnes, S. J. (1981). CPSI: The general system. In W. Barbe & J. Renzulli (Eds.), *Psychology and education of the gifted* (3rd. ed.) (pp. 304–314). New York: Irvington Publishers.

Passow, A. H. (1972). The gifted and the disadvantaged. *The National Elementary Principal, 51*(5), 24–31.

Payne, J. (1981). The mathematics curriculum for talented students. *Arithmetic Teacher, 28*(6), 18–21.

Pedriana, A. J., & Bracken, B. A. (1982). Performance of gifted children on the PPVT and PPVT-R. *Psychology in the Schools, 19*(2), 183–185.

Pegnato, C. W., & Birch, J. W. (1959). Locating gifted children in junior high school. *Exceptional Children, 25*(7), 300–304.

Pendarvis, E. (1983). *The written language of gifted children*. Unpublished doctoral dissertation, University of Kentucky, Frankfurt.

Pendarvis, E. (1985). Gifted and talented children. In A. Blackhurst & B. Berdine (Eds.), *Teaching exceptional students*. Boston: Little, Brown.

Perrone, P. A., & Male, R. A. (1981). *The developmental education and guidance of talented learners*. Rockville, MD: Aspen Systems Corporation.

Peterson, A. (1972). *The international baccalaureate*. London: George G. Harrap.

Petzold, R. G. (1978). Identification of musically talented students. In E. Larsh (Ed.), *Someone's priority* (pp. 58–64). Denver: Colorado State Department of Education. (ERIC Document Reproduction Service No. ED 181 663)

Pfeiffer, S. (1980). The school-based interprofessional team: Recurring problems and some possible solutions. *Journal of School Psychology, 18*(4), 388–394.

Phenix, P. H. (1968). The use of the disciplines as curriculum content. In F. L. Steeves (Ed.), *The subjects in the curriculum* (pp. 1–9). Indianapolis, IN: Odyssey Press.

Piaget, J. (1970). *Science of education and psychology of the child* (D. Coltman, Trans.). New York: Orion Press.

Pirozzo, R. (1982). Gifted underachievers. *Roeper Review, 4*(4), 18–21.

PL 94-142. The Education of All Handicapped Children's Act of 1975. (codified at 20 USC 1401-1461 [1978])

PL 95-561. Financial Assistance to Local Educational Agencies (Education Amendments of 1978). (20 USC 13, sections 236-246)

Poland, S., Thurlow, M., Ysseldyke, J., & Mirkin, P. (1982). Current psycho-educational assessment and decision-making practices as reported by directors of special education. *Journal of School Psychology, 20*(3), 171-179.

Popkewitz, T., & Tabachnick, B. (1982). Themes in current Soviet curriculum reform. *Educational Leadership, 39*(6), 420–424.

Popkewitz, T., Tabachnick, B., & Wehlage, G. (1982). *The myth of educational reform.* Madison, WI: University of Wisconsin Press.

Porter, R. M. (1968). *A decade of seminars for the able and ambitious.* Oneonta, NY: Catskill Area School Study Council. (ERIC Document Reproduction Service No. ED 027 099)

Porter, R. M. (1978). The Catskill Saturday seminars updated. *Gifted Child Quarterly, 22*(3), 361–373.

Postman, N., & Weingartner, C. (1969). *Teaching as a subversive activity.* New York: Dell.

Poulantzas, N. (1975). *Class in contemporary capitalism* (D. Fernbach, Trans.). London: Verso. (Original work published 1974)

Prescott, G. A., Balow, I. H., Hogan, T. P., & Farr, R. C. (1978). *Metropolitan achievement tests: Survey battery.* New York: Psychological Corporation.

Pressey, S. L. (1955). Concerning the nature and nurture of genius. *Scientific Monthly, 81,* 123–129.

Pressey, S. L. (1967). Fordling accelerates: Ten years after. *Journal of Counseling Psychology, 14*(1), 73–80.

Pringle, M. K. (1970). *Able misfits.* London: Longman.

Puravs, O. (1973). Criticism and experience. *Journal of Aesthetic Education, 7*(1), 11–22.

Quilter, A. (1977). Education for the musically gifted. *Trends in Education, 2*(Summer), 4–9.

Raph, J. B., Goldberg, M. L., & Passow, A. H. (1966). *Bright underachievers.* New York: Teachers College Press.

Raser, J. R. (1969). *Simulation and society.* Boston: Allyn and Bacon.

Raths, L. E., Harmin, M., & Simon, S. B. (1966). *Values and teaching: Working with values in the classroom.* Columbus, OH: Charles E. Merrill.

Raven, J. C. (1938). *Progressive matrices.* London: Lewis.

Read, H. (1959). *A concise history of modern painting.* London: Thames & Hudson.

Read, H. (1960). The third realm of education. In *The creative arts in American education: The Inglis and Burton lectures.* Cambridge: Harvard University Press.

Reeve, R., Hall, R. J., & Zakreski, R. S. (1979). The Woodcock-Johnson tests of cognitive ability: Concurrent validity with the WISC-R. *Learning Disability Quarterly, 2*(2), 63–69.

Reid, D. K., & Hresko, W. P. (1981). *A cognitive approach to learning disabilities.* New York: McGraw-Hill.

Reid, D. K., Hresko, W. P., & Hammill, D. (1983). *Test of early reading ability.* Los Angeles: Western Psychological Services.

Reisman, F. K. (1981). Performance on Torrance's thinking creatively in action and movement as a predictor of cognitive development of young children. *Creative Child and Adult Quarterly, 6*(4), 205–209, 233.

Renzulli, J. S. (1973). *New directions in creativity.* New York: Harper & Row.

Renzulli, J. S. (1975). *A guidebook for evaluating programs for the gifted and talented.* Ventura, CA: Office of the Ventura County Superintendent of Schools.

Renzulli, J. S. (1977). *The enrichment triad model: A Guide for developing defensible programs for the gifted and talented.* Wethersfield, CT: Creative Learning Press.

Renzulli, J. S. (1978). What makes giftedness? *Phi Delta Kappan, 60*(3). 180–184, 261.

Renzulli, J. S. (1980). What we don't know about programming for the gifted and talented. *Phi Delta Kappan, 61*(9), 601–602.

Renzulli, J. S. (1982). What makes a problem real: Stalking the illusive meaning of qualitative differences in gifted education. *Gifted Child Quarterly, 26*(4), 147–156.

Renzulli, J. S., Reis, S. M., & Smith, L. M. (1981). *The revolving door identification model.* Mansfield Center, CT: Creative Learning Press.

Renzulli, J. S., & Smith, L. H. (1977). Two approaches to identification of gifted students. *Exceptional Children, 43*(6), 512–518.

Renzulli, J. S., & Smith, L. H. (1978). *The strength-a-lyzer.* Mansfield Center, CT: Creative Learning Press.

Renzulli, J. S., & Smith, L. H. (1981). A practical model for designing individualized educational programs (IEP) for gifted and talented students. In W. Barbe & J. Renzulli (Eds.), *Psychology and education of the gifted* (3rd. ed.) (pp. 335–350). New York: Irvington Publishers.

Renzulli, J. S., Smith, L. H., White, A. J., Callahan, C. M., & Hartman, R. K. (1977). *Scales for rating the behavioral characteristics of superior students.* Mansfield Center, CT: Creative Learning Press.

Rexroth, K. (1966). *An autobiographical novel.* New York: New Directions.

Rice, B. (1980). Brave new world of intelligence testing. In D. M. Jackson (Ed.), *Readings in curriculum development for the gifted* (pp. 93–99). Guilford, CT: Special Learning Corporation.

Richardson, Bellows, Henry & Co., Inc. (1947–1950). *SRA mechanical aptitudes test.* Chicago: Science Research Associates.

Rieck, B. (1977). How content teachers telegraph messages against reading. *Journal of Reading, 20*(8), 646–648.

Riis, J. (1971). *How the other half lives.* New York: Dover Books. (Original edition published 1890)

Rimm, S., & Davis, G. (1976). An instrument for the identification of creativity. *Journal of Creative Behavior, 10*(3), 178–182.

Rimm, S., & Davis, G. (1980). Five years of international research with GIFT: An instrument for the identification of creativity. *Journal of Creative Behavior, 14*(1), 20–24.

Riner, P. S. (1983). Establishing scientific methodology with elementary gifted children through field biology. *G/C/T* (28), 46–49.

Risley, T. (1970). Learning and lollipops. In P. Cramer (Ed.), *Readings in developmental psychology today* (pp. 139–148). Del Mar, CA: CRM Books.

Robinson, A., & Feldhusen, J. (1984). Don't leave them alone: Effects of probing on gifted children's imaginative explanations. *Journal for the Education of the Gifted, 7*(3), 156–163.

Robinson, R., & Kelley, J. (1979). Class as conceived by Marx and Dahrendorf: Effects on income inequality and politics in the United States and Great Britain. *American Sociological Review, 44,* 38–58.

Roe, A. (1981). A psychologist examines 64 eminent scientists. In W. Barbe & J. Renzulli (Eds.), *Psychology and education of the gifted* (3rd ed.) (pp. 103–110). New York: Irvington Publishers. (original article published 1952)

Roedell, W. C., Jackson, N. E., & Robinson, H. B. (1980). *Gifted young children.* New York: Teachers College Press.

Rogers, C. R. (1969). *Freedom to learn.* Columbus, OH: Charles E. Merrill.

Rose, R. (1979). A program model for altering children's consciousness. *Gifted Child Quarterly, 23*(1), 109–117.

Rosenbaum, J. (1975). The stratification of the socialization process. *American Sociological Review, 40,* 48–54.

Rosenshine, B. (1981). How time is spent in elementary classrooms. *Journal of Classroom Instruction, 17*(1), 16–25.

Ross, J. D., & Ross, C. M. (1976). *Ross test of higher cognitive process, administration manual.* San Rafael, CA: Academic Therapy Publications.

Roth, R. M., & Puri, P. (1967). Direction of aggression and the underachievement syndrome. *Journal of Counseling Psychology, 14*(3), 277–281.

Rowe, M. (1973). *Teaching science as continuous inquiry.* New York: McGraw-Hill.

Rubenzer, R. (1979a). Identification and evaluation procedures for gifted and talented programs. *Gifted Child Quarterly, 23*(2), 304–316.

Rubenzer, R. (1979b). The role of the right hemisphere in learning and creativity implications for enhancing problem solving ability. *Gifted Child Quarterly, 23*(1), 78–100.

Runions, T. (1980). The Mentor Academy Program: Educating the gifted/talented for the 80's. *Gifted Child Quarterly, 24*(4), 152–157.

Russell, B. (1919). *Introduction to mathematical philosophy.* London: G. Allen & Unwin.

Rust, J. O., & Lose, B. D. (1980). Screening for giftedness with the Slosson and the Scale for Rating Behavioral Characteristics of Superior Students. *Psychology in the Schools, 17*(4), 446–451.

Ryan, W. (1976). *Blaming the victim.* New York: Vintage Books.

Saigh, P. A. (1981). The validity of the WISC-R examiner verbal praise procedure as a concurrent predictor of the academic achievement of intellectually superior students. *Journal of Clinical Psychology, 37*(3), 647–649.

Salome, R. A. (1974). Identifying and instructing the gifted in art. *Art Education, 27*(3), 16–19.

Salvia, J., & Ysseldyke, J. E. (1981). *Assessment in special and remedial education* (2nd. ed.). Boston: Houghton Mifflin.

Samuda, R. J. (1975). *Psychological testing of American minorities: Issues and consequences.* New York: Dodd, Mead.

Sanders, J. (1981). Research on selection methods and programming for advanced black students at the secondary level of education. Final Report. Shaker Heights City School District. (ERIC Document Reproduction Service No. ED 215 047)

Sanders, N. M. (1966). *Classroom question: What Kinds?* New York: Harper & Row.

Sapon-Shevin, M. (1982). Mainstreaming the handicapped, segregating the gifted: Theoretical and pragmatic concerns. Paper presented at the Annual Meeting of the American Educational Research Association, New York City, March 19–23, 1982. (ERIC Document Reproduction Service No. ED 218 835)

Sattler, J. M. (1982). *Assessment of children's intelligence and special abilities* (2nd ed.). Boston: Allyn and Bacon.

Saunders, R. J. (1982). Screening and identifying the talented in art. *Roeper Review, 4*(3), 7–10.

Saxon, J. (1979). *Algebra, an incremental approach.* Englewood Cliffs, NJ: Prentice-Hall.

Saylor, J., Alexander, W., & Lewis, A. (1981). *Curriculum planning for better teaching and learning.* New York: Holt, Rinehart & Winston.

Scarr, S. (1971). Race, social class, and IQ. *Science, 174,* 1285–1295.

Scarr, S. (1981). *Race, social class, and individual differences in IQ.* Hillsdale, NJ: Lawrence Erlbaum Associates.

Scarr, S., & Weinberg, R. A. (1976). IQ test performance of black children adopted by white families. *American Psychologist, 31,* 726–739.

Schaffarzick, J., & Hampson, D. (1975). *Strategies for curriculum development.* Berkeley, CA: McCutchan.

Schlechty, P., & Vance, V. (1983). Institutional responses to the quality/quantity issue in teacher training. *Phi Delta Kappan, 65*(2), 94–101.

Schlemmer, P. (1981). The Zoo School: Evolution of an alternative. *Phi Delta Kappan, 62*(8), 558–560.

Schmidt, L. (1981). Gifted programs in music: A nuclear model. *Roeper Review, 3*(3), 31–34.

Schmidt, M. (1981). *Kindergarten early entrance identification manual.* Olympia, WA: Washington Office of the State Superintendent of Public Instruction, Division of Instructional and Professional Services. (ERIC Document Reproduction Service No. ED 214 674)

Schubart, M. (1972). *Performing arts institutions and young people: Lincoln Center's study: The hunting of the squiggle.* New York: Praeger.

Schwarz, A. (1975). *The schools and socialization.* New York: Harper & Row.

Schwartz, L. L. (1980). Advocacy for the neglected gifted: Females. *Gifted Child Quarterly, 24*(3), 113–117.

Science Research Associates. (1974). *Think-lab.* Toronto: Science Research Associates.

Scriven, M. (1967). The methodology of evaluation. In R. G. Stake (Ed.), *Curriculum evaluation* (American Educational Research Association Monograph Series on Evaluation, No. 1). Chicago: Rand-McNally.

Seashore, C., Lewis, D., & Saetveit, J. (1960). *Seashore measures of musical talents.* New York: Psychological Corporation. (Test first published 1919)

Selden, S. (1983). Biological determinism and the ideological roots of student classification. *Journal of Education, 165*(2), 175–191.

Sellin, D. F., & Birch, J. W. (1980). *Educating gifted and talented learners.* Rockville, MD: Aspen Systems Corporation.

Shaw, M. C., & Grubb, J. (1958). Hostility and able high school achievers. *Journal of Counseling Psychology, 5*(4), 263–266.

Shaw, M. C., & McCuen, J. T. (1960). The onset of academic underachievement in bright children. *Journal of Educational Psychology, 51*(3), 103–108.

Shelley, M. (1968). *Frankenstein.* New York: Lancer Books. (Original work published 1818)

Shufelt, G. (1981). Providing for able students at the local school level. *Arithmetic Teacher, 28*(6), 44–46.

Shugrue, M. F. (1981). *The essay.* New York: Macmillan.

Silberman, C. (1970). *Crisis in the classroom.* New York: Random House.

Silverman, L. (1980). Secondary programs for gifted students. *Journal for Education of the Gifted, 4*(1), 30–42.

Simpson, R. G. (1982). Correlation between the general information subtest of the PIAT and full scale IQ of the WISC-R. *Educational and Psychological Measurement, 42*(2), 695–699.

Sisk, D. A. (1978). Centering activities for gifted/talented children. *Gifted Child Quarterly, 22*(1), 135–139.

Sisk, D. A. (1979). Unusual gifts and talents. In M. S. Lilly (Ed.), *Children with exceptional needs* (pp. 362–397). New York: Holt, Rinehart & Winston.

Sisk, D. A. (1981). The use of creative activities in leadership training. In W. Barbe & J. Renzulli (Eds.), *Psychology and education of the gifted* (3rd ed.) (pp. 327–334). New York: Irvington Publishers.

Sisk, D. A. (1982). Caring and sharing: Moral development of gifted students. *Elementary School Journal, 82*(3), 221–229.

Sisk, D. A., & Bierly, K. (1979). Every child in a gifted program? *Instructor, 88*(9), 84–86, 90, 92.

Sizer, T. (1984). *Horace's compromise.* Boston: Houghton Mifflin.

Slavin, R. E. (1981). Synthesis of research on cooperative learning. *Educational Leadership, 38*(8), 655–660.

Slosson, R. L. (1971). *Slosson intelligence test.* East Aurora, NY: Slosson Educational Publications.

Smilansky, M., & Nevo, D. (1978). A longitudinal study of the gifted disadvantaged. In National/State Leadership Training Institute on the Gifted and Talented (Ed.), *Advantage: Disadvantaged gifted* (pp. 63–76). Ventura, CA: Office of the Ventura County Superintendent of Schools.

Smilansky, M., & Nevo, D. (1979). *The gifted disadvantaged: A ten year longitudinal study of compensatory education in Israel.* New York: Gordon & Breach.

Smith, P. L. (1977). The liberating arts and career education. *Educational Forum, 41*(3), 317–328.

Smith, R. A. (1973). Teaching aesthetic criticism in the schools. *Journal of Aesthetic Education, 7*(1), 38–49.

Smolak, L. (1982). Cognitive precursors of receptive vs. expressive language. *Journal of Child Language, 9*(1), 13–22.

Snow, C. P. (1969). Elitism and excellence. *The Mathematics Teacher, 62*(6), 505–509.

Snow, R. E. (1980). Consequences for instruction: The state of the art of individualizing. In R. Piazza & I. Newman (Eds.), *Readings in individualized educational programs* (pp. 90–97). Guilford, CT: Special Learning Corporation.

Solano, C. (1976, September). Teacher and pupil stereotypes of gifted boys and girls. Paper presented at the Eighty-Fourth Annual Conference of the American Psychological Association, Washington, D.C., September 3–7, 1976. (ERIC Document Reproduction Service No. ED 137 667)

Solano, C., & George, W. (1976). College courses and educational facilitation of the gifted. *Gifted Child Quarterly, 20*(3), 274–285.

Southern Regional Education Board. (1982). *Regional Spotlight, 14*(3), 2–3.

Spearman, C. (1904). General intelligence objectively determined and measured. *American Journal of Psychology, 15,* 201–293.

Spearman, C. (1927). *The abilities of man: Their nature and measurement.* New York: Macmillan.

Spencer, H. (1963). *Education: Intellectual, moral and physical.* Patterson, NJ: Littlefield Adams. (Original edition published 1860)

Spring, J. (1982). The evolving political structure of American schooling. In R. Everhart (Ed.), *The public school monopoly: A critical analysis of education and the state in American society* (pp. 77–108). Cambridge, MA: Ballinger.

Springer, S., & Deutsch, G. (1981). *Left brain, right brain.* San Francisco: W. H. Freeman.

Stanley, J. (1964). *Measurement in today's schools* (4th ed.). Englewood Cliffs, NJ: Prentice-Hall.

Stanley, J. (1974). Intellectual precocity. In J. Stanley, D. Keating, & L. Fox (Eds.), *Mathematical talent: Discovery, description, and development.* Baltimore: Johns Hopkins University Press.

Stanley, J. (1976). Brilliant youth: Improving the quality and speed of their education. Paper presented to the Eighty-fourth Annual Conference of the American Psychological Association, September, 1976. (ERIC Document Reproduction Service No. ED 136 536)

Stanley, J. (1977). The predictive value of the SAT for brilliant seventh- and eighth-graders. *The College Board Review,* (106, Winter, 1977–1978), 31–37.

Stanley, J. (1981). Rationale of the study of mathematically precocious youth (SMPY) during its first five years of promoting educational acceleration. In W. Barbe & J. Renzulli (Eds.), *Psychology and education of the gifted* (pp. 248–283). New York: Irvington Publishers.

Stanley, J., & Benbow, C. (1982). Using the SAT to find intellectually talented seventh graders. *College Board Review,* (122, Winter, 1981–1982), 2–7, 26–27.

Stanley, J., Keating, D., & Fox, L. (Eds.). (1974). *Mathematical talent: Discovery, description, and development.* Baltimore: Johns Hopkins University Press.

Stedman, L. (1924). *Education of gifted children.* Yonkers-on-Hudson, NY: World Book.

Stephens, T. M., Blackhurst, A. E., & Magliocca, L. A. (1982). *Teaching mainstreamed students.* New York: Wiley.

Sternberg, R. J. (1977). *Intelligence, information processing, and analogical reasoning: The componential analysis of human abilities.* Hillsdale, NJ: Lawrence Erlbaum Associates.

Sternberg, R. J. (1982). Nonentrenchment in the assessment of intellectual giftedness. *Gifted Child Quarterly, 26*(2), 63–67.

Sternberg, R. J. (1984). Testing intelligence without IQ tests. *Phi Delta Kappan, 66*(10), 694–698.

Stewart, E. D. (1981). Learning styles among gifted/talented students: Instructional technique preferences. *Exceptional Children, 48*(2), 134–137.

Stinard, T. A., & Dolphin, W. D. (1981). Which students benefit from self-paced mastery instruction and why. *Journal of Educational Psychology, 73*(5), 754–763.

Stoddard, E. P., & Renzulli, J. S. (1983). Improving the writing skills of talent pool students. *Gifted Child Quarterly, 27*(1), 21–27.

Storms, W. (n.d.). Cost effectiveness for gifted and talented educational programs (Report funded by Title V, section 505, grant, Region V Interrelated State Education Design for the Gifted, Ohio Component). Columbus, OH: State Department of Education.

Stroh, C. (1974). Art in the general curriculum: A plea for emphasis on the cognitive. *Art Education, 27*(9), 20–21.

Suchman, R. (1975). A model for the analysis of inquiry. In W. Barbe & J. Renzulli (Eds.), *Psychology and education of the gifted* (2nd ed.) (pp. 336–345). New York: Irvington Publishers.

Suran, B. G., & Rizzo, J. V. (1983). *Special children: An integrative approach* (2nd ed.). Glenview, IL: Scott Foresman.

Swanson, H. L., & Watson, B. L. (1982). *Educational and psychological assessment of exceptional children: Theories, strategies, and applications.* St. Louis: C. V. Mosby.

Sward, K. (1933). Jewish musicality in America. *Journal of Applied Psychology, 17*(6), 675–712.

Swing, S. F., & Peterson, P. L. (1982). The relationship of student ability and small-group interaction to student achievement. *American Educational Research Journal, 19*(2), 259–274.

Szekely, G. (1981). The artist and the child: A model program for the artistically talented. *Gifted Child Quarterly, 25*(2), 67–72.

Taba, H. (1962). *Curriculum development: Theory and practice.* New York: Harcourt, Brace & World.

Taba, H. (1965). Learning by discovery: Psychological and educational rationale. In J. J. Gallagher (Ed.), *Teaching gifted students: A book of readings* (pp. 177–186). Boston: Allyn and Bacon.

Taba, H. (1975). Learning by discovery: Psychological and educational rationale. In W. B. Barbe & J. S. Renzulli (Eds.), *Psychology and education of the gifted* (2nd ed.) (pp. 346–354). New York: Irvington Publishers.

Tannenbaum, A. (1962). *Academic attitudes toward academic brilliance.* New York: Bureau of Publication, Teachers College, Columbia University.

Tannenbaum, A. (1981). Pre-Sputnik to post-Watergate concern about the gifted. In W. Barbe & J. Renzulli (Eds.), *Psychology and education of the gifted* (3rd ed.) (pp. 20–37). New York: Irvington Publishers.

Tannenbaum, A. (1983). *Gifted children: Psychological and educational perspectives.* New York: Macmillan.

Taylor, C. W. (Ed.). (1978). *Creativity across education: Selected papers from five annual creativity workshops held at the University of Utah.* Salt Lake City: University of Utah Press.

Taylor, C. W., & Ellison, R. (1966). *Biographical inventory.* Salt Lake City: Institute for Behavioral Research in Creativity.

Tempest, N. R. (1974). *Teaching clever children, 7–11.* London: Routledge & Kegan Paul.

Terman, L. (1925). *Mental and physical traits of a thousand gifted children* (Vol I of *Genetic studies of genius*). Stanford, CA: Stanford University Press.

Terman, L. (1973). *Concept mastery test.* New York: Psychological Corporation.

Terman, L. M., & Merrill, M. A. (1973). *Stanford-Binet intelligence scale: Manual for the third revision, form L-M.* Boston: Houghton Mifflin.

Terman, L., & Oden, M. (1947). *The gifted child grows up* (Vol. IV of *Genetic studies of genius*). Stanford, CA: Stanford University Press.

Terman, L., & Oden, M. (1959). *The gifted group at mid-life* (Vol. V of *Genetic studies of genius*). Stanford, CA: Stanford University Press.

Thelen, M. H., Frautschi, N. M., Roberts, M. C., Kirkland, K. D., & Dollinger, S. J. (1981). Being imitated, conformity, and social influence: An integrative review. *Journal of Research in Personality, 15,* 403–426.

Thiagarajan, S., Semmel, D. S., & Semmel, M. I. (1974). *Instructional development for training teachers of exceptional children: A sourcebook.* Minneapolis, MN: Leadership Training Institute/Special Education.

Thiagarajan, S., & Stolovitch, H. D. (1980). Frame games: an evaluation. In R. E. Horn & A. Cleaves (Eds.), *The guide to simulations/games for education and training* (4th ed.) (pp. 98–107). Beverly Hills, CA: Sage Publications.

Thomas, R. (1982). *Discover BASIC: Problem solving with the Apple II Computer* [Computer program with teachers' guide and support materials]. Austin, TX: Sterling Swift.

Thomson, V. (1962). *The state of music.* New York: Vintage Books.

Thorndike, R. L. (1973). *Reading comprehension in fifteen countries: International studies in evaluation* (Vol. III). New York: Wiley.

Thorndike, R., Hagen, E., & Lorge, I. (1974). *Cognitive abilities test.* Boston: Houghton Mifflin.

Thurstone, L. L. (1938). *Primary mental abilities* (Psychometric Monographs No. 1). Chicago: University of Chicago Press.

Thurstone, L. L., & Thurstone, T. (1962). *Primary mental abilities test.* Chicago: Science Research Associates.

Tidwell, R. (1980). A psycho-educational profile of 1,593 gifted high school students. *The Gifted Child Quarterly, 24*(2), 63–68.

Toffler, A. (1970). *Future shock.* New York: Random House.

Toffler, A. (1979). *The third wave.* New York: Bantam Books.

Tomlinson, P. D., & Hunt, D. E. (1971). Differential effects of rule-example order as a function of learner conceptual level. *Canadian Journal of Behavioral Science, 3,* 237–245.

Torrance, E. P. (1962). *Guiding creative talent.* Englewood Cliffs, NJ: Prentice-Hall.

Torrance, E. P. (1963). *Education and the creative potential.* Minneapolis: University of Minnesota Press.

Torrance, E. P. (1965). *Rewarding creative behavior.* Englewood Cliffs, NJ: Prentice-Hall.

Torrance, E. P. (1974). *Torrance tests of creative thinking.* Princeton, NJ: Personnel Press.

Torrance, E. P., & Myers, R. E. (1971). *Creative learning and teaching.* New York: Dodd.

Treffinger, D. J. (1975). Teaching for self-directed learning: A priority for the gifted and talented. *The Gifted Child Quarterly, 19*(1), 46–59.

Treffinger, D. J. (1982). Gifted students in regular classrooms: Sixty ingredients for a better blend. *The Elementary School Journal, 82*(3), 267–272.

Tremaine, C. D. (1979). Do gifted programs make a difference? *The Gifted Child Quarterly, 23*(3), 500–517.

Tsai, S. W., & Pohl, N. F. (1981). Computer-assisted instruction augmented with planned teacher/student contacts. *Journal of Experimental Education, 49*(2), 120–126.

Turnbull, A. P., Strickland, B. B., & Brantley, J. C. (1982). *Developing and implementing individualized education programs.* Columbus: OH: Charles E. Merrill.

Turnbull, H. R., & Turnbull, A. P. (1978). *Free appropriate public education: Law and implementation.* Denver: Love.

Turner, J., & Starnes, C. (1976). *Inequality: Privilege and poverty in America.* Santa Monica, CA: Goodyear.

Tymitz-Wolf, B. (1982). Guidelines for assessing IEP goals and objectives. *Teaching Exceptional Children, 14*(5), 198–201.

United States Employment Service (1946–1973). *General aptitude test battery.* Washington, DC: U.S. Government Printing Office.

Vacca, R. (1981). *Content area reading.* Boston: Little, Brown.

Van Der Linden, W. J. (1981). Using aptitude measurements for optimal assignment of subjects to treatments with and without mastery scores. *Psychometrika, 46*(3), 257–274.

Van Tassel-Baska, J. (1981). A comprehensive model of career education for the gifted and talented. *Journal of Career Education, 7,* 325–331.

Vernon, P., Adamson, G., & Vernon, D. (1977). *The psychology and education of gifted children.* Boulder, CO: Westview Press.

Vida, L. (1979). Children's literature for the gifted elementary school child. *Roeper Review, 1*(4), 22–24.

Voorheis, G. (1979). Concurrent high school-college enrollments. *Educational Record, 60*(3), 305–311.

Walker, J. (1982). The counselor's role in educating the gifted and talented. *The School Counselor, 28,* 362–370.

Walker, L. (1980). A university/community children's art program. *School Arts, 79*(9), 69.

Wallace, D. (1983). Forging a first: The Oxford curriculum. *English Journal, 27*(4), 57–59.

Wallach, M. A. (1970). Creativity. In P. H. Mussen (Ed.), *Carmichael's manual of child psychology* (pp. 1211–1272). New York: Wiley.

Ward, M. (1982). Myth: The "ostrich syndrome": Do gifted programs cure sick regular programs? *Gifted Child Quarterly, 26*(1), 34–36.

Watson, G., & Glaser, E. M. (1964). *Watson-Glaser critical thinking appraisal.* New York: Harcourt Brace Jovanovich.

Watt, I. (1957). *The rise of the novel.* London: Chatto and Windus. (Paperback edition published 1967 by the University of California Press)

Weber, M. (1958). *The Protestant ethic and the spirit of capitalism* (T. Parsons, Trans.). New York: Scribner's. (Original work published 1920)

Wechsler, D. (1949). *Manual for the Wechsler intelligence scale for children.* New York: Psychological Corporation.

Wechsler, D. (1955). *Manual for the Wechsler adult intelligence scale.* New York: Psychological Corporation.

Wechsler, D. (1967). *Manual for the Wechsler preschool and primary scale of intelligence.* New York: Psychological Corporation.

Wechsler, D. (1974). *Wechsler intelligence scale for children—revised.* New York: Psychological Corporation.

Wechsler, D. (1981). *Manual for Wechsler adult intelligence scale—revised.* New York: Psychological Corporation.

Weiler, D. (1978). The alpha children: California's brave new world for the gifted. *Phi Delta Kappan, 60*(3), 185–187.

Weise, P., Meyers, C., & Tuel, J. (1965). PMA factors, sex, and teacher nomination in screening kindergarten gifted. *Educational and Psychological Measurement, 25,* 596–603.

Weiss, D. S., Haier, R. J., & Keating, D. P. (1974). Personality characteristics of mathematically precocious boys. In J. C. Stanley, D. P. Keating, & L. H. Fox (Eds.), *Mathematical talent: Discovery, description, and development.* Baltimore, MD: Johns Hopkins University Press.

Welsh, G. S., & Barron, F. (1963). *Barron Welsh art scale.* Palo Alto, CA: Consulting Psychologists Press.

Wenner, G. C. (1973). Project IMPACT. *Music Education Journal, 59*(5), 26–31.

Wertheimer, M. (1959). *Productive thinking.* New York: Harper.

West Virginia Department of Education. (1982). *Proposed draft regulations for the education of exceptional students.* Charleston, WV: Bureau of Learning Systems.

West Virginia State Department of Education. (1983). *Regulations for the education of exceptional students.* Charleston, WV: Office of Special Education Administration.

West Virginia State Superintendent of Schools Decisions. (1982, September 30). *Jawa v. Drossick.* Charleston, WV: West Virginia State Department of Education.

WGBH Educational Foundation–British Broadcasting Corporation. (1983). *The pleasure of finding things out* [Interview with physicist R. Feynman]. Co-produced by B. Nixon (WGBH) and C. Sykes (BBC-TV). *Horizon* television program originally broadcast November 23, 1981 in the U.K. *Nova* television series originally broadcast January 25, 1983 in the U.S. Boston: WGBH transcript for program #1002. Transcript emended by R. Feynman.

White, M. A. (Ed.). (1966). *School disorder, intelligence, and social class.* New York: Teachers College Press.

White, S. H. (1977). Social implications of IQ. In P. Houts (Ed.), *The myth of measurability* (pp. 23–44). New York: Hart.

Whitfield, R. (1971). Curriculum in crisis. In R. Whitfield (Ed.), *Disciplines of the curriculum* (pp. 1–31). London: McGraw-Hill.

Whiting, B. G. (1976). How to predict creativity from biographical data. In A. Bondi & S. Parnes (Eds.), *Assessing creative growth: Measured changes* (pp. 233–241). Buffalo, NY: Creative Education Foundation.

Whitmore, J. (1980). *Giftedness, conflict, and underachievement.* Boston: Allyn and Bacon.

Whitmore, J. (1981). Gifted children with handicapping conditions: A new frontier. *Exceptional Children, 48*(2), 106–113.

Whitmore, J. (1982). Recognizing and developing hidden giftedness. *Elementary School Journal, 82*(3), 274–283.

Whitmore, J. (1983). Changes in teacher education: The key to survival for gifted education. *Roeper Review, 6*(1), 8–13.

Whitt, J. (1979). Toward a class-dialectical model of power: An empirical assessment of three competing models of political power. *American Sociological Review, 44,* 81–100.

Wiener, N. (1950). *The human use of human beings: Cybernetics and society.* Boston: Houghton Mifflin.

Wiener, N. (1954). *The human use of human beings: Cybernetics and society* (rev. ed.). New York: Avon.

Wiener, N. (1956). *I am a mathematician.* Garden City, NY: Doubleday.

Wilcox, K. (1982). Differential socialization in the classroom: Implications for equal opportunity. In G. Spindler (Ed.), *Doing the ethnography of schooling* (pp. 268–309). New York: CBS College Publishing.

Wilcox, K., & Moriarity, P. (1977). Schooling and work: Social constraints on equal educational opportunity. *Social Problems, 24*(2), 204–213.

Williams, F. (1970). *Classroom ideas for encouraging thinking and feeling.* New York: DOK Publishers.

Williams, F. (1972). *A total creativity program.* Englewood Cliffs, NJ: Educational Technology Publications.

Williams, T. (1983). Some issues in the standardized testing of minority students. *Journal of Education, 165*(2), 192–208.

Williams, W. (1966). *The contours of American history.* Chicago: Quadrangle.

Williams, W. (1969). *The roots of the modern American empire.* New York: Vintage.

Winne, P., Woodland, M., & Wong, B. (1982). Comparability of self-concept among LD, normal, and gifted students. *Journal of Learning Disabilities, 15*(8), 470–475.

Wirszup, I. (1981). The Soviet challenge: The new mathematics curriculum required of all students in the USSR is superior to that of any other country. *Educational Leadership, 38*(5), 358–360.

Witkin, H. (1973). The role of cognitive style in academic performance and in teacher-student relations. Unpublished report, Educational Testing Service, Princeton, NJ.

Witters, L., & Vasa, S. (1981). Programming alternatives for educating the gifted in rural schools. *Roeper Review, 3*(4), 22–24.

Wold, S., & Hastie, W. (1965). From research and theory to teaching practice. In W. R. Hastie (Ed.), *Art education* (Sixty-Fourth Yearbook of the National Society for the Study of Education, Part II) (pp. 326–346). Chicago: University of Chicago Press.

Wolf, J., & Gygi, J. (1981). Learning disabled and gifted: Success or failure? *Journal for the Education of the Gifted, 4*(3), 199–206.

Wolf, J., & Stephens, T. (1979). Individualized educational planning for the gifted. *Roeper Review, 2*(2), 11–12.

Wolf, J., & Troup, J. (1980). Strategy for parent involvement: Improving the IEP process. *Exceptional Parent, 10*(1), 31–32.

Wolynski, M. (1981). Confessions of a misspent youth. In J. M. Wasson (Ed.), *Subject and structure: An anthology for writers* (pp. 110–113). Boston: Little, Brown.

Woodcock, R. (1973). *Woodcock reading mastery tests.* Circle Pines, MN: American Guidance Services.

Woodcock, R., & Johnson, M. (1977). *Woodcock-Johnson psychoeducational battery.* Boston: Teaching Resources.

Worcester, D. (1956). *The education of children of above average mentality.* Lincoln, NB: University of Nebraska Press.

Wright, E. (1979). *Class structure and income determination.* New York: Academic Press.

Wright, F. (1932). *An autobiography.* London: Longmans, Green.

Yeatts, E. H. (1980). The professional artist: A teacher for the gifted. *Gifted Child Quarterly, 24*(3), 133–137.

Yoshida, R. K., Fenton, K. S., Kaufman, M. J., & Maxwell, J. P. (1978). Parental involvement in the special education pupil planning process: The school's perspective. *Exceptional Children, 44*(7), 531–534.

Young, M. (1958). *The rise of the meritocracy.* London: Penguin.

Ysseldyke, J., & Algozzine, B. (1982a). Bias among professionals who erroneously declare students eligible for special services. *Journal of Experimental Education, 50*(4), 223–228.

Ysseldyke, J., & Algozzine, B. (1982b). *Critical issues in special and remedial education.* Boston: Houghton Mifflin.

Ysseldyke, J. E., & Salvia, J. (1974). Diagnostic-prescriptive teaching: Two models. *Exceptional Children, 41*(3), 181–185.

Ysseldyke, J. Algozzine, B., & Mitchell, J. (1982). Special education team decision making: An analysis of current practice. *Personnel and Guidance Journal, 60*(5), 308–313.

Ysseldyke, J., Algozzine, B., Rostollan, D., & Shinn, M. (1981). A content analysis of the data presented at special education placement team meetings. *Journal of Clinical Psychology, 37*(3), 655–662.

Yunghans, M. (1981). A pull-out program for gifted elementary students. *School Arts, 80*(8), 50–51.

Ziegfeld, E. (Ed.). (1961). *Art for the academically talented student in the secondary school.* Washington, DC: National Education Association.

R. L. Zweig & Associates. (1971). *Fountain Valley teacher support system in reading.* Huntington Beach, CA: Richard L. Zweig Associates.

Author Index

Subject Index